FIRST COURSE IN DATA PROCESSING WITH BASIC, COBOL, FORTRAN AND RPG

FIRST COURSE IN DATA PROCESSING WITH BASIC, COBOL, FORTRAN AND RPG

SECOND EDITION

J. DANIEL COUGER, D.B.A.
University of Colorado

FRED R. MCFADDEN, Ph.D.
University of Colorado

JOHN WILEY & SONS

New York · Chichester · Brisbane · Toronto · Singapore

Cover Photo: Small section of computer printed circuit 100x Copyright 1981 Image Bank/Phillip A. Harrington

Inside Cover: Courtesy of MIC
140 Barclay Center
Cherry Hill, N.J. 08084

Library of Congress Cataloging in Publication Data

Couger, J   Daniel.
    First course in data processing with BASIC, COBOL, FORTRAN, RPG

    Published in 1977 under title: A first course in data processing.
    Includes index.
    1. Business—Data processing.   2. Electronic data processing.   I. McFadden, Fred R., 1933– joint author.   II. Title.

HF5548.2.C68   1980b   001.64   80-22129
ISBN 0-471-05581-6

Printed in the United States of America

10 9 8 7 6 5 4

DEDICATED TO OUR PARENTS

Mr. and Mrs. J. L. R. Couger

Mrs. Genevieve McFadden
and the late T. R. McFadden

ABOUT THE AUTHORS

J. Daniel Couger is Professor of Computer and Management Science at the University of Colorado, where he obtained his doctorate. In addition to his 15 years as a teacher, he has 13 years experience in industry, in a variety of managerial positions. He has been directly associated with the computer field for 25 years. He has designed and implemented management information systems, as well as supervised such activities.

Dr. Couger has been a computer consultant to more than 25 organizations, including IBM, NCR, Control Data and Hewlett Packard and has lectured in 50 countries on 6 continents. He has served as an international officer in three professional societies. He is the author/co-author of 12 books and more than 40 publications in the computing field. He is founder and editor of *Computing Newsletter for Schools of Business*. In 1977, he was selected as U.S. Computer Science Man of the Year.

Fred R. McFadden is a Professor of Management Science at the University of Colorado in Colorado Springs. Dr. McFadden has instructed graduate and undergraduate courses in information systems, operations management, management science, and business policy during his career. He has also instructed in a large number of management development programs, including courses in computer based information systems, structured program design, data base management, quantitative analyses for managers, and bank management simulations.

A native of Michigan, Professor McFadden earned his Ph.D. in industrial engineering from Stanford and his MBA from UCLA. He is an active member of the American Institute for Decision Sciences and the American Production and Inventory Control Society. He has written a number of articles that have appeared in professional journals and is co-author of the text *Introduction to Computer-Based Management Information Systems*.

The author is an active consultant to a number of business firms. In particular, he has assisted a number of smaller business firms in evaluating and installing computer information systems. He has tested the ideas in this book both in the classroom and in business practice.

PREFACE

The economist Kenneth Boulding is an internationally recognized thought-provoker. For example, consider his statement:

> The world of today . . . is as different from the world in which I was born as that world was from Julius Caesar's. I was born in the middle of human history. . . . Almost as much has happened since I was born as happened before.

Alvin Toffler, author of *Future Shock,* explains Boulding's enigmatic observation:

> If the last 50,000 years of man's existence were divided into lifetimes of approximately sixty-two years each, there have been about 800 such lifetimes. Of these 800, fully 650 were spent in caves. Only during the last seventy lifetimes has it been possible to communicate effectively from one lifetime to another—as writing made it possible to do. Only during the last six lifetimes did masses of men ever see a printed word. Only during the last four has it been possible to measure time with any precision. Only in the last two has anyone anywhere used an electric motor. And the overwhelming majority of all the material goods we use in daily life today have been developed within the present, the 800th, lifetime.

Perhaps the best example of the acceleration of technological development is the computer, another 800th-lifetime invention. It may produce the greatest impact of all technological innovations. Barely 25 years have elapsed since the introduction of the first business-oriented computer. Even the innovators failed to recognize the computer's potential. In 1950, a computer scientist for IBM speculated that a "dozen or so" large-scale computers would be able to handle all the computational needs of the United States in the 1970s. As this preface is written, there are more than 50,000 computers installed in this country with a capacity greater than the large-scale computers envisioned by this scientist. Early computer scientists did not foresee the computer's use in such a diversity of activities — ranging from use by professional football scouts to areas previously considered sacrosanct, such as composing music.

"Within two decades," says Max Ways, editor of *Fortune Magazine,* "these new information technologies have become an indispensable part of the web that holds society together. If it had to get along without these technologies, the business life of the United States would be imperiled to the point of disaster."

The computer has social and cultural impact, as well as economic impact, on each of us. Little wonder that computer courses are now offered at virtually every college in the country.

OBJECTIVES OF THE FIRST COURSE IN DATA PROCESSING

Although lagging behind industry and government, academia has changed its approach to education concerning the computer. For example, in 1967 only 11 percent of accredited schools of business required students to learn how to program a computer. By 1979, more than 95 percent of these schools had established such a requirement.

Also, course objectives have changed. In the late 1960s, introductory courses concentrated primarily on understanding how the computer works. Today that material is still included, but the primary emphasis is on how the computer is used. System analysis, design, and programming are all introduced in the first course.

The first edition of this book was prepared to meet this new set of objectives. This second edition, while retaining the informal and lively writing style of the original version, has been updated with respect to technical content and has been improved further as a teaching device. The special teaching features are described below.

TEACHING APPROACH

The instructor can make reading assignments and expect students to comprehend much of the material in the book prior to class. Self-study is facilitated through three devices: (1) periodic reinforcement questions, after each micromodule of material (2) exercises, after each macromodule of material, and (3) chapter examinations. The chapter examinations include questions requiring both descriptive and quantitative responses.

Each chapter is specially structured to aid learning. That structure is as follows:

1. *Chapter Overview.* Chapter objectives and a synopsis of chapter contents are provided.
2. *Charts and Tables.* Narrative material is expanded and reinforced by visual representation.
3. *Photographs.* All photographs are closely tied to narrative material, to enhance the learning process.
4. *Highlight on Principles and Concepts.* When a new term, principle, or concept is introduced, it is highlighted by boldface type.
5. *Examples.* After principles and concepts are introduced, examples are provided.
6. *Periodic Reinforcement Questions.* After each micromodule of material, a question is provided to enable students to evaluate their understanding.
7. *Exercises.* After each macromodule of material, an exercise is given. Answers are provided at the end of the chapter.
8. *Summary.* Key points in the chapter are reviewed in the chapter summary.
9. *Chapter Examination.* In-depth understanding of the chapter materials is tested through a comprehensive examination. More than one question is included on each important chapter topic, to enable the instructor to assign different questions in subsequent terms.

OTHER STUDENT AIDS

In addition to the above features of each chapter, the book includes the following learning aids:

1. *Glossary.* Definition of key terms in the book.

2. *Index.* Assists students both in locating the original explanation of a topic and also in identifying additional explanation in later sections of the book.

3. *Student Workbook.* A supplemental workbook is available. To whet student interest it contains a variety of question types: (a) matching terms with definitions, (b) true/false, (c) multiple choice, (d) questions on key illustrations, and (e) short cases. Answers to all questions are printed at the end of each chapter of the student workbook.

INSTRUCTOR AIDS

1. Two one-half hour *color videotapes* (cassette and reel) cover computing concepts, system analysis, and data base implementation in a real company. These are available from the Audio Visual Department, University of Colorado, Colorado Springs, Colorado 80907.

2. Over 150 *transparencies* are provided to adopters for classroom instruction.

3. A *test bank* is available for an instructor's use in developing quizzes and exams.

4. An *adopter's newsletter* provides fresh teaching illustrations and cartoons.

5. The *instructor's manual* provides considerably more pedagogical aid than the traditional IM. For each textbook chapter, the instructor's manual includes the following materials:
   a. *Objectives.* The educational objectives for that chapter.
   b. *Suggestions for Teaching.* Possible teaching approaches and additional resources for lectures, including transparency masters.
   c. *Interesting Tidbits.* Some insight on the writing of the book, to enable the instructor to personalize the textbook for students.
   d. *Answers to Chapter Examinations*
   e. *Answers to Test Bank Questions*

TWO VERSIONS OF THE BOOK

This second edition is available in two versions. This version includes chapters on each of the following computer programming languages: BASIC, FORTRAN, COBOL, and RPG. The problem of student fee determination is used to illustrate each language, so students can see the exact differences in programming languages.

The other version includes only one programming language, BASIC. It is covered in an appendix so the book can be used by schools which include computer programming in the course, as well as those schools which do not.

Both versions provide a brief overview of five programming languages (BASIC, FORTRAN, COBOL, RPG and PASCAL) in Chapter 10, so that the instructor can compare and contrast these languages.

ACKNOWLEDGMENTS The authors express their appreciation to the individuals who helped in the preparation of this book. The following served as reviewers, providing valuable suggestions: Bill Bearley, Bill Charlton, Ken Heideman, Benn Konsynski, Jean Longhurst, Richard Lott, Harice Seeds, David Whitney, and Claude Wiatrowski. Our appreciation also goes to our typists Kathy Abeyta and Elaine Schantz. Last and most important, we thank our students, who were our debuggers.

J. Daniel Couger
Fred R. McFadden

CONTENTS

PART TWO
Computing Concepts and Hardware

CHAPTER 4
Representing Data in the Computer   64

CHAPTER 5
Storage Concepts and Devices   85

PART FOUR
System Analysis, Design and Implementation

PART ONE

INTRODUCTION TO THE COMPUTER FIELD

Part I introduces you to the computer field—covering the widespread use of computers from simple applications such as payroll computation to complicated applications such as diagnosis of medical problems. The rate of growth of computers has surpassed all expectations. In 1974 there were 162,000 computers in operation in the United States. By 1980 the number climbed to more than a million according to the International Data Corporation, the highly respected market research firm in Waltham, Massachusetts.

In addition to sheer quantity of computers, internal speeds have increased spectacularly. Operations were performed in milliseconds (thousandths of a second) in the first generation of computers in the 1950s. Speed increased by a factor of 1000 by the 1960s when the third generation was introduced—operating in microseconds (millionths of a second). Speed increased by another factor of 1000 with the introduction of fourth generation in the 1970s, operating in nanoseconds (billionths of a second). Now, in the 1980s, the fifth generation is operating at speeds of one-trillionth of a second (picoseconds), another increase by a factor of 1000 over the previous generation.

In fact, those terms for speed comparison are rarely used any more. A better mode of comparison is to identify how many millions of instructions a given machine can perform *per second.* Examples of such instructions are additions, multiplications, and comparing numbers. The fifth generation small-scale computers are operating at speeds of 3 to 5 MIPS (million instructions per second), while large scale computers are operating in the range of 10 to 50 MIPS.

Accompanying the growth of the electronic industry is the expansion of the computer manufacturers. The inside cover of this book depicts that growth, in the form of the "Computer Tree." IBM is shown as the lower right-hand branch of the tree. It is easily seen that the "IBM branch" constitutes a smaller contribution to the growth of computers than its market share might indicate.

Improvement in electronic design and manufacturing brought about the increase in speed. It also produced a dramatic reduction in cost. Manufacturing costs have declined by 20 percent per year, making computers affordable for the very small business—and for the home.

CONTENTS OF PART ONE

Chapter 1 of this section is entitled "Computers and Society." As the title implies, this chapter covers the impact of computers on society in general and on individual members of society in particular. By analyzing some of the negative results of computer use, we can learn how to avoid these pitfalls. The objective of this course is for you to feel comfortable in the use of the computer rather than feeling threatened. Some of the myths of computers are analyzed to show their fallacies and to pave the way for increasing your positive feelings about computers.

Chapter 2 examines current applications of the computer: in sports, in education, in government, in anthropology and archeology, in the courts, in energy development and control, and in business. The objective is to show the widespread use of computers—how they have been used in the humanities as well as in business and engineering.

Chapter 3 introduces you to how computers work. We explain enough of the internal operation to enable you to understand how data is processed and transformed into information. After a brief history of the development of computers, the basic components are described. The operation of a computer is explained next. Then the characteristics that distinguish small-, medium-, and large-scale computers are compared.

**OBJECTIVE OF
THE PART**

The intent of Part One is to demonstrate the capability and the potential of computers. The computer is just a tool. Since the beginning of mankind, people have used tools as an extension of their hands. Tools facilitate and enhance manual capabilities. The computer is used in a similar manner—as an extension of a person's mental capacity. As is shown in the photograph, a manager can call up and display information to provide a better basis for decision making. Although the power of this new tool enhances a manager's thought process, it is merely an extension of that process. People and computers together can produce a synergistic effect—where the end result is equal to more than the sum of the parts.

1 COMPUTERS AND SOCIETY

OVERVIEW. This chapter concentrates on the "why" of computers. The remainder of the book concentrates on the "how" of computers. Statistics are given on the improvement of computers, and some beneficial uses are discussed. Quotations from experts in the field explain the potential of computer use.

This chapter also discusses some fears associated with the growth in computer use. We show that there is little to fear, so long as knowledge of computers is not confined to a few specialists. If U.S. citizens learn about computer capabilities and limitations, the democratic process will provide controls on computer use, as it has for other inventions. With not too great an investment in time, you can gain enough computer background to be able to *contribute* to beneficial use of computers.

This chapter also introduces you to the objectives of this book.

1. To provide a foundation to enable students to use the computer in their own academic programs.

2. To provide a foundation for a person who plans to become an information analyst, the link between the computer department and a department using the computer's services.

3. To provide the prerequisite knowledge for a person who plans to enter a degree program to become a programmer or designer of computer applications.

DRAMATIC GROWTH IN COMPUTER USE

As recently as 10 years ago, the average person rarely had direct contact with a computer system. Typically, payroll was computer processed. Grades were processed and printed on computer forms. Some retail stores had computerized billing systems.

The situation has changed dramatically. Over 50 percent of the U.S. labor force is now in information occupations — jobs that "create, manipulate or use information or work with technologies which do these things," according to the National Science Foundation. This compares with 35 percent in manufacturing, 5 percent in agriculture, and 10 percent in service occupations.

Information about each of us is entered, stored, and processed by computers in the schools where we are educated, in the stores where we buy on credit, in the companies that employ us, and in the agencies of state and national governments of which we are citizens. In addition, the computer is used by churches, by recreational organizations, by doctors, and by hospitals. Some people even use it for selecting dates and prospective spouses.

Today we are affected by computer systems in almost every part of our lives—educational, business, social, service, religious, and recreational. Although the rapid growth demonstrates widespread acceptance of the computer's advantages, some people still consider the computer a threat.

COMPUTERS: FRIEND OR FOE?

The question of whether the computer is "friend or foe" is realistic for many persons. One who feels apprehensive about computers is not comforted by cartoons like the following one.

"People used to be great fun.... I really miss them."

(Copyright © 1960 United Feature Syndicate, Inc. Reprinted by permission of United Feature Syndicate.)

A recent survey by well-known pollster Louis Harris revealed that 63 percent of Americans believe that computers are a threat to personal privacy. In 1976, a similar poll produced this response from only 34 percent of the survey participants.

Alan F. Westin, law professor at Columbia University, commented on the poll at a National Computer Conference. "The average American is willing to provide personal information if it is relevant to a particular end, but opposes the intrusiveness and expanded government that are part of an information society."[1]

On the other hand, 60 percent of those polled by Harris believe computers

---

[1]"Panel Cites Snowballing Fear of DP," *Computerworld*, June 11, 1979, p. 1.

have improved the quality of life. These figures show the average citizen feels the computer to be a Dr. Jekyll/Mr. Hyde — friendly at times but unpredictably unfriendly at other times.

Max Ways, editor of *Fortune Magazine,* gives some good insight on both sides of the question, Is the computer a curse or a blessing?

Already information technology has raised in the public mind (and even among leadership groups) grave questions, doubts, misunderstandings, fears, and hostilities. Not long ago, I talked with a young American widow who had been living for several years with her children in a small Arab town where conditions of comfort, hygiene, and safety were below levels most of us would regard as satisfactory. On returning to the United States she had taken her children on a camping trip in the remote mountains of California, cheerfully surviving formidable adventures with weather and wild animals. At the time I talked with her she had just decided against resettling in the United States. She was returning to the Middle East because, she said, she could not face the dangers of allowing her children to grow up in a society dominated by computers.[2]

While computer development may be threatening to some, it is also an important achievement.

Advances in the storage, retrieval, processing, and distribution of information make up the central technological achievements of the twentieth century's third quarter. Within two decades these new information technologies have become an indispensable part of the web that holds society together. If it had to get along without these technologies, the business life of the United States would be imperiled to the point of disaster. The new ways of handling information have brought about fundamental changes in governmental and political processes. They have altered the psychological and cultural attitudes of hundreds of millions who have only the haziest notions of how the new technology works. No wonder many thoughtful people believe that the new information technology will prove as important to human development as all the inventions and innovations introduced during the first 150 years of the Industrial Revolution.[3]

These are examples of the beneficial ways in which most of us have been affected by the computer. Some of us have had some negative interactions with a computerized system. Although the positive results far exceed the negative, the psychologists tell us it is human nature to dwell on the negative. At the time this was being written, I experienced one of these occurrences. A payment was lost, either by the bank or by the credit-card firm. As a result, I received notice that my card was being canceled. Resisting the urge to write a nasty letter, I wrote an objective one. A copy of my authorization for the bank to stop payment on the check was enclosed with the letter. I received a telephone call from a customer representative — thanking me for my letter and assuring me that the account was reopened. Such lucidity does not always occur — you'll read later in the chapter how I angrily handled another situation where all I had received were computer-printed, standard letters answering my complaint. That second company provided no human contact in the procedure and as-

---

[2]Max Ways, "Can Information Technology be Managed?" *Information Technology,* 1972, The Conference Board, Inc., New York, p. 4.

[3]Ways, p. 3.

sumed that "the customer is always wrong" — just the opposite of the slogan and policy of many companies.

Explaining how to resolve a disagreement over a computerized account discrepancy is one of the ways we will introduce you to the behind-the-scenes procedures used in computer applications. Before that explanation, let's examine some of the views of the average person concerning the computer and what may have produced those conclusions. Max Ways is not alone in forecasting the increasing impact of the computer on individuals and on society. Irene Taviss' *The Computer Impact* is filled with other examples. Taviss' book also shows some humorous situations. In one case, a woman tries to return $86.16 that was refunded to her in error by the Internal Revenue Service. She is told that the computer cannot be wrong, that it must be her mistake because "to err is human."[4]

At the beginning of this chapter, we provided some data concerning the percent of the labor force now in information-related occupations. The fact that more than 50 percent of the labor force is now involved in these activities does not mean that they are knowledgeable about the computer. Although most of these persons have firsthand experience with computer input or output, many are ignorant about the capabilities and limitations of computers. They are not computer literate.

The term **computer literacy** is commonly used today to distinguish those persons who have a solid foundation in computing concepts. Some states, such as Minnesota, are requiring computer literacy of grade school graduates. Computer literacy removes the fear of the unknown that many people have about the computer.

REMOVING APPREHENSION ABOUT THE COMPUTER

Have you ever had to consult with a doctor about some ailment that you could not remedy on your own? In some cases you had strong apprehension about what the doctor would tell you. Most of the time he was able to explain the results of his tests in a way you understood. He translated the technical terms into everyday language — but also assumed some knowledge on your part of basic physiology and biology. After the explanation, you usually understood the true nature of your ailment.

The same situation applies to the computer field. With a basic background of computing concepts, computer programming, system analysis, and design you can communicate with the experts. You can get across your needs — as a user of computers — so they can implement them properly.

However, computer practitioners are rarely as good as physicians in explaining technology to us, the user. One reason is our willingness to let them get away with using overly technical language. (The other reason is their assumption of basic knowledge on our part; we will analyze that problem shortly.) We would not allow the doctor to talk "over our heads" — unless we didn't really want to know how bad off we were. In most cases we would insist that the doctor explain the problem in terms we understand. Many lay people haven't been as forceful with their system designer as with their physician. The following incident illustrates this situation.

THE BUSY BANK PRESIDENT

A small suburban bank near one of your author's home decided to computerize its operations. Customers were notified through a form letter from the bank

---

[4]Irene Taviss, ed., *The Computer Impact*, 1970, Prentice-Hall, Inc., Englewood Cliffs, N.J., p. 296.

president. We were told that our service would be improved as a result of conversion of the bank's operations to the computer.

Nevertheless, my first month's bank statement was incorrect. In addition to informing me that my loan payment was late, I was given a two-dollar penalty "because of the extra handling required in processing" my late payment, due on the tenth of the month. Customers had not been charged for late payments previously. Also—my payment was not due on the tenth as noted on the statement. It was due on the twentieth!

So I wrote the bank president. First, I indicated little cause for concern about the error on my payment due date. It was undoubtedly a key entry error. What really concerned me was the penalty assessment. I reminded the president, Mr. Johnson, of his previous letter where he promised "improved service." To get his attention, I enclosed my monthly loan payment—less five dollars, for what I called, "additional harassment" due to his new computer system.

Surprisingly, Mr. Johnson wrote back immediately, saying he would accept my "penalty assessment" of five dollars. He also asked me to drop by and let him explain the situation that caused the problem. Obviously, I was quite interested and visited him the same week. He told me that my letter was his first clue that the bank had instituted the two-dollar penalty assessment.

He explained that he had hired an experienced system designer "because we were already behind the big banks and wanted to catch up as quickly as possible." The first week on the job, the designer asked for an appointment with Mr. Johnson, to "define his needs for his management information system." That was exactly what should have been done; however, the approach was wrong. "After a few minutes I began to be snowed by the technical terminology," Mr. Johnson said. Finally, he told him "Look, I hired you because you are experienced. Just get our demand deposit accounting (checkbook) system going, and talk to me later about my management information system."

A short time later, in the midst of system development, the designer found that customers sometimes made late payments without any penalty. He could easily add logic to his program to detect those situations. He decided to follow Mr. Johnson's instructions "to the letter"—so didn't ask whether the penalty assessment should be implemented.

"Your letter brought this situation to my attention—and I was furious," Mr. Johnson said. "However, when I called the designer in to reprimand him, he reminded me that I made it clear that I didn't want to be bothered with all the technical details. He was wrong in making a policy decision for the bank—but I was also wrong in delegating the system entirely to him."

What he should have said in his initial discussion with the designer, Mr. Johnson explained, was "Look, fellow, you work for me—not the opposite; so, translate those technical terms into banking terminology, so I can understand it."

This incident illustrates that some of our apprehension about computers and computerized systems is our fault—we should insist that technicians explain things in commonly used terminology. We require it of our doctor, our lawyer, our income tax accountant—all the other technicians. We should not be awed by the mystique of the computer any more than by that of any other technical area.

ACQUIRING A COMPUTER LITERACY

The second point to be emphasized, by the explanation of the bank incident, is the need for a basic understanding of computer technology. We can comprehend our doctor's or accountant's explanations because of some fundamentals we acquired through schooling or through self-study. We have a layman's literacy in these areas; thus, we need equivalent literacy in the computer area. This book has computer literacy as one of its objectives.

In *Future Shock,*[5] Alvin Toffler shows why we need to become proficient in use of the computer. He describes the accelerating pace of social and technological change. He shows how that pace will be intensified, producing a shock effect that some people will be unable to overcome. The computer will be the major factor in accelerating change, in his view.

Another objective of computer literacy is to make people feel more comfortable in an increasingly computer-oriented world. If people are comfortable and literate about a subject, they can not only cope with the situation, they can contribute to its improvement.

It is possible to avoid a negative shock effect. However, merely trying to cope with change is not enough. By acquiring computer literacy, a person will be able to feel comfortable in our changing environment, but this goal seems shortsighted. Rather than merely trying to cope or feel comfortable, shouldn't a person attempt to contribute something to society? The computer is already an essential component of our changing environment and will be even more prominent in the future. Gaining proficiency in use of the computer should enable a person to be involved, to contribute. Few of us can be a principal contributor, such as the President's economic advisor. However, as we have seen in the civil rights and the Vietnam peace movements, motivated individuals uniting in a common cause can make an impact. Some of the possibilities of contributing are discussed next.

THE MAJOR THREAT OF COMPUTERS

In the National Computer Conference discussion described above, Professor Westin declared, "because of this deep seated fear that computer use is not sufficiently controlled we have to look forward to a period of high skepticism on the part of the American public." The Harris poll indicated that 80 percent of those surveyed think computers make it easier for someone to obtain confidential information about an individual improperly.

A specific issue is the question of citizen privacy versus the national data bank. Government officials are considering the development of several new federal data banks. One, the criminal data bank, would permit law enforcement officials to control crime more effectively. All agencies — federal, state, local — would have electronic access. Criminals could be detected and apprehended more easily.

The proper use of such a data bank requires procedures to insure that information is accurate. A Senate committee, until recently headed by the Honorable Sam Ervin, is charged with protecting the rights and privacy of citizens in development of national data banks.

Senator Ervin's committee discovered 858 federal data banks containing over 1 billion records on U.S. citizens. Eighty-six percent of these data banks are computerized. Senator Ervin revealed that some agencies have records with sensitive information on race, drug addiction, and salary "but do not regard this as personal information." Twenty-nine of the 858 data banks contain primarily "derogatory information, including agency black lists, look-out files, intelligence and civil disturbance files, kept in such agencies as the departments of Agriculture, Justice, Defense, Treasury, Housing and Urban Development, as well as the Small Business Administration and Government Supply Agency."[6]

[5]Alvin Toffler, *Future Shock*, 1970, Random House, New York.

[6]Nancy French, "858 Data Banks Show Regulation a Must," *Computerworld*, June 26, 1974, pp. 1–2.

QUESTION: Can you think of some procedures to insure that your rights as a citizen are protected in the design of a national criminal data bank?

1. _____

_____

2. _____

_____

ANSWER:
1. Your right of access to data in the data bank would be an important one. If you could check the information periodically, you would probably feel more confident about the government's having such a system.
2. Your right to say which data were included would also be important. For example, is there a need to include criminal records more than three years after the sentence is completed? A person should be completely rehabilitated by that time.

TAKING A STANCE

One can take the position that computerized data banks are more harmful than beneficial. That is frequently the stance of the person who knows little about the computer.

Lack of understanding can also lead to the opposite conclusion, that computerized data banks offer *no* threat to privacy. One of the authors was in England when a Parliamentary committee decided on its position regarding the British data bank. The committee concluded that there was little to fear from a national data bank because there were no instances of misuse of data from existing data banks.

Serving as an expert witness before a Swedish Parliamentary subcommittee, the author labeled the British attitude the "ostrich approach." The British legislators were "sticking their heads in the sand" for fear of seeing what might happen.

The Swedes were the first to have national data banks. Members of the Royal Parliamentary Investigation Committee took responsibility to become educated concerning computer capabilities and limitations. As a result the Swedish Data Act is a model for countries considering development of data banks.

A person who understands the limitations *and* the capabilities of computers can make a proper evaluation of a data bank. A computer-knowledgeable person could determine the benefits and shortcomings of such a system. For example, one U.S. congressman proposed a quarterly computer printout of data bank data on each citizen, to be sent to that person four times per year. A person knowledgeable about computing would recognize that such an approach would be too costly.

Use of the concept of **management by exception** is more appropriate. A person would be sent a printout when his or her name was added to the data bank. Thereafter, printouts would be provided only under "exceptional" circumstances, as defined by law. Notification would occur only when changes were made to "sensitive" data elements. For example, the citizen would not be notified when an employment record was updated but would be notified if an income tax record were changed.

QUESTION: The example above shows that computer-knowledgeable people can suggest ways that a computer can be used to benefit federal agencies without infringing on the individual's right to check the _____ of personal data.

ANSWER: accuracy

CONTRIBUTING TO SOCIETY THROUGH COMPUTER KNOWLEDGE

After reviewing the examples of national data banks, the student can better understand how he or she might contribute to society through proficiency in use of computers.

Let's continue along the same vein to make sure that accelerating computer technology has beneficial impact on our society. Three possible responses to a local data bank are given in Table 1-1.

The fact that you are enrolled in a course using this textbook probably shows that you would like to be in the third category, that is, to make a contribution. You may prefer to use the computer capability you acquire in this course in some other areas. Examples of areas where such an ability would be welcomed are:

1. Service on the school board—helping decide how to better utilize the computer as a teaching aid, and how school administrators can use it to expand services in a period of tightening budgets.
2. Service on the hospital board—helping decide how to better utilize the computer to improve patient care, while reducing the costs of billing and servicing the customer.
3. Service for the church—helping with computer use in the church's education program and administration.

A number of service organizations are presently benefiting from computer use. That number will expand rapidly as computer costs continue to decline. The reduction in cost and expanded capabilities of small-scale computers permit organizations, large and small, to acquire a computer. In just three generations of computer technology, cost has been reduced significantly, as shown in Figure 1-1. The figure shows that price of storage in the central processor unit is less.

TABLE 1-1 THREE POSSIBLE RESPONSES TO ACCELERATING COMPUTER TECHNOLOGY

1.	*Capitulation*	"This is the last blow! The City Council is depersonalizing all of us. I'm going to be just a number in a data bank. And any crank who wants to find anything out about me can just go down to the City Hall and get the computer to regurgitate."
2.	*Coping*	"Well, at least I know it's going to be too expensive for the city to store everything about me. I've got confidence that George Johnson knows enough about the computer to tell other City Council members what procedures ought to be set up. He'll make sure access is limited to only those who have a need to know."
3.	*Contributing*	"Guess I'll volunteer to work on a committee to evaluate the data bank system to make sure my rights are safeguarded."

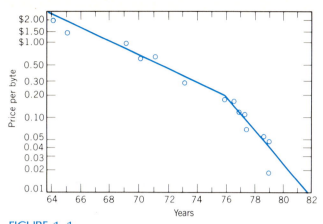

FIGURE 1-1
Reduction in price per byte of central processor memory for IBM computers. (Courtesy of EDP Industry Report.)

than one hundredth of the 1964 value. The figures are for IBM but are representative for the industry as a whole — especially when one considers that IBM has the majority of the market. IBM's revenues in 1979 were almost nine times higher than that of the number-two firm, the Burroughs Corporation.

COMPUTER IMPACT ON LAY PEOPLE

Now that we have discussed how computer capability would enable us to contribute to computer-related projects on a local, state, or national basis, let us examine some more personal benefits.

As computer technology improves, the daily impact of computers on our lives will become more noticeable. The **cashless–checkless** society has been discussed for years; few know it is already in operation in test areas. The Hempstead Bank in Syosset, New York, has a system to process transactions automatically for 3000 customers making purchases at more than 30 participating stores. The customer's credit card is inserted into a terminal at each stop, and purchases are keyed in by the clerk. The information is electronically transmitted to the bank's computer, where the merchant's account is automatically credited and the customer's account is automatically debited. However, customers have an option to delay debiting for 35 days. If the customer's account is overdrawn, the overdraft is automatically converted into a bank loan at the prevailing annual rate of interest.

QUESTION: The cashless–checkless society is one where the computer keeps record of all

_____ transactions, eliminating use of money and checks.

ANSWER: financial

Understanding the computer's capabilities and limitations will aid us in dealing with organizations that provide us goods and services. This knowledge will help us separate the "corn from its husk." Three examples are cited.

THE *READER'S DIGEST* INCIDENT

A recent issue of *Reader's Digest* had an editorial comment that attempted to pass the buck to the computer for a management problem. The editor's comments were repeated in the final exam for a course using this textbook. By that time, students had the knowledge to recognize the editor's lack of understanding (or deliberate attempt to mislead his customer!). The editor's statement is quoted below.

Because the computer also uses parts of your address to distinguish between subscribers, even a slight variation here can also result in duplicate copies. This happens when a subscriber . . . writes 10 3rd Avenue, then 10 Third Avenue. A computer doesn't realize that these are not the same address.

A computer-knowledgeable subscriber would recognize the error in this statement. A computer follows the logic programmed into it. The logic for the *Reader's Digest* system was inadequate, since the programmer could have included logic to compare numerical addresses with alphabetic addresses, so the difference would have been detected and a duplicate subscription avoided.

QUESTION: The editor's error was in saying, "A computer doesn't realize. . . ." He should have said: _____

ANSWER: "Our programmers did not include logic to detect differences in alphabetic and numeric street addresses."

THE PAYROLL INCIDENT   The following cartoon depicts a situation that might well have occurred in the early days of the computer. In fact, there are several recorded instances of a million-dollar check erroneously produced by the computer. The probability that the error was caused by a computer malfunction is less than one tenth of one percent. If the computer malfunctions, the probability is high that the printing on the check will be gobbledegook. It will be a mixture of alphabetic and numeric data that makes no sense, such as "A.24Z = RO@." The error is in the logic developed by the system designer or in the program prepared by the computer programmer. A simple logic check could be added to the payroll program to prevent a large-value paycheck. The logic would go something like this: "Compare the amount of this payroll calculation to that the employee received last pay period. If the difference is plus or minus 15 percent, print a notice to the payroll supervisor for examination before releasing the check."

(Reprinted by permission of the Chicago Tribune — New York News Syndicate, Inc.)

QUESTION: Write a similar logic statement for the payroll program for a *new* employee, one who does not have a pay history for comparison.

_____

_____

_____

ANSWER: "Compare the amount of this payroll calculation with that of another employee in this payroll classification or compare this calculation with the maximum amount allowed for any employee in this payroll classification." There are a variety of ways to perform the comparison to insure an unreasonable amount is not paid.

THE CONTINENTAL AIRLINES INCIDENT

A more frequent problem is that of dealing with a company that has sent you an incorrect bill. This situation is corrected more easily when the customer has a knowledge of computer capability. An example occurs in the billing procedure of Continental Airlines. Customers are invoiced each month, and a delinquent notice is sent out if the bill is not paid within 30 days. As a customer of Continental, one of the authors ignored the delinquency notice when the balance was a few dollars. The cost of the postage was more than the interest charge, since the amount owed was small. This approach backfired once, however. While I was away for an eight-week European trip, delinquency notices began to pile up. Each notice got more demanding.

What do you do in a case like this? None of us wants a bad credit rating. I wrote the credit manager, explained the situation, and requested that my account record not indicate poor-payment history. I also suggested that the invoicing procedure be revised for sending delinquency notices only when the amount owed was significant. Again, the additional programming logic to accomplish this action is very simple. Admittedly, it takes more computer time to process this additional logic. Although my credit record was cleared, the credit manager apparently could not get priority for such a change from the computer department — the procedure has not been revised.

COMMUNICATING WITH THE COMPUTER

Numerous references advise readers to mutilate computer invoice cards in order to get the attention of the humans. Since the computer cannot process mutilated cards, an operator must become involved. However, this procedure is no guarantee that corrective action will occur. Operators do not open mail. The person who takes the card from your envelope is the key to corrective action. Only a responsive, customer-oriented policy will encourage that person to take action. If comments written on the invoice produce no results, the customer is better off writing the credit manager than trying to communicate with the computer directly.

In any event, a knowledge of computer capabilities enables a customer to identify the source of the problem. He or she can then communicate with the proper person to resolve the problem and avoid having to mutilate cards.

The feeling of helplessness in dealing with computer systems should lessen early in this course. Dr. Ulrich Neisser has studied some 60 student users of the computer at MIT and reports an absence of anxieties about the machine. This leads him to believe that uneasiness about computers is simply a passing phase.

As we come into closer everyday contact with computers, we come to accept them with psychological comfort as we accept many other modern inventions.[7]

QUESTION: Success in dealing with computer billing systems is enhanced by determining the cause of the problem, then _____

ANSWER: communicating with the proper person, showing your understanding of the situation.

OTHER EXAMPLES Some of the problems of computer use were described in a column published in the *Honolulu Star-Bulletin*. However, some of the incidents described could not have happened. The columnist either was pulling the reader's leg or did not know that some of the situations he described were untrue. Read the column, reproduced in Figure 1–2, and try to decide which of the incidents could not have happened.

It had to happen. A mill worker in Naturita, Colo., which sounds like a fictitious place but isn't, worked 40 hours.

His hourly pay rate was fed into a computer which multiplied it by 40, and then began to take out the deductions for income tax, state tax, Naturita tax, social security, pension, medical, parking, credit union, three kinds of insurance and six sorts of miscellany.

And when all the subtraction was done — you guessed it — the fellow broke out even, exactly.

The computer reared back and wrote him a check for $000.00 for the week.

At that, I suppose the man should be thankful. He came out even in this machine age.

A fellow in England wasn't so lucky.

He came out even with the gas company because he had been away from home for three months. A bill came for zero.

The man ignored it. The computer billed him again, for zero.

Still ignored, the computer got mad. It began to spin out nasty notices that unless the man paid his bill — of nothing — he would find himself gasless.

Finally, the man sent the computer a check for zero, and solved that.

But — he got his own bank angry at him. "Our computer went up in smoke trying to handle your check for nothing," he was told by an irate bank manager.

These two examples of the machine at work in our troubled times popped out of my Labor Day mail, and seemed appropriate to the season.

So does the story of the man in Albany who was picked up for stealing his own car, thanks to the Police Department computer.

[7]Robert S. Lee, "The Computer's Public Image," in Taviss, p. 274.

It seems his previous car had been stolen the year before, and wrecked. Only the license plates were saved, and he was allowed to put them on his new car.

Somebody forgot to tell the computer, however, and it put out a call to arrest that man. He finally talked his way out of the mess.

An airman was able to explain his way out of a discharge from the Royal Air Force, too, after its new $2.4 million computer in Gloucester, England, had advised the authorities that he was pregnant and should be separated from the service.

But no amount of talking could stop a New York publishing house from billing the Chesapeake Public Library for a bill that the library had paid in advance. The publishing house freely and frequently admitted that the bill had been paid, but it said it simply could not get the message across to its computer.

At last report the billing had been going on for 44 months.

It might help if that publishing house computer would meet the man from San Antonio, who fought a computer with a computer.

The man was a computer programmer himself, and he began to receive a series of dunning notices from a book club computer. Pleas failed to right the situation, so he took the book club's computerized statement to his office and key punched it with holes that meant: "Correction needed on account."

The computer got the word.

The cops got the word in New York City when their computer notified a woman in Dolgeville, N.Y., that she had ignored more than 60 city traffic tickets. The woman had never been in New York City in her life.

And so goes life on the billing machine front, to which I will add one more story, which comes from a reader via something called Datamation magazine.

The clipping announces something called Autocom, which is an automatic warning device which telephones pre-recorded requests for assistance, according to the magazine, "when a dangerous condition develops." (Whatever that means.)

Apparently this thing can be set up so that if an "unacceptable condition" — let's put that into English for Datamation magazine; they must mean a fire or something — develops, the thing will telephone for help in prerecorded words.

It can even be arranged to make the machine make a priority call, although it doesn't say what will happen if the machine happens to get another on the line.

And guess who ordered the first one of these things? The Hawaiian Telephone Company, that's who.

"And two bits says it will get the wrong number," wrote the reader, but I think that's a little cruel.

FIGURE 1-2
A columnist's list of some problems in computer use. (Courtesy Jim Becker, *Honolulu Star-Bulletin.*)

Most beginning students recognize that one of these incidents could not have happened, according to our experience in using this editorial in the first class each semester. Through the informal education described earlier in this chapter, the average person recognizes that the story about the Chesapeake Public Library is suspect. Even if the procedures for inputting corrections to the computing system had been lost or destroyed, they could be reconstructed.

How would you respond if you were on the receiving end of each of the problems cited in Mr. Becker's column? By the end of this course, you should have the knowledge to determine the cause of each of these problems. Also, you should be able to determine the best method of getting corrective action.

OBJECTIVES IN DESIGNING THIS COURSE

Solving problems arising from a lay person's contact with the computer is one of the objectives for which this textbook was designed.

In today's business environment, all employees need to know more about the computer. To fully utilize the computer in any profession, a person needs a thorough understanding of the inner workings of a computer system.

OBJECTIVE 1: THE FIRST COURSE FOR AN EFFECTIVE COMPUTER USER

Just five years ago a course of this type was taught to college seniors; it is now being taught to freshmen and sophomores. The purpose five years ago was to educate the student about the use of the computer in that student's chosen profession. That purpose has not changed, but it has been enlarged. The course is now designed to enable the students to use the computer in their own academic programs while in school, as well as in their professions after completing school. By gaining such a capability at the freshman level, students can use the computer to gain more depth and to perform more analysis in other courses.

OBJECTIVE 2: THE FIRST COURSE FOR AN INFORMATION ANALYST

Other students completing this course will be attracted to a new profession, that of the information analyst. This person will be employed in one of the user areas, such as marketing or hospital administration. The **information analyst** functions as a link between the using department and the computer department. He or she will determine the informational needs of the organization based on a knowledge of its functions and upon interaction with the various managers of the organization. In cooperation with the system designer, the analyst will translate informational needs into a set of specifications for conversion to the computer.

To prepare to be an information analyst, the student takes four to six computer courses in addition to the courses required in the major field. Most colleges allow more than enough elective credits so that this double major does not lengthen the degree program.

OBJECTIVE 3: THE FIRST COURSE FOR A COMPUTER PROFESSIONAL

The person who is attracted to a degree in the computer field will find that the course is a prerequisite for entry in such a program.

SUMMARY

Upon completion of this book, the reader will view cartoons such as the one on page 4 with humor rather than fear. We need not look at the computer as a threat but as an ally, if we are properly educated concerning computing concepts, capabilities, and limitations.

We'd like to use another cartoon to summarize our objectives, the Charlie Brown cartoon below.

(Copyright © 1960 United Feature Syndicate, Inc. Reprinted by permission of United Feature Syndicate)

The graduate of the course for which this book is designed should no longer feel "out of place" in dealing with the computer and with computer professionals. On the contrary, he or she should feel comfortable in use of the computer throughout the academic program and in his or her chosen profession.

CHAPTER EXAMINATION

1. Match the following.

    ____ Link between users and designers

    ____ Understands computing concepts

    ____ Person for whom computer application designed

    ____ Computerized files of information

    ____ Learning through everyday contacts

    ____ Ignores the problem

    ____ Inability to avoid future shock

    ____ Unable to cope with change

    ____ Considers only exceptional circumstances

    ____ Learning through college courses

    ____ Result of computer processing

    ____ Programmer or system designer

    ____ Protection of citizen rights

    ____ Feels out of place

    ____ Folding, spindling, or mutilating

    a. Informal computer education

    b. Formal computer education

    c. Information analyst

    d. Ostrich approach

    e. Computer literacy

    f. Computer illiteracy

    g. Those subject to "future shock"

    h. Privacy

    i. Data bank

    j. Management by exception

    k. Capitulation

    l. Computer professional

    m. Output

    n. User

    o. Charlie Brown

2. The price of the central processor in 1980 was _____ percent of the 1964 price (see Figure 1–1).

3. Why is a course using this textbook taught to freshmen or sophomores when five years ago it was taught to college seniors?

    _____

    _____

4. Who is an effective computer user? _____

    _____

    _____

5. What comprises the informal education that lay people receive about computers? _____

    _____

    _____

6. What should be provided in a formal education concerning the computer? _____

    _____

    _____

    _____

7. What tasks are performed by a person in the new profession, information analysis? _____

    _____

    _____

8. What two categories of knowledge must the information analyst possess to function effectively? _____

    _____

    _____

9. What brought about the recognition of the need for the new position? _____

    _____

    _____

    _____

10. Why were the Swedes able to develop a Data Act that serves as a model for developing federal data banks?

    _____

    _____

11. What does the term "management by exception" mean? _____

    _____

    _____

12. What is the concept of the "cashless-checkless" society? _____

_____

_____

_____

13. What problems need to be anticipated and resolved prior to adoption of a cashless–checkless system? _____

_____

_____

_____

_____

14. What prerequisite knowledge in the computer area is required of a person who plans to enter a degree

program in information systems? _____

_____

_____

15. Instead of Charlie Brown's feeling of being out of place, the person who completes this textbook should feel:

_____

_____

_____

16. At the end of this course, we discuss each of the incidents described in the _Honolulu Star-Bulletin_ (Figure 1-2). Examine each incident below and suggest what might have caused the problem, based on your present knowledge.

a. It had to happen. A mill worker in Naturita, Colo., which sounds like a fictitious place but isn't, worked 40 hours.

His hourly pay rate was fed into a computer which multiplied it by 40, and then began to take out the deductions for income tax, state tax, Naturita tax, social security, pension, medical, parking, credit union, three kinds of insurance and six sorts of miscellany.

And when all the subtraction was done—you guessed it—the fellow broke even, exactly.

_____

_____

_____

_____

_____

b. _A fellow in England wasn't so lucky._

He came out even with the gas company because he had been away from home for three months. A bill came for zero.

_____

_____

The man ignored it. The computer billed him again, for zero.

Still ignored, the computer got mad. It began to spin out nasty notices that unless the man paid his bill — of nothing — he would find himself gasless.

Finally, the man sent the computer a check for zero, and solved that.

But — he got his own bank angry at him. "Our computer went up in smoke trying to handle your check for nothing," he was told by an irate bank manager.

c.   *So does the story of the man in Albany who was picked up for stealing his own car, thanks to the Police Department computer.*

It seems his previous car had been stolen the year before, and wrecked. Only the license plates were saved, and he was allowed to put them on his new car.

Somebody forgot to tell the computer, however, and it put out a call to arrest that man. He finally talked his way out of the mess.

d.   An airman was able to explain his way out of a discharge from the Royal Air Force, too, after its new $2.4 million computer in Gloucester, England, had advised the authorities that he was pregnant and should be separated from the service.

e.   But no amount of talking could stop a New York publishing house from billing the Chesapeake Public Library for a bill that the library had paid in advance. The publishing house freely and frequently admitted that the bill had been paid, but it said it simply could not get the message across to its computer.

At last report the billing had been going on for 44 months.

f.   It might help if that publishing house computer would meet the man from San Antonio, who fought a computer with a computer.

The man was a computer programmer himself, and he began to receive a series of dunning notices from a book club computer. Pleas failed to right the situation, so he took the book club's computerized statement to his office and key punched it with holes that mean: "Correction needed on account."

g.   *The computer got the word.*

The cops got the word in New York City when their computer notified a woman in Dolgeville, N.Y., that she had ignored more than 60 city traffic tickets. The woman had never been in New York City in her life.

17. The case of the Busy Bank President illustrated the need for managers to _____

_____

18. Define computer literacy. _____

_____

19. In 1967 only 11 percent of accredited schools of business required computer literacy of students. Today

more than _____ percent have such a requirement. What do these requirements encompass? (See
the Preface.)

20. Self-study in this book is facilitated through three devices. (See the Preface.) List them below.

a. _____

b. _____

c. _____

21. Early innovators failed to recognize the computer's potential. In the 1950s an IBM scientist estimated that

_____ large scale computers would handle the needs of the U.S. in the 1970s. Now, more than

_____ large scale computers are in use. (See the Preface.)

2 CURRENT APPLICATIONS OF THE COMPUTER

OVERVIEW. Colleges have revised requirements today so that students take more courses outside their major fields. While specialization was emphasized in earlier years, breadth is emphasized today. Breadth has two purposes: to prepare a student for living and for earning a living.

The same philosophy applies to education concerning the computer. The material in Chapter 1 illustrated that knowledge about the computer better prepares a person for living—in an increasingly computer-oriented world. This chapter discusses how knowledge of the computer will better prepare a person for earning a living.

We hope you will not just thumb through the material and read only the section that applies to your chosen field. Although that section will explain how knowledge about the computer will aid you in earning a living, the other sections will help you prepare for life in a computer-oriented world. The first section provides an overview of computer use; it is followed by descriptions of major applications in government and industry.

WHAT ARE COMPUTER SYSTEMS?

The term "computer systems" is used in Chapter 1 as it is used in everyday English. Actually, the term **computer application** would have been more correct. Payroll processing is an application of the computer. The **computer system** is the set of hardware and software through which the application is processed. As the name implies, **hardware** is physical equipment, such as the mechanical, electronic, and magnetic units in a computer. **Software** is the set of computer programs that causes the computer to produce the desired results.

Philip Jordain provides a good way to distinguish hardware from software: "If a human being were born fully grown physically, he would be analogous to a computer without software: all potential, but no performance. Education (formal or otherwise) enables man to function; software enables computers to function."[1] However, in this chapter we are interested more in providing an overview of computer uses than in defining terms. Only terms necessary to this objective will be introduced.

---

[1]Philip B. Jordain, *Condensed Computer Encyclopedia*, 1969, McGraw-Hill Book Company, New York, p. 47.

WHAT ARE BUSINESS INFORMATION SYSTEMS?

Although the computer field has been analyzed in a variety of ways, the most common approach is by area of application. At the top of the hierarchy are three categories: science/engineering, humanities, and business (administrative) applications. The total number of different applications has increased by a factor of 10 each decade—from 300 in 1960 to over 3000 in 1970 and to more than 30,000 in 1980.

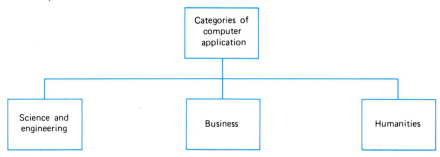

Examples of scientific applications are: testing airplane stress, guidance and flight control, spectrum analysis, shoreline erosion studies, seismic reading for earthquake detection, matrix inversion, blood count analysis, metal alloy calculations, voice print identification, and solution of differential equations.

Examples of business or administrative applications are: billing and invoicing, accounting, order processing, payroll, stolen automobile identification, church information systems, economic forecasting, garbage truck scheduling, stock market analysis, insurance premium accounting, inventory control, job placement, farm management, college course scheduling, bank check processing, and labor union bargaining strategy analysis.

Examples of applications in the humanities are: artifact classification, computer art design, map reproduction, historical research, language syntax pattern analysis, poetry style analysis, concordance construction, music composition, and harmonics analysis.

QUESTION: Which application in each category was most surprising to you?

Science _____

Business _____

Humanities _____

ANSWER: In the past our students have been most surprised to learn that the computer could: identify voice prints, analyze labor bargaining strategies, and compose music.

Figure 2-1 provides a summary of applications in the two major categories, science/engineering and business.[2] The number of applications in the human-

[2]Projections are based on extrapolations of the trends first reported in *Computer Directory and Buyer's Guide*, 1974, Berkeley Enterprises, Inc., Newtonville, MA, and modified by data on computer industry trends published monthly in *EDP Industry Report*, Waltham, MA.

ities is quite small, estimated to be less than 10 percent of the combined total for the other two categories.

```
                    ┌─────────────────┐
                    │  Applications   │
                    │ of the Computer │
                    └─────────────────┘
```

Scientific Applications		Business Applications	
Field of Application	Percent of Total	Field of Application	Percent of Total
1. Aeronautics and space engineering	13.73	1. Business	
2. Astronomy	1.74	1. Office	7.24
3. Biology	3.27	2. Plant and production	4.73
4. Botany	.33	3. Advertising	1.32
5. Chemical engineering and chemistry	3.92	4. Automotive industry	3.23
6. Civil engineering	9.70	5. Banking	2.75
7. Ecology and energy	1.09	6. Educational and institutional	6.04
8. Economics	.87	7. Farming	2.63
9. Electrical engineering	3.92	8. Finance	2.45
10. Geology	1.53	9. Government (local, state, federal)	12.57
11. Geophysics	.76	10. Health and medical facilities	5.33
12. Hydraulic engineering	2.94	11. Insurance	2.63
13. Marine engineering	3.38	12. Labor unions	.66
14. Mathematics	4.79	13. Law	1.85
15. Mechanical engineering	4.03	14. Libraries	.72
16. Medicine and physiology	20.81	15. Magazine and periodical publishing	1.56
17. Metallurgy	.33	16. Military	.72
18. Meteorology	2.27	17. Oil industry	4.97
19. Military engineering	4.14	18. Police	1.73
20. Naval engineering	.76	19. Public utilities	3.47
21. Nuclear engineering	2.07	20. Publishing	.66
22. Oceanography	2.51	21. Religious organizations	3.71
23. Photography	1.63	22. Sports and entertainment	5.15
24. Physics	2.61	23. Steel industry	1.85
25. Psychology	2.94	24. Telephone industry	1.26
26. Sociology	.54	25. Textile industry	.96
27. Statistics	2.94	26. Transportation	10.41
		27. Miscellaneous	9.40
TOTAL	99.55%	TOTAL	100%

FIGURE 2-1

Categories of applications of the computer. (Source: Computer Directory and Buyers Guide, published in Newtonville, MA.)

QUESTION: Examine Figure 2-1. Which field within each of the two major categories has the largest percentage of applications?

Business applications _____

Scientific applications _____

ANSWER: Business applications: government, (12.57 percent); scientific applications: medicine and physiology, (20.81 percent).

With this background, we are now ready to tackle the question, What are business information systems? In one sense, all applications are information systems. A **system** consists of input, processing, and output. Both scientific and business systems have these characteristics. Also, both process information. For example, one of the scientific systems that supports space flights is the guidance system. Radar data are continuously collected and fed to the guidance computer system. These data are then processed through the guidance computer program and compared against the flight plan. The output of the system is automatic correction to maintain the flight plan. Of course, the system provides for manual override of automatic guidance by the astronauts when special circumstances arise.

Also associated with the space flights are many business systems. For example, data are collected on costs, fed into the accounting system, and processed according to the accounting computer program. The output of the system is a series of reports on performance against budget.

In some cases both scientific and business applications share the same input. For example, sensors are attached to the astronauts, primarily to monitor physical condition — a scientific application. However, these same data are collected for later processing in an administrative application, to determine costs of providing each astronaut with the proper life-support environment.

QUESTION: Scientific and business applications of the computer have several things in common. Both consist of _____ _____ , and _____ ; both

process _____

ANSWER: input, processing, output; information

Despite similar basic characteristics, scientific and business systems generally serve very different masters. Output of scientific computer applications is for engineers and scientists of the organization. Output of business applications is for managers of the organization. Another way of looking at the distinction is to relate it to the product of an organization. We can generalize that scientific applications are used in the design of the product. Business applications are used to insure that the correct quantities of products are manufactured and that the products get to consumers efficiently and economically.

QUESTION: _____ applications are used in the design of the product, and

_____ applications are used in the administration of the enterprise.

ANSWER: Scientific, business

DIFFERENCE BETWEEN SYSTEMS AND APPLICATIONS

The terms "applications" and "systems" were used interchangeably in the preceding section. Both consist of input, processing, and output. However, there is a major distinction between systems and applications. Systems existed long before computers were invented. The Bible describes many business systems. For example, in the book of Numbers, Moses organized the 600,000 adult Israelites by a numbering system that distinguished warriors (those over 20 years of age) and that established armies with a chain of command.

We have also implied that the information processed by systems exists in some physical form, such as punched cards. Figure 2–2 illustrates a **cybernetic system.** The input to this system has no physical form. The external stimulus (input) is processed against the internally stored program. Although the mechanism and procedure for processing are inherent, results vary greatly, depending on the comparison of input data against those in the memory bank. Following upon the analogy used earlier in this chapter, if two human beings were born fully grown, the program for processing could be expected to be similar. It is the data in the memory bank that affect the output significantly. A set of data passed through the cybernetic systems of two humans born fully grown should produce essentially the same results — for the first few cycles. Thereafter, only in a completely controlled environment could we be assured of similar results. The memory banks of two normally reared adults contain different data, resulting from different environments. Despite identical input, output varies significantly.

FIGURE 2–2
Cybernetic system.

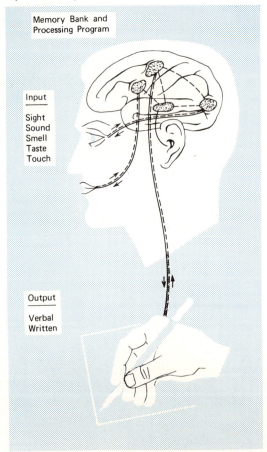

Memory Bank and Processing Program

Input

Sight
Sound
Smell
Taste
Touch

Output

Verbal
Written

The situation is similar in business. Two identical computerized forecasting systems could produce opposite results, depending upon the data banks utilized. On the other hand, rarely are systems designed identically. These two reasons account for the great differences in results of computer use.

The foregoing should have clarified the concept of a system. Any system can be computerized if the processing rules can be defined, even the cybernetic system just described. However, it may not be feasible to computerize the system. Later, we show how to determine when computerization is feasible and also discuss the techniques of computerization, concentrating on business information systems. A system that is converted to the computer is a **computer application.** The next section gives examples of a variety of computer applications.

QUESTION: (True or False) If managers can explain their decision rules, the task of the

manager can be computerized._____

ANSWER: True. However, many of the decision rules are not clear, so we are a long way from being able to transfer the manager's task to the computer.

COMPUTERS IN EDUCATION

Computers are widely used in the educational field, not only for instruction and for administration but for many other activities as well. The versatility of computer use in education is illustrated by the following applications.

COUNSELING

There is only one guidance counselor for every 420 high school students in the United States, according to Stephen M. Raucher, a national consultant to secondary education for IBM. "During their high school years, students spend only four hours with a counselor, and three of those hours will be spent discussing and changing class schedules. This leaves an hour for students to discuss their interests, problems and ambitions, and to plan for any additional education and training needed to reach their goals."

Now available to augment career guidance services for grades 7 through 12 is "Discover," a career guidance system. Using a computer terminal, a student can quickly review data on occupations, colleges, financial aid, military training, and apprenticeship programs. The computer-stored information can be updated and made available for quick reference, allowing counselors to keep up with changes in career fields and education programs.

The Discover system is divided into 12 modules, with the entry module introducing the student to the system and the use of an IBM 3270 display terminal. In addition, the entry module performs the record-keeping functions of the system. The remaining 11 modules fall into three major categories: values and decision-making education, relating and exploring occupations, and career planning.

The system combines the occupational or educational characteristics desired by the student, searches through the appropriate data file, and quickly retrieves the relevant information. Because the system can store vocational information about each student, it can relate personal preferences of the user to data about a given occupation, program, or school.

"With less time spent on searching for information, counselors have more opportunities to discuss problems and alternatives with students," says Mr. Raucher.

INSTRUCTION   Although counseling assistance is a good example of using the computer for the education field, its primary use is in instruction.

Colleges view use of computers not so much as a means to reduce cost but as a means to improve the quality of education. The computer is freeing faculty members to give more individual attention to students. It also allows students to work at their own pace and makes it possible for more students to take courses.

Through **computer-assisted instruction (CAI)** students receive help in such subjects as biology, accounting, chemistry, agricultural economics, home economics, business administration, genetics, logic, German, and teacher education.

Most of the CAI supplements regular classes and textbooks, with the instructors determining the amount of computer teaching. One course, in medical terminology, is taught entirely by computer. This enables the instructor to function more as an educational consultant.

Using faculty-written programs, students are able to engage in a tutorial dialogue at the computer terminal. They receive corrective feedback when they make mistakes and reinforcing feedback when they provide correct answers. The computer stores records of all student interactions with these programs, and, from these, instructional management reports are generated for faculty use. An instructional system is illustrated in Figure 2–3. The student is using a "light pen" to indicate his answer to the problem.

FIGURE 2–3
The IBM data acquisition and control system connects Ohio State University students with a desired course, monitors the network of some 400 listening and viewing stations, and terminates each tape as the last student disconnects. (Courtesy IBM.)

QUESTION: The student's education is improved by the computer system because

ANSWER: they receive immediate response to their work and can move at their own pace.

QUESTION: The instructor's task is improved by the computer system because

ANSWER: instead of repeating lectures, the instructor is giving students individual attention.

Audio input and output systems are now available for all fields of computer application. An example in the education field is a unit to aid elementary school students in spelling. The unit is marketed under the name Speak and Spell® and evaluates spelling that students have keyed in to the unit. It correctly pronounces as well as prints the correct version of misspelled words. It gives visual and verbal praise to the child when words are spelled correctly. It costs less than $50 per unit.

COMPUTERS IN SPORTS

Almost every area of athletics now has some form of computerization. Representative applications are described below, for football, baseball, and track.

FOOTBALL The computer has changed football coaching radically — it has become an indispensable tool. Under the National Football League film exchange system, each team must be provided films of its next opponent's last three games. For years, coaches attempted to handle manually the statistical data compiled from the films. The variety of game situations often left just a day or two between the availability of the last game's film and the deadline for development of the next game's strategy.

Play analysis from the previous Sunday's contest must be ready no later than Tuesday so that a game plan for the coming Sunday is ready by Wednesday for the players.

The situation has improved significantly with the introduction of a new computer, the Datapoint 1500®. The system was developed through a collaboration of three companies: Sports Data, Inc., of Los Angeles, Quanex Management Sciences of Detroit, and Datapoint Corporation of San Antonio. There are 18 NFL teams now using this system, along with Southern California, UCLA, and several other colleges.

Sports Data can furnish more than 300 reports on any team. However, most coaches make a fairly limited selection, requesting only the data they feel is most meaningful. Coaches also request analysis of their own games, to see if they are falling into patterns that opponents can identify and use to their advantage.

Other computer applications print tickets, handle the payroll and control season-ticket sales.

QUESTION: The computer's principal advantage for professional football coaches is capturing large amounts of data about players and game performance and processing

these data quickly enough to _____

ANSWER: allow them to prepare a game plan early in the week.

BASEBALL   Professional baseball has also changed due to the computer. Most of the big league teams get more scouting done for less money by using the Major League Scouting Bureau (MLSB).

Scouts from five regions attend games of high school, college, and minor league teams during their playing seasons. On a standardized report form the scout indicates the player's vital statistics including name, phone number, address, weight, height, and the number of games and innings in which he was observed. Beyond that, the scout evaluates the player's baseball skills in five categories, using a rating system of two through eight (eight being the highest score for the particular skill being measured).

Once scores are entered for hitting ability, throwing accuracy, fielding range, baseball instinct, and other parameters outlining the player's skill, the scout then enters comments on physical characteristics, abilities, and weaknesses and provides a summary. Finally, the scout determines how much money he thinks the player should be paid and what he thinks it might take to sign him.

The report is then sent to MLSB, where it is entered onto a cassette, then into the Honeywell, Inc., Datanetwork service headquartered in Minneapolis. Client teams, using either CRT terminals or teletypes, dial into Honeywell's large-scale three-processor system. They request player profiles by name, position, location, or ranking. Datanetwork's dial-in access and simplified procedures make it easier for nontechnical users to process all this information.

The bureau is run by former major league pitcher Jim Wilson, who employs 60 scouts, most of whom once worked for the teams that now subscribe to the scouting service. Wilson says, "Relying on Honeywell's service allows us to work with the information without installing a complete computer system and then spending a lot of time learning how to use it."

TRACK   U.S. athletes' preparation for the ill-fated 1980 Olympics was assisted by a performance diagnostic system developed by Dr. Gideon Ariel, Amherst, Massachusetts. Founder of Computerized Biomechanical Analysis, Inc., Ariel is credited with helping Mac Wilkins win the 1976 Olympic gold medal in the discus throw and Terry Arbritton set the world record in the shot put.

"Until 1964, talent alone was good enough to win," Ariel said. "Since then, however, sport has become a science, not an art. We have the best scientific know-how in the world, and can provide our coaches with the best training tools. Why not use them?"

Dr. Ariel's system involves taking a high-speed film of an athlete, digitizing those movements into stick figures on a television-like display screen developed by Megatek, and then analyzing the movements with the Data General computer. From the computer readout Ariel is able to suggest ways an athlete can improve. In Wilkins' case, for example, he won the Olympics with a throw of more than 232 feet after working with Ariel. He previously had been throwing the discus less than 220 feet.

In Figure 2–4, Dr. Ariel is analyzing movement patterns of an athlete on his CRT terminal.

QUESTION: The computer enables baseball managers to obtain data about players and reports on comparative analysis of players. In track, the computer enables athletes to improve their efficiency by analyzing their _____ via a CRT terminal.

ANSWER: movements

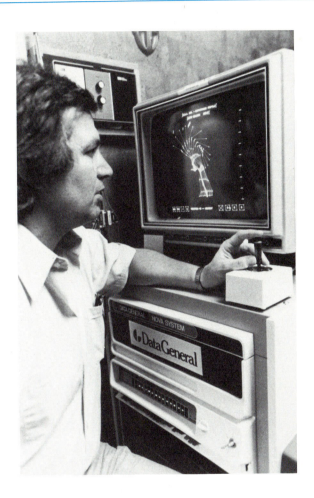

FIGURE 2–4
COMPUTER AIDS ATHLETES—Dr. Gideon Ariel of Amherst, Mass. has developed a computerized system that is being used by the United States Olympic Committee to help train American athletes. Dr. Ariel films an athlete performing in his particular sport, breaks down these movements on individual frames and digitizes them to show stick-like figures on a computer terminal. A Data General computer analyzes these movements to identify the athlete's strengths and weaknesses and provide further information from which Dr. Ariel can suggest how the athlete can improve. (Courtesy Data General.)

COMPUTERS IN GOVERNMENT

Television and newspaper coverage provides the average person with some background of computer uses in the federal government. Much less is known about computer applications in local government.

The Sunnyvale, California, city government system produced a savings of more than a million dollars over a four-year period. This community of 100,000 claims the smallest city staff per 1000 population of the five cities in Santa Clara County.

In addition to the direct cost savings, there are many other benefits, such as improved management information. Detailed financial breakdowns show the status of managers' budgets and pinpoint the effects of their policies. Each manager can do budget planning for several years ahead, within the context of a total city budget projection.

Citizens as well as the managers benefit from budget breakdowns that are clearly developed, both graphically and in tables. These include three years of past data and six years of future projections of each program, both by totals and per unit.

Data are collected from 35 terminals located at such places as police and fire headquarters and the city hall accounting office. The on-line approach permits all files to be updated daily; most files are updated continuously. As data enter the system, several validity checks are performed, and error messages are immediately sent back while source documents are at hand. The general ledger operates on a positive accounting principle; that is, transactions must have valid credit and debit accounts before the computer will accept them. Thus the ledger is always in balance. The total city record is checked several times a day to see that everything is in balance.

The utility billing procedures illustrate some of the benefits of the on-line approach. Sunnyvale bills residents for water, sewage, and garbage collection. An operator uses a terminal in a conversational mode, beginning with an account code indicating whether a payment or a meter reading is being entered. A payment updates the master file immediately. Meter readings enter the master file as "to be billed" indicators for use during a billing run. Billing is on a bimonthly cycle, but a billing run is performed each working day. Historical data for each account are immediately accessible. The last three bills and the last four payments are kept in the master file, for instance. Meter readings are compared against the last month's readings and the prior three-month average, so that abnormal consumption can be checked.

Inquiries can retrieve current financial status of an account, get details on a current or previous bill or payment, or obtain descriptive information on either a customer or a parcel. The inquiry can be by customer number, by account number, or by street address.

A schematic of the Sunnyvale information system is shown in Figure 2-5. The major systems are linked to a pair of DEC 11/70 computers through a communications system. The abbreviation **TDM** on the chart stands for **time division multiplexing.** It means that the communications channel correcting all these devices can be used for multiple transmissions.

QUESTION: Note in Figure 2-5 that the library system is included. By studying patterns of types of books checked out in different areas, the computer recommends locations for mobile libraries and the selection of books at each location. With what other major systems would the library system interact most often? Why?

ANSWER: Accounting/general ledger: keeping track of costs per library and per user; or inventory/purchasing: keeping control of purchases and book inventories.

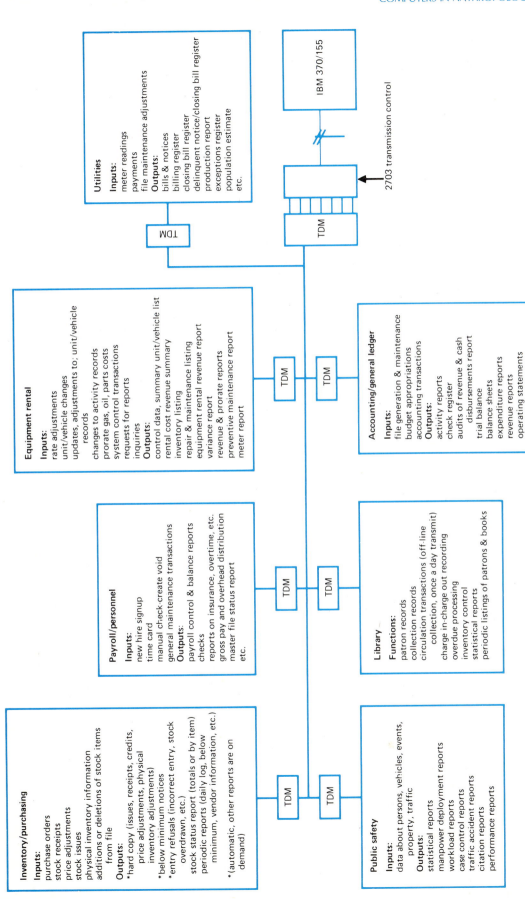

Inventory/purchasing

Inputs:
purchase orders
stock receipts
price adjustments
stock issues
physical inventory information
additions or deletions of stock items
    from file
Outputs:
*hard copy (issues, receipts, credits,
    price adjustments, physical
    inventory adjustments)
*below minimum notices
*entry refusals (incorrect entry, stock
    overdrawn, etc.)
stock status report (totals or by item)
periodic reports (daily log, below
    minimum, vendor information, etc.)
*(automatic, other reports are on
    demand)

Payroll/personnel

Inputs:
new hire signup
time card
manual check-create void
general maintenance transactions
Outputs:
payroll control & balance reports
checks
reports on insurance, overtime, etc.
gross pay and overhead distribution
master file status report
etc.

Equipment rental

Inputs:
rate adjustments
unit/vehicle changes
updates, adjustments to; unit/vehicle
    records
changes to activity records
prorate gas, oil, parts costs
system control transactions
requests for reports
inquiries
Outputs:
control data, summary unit/vehicle list
rental cost revenue summary
inventory listing
repair & maintenance listing
equipment rental revenue report
variance report
revenue & prorate reports
preventive maintenance report
meter report

Utilities

Inputs:
meter readings
payments
file maintenance adjustments
Outputs:
bills & notices
billing register
closing bill register
delinquent notice/closing bill register
production report
exceptions register
population estimate
etc.

Public safety

Inputs:
data about persons, vehicles, events,
    property, traffic
Outputs:
statistical reports
manpower deployment reports
workload reports
case control reports
traffic accident reports
citation reports
performance reports

Library

Functions:
patron records
collection records
circulation transactions (off-line
    collection, once a day transmit)
charge in-charge out recording
overdue processing
inventory control
statistical reports
periodic listings of patrons & books

Accounting/general ledger

Inputs:
file generation & maintenance
budget appropriations
accounting transactions
Outputs:
activity reports
check register
audits of revenue & cash
    disbursements report
trial balance
balance sheets
expenditure reports
revenue reports
operating statements

TDM

IBM 370/155

2703 transmission control

FIGURE 2–5
Local government computer system, Sunnyvale, California.

COMPUTERS IN ANTHROPOLOGY/ ARCHEOLOGY

A 1400-year-old architectural puzzle is being solved with the aid of a computer at the University of South Florida in Tampa. Dr. James F. Strange, who teaches biblical archeology, is working on the reconstruction of a synagogue that was destroyed in Galilee, probably by an earthquake, about 550 A.D. Until recently the synagogue and the surrounding village were buried under layers of soil. Dr. Strange is a member of a team that has been conducting excavations at the site, an Israeli village called Khirbet Shema about 90 miles north of Jerusalem.

No positive clues to the building's construction have been found at the site, so Dr. Strange has been using the computer to help find the answer. With most of the dimensions of the building known, engineering calculations can be made to determine the missing structural parameters. Data will be processed statistically, allowing the researchers to compare various roof styles and explore alternative designs. "From this information, we will be able to mathematically predict what the entire building probably looked like," says Dr. Strange. "Using the computer to produce perspective drawings, we will literally be able to reconstruct the building." (Figure 2–6 illustrates perspective drawings produced by a computer.)

FIGURE 2–6
Computer plot of elevation contours. (Courtesy Disspla.)

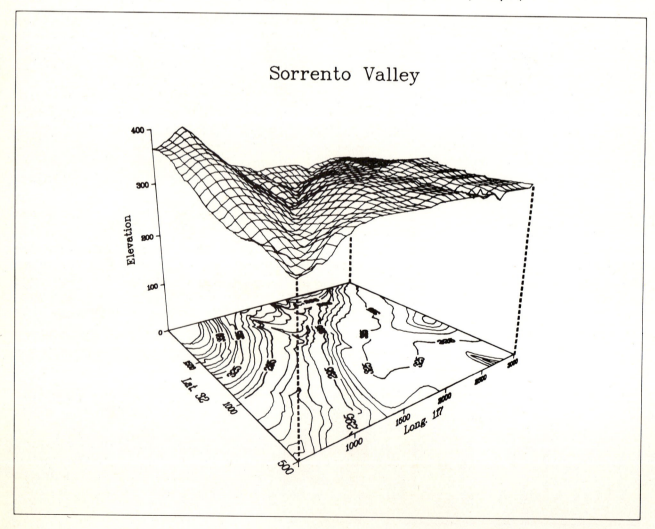

The computer also will play a major role in determining what the social and economic makeup of the village was like. Some 4000 artifacts have been found in the excavations, including worked bone, ceramic and plaster objects, coins, examples of jewelry, and some organic materials. Information about each artifact—its description, and where it was found—is punched into cards and entered into computer storage.

"Using statistical analysis, and comparing data derived from other excavated sites in the area," says Dr. Strange, "the computer is helping us find patterns in the cultural composition of Khirbet Shema. It helps us eliminate alternatives that would take years to explore manually, and it enables us to determine whether our conclusions make sense archaeologically."

QUESTION: Archeology has been a slow, painstaking task. How has the computer enhanced

this activity? _____

_____

ANSWER: By performing analyses to eliminate alternatives previously explored manually.

COMPUTERS IN THE COURTS

As a number of other jurisdictions are doing, Wisconsin's Milwaukee County is using the computer to cut through the paperwork that can hamper the efficient administration of justice, especially in an era of increasing case loads. The county developed an on-line record-keeping system called JUSTIS, an acronym for Justice Information System. It serves the criminal justice agencies of Milwaukee County, including the courts, the clerk of courts, the sheriff's department, and the district attorney's office. More than 170 items of information for every case undergoing criminal justice procedures are entered onto JUSTIS files. These fall into four major categories.

☐ Information regarding the criminal incident or event—time, nature of crime, injuries incurred.

☐ Information on the defendant—detailed identification, aliases, other pending cases, case status.

☐ Information surrounding the case and its progress—the arrest and its circumstances, charges issued, court events or transactions with results (hearings, continuances, and trials), including date, time, action taken, reason for action, party requesting action, disposition, and sentence.

☐ Information on participants—victims and witnesses, police officers and special personnel involved, prosecutors and defense attorneys, judges, court reporters, and clerks.

With the job of filing records concerning more than 35,000 cases that develop each year, Milwaukee County's clerk of courts was one of the first to feel the impact of JUSTIS.

Louis A. Metz III, judicial information systems coordinator for Milwaukee County, says that benefits of the system all derive from one primary aspect of automation—computers are "infinitely well adapted to perform repetitive actions, therefore lending themselves admirably to the recordkeeping process."

He continues:

Entering case data—such as offense, arrest, arraignment, continuance, disposition, and sentencing information—in the court minute record and asking the computer to store it and make use of it in appropriate ways is the type of job for which the computer is well suited.

Concerning the previous manual system, Mr. Metz says:

If we were lucky, we could usually get the data we wanted within an hour, after having searched cross-reference cards and other pointers. Now, with on-line visual display terminals, we can get the same information within seconds. By improving communication between agencies involved in criminal case processing, we cut down on the number of man-hours necessary to keep everyone informed. We also eliminate a lot of duplicate effort when we enter case data that is shared by common-purpose agencies. Shared data is entered into the computer files only once, and it is available to all users thereafter upon inquiry.

In summary, the system indexes people and cases, prepares calendars, and prepares and records subpoenas.

QUESTION: Although record keeping was simplified and cost was reduced, the new computer system also improved the quality of the justice system by providing

_____ the information for every case to the concerned parties.

ANSWER: all

COMPUTERS IN ENERGY CONTROL

The computer has become a major tool in energy control. It is used by industries as a whole or by individual firms, like the Broadmoor Hotel in Colorado Springs, Colorado. The Broadmoor reduced energy consumption 20 percent by installing a computer just to control heat and lighting. Other examples are provided below, for solar energy and oil exploration.

SOLAR ENERGY

With oil supplies rapidly diminishing, a practical alternative to fossil fuels must be found. Sandia Laboratories of Albuquerque, New Mexico, is studying the potential of solar energy and uses an HP-1000® distributed processing network to operate the world's largest solar test facility. During a four-hour test period, Sandia's facility is capable of receiving 5 million watts of solar energy. If converted to electrical power, this would be enough to support a community of 1000 homes. The facility also provides experimental engineering data for the design, construction, and operation of proposed solar thermal electric plants.

The facility covers 10 acres and consists of a tower, a control building, and a field of 222 heliostats (sun-tracking mirrors) (Figure 2–7). A computer network controls these heliostats to concentrate a single beam of solar radiation. Directed to a receiver on the tower, this beam heats up an energy absorber in the receiver to produce useful energy.

Five HP-1000 computers manage the operation, which includes data management, collection, control, analysis, and display. The system has proven so successful that many of its features will be incorporated into a pilot solar plant under construction near Barstow, California.

Dave Darsey, automated control system project leader, states:

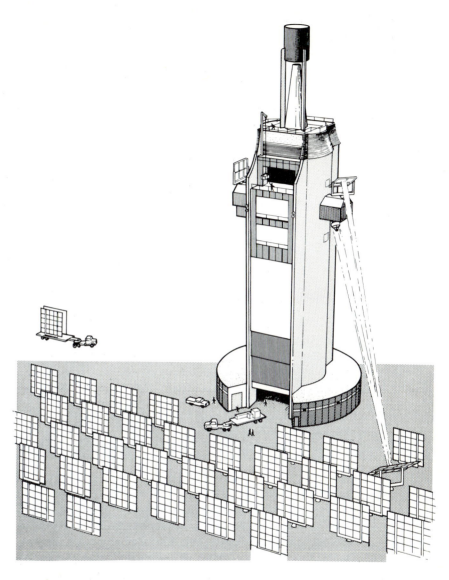

FIGURE 2-7
World's largest solar test facility, controlled by a network of Hewlett-Packard HP-1000 computers.

Though the use of solar energy has many advantages, there are still problems and techniques to be worked out. The HP-1000's excellent networking capabilities, sophisticated control, and data communications make it an excellent tool to assist us in exploring these areas and finding the best solutions.

OIL EXPLORATION   A major oil-exploration company has been achieving dramatic savings with a terminal that accepts verbal input and provides audio output. The company's geophysicists utilize ordinary telephones in cities around the United States to enter data directly located at the company's home-office data center. Faced with complex computer codings, batch-processing problems, and hundreds of geological terms, these scientists now enter complicated well-hole and formulation data into the computer using natural language. The terminal's voice synthesizer literally "talks back" to the caller, verifying words and figures in the geophysicist's scientific terminology.

With a vocabulary of 900 words, the accuracy of the terminal is in excess of 99 percent.

The "hands-off" system, designed by Interstate Electronics Corp., Anaheim, California, is basically a terminal that automatically encodes the spoken information into computer language in whatever format the host computer normally uses. The basic, single-station terminal costs less than $20,000 including software and documentation. In a multistation configuration, the cost is less than $11,000 per station.

Moreover, IBM has a system that can handle sentences seven to nine words in length. The accuracy is 100 percent if the speaker is careful. At present it has only a 250-word vocabulary, which sounds very limited. However, 14 million sentences can be constructed from such a system, according to IBM.

QUESTION: Not only does audio input reduce cost and speed up processing, it improves

accuracy of input because the person can _____

_____

ANSWER: listen to a replay of input to verify words and figures.

COMPUTERS IN BUSINESS

As Figure 2–1 indicated, the number of uses of computers grows so quickly that this growth is difficult to track. A few examples are provided below, to demonstrate the value of computers in vastly different types of business.

RETAIL STORE APPLICATIONS

The adoption of the **Universal Product Code (UPC)** has ushered in a new era for the food industry. The combination of the UPC and scanning systems to read the code provides benefits to the consumer, the supermarket operator, employees, and the food manufacturer.

The UPC code for grocery items consists of a number of 10 digits plus a check digit. The first 5 digits represent the manufacturer and the next 5 digits represent the item. This system is called **source symbol marking.**

In-store labeling devices for variable-measure items such as prepackaged meats and produce are now available. These label makers are electronically interfaced with scales in the back rooms of the supermarkets. While the conventional label is being attached to the top of a package of meat, for example, a scannable symbol will be put on the bottom of the package.

Why is the supermarket operator interested in the installation of automated check stands? The benefits to the store owner fall into two categories. The industry calls these "hard" benefits and "soft" benefits.

Hard benefits are measurable savings generated in the store itself by the installation of scanning systems. Soft savings will be developed over time by the use of the data generated to provide better inventory, merchandising, and management controls.

Hard savings include:

1. Productivity gains at the checkout.
2. Elimination of price marking on individual items.
3. Reduced training of checkers.

4.   Greater accuracy.

5.   Office labor savings in bookkeeping.

The following results have been produced by grocery stores where a Univac system was introduced.

1.   The scan-and-bag procedure was 45 percent faster than the ring-and-bag system.

2.   Checkers made 75 percent fewer mistakes.

3.   New checkers achieved an acceptable level of performance with a minimum of training. There was no measurable learning curve.

Many chain operators believe that the soft benefits will eventually equal or surpass the in-store hard benefits. More accurate and timely item movement data, for example, could change present merchandising concepts. The product selection in specific stores could be more finely tuned to the demographics and shopper preferences in that particular store. A more accurate job of shelf allocation could maximize profits and customer satisfaction.

The consumer will also benefit from the installation of this system. Better merchandising techniques will permit the grocer to be more responsive to the shopper's product needs. Better inventory control at the store will reduce deficiencies in stock, so the customer will be able to find and purchase the product he or she wishes.

Checkout through the front end is faster (see Figure 2–8). In a test at Kroger

FIGURE 2–8
Checkout operations at supermarkets are speeded by an optical scanner within the X-shaped slot that automatically reads Universal Product Code (UPC) symbols on products. The system's minicomputer immediately displays and prints the price and description of the item. The checkout clerk has both hands free to pass items across the slot and bag them in the same motion.

grocery stores, the shopper waiting time at the check stand, presently one of the major consumer complaints, decreased 40 percent.

The more recent versions of the system include **point-of-sale** (POS) devices to replace the cash drawer with a full-service "total teller." This unit handles deposits, account transfers, and utility bill paying, as well as cash dispensing.

Finally, the customer receipt provides the customer with much more information than it previously did. It includes the item price, store department, a taxable indicator, multiple-item purchase, credit type (refund, store coupon, etc.), amount and method of payment (cash, check, etc.), amount of change, and, for each item, either the last five digits of the UPC number for specific positive correlation or an alphabetic descriptor for each item.

The store checkers prefer the automated scanning check stand also. It makes their jobs easier — they have to remember fewer data. This gives them more time to chat with the customer, which both the checker and the customer enjoy. Shopping and checking out become more pleasant experiences for everyone concerned.

QUESTION: "Soft" benefits derived from this system were:

ANSWER: merchandising data, product selection tuned to demographics and shopper preference, shelf allocation improvements.

BANKING Customer service has been increased and costs lowered through expanded use of computers in banking. Three basic types of terminals are used: (1) teller terminals that put remote branch tellers directly in contact with the main computer, (2) audio response units for balance inquiry and credit authorization, and (3) visual information terminals for instant access to data stored in the main computer facility.

The teller terminal system puts tellers directly in touch with computer files. Any service offered a customer at one branch can be made available to that same customer at all locations. The response is instantaneous to inquiries for the most current information.

Employing a blend of on-line and off-line processing, the system performs the following accounting applications: savings (both regular and day-of-deposit to day-of-withdrawal accounts); Christmas, Hanukkah, and vacation clubs; time savings; and lease security. Additionally, the system handles repayment of demand loans; interest saving loans; on-line name and address updates; and on-line money orders and teller's checks.

The bank management information system provides the answer to data collection and reporting problems with an on-line centralized information file capability. The system can accommodate large transaction volumes and insure up-to-date decision-making data. It offers demand deposit accounting, savings accounting, installment loan accounting, commercial loan accounting, certificate-of-deposit accounting, mortgage loans, and general ledger financial management.

QUESTION: Examine the banking terminal shown in Figure 2–9. At the time she enters the savings account deposit, the teller is sending data to another banking system called **total deposit accounting.** With information on deposits, loan officers

know the availability of bank funds for _____ to customers.

ANSWER: loans

FIGURE 2-9
This teller terminal can be used for updating passbook savings accounts on line
to a computer, and for various off-line work. (Courtesy Honeywell.)

SUMMARY   Almost every profession uses computers today. The variety of computer applications is growing in each profession as well. Therefore, the person who acquires an understanding of computers during college is better prepared to move ahead in his or her profession.

The authors are frequently asked by students in the first course in data processing, "Can computers think?" The response is, "If you can define the process by which you think, it can be computerized." Any system can be computerized if the processing rules can be defined. And, because technology improvements are reducing the cost of computing so fast, many activities previously uneconomical for computers now are feasible. Already the computer affects each of us in a variety of ways. Only a few applications were described to show the impact of computers on specific and varied activities. The widespread growth of computer applications will expand that impact. We need to become knowledgeable about computers to better prepare us both for living and for earning a living in an increasingly computer-oriented world.

CHAPTER EXAMINATION

1. The purpose of this chapter is to discuss how knowledge of the computer better prepares a person for _____

2. The preceding descriptions touched only a few of the categories of computer applications in business. Look back at Figure 2–1 and identify the specific fields that were illustrated.

Application	Specific Field
a. National data bank	Example: Government (federal)
b. Sandia system	
c. Sunnyvale, California, system	
d. UPC system	
e. "Discover" system	
f. MLSB system	
g. JUSTIS system	
h. Teller terminal system	
i. Dr. Ariel's system	
j. Dr. Strange's system	

3. Classify the following applications.

	Science/ Engineering	Business	Humanities
a. Steel industry			
b. Advertising			
c. Banking			

d. Ecology   _____   _____   _____

e. Publishing   _____   _____   _____

f. Photography   _____   _____   _____

g. Art design   _____   _____   _____

h. Music composition   _____   _____   _____

i. Blood count analysis   _____   _____   _____

j. Garbage truck scheduling   _____   _____   _____

4. Distinguish business from scientific applications. _____

5. Several items listed under scientific applications in Figure 2–1 might be just as easily listed as business applications. Identify two.

a. _____

b. _____

6. Define hardware. _____

7. Define software. _____

8. Explain Jordain's analogy distinguishing hardware from software. _____

9. A system consists of _____

10. What is a cybernetic system? _____

11. Apply the three possible responses to accelerating computer technology in Table 1–1 to the situation of the manager of a grocery store, confronted with competitors like Kroger with its new computer system.

    a. Capitulation: _____

_____

_____

_____

    b. Coping: _____

_____

_____

_____

_____

    c. Contributing: _____

_____

_____

_____

12. Apply the same process to the situation of the checkout clerk presently working in a store that decides to adopt the Kroger system.

    a. Capitulation: _____

_____

_____

_____

    b. Coping: _____

_____

_____

_____

    c. Contributing: _____

_____

_____

_____

13. Draw a diagram of the JUSTIS system of Milwaukee County, Wisconsin similar to Figure 2-5, which was developed to illustrate the Sunnyvale, California, city government system.

14. Draw a diagram similar to Figure 2-5 for the Kroger system.

15. Analyze the university CAI system and describe how a similar system might be set up for a course using this book.

_____

_____

_____

_____

_____

_____

_____

_____

16. Use a library reference, or talk to a local practitioner, to describe how the computer is presently being used in your major field. If you've not selected a major, use the accounting field.

_____

_____

_____

_____

_____

_____

_____

_____

_____

_____

17. Find out how the computer is being used to aid the administrative (not the educational) process in your college. List the applications and give a one-sentence description of each.

a. _____

_____

_____

_____

b. _____

_____

_____

_____

c. _____

_____

_____

_____

d. _____

_____

_____

_____

18. Can computers think? _____ Explain. _____

_____

_____

_____

19. Find out how the computer is being used in your city government. On a separate sheet of paper, prepare a schematic similar to the one used for Sunnyvale (Figure 2–5). Identify computer applications with an asterisk; manual applications with a dot.

20. A system is comprised of input, processing, and output. Describe what is input, what is processing, and what is output for the following systems illustrated in the chapter.

System	Input	Processing	Output
CAI	_____	_____	_____
	_____	_____	_____
	_____	_____	_____
Kroger	_____	_____	_____
	_____	_____	_____
	_____	_____	_____

3

INTRODUCTION TO COMPUTERS

OVERVIEW. To be an effective computer user, you must understand the basic computer functions and operations. As a business manager or staff person, you will need this knowledge to communicate effectively with data processing specialists. If you wish to become a computer specialist—system designer, programmer, or data processing manager—you will need to acquire additional knowledge and experience. This chapter presents an introduction to computers, how they work, and how they are used in business.

The type of computer used in business applications is an electronic digital computer. This type of computer processes digital data, such as numbers and letters. Another type of computer (used almost exclusively for scientific and engineering applications) is an analog computer, which measures continuous electrical or physical magnitudes. Digital computers are especially suited to business applications because of their accuracy, high speed, and large internal storage capacity.

Digital computers range in size from small microcomputers costing a few hundred dollars to giant supercomputers costing several million dollars. All of these computers perform the same basic functions—data input, storage, control, processing, and output. The computer performs these functions by automatically executing a set of instructions called a program that has been written by a programmer (or other computer user) and stored in computer memory.

EARLY COMPUTING DEVICES

As soon as commerce developed in early societies, people recognized the need to calculate and to keep track of information. They soon devised simple computing devices and bookkeeping systems to enable them to add, subtract, and record simple transactions. However, many centuries elapsed before technology was sufficiently advanced to develop mechanical calculators.

Four of the important calculating devices that preceded the modern computer are shown in Figure 3–1 and described below.

The **abacus** was one of the earliest computing devices; it appeared both in ancient Egypt and in China. An abacus consists of rows of beads strung on wires set in a rectangular frame (see Figure 3–1a). The beads are used to represent "place values" such as units, tens, hundreds, and so on. The abacus may be used to add, subtract, multiply, and divide. In the hands of a competent operator,

FIGURE 3-1
Early calculating devices. (*a*) Abacus. (*b*) Pascal's calculator. (*c*) Babbage's difference engine. (*d*) Hollerith's tabulating machine.

this ancient device can still compete favorably in speed with a pocket or desk calculator.

The first mechanical **adding machine** was developed in 1642 by French philosopher and scientist Blaise Pascal. Pascal's adding machine used gears with teeth to represent numbers. Some 50 years later, German mathematician Gottfried Liebnitz introduced the first mechanical **calculating machine.** This device could multiply and divide as well as add and subtract numbers.

An important forerunner of the modern computer was the **difference engine,** devised by Charles Babbage in the early 1800s. Babbage was professor of mathematics at Cambridge University. The important contribution of Babbage's remarkable difference engine was its ability to perform computations and print results without human intervention. The difference engine was used to automatically compute and print out mathematical tables that were accurate to five significant digits.

Babbage also conceived (but never built) an **analytical engine,** which was to have a memory unit, a "mill" or arithmetic unit to perform computations, and a punched card input system. The analytical engine was far too advanced for its time, and the necessary parts could not be manufactured for it. Babbage's work was essentially forgotten for nearly a century, but his concept of a machine with a stored program anticipated the modern computer.

In the 1880s, Dr. Herman Hollerith developed a punched card **tabulating machine** (see Figure 3–1*d*) to process U.S. census data. This device reduced the time required to process the 1890 census from about $7\frac{1}{2}$ years to $2\frac{1}{2}$ years. Hollerith founded the Tabulating Machine Company in 1896 to manufacture and market punched card equipment. Several years later this company was merged with 12 others to form International Business Machines Corporation (IBM).

TYPES OF COMPUTERS

The Latin word **computare** means "to compute." Therefore, any device that helps one compute — such as a slide rule, adding machine, or pocket electronic calculator — might technically be called a computer. However, in today's world the word "computer" is almost always used (and is used in this text) to refer to a stored-program electronic digital computer.

The features that distinguish an electronic computer from other computing devices are speed, internal memory, and automatic execution of a program stored in computer memory. The speed of an electronic computer is achieved by the use of electronic circuitry. Other devices such as electric desk calculators depend on electrical and mechanical components, which severely limit the speed of operation.

The internal memory of an electronic computer is used to store both data and instructions. A sequence of instructions (including input, processing, and output), is carried out automatically, without human intervention. In contrast, a device such as a desk calculator requires human direction (by means of a keyboard) at each step in a computational routine.

The more expensive pocket electronic calculators have a memory and can accept and store a program. Are these devices tiny digital computers? According to the commonly accepted definition, a programmable calculator is not a true computer. Although it can accept and store a program, a calculator does not have memory for data storage (only special-purpose areas called "registers" are available). Also, a programmable calculator cannot automatically "read" data from an input device (data is entered a step at a time by an operator). The smallest true computers today are the microcomputers or "personal" computers offered by electronics and hobby shops. In the future we may expect to see true hand-held computers with data memory and the ability to input data automatically from miniature input devices.

QUESTION: A programmable pocket-size electronic calculator today (is, is not) a true digital computer.

ANSWER: is not

There are two basic types of computers: analog computers and digital computers. Analog computers **measure** (electrical or physical magnitudes), while digital computers **count.** Therefore, analog computers are not appropriate for business applications. They are described briefly below because of their importance in other applications.

ANALOG COMPUTERS An automobile gasoline-level measuring system is a simple analog computing device. It is an electromechanical device that measures the level of gasoline in a tank, converts the measurement to an electrical signal, and displays the level on a dashboard gauge.

In a similar manner, an electronic analog computer uses electrical components and circuits to measure electrical or physical quantities. The advantage of an analog computer is that it can easily be used to model or analyze a dynamic process such as a chemical reaction or an electrical flow. The advantage of modeling on an analog computer is that we can find simple and inexpensive solutions to dynamic problems in the laboratory before going into the real world.

DIGITAL COMPUTERS An analog computer operates on data that vary continuously, such as voltage, pressure, and temperature. In contrast, a **digital computer** is basically a counting device that operates on discrete data or numbers. Since most business data are in discrete form (either numerical or alphabetical), the digital computer is readily adaptable to business data processing applications.

QUESTION: _____ computers operate on discrete or numerical data, while

_____ computers operate on continuous or measurable data.

ANSWER: Digital, analog

A **hybrid computer** is a combination analog and digital computer. Hybrid computers are used in research and in some applications such as process control.

GENERATIONS OF COMPUTERS

Modern electronic computers were first developed during the 1940s. The earliest models were essentially one-of-a-kind machines that, although experimental in nature, were used for practical applications. The more important of these early computers were the following.

MARK I—Developed by Howard Aiken at Harvard University (1937 to 1944). A very large electromechanical calculator that operated according to a program punched on paper tape, resembling a player-piano roll. After a century had elapsed, Babbage's dream of an automatic digital computer was finally realized with the completion of the MARK I computer.

ENIAC (Electronic Numerical Integrator and Calculator)—Developed by Eckert and Mauchly at the University of Pennsylvania (1943 to 1946). This was the first all-electronic calculator (electronic tubes were used instead of relays). The ENIAC did not use an internally stored program—programs were wired on boards similar to a telephone switchboard. However, the ENIAC is often mentioned as the first electronic digital computer.

EDVAC, EDSAC (Electronic Delay Storage Automatic Computer)—These were the first true electronic computers with internally stored programs. The EDVAC was developed at the University of Pennsylvania, the EDSAC at Cambridge, England (1949).

The first commercially available computer was the UNIVAC I, produced by the UNIVAC division of Remington Rand (later Sperry–Rand Corporation). Although slow by today's standards, the UNIVAC I had self-checking circuitry and a high-performance magnetic tape system for input and output of data. The first UNIVAC I was delivered to the Bureau of the Census in 1951, where it was used for tabulating census data. The first computer used for business data processing was a UNIVAC I delivered to General Electric at its Louisville plant in 1954.

Further, IBM installed its first commercial computer, an IBM 650, in 1954. However, IBM's dominant position in the data processing industry began with the introduction of its 1401 computer in the 1960s. This was followed by the popular 370 series of computers, introduced during the late 1960s.

The first commercially available computers (such as the UNIVAC I and IBM 650) were referred to as *first-generation computers*. Subsequent improvements in technology led to second, third, and fourth generation computers. The major characteristics that distinguish the various generations are the following.

☐ Dominant type of electronic circuit elements used.

☐ Major secondary storage media used.

☐ Computer languages used.

☐ Type or characteristic of operating system used.

☐ Memory access time (time to store or retrieve a word of data from memory).

The characteristics that appeared in each generation are summarized in Table 3–1 and described below.

First-generation computers used vacuum tubes as the principal electronic components. Memory access times were expressed in **milliseconds** (a millisecond is one thousandth of a second). Punched cards were the primary medium used to store data files and input data to the computer. Computer languages were primitive, consisting of machine language in the earliest computers, followed by assembly language (computer languages are described in Chapter 10). Computer operating systems were also primitive, and jobs were processed sequentially under manual control of the computer operator.

First-generation computers demonstrated the usefulness of computers in data processing applications. However, they had a number of disadvantages: they were expensive, relatively slow and unreliable, and required extensive

TABLE 3–1 SUMMARY OF FOUR COMPUTER GENERATIONS

Generation	Circuit elements	Secondary storage media	Languages	Operating system	Typical access time
First	Vacuum tubes	Punched cards	Machine and assembly	Operator-controlled	1 millisecond
Second	Discrete transistors	Magnetic tape	COBOL, FORTRAN, assembly	Batch	10 microseconds
Third	Integrated circuits	Magnetic disk	Structured languages	Interactive (time-sharing)	100 nanoseconds
Fourth	VLSI	Mass storage hierarchy	Applications-oriented	Virtual	1 nanosecond

air conditioning to dissipate the heat generated by a large number of vacuum tubes.

Second-generation computers (introduced in 1959 to 1960) replaced vacuum tubes with discrete solid-state devices, principally transistors. Transistors offered three important advantages over vacuum tubes: smaller size, reduced power requirements and heat generation, and greater reliability. While vacuum tubes become less reliable with age, transistors tend to remain as reliable after a period of usage as when they were first installed. With transistors, memory access times were expressed in **microseconds** (millionths of seconds). Ten microseconds was a typical memory access time, an improvement of a factor of 100 over first-generation memories.

Magnetic tape was the dominant form of secondary storage. This medium permitted much greater storage capacity and faster data input rates than punched cards. High-level languages such as COBOL and FORTRAN were introduced during this period. Batch operating systems were used that permitted rapid processing of magnetic tape files.

Third-generation computers were introduced about 1965. In these computers, discrete electronic components such as transistors were replaced with **integrated circuits.** With integrated circuits, thousands of transistors are fabricated on the surface of a silicon chip less than one-tenth the size of a postage stamp. Until about 1970 these integrated circuit (or IC) chips were used mostly to replace discrete transistors in computer logic circuits. After 1970, the IC chips were also used to replace magnetic core memories that had been used in computers since the late 1950s. In early third-generation computers (until about 1970) fewer than 1000 circuits were integrated on a single circuit chip. This technology was referred to as **small-scale integration** (SSI). During the1970s, up to 65,000 components were combined on a single chip; this technology was referred to as **large-scale integration** (or LSI).

With IC circuits, third generation computers were smaller, faster, and more reliable than earlier computers. Access times in these computers are measured in **nanoseconds** — billionths of a second. Typical memory access time in third-generation computers was 100 nanoseconds — an improvement by another factor of 100 over second generation.

Other significant improvements were made in third-generation computers. Magnetic disk storage became popular and provided direct access to very large data files. Structured programming languages were introduced that improved programming productivity. With the shift to magnetic disk files, interactive operating systems were introduced that allowed individual users to access their data files.

Fourth-generation computers were first introduced during the late 1970s and continue to be introduced today. The main distinction of these computers is the introduction of **very large scale integration,** or VLSI. With this technology, circuit densities approaching 100,000 components per chip and more are being used. Access time in fourth-generation computers is approaching one nanosecond — another 100-fold improvement from the previous generation. A variety of mass storage devices (described in Chapter 5) is being introduced for the storage of programs and data bases. New user-oriented and applications-oriented languages are being introduced. Virtual operating systems are used that permit many users to share the use of the computer while simplifying the programming task.

Fifth-generation computers are now being developed and will probably be introduced beginning about the mid-1980s. With these computers, new techniques for fabricating integrated circuit chips such as electron beams and X rays will be used, and circuit densities may increase by a factor of 100 over today's chips. Also, new memory devices such as tunnel junctions that operate at temperatures near absolute zero are expected to be introduced. These memories will operate at speeds from 10 to 100 times faster than today's memories. Access times will be expressed in **picoseconds** — trillionths of a second.

A summary of the circuit elements, memory devices, and access times for the generations of computers is shown in Figure 3-2.

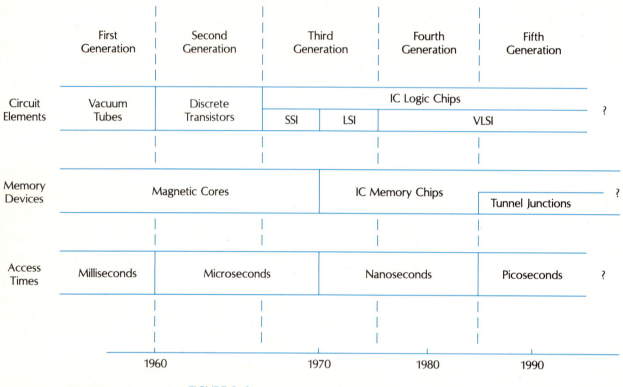

FIGURE 3-2
Summary of computer generations.

1. Refer to Figure 3-2. Summarize the four generations of computers by filling in the following table.

Computer generation	Circuit elements	Memory devices	Access times
First	——————	——————	——————
Second	——————	——————	——————
Third	——————	——————	——————
Fourth	——————	——————	——————

2. Name two advances in computer technology that are likely to be introduced in the fifth generation of computers.

a. _____

b. _____

THE MICROELECTRONIC REVOLUTION

In the past 20 years the speed at which calculations can be performed has increased by over 1 million times. During the same period, the cost of computation has fallen dramatically. Microcomputers available today for less than $1000 have nearly the capabilities of machines that cost several million dollars 15 years ago. By 1985, a medium-scale computer may cost less than $100 and may fit in a shoe box or even in one's pocket.

This rapid increase in our ability to process information is being referred to as a *second industrial revolution*. The advances in computer technology have far outstripped those of nearly every other field. For example, it is sometimes stated that, if the automobile industry had been able to advance its technology as rapidly as the computer industry, a Rolls Royce today would cost $2.50 and would get 2 million miles per gallon!

The revolution in computer technology has been made possible largely by the remarkable advances in fabricating microelectronic circuits. The electronics industry has learned to fabricate tens of thousands of circuit elements on a silicon chip less than one-quarter of an inch on a side. In fact, the number of electronic components on an integrated circuit chip has doubled nearly every year since 1960. At the same time, the cost of these circuits has been declining.

In this section we will present a brief introduction to microelectronic components and how they are made.

SEMICONDUCTORS   Integrated circuit (or IC) chips are made up of tens of thousands of tiny devices called semiconductors. A **semiconductor** is an electronic device that is normally not in a conducting state. However, when a small voltage is applied to a semiconductor device, it readily conducts electricity.

By far the most important type of semiconductor device on an IC chip is the **transistor.** The property of transistors that makes them important in microelectronics is their capacity for gain, or amplification; that is, a transistor can readily transform a low-power signal into a high-power signal. Previously, this function was performed by vacuum tubes, which were bulky, expensive, and consumed large amounts of power.

Semiconductor devices (such as transistors) are made by introducing controlled quantities of impurity atoms into a pure silicon crystal. This process is called *doping*. Silicon doped with phosphorus results in what is called an *n*-type semiconductor, since excess negative electrical charges (or electrons) are introduced. Doping with a substance such as boron gives rise to a *p*-type semiconductor, with excess positive charges.

A transistor is made by alternating *p*-type and *n*-type regions in the silicon base. For example, Figure 3–3 shows a simple transistor with a *p*-type region sandwiched between two *n*-type regions. One of the *n*-type areas is called the **emitter** and the other the **collector.** The *p*-type area is called the **base.**

This transistor can be made to function in the following way. If the voltage applied to the base is zero (or negative), no current flows from the emitter to the collector. If a small positive voltage is applied to the base, a large current flows from the emitter to the collector. The "gain" is the ratio of the collector current to the base current and is commonly as high as 100. Thus the transistor can function both as a **switch** (to turn current on or off) and as an **amplifier** (to amplify a low-power signal).

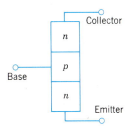

FIGURE 3–3
Simple transistor.

QUESTION: Examine Figure 3–3. To switch the current off, a voltage of _____ is

applied to the _____ When the voltage applied to the base is positive, the current flow at the collector is (greater than, less than) that at the base.

ANSWER: zero, base, greater than

HOW IC CHIPS ARE MADE   In today's integrated circuit chips, over 100,000 tiny transistors and other semiconductor devices are commonly fabricated on a single chip less than one-fourth of an inch on a side. These chips are fabricated in "clean room" environments since a single particle of dust can cause a defect that will result in a circuit malfunction. Special clothing is worn by the human operators and the air is continuously filtered and recirculated to keep the dust level at a minimum.

The basic steps in fabricating an IC chip are illustrated in Figure 3–4 and described below.

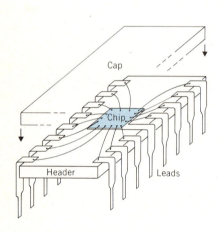

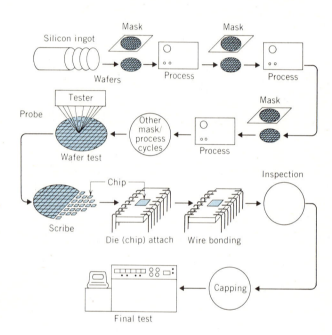

FIGURE 3–4
How IC chips are made (Source: Monte Phister, Jr., *Data Processing Technology & Economics,* 2nd Ed., Digital Press, Bedford, Mass.)

1. The microcircuit is designed with the aid of a computer. Typically the circuit design is displayed on a cathode ray tube and the designer can alter the design by typing in commands or redrawing with a "light pen"—a photoelectric device that allows persons to trace designs on a display screen.

2. From the circuit design stored in computer memory, a pattern or **photomask** is generated on a plate. Several such masks are required for each IC chip, one for each layer of the circuit.

3. A cylinder-shaped ingot of silicon (containing the desired dopant or impurity atoms) is withdrawn from a crucible of pure molten silicon.

4. Thin wafers of silicon are sliced from the ingot using a diamond-edged circular saw. Each wafer is polished, inspected, and heated in a furnace to oxidize its surface. The wafer is then coated with a thin film of a light-sensitive material called **photoresist.**

5. The coated wafer is then exposed to ultraviolet light through the photomask. This process, called **photolithography,** transfers the im-

age of the circuit to the wafer. The wafer is then washed in a developer solution and immersed in an acid solution to etch the circuit pattern on the wafer surface. This process is repeated for a succession of several masks as the circuit is formed.

6. The wafer is then scored and broken into individual chips, called **dice.** Several hundred IC chips are commonly formed on the surface of each silicon wafer.

7. In the final steps, the dice are assembled into "packages" and tested.

QUESTION: The process of forming circuit patterns on the surface of silicon wafers is referred to as _____. The circuit patterns are formed on a plate called a _____

ANSWER: photolithography, photomask.

Electron beams and X rays are also used (instead of ultraviolet light) in the lithographic process.

COMPUTER FUNCTIONS AND ORGANIZATION

In this section we will describe the major functional components or units of a computer. To understand the purpose of each of these units, you must know what operations a computer must perform in order to solve a problem.

Suppose that you wish to compute the arithmetic mean of two numbers. To accomplish this task manually, you might perform the following steps.

1. Write the two numbers on a sheet of paper.
2. Add the two numbers together to obtain their sum.
3. Divide the sum by two to obtain the mean of the numbers.
4. Record the answer or communicate it to someone else.

Now let us speculate how a computer might accomplish the task, without any outside assistance or intervention during the calculations. First, there are three steps that would have to be performed by a human being.

1. A set of instructions would have to be prepared to direct the computer to perform each step in the calculation. Such a set of instructions is called a **program.** The program must be prepared in a language or form that the computer can understand.

2. The two numbers would have to be prepared or made available in a form suitable for entry into the computer. (For example, they might be punched into cards or entered on a terminal keyboard.)

3. The person would have to specify where and in what form the output or results are to appear.

To solve a problem on the computer, it is necessary to create a computer program, prepare the input data, and specify the output format. These three steps are described in detail in later chapters.

Now let us suppose that a program has been prepared to compute the arithmetic mean of two numbers and that this program has been stored in the computer. The program will direct the computer to perform the following steps.

1. Read the two numbers into the computer.
2. Compute the sum of the numbers.
3. Divide the sum by 2.
4. Write or display the result.

A diagram showing these steps — called a *flowchart* — is shown in Figure 3-5. The flowchart consists of a series of blocks, each of which represents a step in the problem-solving process. Shown alongside each block is a computer instruction to perform that step, written in a language called BASIC described later in this text. You will learn to flowchart and write programs in later chapters.

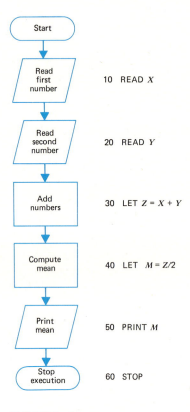

Start	
Read first number	10 READ X
Read second number	20 READ Y
Add numbers	30 LET $Z = X + Y$
Compute mean	40 LET $M = Z/2$
Print mean	50 PRINT M
Stop execution	60 STOP

FIGURE 3-5
Flowchart and program for averaging two numbers.

QUESTION: Examine Figure 3-5. Suppose the first number (X) has the value 100, while the second number has the value 80. The result that should be printed out for the result (M) is _____

ANSWER: 90.

From this simple program, you can see that the computer must be able to **read** or **input** data, and it must be able to **write** or **output** results. It must have a

memory to store program instructions as well as the data that are being processed. Since the computer is directed by a program, it must have a unit that interprets the program instructions and supervises their execution. These functions are supervised by a **control unit.** Finally, the computer requires a unit that can perform additions, divisions, and other arithmetic operations. This unit is called the **arithmetic/logical unit,** since it can also perform logical operations such as comparing the magnitude of two numbers.

The relationships among the various functional units of a computer are shown in Figure 3–6. The flow of data is shown by solid lines, while the dashed lines show the flow of control information. It is important to understand that all computers, regardless of size or complexity — from microcomputers to supercomputers — have the functional components shown in Figure 3–6.

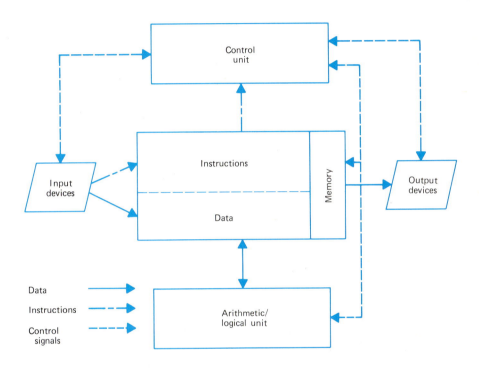

FIGURE 3–6
Functional components of a computer.

EXERCISE 3–2   Examine Figures 3–5 and 3–6 and answer the following questions.

1. Computing an arithmetic mean is carried out by instructions stored in _____ The various operations are coordinated by the _____ unit.

2. The instruction READ X causes a number to be read from an _____ device into _____

3. To compute the total of two numbers using the instruction LET

$Z = X + Y$, data are transferred from _____ to the _____ unit.

4. The arithmetic mean is computed in the _____ unit using the instruction $M = Z/2$. The result (M) is then stored in _____.

5. The result M is then displayed for the user using the instruction PRINT M, which causes M to be transferred from _____ to an _____ device.

CENTRAL PROCESSING UNIT

In Figure 3–6, the computer control unit and arithmetic/logical unit are shown as two physically separate devices. Although they perform different logical functions, these devices are actually integrated into a single physical unit called the **central processing unit.** The central processing unit (or **CPU**) is the "brain" or nerve center of a computer. It controls the operation of the computer (through the control unit) and performs arithmetic and logical operations (through the arithmetic/logical unit).

CONTROL UNIT

The control unit supervises all operations of the computer, under the direction of a stored program. First, the control unit determines which instruction is to be executed next by the computer. The control unit then fetches this instruction from main memory and interprets the instruction. The instruction is then executed by the other computer units, under the direction of the control unit.

ARITHMETIC/LOGICAL UNIT (ALU)

The arithmetic/logical unit of the CPU performs arithmetic operations, as directed by the control unit. For example, the program in Figure 3–5 causes two numbers (X and Y) to be added together. This addition is carried out in the computer ALU. Also, the division of this result by 2 to compute the mean is performed within the arithmetic/logical unit.

The arithmetic/logical unit also performs logical operations. A typical logical operation involves comparing two numbers, then selecting one of three program paths depending on the result of the comparison. For example, suppose that you wish to extend the program in Figure 3–5 to compute and print out the mean of 10 numbers. You would need to insert a logical step to determine whether 10 numbers had been read into the computer. In a program flowchart, a logical operation is represented by a diamond (see Figure 3–7). In this figure, a variable (N) is used to count the numbers as they are read. After each number is read, N is incremented and compared to 10. If N is less than 10, the program branches to read another number. If N equals 10, the arithmetic mean is computed and printed.

Acting in harmony with the control unit, the arithmetic/logical unit can test the two numbers (the variable N and the constant 10) and cause the computer to branch to one of two possible program paths. This ability to **test** (or compare) two numbers and to **branch** to one of several paths depending on the result of the comparison gives the computer great power and flexibility. It is a major reason for the usefulness of digital computers in many different applications.

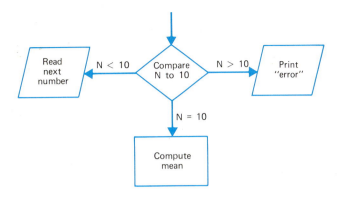

FIGURE 3–7
Example of logical operation.

QUESTION: If you wished to print out a different set of information for employees who are age 55 or older than for employees who are age 54 or under, you would use

the computer's ability to ＿＿＿＿＿ and ＿＿＿＿＿

ANSWER: test (or compare), branch

The basic building block of a computer central processing unit is the integrated circuit **logic chip.** A typical logic chip is about one tenth of an inch on a side and contains a number of logic circuits. Logic circuits consist of switching devices that carry out fundamental computer operations such as interpreting instructions and performing arithmetic operations.

Logic chips are mounted onto larger units called **logic boards.** An example of a logic board is shown in Figure 3–8. This board measures about six inches by eight inches and contains over 100 integrated circuit chips.

FIGURE 3–8
CPU logic board. (Courtesy Computer Automation.)

Depending on its size, a computer central processing unit may contain a number of logic boards such as the one shown in Figure 3–8. For example, the CRAY-1 supercomputer (pictured later in this chapter) contains over 1000 logic boards in its central processing unit. On the other hand, a small minicomputer may contain only one (or at most a few) logic boards. Regardless of the number of logic boards, a computer CPU is almost always contained in a single physical cabinet.

QUESTION: A computer CPU normally consists of a number of logic _____. On

each logic board are mounted many integrated circuit logic _____.

These chips contain the necessary logic _____ to carry out the functions of the CPU.

ANSWER: boards, chips, circuits

MICROPROCESSORS   Large-scale integration of electronic circuits has resulted in a continuing increase in the number of logic circuits that can be placed on a single chip. This has made possible the development of tiny central processing units contained on a single semiconductor chip. In other words, instead of a logic board with many chips such as the one shown in Figure 3–8, the CPU is contained on a single chip. These miniature CPUs are called **microprocessors.**

An example of a microprocessor is shown in Figure 3–9. This unit contains a miniature central processing unit and memory and (except for an input/output section) is truly a tiny general-purpose computer on a single chip. The chip is about the size of the first three letters of the word ENIAC. Yet this tiny computer can perform calculations many times faster than could the ENIAC, which weighed about 30 tons and occupied 1500 square feet of floor space.

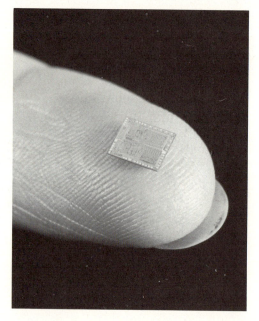

FIGURE 3–9
Microprocessor chip. (Courtesy Intel.)

Microprocessors like the one shown in Figure 3–9 are creating a revolution in consumer and industrial products.

Some typical applications are the following.

Hand-held calculators.

Television games.

Automobiles (carburetion, ignition).

Appliances (radar ranges, ovens).

Traffic lights (optimum traffic flow).

Medical instruments (measuring blood pressure).

Intelligent computer terminals.

MAIN MEMORY   Thus far we have described the computer central processing unit, or CPU. Referring to Figure 3-6, you will recall that a computer must also have a memory for storage of data and instructions. Data and instructions are stored in areas called **locations;** each location in main memory has an **address** so that data can be located. The capacity of main memory depends on the size of the computer. A microcomputer would have several thousand locations, while a large-scale computer may have several million locations in its memory.

Actually, in most computers memory is divided into several levels or sections. For example, there is often a division between **random access memory** (or RAM) and **read-only memory** (or ROM). In addition, main memory is often supplemented by low-cost **secondary storage** devices such as magnetic disks. Devices used for main memory and secondary storage are described in detail in Chapter 5.

The basic building block of computer main memory is the integrated circuit **memory chip.** Each such chip contains thousands of tiny transistors that function as switches in representing the binary digits zero and one. A typical memory chip is shown in Figure 3-10. This chip has a capacity of storing about 64,000 "bits" (or binary digits) equivalent to about 8000 characters of information.

FIGURE 3-10
Integrated circuit memory chip. (Courtesy IBM.)

MICROCOMPUTERS   As you have seen, there are two basic building blocks for the electronic components of modern computers: logic chips and memory chips. With continuing advances in microelectronics, you may wonder whether both logic circuits and memory circuits can be combined on a single semiconductor chip. In fact, the microprocessor chip shown in Figure 3–9 contains both logic circuits and memory circuits. A **microcomputer** is a miniature computer contained on a single semiconductor chip.

Bell Labs has developed a microcomputer (called the MAC-4) that will be used to bring "intelligence" to telephones and telephone switchboards. The MAC-4 incorporates a central processor, memory, and input-output circuitry on a single chip less than one-tenth the size of a postage stamp. Unlike a microprocessor, which requires additional chips for memory storage, the microcomputer is self-contained on a single silicon chip. Along with the CPU, the chip includes enough memory to store operating instructions as well as to provide for added features such as self-diagnosis when equipment malfunctions.

QUESTION: The main difference between a microprocessor and a microcomputer is that, in addition to a CPU, a microcomputer includes _____ on the same semiconductor chip.

ANSWER: memory

COMPUTERS USED IN BUSINESS

Until about 1970 the high cost of computers restricted their use to relatively large firms — say those with annual sales of $25 million or more. With the advent of minicomputers and small business computers, much smaller firms (for example, with annual sales of $5 million or less) could often justify owning their own computers. Today, with business microcomputers costing only a few thousand dollars, even much smaller firms can afford a computer.

This section describes the various types of computers and computing devices that are commonly used in business applications today. These range from microcomputers (or "personal computers") to supercomputers, as shown in Figure 3–11. Microcomputers and minicomputers are used in so many different applications that they are described in detail in Chapter 7.

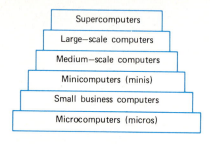

FIGURE 3–11
Computers used in business applications.

MICROCOMPUTERS

Microcomputers (or **micros**) represent perhaps the fastest growing segment of the computer industry. As you would expect, many of these computers are used as "personal" computers — in homes, hobby applications, and so on. However, what is surprising is how rapidly microcomputers are being adopted for business applications. For example, in the first two years after introduction, Radio Shack sold over 100,000 of its TRS-80 micros. A substantial percentage of these computers is being used for billing, accounts receivable, payroll, and other business applications in small businesses.

A microcomputer is a tiny computer whose central processing unit is contained on a single IC chip. For business (and similar) applications, micros are generally packaged in a console with a keyboard and display. They are also usually equipped with printers and with "floppy disks" for storage of data files. Each floppy disk can store up to several hundred thousand characters of information (these devices are described in detail in Chapter 5).

The TRS-80 Model II microcomputer for business applications is shown in Figure 3–12. Notice the keyboard, display, printer, and slots for inserting floppy disks. Application programs are available for this computer for accounting applications such as accounts receivable, inventory, and general ledger. A microcomputer like the one shown is suitable for small businesses such as retail stores, small construction firms, and small accounting and brokerage firms.

FIGURE 3–12
Business microcomputer. (Courtesy Radio Shack.)

There is an explosion of firms manufacturing microcomputers and related products and services. Among the more important of these are Apple Computer, Computer Devices, Cromemco, Digital Equipment, Heath, North Star, Ohio Scientific, and Radio Shack (Division of Tandy Corporation).

SMALL BUSINESS COMPUTERS
These computers are designed for business applications in smaller companies. Small business computers range in power between microcomputers and minicomputers. There are two basic types of small business computers.

1. Micros and minis that have been configured and supplied with software (such as application programs and data base management systems) for business applications.
2. Scaled-down versions of larger computers made by "mainframe" manufacturers such as IBM, Burroughs, and others.

An example of a small business computer is the IBM System/38, shown in Figure 3–13. This computer uses 64K-bit memory technology and has many

FIGURE 3-13
Small business computer. (Courtesy IBM.)

functions of the operating system "built in" in the form of microcode (these concepts are described in later chapters).

Important manufacturers of small business computers include Basic Four, Burroughs, Datapoint, Hewlett-Packard, Honeywell, IBM, Microdata, NCR, and Univac.

MINICOMPUTERS

Minicomputers (or **minis**) are general-purpose computers whose central processing units are contained on a single logic board, or at most, a few boards. Compared to micros, minis are larger and more powerful. They can be used with a wider variety of input-output devices and contain more memory and storage capacity. Also, while micros can often process only one user problem at a time, minis can generally process two or more problems at the same time. However, today's micros are so powerful it is often difficult in practice to distinguish between micros and smaller minis.

Minis are used in a wide variety of applications in business, engineering, communications, and so on (typical applications are described in Chapter 7). For business applications, minis are "configured" with displays, line printers, and mass storage devices such as the magnetic disk. A typical minicomputer configuration is shown in Figure 3-14.

The mini in Figure 3-14 is manufactured by Data General Corporation. Other important mini makers include Digital Equipment Corporation, Hewlett-Packard, Honeywell, IBM, Perkin-Elmer, Prime, Texas Instruments, and Univac.

MEDIUM-SCALE COMPUTERS

Medium-scale computers provide greater storage capacity and a wider range of input/output devices than small business computers. Also, these systems provide greater capacity for communicating with remote terminals. These computers are often used by intermediate-size organizations and by divisions of large corporations.

FIGURE 3-14
Minicomputer. (Courtesy Data General.)

FIGURE 3-15
Medium-scale computer. (Courtesy NCR.)

An example of a medium-scale computer (NCR 8500) is shown in Figure 3-15. The operator console is shown at the center, central processing unit in the back (cabinet labeled "8500"), magnetic disk drives to the left, line printers to left of CPU, and magnetic tape drives to the right of the picture.

Important manufacturers of medium-scale computers include Burroughs, Digital Equipment Corporation, Honeywell, IBM, NCR, and Univac.

LARGE-SCALE COMPUTERS

Large-scale computers are used primarily by large corporations and government organizations and by computer service organizations such as service bureaus. Such systems provide very large storage capacity: several million characters of main memory and vast quantities of mass storage. Also, large systems can accommodate a large number and variety of peripheral units—magnetic tape, optical readers, displays, and communications terminals.

An example of a large-scale computer (Honeywell DPS 8) is shown in Figure 3–16. Other important manufacturers of large-scale computers are Amdahl, Burroughs, Control Data, IBM, NCR, and Univac.

FIGURE 3–16
Large-scale computer. (Courtesy Honeywell.)

SUPERCOMPUTERS

A few organizations require extraordinary amounts of computing power. These include the U.S. Weather Service, certain scientific laboratories, airline reservation systems, and large time-sharing networks. In these organizations, vast amounts of information must be processed in a short time to provide fast response to users. For example, centralized airline reservation systems must process reservation and ticketing information from a host of locations throughout the country.

These relatively few organizations rely on **supercomputers,** the largest, fastest, and most expensive computers available. These computers can store several million characters of data in main memory and have computing speeds several times faster than other large-scale computers. The cost of a supercomputer may exceed $5 million.

An example of a supercomputer is the CRAY-1, shown in Figure 3–17. This computer has over 1000 logic circuit boards and a total memory capacity of up to 5 megabytes (5 million characters). Memory access time for the CRAY-1 is 12.5 nanoseconds.

SUMMARY

In this chapter you have studied the basic components of all computers. These are the following.

1. Input/output devices for reading data into the computer and producing output.

FIGURE 3-17
Supercomputer. (Courtesy Cray Research.)

2. A control unit that supervises all activities of the computer by interpreting a stored program.

3. An arithmetic/logical unit that performs all calculations and carries out logical operations specified in the program.

4. A main memory that contains program instructions and data to be processed by the program.

Computing devices used in business applications range from microcomputers to giant supercomputers. In fact, tiny microcomputers no larger than a pencil eraser are becoming common in business applications, especially as components of other devices such as terminals and printers. These devices are revolutionizing the operation of automobiles and household devices as well as industrial products.

In the next four chapters you will study the concepts and devices introduced in this chapter in greater detail.

ANSWERS TO EXERCISES

EXERCISE 3-1

1.

Computer Generation	Circuit Elements	Memory Devices	Access Times
First	Vacuum tubes	Magnetic cores	Milliseconds
Second	Discrete transistors	Magnetic cores	Microseconds
Third	IC logic chips	IC memory chips	Nanoseconds
Fourth	IC logic chips	IC memory chips	Nanoseconds

2. a. Higher-density IC chips made possible by new fabrication techniques (electron beams, X rays).
    b. Introduction of tunnel junction memory devices.

EXERCISE 3-2

1. memory, control   2. input, memory   3. memory, arithmetic/logical
4. arithmetic/logical, memory   5. memory, output

CHAPTER EXAMINATION

1. Match each of the following terms with the most appropriate definition.

   ____ Analog   a. Performs arithmetic operations and comparisons.

   ____ Digital   b. Operation in which computer selects one of two paths.

   ____ Transistor   c. Computer-on-a-chip.

   ____ Branch   d. Performs both analog and digital operations.

   ____ Microcomputer   e. Functions as switch or amplifier.

   ____ ENIAC   f. Computer that processes measurable data.

   ____ Hybrid   g. Ancient computing device.

   ____ Control unit   h. Computer that processes numerical data.

   ____ Arithmetic/logic unit   i. First all-electronic calculator.

   ____ Abacus   j. Supervises computer operations.

2. Briefly describe the four major functional units or sections of a digital computer.

   a. _____

   b. _____

   c. _____

   d. _____

3. What is a microprocessor? How is it used?

   _____

   _____

   _____

   _____

4. Describe the three major functions of the central processing unit.

   a. _____

   b. _____

   c. _____

5. You are asked to comment on whether a computer can make decisions. How would you reply?

   _____

   _____

6. Briefly list seven major steps in fabricating semiconductor chips.

   a. _____

   b. _____

   c. _____

   d. _____

   e. _____

   f. _____

   g. _____

7. Briefly define each of the following terms.

   a. Semiconductor _____

   _____

   b. Transistor _____

   _____

   c. Doping _____

   _____

   d. Clean room _____

   _____

8. Mark each of the following statements true or false.

   ____ a.   Hybrid computers are widely used in business information systems.

   ____ b.   The basic processing functions in a small digital computer are different from those in a large computer.

_____ c.   Although under development, a computer on a single chip is several years from reality.

_____ d.   Small business computers often use minicomputer central processing units.

_____ e.   If a pocket electronic calculator is designed to accept a small stored program, it might properly be termed a computer.

_____ f.   There are clear distinctions between small-, medium-, and large-scale computer systems.

_____ g.   Most business computers are special-purpose digital computers.

_____ h.   The term "computer" is generally used to refer to a general-purpose electronic digital computer.

9. List and briefly describe four early computing devices.

a. _____
    _____

b. _____
    _____

c. _____
    _____

d. _____
    _____

10. What is the flowchart symbol for a logic operation? How many paths can normally be taken from such a logic block?

    _____
    _____

11. What are the principal characteristics of four generations of computers?

a. First generation _____
    _____

b. Second generation _____
    _____

c. Third generation _____
    _____

d. Fourth generation _____

12. List and briefly describe three pre-first-generation computers.

    a. _____

    _____

    b. _____

    _____

    c. _____

    _____

13. How do analog, digital, and hybrid computers differ?

    _____

    _____

    _____

    _____

14. What new features will be found in fifth-generation computers? _____

    _____

    _____

15. List five future applications of microprocessors.

    a. _____

    b. _____

    c. _____

    d. _____

    e. _____

16. What is a supercomputer? What type of organization might use one? _____

    _____

    _____

    _____

17. List five vendors of each of the following types of computers.

    a. Microcomputers _____

    _____

    b. Small business computers _____

    _____

    c. Minicomputers _____

    _____

    d. Medium-scale computers _____

    _____

    e. Large-scale computers _____

    _____

18. Distinguish between each of the following.

    a. Small-scale versus large-scale integration _____

    _____

    _____

    b. Microprocessors versus microcomputers _____

    _____

    _____

    c. *n*-type versus *p*-type regions _____

    _____

    _____

    d. Logic chips versus memory chips _____

    _____

19. Name five types of peripheral devices (input/output and storage) commonly used with computers.

    a. _____

    b. _____

    c. _____

d. _____

e. _____

20. Describe briefly how a transistor works. _____

_____

_____

21. What is the difference between minicomputers and small business computers? _____

_____

_____

22. In the past 20 years the speed at which calculations can be performed has increased by a factor of at least one

_____ times. It is expected that by 1985 a medium-scale computer may cost less than _____
dollars.

23. Why are transistors the most important type of semiconductors used in computers? _____

_____

_____

_____

24. The revolution in computer technology can be attributed largely to advances in what factor? _____

_____

25. The CPU contains two major units: a _____ unit and an _____ unit.

PART TWO

COMPUTING CONCEPTS AND HARDWARE

Ten years ago many schools used the "black box" approach to teaching computer subjects. The approach was to treat the computer as a black box whose contents were unimportant. Importance was placed on the output of the box. Students were told that "there will be specialists in your firm to worry about what is in the black box; managers do not need to concern themselves with that level of detail."

When these students became managers, they had little ability to evaluate what computers could or could not do. Their predicament is well illustrated by the following cartoon.

DUNAGIN'S PEOPLE

"IT SAYS IT DOESN'T KNOW."

(Reprinted by permission of Field Newspaper Syndicate.)

Few schools use the black box teaching approach today, for two reasons:

1. Managers want to evaluate the process by which their information is produced—to ensure the validity of output.

2. Managers want to be assured that the cost of producing their output is reasonable.

To achieve these two goals, managers are taking positive steps to understand the internal operations of computers. Schools of management are following suit. Let us examine the reasons in more detail.

Speaking to reason number two, Hillel Segel, president of the Association of Computer Users, recently reported, "We find vast differences between machinery that's similar in cost and similarly configured. I'm not talking about differences of 10 or 20 percent. I'm talking about differences of 20 to one in time taken to run certain programs."

Although the cost per calculation is declining significantly, the total cost of computer use in a company typically increases at a rate of 10 to 15 percent annually. The reason is the expansion in computer use. Twenty years ago, the accounting department was the only department using computers. Ten years ago it was being used in most production departments as well. Today, the marketing and personnel departments are also heavy users of computers. That is a horizontal expansion—across departments. A vertical expansion has also occurred. Twenty years ago computers were used mostly for nonsupervisory tasks, such as payroll preparation. Ten years ago, production departments began using it for inventory control. Now it is also used by managers, at all levels. Not only are managers receiving regular reports on all activities of the firm, many are interacting directly with the computer through terminals. The computer is becoming an integral part of the decision-making function for many managers.

Now that computer cost is a significant item in the company budget, managers want to make certain that those costs are properly controlled. To properly control these operations, they must better understand how computers work and how applications are developed.

Also, now that computers are being used as an integral part of the managerial process, the effect of a system error is substantial. Managers want to reduce the risk of errors occurring. If they understand how systems are developed and processed, they can be involved in the development of their systems to be assured that errors are minimized. Section Two covers computing concepts and hardware and helps prepare you for becoming one of these computer-knowledgeable managers.

CONTENTS OF PART TWO

Chapter 4 explains how data is represented internally in the computer. The decimal numbering system used by humans must be translated into a numbering system that is appropriate for machine processing. Not all computer manufacturers use the same internal numbering system. The chapter explains and compares the more important methods for representing data internally for each major computer type.

Storage concepts and devices are explained in Chapter 5. A large variety of devices are available for storing data in computer-acceptable form. Some are inexpensive but slow. Others are quite fast but expensive. Companies typically use several types of storage devices, since some systems require immediate response whereas others are processed each evening, or perhaps weekly or monthly. The differences in storage devices are analyzed.

Chapter 6 covers input and output (I/O) devices. Like storage devices, I/O devices vary greatly in speed and capability. The typical company uses a variety of both input and output devices. I/O devices appropriate for various computer applications are discussed.

Microcomputers and minicomputers are discussed in Chapter 7. Many of today's micros are capable of performing functions previously handled by more expensive minicomputers. The capabilities are compared for these two types of computers. A special category of microcomputers is the personal computer. They are given this title because of their use by individuals like you and me in hobby types of applications (such as games) as well as home-related applications (such as checkbook accounting). The capabilities of personal computers are accelerating rapidly compared to cost. Within a short time you will be able to afford your own personal computers, one for home and one for work. The one at work will communicate with the large, central system of the firm. The means through which this communication occurs is the subject of Chapter 8. Data communications covers a vast range of communication approaches—via telephone lines, microwave units, and space satellites.

Chapter 9 covers the special concepts of data processing—for capturing, classifying, sorting, and calculating. Approaches to organizing data into files and data bases are described and evaluated.

Upon completion of Part Two you will have a good foundation for use of the computer—for deciding what type you want for your personal use as well as for assisting in the selection of a computer for your professional activities.

4

REPRESENTING DATA IN THE COMPUTER

OVERVIEW. As you read this page, you are storing information in your memory for later recall. The human brain is a marvelous, complex organism. It requires only about 100 cubic inches of space and uses only a small amount of energy. Yet, the human memory has the capacity of storing billions of "bits" or elementary pieces of information. Further, humans can associate and recall this information in complex and creative ways.

A computer also has a "brain," usually called memory **(the term "storage" is also frequently used). The size of computer memory ranges from a few dozen characters in a simple electronic calculator to several million characters in a larger computer. Computer memory is used for storing data and for storing instructions that are used to manipulate that data.**

The human brain can accept a wide variety of information from the various senses. Digital computers are much more limited in the information they can accept. Every computer has a character set—**the set of characters that the computer can recognize and store in its memory. A simple pocket electronic calculator can only accept and store the digits 0 through 9 plus decimal point and minus sign. However, in data processing applications a computer must be able to accept and process** alphanumeric data—**combinations of numbers, upper- and lowercase letters, and special characters such as commas, periods, and parentheses. Most computers can recognize and store over 100 distinct characters; some can accept over 200 different characters.**

Computer storage today consists of a vast number of elementary electronic semiconductor devices. Each semiconductor device can be in one of two possible states, **similar to a wall switch that is either "on" or "off." These states are used to represent two symbols, the digits 0 and 1. The digits 0 and 1 are called** binary digits, **or** bits. **A binary digit is the smallest unit of information that can be recognized by the computer.**

How can a computer, which recognizes only the symbols 0 and 1, store and manipulate over 200 different characters?

This is accomplished by a coding scheme in which each character (such as a number or letter) is represented by a particular combination of binary digits. For example, in some computers the letter A is represented by the bit combination 1100 0001. For most computers used in data processing each character is represented by a combination of either seven or eight bits.

When a number or letter (or other character) is read into the computer, the computer system converts this character into the correct internal binary code. The same process is repeated in reverse when a character is output from the computer. As a result, you can use a computer without understanding its internal data representation. Nevertheless, this understanding is important if you wish to appreciate fully the capabilities and limitations of a computer. It is especially important in comparing computers, since different internal coding systems are used in different computers. These coding systems affect the performance, ease of use, and capacity of computers.

REPRESENTING NUMBERS IN A COMPUTER

Suppose that when using an electronic calculator you depress any key, say the "7" key, and enter this number into the machine. Obviously the calculator somehow represents and "stores" the number 7. Numbers are represented in machines by the **states** (or positions) of mechanical or electronic devices.

Most of you are familiar with an odometer, which shows the total mileage accumulated on an automobile. In this mechanical device, a series of adjacent wheels is used to represent decimal numbers (see Figure 4–1). Each wheel has ten spaces (numbered 0 through 9) on the rim. The rotational position of the wheel is used to represent a particular number. Adjacent wheels are used to represent the units position, tens position, hundreds position, and so on. The wheels are connected so that when the units wheel turns past 9 it moves the tens wheel one position, and so on.

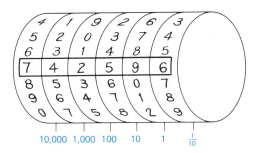

10,000 1,000 100 10 1 $\frac{1}{10}$

FIGURE 4–1
Ten-state device (automobile odometer).

QUESTION: Each wheel in Figure 4–1 can assume _____ different states or positions, corresponding to the _____ number system. The mileage represented by the wheels shown in the figure is _____ .

ANSWER: ten, decimal, 74259.6

In contrast to an odometer, whose wheels are ten-state devices, the storage elements in an electronic computer are two-state electronic devices. Two-state memory devices are used in computers because they operate very rapidly, are highly reliable, and require a minimum amount of space and energy. For example, a common form of computer memory before 1970 consisted of ferrite cores, which are magnetized by applying an electric current. The polarity (or state) of each core is in one of two directions, depending on the direction of the magnetizing current. Thus, the core is similar to a switch that is in either the "on" or "off" position (see Figure 4-2). The speed of modern computers is largely due to the speed with which such switching operations are performed.

 (a)   (b)

FIGURE 4-2
Two-state device (magnetic core). (*a*) (binary 1). (*b*) (binary 0).

As shown in Figure 4-2, each magnetic core has two possible states and therefore can be used to represent the digit 0 ("off" state) or 1 ("on" state). These two digits, **binary digits** or **bits,** are the basis for the binary number system used in all digital computers.

QUESTION: The device shown in Figure 4-2 can represent _____ different states,

corresponding to the _____ number system.

ANSWER: two, binary

In today's computers, magnetic core memory has been replaced by semiconductor memory. A **semiconductor memory chip** is a storage device that uses thousands of tiny memory cells integrated on a silicon chip measuring about one-eighth inch on a side. For example, the memory chip shown in Figure 4-3 is capable of storing over 65,000 binary digits (or bits) of information.

Each miniature memory cell is made up of a circuit that contains two main components: a capacitor and a transistor. A **capacitor** is an electronic component that is capable of holding an electrical charge. As shown in Figure 4-4, the presence of a charge on a capacitor is used to represent a binary 1, while the absence of a charge represents a binary 0. Thus the capacitor functions as a two-state device, much like a magnetic core.

The **transistor** in each memory cell functions as a tiny switch. When the switch is "on" the computer can sense whether there is a charge (binary 1) or no charge (binary 0) in the memory cell. The charge is placed in the memory cell by a computer "write" operation; this process is described in Chapter 5. Semiconductor memories have replaced magnetic core memories because they are faster, cheaper, and much more compact.

FIGURE 4-3
Semiconductor memory chip. (Courtesy IBM.)

FIGURE 4-4
Semiconductor memory cell. (*a*) No charge (binary 0). (*b*) Charge (binary 1).

QUESTION: In the early 1970s, the basic storage element in most electronic computers was

a magnetic _____ In 1980, computers use _____

memory where the basic storage element is a tiny _____

ANSWER: core, semiconductor, capacitor

NUMBER SYSTEMS To understand how numbers (and other data) are represented in a computer, it is necessary to understand the binary number system. A brief review of the decimal number system will aid in understanding other systems.

Suppose that an individual weighs 165 pounds. This individual's weight could be represented by one 100-pound weight, six 10-pound weights, and five 1-pound weights (see Figure 4-5).

Each of the weights in Figure 4-5 is referred to as a **place value.** Notice that each place value in the decimal number system has a magnitude equal to a power of 10. A decimal number is then expressed as a sum of digits multiplied by corresponding place values. For example, the number 165 really means the following.

$$165 = (1 \times 10^2) + (6 \times 10^1) + (5 \times 10^0)$$

The decimal number system is derived from the Latin "decem," meaning "ten," which is the **base** of the system. There are ten values in the decimal

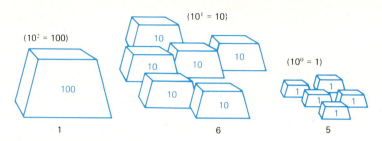

FIGURE 4–5
Representing a decimal number.

system, represented by the digits 0 through 9. Any number can be written as a sum of these digits multiplied by powers of 10, as in the above example.

BINARY NUMBER SYSTEM   In contrast to the decimal number system, the binary number system has base 2. Thus, there are two digits in the binary system, represented by the binary digits 0 and 1. A binary number therefore consists of a string of 0s and 1s, for example 101011. The term "bit" is often used as an abbreviation of binary digit.

QUESTION: The number 10201 (could, could not) be a binary number.

ANSWER: Could not, since only the binary digits (bits) 0 and 1 are used in the binary number system.

A binary number may be interpreted as a set of weights, except that each weight (or place value) is a power of 2. For example, the binary number 1011 is represented in Figure 4–6.

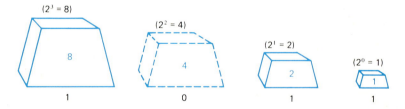

FIGURE 4–6
Representing a binary number.

QUESTION: Suppose that another weight were placed to the left of the eight-pound weight

in Figure 4–6. What would be its weight? _____

ANSWER: 16 (obtained from 2^4)

The decimal equivalent of the binary number 1011 may be found by adding the weights used in Figure 4–6. Since one 8-pound weight, one 2-pound weight, and one 1-pound weight were used, the decimal equivalent is $8 + 2 + 1$ or 11. This computation may also be shown as follows.

$$1011 = 1 \times 2^3 + 0 \times 2^2 + 1 \times 2^1 + 1 \times 2^0$$
$$= 8 + 0 + 2 + 1$$
$$= 11 \text{ (decimal)}$$

A decimal number may be represented in the computer by using two-state devices (such as semiconductors) to represent its binary equivalent. For example, the equivalent of the decimal number 37 is the binary number 100101. This number may be represented by six devices, as shown in Figure 4–7.

Device	●	○	○	●	○	●	Code
Positional value	2^5 (32)	2^4 (16)	2^3 (8)	2^2 (4)	2^1 (2)	2^0 (1)	● device "on" (1 bit) ○ device "off" (0 bit)

FIGURE 4–7
Representing a decimal number with two-state devices.

QUESTION: What is the largest decimal number that may be represented by the six devices shown in Figure 4–7?

ANSWER: 63 (all devices "on")

Sometimes it is necessary to convert a decimal number to its binary equivalent. This may be accomplished by successive divisions by 2, recording the remainder from each division. As shown in Figure 4–8, applying this procedure to the decimal number 37 yields the binary equivalent 100101.

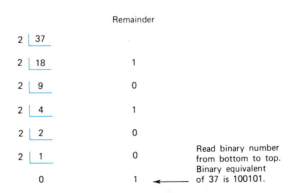

FIGURE 4–8
Converting a decimal number to binary by successive division by 2.

QUESTION: In the above example, the number 37 is first divided by 2. The quotient is _____ and the remainder is _____. Next, the number 18 is divided by two; the quotient is _____ , with the remainder

_____

ANSWER: 18, 1; 9, 0

EXERCISE 4-1   1.   An individual weighs 165 pounds. Convert his weight to a binary number, using the procedure shown in Figure 4-8.

_____

2.   Check your answer in problem 1 by converting the binary number back to decimal (use a system of weights, as shown in Figure 4-6). _____

3.   What decimal number is represented by the following two-state devices?

○   ○   ○   ○   ●   ○   ●   ●

A shaded circle represents the 1 bit; an empty circle the 0 bit. _____

HEXADECIMAL NUMBER SYSTEM   The hexadecimal number system is of importance in many of today's computers.

The hexadecimal number system has base 16 (hexa stands for 6, decimal for 10; 6 + 10 = 16). Therefore, there are 16 values in the system, ranging from 0 to 15. The first 10 of these values are represented by the digits 0 through 9, as for the decimal system. The last six values have been assigned the letters A through F. The decimal equivalents of these letters are: A = 10, B = 11, C = 12, D = 13, E = 14, and F = 15.

The place values in the hexadecimal number system are powers of 16. To convert a hexadecimal number to its decimal equivalent, it is only necessary to multiply by powers of 16 and then add. For example, suppose that you wish to convert hexadecimal A5 to decimal. First note that A stands for the decimal value 10.

$A5 = 10 \times 16^1 + 5 \times 16^0$
$= 160 + 5$
$= 165 \text{ (decimal)}$

Therefore, an individual who weighs 165 pounds may be said to weigh A5 pounds in hexadecimal notation (a good method of concealing weight!).

The hexadecimal and binary number systems are closely related, since 16 (the base of the hexadecimal system) is equal to 2^4. As a result, any four-digit binary number can be expressed as a single hexadecimal digit. Table 4-1 shows the relationship between the hexadecimal, decimal, and four-digit binary numbers.

QUESTION: Examine Table 4-1. The decimal equivalent of hexadecimal D is _____

The equivalent four-digit binary number is_____

ANSWER: 13,1101

TABLE 4-1   RELATIONSHIP AMONG HEXADECIMAL, DECIMAL, AND BINARY NUMBERS

Hexadecimal Numbers	Decimal Equivalent	Binary Equivalent
0	0	0000
1	1	0001
2	2	0010
3	3	0011
4	4	0100
5	5	0101
6	6	0110
7	7	0111
8	8	1000
9	9	1001
A	10	1010
B	11	1011
C	12	1100
D	13	1101
E	14	1110
F	15	1111

The hexadecimal system is used primarily as a shorthand notation for binary numbers. Table 4-1 shows that any group of four binary digits can be replaced by a hexadecimal number. To use hexadecimal as a shorthand for binary, the procedure is to mark off groups of four binary digits, starting at the right-most position, and write down the hexadecimal equivalents. Following is an example for the binary number 10101110.

Binary	1010	1110
Hexadecimal	A	E

Therefore, hexadecimal AE is equivalent to binary 10101110. In some computers, the contents of memory positions are printed out or displayed in the form of hexadecimal numbers.

EXERCISE 4-2   1.   Convert hexadecimal B7C to decimal. _____

2.   Express the following binary numbers in hexadecimal notation.

a.   10010011_____

b.   11011001_____

c.   11111111_____

COMPUTER DATA CODES

You now have been introduced to the means by which numbers are stored and represented in a computer. Decimal numbers—familiar to humans—may be represented in straight binary form in a computer. For example, the number 165 may be represented in the computer as the binary number 10100101. This number in turn can be represented by the shorthand hexadecimal number A5.

This leaves an important question unanswered—how is nonnumeric data represented in a computer? In addition to numeric data, a computer must be able to process alphabetic characters, perhaps lowercase as well as uppercase. Also, the computer must be able to accept special characters such as the following: $, \, (). A combination of any of these three types (numeric, alphabetic, special) is referred to as **alphanumeric characters.** Following are some examples of expressions using alphanumeric characters.

1185 Baker St. Apt. 2
January 25, 1983
DC-10

Each alphanumeric character is represented in a computer by a specific combination of binary digits; that is, an internal **code** is used to represent these characters. Before we examine internal computer codes, it will be helpful to you to understand how characters are coded on a punched card before being read into a computer.

HOLLERITH CODE   Numbers, letters, and a variety of special characters are encoded on punched cards using a code called the **Hollerith code.** The punched card that is most commonly used is laid out in 12 horizontal rows and 80 vertical columns (see Figure 4-9). The top three rows (12, 11, and 0) are called "zone rows," or simply "zones." Rows 0 through 9 are called "numeric rows" (note that row 0 may be either a zone or numeric row).

Any numeric digit 0 through 9 is encoded in a card column by punching a hole in the corresponding row. For example, the digit 3 is represented by a punch in the 3-row; all other rows in the selected column (including zone rows) are left blank.

An alphabetic character is encoded in a particular column as a combination of one zone punch plus one numeric punch. For example, referring to Figure 4-9, the letter K is encoded as the combination of two punches: 11-zone and numeric row 2.

Special characters are represented by unique combinations of zone and numeric punches. For example, the dollar sign ($) in Figure 4-9 is represented by three punches: 11-zone, and numeric rows 3 and 8.

QUESTION: Examine Figure 4-9 and record the punching combinations for each of the following.

a.   letter W _____

b.   percent (%) _____

ANSWER: a.   0-zone, numeric 6
b.   0-zone, numeric 4 and 8

Not all of the special characters in the Hollerith code are shown in Figure 4-9. Among the commonly used characters not included in the figure are parentheses (left and right), equals sign, and plus sign.

The holes in a punched card might be thought of as representing binary

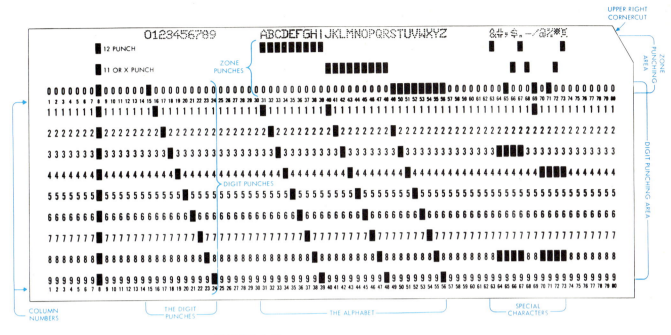

FIGURE 4-9
Hollerith code.

digits; a punch represents a 1-bit; no punch a 0-bit. The Hollerith code could theoretically be used in a computer, so that Hollerith characters on punched cards would be stored using the same bit combinations in the computer. However, to represent each character in computer memory by a 12-bit code would waste storage. Therefore, input data in Hollerith code are automatically converted to one of several possible internal codes before they are stored in the computer. These internal codes are generally referred to by some variation of the term "binary coded decimal." However, the term "binary coded character" would be more descriptive since the codes are used for alphabetic and special characters as well as numeric data.

THE 4-BIT BCD   The 4-bit **binary coded decimal** (BCD) is one of the earliest computer codes. With this code, a group of four binary digits is used to encode each digit of a decimal number. For example, suppose the decimal number 437 is to be represented in a computer using 4-bit BCD. Each digit of this number (4, 3, and 7) is represented by its 4-bit binary equivalent, as follows.

4	3	7	Decimal number
0100	0011	0111	4-bit BCD code

It is important that you understand the difference between straight binary representation of a number and its BCD equivalent. A comparison of the decimal number 437 represented in straight binary and in 4-bit BCD is shown below.

110110101	Binary representation	decimal 437
0100 0011 0111	4-bit BCD representation	

Notice that the binary representation of this number requires 9 bit positions, whereas the 4-bit BCD representation requires 12 bit positions. Since a computer can represent numbers and perform arithmetic using the straight binary notation, why is the BCD representation necessary for numeric data? The answer is that each type of representation has advantages and disadvantages.

1. In addition to requiring fewer bit positions, straight binary representation affords faster arithmetic calculations. However, it introduces the possibility of *rounding errors* where some accuracy is lost in performing these calculations.
2. Since the BCD code keeps track of each decimal digit (including fractions), it eliminates the possibility of rounding errors at the expense of slower arithmetic calculations and increased bit positions.

Since accuracy is important in data processing applications, most business-oriented computers use (or include) some form of BCD representation for numerical data. Some computers permit either straight binary or BCD representation of numerical data, at the option of the user.

The major disadvantage of the 4-bit BCD code is that, since only four bits are used to represent each character, only 2^4 or 16 distinct characters can be represented. After the ten decimal digits 0 through 9, this leaves room for only six additional characters. A few special characters (zero, comma, period, minus, etc.) could — and sometimes are — represented using the 4-bit BCD code. However, the alphabetic characters cannot be represented using this code. As a result, the 4-bit code has very limited usefulness in computers for data processing applications. Instead, an extended BCD code is used in most computers today.

THE 6-BIT BCD CODE   In this coding system two additional bits (called the **zone** bits) are added to the four numeric bits. With six bits to represent each character, a total of 2^6 or 64 characters can be represented. Thus the 6-bit BCD system can be used to encode the 10 decimal digits, 26 alphabetic characters, and up to 28 special characters.

The zone bit positions in this code (called positions A and B) are used in much the same way as the zones on punched cards. To represent numeric data, the zone bits are set to 0. Decimal numbers 0 through 9 are then represented by combinations of four binary digits (as for the 4-bit BCD code). For example, the numbers 3 and 9 are represented in 6-bit BCD as follows.

Bit positions						Decimal number
B	A	8	4	2	1	
0	0	0	0	1	1	3
0	0	1	0	0	1	9

Alphabetical and special characters are represented in 6-bit BCD by combinations of zone and numeric bits. For example, the letters A and R and the special character "$" are coded as shown in Figure 4–10.

QUESTION: Examine Figure 4–10. Can you guess the 6-bit BCD code for the letter

B? _____

ANSWER: 110010. The zone bits are the same as for the letter A. The numeric 1-bit is moved from the one position to the two position.

Bit positions						Character
B	A	8	4	2	1	
1	1	0	0	0	1	A
1	0	1	0	0	1	R
1	0	1	0	1	1	$

FIGURE 4–10
Examples of 6-bit BCD codes.

In addition to the six bit positions for encoding data, a seventh bit (called a **check bit** or **parity bit**) is often added for checking purposes in this code. This check bit has no significance as far as encoding a character but is used by the computer to check the validity of data. This is done automatically by internal computer circuitry through a system called **parity checking.** With the addition of the check bit, the 6-bit BCD code appears as follows.

Check bit	Zone bits		Numeric bits			
C	B	A	8	4	2	1

Depending on the computer, the parity check may be for even or odd parity. Assume that the computer uses an odd parity check. When a character is stored in the computer in 6-bit BCD code, the number of 1-bits in the first six bit positions is counted. If this number is even, a 1-bit is stored in the C position; if it is odd, a 0-bit is stored in this position. As a result, the seven bit positions of a BCD character always have an odd number of 1-bits. If an even parity check is used, the procedure is reversed.

To illustrate, following are the representations for the number 3 and the letter A, in a computer using odd parity checking.

BCD position							Character
Check	B	A	8	4	2	1	
1	0	0	0	0	1	1	3
0	1	1	0	0	0	1	A

QUESTION: How would the above codes change for a computer that uses an even parity check?

ANSWER: The check bit would be reversed—the C position would contain a 1 for the letter A; 0 for the digit 3.

Whenever data are transmitted from one storage location to another in the computer, the computer checks to determine if the necessary odd (or even) number of bits is present. If a bit has been changed during transmission, a parity error condition will occur and processing will be terminated. It is possible that two or more transmission errors will occur so that the parity check will fail to detect an error condition, but this is extremely unlikely. Inclusion of a parity check results in detecting hardware "faults" that can occur even in the most reliable of systems.

The 6-bit BCD code described in this section was widely used in earlier computers and is still found in a few computers today. However, the limitation of 2^6 or 64 characters in this code is a strong disadvantage in business data processing applications. For example, it is not possible to represent both upper- and lowercase alphabetic characters in 6-bit BCD. As a result, most computers today use either the 7-bit or 8-bit codes described in the following sections.

THE ASCII CODE   The term ASCII stands for American Standard Code for Information Interchange. This code was developed under the guidance of the American National Standards Institute (ANSI) as an attempt to standardize the code used in computers and in data transmission.

There are two versions of the ASCII code: a 7-bit version and an 8-bit version. The ASCII-7 code was developed in the late 1960s. This code permits 2^7 or 128 distinct characters to be represented. The ASCII-7 code includes upper- and lowercase alphabetic characters as well as a number of special codes that are used as control characters in data communications.

The ASCII-7 code employs three zone bits and four numeric bits to represent characters. Following is the ASCII-7 format, with an eighth bit added for parity checking. The example shows the number 7, the lowercase letter c, and the special character ? represented in ASCII-7, with even parity checking.

Check bit (even)	Zone bits			Numeric bits (place values)				
	C	B	A	8	4	2	1	
1	0	1	1	0	1	1	1	= 7
0	1	1	0	0	0	1	1	= c
0	0	1	1	1	1	1	1	= ?

QUESTION: From this example, can you guess the ASCII-7 code for lowercase b? Include the even parity bits.

ANSWER: 11100010 (the zone bits are the same as for lowercase c; the numeric bits are set to the value 2 instead of 3).

A more recent version of the ASCII code uses eight (rather than seven) bits. The ASCII-8 code was also developed under the auspices of the American National Standards Institute and permits the representation of 2^8 or 256 separate characters. The format is essentially the same as ASCII-7, with the addition of an extra (or fourth) zone bit.

THE EBCDIC CODE   The Extended Binary Coded Decimal Interchange Code (or EBCDIC) was developed by IBM. Like ASCII-8, this code is an 8-bit code that permits representing 256 distinct characters. However, the bit patterns for EBCDIC characters are different from the bit patterns for corresponding ASCII-8 characters. The EBCDIC code is widely used throughout the lines of IBM computers and communications devices.

In the EBCDIC code, alphanumeric characters are represented by a combination of four zone bits and four numeric bits. Following is an example of the EBCDIC format, showing the number 7, lowercase letter c, and special character ? in EBCDIC code. For simplicity, a check or parity bit has been omitted. However, a ninth bit would normally be included for parity checking.

Zone bits				Numeric bits				
Z	Z	Z	Z	8	4	2	1	
1	1	1	1	0	1	1	1	= 7
1	0	0	0	0	0	1	1	= c
0	1	1	0	1	1	1	1	= ?

QUESTION: Examine the EBCDIC format above. Can you guess the EBCDIC code for the lowercase letter b? _____

ANSWER: 10000010

In computers that use the EBCDIC code, each addressable unit of storage is eight bits in length and is referred to as a **byte.** As you can see, each 8-bit EBCDIC character (such as those in the above example) can be stored in one byte of computer memory.

The EBCDIC format shown in the above illustration is referred to as **zoned decimal,** since each character is stored in one byte and is represented as a combination of four zone and four numeric bits. Notice that the four zone bits in the code for the decimal number 7 are 1111. This bit combination in EBCDIC zoned decimal indicates that a number is *unsigned*—that is, neither positive nor negative.

Recall from our discussion of 4-bit BCD that the decimal numbers 0 through 9 can be represented with only four binary bit positions. Therefore, it is wasteful to store purely numeric data in zoned decimal format, one decimal digit per byte. Instead, purely numeric data is generally stored in EBCDIC **packed decimal** format, with two decimal digits packed into each 8-bit byte. The packed decimal format is shown below, illustrating the representation of the number 75.

Numeric bits				Numeric bits			
8	4	2	1	8	4	2	1
0	1	1	1	0	1	0	1

7   5

Notice that, with the above format, the decimal number 75 is stored in one 8-bit byte or computer storage location. However, the number contains no sign. For arithmetic operations, it is necessary to store the sign (plus or minus) of a number, as well as its magnitude. In EBCDIC packed decimal, the sign of a number is stored in the right-most four bit positions of the EBCDIC decimal "character string." A bit pattern of 1100 represents a positive number, while 1101 represents a negative number. In the following example, the decimal number −597 is shown in packed decimal format.

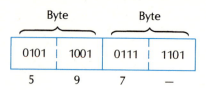

	Byte			Byte	
0101	1001		0111	1101
5	9		7	−

QUESTION: To represent the number +597, the right-most bit positions would contain the

bit pattern _____

ANSWER: 1100

The storage capacity of memory devices for numerical data is nearly doubled when using the packed decimal format. As a result, most computers that use the EBCDIC code have instructions for packing numerical data and for performing arithmetic operations using this format.

In studying the hexadecimal number system, you learned that hexadecimal is often used as a shorthand for binary numbers. In particular, hexadecimal numbers are often associated with the EBCDIC code. The reason for this is that two hexadecimal digits can be used to represent each 8-bit EBCDIC character. For example, following is the EBCDIC code for the question mark character (?). Dividing this bit string into groups of four and writing down the hexadecimal equivalents, you can see that 6F is the hexadecimal equivalent for this character.

0110	1111	EBCDIC code for ?
6	F	Hexadecimal equivalent

SUMMARY OF DATA CODES   Figure 4–11 provides a comparison of the major data codes (except ASCII-8) described in this chapter. The parity check bits normally included with each of these codes are omitted for simplicity.

Table 4–2 provides a comparison of the ASCII-7 and EBCDIC codes for the capital letters and decimal numbers.

ORGANIZATION OF COMPUTER STORAGE   Main memory is used to store data and instructions currently being used by the computer. The above discussion of data codes describes how this data is represented in memory. However, the computer must be able to locate data before it can be stored or retrieved. To achieve this, memory is divided into a series of storage **locations,** each within a unique **address.** Each location represents a certain number of bit positions, depending on the computer and the type of instructions used. For example, in a microcomputer each location most often consists of 8 bits. In larger computers, a location may consist of 60 bits or more. An address associated with each storage location permits the computer to directly reference that location.

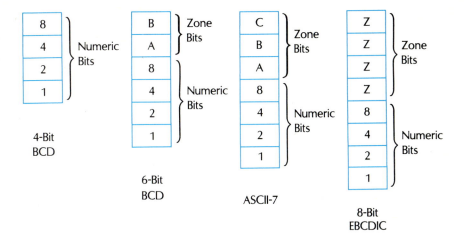

FIGURE 4–11
Comparison of computer codes.

A **storage address** serves much the same function as a mailbox number in a post office. To store or retrieve mail, a person identifies the location by the box number. In the same way, each computer storage location has an address or "box number" (see Figure 4–12).

There is an important difference between a mailbox and a computer memory location in the way information is stored and retrieved. When the contents of the mailbox are removed, the box is emptied. However, when the contents of a memory location are read by the computer, the contents remain in that location. In other words, the computer *copies* rather than removes the contents during a *read* operation. For this reason, the read operation is said to be **nondestructive.** On the other hand, when a new letter is inserted into a mailbox, the previous contents remain undisturbed. However, when the computer stores (or *writes*) new information in a storage location, the previous contents are completely replaced. Therefore, the write (or store) operation is said to be **destructive.**

TABLE 4–2   ASCII-7 AND EBCDIC REPRESENTATION OF CAPITAL LETTERS AND DECIMAL NUMBERS

Character	ASCII-7	EBCDIC	Character	ASCII-7	EBCDIC
A	1000001	1100 0001	S	1010011	1110 0010
B	1000010	1100 0010	T	1010100	1110 0011
C	1000011	1100 0011	U	1010101	1110 0100
D	1000100	1100 0100	V	1010110	1110 0101
E	1000101	1100 0101	W	1010111	1110 0110
F	1000110	1100 0110	X	1011000	1110 0111
G	1000111	1100 0111	Y	1011001	1110 1000
H	1001000	1100 1000	Z	1011010	1110 1001
I	1001001	1100 1001	0	0110000	1111 0000
J	1001010	1101 0001	1	0110001	1111 0001
K	1001011	1101 0010	2	0110010	1111 0010
L	1001100	1101 0011	3	0110011	1111 0011
M	1001101	1101 0100	4	0110100	1111 0100
N	1001110	1101 0101	5	0110101	1111 0101
O	1001111	1101 0110	6	0110110	1111 0110
P	1010000	1101 0111	7	0110111	1111 0111
Q	1010001	1101 1000	8	0111000	1111 1000
R	1010010	1101 1001	9	0111001	1111 1001

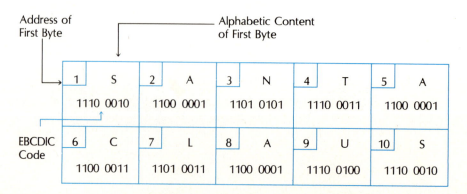

Set of cores

(a)   (b)

FIGURE 4-12
Comparison of addresses for computer storage and mailboxes. (*a*) Each set of cores has an address. (*b*) Each mailbox has an address.

It is important that you recognize the difference between the **address** of a storage location, and the **contents** of that location. In Figure 4-13, the letters SANTACLAUS are stored in consecutive storage locations. In this example, each location consists of one 8-bit byte and the locations have addresses 1 through 10. The contents of the locations are shown both as alphabetic characters and as the corresponding EBCDIC code representation of the letters.

QUESTION: Examine Figure 4-13. Write down the address of each storage location that has

the letter A as its contents. ——————————————————————————————
What is the EBCDIC code for this letter?

ANSWER: 2, 5, 8   1100   0001

FIXED VERSUS VARIABLE WORD LENGTH   We have now established that each storage location is referred to by its address. However, we have not yet specified the **length** of each storage location.

FIGURE 4-13
Ten storage locations (bytes) and their contents.

Address of First Byte ——————   ———————— Alphabetic Content of First Byte

1	S	2	A	3	N	4	T	5	A
1110 0010		1100 0001		1101 0101		1110 0011		1100 0001	

EBCDIC Code

6	C	7	L	8	A	9	U	10	S
1100 0011		1101 0011		1100 0001		1110 0100		1110 0010	

In some computers, each storage location consists of a fixed number of binary digits or bit positions. Whenever a computer instruction references a storage location, it refers to this fixed-length location, called a **word.** This type of organization is called **fixed word length.** For example, a typical minicomputer has a 16-bit word length.

In other computers, each address refers to a single byte or character. These computers are said to be **character-addressable** or **byte-addressable.** Figure 4–13 shows such a storage organization, since each of the 10 bytes is individually addressable.

Computers that are character-addressable are often referred to as **variable word length** machines. The reason for this terminology is that a given computer instruction (such as an "add" or "move") will operate on a variable number of characters. In contrast to a fixed word length computer, the number of characters is specified in the instruction itself.

A comparison of fixed and variable word length storage organizations is shown in Figure 4–14. Figure 4–14*a* shows a fixed word length organization, in which each word can store four characters. Notice with this organization that, although groups of four characters are addressable, each individual character cannot be addressed. In the character-addressable or variable word length organization (Figure 4–14*b*), the computer can address each character.

In Figure 4–14*b*, suppose that it is desired to retrieve the first five characters (the letters SANTA). To achieve this, it might seem that five separate references would be required. However, this is unnecessary. The variable word length instructions permit accessing all of the characters in a group by specifying only the address of the starting character, plus the number of characters in the group. For example, in Figure 4–14*b* an instruction to retrieve the letters SANTA would specify the first location (001) and the number of locations (5) to be retrieved.

FIXED–VARIABLE COMBINATION   The principal advantage of the variable word length organization is storage efficiency; that is, only the required number of character positions is used to represent a group of characters. On the other hand, fixed word length tends to be wasteful of storage space. For

FIGURE 4–14
Comparison of fixed length and variable length organizations. (*a*) Fixed word length organization. (*b*) Variable word length organization.

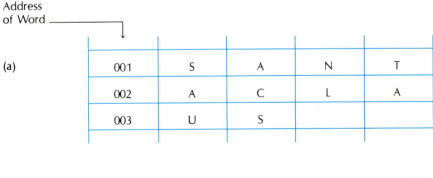

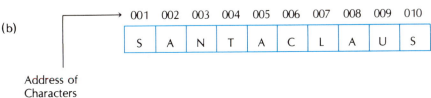

example, in Figure 4–14*a* the third word (address 003) is only half utilized; the second half of this word is not used.

The principal advantage of the fixed word length organization is speed in performing arithmetic operations. The reason for this is that arithmetic operations are performed in parallel on complete words; that is, all binary positions of digits to be processed (including carries) are added at the same time, in one step. In contrast, with variable word length, characters are added **serially,** one at a time — much like performing addition with paper and pencil.

Considering these advantages and disadvantages, fixed word length organization is used largely for scientific computations, where computational speed is important. On the other hand, variable word length is preferred for data processing applications where large quantities of alphanumeric data must be processed. For example, variable word length would be more appropriate for payroll, inventory, and accounts receivable applications.

Fortunately, today's computers can often be operated either as fixed or variable word length machines. These general-purpose computers have one set of instructions for fixed word length operations and another for variable word length operations. The user is therefore free to select the type of operation that is most appropriate.

EXERCISE 4–3

1. State whether each of the following codes represents a character in 4-bit BCD, 6-bit BCD, ASCII, or EBCDIC. If the code is 4-bit BCD or EBCDIC, express its hexadecimal equivalent.

   a. 111111 _____

   b. 10100110 _____

   c. 1011 _____

   d. 0110011 _____

   e. 1010 _____

   f. 11110111 _____

2. Suppose that for a particular computer code all characters are encoded using five bit positions. How many distinct characters can be represented using this code? _____

SUMMARY

In this chapter you have learned the basic techniques for representing data in a computer. A knowledge of these techniques is important in using computers and understanding the differences among computing systems.

In human communication we normally use the decimal number system and alphabetic characters and other symbols. In the computer all symbols are represented as combinations of binary digits or bits. Each binary digit is in turn represented by two-state semiconductor devices.

Numerical data may be represented in the computer using straight binary notation. However, alphanumeric data (combinations of numbers, letters, and special characters) are expressed using a binary coded decimal (BCD) format such as ASCII or EBCDIC. Both fixed word length and variable word length organizations are used in computers.

A variety of the codes described in this chapter is used in a typical computer system. Some of the more important uses of codes are shown in Figure 4–15.

In Chapter 5 you will study the various commonly used types of computer storage devices.

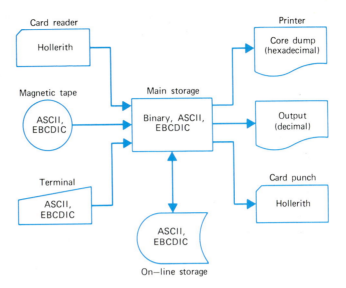

FIGURE 4-15
Some uses of codes in a typical computer system.

ANSWERS TO EXERCISES

EXERCISE 4-1

1.
2	165	Remainder
2	82	1
2	41	0
2	20	1
2	10	0
2	5	0
2	2	1
2	1	0
	0	1

Answer: 10100101

2. $1 \times 2^7 + 0 \times 2^6 + 1 \times 2^5 + 0 \times 2^4 + 0 \times 2^3 + 1 \times 2^2 + 0 \times 2^1 + 1 \times 2^0$
    $= 128 + 32 + 4 + 1$
    $= 165$

3. $2^3 + 2^1 + 2^0 = 11$

EXERCISE 4-2

1. $B7C = 11 \times 16^2 + 7 \times 16^1 + 12 \times 16^0$
    $= 2816 + 112 + 12$
    $= 2940$ (decimal)

2. a. 10010011 (Binary)
           9   3 (Hexadecimal)

    b. 11011001 (Binary)
           D   9 (Hexadecimal)

    c. 11111111 (Binary)
           F   F (Hexadecimal)

EXERCISE 4-3

1. a. 6-bit BCD
    b. EBCDIC; A6
    c. 4-bit BCD; B
    d. ASCII
    e. 4-bit BCD; A
    f. EBCDIC; F7

2. 2^5 or 32

CHAPTER EXAMINATION

1. Describe each of the following codes.

    a. Hollerith _____

    _____

    b. ASCII-7 _____

    _____

    c. EBCDIC _____

    _____

    d. 6-bit BCD _____

    _____

2. Convert each of the following decimal numbers to binary.

    a. 9 _____

    b. 15 _____

    c. 127 _____

3. Convert each of the following binary numbers to decimal.

    a. 1101011 _____

    b. 11110011 _____

4. John Klipp, a tackle on the football team, weighs 256 pounds. Express his weight in hexadecimal notation. ___

5. Explain briefly the main advantage of each type of memory organization.

    a. Fixed word length _____

    _____

    b. Variable word length _____

6. Following are the EBCDIC codes for several characters. Assuming that a computer uses an odd parity check, what binary digit would appear in the check bit position for each of these characters?

Character	EBCDIC Code	Check Bit
E	1100 0101	_____
R	1101 1001	_____
4	1111 0100	_____
+	0100 1110	_____
b (blank)	0100 0000	_____

7. Use hexadecimal notation to represent each of the EBCDIC bit configurations in problem 6.

E _____   4 _____   b _____

R _____   + _____

8. Mark each of the following statements true or false.

_____ a.   The hexadecimal number system uses eight digits (0 through 7).

_____ b.   The largest number that could be represented by three "on-off" devices is 7.

_____ c.   A decimal number may be converted to binary by successive division by 8, saving the remainder from each division.

_____ d.   The hexadecimal number system is a shorthand notation for groups of four binary digits.

_____ e.   The EBCDIC code is limited to a representation of 128 distinct characters.

_____ f.   Hollerith code is widely used as an internal computer code.

_____ g.   Variable word length organization has the advantage of faster computational speeds.

_____ h.   The most commonly used internal computer codes today are ASCII and EBCDIC.

9. Match each of the following terms to the most appropriate definition.

_____ State   a.   Both 7-bit and 8-bit versions are used.

_____ Base   b.   Coding system used for punched cards.

_____ Bit   c.   Position or characteristic of a device.

_____ Parity   d.   Code based on four binary positions.

____ASCII   e.   Number of absolute values in a numbering system.

____4-bit BCD   f.   Storage location containing eight bits.

____Hollerith   g.   Binary digit, represented by 0 or 1.

____EBCDIC   h.   Code based on eight binary positions.

____byte   i.   Check for validity of data.

10. You observe a printout of computer memory (called a **core dump**). The printout consists entirely of the digits 0 through 9 and the letters A through F. What notation is being used? _____

11. Explain why it is convenient to represent EBCDIC characters using hexadecimal notation. _____

_____

_____

12. What binary number is represented by each of the following two-state devices? A shaded circle represents the 1-bit; an empty circle the 0-bit.

a.   ● ○ ○ ○ ○ ○   _____

b.   ● ○ ○ ○ ○ ●   _____

c.   ● ○ ● ○ ● ○   _____

d.   ● ● ● ● ● ●   _____

13. Convert each of the following decimal numbers to binary.

a. 37 _____

b. 476 _____

14. Convert each of the following hexadecimal numbers to decimal.

a. 9A _____

b. F3D _____

15. Explain the meaning of the term "byte." _____

_____

_____

16. In electronic computers the following devices are used. _____

_____

a. Ten-state devices   c. Zero-state devices
b. Two-state devices   d. Combinations of the above

17. The following code is used in punched cards. _____
    a. EBCDIC   c. 6-bit BCD
    b. 4-bit BCD   d. Hollerith

18. What is the base for each of the following number systems?

    a. Decimal   _____

    b. Binary   _____

    c. Hexadecimal   _____

19. Explain how parity checking is used. _____

    _____

    _____

20. Express the decimal number 112 using each of the following.

    a. Binary number system   _____

    b. 4-bit BCD code   _____

    c. 6-bit BCD code   _____

21. Show how each of the following decimal numbers would be coded in EBCDIC packed decimal format.

    a. −473   _____

    b. +99   _____

    c. 1984   _____

22. State the main advantage of BCD code over straight binary representation.

    _____

    _____

23. Why is EBCDIC zoned decimal inefficient for numerical data?

    _____

    _____

24. What is meant by the term "byte-addressable"?

    _____

    _____

    _____

25. Distinguish between the following terms.

    a.   Nondestructive versus destructive _____

        _____

    b.   Fixed versus variable word length _____

        _____

        _____

    c.   Address versus contents _____

        _____

        _____

    d.   Packed decimal versus zoned decimal _____

        _____

5

STORAGE CONCEPTS AND DEVICES

OVERVIEW. In Chapter 4, you learned how data are stored and represented in the computer. You should now be familiar with the binary number system and the various codes that are used to represent numbers, letters, and other characters. In this chapter you will study the devices that are actually used—and will be used in the future—to store data.

Computer storage may be classified according to a hierarchy, as follows: main memory, paging memory, data base storage, and archival storage. The central processor executes instructions and processes data that are stored in main memory. Paging memory is used for currently inactive program segments that are brought into main memory as needed. Secondary storage is used for the organization's current data base, while historical data is stored in archival storage.

Large-scale integrated semiconductor devices are used for main memory in today's computers. These devices replaced the magnetic core memories used in earlier computers. Two types of devices are used for secondary storage: magnetic tape and direct access storage devices (DASDs) such as magnetic disk, drum, and diskette. The DASDs are also used for paging memory, but these devices are being replaced by new types of memory such as magnetic bubbles and charge-coupled devices to achieve faster access times. Memory devices under development (such as tunnel junctions) may result in a new generation of supercomputers during the 1980s.

CLASSIFICATION OF COMPUTER STORAGE

Every computer has a central storage unit, usually called **main memory** (or primary storage). Main memory is the computer's workshop—it is where data and instructions are stored that are actively being processed by the computer.

Actually, computer main memory is used for a variety of functions. As Figure 5-1 shows, main memory may be visualized as being divided into several areas that are used for the following purposes.

1. Operating system—controls the operation of the computer (described in detail in Chapter 10).

2. Input area—area where data is stored when it is read into the computer (for example, time card information).

85

| Operating System |
| Input Area |
| Application Program |
| Working Storage |
| Output Area |

Main Memory

FIGURE 5-1
Uses of main memory
in a computer.

3. Application program—area where a user program resides (for example, a payroll program).
4. Working storage—area for computations and temporary storage of data.
5. Output area—area where data is stored prior to output (for example, payroll data used to print checks).

Although computer main memory can generally be expanded within limits, it is expensive and does not provide sufficient storage capacity for all of an organization's data. Instead, main memory is generally supplemented by some form of **secondary** (or **auxiliary**) storage. Secondary storage in a computer is used for data and programs that are not currently needed in main memory. Secondary storage is most often used for the following purposes.

1. Large data files (such as files of personnel records or inventory records).
2. Programs (or portions of programs) that are not currently being executed by the computer.
3. Areas for temporary storage of input and/or output data.

Secondary storage cannot be directly addressed by the computer central processing unit (CPU). Therefore, before programs that are stored in secondary storage can be executed by the computer, they must be read into main memory. Also, data contained in secondary storage must be read into main memory before it can be processed by the CPU.

The division between main memory and secondary storage is illustrated in Figure 5-2 for a microcomputer. Programs and data are stored on **floppy disks,** a form of secondary storage described later in this chapter. For example, one floppy disk might contain medical records for a physician's patients. A second floppy disk might contain a program that is used by the microcomputer to update the patient's records. When the program and/or data are required by the computer, the user inserts the appropriate floppy disk into a disk drive (illustrated in Figure 5-2). The program and/or data are then read into main memory so that the patient records can be updated.

Why is there a distinction between main memory and secondary storage? The reasons have to do with the relationships between the cost, storage capacity, and speed of various memory devices. The computational speed of a computer depends to a large extent on the speed of its main memory. Therefore, the fastest devices (semiconductor chips) are used for main memory. Although

FIGURE 5-2
Types of storage in a microcomputer.

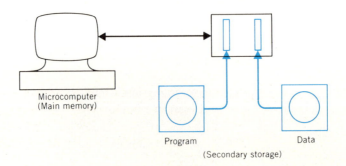

Microcomputer
(Main memory)

Program

Data

(Secondary storage)

the cost per bit of semiconductor memory is decreasing rapidly, it is still much higher than that for secondary storage devices such as magnetic disk, which have enormous storage capacity at a low cost per character.

STORAGE HIERARCHY   Although still valid, the classification of computer memory into main memory and secondary storage is somewhat oversimplified today. In fact in today's computers (especially larger computers) it is more accurate to visualize a storage hierarchy (see Figure 5-3). The four storage levels shown in Figure 5-3 and their main usages are as follows.

1. Main memory—used to store programs (or program segments) that are currently being executed by the computer and data that are currently being processed by these programs.

2. Paging memory—used primarily to store on-demand program segments that are not currently being executed by the computer but are likely to be requested by the central processing unit within a short period of time. The term "paging" refers to the fact that program segments (or other data) are read in frames called "pages" (described in more detail below). Paging memory is designed to provide fast access to frequently used programs, thereby improving computer performance.

3. Data base storage—used for storing the current data base or files of data used by the organization.

4. Archival storage—used for storing historical data, for reference or legal purposes. Archival storage provides adequate access to very large files of historical data.

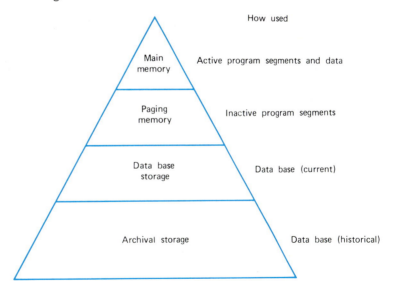

FIGURE 5-3
Hierarchy of computer storage.

An overview of the major storage devices used in the storage hierarchy is shown in Table 5-1. This table shows the major devices used, together with typical access times and range of storage capacity. **Access time** is the time interval between the instant when the control unit issues a call for data and the instant at which delivery of that data is completed. Access time is an important

TABLE 5–1   TYPES OF STORAGE DEVICES USED IN COMPUTERS

Type of memory	Devices used	Typical access times	Typical capacity range (bytes)
Main	Semiconductors	100 nanoseconds or less	4K to 10M
Paging	Fixed-head disk Magnetic drum Semiconductor Magnetic bubble Charge-coupled	5 milliseconds 2 to 5 milliseconds 0.2 milliseconds 0.3 milliseconds 0.7 milliseconds	10M to 100M
Data base	Moving-head disk Floppy disk Magnetic tape	15 to 30 milliseconds 100 milliseconds seconds or minutes	1M to 1000M
Archival	Magnetic cartridge Video disk	2 to 5 seconds 150 milliseconds	Up to one trillion bytes

factor in selecting storage devices, since it dictates the speed of information storage and retrieval.

Storage capacity is most often stated in terms of the number of bytes (or alphanumeric characters) that can be stored on the device. Two terms are frequently used when referring to storage capacity: K (for *kilo,* meaning one thousand) and M (for *mega,* meaning one million). Thus one might refer to a main storage capacity of 200K, or a secondary storage capacity of 100M.

When referring to storage capacity, the term K actually means 2 raised to the tenth power, or 1024. Thus a microcomputer that has 4K main storage capacity actually has 4096 (4 times 1024) positions. Similarly, the term M means 2 raised to the twentieth power, or 1,048,576. Thus a small business computer that has 10MB (10 megabytes) of disk storage actually has a capacity of 10,485,760 bytes of disk memory.

QUESTION: A medium-scale computer has a main memory with storage capacity of 256K and magnetic disk storage capacity of 100MB. What is the actual storage capacity of each type of storage (bytes)?

Main _____

Disk _____

ANSWER: 262,144; 104,857,600

EXERCISE 5–1   1. Refer to the storage hierarchy (Figure 5–3). What type of storage would be used for each of the following?

a.   File of current student records _____

b. Portion of a program to update student records that is currently being executed by the computer _____

_____

c. Portion of a program to update student records that is currently inactive but on call to the computer _____

_____

d. Historical file of previous students, maintained for reference purposes

_____

2. Refer to the types of storage devices used (Table 5–1). For each of the types of memory, enter the fastest device (smallest access time) and slowest device (largest access time) shown in the table.

Type of Memory	Fastest	Slowest
Main	_____	_____
Paging	_____	_____
Secondary	_____	_____
Archival	_____	_____

MAIN MEMORY

The important concepts and devices used for main memory are described below.

TYPES OF MAIN MEMORY

There are two basic subdivisions or types of main memory in today's computers—random access memory and read-only memory.

Random access memory (or RAM) is used for temporary storage of data and/or program instructions. The contents of RAM can be modified by a user program; that is, data and/or program instructions can be written into or read from random access memory. The access time to any one location in RAM is the same as the access time to any other location.

Read-only memory (or ROM) is used to store program instructions and/or data that are permanent or rarely altered. This information is generally placed on the storage chip when the chip is manufactured, and the contents of ROM cannot be modified except under special circumstances. Thus the computer processor can read information stored in ROM but cannot write information to this type of memory.

Information stored in ROM is **nonvolatile;** that is, it is not lost when external power is removed from the computer. In contrast, RAM memory is volatile in that information is generally lost when power is removed.

CAPACITY OF MAIN MEMORY

Two types of addressing are used in computer main memory: byte addressing and word addressing (you may want to review these terms in Chapter 4). For computers that use byte addressing (including most IBM computers), the capacity of main memory is stated in terms of the number of 8-bit bytes that can be stored. For computers that use word addressing, capacity is stated in terms of number of fixed length words. Common word lengths are 16, 32, 36, 48, and 64 bits (minicomputers generally have either 16- or 32-bit word lengths). One must be cautious in comparing the storage capacities of byte-addressable and word-addressable computers, since more information can generally be stored in a word than in an 8-bit byte.

QUESTION: Computer A has 256K 8-bit bytes of main memory, while Computer B has 256K words of 32 bits each. Which computer main memory has the greater storage

capacity? _____

ANSWER: Computer B. (However, the capacity is not four times greater because the longer words cannot always be packed full of information.)

The total capacity of main memory is often not as important as how efficiently that capacity is utilized. If you review Figure 5–1 you will recall that main memory is used for the computer operating system as well as for user programs. Often the computer operating system may require one-half (or more) of the capacity of main memory. An important question in judging the capacity of main memory concerns how much space is available for each individual user. Thus, it is not unusual for a large computer to have 1 million bytes (1MB) or more of main memory capacity, but for each user to be allocated a much smaller partition (say 8K) of memory capacity for a particular program. A **partition** is an area of main memory allocated to a particular program or task (described below).

Two types of electronic devices have been used for computer main memory in modern computers—magnetic cores and semiconductors. Semiconductor memories have completely replaced magnetic cores in recent computers because of their faster access times, lower cost, and reduced space and power requirements. However, magnetic cores are described briefly below because of their historical importance.

MAGNETIC CORE MEMORY   A single **magnetic core** is a tiny doughnut-shaped element about the size of a grain of salt. It is molded from a magnetic

FIGURE 5–4
Magnetic core plane.

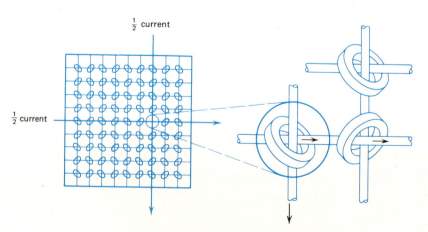

material such as ferrite. Cores are strung like beads on intersecting wires to form a **core plane,** as shown in Figure 5-4.

The important property of a magnetic core element is that it can be **polarized** in one of two directions, clockwise or counterclockwise. A core that is polarized in a clockwise direction is said to be "on," while a core polarized in the counterclockwise direction is said to be "off." Thus a core is a two-state element that can represent the binary digits 0 and 1, as you learned in Chapter 4.

A magnetic core is polarized by sending one-half of a required amount of current along each of the two wires intersecting at its center (see Figure 5-4). The polarity (or direction of magnetization) then remains fixed until it is "flipped" (or reversed) by sending a flow of current through each of its intersecting wires in the opposite direction. The technique of sending one-half of the necessary current through each of the two intersecting wires allows the polarity to be reversed for the desired core element without disturbing any other element in the core plane.

The above description concerns "writing" or storing information in cores. Provision must also be made for the computer to "read" or sense the polarity of a core. Sensing is accomplished by using two additional wires (called the sense and inhibit wires) through each core. Simply stated, these wires used with logical

FIGURE 5-5
Representation of a character in magnetic core storage.

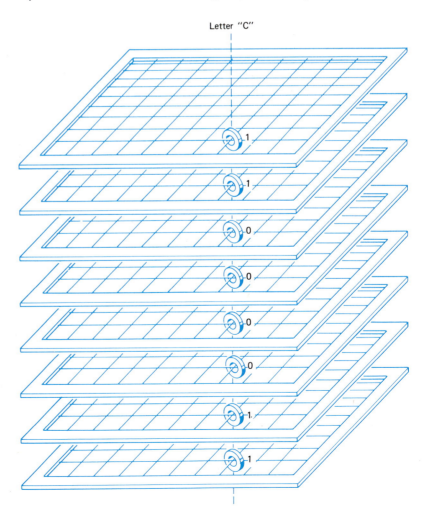

Letter "C"

circuitry permit the computer to sense the "on" or "off" condition of each magnetic core element.

Magnetic core planes are stacked to form core stacks as shown in Figure 5-5. Cores in the same location on adjacent planes are then used to form bit combinations to represent numbers and characters. For example, in EBCDIC notation the letter C is represented by the binary code 11000011. Figure 5-5 shows how adjacent cores are used to represent this character.

SEMICONDUCTOR MEMORY   Since about 1970, magnetic core memory has been replaced by semiconductor memory, in which many thousands of microscopic memory cells are emplaced on a tiny chip of silicon. These memory devices provide faster data access, much smaller physical size, lower power consumption, and significantly reduced cost compared to earlier core memories.

As you learned in Chapter 4, each semiconductor memory cell is made up from two principal components, a capacitor and a transistor (see Figure 4-4). The capacitor is a two-state device that stores a tiny electrical charge (corresponding to the "1" bit) or no charge ("0" bit). The transistor functions as a switch to determine whether the capacitor is charged.

A **semiconductor memory chip** is made up of thousands of such cells organized into a rectangular array of rows and columns. For example, Figure 5-6 shows a simple eight-by-eight array for the storage of 64 bits of information. Each row and each column is numbered from 0 to 7 (both decimal and binary numbers are shown). Thus the row and column numbers specify the address of the memory cell located at the intersection of each row and column.

By activating a particular row and column the computer logic selects a particular memory cell for a read or write operation. In Figure 5-6 the memory cell at row 5, column 4 (address 54) has been selected. The computer can then read the information (binary 0 or 1) stored at that location or can store new information in the cell. Decimal numbers, alphabetic characters, and special symbols are represented by a combination of 0s and 1s stored in adjacent cells in the memory array, similar to the procedure for magnetic core memory.

FIGURE 5-6
Random access memory array.

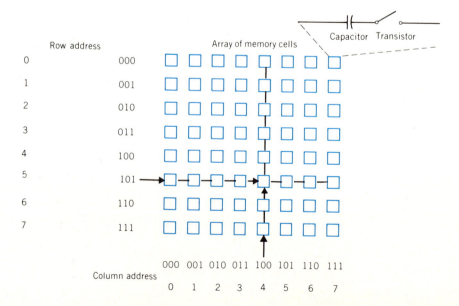

QUESTION: A byte is a sequence of eight bit positions used to store data in a computer.
a.   How many bytes can be stored in each row of the memory array shown in

Figure 5–6? _____

b.   How many bytes can be stored in the entire array? _____

ANSWER: a.   one   b.   eight

Of course in today's semiconductor memory chips, the storage capacity is far greater than 64 bits. The 1980 industry standard was 65,536 bits (referred to as a 64K-bit chip). An example of a 64K-bit chip is shown in Figure 5–7. In the early 1980s the computer industry standard became 256K-bit chips (the chips are the same size — the storage density is four times as great).

FIGURE 5–7
Semiconductor memory chip. (Courtesy IBM.)

As you learned in Chapter 3, the large-scale integration of semiconductor memory circuits has been one of the most significant factors in reducing the cost of computers. Figure 5–8 shows how the cost per bit of computer memory has declined over a 10-year period. The figure shows the cost per bit for increasingly high-density chips, including the 64K-bit chip shown in Figure 5–7. This trend in the declining cost of semiconductor memory is expected to continue at least until the late 1980s.

QUESTION: Examine Figure 5–8. In 1981 the cost per bit for a 64K memory chip is about

_____ cents. Thus the cost for one byte of capacity (or 8 bits) is about

_____ cents. The cost for the entire 64K-bit chip is _____ cents

or _____ dollars.

ANSWER: .03, .24, 1966, 19.66

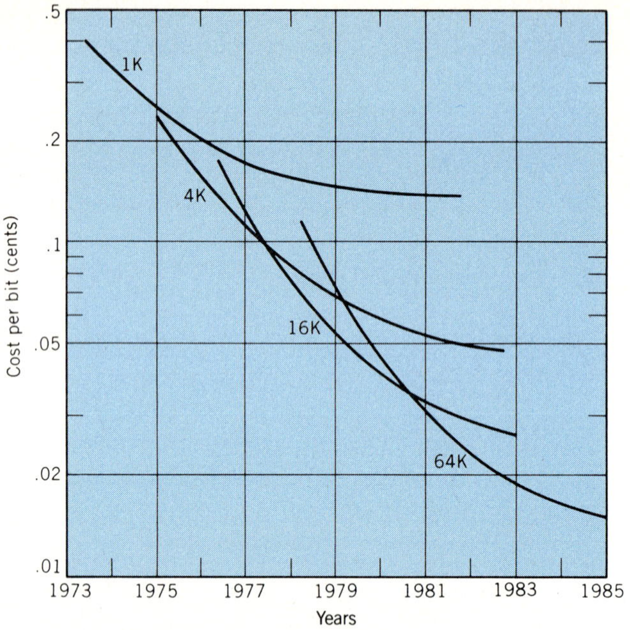

FIGURE 5-8
Cost of computer memory.

Two types of semiconductor chips are used in most computers — metal oxide semiconductor (or MOS) and bipolar semiconductor. Bipolar semiconductor devices are faster but more expensive than are MOS devices. Access times for bipolar devices range from 10 nanoseconds (10 billionths of a second) to 100 nanoseconds. The MOS devices have access times ranging from 100 nanoseconds to one microsecond. The faster bipolar devices are used in some computers for **cache memory,** a subdivision of main memory used for fast execution of program instructions.

PAGING MEMORY AND VIRTUAL STORAGE

A typical organization uses its computer (or computers) for a variety of purposes. For example, the computer might be employed to maintain personnel records, bill customers, solve engineering problems, and maintain car pool information. Often the various users contend for the use of the computer at the same time.

MULTIPROGRAMMING

If the computer were only able to process one job or task at a time, users would have to queue their jobs at the computer, similar to the situation with a copy machine. Fortunately, most computers today (except for the smallest micros) are able to process two or more jobs at the same time. **Multiprogramming** is the concurrent execution of two or more computer programs by the computer. Using this approach speeds the completion of tasks and makes more efficient use of computer resources.

With multiprogramming, computer users are each allocated a "slice" of main memory for their programs. This subdivision of main memory is referred to as a **partition.** The size of a user partition depends on a number of factors, including the size of main memory, the amount of memory required by the operating system, and the number of user programs contending for main memory at a given time.

VIRTUAL STORAGE   Very often, a user program will exceed the size of the memory partition allocated to that user. For example, User A might be allocated a partition of 8K bytes, while User A's program might require a total of 24K bytes. How will User A's program be stored in main memory? It will be split into segments called pages (see Figure 5–9). A **page** is a block of instructions or data (or both) that can be transferred as a unit between secondary storage and main memory. Each page is limited to the size of the user partition. In the above example, the 24K program could be segmented into three 8K pages as shown in Figure 5–9.

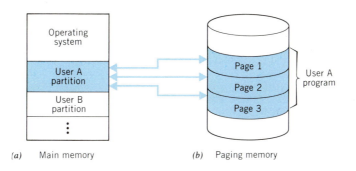

(*a*)   Main memory   (*b*)   Paging memory

FIGURE 5–9
Paging memory and virtual storage. (*a*) Main memory. (*b*) Paging memory.

The program segments or pages are stored on some form of fast secondary storage, often called **paging memory** (see Figure 5–9*b*). Each page is transferred from paging memory to the user partition in main storage as it is needed by the central processing unit. For example, in executing User A's program the CPU might request page 1, followed by page 2, then page 1 again, and so on.

It might seem that the necessity of segmenting programs into pages would complicate the programming task. However, this is not generally the case. Using the concept called **virtual storage,** programmers simply pretend in writing their programs that they have available an unlimited (or at least very large) partition of main memory. The computer automatically controls the segmentation of the programs into pages and the transfer (or **paging**) of these segments between main memory and secondary storage.

Fast access to paging memory is essential, or else the computer will be slowed by the transfer or paging of program segments. Magnetic drums and fixed-head magnetic disks are widely used for paging memory, since they provide relatively fast access at a reasonable cost. However, semiconductor memories and newer devices such as magnetic bubble memories are rapidly replacing these slower devices today since they provide much faster access times. All of these devices are described below.

SECONDARY STORAGE   We now turn our attention to secondary storage devices. These devices are used to store programs and/or data that are not currently needed in main memory. Secondary (or auxiliary) storage devices are on line to the computer and may be accessed by the computer with little or no operator intervention. However, the access time for data in secondary storage is slower than for data in main memory; how much slower depends on the type of device used.

DIRECT VERSUS   There are two basic types of secondary storage devices: sequential access de-
SEQUENTIAL ACCESS   vices and direct access devices.

Sequential access devices are those whose storage locations cannot be addressed. Data records are simply stored from beginning to end on the storage medium. To retrieve a record, it is necessary to start at the beginning and search all records until the desired record is located. Magnetic tape is the principal form of sequential access storage used in computers.

In contrast, **direct access** storage devices (or DASDs) have addressable storage locations. Thus if it is known that a particular data record is stored at a given address, the record can be retrieved at that address without searching intervening records. This is an important feature if records must be updated when changes occur, or if frequent inquiries are addressed to individual records. For example, a retail credit system would require direct access if frequent credit checks were made against customer account records. The most common type of direct access storage device at present is magnetic disk.

QUESTION: Magnetic tape is an example of a _____ access medium, while magnetic

disk is an important type of _____ access device.

ANSWER: sequential, direct

The contrast between direct and sequential access is illustrated in Figure 5-10. In this example, several records are stored on each type of device. Suppose it is desired to access record number 19 from among these records. In the direct access device (Figure 5-10a), suppose that it is known that record number 19 is stored at location 004. The computer can access this location and its contents directly, without referencing any of the other locations. On the other hand, with the sequential access device (Figure 5-10b) the computer must search each location until the desired record is located.

The distinction between sequential and direct access is similar to that for music recorded on a cassette tape versus music recorded on a phonograph record. To locate a particular selection on a cassette tape, one must play the tape from the beginning until the desired selection is located. For a phonograph record the stylus can be lowered at the desired location without playing preceding selections.

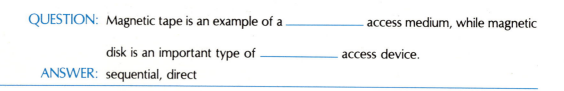

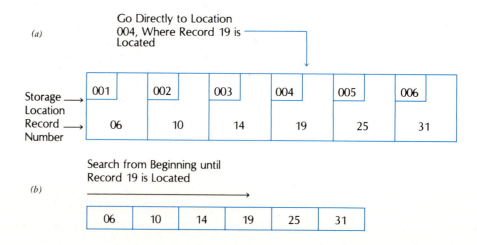

FIGURE 5-10

Comparison of direct and sequential access. (*a*) Direct access. (*b*) Sequential access.

MAGNETIC TAPE   Magnetic tape is used extensively in data processing, primarily for storing large sequential data files. Its principal applications are the following.

1. Off-line secondary storage of large sequential data files. Tapes are kept in storage racks and are mounted on tape drives and processed as they are needed.

2. Backup storage for on-line magnetic disk files. To prevent loss of data, disk files are "dumped" periodically (often once per day) to magnetic tape, which is placed in protected storage.

3. Medium for key-to-tape data entry operations (magnetic disk is more commonly used for this purpose today).

PHYSICAL CHARACTERISTICS   Magnetic tape is a sequential medium; that is, data records are stored in sequence from beginning to end of the tape. Individual locations on tape are not addressable, so that it is possible to locate a particular record only by searching through preceding records on the tape.

Magnetic tape is made of a plastic base (such as Mylar®) coated with a metal oxide film. The film becomes magnetized when an electric field is applied. Data are recorded as a series of magnetized "spots," or 1-bits. A reel of tape is mounted on a tape drive that moves the tape past read/write heads for reading or recording. Writing on tape destroys the previous contents. However, reading from the tape is nondestructive so that the contents may be read repeatedly. Some magnetic tape units will read only when the tape is moving in the forward direction, while other units will read in both the forward and reverse directions. Standard magnetic tape is one-half inch wide. However, tape widths may range from about one-fourth inch for cassettes to one inch for high-capacity tape. A standard reel of tape is 2400 feet long, but smaller and larger sizes are also common.

RECORDING ON TAPE   Data is recorded in a binary coded decimal format on magnetic tape. The tape width is divided into a series of channels (see Figure 5–11). The most common coding schemes are 7-channel (ASCII) and 9-channel (EBCDIC). The EBCDIC format is shown in Figure 5–11. Each character is recorded across the tape width in a row called a **frame**. Figure 5–11 illustrates the recording of the letter C and the number 7 on nine-channel tape in EBCDIC code.

The bit patterns for ASCII and EBCDIC codes are the same on magnetic tape as corresponding internal computer codes. In Figure 5–11, the ninth channel is a **parity** channel. A parity (or check) bit is used in this channel to check the validity of data as it is read or recorded. Figure 5–11 shows an odd parity bit (some systems use an even parity check).

FIGURE 5–11
Representing data on magnetic tape.

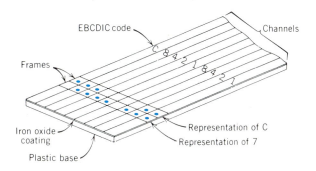

The density of data storage on magnetic tape is measured in characters per inch or bytes per inch (BPI). Common storage densities are 556, 800, and 1600 BPI. Some high density tapes can record at 6250 BPI.

TAPE RECORDS   Data is recorded on magnetic tape in the form of physical records called **blocks.** Blocks are separated by gaps, called **interblock (or interrecord) gaps** (see Figure 5–12). A typical interblock gap is one-half inch or three-fourths inch wide.

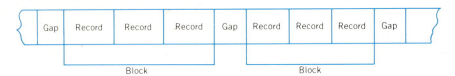

FIGURE 5–12
Blocking of records on magnetic tape.

When a tape "read" instruction is given, the entire block of data is read into computer memory. The interblock gap allows the tape to accelerate to reading speed before it is read and to decelerate when the end of the block is encountered.

In Figure 5–12, there are three logical records per block. For example, each logical record might be an employee record. If so, there are three employee records per block. The number of logical records per data block is called the **blocking factor.** Since the interblock gaps contain no data, increasing the blocking factor increases the effective storage density and, therefore, the rate at which data can be read from tape.

QUESTION: Examine Figure 5–12. The blocking factor is _____

ANSWER: 3

The rate at which data can be read from magnetic tape (called the **transfer rate**) depends on two factors: the recording density and tape speed. As stated above, typical recording densities are 556, 800, 1600, and 6250 bytes per inch. Typical tape speeds are 112.5, 125, and 200 inches per second. A magnetic tape with a rated density of 800 bytes per inch and a speed of 125 inches per second has a transfer rate of 100,000 bytes per second (800 × 125 = 100,000). Actually, this rate would be an instantaneous transfer rate. The average transfer rate is less because the tape spends much of its time starting and stopping at interblock gaps.

EVALUATION OF MAGNETIC TAPE   Magnetic tape offers several important advantages as a secondary storage medium.

1. Speed. The transfer rate is typically 50,000 to 100,000 (or more) characters per second, adequate for many applications.

2. Capacity. A standard reel of tape can hold 10 million or more characters, depending on the blocking factor. Thus tapes can be used for relatively large files or for dumping disk files.

3. Cost. Magnetic tape is the least expensive magnetic medium. A reel of

magnetic tape costs between $20 and $100. One cent buys enough capacity to store tens of thousands of characters of data.

4. Convenience. Tape reels can be easily stored in storage racks. Some organizations have thousands of reels in storage banks.

The major disadvantages of magnetic tape are the following.

1. Since tape is a sequential medium, a particular record can be accessed only by searching from the beginning of the tape. So tape is infeasible for applications requiring direct access to data records.

2. A record on magnetic tape cannot be updated "in place." Records to be updated must be read, updated, and then written on a second tape.

3. Environmental conditions (temperature, humidity, and dust) must be tightly controlled. Failure to control these conditions often results in read errors, or inability to process a tape.

4. Tape has a limited shelf life, perhaps 18 to 24 months for reliable results. As a result, it is not acceptable for long-term storage of historical files. In fact, the IRS will not accept magnetic tape but requires microfilm or other medium for audit trails.

MAGNETIC DISK

The most commonly used form of secondary storage at present is magnetic disk. The reason for this is that magnetic disk storage provides direct access to large data files and data bases at reasonable cost. Newer devices such as magnetic bubble memory and charge-coupled devices (described below) provide better price and performance in some applications. However, magnetic disk memory is itself continually being improved. As a result, it is expected that magnetic disk memory will remain the dominant form of large direct access secondary storage until at least the mid-1980s.

PHYSICAL FEATURES   A magnetic disk file is made up of a stack of rotating metal disks mounted on a spindle. Each disk is a thin metal platter, similar in appearance to a phonograph record. The disks are coated on both sides with a ferrous oxide material. Data are recorded on the disk surfaces in the form of magnetized spots; a spot represents the "1" bit, the absence of a spot the "0" bit.

The surface of each magnetic disk is divided into concentric circular paths called **tracks.** Data are recorded serially on each surface. In some (but not all) magnetic disk units, each track is further divided into pie-shaped segments called **sectors** (see Figure 5–13). The recording density is greater toward the middle of the platter, so that each track contains the same amount of data.

Several disk platters are mounted on a spindle and enclosed in a unit called a **disk module** (also called a pack or cartridge). The module in turn is loaded into a disk **drive,** such as the one shown in Figure 5–14. Although this particular drive has two spindles, some drives have only one spindle while others have multiple spindles. The disk module shown in the right side of this figure has the capacity to store 70 million characters of information.

ADDRESSING DISK STORAGE   Data are read from or written onto the disk surfaces by read/write heads similar to those used in a tape recorder. There is usually one head for each disk surface. The heads are mounted on a movable comb-shaped access mechanism whose access arms move in and out and position the read/write heads at the desired location over the disk surface

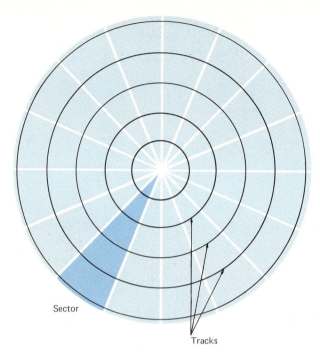

Sector

Tracks

FIGURE 5–13
Tracks and sectors on a disk surface.

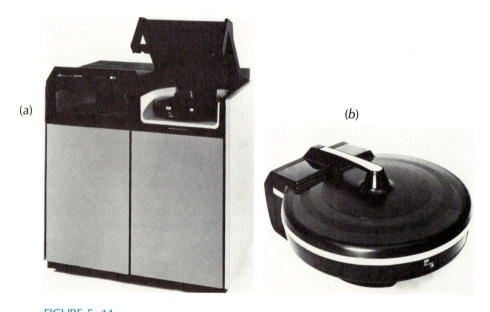

(a)

(b)

FIGURE 5–14
(a) Disk drive and storage module. (b) Disk pack.

FIGURE 5–15
Components of a disk pack.

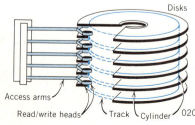

Disks

Access arms

Read/write heads   Track   Cylinder   020

(Figure 5–15). The read/write heads are positioned slightly above the disk surface and do not actually touch the surface.

When the access arms are moved laterally, all of the read/write heads are
moved in unison. Therefore, for any particular setting of the mechanism all of
the read/write heads are positioned over the same track on each recording
surface. The set of tracks under the recording heads forms a vertical **cylinder**
through the disk pack. In Figure 5–15, the read/write heads are positioned over

cylinder 020. If related records are all stored on the same cylinder, they can be accessed without moving the access assembly.

QUESTION: The magnetic disk system shown in Figure 5-15 has 10 recording surfaces.

Therefore, cylinder 020 consists of _____ vertically adjacent tracks.

ANSWER: 10

Since magnetic disk is a direct access form of storage it is possible to access directly any desired record stored on the disk without searching through other records. This is accomplished by specifying the cylinder number, track (or surface) number, and record number. Figure 5-16 shows five records stored on a disk track. The cylinder number is 020 (the same as for Figure 5-15). The track number is 03, indicating the third surface down from the top of the disk pack. Record 4 on this track has address 020034, as shown in the figure.

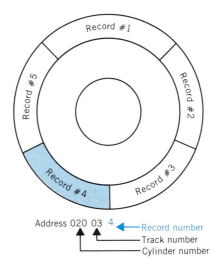

Address 020 03 4 ← Record number
└ Track number
└ Cylinder number

FIGURE 5-16
Addressing records on magnetic disk.

QUESTION: The third record on track 05 of cylinder 030 would have address _____
ANSWER: 030053

For disk units that subdivide tracks into sectors, the sector number (rather than record number) is used as part of the disk address.

Although direct access storage devices permit direct access to individual records, they also permit sequential processing of records if required by the user. In the sequential mode of processing with DASDs, records are processed much as with magnetic tape.

DISK CAPACITY   The storage capacity of a disk pack or module depends on the number of recording surfaces, the number of cylinders, and the recording density (bytes/track). This capacity is stated in terms of megabytes (MB), or millions of bytes. As indicated earlier in the chapter, the term "M" means 2 raised to the twentieth power, or 1,048,576.

A small disk pack for a minicomputer might have a capacity of 5MB, while a disk module for the disk drive of a large computer might have a capacity of over 600MB. The disk module pictured in Figure 5–14b has the following characteristics.

Bytes/track	8368
Tracks/cylinder	12
Cylinders/pack	696

Therefore, the total storage capacity of this module can be calculated as follows.

(12 tracks/cylinder) × (696 cylinders/pack) × (8368 bytes/track)
= 69,889,536 bytes (about 70MB)

Several disk drives can ordinarily be connected to the computer at the same time, so that the total on-line secondary storage capacity may range from 50MB in a smaller computer to several billion bytes in a larger computer.

As you can see in Figure 5–14b, the disk pack for the unit pictured has been removed from the disk drive. **Removable disks** of this kind are used for the storage of most data files in a data processing system. When the data on one disk pack have been processed by a particular application, the pack can be removed and another pack mounted on the same spindle. In some disk drives the disk packs are permanently mounted and cannot be removed. **Fixed disks** are generally used for storing more-or-less permanent data such as portions of the computer operating system (in some computers, fixed disks are also used for data storage).

Another feature of the disk pack shown in Figure 5–14b is that the disks, spindle, and access mechanism are all sealed into the disk module itself. The advantage of this approach is greater reliability since dust and other foreign particles cannot enter the sealed unit. For other systems the disk access mechanism is mounted in the disk drive, rather than within each disk pack. The advantage of these systems is that the disk packs are lighter and considerably less expensive than the sealed units.

DISK PERFORMANCE   Two types of magnetic disk access mechanisms are commonly used—moving-head disks and fixed-head disks. With **moving-head** disks, the access mechanism moves in and out to position the read/write heads at the desired location (this is the type of mechanism illustrated in Figure 5–15). With **fixed-head** (or **head-per-track**) disk units, the access mechanism is stationary and there is a read/write head permanently positioned over each track of the disk module.

The performance of a magnetic disk unit is measured primarily by its access time—the time it takes to access a stored record. There are two sources of delay in accessing a record with moving-head disks.

1. Seek time—the time required to move the access arm to position its read/write head over the track where the record is stored.
2. Rotational delay time (or latency)—the time for the disk to rotate until the desired data record is under the read/write head.

Access time is the sum of seek time plus rotational delay. It depends on the performance of the disk drive itself, and for a particular drive the access time varies from one record to the next. Therefore, the performance of a disk is stated in terms of *average* access time.

Disk spindles commonly rotate at 2400 or 3600 revolutions per minute (rpm). For a disk that rotates at 3600 rpm, the time required for a complete revolution is 16.7 milliseconds, computed as follows.

$3600 \div 60 = 60$ revolutions per second
$1 \div 60 = 0.0167$ seconds (16.7 milliseconds) per revolution

---

QUESTION: For a disk that rotates at 2400 rpm, the time required for a complete

revolution is _____ milliseconds.

ANSWER: 25

On the average, a disk will have to rotate one-half revolution for a selected record to move under the read/write head. Thus the average rotational delay for a disk that rotates at 3600 rpm is 8.4 milliseconds ($\frac{1}{2} \times$ 16.7 milliseconds per revolution).

The seek time for a disk is based on the distance (number of cylinders) the read/write heads must travel to reach the specified cylinder and on the speed of the mechanism itself. If the read/write heads are already positioned over the selected cylinder, the time is zero. Seek time is maximum if the mechanism must be moved across the entire disk surface. Average seek times for disk packs range from 20 to 50 milliseconds.

Finally, the average access time for a disk unit is the sum of seek time plus rotational delay. For a disk that has an average seek time of 25 milliseconds and rotates at 3600 rpm, the average access time is 33.4 milliseconds (25 milliseconds seek plus 8.4 milliseconds rotational delay).

Magnetic disk units are often used to store programs, as well as an organization's data base. However, when magnetic disk units are used for paging memory, the access times for moving-head disk drives are a strong disadvantage. As a result, fixed-head disks are most often used for paging memory. Since the seek time is eliminated, the access time for a fixed-head disk is equal to the rotational delay. The average seek time for this type of magnetic disk ranges from 5 to 10 milliseconds.

ADVANTAGES AND DISADVANTAGES OF MAGNETIC DISK   The principal advantages of magnetic disk are:

1. Data records can be accessed directly, without searching other records.
2. Conversely, a disk file can be organized sequentially and processed like magnetic tape, if desired.
3. Disk packs provide very high capacity storage, at a relatively low cost per character stored.
4. Disk packs are convenient to handle and store.

The principal disadvantages of magnetic disk are:

1. Magnetic disk still costs more than magnetic tape (by a factor of about 10 to 1 per character stored).

2. The time to access records is high compared to nonrotating devices such as magnetic bubble and charge-coupled devices.

3. Disks are somewhat unreliable, being subject to dust, static electricity, head crashes, and other incidents.

Magnetic disk storage is constantly being improved, which will insure its continued importance as a secondary storage medium. Manufacturers are currently introducing **thin film** technology, which will permit faster and larger capacity disks. Thin film coating on disk platters (replacing present oxide coatings) makes it possible to deposit much more information per square inch of disk surface. Thin film heads (made by a semiconductor process), which fly closer to the disk surface, permit reading the bits of information at increased density.

FLOPPY DISKS   With the introduction of minis, micros, and small business computers, a need was recognized for a simple, low-cost form of disk storage. This need led to the development of the **floppy disk** (also called diskette). A floppy disk is a thin, flexible disk made of polyester film coated with a metal oxide compound. The diskette is about eight inches in diameter and resembles a 45-rpm record (see Figure 5–17). It is mounted and rotates freely within a jacket that prevents damage to the diskette. The jacket has access holes to accommodate the read/write head.

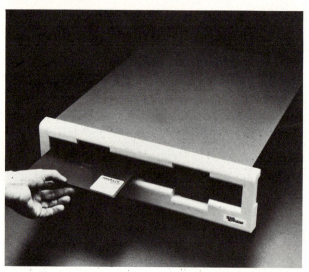

FIGURE 5–17
Floppy disk system. (Courtesy Data Systems Design.)

The capacity of a floppy disk normally ranges from 500K to 1000K bytes of data. The disk is inserted into a floppy disk drive (also shown in Figure 5–17). Average access time for a diskette is about 100 milliseconds.

A miniature floppy disk (referred to as a mini-disk) is often used on microcomputers. Mini-disks are about five inches in diameter and have a storage capacity of up to 100,000 bytes or characters on each disk.

MASS CARTRIDGE   Some organizations need direct (or at least reasonably fast) access to extraordi-
STORAGE   narily large files of data. For example, a large insurance company may have several million policyholders whose records must be kept up to date and avail-

able for reference. Large banks, computer service bureaus, and some government agencies have similar needs for mass data storage.

As you have learned, if records are stored on a reel of magnetic tape they cannot easily be retrieved, since tape is a sequential medium. However, it is possible to use short strips of magnetic tape for data storage, where each strip can be addressed (or selected) and its contents read sequentially by the computer. Two mass storage systems based on this principle have been used in the past: one based on small strips of magnetic tape, the other on small magnetic cards.

The most recent type of mass storage facility of this type uses a small data cartridge that can be held in the palm of one's hand. Each data cartridge contains a strip of oxide-coated magnetic tape, 150 inches long by 2.75 inches wide. The tape in each cartridge has the capacity to store 8 million characters of information. The cartridges are stored in cells in the storage unit or facility, as shown in Figure 5-18.

FIGURE 5-18
Cartridge storage system. (Courtesy Control Data.)

When the computer requires data from the facility, it determines what cartridge contains that data. It then "selects" that cartridge. A transport mechanism removes the selected cartridge from its cell and moves it to a read/write station (see Figure 5-18). At the read/write station the strip of tape is automatically unwound into a vacuum column. The contents of the tape are read (or new data is recorded), and the tape and its cartridge are then returned to the storage cell. The average time to access and read a tape (including mechanical movement) is between two and three seconds. Since this operation is slow compared to computer speeds, data are normally read from the facility and "staged" on magnetic disk storage before entry into the computer.

The storage unit for the mass cartridge system is shown in Figure 5-19. This unit can contain up to 2000 cartridges and has from two to four read/write stations. Since the storage capacity of each cartridge is 8 million characters, the total capacity of the mass storage facility is 16 billion characters of on-line data. Thus this facility, which is a 10-foot-long bank of rectangular cells, has a capacity equivalent to several thousand reels of magnetic tape, or about 200 disk packs of the type shown in Figure 5-14.

FIGURE 5-19
Mass storage facility. (Courtesy Control Data.)

Because of the mechanical movement, magnetic cartridge storage is relatively slow (at least two to three seconds per access). However, it provides the major advantage of magnetic disk storage (direct access to data) at a cost that is comparable to magnetic tape storage.

QUESTION: The advantage of magnetic cartridge storage over magnetic tape is that it provides _____ access to data records. The advantage over magnetic disk storage is the lower _____

ANSWER: direct, cost

OPTICAL DISK SYSTEM A new mass information storage system is based on the use of video disk technology. A special version of the video disk, called the "Philips Air Sandwich," was developed by Philips Laboratories. This device consists of two 12-inch disks stuck together, with tellerium-layer recording surfaces sealed inside the disks. Data is recorded on the disks by a helium–neon laser that burns micron-sized holes in the tellerium recording material.

The present version of the optical disk system has a storage capacity of 2×10^{10} bits (20 billion bits). Once the bits are recorded as holes by the laser they cannot be erased. If the data must be updated, the sector where the original data is stored is tagged with the address of the updated data.

The optical disk system provides direct access to enormous files of data. Since the recording is permanent, it is most appropriate for historical or **archival** data. For example, banks and insurance companies must maintain historical files of customer account data for legal audit trail requirements.

The optical disk system has a number of important advantages over magnetic tape.

1. Higher density—one 12-inch optical disk is equivalent to 25 high-density magnetic tape reels.

2. Lower cost—the optical disk media cost (cents per bit) is about one-tenth that of magnetic tape.

3. Faster access—average access time for the optical disk is less than 150 milliseconds, compared to about 15 seconds for magnetic tape (10,000 times faster).

4. Longer life—magnetic tape has a dependable error-free life of 18 months to two years, while the optical disk has an indefinite life.

Requirements for mass information storage systems are growing, creating a need for systems such as optical disk storage. For example, the annual information storage requirements for U.S. oil exploration by 1983 to 1984 are projected at 2×10^{16} bits. As a result, researchers are developing **terabit** optical disk systems (a terabit is 10^{12} or a trillion bits). For example, Philips is developing a disk pack with terabit capacity that may cost about $150. Capacity could be increased to 10^{15} bits by storing 1000 such disk packs in a 325-square-foot room. The equivalent magnetic tape storage would require an eight-acre building.

SERIAL ACCESS MEMORY   The secondary storage devices we have been discussing (such as magnetic disk) are all rotating or moving surface devices. These devices have proved satisfactory for many applications and are widely used. However, they are shackled with the same limitations associated with all electromechanical devices: limited speed, limited reliability, and relatively high cost. As a result, the computer industry is expending considerable effort to develop all-electronic secondary storage devices, especially for use as paging memory.

Unfortunately, the random access semiconductor devices used for main memory are still expensive for large-capacity secondary storage. However, all-electronic devices can be produced at reasonable cost if a technique known as serial access is used, rather than random access. With **serial access** devices, binary digits (or bits) circulate as if they were in a closed pipeline (see Figure 5–20). When bits are written into the serial access device, they are shifted sequentially through a series of storage locations before they become available for reading.

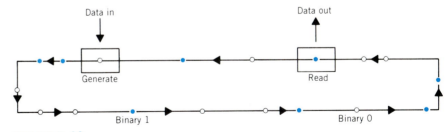

FIGURE 5–20
Serial access device.

The access time for a serial access device depends on the number of storage locations in the storage loop and the rate at which bits are shifted from one location to the next. At present, the storage loops range in length from about 10 locations to over 1000 locations.

QUESTION: In a serial access device, data cannot be read until it has been shifted in storage to a read station. Therefore, the access time is (faster, slower) than for random access memory.

ANSWER: slower

Magnetic bubble memory is one important type of serial access device in use today.

Magnetic bubbles are microscopic spots or regions on a thin magnetic film of garnet. The spots are magnetized in a direction opposite to that of the surrounding film (see Figure 5–21). Without an external magnetic field, areas of opposite magnetization in the film are approximately equal (left). When an increasing magnetic field is applied, the areas of opposite magnetization shrink and form bubbles with a circular cross section of microscopic size (right). The presence of a bubble at a particular location corresponds to a binary 1, and the absence to a binary 0. The magnetic field is rotated to shift the bubbles in a circulating pattern. The information can then be read at a "read" station, as shown in Figure 5–20.

FIGURE 5–21
Distribution of magnetic bubbles in magnetic film material.

Magnetic bubble memory offers two significant advantages over semiconductor memory.

1. Magnetic bubbles are nonvolatile (data is retained when power is lost).

2. Much higher storage densities can be achieved. In 1979, Intel Corporation introduced a 1M-bit bubble memory unit (one million bits on a chip). This chip (see Figure 5–22) has the capacity to store approximately 50 pages of text from this textbook.

FIGURE 5–22
The 1M-bit magnetic bubble memory chip. (Courtesy Intel Corporation.)

ADVANCED MEMORY SYSTEMS Existing memory systems are continually undergoing improvement. Very large scale integration is permitting ever higher bit densities for semiconductor memories, resulting in lower costs and reduced space and power requirements. Also, magnetic disk and other moving-surface devices are improved each year. These improvements have served as a barrier to the introduction of new memory technology. Over the past 25 years, dozens of new memory technologies have fallen by the wayside in the face of continued improvements in existing technology. Other promising technologies (such as thin film memory and optical beam memories) have not achieved commercial success in spite of extensive research and development and prototype production. Exceptions are the magnetic bubble memory and charge-coupled devices described above.

Despite the competition from existing technology, research is continually underway to develop new memory devices for computers. The most promising area of research at present appears to be in the area of **cryoelectronic memories.** Cryogenics is the study of behavior of materials at temperatures near absolute zero ($-273°$ Celsius).

The particular cryoelectronic memory device under development is referred to as a superconductive **tunnel junction.** "Tunneling" refers to the ability of electrons under low temperature conditions to penetrate energy barriers they would ordinarily not surmount. Tunnel junctions undergo a transition from a superconductive tunneling state to a normal tunneling state when a small magnetic field is applied. In order for the tunnel junction to go into the superconducting state the device must be cooled to cryogenic temperatures by immersion in liquid helium.

QUESTION: A tunnel junction is a two-state device in which the states are referred to as the

_____ tunneling state and the _____ state.

ANSWER: superconducting, normal

Tunnel junctions operate at very low voltages and at temperatures close to absolute zero (about $-269°$ Celsius). They consume from 100 to 1000 times less power than semiconductor circuits. This reduction makes it possible to pack circuits very densely without causing heat dissipation problems. As a result, signal propagation times are reduced and the devices are much faster than conventional circuits. These factors lead experts to predict cryoelectronic memories with extremely high component densities operating at speeds 10 to 100 times faster than today's fastest memories. This speed has the potential of leading to the development of a new generation of superfast computers.

A number of difficult problems must be solved before cryoelectronic memories become practical. The fabrication of tunnel junctions requires a perfect insulating film with a thickness of about two-hundredths the wavelength of blue light. Also, new packaging techniques are required to achieve the extremely high packing densities. Mechanical stresses generated in the devices when temperatures are reduced from room temperature to near absolute zero must be overcome. These factors suggest that several years of development will be required before cryoelectronic computers are commercially available.

QUESTION: Compared with existing memory devices, cryoelectronic memories will be

_____ to _____ times faster and will consume from

_____ to _____ times less power.

ANSWER: 10, 100, 100, 1000

EXERCISE 5-2   1.   Refer to Figure 5-23. The average access time for magnetic bubble mem-

ory is about _____ seconds. This is about _____ times the
average access time for MOS semiconductor memory. However, the cost

of MOS memory is about _____ times that for magnetic bubbles.

2.   Suppose that a magnetic disk storage unit has an average rotational delay
time of 8.4 milliseconds, and an average seek time of 30 milliseconds.
   a.   What is the average access time for this unit?

_____ milliseconds
   b.   How many records can be read from secondary storage per minute
on the average? _____

3.   A data record is located on magnetic disk by means of a disk address. This
address specifies what three factors?

a.   _____

b.   _____

c.   _____

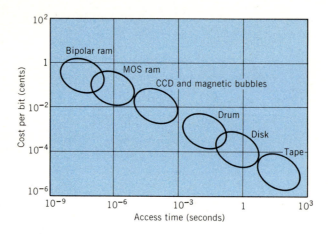

FIGURE 5-23
Access time versus cost for memory devices.

SUMMARY   In this chapter you have studied the various types of memory and storage
devices used in most computers. Two important characteristics of memory
devices (access time and cost) are compared in Figure 5-23 for various devices.

The next decade is expected to bring substantial improvements in all of these devices. Introduction of electron beam and X-ray techniques in the fabrication of semiconductor circuits should make it possible to increase the bit density of these devices by a factor of 100. With the introduction of thin film technology, bit densities of magnetic disks are also expected to increase 100-fold within five years. The price per bit of all of these devices will probably decrease by a factor of 10 or more during the 1980s.

Tunnel junction devices (a form of cryogenic memory) will be introduced by the mid 1980s. These devices may lead to the introduction of computers that are superfast by today's standards.

ANSWERS TO EXERCISES

EXERCISE 5-1

1. a. Data base storage
   b. Main memory
   c. Paging memory
   d. Archival storage

2.

Type of Memory	Fastest	Slowest
Main	Semiconductor	Semiconductor
Paging	Semiconductor	Fixed-head disk
Secondary	Moving-head disk	Magnetic tape
Archival	Video disk	Magnetic cartridge

EXERCISE 5-2

1. 10^{-3} to 10^{-5} (average is 10^{-4})
   100 times (10^{-4} versus 10^{-6})
   10 times (10^{-2} versus 10^{-1})

2. a. 38.4 (30 plus 8.4)
   b. 1,563 (60,000 ÷ 38.4)

3. a. cylinder number
   b. track number
   c. record number

CHAPTER EXAMINATION

1. Explain the purpose of each of the following types of storage and the major types of devices or media used.

   a. Main memory _____

   _____

   _____

   b. Paging memory _____

   _____

   _____

   c. Data base storage _____

   _____

   _____

   d. Archival storage _____

   _____

   _____

2. Match the following terms to the most appropriate definitions.

   ____ Semiconductor   a. Consists of seek time plus rotational delay time.

   ____ Seek time   b. Mass storage for programs and data files.

   ____ Paging   c. Records may be accessed without searching.

   ____ Magnetic bubbles   d. Historical or reference data.

   ____ Access time   e. Moving program segments between main memory and secondary storage.

   ____ Direct access   f. Information is lost when power fails.

   ____ Archival   g. Microscopic spots on thin film.

_____ Secondary storage   h.   Removable pack or cartridge.

_____ Disk module   i.   Circuits integrated on silicon chip.

_____ Volatile   j.   Time to move disk access mechanism.

3. Briefly describe two all-electronic devices used for secondary storage.

a. _____

_____

b. _____

_____

4. Mark each of the following statements true or false.

_____ a. Semiconductor memories are widely used for secondary storage.

_____ b. Programs currently being executed and data being processed are contained in main memory.

_____ c. Semiconductor memories are faster, cheaper, and more compact than magnetic core memories.

_____ d. Disk storage is cheaper than magnetic tape storage.

_____ e. A storage address references a character (or byte) in a variable word length computer, while in a fixed word length computer each address references a full word.

_____ f. A track is a pie-shaped segment on a magnetic disk surface.

_____ g. Magnetic cartridge storage provides low-cost, high-capacity direct access storage with relatively high access times.

_____ h. The time for a magnetic disk to rotate into position is referred to as seek time.

_____ i. Magnetic bubble memory will completely replace magnetic disk storage by 1984.

_____ j. Magnetic drum storage is the most common form of secondary storage at the present time.

_____ k. Tunnel junction devices will operate at about 0° Celsius.

5. Give two advantages of semiconductor memory over magnetic core storage.

a. _____

b. _____

6. Define each of the following terms.

a. Sequential access _____

_____

b.   Direct access _____

_____

c.   Multiprogramming _____

_____

d.   Serial access _____

_____

e.   Virtual storage _____

_____

7   List the principal advantages of each of the following types of secondary storage.

a.   Magnetic disk _____

_____

b.   Magnetic tape _____

_____

c.   Magnetic cartridge _____

_____

8.   Explain the concept of virtual storage. What are its advantages?

_____

_____

_____

9.   Rank each of the following types of memory according to the categories shown below: magnetic disk, magnetic tape, magnetic bubble, MOS RAM, bipolar RAM.

a.   Access time (fastest device to slowest device)

(1) _____

(2) _____

(3) _____

(4) _____

(5) _____

b. Cost per character of capacity (highest to lowest)

(1) _____

(2) _____

(3) _____

(4) _____

(5) _____

10. Explain how data are represented or stored on each of the following.

a. Magnetic core _____

_____

b. Magnetic disk _____

_____

c. Magnetic bubble _____

_____

d. Semiconductor _____

_____

e. Magnetic tape _____

_____

11. What type of organization would consider using magnetic cartridge storage?

_____

_____

12. What is the main advantage of each of the following?

a. Removable disk pack _____

_____

b. Head-per-track disk _____

_____

13. Give at least one type of storage device that might be used for each of the following.

a. Storing programs when not in main memory _____

_____

b. Storing large sequential data files _____

_____

c. Storing large direct access files _____

_____

d. Storing extremely large direct access files _____

_____

14. Briefly describe magnetic cartridge storage. What are its advantages?

_____

_____

_____

_____

_____

15. Describe the primary advantage and the primary disadvantage of magnetic disk storage, compared to magnetic tape.

a. Advantage _____

b. Disadvantage _____

16. From the following list, pick one or more of the most commonly used types of main memory.

_____

a. Magnetic disk   d. Tunnel junction
b. Magnetic bubble   e. None of the above
c. Laser

17. From the discussion of various devices, list typical times for each of the following operations.

a. Access a word of data in main memory _____

b. Access a record in magnetic disk storage _____

c. Access a block of data in magnetic cartridge storage _____

18. Explain the basic principle of tunnel junction devices.

_____

_____

_____

19.   What is the basic purpose of each of the following.

a.   Random access memory _____

_____

b.   Read-only memory _____

_____

20.   For what type of memory are each of the following devices used, and what are their typical access times?

a.   MOS semiconductor _____

_____

b.   Bipolar semiconductor _____

_____

21.   Describe briefly a floppy disk. How is it used?

_____

_____

_____

_____

22.   What is serial access memory? What is its advantage?

_____

_____

_____

_____

23.   An IBM 3330 disk pack has the following characteristics.

411 cylinders   30 millisecond average seek time
19 tracks/cylinder (usable)   3600 rpm rotational speed
13,034 bytes/track

a.   What is the total storage capacity of the disk pack?

_____ M bytes

b.   What is the average access time for the disk pack?

_____ milliseconds

24.   Contrast each of the following.

   a.   Random access memory versus read-only memory _____

   _____

   _____

   b.   Paging memory versus data base storage _____

   _____

   _____

   c.   Kilobyte versus megabyte _____

   _____

   _____

   d.   Sequential versus direct access _____

   _____

   _____

25.   State the major advantage of each of the following.

   a.   Fixed-head disk over moving-head disk _____

   _____

   b.   Magnetic cartridge over magnetic tape _____

   _____

   c.   Magnetic bubble memory over magnetic disk _____

   _____

6

INPUT/OUTPUT CONCEPTS AND DEVICES

OVERVIEW. Data processing consists of three fundamental operations: input **of data into the computer,** processing **the data into meaningful forms of information,** and output **of (or communicating) the information to human beings. For example, at the end of each semester, data representing courses and grades is input for each student, the data is processed to update grade point averages and degree plans, and information is output in the form of grade reports.**

Most data processing applications require the preparation and input of large amounts of data resulting from the daily transactions of the organization. These data often must be converted to machine-readable form before they can be input to the computer. As a result, the cost of input data preparation may represent from 25 to 50 percent of the DP operating budget in some organizations.

Rising data preparation costs and the need for improved responsiveness and accuracy have led to a number of improved data entry techniques. Key-to-tape and key-to-disk systems are replacing large keypunch operations. On-line data entry terminals are being placed in remote locations (such as warehouses and sales offices) where user personnel enter data directly into the computer. Optical character recognition equipment and bar code readers are being used to read source data, so that key-entry is eliminated. Also, voice data entry devices are being introduced that permit direct entry of data from the human voice. These improvements are leading to increased accuracy of data entry, as well as reduced data preparation costs.

Methods for output and communication of information to human beings are also undergoing constant improvement. Faster and quieter printers, some of which collate multiple copies of reports, are common. Plotters and graphics terminals communicate digital information in the form of color charts and illustrations. Voice response units are also used in some applications.

The various input/output and secondary storage devices for a computer are referred to as peripherals. **Figure 6–1 illustrates the wide variety of input/output devices that are used**

with computers today. The more important input/output concepts and devices are described in this chapter.

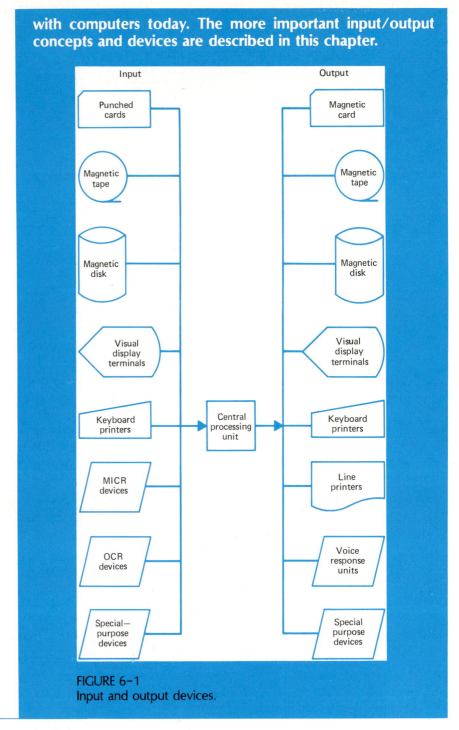

FIGURE 6–1
Input and output devices.

INPUT/ OUTPUT CONCEPTS

In Chapter 3 you learned that every computer has an input and an output section. Before studying the various devices that are used, you should understand the basic steps in the input of data and the output of information. The following steps are normally required.

1. Identifying the sources of data.
2. Converting the data to machine-readable form.
3. Input of data to the computer.
4. Output of information, following internal processing.

When data are entered on-line into the computer (for example, from a video display terminal), steps two and three are accomplished together.

IDENTIFYING SOURCES OF DATA

The data to be processed by a computer system may originate from a number of different sources, depending on the nature of the organization. Much of the data typically results from transactions with customers and suppliers — for example, customer orders, payments on accounts, and receipts of goods. Other data result from activities within the organization — for example, employee hours worked and usage of materials and supplies.

The variety of data sources in different organizations can best be illustrated by several examples.

1. In a hospital, various supplies and services—medicines, X-rays, beds, surgical facilities—are used in patient care. Data concerning the supplies and services used for each patient must be recorded for purposes of billing the patient and updating supply inventory records. Relevant data include the patient name and quantity and unit cost of each supply or service used.

2. In a manufacturing facility, jobs are performed at various work centers. When employees complete a job, they report the following data: work station number, job number, employee number, and time spent on the job.

3. In a bank, checks are presented for payment. Data to be input to the computer include bank identification number, customer account number, and amount of check.

4. In a mail order firm selling stationery, customer orders arrive by mail on a preprinted order form. An example of such a form is shown in Figure 6–2.

QUESTION: Examine Figure 6–2. What are the relevant data for processing the customer

order? _____

ANSWER: Customer name and address, order code, name of article, quantity and price for each item ordered, total amount, total enclosed, and amount charged.

CONVERTING TO MACHINE-READABLE FORM

Before data can be processed by a computer, it must be in machine-readable form. This step is called **data preparation** or **data entry.** Two basic principles should be followed in designing the data entry system.

1. Data should be captured in machine-readable form at the earliest opportunity. Ideally, data are recorded in machine-readable form when they are originated. Often this is not possible, especially when data originate outside the organization. For example, much of the data on the mail order form shown in Figure 6–2 are handwritten by the individual customer. In such cases, the data should be converted to machine-readable form as soon as practicable after they enter the organization. Capturing data in machine-readable form at an early stage reduces manual operations, with the advantages of greater processing speed and reduced error rates.

Order Blank

PLEASE PRINT

Please Use One Name For All Orders In Your Household

TODAY'S DATE 3-1-8X

(Please Do Not Write In This Space)
CH
A/RP ORG
SVC

F

YOUR NAME Mrs. J. Bishnou

ADDRESS 2635 Bitters Rd.

CITY San Antonio STATE Texas ZIP 78217

PRICE SCHEDULE
On orders of 1 to 5 items (any assortment): Retail Price
On orders of 6 or more items (any assortment): Fund Raiser Price
Please add 30¢ Handling Charge on orders under $6.60.

ORDER CODE	HOW MANY ITEMS?	NAME OF ARTICLE	RETAIL PRICE	FUND RAISER PRICE	TOTAL AMOUNT
38	3	Just-A-Note (Butterfly Designs)	$1.00 ea.	$ .55 ea.	1.65
75	1	Farmyard Friends	1.00 ea.	.55 ea.	.55
123		Recipe Cards (Garden Harvest)	1.25 ea.	.70 ea.	
158	5	North American Birds (Ecology Cards)	1.00 ea.	.55 ea.	2.75
159		American Country Cards	1.00 ea.	.55 ea.	
301		Wildwood Stationery (Blue)	2.00 ea.	1.10 ea.	
302		Wildwood Stationery (Yellow)	2.00 ea.	1.10 ea.	
309		Post-A-Notes (Mini Merchants)	1.00 ea.	.55 ea.	
310	2	Pantry Post Cards	1.50 ea.	.85 ea.	1.70

TOTAL ITEMS 11

TOTAL AMOUNT
Total From Above $ 6.65
30¢ Handling Charge On Orders Under $6.60 $
Total Amount $ 6.65

IMPORTANT
Please Do Not Send Stamps or Cash.
We Welcome Your Comments or Suggestions at Any Time.

Please Charge My Order
Add Postage to My Bill
AMOUNT CHARGED
$

MY TELEPHONE IS:
(To Expedite Your Order)
Area Code
Number

Check or Money Order Enclosed
Current Pays the Postage
TOTAL ENCLOSED
$ 6.65

CURRENT, INC., THE CURRENT BLDG., COLORADO SPRINGS, COLO. 80941

FIGURE 6-2
Order form for mail order firm.

2. Constant data should be prerecorded in machine-readable form or entered automatically into the system. For example, in the banking industry the bank identification number and customer number are recorded in magnetic ink characters on the checks by machine before checks are sold or issued to a bank customer. When the customer writes a check, only the amount of the check is encoded by the bank before processing. The use of magnetic ink characters on checks is illustrated later in this chapter.

Entering constant information as prerecorded machine-readable data reduces manual conversion of data and the attendant chances for error. In the banking example, entering the bank and customer number on each check as it is processed would be an extremely inefficient procedure, resulting in a prohibitive amount of manual data encoding and a resultant high error rate.

The method of capturing or converting data to machine-readable form depends on a number of factors such as the source and nature of the data, volume of data, time and accuracy requirements, and cost constraints. There are three basic approaches (see Figure 6–3).

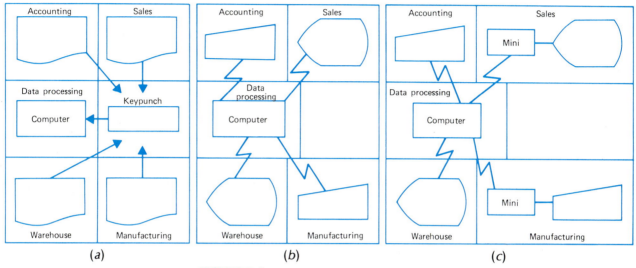

FIGURE 6–3

Alternative approaches to data entry (*a*) Batch data entry. (*b*) On-line data entry, central processing. (*c*) On-line data entry, distributed processing.

1. *Off-line batch data preparation*—source documents from various departments are accumulated into batches and sent to a central key-entry department (illustrated in Figure 6–3a). Professional keypunch operators punch the data into cards. Alternatively, the key-entry operation stores the data on magnetic tape, disk, or diskette. The cards (or magnetic media) are then sent to the computer for processing.

2. *On-line data entry, central processing*—remote terminals (such as video displays) are located in user departments. Users enter data directly into the computer, without converting the data to a medium such as punched cards. Transactions may be entered as they arrive or are created in the departments, rather than being accumulated into batches. This approach is often referred to as **transaction processing.**

    Two types of terminals are illustrated in Figure 6–3b: visual display terminals and printer terminals. The symbols used for these terminals are the following.

3. *On-line data entry, distributed processing*—minicomputers are placed in each of the major departments. Data is entered on line to the minicomputers for processing within the department. Summary data may

be transmitted from each minicomputer to a central computer. This approach is illustrated in Figure 6–3c.

QUESTION: Figure 6–3c represents a distributed data entry and processing system because

there are minicomputers in the _____ and _____ departments, each connected to a central computer.

ANSWER: sales, manufacturing

Figure 6–3 actually depicts the evolution that has occurred (and is occurring) in data processing. Earlier data processing departments relied on batch data entry, with a large keypunch department. Keypunches were then replaced with faster key-to-tape or key-to-disk systems. During the next stage, remote terminals were placed in user departments. Today the trend is to distributed processing systems of the type shown in Figure 6–3c.

EXERCISE 6–1   1. A hospital records the type, amount, and cost of each type of supply and service issued to a patient. At present, data are recorded manually on a worksheet. Suggest a way to capture these data using punched cards that recognizes the basic principles discussed in the previous section.

_____

_____

_____

2. Figure 6–2 shows a customer order form for a mail order firm. Suppose data are to be keypunched for entry into the order processing system. What information from the order form would be keypunched? Is it necessary to keypunch all of the data shown on the form? Explain your reasoning.

_____

_____

_____

INPUT OF DATA INTO THE COMPUTER   When data are prepared off-line for input into the computer they are punched into cards or captured on magnetic tape, disk, or floppy disk. The data may then be read into the computer by means of an input (or input/output) device. The basic input/output devices used for this purpose are card readers, magnetic tape units, magnetic disk units, and floppy disk drives.

THE INPUT/OUTPUT CYCLE   When data are read into the computer, the following sequence of events occurs.

1. A computer "read" instruction is executed, which specifies the address of the device from which the data are to be obtained and the

address of the area in computer memory into which the data are to be read.

2. An electrical signal is sent to the device control unit that activates the transport mechanism for the device. If the device is busy or inoperable, a signal is returned by the control unit to the central processor.

3. The input device reads the contents of the record from the input medium and encodes the data into electrical signals.

4. The device control unit converts the data input code (such as Hollerith) into the internal code for the computer (such as EBCDIC) and transmits the data to main memory via a data channel (discussed below).

5. When the input operation is completed, a signal is transmitted to the central processor. This signal may be used to interrupt the sequence of program instructions.

The sequence of events for the output of data is similar to the input cycle.

DATA CHANNELS   Information is transferred between the computer and its peripheral devices by means of data channels. In a microcomputer or minicomputer the data channel is a simple electrical connection referred to as a **bus,** which connects the peripheral devices to the central processing unit.

In larger computers, the data channel is more complex and in fact is itself a special-purpose micro or minicomputer. The advantage of this type of channel is that it permits input/output operations to be controlled independently of the central processing unit. As a result, the relatively slow input/output operations are scheduled for maximum throughput and are overlapped with internal processing; that is, input/output operations and computations can be performed at the same time. Very often the major difference in capacity between minicomputers and larger computers is not so much in internal processing speeds, but in the fact that the larger computer is less restricted by input and output capacity.

A data channel operates in the following way. When the computer central processing unit (CPU) encounters an input or output instruction coded by the programmer, it activates a channel. After it activates the channel, the CPU is free to continue with other processing tasks. The channel controls the transfer of information to and from the computer. It also provides a buffer or temporary storage capacity for data being transferred. When data transfer is completed, the channel interrupts the CPU so that it may continue with other operations. It will also interrupt the CPU if an error condition occurs.

Most modern computers have a number of channels that can be operated simultaneously. The number and capacity of channels supplied are important considerations in selecting a computer. The number of channels determines the number of devices that can be operated simultaneously, while the capacity limits the rate of data transfer.

Figure 6-4 shows a simplified computer input/output system. A channel is generally connected to a control unit, which in turn is connected to one or more input/output devices. There is often a separate control unit for each type of device, for example printer control unit, magnetic tape control unit, and so on.

QUESTION: Input and output operations are controlled by a _____ that is part of the

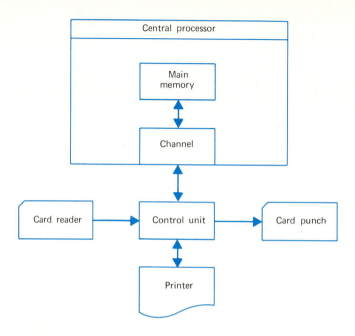

FIGURE 6-4
Simple input/output configuration.

CPU. This unit is connected to a _____ unit that controls one or more

_____ devices.

ANSWER: channel, control, input/output

An important consideration in selecting input/output devices is compatibility. Each device receives and transmits messages in a particular code format, referred to as a **protocol.** Device A can communicate directly with device B only if they "talk the same language;" that is, they have the same protocols. To facilitate the connection of input/output devices to computers there are certain industry standard protocols. A widely used standard protocol is called the **RS232C** standard. Thus, for example, a terminal with the RS232C standard is compatible with any computer that uses this standard.

The manufacture of peripheral devices is a highly competitive aspect of the computer industry. There are many **independent peripheral manufacturers** that produce devices for use on widely used computers. For example, Storage Technology Corporation produces magnetic disk drives for use on IBM computers. Devices that are compatible with the manufacturer's computer are referred to as **plug-compatible** devices; that is, these devices can be used in place of the manufacturer's peripherals without modification to hardware or software.

A logical extension of plug-compatible peripherals is the development of **plug-compatible mainframes.** These are central processing units produced by one manufacturer, designed to be compatible with and to replace the CPU of another manufacturer. Thus, Amdahl Corporation manufactures CPUs that are designed to replace IBM mainframes. The plug-compatible mainframe is compatible with all peripheral devices attached to the CPU it replaces and will execute the user's programs without modification. Plug-compatible products have increased competition in the computer industry, thereby reducing prices and accelerating the introduction of new technology.

OUTPUT OF INFORMATION   The last stage in the processing cycle is the output of information. Information may be stored on a machine-readable medium such as magnetic tape or disk for further processing, or it may be printed or otherwise displayed for persons. In most programs both types of output are produced.

Figure 6-2 showed a customer order form for a mail order firm. Processing the data results in the following types of output information.

1. An updated inventory record for each item, reflecting the amount sold. This information is output on magnetic disk.

2. A shipping notice, used by a clerk to select and pack the order. An example is shown in Figure 6-5. This notice is also used as a customer invoice if the order is not prepaid.

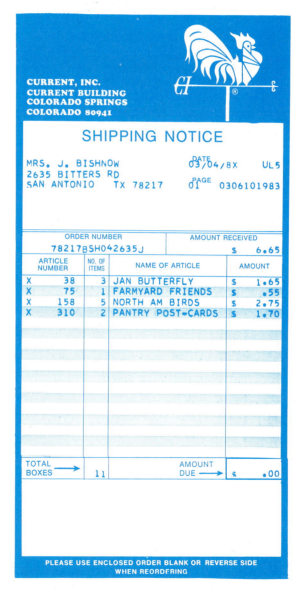

FIGURE 6-5
Customer shipping notice for mail order firm.

EXERCISE 6-2   1. List three functions performed by a data channel.

a. _____

b. _____

c. _____

2. List three alternative approaches to data entry.

a. _____

b. _____

c. _____

3. A computer has two data channels. The first channel is connected to a video display control unit, which has three video display terminals attached. The second channel is connected to a magnetic disk control unit with two magnetic disk drives attached. Draw a configuration diagram (similar to Figure 6-4).

INPUT AND OUTPUT DEVICES

We now turn our attention to the actual devices and media that are used for the input of data to the computer and output of information to the user. We use the term **media** to refer to the punched cards, magnetic tape, paper, or other products on which data are actually transcribed or recorded. On the other hand, we use the term **device** to refer to the input and/or output units that read data from the media used or write data onto the media. For example, punched cards are a form of media while a punched card reader is an input device.

The various input–output devices described in this chapter are classified according to the type of media used, as follows.

1. Paper media—punched card readers and punches, printers (impact and nonimpact), and plotters.
2. Keyboard devices—keyboard printers, visual display terminals, graphics terminals, and key-to-storage devices.
3. Magnetic media—magnetic tape, magnetic disk and diskette, and magnetic ink characters. Magnetic tape, disk, and diskette were described in Chapter 5 since they function as storage media as well as input/output media. Therefore, only magnetic ink character recognition is described in this chapter.
4. Optical media—optical character devices, bar code readers, and computer output microfilm.
5. Voice recognition and response units.
6. Specialized input/output devices—point-of-sale terminals, factory data collection terminals, automated teller machines, and transaction telephones.

DEVICES USING PAPER MEDIA

Paper is widely used for computer input and output in the form of punched cards, printed or plotted output, and character-encoded documents. The major advantage is that it is readily handled and interpreted by humans. On the other hand, paper has low recording density and cannot be reused. Also, since electromechanical devices are used, input and output of data using paper media are comparatively slow. Typical reading rates are 1000 to 2000 characters per second. Another disadvantage is that the cost of paper is increasing rapidly and supplies are sometimes uncertain. As a result, paper media are used in applications where the volume of data to be input or output is relatively low, where data must be in a form readily interpreted by people, where a permanent record is required, and where high speed is not important.

PUNCHED CARDS   Punched cards were the most common form of input medium in early computer systems. In today's systems, emphasis has switched to magnetic media such as magnetic tape, disk, and floppy disk. However, punched cards are still used in some applications. For example, punched cards are widely used as "turnaround" documents in billing and similar applications. Many utilities send monthly bills in the form of cards with prepunched customer number, name and address, month, amount billed, and other information. When the card is returned, the amount paid is punched into the card, and it is used to update the customer's account.

The 80-column Hollerith card (called the "IBM card") is the most popular type of card in use today. This card is laid out in 12 horizontal rows and 80 vertical columns (see Figure 6–6). The top three rows (12, 11, and 0) are called "zone rows" or "zones." Rows 0 to 9 are called "numeric rows." Any digit 0 to 9 is represented in a single column by a single punch in the corresponding row of that column. An alphabetic character is represented by a combination of two punches, one zone and one numeric. Special characters are represented by various punching combinations (see Figure 6–6). Notice that the 0-row is either a numeric or a zone, depending on its use.

Another type of card that is commonly used is a 96-column card. This card was introduced by IBM in 1969 for use with its System/3 computer. This card is much smaller than the 80-column card, measuring $3\frac{1}{4}$ inches wide by less than

FIGURE 6–6
The 80-column Hollerith card.

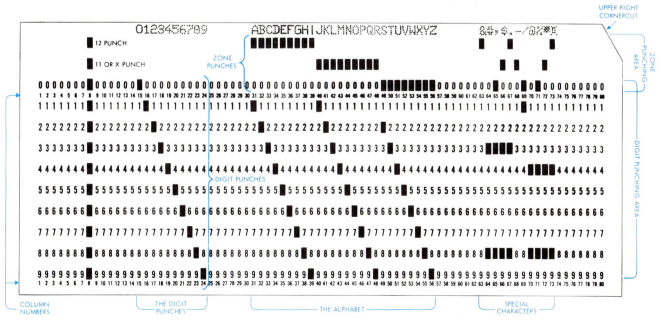

$2\frac{3}{4}$ inches high. The 96-column card has three punching tiers and uses round rather than rectangular punched holes.

Cards are read by a card read unit and punched by a punch unit. For reading, the file of cards is placed in a read hopper. In response to a "read" command, a card is moved past two sensing stations, as shown in Figure 6-7. The sensing stations use either wire brushes or photoelectric cells to sense the presence of card punches. The reason for two stations is to compare the results of the two read operations, to detect possible errors in reading. After the cards are read, they are placed in one or more output stackers.

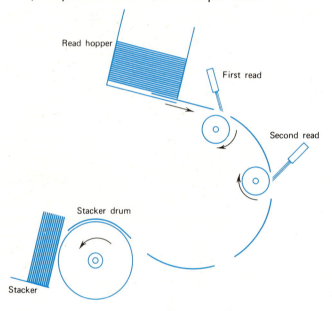

Read hopper

First read

Second read

Stacker drum

Stacker

FIGURE 6-7
Card reader mechanism.

In a card punch unit, blank cards are placed in a read hopper. After they are punched, cards are placed in an output stacker. Card punching is generally only one-fourth to one-half as fast as reading, due to the mechanical action of punching the cards.

In many computer systems, the card reader and punch are combined into a single unit. One such unit is shown in Figure 6-8. This unit reads 80-column cards at 1000 cards per minute and punches at 300 cards per minute.

PRINTED OUTPUT   All of us are familiar with computer-printed documents. Our payroll checks, credit card and utility bills, bank statements, and report cards are all printed by computers. Computer-printed documents in a business include invoices, shipping notices (see Figure 6-5), credit reports, stock status reports, profit and loss statements, and balance sheets. Printed output provides these advantages: ease of distributing multiple copies and a permanent record for audit or legal requirements.

TYPES OF PRINTERS AND MEDIA   There are two basic types of printers—character printers and line printers. A **character printer** prints serially (one character at a time), much like a typewriter. As a result, character printers are generally limited to speeds of from 10 to 150 characters per second. A **line printer** prints an entire line (typically up to 132 characters) at a time and consequently is many times faster than a character printer.

FIGURE 6–8
Combination card read–punch unit. (Courtesy IBM.)

Printers can also be classified by the method on which print characters are transferred to paper. There are two basic approaches: impact printers and nonimpact printers. With an **impact printer,** characters are formed by striking the type against an inked ribbon, which in turn strikes the paper to transfer the type image. A typewriter is an example of an impact printer. **Nonimpact printers** use other techniques such as ink spray, heat, xerography, or laser to form printed copy.

A wide variety of paper is used in computer printers, ranging from inexpensive newsprint to heat-sensitive paper. Paper widths vary from 1 or 2 inches for calculator ribbon up to 15 inches or more for conventional printer stock. Line printers usually require the paper to have sprocket holes at the edges, to ensure proper alignment and feeding of the paper.

Some of the more commonly used types of printer media (illustrated in Figure 6–9) are the following.

1. Stock tab—simple lined or shaded-band paper, most often used to produce listings of computer programs.
2. Roll paper—used in calculators and printing terminals.
3. Continuous forms—preprinted forms (such as checks, invoices, etc.) with company logo, address, and so on. Only variable information (such as customer name and address) is printed by the computer.

4. Continuous form card stock—punched cards or postcards in continuous form, for applications such as utility billing.

QUESTION: Which of the above four types of paper would a bank use to produce monthly

bank statements for its customers? _____

ANSWER: Continuous preprinted forms.

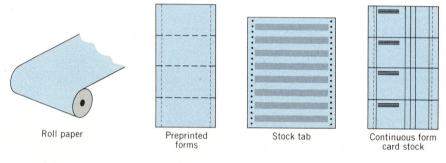

Roll paper   Preprinted   Stock tab   Continuous form
                    forms   card stock

FIGURE 6-9
Commonly used printer media.

FIGURE 6-10
Dot matrix printer.

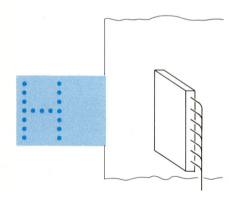

IMPACT PRINTERS

Impact printing techniques are used both for character and line printers. Both types are described below.

Character Printers. Character printers are used where the volume of printing is relatively small. They are especially common with micros and small minis but are also used as printing terminals on larger computers.

There are two basic types of impact character printers — dot matrix printers and those that use a moving print head such as a ball or wheel.

A **dot matrix** printer prints a pattern of dots in the shape of the desired character. A "five-by-seven" dot matrix printer would have a set of seven vertically arranged wires that strike the print ribbon, transferring the image to the paper (see Figure 6-10). The letter is formed, as a series of five strikes by the wires. Some printers use a "seven-by-nine" matrix. The advantage of a dot matrix printer is that it can achieve print speeds up to 165 characters per second (CPS). The disadvantage is that the print characters are of somewhat lower quality than full-strike characters.

A **ball** printer uses a rotating and/or pivoting ball as a print head. The printing characters are on the face of the ball. When the ball strikes the ribbon, the print character is transferred to the paper behind the ribbon (see Figure 6-11). The IBM Selectric Typewriter is the most commonly used ball printing device.

In a **wheel** printer, a wheel is used as a print head rather than a ball. The print characters form a band around the circumference of the print wheel (see Figure 6-12). The wheel rotates and moves from left to right across the paper. As the desired character on the wheel rotates past the print position, the hammer strikes the back side of the paper and presses it against the inked wheel.

Some ball and wheel-type printers print from left to right on one line, then print right to left on the next line. This increases the effective print speed since the lost motion of returning the print mechanism is eliminated. These printers have printing speeds of from 10 to 50 CPS. The main advantage of this type of

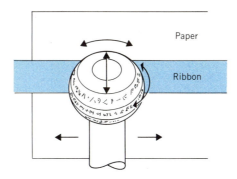

FIGURE 6-11
Ball printer.

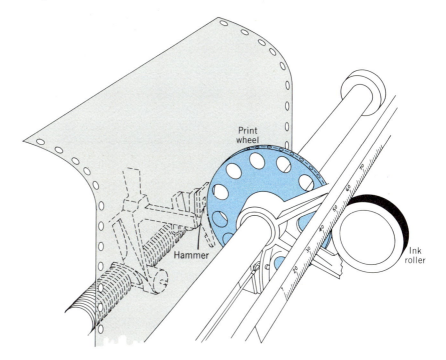

FIGURE 6-12
Wheel printer.

printer is that it produces full-strike (or "letter quality") characters, like those of an electric typewriter.

Line Printers. With impact line printers, print characters are mounted on a moving chain or belt or engraved on the face of a rotating drum. Print hammers press the paper and print ribbon against the selected type characters as they pass in front of the paper at high speed. Line printers produce printed output at a rate of from 200 to 3000 lines per minute. Multiple copies can easily be produced and characters are of full-strike quality. Examples of line printers are shown in Figure 6-13.

NONIMPACT PRINTERS   Much effort today is directed to developing nonimpact printers. These printers have two major advantages over impact printers: much quieter operation and much faster printing speeds. On the other hand, nonimpact printers have a higher purchase cost and many require a spe-

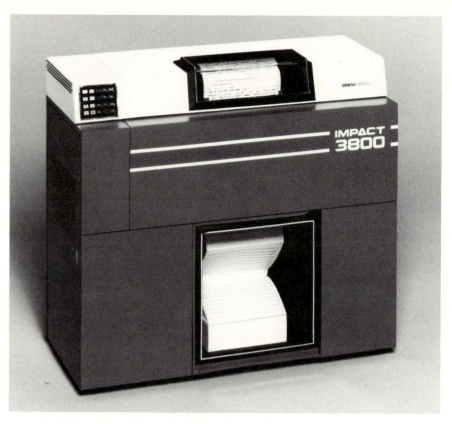

FIGURE 6-13
Impact line printer. (Courtesy Documentation, Inc.)

cial type of paper that costs more than paper used in impact printers. Also, many nonimpact printers do not permit multiple copies to be produced.

A variety of approaches is used for nonimpact printing. The most common of these are thermal, electrostatic, magnetic, xerographic, and laser printing. Each of these approaches is described briefly below.

Thermal printers are character printers, operating in the range of 10 to 30 CPS. The print image is created on a special heat-sensitive paper by heated wires in the print head. The heated wires form an array and produce a dot-type character, similar to the dot matrix impact printer.

An **electrostatic printer** places electrostatic charges in the shape of the desired character on a sensitized paper. The paper is then passed through a toner or solution containing ink particles of the opposite charge. These particles adhere to the charged spots on the paper, yielding the print image (see Figure 6-14). Electrostatic printers operate up to speeds of 3000 lines per minute or more. As with thermal printers, the print character is in dot matrix form.

A **magnetic printer** operates much like an electrostatic printer, except that the magnetic charges are placed on a belt rather than on sensitized paper. The belt then passes through a toner and the ink particles adhere to the belt where the print image is recorded. The belt is then pressed against heated paper, causing the ink to fuse to the paper. Magnetic printers are much slower than electrostatic printers (up to 200 lines per minute) but do not require special paper.

A **xerographic printer** is an adaptation of a Xerox office copier. A powerful light source is located in the center of a rotating drum. The drum has holes in the form of character images around its surface. As the drum rotates, the light

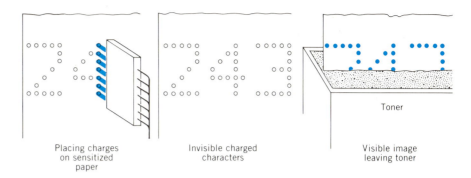

Placing charges on sensitized paper | Invisible charged characters | Visible image leaving toner

Toner

FIGURE 6-14
Electrostatic printing process.

energy is projected through the stencil-like openings, through a lens system, and onto the surface of a drum coated with a light-sensitive material. The drum is electrically charged and dusted with a powder ink. The drum is then rolled against paper and the print image is transferred and fixed by a combination of heat and pressure.

The xerographic printer produces sharp character images on letter-sized paper. The printer has a built-in minicomputer and can produce and collate multiple copies. The printer operates at about 4000 lines per minute.

The **laser printer** is the newest technology for very high speed computer printers. Thus, IBM introduced its 13,360 line-per-minute laser electrophotographic printer in 1975. In this printer, a laser beam (very intense light) forms character images on the surface of a rotating drum. A powder toner that adheres to the light images is then transferred to paper.

Xerox introduced its Model 9700 laser light printer in 1977. The printing process generates character patterns on a moving belt by means of a minicomputer-controlled laser light. Electrically charged toner particles are attracted to the light patterns on the belt and are then transferred to letter-sized paper. The Xerox printer prints at from 8000 to 18,000 lines per minute (LPM) and can operate either off-line or on-line to a computer. Honeywell's Page Processing System contains an integral minicomputer and is capable of printing at speeds from 2000 to 18,000 lines per minute (see Figure 6-15).

FIGURE 6-15
Laser printer. (Courtesy Honeywell.)

CONSIDERATIONS IN PRINTER SELECTION   The major considerations in selecting a printer are the following.

1. Speed—the required printing speed depends on the total volume of output, which can be estimated by systems analysts. Sufficient printer capacity must be provided, or else the computer will be "print bound" (printing is the limiting operation).

2. Cost—there are two cost factors, the initial cost and the recurring cost of paper and other supplies. Printers range in cost from less than $1000 for a slow character printer, to nearly $300,000 for a laser printer.

3. Reliability and ease of maintenance.

4. Print quality—readability and neatness of printed output.

5. Multiple copy capability, if required.

6. Line width—normal range is 72 to 132 characters.

7. Compatibility with computer and/or communications devices.

EXERCISE 6-3

1. What type of printer would you recommend for each of the following?
   a. Printer for microcomputer with capacity of up to 50 full-strike characters per second. _____

   b. Printer for microcomputer with capacity of 150 characters per second, full-strike characters not required. _____

   c. Printer for microcomputer with capacity of up to 30 CPS; must operate quietly in an office environment. _____

   d. Printer for medium-sized computer, 1000 lines per minute, multiple copies required. _____

   e. Printer for large-scale computer; must be able to print at least 10,000 lines per minute and collate multiple copies. _____

2. Name three advantages of impact printers over nonimpact printers.

   a. _____

   b. _____

   c. _____

PLOTTERS   It is often easier for humans to visualize data after they have been plotted rather than printed in numerical form. For example, a plot of sales versus months or of foreign oil imports as a percentage of total oil consumption is more readily grasped by humans than the same information obtained by reading through the corresponding statistical data.

A **plotter** is a device that converts digital computer output into illustrations. The illustrations may be in the form of graphs, bar charts, pie charts, maps, engineering drawings, and so on. Plotted output can be in color (up to three different colors is common), and three-dimensional figures can be simulated.

A plotter operates by converting digital coordinate data into pen movements. There are two basic types of plotters, flatbed plotters and drum plotters. In a **flatbed** plotter the paper remains stationary on a flat table or bed and the writing pen moves across the paper. In a **drum** plotter a roll of paper is moved back and forth while the pen moves across the paper. A drum plotter and some of its typical output are shown in Figure 6–16.

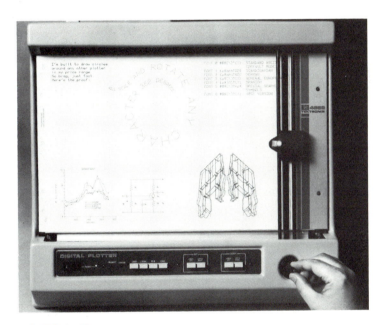

FIGURE 6–16
Drum plotter and output. (Courtesy Tektronix.)

A plotter may be connected on-line to the computer or it may be driven off-line by data stored on magnetic tape. Some firms package plotters, minicomputers, and prewritten software into self-contained **graphics systems.** These systems relieve the user of the tedious and time-consuming task of writing programs to plot digital output.

KEYBOARD DEVICES   Keyboard terminals and similar devices are used in many computer systems for on-line entry of data or inquiries. These are generally combination input/output devices, with keyboard input and printed or video display output. Keyboard devices are often used in locations remote from the computer and are limited to relatively low input volumes since input occurs at typewriter speeds. The use of terminal devices in data communications systems is described in Chapter 8.

KEYBOARD PRINTERS   A common type of terminal used in many on-line applications is the keyboard printer. These devices provide a versatile means of transmitting messages and data between a remote user and the computer. Input data are entered on a typewriter-like keyboard and output is printed on a character printer.

A standard printer terminal for many years has been the Teletype KSR-33 (often referred to as a teletypewriter). These devices have a standard keyboard and slow-speed (10 CPS) character printer. Some Teletype machines (and similar keyboard terminals) are equipped to transmit or receive data recorded on punched paper tape or magnetic tape cassette.

A sophisticated printer terminal is the Texas Instruments Model 763 Memory Terminal (see Figure 6–17). This terminal is the first to employ magnetic bubble memory (described in Chapter 5). Magnetic bubble memory has several advantages: it is nonvolatile (data is retained when power is turned off), consumes little power, and permits fast access to data stored in memory.

FIGURE 6-17
Printer terminal with bubble memory. (Courtesy Texas Instruments.)

With this terminal, prompting and operator lead-through can be developed to facilitate data entry; that is, the terminal provides instructions to the operator indicating what action is to be performed at each step. A file management system is provided that allows the operator to locate any indexed record in the terminal memory in less than 15 milliseconds (a comparable search with cassette tape might take several minutes). The terminal permits editing data including deleting and inserting characters and lines. The terminal has a standard keyboard and standard automatic send/receive functions. It has a 30-CPS thermal printer that permits quiet operation in an office environment. A portable version (Model 765) weighing 17 pounds is also available.

VISUAL DISPLAY TERMINALS   A visual display terminal (VDT) is a combination input/output device. Data are entered (or input) by means of a typewriter-like keyboard. Information is displayed (or output) on a television-like screen, usually a cathode ray tube (CRT).

Visual display terminals are widely used in a number of important on-line computer applications.

1.   Data entry—input of data to the computer.

2. Inquiry/response—entry of a request for information; display of the resulting message on the screen.

3. On-line programming—computer instructions are entered directly into the computer, which provides immediate feedback of syntax errors.

4. Computer-assisted instruction—VDT displays test questions; student enters responses on the keyboard.

The CRT screen in a visual display device consists of a screen coated with a substance called "phosphor." When a beam of electrons strikes the phosphor, a bright spot is produced. The beam scans the screen from left to right and from top to bottom at a rate of about 60 times per second. Characters are formed by turning on the beam at selected spots, analogous to forming characters with a dot matrix printer.

There are two basic types of visual display terminals.

1. "Dumb" terminals, with a conventional control unit. These terminals are used primarily for inquiry/response and timesharing applications.

2. "Smart" terminals, with a built-in microprocessor control unit and memory. Smart VDT terminals are programmable and offer features such as the display of input forms and the ability to edit input data and back space or delete characters or lines. Smart terminals are used primarily for data entry applications.

A typical visual display terminal (Hewlett-Packard 2621) is shown in Figure 6-18. This VDT can display 24 lines of data, 80 characters per line, or a total of 1920 characters. Both upper- and lower-case characters can be displayed, and characters can be underlined. The display has a built-in memory of 4096 bytes, corresponding to two full pages (full screens) of information. With this feature, the contents of memory can be viewed with "roll-up" and "roll-down" keys.

FIGURE 6-18
Visual display terminal. (Courtesy Hewlett-Packard.)

The display has a built-in 120-CPS thermal printer that will produce a hard copy of the full screen in 16 seconds.

Visual display terminals offer a number of important advantages over keyboard printers.

1. A formatted screen can be provided for data entry applications, so the operator "fills in the blanks."
2. Immediate sight verification is provided to the operator as data is entered.
3. Data can easily be edited on-line (by character or by line) before it is transmitted to the computer.
4. On output, a VDT is much faster than a printer. It displays a full page of information in an instant.

QUESTION: In an inquiry/response application (such as a hotel reservation system), the main

advantage of a visual display terminal is that it is much _____ than a printer terminal.

ANSWER: faster

GRAPHICS TERMINALS   Rather than display alphanumeric characters, visual display terminals can be used to display charts, graphs, maps, drawings, and other graphical images. Special **graphics terminals** are often used for this purpose. These are generally sophisticated display terminals with built-in microcomputers or minicomputers and come equipped with special graphics software. Graphics terminals can display objects in several different colors and light intensities. Often the terminals allow the use of a light pen by which an operator can trace an object on the screen. A **light pen** is a pen-shaped device with a photoelectric cell at its end, used to draw lines on a visual display screen. The characteristics of the object are then stored in the computer. The operator can then rotate or change the displayed object with the light pen.

Graphics terminals are used for two primary types of applications.

1. Displaying digital data in the form of graphs, charts, maps, and so on.
2. Engineering design of components and objects such as electronic circuits, automobiles, and others.

A graphics terminal is shown in Figure 6–19.

KEY-TO-STORAGE SYSTEMS   Often the preparation of input data is the bottleneck in the entire computer operation. Keypunching and verifying data are relatively slow and tedious operations and are vulnerable to error. Newer computers are faster and more powerful than ever before. Unless care is taken, the input operation can limit throughput and cause gross underutilization of the computer.

Many organizations facing the problem of speeding up data preparation are replacing conventional keypunches with **key-to-storage** systems. There are two basic types: **key-to-tape** and **key-to-disk** systems. Such systems consist of a number of key-stations (visual display terminals) connected to a minicomputer.

FIGURE 6-19
Graphics terminal. (Courtesy Tektronix.)

Operators enter data into the CRT units under control of the minicomputer. The data are then edited and stored on magnetic tape, disk, or flexible disk for processing by the organization's mainframe computer.

A typical key-to-storage system provides the following functions.

1. The minicomputer prompts the operator to enter the correct data at each step.
2. The CRT key-station provides sight verification to the operator; if an input error is made, back spacing and deletion allow the operator to correct the error immediately.
3. The keyed-in data is input to an edit program to filter out most errors. The mini can make checks for the reasonableness of input data.
4. Data from all of the key-stations are sorted and merged to produce a disk (or tape) file for further processing.
5. The system monitors operator performance and maintains statistics that are useful in improving productivity.

An example of a firm that has realized benefits from a **key-to-disk** system is Looart Press, a mail order firm that markets stationery and other paper products. During its peak selling season this firm processes between 15,000 and 20,000 customer orders daily. You saw a typical customer order in Figure 6–2. The firm has up to 24 key-stations in which operators key in data from the customer order for processing by a larger computer.

The benefits that Looart Press and other firms are realizing from key-to-disk (or key-to-tape) systems are the following.

1. Significant increase in productivity in preparing input data (25 to 75 percent improvement).
2. Reduced errors due to editing and operator prompting and sight verification.
3. Job enlargement effect due to elimination of menial tasks such as handling cards and also due to reduced noise levels.

4. Reduced load on mainframe computer, since input functions are handled off-line by a minicomputer.

A low-cost variation of **key-to-disk** systems is the **key-to-diskette** system. In this system, data that are entered in the key-station are recorded on floppy disks for further computer processing (see Figure 6–20). Floppy disks (or diskettes) are described in Chapter 5.

FIGURE 6–20
Key-to-diskette system. (Courtesy Mohawk Data Sciences.)

DEVICES USING MAGNETIC MEDIA

Both keyboard devices and devices using paper media have relatively slow input and output speeds. If large volumes of data must be input to or read from the computer, the data are often transcribed or recorded on a magnetic medium. The principal magnetic media are magnetic tape, magnetic disk and diskette, and inscribed magnetic characters. All of these media except magnetic ink characters are described in Chapter 5, since they are used as storage devices as well as input/output devices.

The principal advantage of the magnetic media is high recording density, resulting in compact storage and high input/output speeds. Also, magnetic media can be repeatedly erased and reused.

MAGNETIC INK CHARACTER RECOGNITION   In 1952, some 8 billion checks were written and processed in the United States. By 1960 this figure had grown to 13 billion, and at present over 30 billion checks are processed annually. Faced with this growth of paperwork, the American banking industry pioneered the development of magnetic ink character recognition, or MICR. Today almost all checks, deposit slips, and related documents are encoded with magnetic ink characters and processed with MICR equipment.

With MICR, characters are inscribed on documents with magnetic ink containing particles of iron oxide. The document reader senses the magnetic pattern formed by the characters. Only 14 characters are used in MICR—the 10 digits 0 through 9, plus four special characters. These characters are standard throughout the banking industry.

Constant information is recorded on the check in magnetic characters before it is issued to the bank customer. This includes the check routing symbol, transit number, and customer account number (see Figure 6-21). After the check is cashed, the amount is inscribed in the lower right-hand corner. All of the data inscribed on the check are read by a document processor at speeds comparable to a punched card reader.

FIGURE 6-21
Check inscribed with magnetic ink characters.

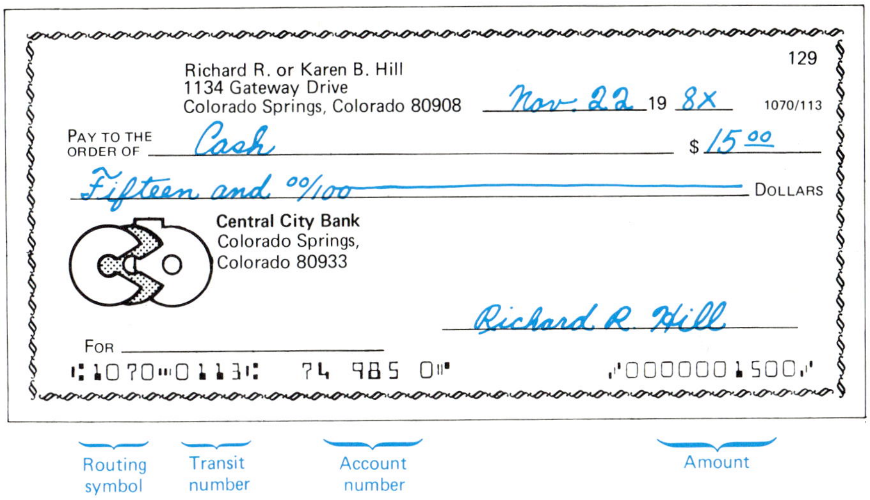

QUESTION: Examine Figure 6-21. The check routing symbol and transit number are preprinted in the upper right-hand corner of the check and inscribed in the lower left-hand corner. The check amount is inscribed in the lower right-hand corner. Identify these three quantities for the check shown: (a) routing symbol _____ , (b) transit number _____ , (c) amount _____

ANSWER: (a) 1070, (b) 113, (c) 1500 (interpreted as $15.00)

DEVICES USING OPTICAL MEDIA

Thus far we have discussed the following devices and media for data entry: punched cards, keyboard terminals, and key-to-tape and key-to-disk systems. Although each of these approaches has its advantages, they all rely on the manual manipulation of a keyboard. With optical reading devices, the key-entry operation is eliminated. Documents or items are marked or labeled with characters, marks, or special codes that can be read directly by a special optical reading device.

Three types of optical devices are described in this section: optical character readers, bar code readers, and computer output microfilm devices.

OPTICAL CHARACTER RECOGNITION   The reading of printed data using optical scanning equipment is called **optical character recognition** (OCR). Characters are imprinted or embossed on documents that are then read by optical character readers, so that keying operations are eliminated.

The OCR equipment is used for a wide range of applications and media. For example, in credit card sales the customer account number is embossed on the credit card invoice from the customer's credit card. The amount of the sale is dialed into the machine and also embossed on the sales slip. These data are then processed by OCR equipment. Other applications include·utility bills, retail price tags, and federal tax returns.

The most common type font (or character set) used in OCR is called **OCR-A** (see Figure 6–22). This font is a voluntary standard used by a number of organizations. For example, the National Retail Merchants Association (NRMA) has adopted the OCR-A font as its standard code for marking price tags in retail stores. However, a number of other character fonts are also in use for OCR applications.

FIGURE 6–22
OCR-A type font.

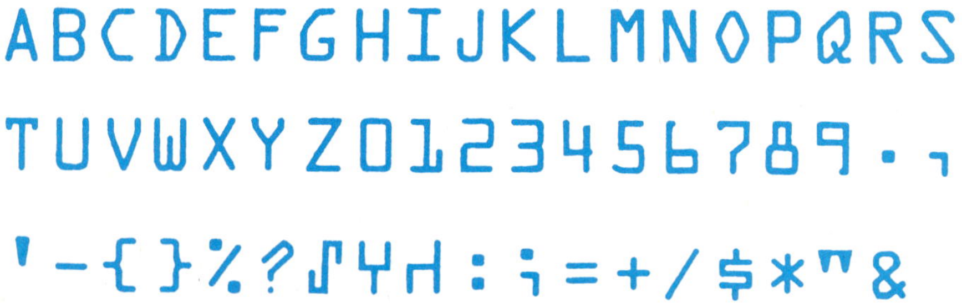

ABCDEFGHIJKLMNOPQRS
TUVWXYZ0123456789.,
'-{}%?♩Чн:;=+/$*"&

Documents imprinted with optical characters are read by an optical character reader/sorter (see Figure 6–23). The characters to be read are scanned by a photoelectric device that converts the characters to electric signals. The signals

FIGURE 6–23
Optical character reader/sorter. (Courtesy IBM.)

are then matched against internally stored reference patterns for the given font. Patterns that cannot be read cause the document to be rejected. Data that are accepted are either read directly into the computer or recorded on magnetic tape or disk for further processing. After having been read, the documents can be sorted into one of several pockets. The OCR readers are capable of reading from 100 to 1500 documents per minute, depending on the type of document and type font used.

Some optical character readers are equipped to handle multiple fonts and even carefully formed hand-printed characters. However, devices that handle only one standard font (such as OCR-A) are generally less expensive and can read documents much faster than the more complex devices.

Reliability is an important consideration in selecting an OCR application. Two measures of reliability are the **reject rate** and the **error rate.** The reject rate is the percent of documents that cannot be read by the reader. Depending on the application, this currently ranges from 1 to 10 percent. The error rate is the percent of documents read on which one or more characters are incorrectly identified; at present, the error rate is less than 1 percent.

QUESTION: Two measures of reliability in OCR are the _____ rate and the

_____ rate.

ANSWER: reject, error

Evaluation of OCR. The major advantages of OCR are the following.

1. Key-entry operations are eliminated. This increases throughput and reduces costs and input errors.
2. Optical characters can be read by humans.
3. Data are captured in machine-readable form at the earliest opportunity.

The disadvantages of OCR are the following.

1. Document readers are relatively expensive (lower cost devices have lower throughput and are limited to a single font).
2. Document design must follow a rigid format (installing OCR equipment usually requires forms redesign).
3. Reject rate is sensitive to the quality of the document (for example, creased paper and smudges).
4. There is no universal standard type font.

The cost and performance of OCR equipment is improving, so that the use of this technology seems certain to increase in the future.

BAR CODE READERS   Another approach to optical character recognition is to use a bar code rather than optical characters. A **bar code** is a series of vertical lines of varying widths and/or colors used to encode information. The most familiar example of a bar code is the **Universal Product Code (UPC)** used by the grocery and drug industries. Each package or item is marked with the UPC, which provides a unique identification for the item. Also, the shelves where the items are displayed are often labeled with the UPC. A schematic of a computerized checkout system with an example of the UPC is shown in Figure 6-24.

The UPC is the basis for the computerized checkout system now used in many supermarkets. As each grocery item is checked it passes over a reading slot where the scanner mechanism optically reads the product code and transmits the information to the computer. Upon recognizing the code, the computer looks up the current price for the item and prints or displays the information on the cash register. When checkout is completed, the cash register computes the total and prints out a customer receipt. At the computer, data are collected to maintain inventory and provide management information.

QUESTION: Examine Figure 6-24. The principal elements of the computer checkout system

are an optical _____ , a modified _____ , and a

_____ processor.

ANSWER: scanner, cash register, computer

An example of a supermarket terminal is shown in Figure 6-25. A computerized checkout system speeds customer service, reduces costs, and provides

FIGURE 6-24
Computerized grocery checkout system.

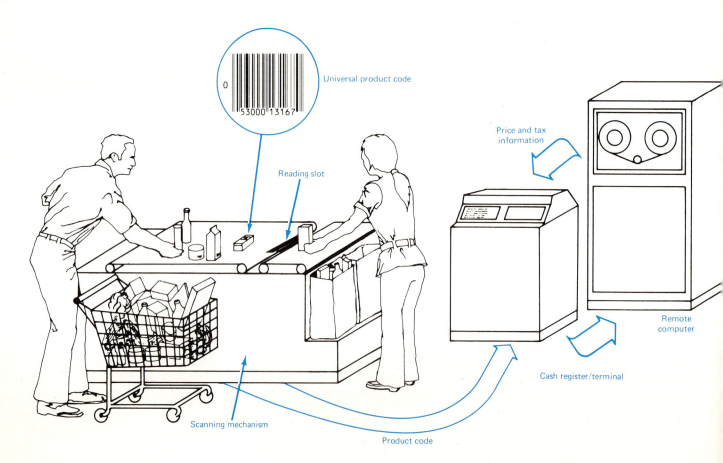

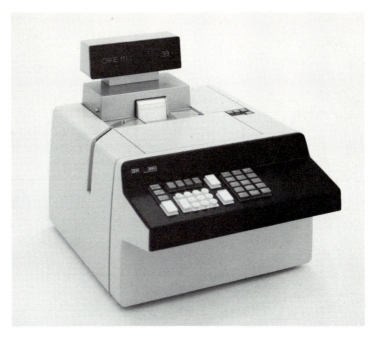

FIGURE 6-25
Supermarket terminal. (Courtesy IBM.)

timely information for sales analysis and inventory management. The main barrier to the introduction of these systems appears to be the controversy over price marking of individual items (see Figure 6-26). The food industry maintains that individual items need not be price marked, since unit prices are on the

FIGURE 6-26
Universal Product Code trouble. Copyright 1979 Los Angeles Times Syndicate. Reprinted with permission.

shelf labels as well as being stored in the computer. However, consumer groups advocate the retention of individual price markings to facilitate item comparisons.

Bar codes are used in other applications. For example, they are placed on the outside of cardboard boxes to identify the items and/or to route the boxes on conveyors.

COMPUTER OUTPUT MICROFILM   In many computer applications, large quantities of data must be retained for reference or legal purposes. For example, a bank must maintain voluminous records of customer account information. A manufacturing firm must maintain historical information concerning products shipped, to answer customer inquiries and to provide service under warranty. Printed output for such large files is bulky, slow, and costly to access.

An alternative for such applications is to use **computer output microfilm (COM)**. A COM device displays data on a CRT screen, which is then projected onto microfilm. The device may display data on-line from the computer, or (more often) off-line from magnetic tape. The computer also produces an index to locate the proper roll and frame for a given output.

The microfilm output is either in the form of roll film or microfiche. Of these, microfiche is by far the more popular medium. **Microfiche** is a microfilm card on which data images are arranged in a grid pattern. The microfiche is easily stored in a file drawer and is easily displayed on a microfilm reader. A printer can be attached to the reader to produce a hard copy of any document.

COM offers the following advantages.

1. Recording on COM is much faster than printing (from 25 to 50 times faster).
2. The cost of microfilm is less than that of an equivalent amount of paper.
3. Microfilm is much more compact than hard-copy storages; vast quantities of data can be stored in a small space.
4. Microfilm is much easier to access. In some systems, desk-top inquiry stations can be used to retrieve and display microfilm data in seconds.
5. Whereas magnetic tape deteriorates over time, microfilm will last indefinitely.

The disadvantages of COM are:

1. The COM equipment is relatively expensive, compared to a printer.
2. Microfilm records cannot be read by a computer or easily updated.
3. A microfilm reader is necessary for access by people.

VOICE RECOGNITION/ RESPONSE   Since the inception of computers, scientists and engineers have been seeking a way to "talk to the computer," to feed instructions and data directly into the computer by human voice. Until recently, to communicate with a computer, man had to learn and use the language of the machine — instructions are written in a machine-oriented language, and data is manually keyed into machine-readable form. Voice recognition units are now available that permit direct verbal communication with the computer using a limited, standard vocabulary. Also, voice response units that create output in the form of prerecorded human voice are widely used.

VOICE DATA ENTRY   A voice data entry terminal (Threshold 500) is shown in Figure 6-27. The terminal is about the size of a desk-top office copier. It consists of a microphone headset, a preprocessor, and a minicomputer. Depending on the application the system may also include a visual display, printer, and data link to a central computer.

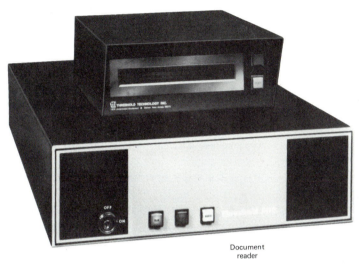

Document
reader

FIGURE 6-27
Voice data entry terminal. (Courtesy Threshold Technology.)

To use the system, a vocabulary is first established that is required for the intended application. In most applications the vocabulary consists of from 30 to 50 words or short phrases. However, the system can handle a larger vocabulary (over 200 words) by adding more memory. Individual words can be added or changed as necessary and the entire vocabulary may be changed within minutes.

When operators use the system for the first time, they train it to recognize their voices by repeating each word in the vocabulary about 10 times. The parameters of the operator's pronunciation of each word are averaged and filed in the processor's memory for later matching and identification. Once they have provided these initial reference data, the operators need not retrain the system. They simply dial in their identification numbers when they start work, and the voice terminal accesses the voice reference data from the central computer and transfers it to the voice terminal memory.

In using the terminal, the operator simply speaks the words of the established vocabulary into the microphone. The recognition device analyzes the spoken word pattern and selects the corresponding vocabulary word. The word is then displayed on a visual display, so that the operator can verify its corrections. If a mistake has been made, the operator simply says "erase" and repeats the correct word. When a correct message has been entered, the operator says "go" or "OK" and the message is transferred to the computer. A block diagram of the internal structure of the voice recognition terminal is shown in Figure 6-28.

Dialects, languages, and even different languages pose no problem, since the system is trained for each operator's voice. For example, a Spanish-American operator can train the system to recognize his "ocho" for the vocabulary word "eight." Also, because the system recognizes basic speech components, abnor-

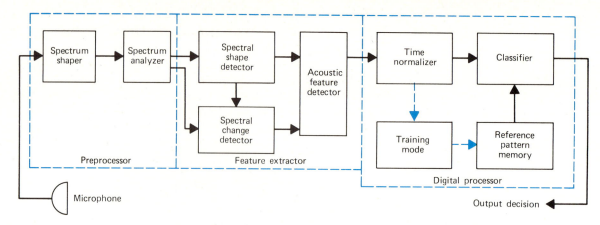

FIGURE 6-28
Block diagram of voice recognition system. (Courtesy Threshold Technology.)

malities such as head colds or hoarseness normally will not affect speech recognition.

There are several obvious advantages to a voice data entry system.

1. Key-entry of data is eliminated.
2. Accuracy is increased. The inherent accuracy rate is over 98 percent. Also, the operator sees his data entered by voice on a display before transmitting it to a computer by a control word.
3. The operator can enter data while his or her hands and/or eyes are busy handling documents or products.
4. The operator can enter data while moving around, since a wireless microphone can be used.
5. As a result of the above, throughput is increased—often by 25 to 50 percent.

A number of organizations are already using the voice data entry terminal for a variety of applications. Some examples are the following.

1. Automated materials handling—at S. S. Kresge, parcels arrive at an operator's station where he or she simply speaks into the microphone headset the destination code for each carton. The code is recognized and the conveyor system routes the parcel to its destination.
2. Quality control—at Continental Can, the voice data entry terminal is used for reporting the results of quality control inspection. A visual display guides the operator and prompts him or her through the inspection sequence. The operator's hands are free to carry out the inspection steps, while the result of each step is entered verbally. Tolerances are stored in the computer. The operator is alerted with a "reject" light and an audio "beeper" when an out-of-tolerance measurement is entered.
3. Stock prices—commodity exchanges must report changing commodity prices quickly and accurately. At the Chicago Mercantile Exchange the price reporter, wearing a small wireless microphone, enters price change information by voice as transactions occur.
4. Programming machine tools—sophisticated machine tools must be programmed, a task performed in the past by skilled computer pro-

grammers. Use of voice programming makes it possible for factory supervisory personnel to program the machines and exercise better control over the processes.

An important prospective application of voice recognition is in security and access control. Each person has a unique "voiceprint" that can be used to identify persons positively. This approach may well be used to provide security in electronic funds transfer systems, among others. In fact, as the technology of voice recognition improves and costs are reduced, applications seem certain to explode in the future.

AUDIO RESPONSE   In addition to recognizing speech, the computer can also be made to produce output or response in the form of human voice. On some units spoken words and phrases forming a prerecorded vocabulary are stored on a magnetic tape or drum, much like recording voice on a cassette tape. The computer forms a digital response, then transmits it to the audio response unit. The unit selects words and phrases from the audio response unit and forms a spoken reply. On other units, the computer synthesizes the human voice rather than selecting from a prerecorded vocabulary.

Audio response units are most often used in replying to inquiries over the telephone. Typical applications include stock quotations, credit inquiries, and checking account status.

SPECIALIZED INPUT/OUTPUT DEVICES

In this chapter we have described input/output devices that are adaptable to a wide variety of applications. In many cases, input/output terminals are specialized for use in a particular industry or type of application. Following are several examples.

Point-of-sale (POS) **terminals** are used extensively in the retail merchandise industry to process transactions and capture sales data. A typical point-of-sale terminal (serving as both a modified cash register and computer terminal) is shown in Figure 6–29a. In a cash transaction, the salesperson passes a hand-held "wand" (shown in the picture) over a bar code or other machine-readable code on the price tag, without removing the tag from the merchandise. The terminal reads the price and identifying information from the tag, records and prints this information, and displays the price on a lighted panel. It also computes the amount due including taxes, calculates and returns change, and prints a cash receipt. The terminal then forwards this data to the central computer, where it is used for inventory control and sales analysis.

In a credit transaction the wand can be used to read a customer's credit card and initiate a credit check. The terminal also contains a keyboard for entry of data or messages. For example, the salesperson can enter a request to locate and reserve a "big-ticket" item such as a refrigerator of a certain model and color.

QUESTION: From the point of view of the customer, describe two advantages of the terminal in Figure 6–29a over a conventional cash register.

a. _____

b. _____

ANSWER: (a) speedier sale (less waiting), (b) fewer errors

(a)

(b)

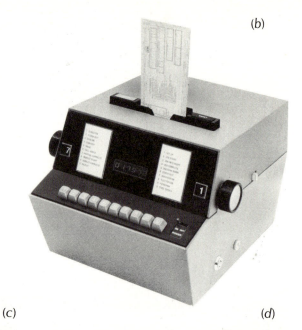

(c)

(d)

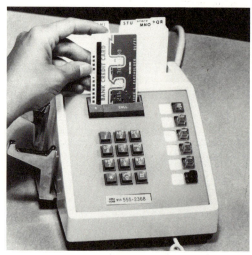

FIGURE 6-29
Specialized input/output devices. (*a*) Point-of-sale terminal. (Courtesy NCR.) (*b*) Data collection terminal. (Courtesy IBM.) (*c*) Automated teller machine. (Courtesy IBM.) (*d*) Transaction telephone. (Courtesy AT&T.)

Factory data collection terminals are used to collect data regarding employees, products, and machines on the factory floor and transmit the data to a computer. A typical data collection terminal is shown in Figure 6-29*b*. As jobs are completed, the operator inserts a punched card containing his employee number and other identifying information. Variable information such as the number of units completed is entered by setting the dials and depressing the keys on the unit. Data are then transmitted to a central computer and used for production scheduling, inventory control, and other applications.

QUESTION: The data collection device shown in Figure 6-29*b* employs two types of media:

_____ (punched cards) and _____ (keys and dials).

ANSWER: paper, keyboard

Automated teller machines (ATMs) are customer-operated terminals that dispense cash, receive deposits, and handle other routine financial transactions. The ATMs may be located either on the bank premises or at remote locations such as retail stores. An ATM is normally activated by inserting a credit card with a magnetic strip containing the customer identifying number. The ATM leads the customer through the transaction steps by illuminated function keys or by displaying instructions. A typical ATM is shown in Figure 6–29c.

The main advantages of ATMs are 24-hour banking services for customers, while retailers are relieved of the burden of cashing checks. The growth of ATMs has been limited to date by legal issues concerning whether ATMs constitute branch banking and, therefore, may be illegal in states that prohibit this activity.

Transaction Telephones developed by AT&T are used for credit-checking applications. The Transaction Telephone resembles a conventional push-button phone but has an integral magnetic strip reader (see Figure 6–29d). To check a customer's credit, a retailer or banker inserts the customer's credit card into a slot in the phone. The magnetic strip reader reads the customer ID on the back of the credit card. The phone automatically dials the credit card company's computer. The system guides the device's operator by means of instruction lights on the phone. The credit status of the cardholder is returned either by audio response or by a visual display on the front of the telephone.

EXERCISE 6–4   1. Explain the difference between optical character recognition (OCR) and magnetic ink character recognition (MICR).

2. Give two reasons why optical character recognition is not more widely used for data entry applications.

   a. _____

   b. _____

3. Give four advantages of visual display terminals over keyboard printers.

   a. _____

   b. _____

   c. _____

   d. _____

SUMMARY

A wide variety of devices are used for preparation and input of data and output of information. The more important of these devices, discussed in this chapter, are summarized in Table 6-1.

In this chapter, the input/output devices were classified according to the media used — paper, keyboard, magnetic, voice, optical. Another method of classification is according to input and output rates. As a general rule, devices that depend on human manipulation of a keyboard — keypunches, key-to-tape and key-to-disk systems, and keyboard terminals — can be operated (at best) at a few hundred characters per minute. Devices that manipulate paper documents — card readers, line printers, optical character readers, and magnetic ink document processors — can process data at rates up to several thousand characters per second. Devices that process magnetic media (tape or disks) can read or output data at up to several hundred thousand characters per second.

Input/output and secondary storage devices represent the means by which data are input, stored, retrieved, and output from the computer. Taken to-

TABLE 6-1   PRINCIPAL INPUT/OUTPUT DEVICES

Device	Purpose	Typical Application
Card punch and reader	Input and output of data on 80-column or 96-column punched cards	Low-volume batch processing applications — small business systems, turnaround documents
Magnetic tape unit	Storage and high-speed input/output of large sequential files	High-volume batch processing applications, backup of on-line disk files
Printer	Recording output information on paper	All applications requiring printed output — operating documents and management reports
Visual display	Keyboard entry of data and inquiries; video display of alphanumeric and graphical output	On-line inquiries and updating — time-sharing, reservations systems
Optical character reader	Reading printed data directly from documents without keyboard entry	High-volume input where data is in standard printed form — processing airline tickets, invoices, utility billing, and others
Magnetic ink character reader	Reading documents inscribed with magnetic ink characters	Banking industry — reading checks and deposit slips
Voice recognition/response	Direct voice input and response	Quality control, materials handling, credit checking
Special-purpose terminals	Tailored to particular applications	Point-of-sale, banking, credit checking, manufacturing, and others

gether, these devices are often referred to as computer peripherals. In the past few years, peripherals have been among the fastest growing areas of the computer industry. Intense competition has improved performance, has reduced cost, and has led to "mixed" systems in which a central processing unit from a major manufacturer is surrounded by peripherals produced by several smaller manufacturers. This type of competition has undoubtedly been healthy for the industry, as well as beneficial to the user.

In many computer applications, input and output devices are located at some distance from the central computer. Communications channels and devices are used to link the computer with these remote devices. In Chapter 8 you will study devices for data communications.

ANSWERS TO EXERCISES

EXERCISE 6-1

1. Each department could be issued prepunched cards for the various services or supplies that it dispenses. Each card would contain a stock number, description of the supply or service, and unit cost. For example, the X-ray department could have cards for each major type of X-ray. As various services are performed and supplies are issued, cards are assembled for the patient. Processing the cards would then provide patient billing.

2. It is necessary to keypunch only customer name and address and, for each item, the order code and quantity ordered. The name and price of each article are constants that can be stored in the computer system (for example, on magnetic tape or disk). The computer multiplies unit price by quantity to obtain the total for each item and computes the total amount for the order.

EXERCISE 6-2

1. a. Controls the flow of information between the computer and input/output devices.
   b. Provides a buffer or temporary storage capacity.
   c. Interrupts the CPU when a data transfer is completed or when an error condition is encountered.

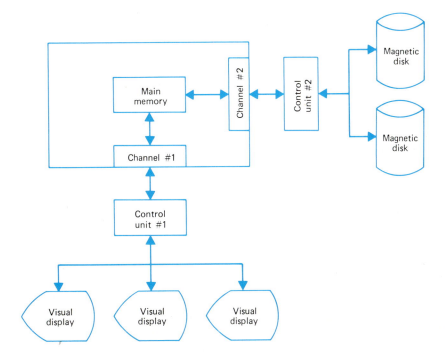

2. a. Batch data entry.
   b. On-line data entry, central processing.
   c. On-line data entry, distributed processing.

3. Diagram for two data channels.

EXERCISE 6-3
1. a. Ball printer
   b. Dot matrix printer
   c. Thermal printer
   d. Drum printer
   e. Laser printer
2. a. Full-strike characters
   b. Multiple copies
   c. No special paper

EXERCISE 6-4
1. OCR uses optical characters that are printed on documents, while MICR uses characters that are inscribed on documents using a special magnetic ink.
2. a. OCR equipment is expensive, although costs have been declining.
   b. OCR requires a special font or, in the case of hand-printed characters, very close control over character format.
3. a. Formatted screen for data entry
   b. Immediate sight verification
   c. On-line editing of data
   d. Faster output of data

CHAPTER EXAMINATION

1. Define each of the following abbreviations.

   a. MICR _____

   b. COM _____

   c. OCR _____

   d. CRT _____

2. Match each application in the first column with the most appropriate input/output device or medium.

   ____ Backup of magnetic disk files

   ____ Processing checks

   ____ Capture of sales data in
   a retail store

   ____ Low-volume input of data in a small
   business system

   ____ Storing large-volume output for ease of
   visual retrieval

   ____ Direct input of large volumes of data recorded
   in a special printing font

   ____ On-line display of inventory status

   ____ Output of a 1000-item stock status report

   a. Visual display unit (CRT)

   b. Optical character recognition

   c. Computer output microfilm

   d. Line printer

   e. Magnetic tape

   f. Point-of-sale terminal

   g. Magnetic ink character recognition

   h. Punched cards

3. Define each of the following terms.

   a. Graphics _____

   b. Bar code _____

   c. Channel _____

   e.   OCR-A _____

4.   Mark each of the following statements true or false.

   ____ a.   Data preparation generally accounts for less than 10 percent of the data processing budget.

   ____ b.   Ideally, data are recorded in machine-processable form when they are originated.

   ____ c.   Data channels make possible the overlapping of input/output and processing.

   ____ d.   Constant information (routing symbol, transit number, and account number) are inscribed on checks after they are cashed.

   ____ e.   For high input/output rates (say, 100,000 characters per second), magnetic media must be used.

   ____ f.   Reading rates for optical character devices are significantly higher than for punched cards.

   ____ g.   Compared with printers, visual display devices offer the advantages of faster output rates and the ability to display graphical information.

   ____ h.   Although computer output microfilm provides very compact information storage, it has the disadvantage of slower output than that of printed output.

   ____ i.   Data collection devices make it possible for the user to capture data in machine-processable form at various activity centers.

   ____ j.   Present-day optical character readers can read handwritten data.

5.   List four basic steps in the input and output of information.

   a.   _____

   b.   _____

   c.   _____

   d.   _____

6.   Calculate the data rates (characters/second) for each of the following.

   a.   Punched card reader that reads 1000 cards per minute (80 characters/card) _____
   b.   Optical character reader that reads 500 documents/minute (average 200 characters/document)

   _____

   c.   Magnetic ink document reader that processes 600 checks/minute (average 35 characters/check)

   _____

   d.   Line printer that prints 1200 lines per minute (132 characters/line)

   _____

7. Explain briefly how a voice data entry terminal works.

_____

_____

8. List three examples of each of the following?
   a. Devices using paper media

   _____

   b. Devices using magnetic media

   _____

   c. Devices using optical media

   _____

   d. Devices using key-entry

   _____

9. List three advantages of optical character recognition.

   a. _____

   b. _____

   c. _____

10. Give four advantages of computer output microfilm over printed output.

   a. _____

   b. _____

   c. _____

   d. _____

11. Define the following.

   a. Reject rate _____

   _____

   b. Error rate _____

   _____

12. Describe the function of a data channel.

   _____

   _____

_____

13. Describe three basic approaches to data entry.

   a. _____

   _____

   _____

   b. _____

   _____

   _____

   c. _____

   _____

14. Briefly describe the following.

   a. Audio response unit _____

   _____

   b. Graph plotter _____

   _____

15. What is a bar code?

   _____

   _____

16. List five functions of a key-to-disk system.

   a. _____

   b. _____

   c. _____

   d. _____

   e. _____

17. Why are optical character recognition devices not more widely used?

   _____

   _____

18. Describe briefly how each of the following devices works.
    a. Dot matrix printer

    _____

    _____

    b. Ball printer

    _____

    _____

    c. Drum printer

    _____

    _____

    d. Electrostatic printer

    _____

    _____

    e. Laser printer

    _____

    _____

19. List seven factors to consider in selecting a printer.

    a. _____

    b. _____

    c. _____

    d. _____

    e. _____

    f. _____

    g. _____

20. Describe briefly the difference between the following.
    a. Flatbed plotter and drum plotter

    _____

    _____

    b. "Dumb" terminal and "smart" terminal

    _____

c. Microfiche versus microfilm roll

_____

_____

21. List four benefits in using a key-to-disk system.

a. _____

b. _____

c. _____

d. _____

22. List four types of paper used in printers.

a. _____

b. _____

c. _____

d. _____

23. List four important applications of visual display terminals.

a. _____

b. _____

c. _____

d. _____

24. How are each of the following devices used?
a. Light pen

_____

_____

b. Hand-held wand

_____

_____

25. What are the major barriers to more widespread use of each of the following?
a. Automated teller machines

_____

b. Optical character readers

c. Supermarket terminals

7

MICRO/MINI COMPUTERS AND PERSONAL COMPUTING

OVERVIEW. Most of today's top-level executives began their careers before the first business computer was designed. Those persons were in mid-career when General Electric installed its UNIVAC 1 computer in 1954. The microcomputer, at a cost of less than $300, has more computing capability than the UNIVAC 1. It is 20 times faster, has a larger memory, is thousands of times more reliable, consumes the power of a light bulb rather than that of a locomotive, occupies 1/30,000 the volume and costs 1/10,000 as much. It is available by mail order or at your local computer store.

Many of the companies where today's executives work could not justify the high cost of computers, as recently as 15 years ago. Now a one-person company can afford a computer. And—that computer can be linked through a telephone to other companies or to data bases.

This chapter covers the operation and characteristics of microcomputers (micros) and minicomputers (minis). A minicomputer has more capacity and capability and is required for more complex business activities.

The purpose of this chapter is threefold: (1) to build on the material of previous chapters to explain how computers work; (2) to compare the capabilities of micros and minis; and (3) to give examples of the applications of these two categories of computers.

MICROCOMPUTER CONCEPTS

WHAT IS A MICROCOMPUTER?

A **microcomputer** is the smallest version of a computer—both in size and capability. It is comprised of a microprocessor, storage, input/output units, and the interconnecting circuitry.

The **microprocessor** is equivalent to the central processing unit described in Chapter 3. It is typically manufactured on a single silicon chip—only $\frac{1}{4}$-inch square. The microprocessor contains an arithmetic/logic unit (ALU) and a control unit (CU). Arithmetic and logical operations are performed by the ALU on data received from memory or input devices. The CU controls the flow of data and instructions. It activates the appropriate circuitry and controls the interaction of all units.

As in the central processing unit (CPU) of a larger computer, the task of the microprocessor is to receive data in the form of strings of binary digits (0s and 1s), to store the data for later processing, to perform arithmetic and logic operations on the data in accordance with previously stored instructions, and to deliver the results to the user through an output mechanism such as an electric typewriter or a cathode ray tube (CRT) display.

The microcomputer is now performing jobs previously performed by its elder brother—the minicomputer. Because of the micro's low cost, many applications previously uneconomical for computing can now be computerized.

However, microcomputers are still limited in capability, so they have not replaced the minicomputer. Instead, they should be viewed as the starting level for business computing.

ELECTRONIC CHARACTERISTICS OF MICROS

The small size and low cost characteristics of microcomputers have resulted from the enormous improvements in electronics technology. A review of the rapid advances in the electronics field will set the stage for understanding the amazing capabilities of such compact devices.

Microprocessors are inexpensive to produce because they can be manufactured in mass production. They require little power (many use less power than a 20-watt light bulb). They are small, as shown in Figure 7-1.

In addition to serving as the integral unit in a microcomputer, microprocessors are the fundamental unit in the architecture for the future generation of large-scale computers.

As described in Chapter 3, the present day manufacturing process of microminiaturization integrates thousands of components onto a single chip by sandwiching them into ultrathin layers. Each chip is a thin piece of silicon schematically designed to connect diodes, transistors, resistors, and other electronic components.

Complex circuits are formed a layer at a time. Light is flashed onto a tissue-thin piece of silicon through a glass negative containing an image of part of the circuit. That pattern is etched into the silicon. Additional patterns are etched with additional light exposures until the circuit is complete.

The overwhelming difference between this process and previous technology is the minute size of the circuits. The silicon chip shown in Figure 7-1 contains 64,000 bits of information. By the mid-1980s technology is expected to improve such that 256,000 bits can be manufactured on a chip of that size, and by 1990 ten times that many.

In 1960, before any production of integrated circuits, about 500 million transistors were made. Assuming that each transistor represents one circuit function, which can be equated to a logic "gate" or to one binary digit (bit) of memory in an integrated circuit, annual usage has increased by 2000 times, or has doubled 11 times in the past 17 years. This stunning increase promotes continual cost reductions.

The reduction in size of the circuit elements not only reduces the cost but also improves the basic performance of the device. Delay times are directly proportional to the dimensions of circuit elements, so that the circuit becomes faster as it becomes smaller. Similarly, the power is reduced with the area of the circuits. The linear dimensions of the circuit elements can probably be reduced to about a fifth of the current size before any fundamental limits are encountered.

Over the past decade operating speed and reliability have increased by at least 10 times as physical size, power consumption, and cost per bit of storage have been reduced by factors ranging from 100 to 1000.

By 1990 the number of electronic functions incorporated into a wide range of products each year can be expected to be 100 times greater than it is today. The experience curve predicts that the cost per function will have declined by then to a twentieth of the 1980 cost, a reduction of 25 percent per year. At such prices, electronic devices will be exploited even more widely, augmenting

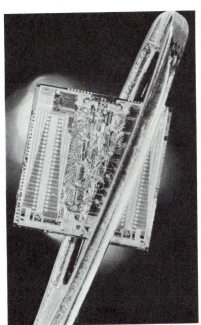

FIGURE 7-1
This 64,000-bit microprocessor chip is small enough to pass through the eye of a common needle. (Courtesy IBM.)

mail service, expanding the library and making its contents more accessible, providing entertainment, disseminating knowledge for educational purposes, and performing many more of the routine tasks in the home and office. It is in the exponential proliferation of products and services dependent on microelectronics that the real microelectronics revolution will be manifested.

One of the many present-day applications of microprocessor systems is in aircraft operations. There are nine microprocessors in the Boeing 747, illustrated in Figure 7–2, for aid in control of navigation, communication, passenger comfort and safety, engine control, and the control of aerodynamic surfaces.

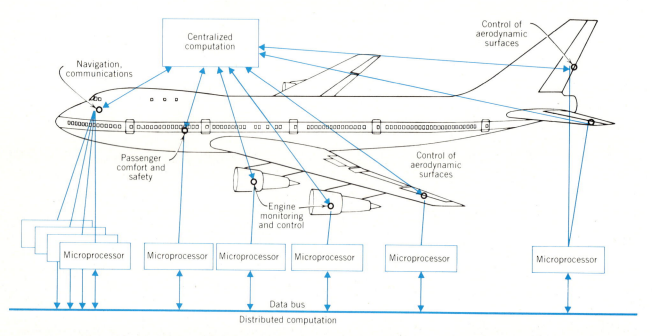

FIGURE 7–2
Use of microprocessors in the Boeing 747. (Courtesy *Scientific American*.)

QUESTION: Over the past decade, operating speed and reliability have increased _____ times and are expected to be _____ times greater by 1990.

ANSWER: 10, 100

The following examples show the variety of activities being performed by microcomputers today.

1. Microprocessor chips are now installed in automobiles to direct air and fuel mixtures, govern speed, and signal when antifreeze is low or when to add oil. They shift gears and balance suspension on corners, increase performance, and save on gas.

2. A micro-controlled mannequin for instructors in anesthesiology is used at the University of Southern California Medical School. It is a human simulator, called "Sim One," which is under control of the instructor. However, it responds to students' actions by changes in respiration

rate, temperature, blood pressure, and heart rate. Contraction and dilation of the pupil of the eye and other physiological events can also be induced.

3. The Apple II microcomputer is programmed to accept voice input. One program controls home security and comfort. Sitting in your easy chair, you can pick up the input transmitter and speak the command, "Lower thermostat 2°" or "Open north bedroom window." If you had a telephone unit in your car, or were out of town, you could dial your Apple II in the evening and command, "Turn on living room lights and TV." The system has a color TV display that shows your home and the results of each of these commands. For example, the command "Open garage" causes the door pictured on the video screen to raise at the same time the actual garage door is being raised.

EXAMPLE OF STORED-PROGRAM MICROCOMPUTERS

Anatoli Karpov, world chess champion, has played chess against one of the chess microcomputers. These units sell for less than $100 and play at a level set by the challenger—from 1 to 10 levels of complexity. Karpov found the top level "to be a challenge even for me."

As shown in Figure 7-3, a chess computer is lightweight (a few ounces) and compact (two by four by nine inches).

FIGURE 7-3
Chess microcomputer. (Courtesy Fidelity Electronics.)

We will use the chess computer to illustrate how a microcomputer works. There are several versions on the market. The program for responding to your moves is stored in the microcomputer memory. You enter your moves through a keyboard. Moving a piece from location D2 to D4 would be accomplished by entering D2D4 and hitting the "play" key.

The micro analyzes your play by processing that entry (data) through its program. Each play activates program logic that analyzes alternative moves (processing). The best alternative is selected and is displayed on the screen (output).

Authorities generally agree that human chess masters look ahead only four moves. The chess computer can consider many more moves, depending on the amount of logic built into the program and stored in memory. The more possibilities considered (the more instructions processed), the longer the response.

One version has a timer that can be set from one second to 100 hours. The higher settings allow for more alternatives to be considered. The same micro responds to your play by displaying remarks such as "Hooray" or "Ready to resign?" More than 80 responses (outputs) are programmed into the system.

Another version has a special feature called "survival" mode. It will randomly select one of 1500 possible middle-game positions, playing at the level selected by its human opponent.

Shelby Lyman, an expert in chess microcomputers, says that the machines improve a player's tactical capability. He illustrates through the story of a four-year-old boy who became a good chess player through competition with one of the chess micros. Incidentally, the boy always insisted on another person being in the room with him whenever he played against the microcomputer!

Lyman says that there is still a long way to go from the present-level chess computers to Star Wars droids like R2D2®, but that "90 percent of the 40 million Americans who play chess can be easily beaten" by today's good micro chess computers.[1]

QUESTION: The chess machine utilizes the three functions necessary for classification as a system: input, processing, output. It best illustrates the function of stored logic used in electronic computers. The computer program to analyze alternative strategies is quite complex. However, the amount of logic (program instructions)

used depends upon _____ selected by the player.

ANSWER: the level of complexity

HOW MICRO-COMPUTERS WORK

You may have heard or seen references to a computer's capacity in terms like "32K." In the metric system the letter K (kilo) represents 1000. When used with computers, the symbol "K" always represents 1024, which is 2 to the tenth power. A computer with a memory capacity of 32K can store 32,768 bytes of data.

When you enter data to a computer through a keyboard, the system **decodes** your alphabetic or decimal representation into an electrical representation. Likewise, when the computer is ordered to print out the results of processing, it must translate the electronic representation back into an English representation.

Data representation was explained in detail in Chapter 4. With that background, you have the knowledge to understand how microcomputers work.

TWO COMPONENTS OF MICROPROCESSOR MEMORY

There are two basic types of memory internal to a microcomputer: (1) read-only memory (ROM) and (2) read-and-write memory (RWM). (Instructions are usually stored in read-only memory and read into the processor for execution.) Unfortunately, the industry uses the term RAM for the latter type of memory, so the abbreviation is not as easy to interpret. However, RAM stands for random access memory—meaning that each area of memory is directly accessible, as opposed to sequential memory (like a magnetic tape), where

[1]Shelby Lyman, "PM Crowns the Computer Chess Champ," *Popular Mechanics*, May, 1979, pp. 118–119, 284–286.

records must be processed in sequence to reach the one desired. Intermediate values and results of computations are stored in and read from RAM by the processing unit.

The way to distinguish ROM from RAM is to remember that the contents of RAM are continuously being changed. The contents of ROM remain fixed. Typically, ROM is used to store programs that will be used repeatedly. Since you do not want to modify these programs, you record them in a read-only device.

Reading from ROM is similar to use of an audio tape unit that is a "play only" unit. Playing (reading from) does not destroy the contents of the tape. Only when you activate the RECORD button on a combination tape player/recorder do you wipe out the previous contents of a tape. This latter action is similar in function to a RAM—you can read from it or write into it.

Figure 7-4 illustrates the interaction of RAM and ROM. The computer program (complete set of instructions for accomplishing a task) is stored on ROM. The operator key-enters data to be processed. For example, assume a person wishes to obtain the square root of a number. The logic for computing square root is accomplished in a set of instructions stored on ROM. The value from which the square root is to be derived (e.g., the number 38,025) is entered to RAM via the keyboard. The instructions in ROM are executed by the microprocessor in sequence until the result (195) is obtained. The result is then output on the typewriter device.

QUESTION: Another way of defining RAM is that memory access time is independent of the memory location being accessed. In a 64K memory, the last location can be

accessed _____ as the first location.

ANSWER: as quickly or in the same amount of time

FIGURE 7-4
Typical interaction between RAM, ROM, and microprocessor.

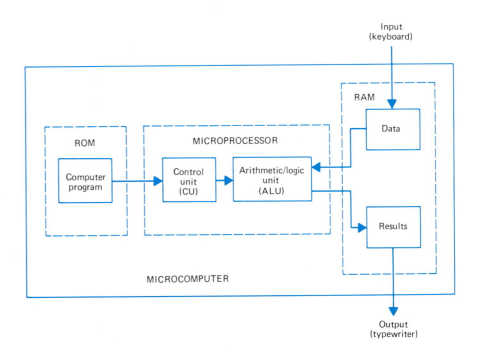

Although the example problem illustrates the operation of a microcomputer, square root extraction is more economically performed on a hand-held calculator. So, we will expand the illustration to a typical microcomputer application. Several automobile manufacturers now have a microcomputer to control ignition timing of an engine's distributor. Data on the engine's condition—load acceleration and engine revolutions—are read into the micro's RAM. The microprocessor processes the data from the RAM according to the instructions from the ROM. The engine's timing is adjusted automatically (output data is sent electronically to control mechanisms). Such a system can reduce exhaust emission by 5 to 10 percent. Combined with fuel injection systems, these ignition systems save up to 40 percent in fuel consumption. Figure 7-5 shows the RAM and ROM units as they actually appear on a microprocessor chip.

FIGURE 7-5
Magnified photograph of components of a microprocessor. (Courtesy Rockwell International Corporation.)

QUESTION: Examine Figure 7-4. Computer instructions are pulled from the _____ as needed for processing data in the _____.

ANSWER: ROM, RAM

PROGRAMMING A MICROCOMPUTER

ROMs typically store two of the three types of programs (software) used in a microcomputer system. The **operating system** (OS) program is stored on ROM. As implied by its name, the operating system is a supervisory program that controls the interaction of all devices. Its function is similar to that of the human brain, which controls muscles and nerve centers. The operating system is provided by the manufacturers (it is written by their programmers, not ours).

A second category of software typically stored in ROM is the **compiler.** The compiler translates instructions written in English-like terminology to a form the microprocessor understands — binary representation. It is called a compiler because it compiles a set of machine language (binary) instructions from our English-like instructions. For example, in the high-level language PL/M, the programmer could write the instruction:

if $X > Y$, then $Z = X$; else $Z = Y$

That is very close to the English version of: "If the value of variable X is greater than the value of variable Y, then assign the same value to Z; otherwise, assign the value of Y to Z."

The machine language version of that instruction consists of a dozen or more instructions, expressed in a form that a machine can interpret. An example of a machine language instruction would appear as follows (where the first set of bits represents the operation "add" and the second and third set represent memory locations of the numbers to be added).

000001011   011000001   001110001

Programming a micro would be tedious and time consuming at the machine language level. Use of a high-level (English-like) language allows you to write instructions in notation similar to your normal expression. The compiler translates the high-level language to machine language. Compilers are usually stored in ROMs and are provided by the supplier along with the microcomputer.

A third category of software is the **application program.** It is the system to which the microcomputer is applied. Unlike the ignition system program discussed above, the typical application program changes from time to time. For example, a company's inventory program may change when company procedures or policies change. It would not be practical to store this type of software in read-only memory.

Finally, the usages of ROM and RAM are sometimes blurred. Operating systems and compilers may sometimes be stored in RAM, especially if several different operating systems or compilers must be used. Similarly, application programs are sometimes stored in ROM when no changes are anticipated.

QUESTION: The software that translates your English-like programming statement into machine language is called a _____.

ANSWER: compiler

EXAMPLE OF PROCESSING A TYPICAL APPLICATION PROGRAM

Figures 7–6 and 7–7 illustrate the interaction of the three types of software and associated storage media. Examine Figure 7–6 first.

During the development and testing of a program, the compiler ROM is utilized. The programmer command LOAD causes the operating system to read the high-level language program (typically from a cassette tape or magnetic disk) into a module of RAM. When the programmer types in the command COMPILE, the operating system directs the compiler to analyze each high-level instruction and convert it to the corresponding machine language instructions. These instructions are loaded into a second area of RAM. Upon completion of this process, the operating system notifies the operator that the system is ready to process data. The video unit would display the word READY.

Only during development of the program is the compiler needed. Once the program is completed, the machine language version is used in processing.

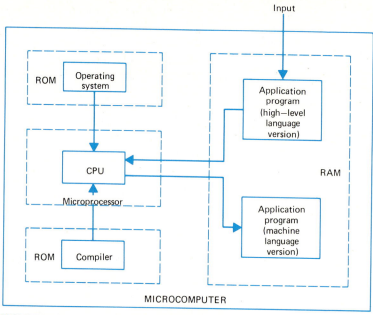

FIGURE 7-6

Interaction of RAM and ROM in translating a program to machine language.

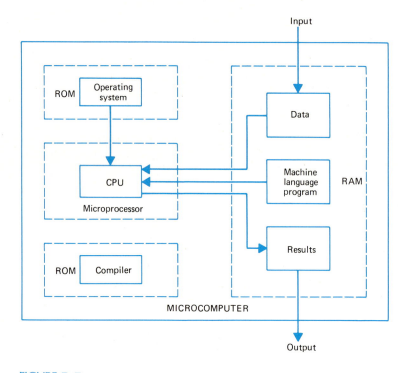

FIGURE 7-7

Processing of the application program.

Figure 7–7 shows the next stage—processing data. The operator enters the data to be processed, that is, order information from which a customer invoice will be prepared. Since the RAM modules previously allocated for program compilation are no longer needed for that purpose, the system would load data into these modules. In essence, data replaces what was there previously. When the data are loaded into RAM, the operating system displays the word READY, informing the operator that the system is ready to process the data.

When the operator enters the command RUN, processing begins. The program is executed, using the data stored. Continuing with the invoicing example — costs are calculated and stored in another section of RAM. The command PRINT causes the output device to print the contents of that storage area onto the invoice form.

Figure 7–7 shows the application program retained on RAM with only data being entered. This situation would apply for a company where orders are processed continuously. An application that is processed less frequently, such as payroll, might be stored on cassette tape and entered onto RAM only at the time payroll is to be processed.

QUESTION: What change would be made to Figure 7–7 to reflect processing of the payroll

application? _____

_____

ANSWER: A line would be added from the input area to the block for the machine language program.

One of the principal advantages of computers is the ability to reuse data without recapturing it a second time. In the above example, both the payroll results and the accounts receivable (invoicing) results would be needed in producing the general ledger each month. That information would be stored in another section of RAM, or be output on a machine-readable medium such as cassette tape. When the time arrives for monthly processing of the general ledger, these data are quickly and inexpensively entered for processing.

QUESTION: Examine Figure 7–7. The compiler is not involved at this stage of processing,

because _____

ANSWER: the program was translated to machine language in the previous step.

Output can be printed or can also be displayed through an inexpensive LED (light emitting diode) — see Figure 7–8. An LED has no memory. It will display data only as long as the segment lines are active. Seven-segment LEDs display the characters shown in Figure 7–8. Dot matrix LEDs can display all the letters of the alphabet as well as numbers. Other display technologies such as plasma and

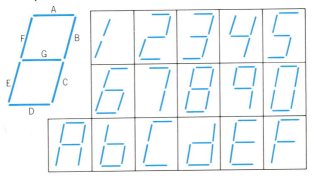

FIGURE 7–8
Characters generated with a 7-segment LED.

liquid crystal (LCD) displays work very much like LED displays. Of course, it is possible to attach a terminal with cathode ray tube screen similar to your television screen. Such terminals are many times more expensive than LED devices.

EXERCISE 7–1   It is important that you understand the internal operations of a microcomputer. Reexamine Figures 7–6 and 7–7 and answer the following questions.

1. When a program is written in an English-like language such as PL/M or

    PASCAL, it must be translated from the _____ _____ ver-

    sion to the _____ _____ version before processing begins.

2. When you type in the command to start the translation process, the

    _____ _____ takes control of the interaction of the var-
    ious units within the microprocessor.

3. The operating system controls the movement of the computer program

    for translation (the compiler) from the _____ unit to the

    _____ unit.

4. The _____ program (written in a high-level language like PL/M or
    PASCAL) is analyzed by the logic of the compiler and is converted to
    machine language.

5. Once the translation procedure is completed, the memory area occupied

    by the _____ and the _____ is no longer needed.

6. The _____ are then entered by the keyboard in preparation for
    processing.

7. After the data are processed, the results are stored in _____ prior
    to printout.

8. The results may be printed out or may be read into another medium, like a

    _____ or a _____, to be used by another application pro-
    gram, such as the general ledger program.

A few versions of micros do not have high-level programming language compilers; therefore, programming cost will be significantly higher. For example, consider the Intel Corporation's comparison of programmer productivity according to language type. Using Intel's PL/M (or National Semiconductor's PL/M "Plus") a programmer can produce 50 times as many instructions per day (each fully debugged) as he/she can with machine language.[2] Of course, there is the

[2]Charles J. Sippl, *Microcomputer Handbook*, Petrocelli/Charter, New York, 1977, p. 155.

additional cost of translating the high-level instruction before processing. This cost is nominal, compared to the cost of programming, however.

There are also macroinstructions available from some vendors. For example, NCR has a low-cost yet comprehensive library of standard accounting applications. The accounts receivable program consists of 46 steps and costs about $100. The 63-step payroll program sells for $150. The NCR representatives will develop programs at a customer site for $4.50 per step. To program such an application, the NCR representative completes a form with one- and two-word answers to questions regarding the functions as operations desired. The typical modification to a standard program takes less than two minutes.[3]

CATEGORIES OF MICROCOMPUTER APPLICATIONS

The following applications are typical of those that microcomputers perform. They are categorized according to the degree of complexity.

SIMPLE APPLICATIONS

Carburetor and timing control in automobiles.

Appliances.

Calculators.

Game machines.

Industrial scales.

Terminals (simple).

INTERMEDIATE- LEVEL APPLICATIONS

Automotive inspection.

Intelligent terminals and instruments.

Point-of-sale terminals.

Traffic controllers.

Teaching machines (basic algebra, etc.).

Accounting systems.

Data acquisition systems.

COMPLEX APPLICATIONS

Numerical control.

Process control.

Communications preprocessors (data concentrators).

Supervisory control (gas, power, water distributions).

Automatic testing systems.

QUESTION: A microprocessor in a microwave oven would be classified as a _____ application while a retail store cash register system would be classified as a

_____ application.

ANSWER: simple (appliance), intermediate (point-of-sale)

[3]Ibid., p. 99.

Robert Mankoff, Saturday Review.

PLEASE STAND BY
WE HAVE TEMPORARILY
LOST YOUR ROAST

WARM
DEFROST
SIMMER
ROAST
REHEAT

MANKOFF

PERSONAL COMPUTING

The previous listing identified the full range of microcomputer applications. We will now concentrate on a category of applications that constitutes only 20 percent of sales of microcomputers but that has the near-term potential for more than 50 percent of the market.

The cost of a microcomputer is now low enough for many persons to be able to acquire their own unit—hence, the term **personal computing.** Unfortunately, the term has been used interchangeably with the term "hobby" computing. This situation has resulted from the huge marketing campaigns for use of micros for game playing. Hundreds of micro-based games are available, from simple games like tic-tac-toe to complex games like chess. Webster defines hobby as "a pursuit outside one's regular occupation, engaged in for relaxation." The use of microcomputers for game playing fits within that definition. However, game playing is probably the least important of the hobby applications of the microcomputer. Performing accounting functions on a micro is part of an accountant's occupation but may be a hobby for a sound system engineer. Conversely, the accountant may be performing microcomputer analysis to balance stereo components—a hobby to anyone but the sound system engineer.

The term personal computing is not only much broader in scope, it also more accurately portrays microcomputer potential. The microcomputer can be used to prepare personal budgets, compute income tax, and carry out many other functions that we, as individuals, must perform.

The home computer fits within this same definition, although for the housewife its applications might be considered more occupationally related. Checkbook balancing, recipe conversion, and telephone message taking are examples of home computer applications.

Individuals working in a company may have some activities that are peculiar to their job alone. They might acquire a microcomputer to perform these functions and, in that sense, it is their personal computer. However, for the purposes of explaining computer applications, we will differentiate **occupation-**

related and personal computing. Occupation-related applications will be discussed in the next section.

In Chapter 3 computers were classified into six categories, depending primarily on the capability of the system. Electronic calculators and microcomputers, the first two categories, would be used in personal computing as well as in occupation-related computing. Checkbook balancing and recipe conversion could be performed on electronic calculators. Also, a number of games have been programmed for electronic calculators.

Income tax preparation would be more appropriate for a microcomputer. Although the individual computations could be made on an electronic calculator, the special income tax formulas and procedures would require more logic and memory capacity than that available in the typical electronic calculator. Likewise, the electronic calculator does not have the more complicated circuitry necessary for telephone message taking.

Another facet of home computing is preschool and primary school education. Educational games are available on hand-held electronic calculators. Hand-held systems are also available for more advanced, special-purpose functions. The spelling computer, described in Chapter 2, is an example. However, the more complex logic of the programmed-instruction educational approach requires a higher capacity system, such as a microcomputer.

An example of a micro-based educational game is GAMBO, developed by Edutek Corporation. There are two players in this computerized/tutorial game. One is the student; the other is "Jody," a computer-simulated player. The computer program also includes logic for a third person, called Gambo — the umpire and scorekeeper for the game. Each player is given an arithmetic problem to solve. The answer is evaluated by the opponent. The umpire then provides the correct answer. The player with a correct answer gets to make a move on a tic-tac-toe board. A tic-tac-toe turn is forfeited if an answer is incorrect. The object of the game is to obtain the highest possible score in a limited amount of time. A player receives 10 points for correctly answering the problem, 5 points for correctly evaluating an opponent's answer, and 15 points for getting three marks in a row on the tic-tac-toe board.

This example shows the potential benefits of home computers for children. The present generation spends more time in front of the television set than in the classroom. Interesting educational games can replace huge amounts of passive, nonproductive time spent by youngsters watching television.

The above examples reveal the vast potential for personal computing. As costs diminish and more programs become available, personal computing will mushroom.

IMPROVEMENTS ANTICIPATED FOR MICROS

The size of the microprocessor is now so small that manufacturers feel the customer will balk at paying several hundred dollars for such a miniaturized system. Some manufacturers package the $\frac{1}{4}$-inch chips in an attractive console two feet or so in diameter. It's quite a shock to open the back of the cabinet and see all the system units packaged in a space a little larger than that required for a wristwatch. In fact, wristwatch computers are already available.

Microcomputers will continue to improve — at a rate faster than the average person's capacity for recognizing how to use the expanded capabilities.

The cost of microprocessors has dropped an average of 40 percent per year over the last seven years. It costs approximately $15 million to set up a semiconductor manufacturing line. So, the quantity of units sold has expanded tremendously to justify such high development cost.

Single-chip microprocessors have expanded computer uses to areas that previously required minicomputers. Radical reduction in cost, coupled with rapidly expanding capability, cause new vistas to continuously open to the application of micros.

MINICOMPUTERS

The industry does not have a standard for distinguishing microcomputers from minicomputers, but micros are usually distinguishable from minicomputers because of their minuteness, minimal power requirements, and low cost. In the near future many of the computer application programs now available on minicomputers will also be developed for micros. The former are used for more complicated applications that require more computing capacity and a variety of input and output devices. The internal operations of a micro, described earlier in this chapter, are similar to those performed on minicomputers and on large-scale computers. Only the devices differ. For example, examine Figure 7-9, a cutaway diagram for a small minicomputer, the Hewlett-Packard 300. In addition to 256K bytes of primary storage (RAM), it has 13MB of secondary storage. For economy, secondary storage is separated into two types — 1 million bytes of flexible disk (removable by operator) and 12 million bytes of fixed disk (nonre-

FIGURE 7-9
Minicomputer with multiple memory devices. (Courtesy Hewlett-Packard.)

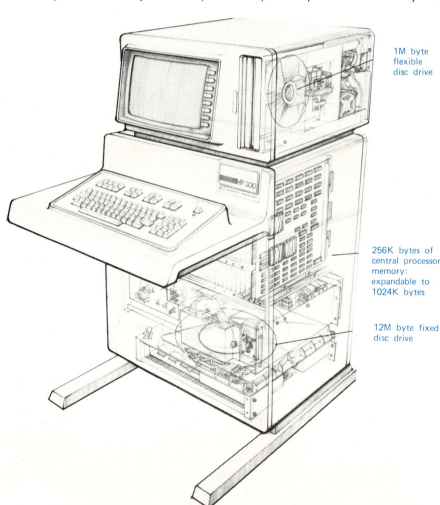

1M byte flexible disc drive

256K bytes of central processor memory: expandable to 1024K bytes

12M byte fixed disc drive

movable by operator). An illustration of the use of the two disk units would be as follows: storing the daily inventory program continuously on the fixed disk while capturing each day's inventory transactions on a flexible disk, which is then taken to the HP 300 for processing. Flexible disks are many times less expensive than fixed disks. However, fixed disks typically have much faster access speed.

Table 7-1 provides a way of comparing micro- and minicomputers. For example, a minicomputer can have half a million bytes of disk storage (0.5-MB capacity) and a printer that operates at 3000 lines per minute (each line contains 132 characters). A minicomputer configuration often includes magnetic tape drives, a card reader, and a variety of terminals, either for input or output.

TABLE 7-1   CLASSIFICATION OF MICRO/MINICOMPUTERS FOR BUSINESS USE

	Micro		Mini
	Personal applications	*Business applications*	*Business applications*
CPU storage (bytes)	4 to 16K	16K to 128K	128K to 2M
Terminals (number of devices)	1	2 to 8	8 to 64
Disk storage on line (millions of bytes)	0.5 to 2	1 to 10	10 to 500
Printers	Character printers (30 to 165 char/sec)	Line printers (100 to 600 line/min)	Line printers (600 to 3000 lines/min)

Other peripherals
  Card reader/punch
  Magnetic tapes
Communications
Terminals
	Not usually available
	Cassette
	None to limited
	CRT or printing
		Available
		Cassette
		Limited to full scale
		CRT or printing
			Available
			Full scale
			Full scale
			All types including cash register

Price range (full system purchase in thousands)	$0.3 to $3	$2 to $20	$20 to $1000

QUESTION: Examine Table 7-1. For a minimal configuration of a business microcomputer indicate whether the following characteristics are true or false.

_____ 1.   price: $200

_____ 2.   disk capacity: 1,000,000 bytes

_____ 3.   central storage capacity: 16,000 bytes

_____ 4.   printer: 30 lines per minute

ANSWER: (1) False ($2000), (2) True, (3) True, (4) False (100 lines/minute)

Table 7-2 compares the software available on the various-sized systems. Only a subset of a high-level language like PL/1 is available on the typical personal microcomputer. A partial implementation of a high-level language makes

TABLE 7-2   MICRO/MINI SOFTWARE FOR BUSINESS

| | Micro | | Mini |
	Personal applications	Business applications	Business applications
Operating systems	Single terminal	Multiterminal Multiprogramming Data base management	Multiterminal Multiprogramming Multitasking Time-sharing Data base management

Languages	Machine
	BASIC
	FORTRAN (Subset)
	PL/1 (Subset)
	PASCAL
		Machine
		Assemblers
		Extended
		    BASIC
		    FORTRAN
		    PASCAL
		COBOL (Subset)
		RPG
		Query (Subset)
			Full version:
			BASIC
			FORTRAN
			PL/1
			COBOL
			RPG
			PASCAL
			GPSS
			Query

Application software	Bookkeeping Home uses	Marketing, manufacturing, accounting/finance	Full range of applications

programming more difficult, and a program often requires more instructions and memory than it would with a full implementation.

Partial language implementations exist for two reasons. The primary reason is that partial implementations are cheaper and faster to build than full implementations. Secondly, many people had the misconception that partial language implementations were sufficient for microcomputing because microcomputers are small. Economics still controls software availability. Large, more expensive computers tend to have better software and a greater variety of software.

Missing software functions may or may not be important. One example is double precision operations. Larger scale computers permit many decimal values of a number (e.g., 32 decimals) to be stored to achieve high precision. For a space shot, such accuracy is essential. For accounting purposes, all those extra decimals are unnecessary. The typical high-level language subset does not provide for double precision operations.

A brief explanation will be provided for each of the characteristics under the operating system category. The more sophisticated an operating system is, the more functions it can handle. An operating system that provides for multiprogramming enables the processing of more than one program at a time. Multitasking is a sophisticated method of multiprogramming—a single copy of a program can be used for more than one task. For example, persons at two terminals could input data to the inventory system. Time-sharing is allocating a portion of central memory to more than one on-line user of the system.

A query language is an extension of another software package, a **data base management system** (DBMS). Data base management is adding or extracting data from the data base, and DBMS software enables these functions to be performed without special programming. A high-level **query language** enables persons to ask questions of the data base in an English-like mode, such as, "What are sales of Product X for March?"

QUESTION: True or False? A minimal configuration business microcomputer would support both machine language and PASCAL for writing programs. A minicomputer might be required to support the full version of COBOL. _____

ANSWER: True. Some micros do not provide for a full version of COBOL, the language most widely used for business applications.

EXAMPLES OF MINICOMPUTER APPLICATIONS

Minicomputers are required when a company's computing needs extend beyond the capabilities of microcomputers. However, as in the case of microcomputers, the cost of minicomputers has been reduced dramatically. Minicomputers often use the same basic components in central memory as microcomputers—the minicomputer just has more of them. For example, a typical minicomputer has 128K bytes of memory compared to a typical microcomputer of 32K. The mini handles larger programs with larger data bases. Users of minis usually desire a variety of output devices: video display units, plotters, high speed printers, and others.

The following examples of minicomputer uses show the wider variety and larger size of applications required by the average customer.

RESTAURANT MANAGEMENT

Carl Junior's with the help of minicomputer systems and POS (point-of-sale) devices at the majority of its more than 200 hamburger outlets in California, has reduced the ordering process to 23 seconds. The cashier does not have to leave his or her station since the order goes electronically from the cashier's terminal to the cook's printer.

The HLx Systems "Star" computer in each restaurant consists of cashier terminals, remote printer in the kitchen, a processor, and a magnetic disk drive.

When a customer places an order at the counter, a cashier touches the appropriate boxes on a terminal keyboard containing: (1) all the menu items, (2) cooking instructions, (3) dining room or carryout keys, and (4) miscellaneous reporting keys. Depositing the money in the cash drawer triggers the system to print the food order on the cook's printer in the kitchen. The terminal totals the sale and adds tax.

Management also relies on the system for inventory management, accounting, and labor monitoring. Individual stores and headquarters use data to analyze food waste and shortage, production cost, profit, and salaries. Every morning, a minicomputer at Carl Junior's headquarters polls the store computers for sales and inventory statistics.

QUESTION: What features of this company's system identify it under the minicomputer classification in Table 7-1?

1. _____   2. _____

ANSWER: (1) Several types of terminals, including cash registers
(2) Full data communications (to all stores)

HEALTH ADMINISTRATION

Recently a Michigan health care firm made the headlines when it requested and received permission from the State Insurance Commission to reduce its subscriber rates by 16 percent. In a decade that has seen health costs soaring above the general increase in the cost of living, the news was startling.

Under the Michigan Health Maintenance Organization (HMO) concept, physicians and other medical specialists under contract to HMO are prepaid for their services to subscribers. The accent is on preventive health care, including regular physical examinations, to avoid the necessity of hospitalization wherever possible. For the premium, the subscriber enjoys access to full health care including prescriptions, hospital room, specialist services, and transportation to a hospital, if necessary, without any additional charges. Currently Michigan HMO has 32,000 subscribers serviced by 36 primary health care centers in the greater Detroit metropolitan area.

One of the major tools helping Michigan HMO control costs is a Univac 90/60 computer, which is now the hub of a total management information system.

The computer files and systems are organized under four basic modules. These consist of a membership file (a complete record of all subscribers), on-line claims processing, financial information, and health care administration. With the on-line claims processing, all manual filing of records and claims was eliminated at a substantial cost saving and much faster processing. Currently about 700 invoices are processed weekly.

Using the terminals, operators handling claims first check the eligibility of the person treated by examining the master membership file. The next step is to check the master patient medical record utilization file to determine if the invoice has already been paid.

At the end of each day all invoices approved for payment or rejection on the processing file are purged and transferred to the financial accounts payable file. At the same time the patient's medical record utilization file is updated. Checks and check vouchers are printed by the computer to reimburse health providers. Under the new computer system, all invoices are processed and checks mailed to health care providers in less than 30 days. Previously under the manual system it could have taken up to 60 days.

Other systems on the computer include a drug profile system, which allows the operator to check prescriptions for duplication, and a financial module that lets administrators monitor health care services and costs. The computer also prepares reports on the number of insured persons admitted to area hospitals, the number discharged, the number of days in the hospital, and an estimate of billings to be received.

Another computer printout lists the names of patients who have received hospital emergency room treatment but have not reported back to the health care center for follow-up care. Monthly reports are also prepared on the utilization of medical services by subscribers, separated by health center, hospital, and age group. "This information is extremely valuable to us. We may find that one of our health centers is hospitalizing patients longer than the average for the other centers. In this case we'll want to find out why," says Bruce Mullican, vice-president. "All of our reports are geared to give us the management information we need to closely monitor the use of all health services."[4]

QUESTION: What four application areas are used by HMO?

1. _____

2. _____

3. _____

4. _____

ANSWER: (1) membership records, (2) claims processing, (3) financial information, (4) health care administration

[4]"Computer Power Limits Spiralling Health Costs," *Infosystems*, October, 1978, pp. 126, 128.

EXAMPLES OF MINICOMPUTER APPLICATIONS

ORDER ENTRY/INVENTORY UPDATE

Until recently, Lipton Tea Company, the big grocery manufacturer, was using a centralized system that processed two batches of orders a day. The system was "adequate," according to Lipton's Director of Operations Systems, Robert C. Savage.[5] "But the error rate was high—about 25 percent—and we wanted to cut the lead time required to get merchandise shipped."

The new system was a distributed network of four DMS-1000 minicomputer systems. The DMS-1000s are used primarily for on-line order entry and inventory update at four Lipton regional offices in Chicago, Memphis, San Mateo, and Rochelle Park, New Jersey. They are linked to a centralized order processing system that is run on an IBM 370/158 at company headquarters in Englewood Cliffs, New Jersey.

In addition to order entry and inventory update, the network is used to generate shipping information, which is sent out over communications lines to 25 warehouses, where shipping documents are printed out on Terminet 30 terminals. The system has not only increased the accuracy of orders and shipments but speeded delivery of merchandise as well.

QUESTION: By decentralizing operation and putting minicomputers in the regional offices, _____ was faster and _____ was improved.

ANSWER: order entry/inventory update, accuracy

EXERCISE 7-2

1. Minicomputers are like microcomputers in structure but have more _____ and _____.

2. Minicomputer applications are more complicated and are available for each of the three major functions of a business: _____, _____, and _____.

3. Examine Table 7-1. If a character printer (typewriterlike device) has a capacity of 60 characters per line, how many lines per minute can be produced by the fastest micro printer? _____

4. Although a personal computer, for playing games and other uses, is available for less than $400, a micro large enough to run business applications usually cost at least $ _____.

5. A minicomputer with "all the bells and whistles" available (data communications, 64 terminals, 3000-line-per-minute printer, 2-MB CPU, etc.) might cost as much as $ _____.

6. The minicomputer could have on-line disk files capable of storing as much as _____ bytes of data and programs.

---

[5]"Distributed Processing Suits Lipton to a T," *Infosystems*, October, 1978, pp. 124, 126.

SUMMARY

Today, with circuits containing 2^{18} (262,144) elements available, we have not yet seen any significant departure from the laws of physics. Nor are there any signs that the process is slowing down, although a deviation from exponential growth is ultimately inevitable. Further miniaturization is less likely to be limited by the laws of physics than by the laws of economics.

The most striking characteristic of the microelectronics industry has been a persistent and rapid decline in the cost of a given electronic function. The hundredfold decline in prices for electronic components since the development of the integrated circuit is unique because, although other industries have shown similar experience curves, the integrated circuit industry has been unique in its annual doubling of output over an extended number of years.

Since microelectronics is used at all levels in computing (micro, mini, maxi), costs are declining throughout the computer industry.

The result is that few activities in industry remain uneconomical for computing. In addition, many areas of our home and recreational life can be enhanced through microcomputers.

And, just to show how flexible the little systems are, the following item appeared in a recent issue of *The Printout:* "A film entitled, 'Commitment to Quality,' illustrated what happened after a flood of the Grand Teton Dam innundated a System 32. IBM assisted the user in washing his floppy discs and using them on a replacement system with almost no loss of data from the files."

ANSWERS TO EXERCISES

EXERCISE 7-1

1. High-level language, machine language
2. Operating system
3. ROM, CPU
4. Application
5. Compiler, high-level language program
6. Data
7. Another section of RAM
8. Cassette tape, disk

EXERCISE 7-2

1. Capacity, capability
2. Marketing, manufacturing, accounting/finance
3. $165 \div 60 = 2.75$ lines/sec $\times 60 = 165$ lines/min
4. $2000
5. $1,000,000
6. One-half billion (500 million)

CHAPTER EXAMINATION

1. Match the following terms to the most appropriate definition.

   ____ Microprocessor

   ____ PL/M or PASCAL

   ____ Macro instruction

   ____ RAM

   ____ LED

   ____ ROM

   ____ Compiler

   ____ Microcomputer

   ____ Machine language program

   ____ Operating system

   ____ LCD

   ____ Application program

   ____ GAMBO

   ____ Maxi computer

   a. Controls the interaction of all devices

   b. CPU for a microcomputer

   c. Memory that can not be recorded on in normal computer operations

   d. An inventory program

   e. Low-level language

   f. Visual as opposed to printed output medium

   g. A form of visual display device

   h. Facilitates program modifications

   i. Smallest version of a computer

   j. Memory that is directly accessible

   k. High-level language

   l. Educational application of a micro

   m. Translates high-level to machine language

   n. Large-scale computer

2. True or False?

   ____ a. Microprocessors are inexpensive because they can be mass produced.

   ____ b. RWM refers to the same type of memory as RAM.

   ____ c. The letter "K" in computer use represents 1024.

   ____ d. ROM may be used to store any type of software.

_____ e.   Microprocessors are the fundamental unit for future generations of large-scale computers.

_____ f.   The microcomputer is capable of using only two of the three types of software.

_____ g.   A minicomputer can be thought of as large-scale microcomputer.

_____ h.   An inventory program is an example of operating system software.

_____ i.   Hobby computing is not a form of personal computing.

3.   True or False?

_____ a.   Microcomputers perform the same basic functions as minicomputers.

_____ b.   RAM may be used to store any type of software.

_____ c.   Only during development of a program is the compiler needed.

_____ d.   A payroll program is an example of application software.

_____ e.   A general ledger program is an example of a program that uses data captured as a by-product of processing other programs.

_____ f.   A personal computer is most often used for bathroom activities.

_____ g.   The hand-held electronic calculator would not be used for occupation-related computing.

_____ h.   Checkbook balancing might be considered as either occupation-related or personal computing.

4.   An application program might be recorded on either RAM or ROM. Explain the characteristics of the program in each case.

a.   ROM _____

_____

b.   RAM _____

_____

5.   Why is the operating system (OS) typically stored on ROM? _____

_____

_____

6.   Why is a compiler typically stored on ROM? _____

_____

_____

7.   Is the analogy of a child versus an adult appropriate to explain the capabilities of microcomputers versus minicomputers? _____ Explain your answer.

_____

_____

_____

8. Match the micro application to its degree of complexity.

		Simple	Intermediate	Complex
a.	Calculator	_____	_____	_____
b.	Automatic testing	_____	_____	_____
c.	Accounting	_____	_____	_____
d.	Game machines	_____	_____	_____
e.	Traffic controllers	_____	_____	_____
f.	Process control	_____	_____	_____

9. Income tax preparation would utilize which — an electronic calculator or a microcomputer? _____

   Explain your answer. _____

   _____

   _____

10. In what area of activities might the microcomputer motivate preschoolers and elementary school children to

    spend their time more productively? _____

    _____

    _____

11. Complete the following sentences.

    a. The cost of microprocessors has dropped an average of _____ percent per year over the last
       seven years.

    b. Instructions cannot be processed on a compiler without _____

       _____ .

    c. The letter "K" in computing represents the number _____ .

    d. Micros are distinguishable from minicomputers because of their _____ , _____ , and

       _____

12. Complete the following sentences.

a. Over the past decade operating speed and reliability have increased at least _____ times as physical size; power consumption and cost per bit of storage have been reduced by factors ranging from

_____ to _____

b. Twelve "K" of computer storage would represent _____ bytes.

c. The Michigan HMO reduced subscriber rates _____ percent by changing to a computerized system.

d. A multiprogramming system can operate on more than _____

13. Could the chess computer be programmed for a hand-held electronic calculator? _____ Explain your

answer. _____

_____

14. Figure 7–9 illustrates two types of disk storage. Explain the reason for the two types. _____

_____

_____

15. Indicate which of the following characteristics are representative of a personal computer.

____ a. Price: $400

____ b. Disk capacity: $1\frac{1}{2}$ megabytes

____ c. CPU storage capacity: 12,288 bytes

____ d. Typewriter input and CRT output (be careful on this one!)

____ e. Cassette tape reader

16. Could a micro be coupled to a minicomputer? (Use Table 7–1 as a basis for your answer.) _____

Explain. _____

_____

_____

17. Indicate which of the following characteristics are representative of a minicomputer.

____ a. Price: $0.5 million

____ b. CPU capacity: 2,000,000 bytes

____ c. Following I/O devices: CRT terminal, cash register, line printer, tape drive

_____ d.   Data communications: interaction with a maxicomputer as well as with other minicomputers

_____ e.   Disk capacity: 0.5 megabytes

18.   Indicate which of the following software would be available for a business microcomputer.

_____ a.   COBOL (full version)

_____ b.   Facility for two persons on different terminals using different programs.

_____ c.   Accounts receivable program

_____ d.   Market analysis program

_____ e.   Restaurant management program

_____ f.   Query language (full version)

19.   Match the following terms to the most appropriate definition.

_____ DBMS   a.   Macrolike language

_____ COBOL   b.   Business-oriented language

_____ Multiterminal OS c.   Video display output

_____ Query language   d.   Not removable by operator

_____ CRT   e.   Software for updating data base

_____ Fixed disk   f.   Operating system enabling multiple users

_____ Flexible disk   g.   Removable

20.   Distinguish each of the functions performed by the operating system for a minicomputer.

a.   Multiterminal _____

_____

b.   Multiprogramming _____

_____

c.   Multitasking _____

_____

d.   Time-sharing _____

_____

e.   Data base management _____

_____

21. Examine the description of Carl Junior's restaurant management system. Identify which of the features in Tables 7-1 and 7-2 are used by this company's minicomputer system. You may not have enough information to determine if every feature exists. Explain each of your choices.

Multiterminal _____

_____

Multiprogramming _____

_____

Multitasking _____

_____

Time-sharing _____

_____

Data base management _____

_____

Query _____

_____

22. Examine the description of the Michigan Health Administration System. Identify which of the features on Table 7-1 and 7-2 are used by this company's minicomputer system. You may not have enough information to determine if every feature exists. Explain each of your choices.

Multiterminal _____

_____

Multiprogramming _____

_____

Multitasking _____

_____

Time-sharing _____

_____

Data base management _____

_____

Query _____

_____

8

DATA COMMUNICATIONS

OVERVIEW. In Chapter 6 you studied devices and techniques for data input and output. Often the user is some distance from the computer—perhaps in another room, or even in a different city or country. In such situations, a data communications system may be used for transmitting data to and from the computer. In this chapter you will study the major elements of such a system.

A data communications **(or** datacom) system **consists of terminals, communications equipment and channels, and related computer programs. It links together the various elements of a data processing system, primarily terminals and computers. It may consist simply of a terminal in an executive's office, connected to a computer in another part of the building. On the other hand, a data communications system may consist of a nationwide network of interconnected computers and terminals. A properly designed data communications system can improve response to the user, reduce errors, improve the utilization of data processing facilities, and save energy.**

The data communications industry is perhaps the fastest growing segment of data processing. In 1980, the total expenditure by all firms in the United States on data communications products and services exceeded $3 billion. Millions of remote terminals in banks, retail stores, supermarkets, hospitals, plants, sales offices, and other organizations are connected to computers by data communications. In the future, the use of data communications is expected to explode as new products and services are introduced. On a national scale this explosion is likely to change our life-styles as home computers and terminals linked to various data bases become economically feasible.

APPLICATIONS OF DATA COMMUNICATIONS

Data communications systems are used in a variety of modes. The most important applications or modes of use can be summarized in the following categories.

☐ Inquiry/response.

☐ On-line data entry (also called *transaction processing*).

☐ Remote job entry.

☐ Conversational time-sharing.

☐ Distributed processing.

You studied two of these applications briefly in Chapter 6 — on-line data entry and distributed processing (see Figure 6–3). The five categories of usage are described below and are illustrated in Figure 8–1.

INQUIRY/RESPONSE In this type of application, users at various locations require access to a remote computer data base. The user typically uses a video display terminal and requires a response to an inquiry for information within a few seconds. Examples include credit checking, library reference, and law enforcement.

ON-LINE DATA ENTRY The user enters transaction data at a remote terminal as the transactions become available. This mode is also referred to as **transaction processing** and was described in Chapter 6.

On-line data entry is required where the computer data base must be maintained up to the minute, and where rapid response is required. Typical applications of transaction processing include the following.

1. Airline reservations systems. A clerk presses buttons on a terminal to request the availability of a certain flight. A central computer thousands of miles away checks the status of that flight and flashes back an answer almost instantly. The reservations clerk then keys in the information needed to make the reservation, and the computer updates its file. Similar reservations systems are used by hotels and rental car agencies.

2. Banks and savings institutions. Tellers can insert a depositor's passbook into a terminal and give the customer an up-to-date balance including accrued interest. Transactions such as deposits and withdrawals are posted instantly to the customer's account, maintained by a remote computer.

3. Insurance companies. All agents in branches throughout the country can access and update the company's huge central computer policy file in seconds.

4. Manufacturing companies. For example, one company uses an on-line system that links more than 350 factories, offices, and warehouses. Several thousand orders are received and processed daily. For most of these orders, shipping instructions are printed on a terminal in the warehouse nearest the customer within seconds after the order is received.

REMOTE JOB ENTRY With this mode, a remote terminal that is equipped with a high-speed card reader and line printer is linked to a central computer. Data processing "jobs" (programs and data) are entered at the remote terminal and transmitted to the central computer for processing. Output is transmitted back to the remote site for printing.

CONVERSATIONAL TIME-SHARING This data communications application allows a number of remote users to solve problems simultaneously on a central computer. The computer allocates its resources to each of its current users, so that to each user it appears that he alone is using the computer. Applications include engineering design, management science, and text editing.

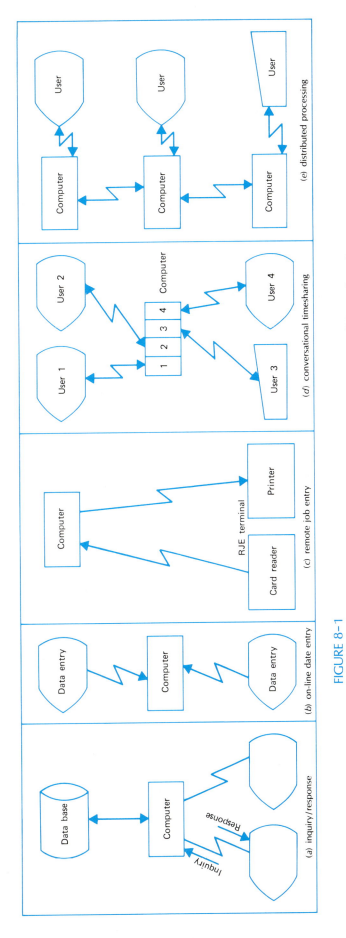

FIGURE 8-1
Modes of data communications usage. (*a*) Inquiry/response. (*b*) On-line data entry. (*c*) Remote job entry. (*d*) Conversational time-sharing. (*e*) Distributed processing.

DISTRIBUTED PROCESSING   This mode was also described in Chapter 6. Rather than using a large central computer, companies disperse smaller computers throughout the organization. The computers are often linked together by data communications and may share data bases. An example of distributed processing is a network of mini-computers in a large bank, with each mini performing specialized functions within a department. These minis may support time-sharing, inquiry/response, transaction processing, and remote job entry.

QUESTION: Some applications require two or more modes of data communications. What two modes are used by airline reservations systems as described in the above paragraphs?

a. _____

b. _____

ANSWER: inquiry/response, on-line data entry

ADVANTAGES OF DATA COMMUNI- CATIONS

A well-designed data communications system provides some or all of the following advantages.

1. Capture of data in machine-processable form at the point of origin. For example, in a retail store using point-of-sale recorders, sales data for each customer is recorded by a terminal and transmitted to a central computer. By reducing the number of times and places at which data is manually handled, one reduces clerical costs and chances for error.

2. Prompt collection of data and dissemination of information. Data is transmitted at electronic speeds, rather than by mail or other comparatively slow methods. This permits a company to keep in close touch with plants, warehouses, sales offices, and other units, as well as customers and suppliers. Overall planning and control is based on current, accurate information.

3. Reduced operating costs. A company with data communications has the choice of processing the data centrally, thereby taking advantage of economies of scale. Alternatively, the company can distribute its processing to remote sites, thereby providing better service to its users while at the same time retaining centralized control.

4. Backup data processing capacity. In larger systems, two or more computers are often connected by a data communications system. This permits priority jobs to be routed to another computer if the primary computer is busy, or if one of the computers fails.

5. Reduced energy consumption. Data communications replaces courier services and often can eliminate the need for meetings and conferences.

COMMUNI- CATIONS CONCEPTS

Data is communicated from a source to one or more destinations in the form of messages. A **message** generally consists of three parts (see Figure 8-2).

1. A header, which indicates start of message, destination, and perhaps other information such as source, date, and routing.

2. The body of the message, containing one or many characters of information.

3. End-of-message indicator.

FIGURE 8-2
Format of a message.

MODES OF TRANSMISSION There are two basic modes of transmitting data—asynchronous and synchronous.

Asynchronous transmission is known as start–stop transmission. As each character of information is made ready by the transmitting device, it is sent to the receiving device. Characters can be sent at irregular intervals. This mode of transmission is appropriate for slow-speed keyboard terminals where, for example, a person might type two characters in 1 second, then wait 10 seconds before the next character is entered.

To enable the receiver to recognize a character, in asynchronous transmission each character has its own start and stop bits. For example, the most commonly used code for data transmission is the ASCII code (American Standard Code for Information Interchange). This code uses seven bits per character, plus parity bit (an 8-bit ASCII is also available). Figure 8-3 represents the transmission of the character A, followed by the character Z, in ASCII code. Each character is represented by a start bit, followed by eight signal bits, then two stop bits.

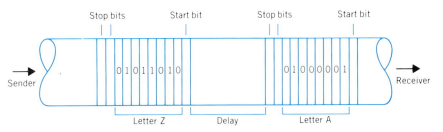

FIGURE 8-3
Asynchronous transmission of ASCII characters.

QUESTION: In asynchronous transmission using the ASCII code, how many bits are required

for each character? _____

ANSWER: 11

With **synchronous** transmission, start and stop bits are not required for each character. Instead, the sending and receiving devices are synchronized by exchanging a predetermined set of "sync" characters either periodically or before the transmission of each message. With synchronous transmission, the sending device transmits a long stream of characters without start/stop bits. The receiving device counts off the first eight bits (assuming an ASCII code), assumes this is the first character and passes it on to the computer. It then counts off the second character and so on until the message is completed.

Figure 8–4 portrays the transmission of the message AZ in ASCII code using synchronous transmission.

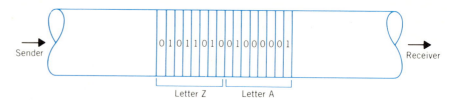

Sender   0 1 0 1 1 0 1 0 0 1 0 0 0 0 0 0 1   Receiver

Letter Z   Letter A

FIGURE 8–4

Synchronous transmission of ASCII characters.

Asynchronous transmission is favored for slow-speed terminals that are operated by persons since it permits characters to be transmitted at irregular rates. The disadvantage is that transmission is less efficient, since each character must have start and stop bits. For example, with ASCII code each 8-bit character of information requires a total of 11 bits in transmission. Thus, the efficiency is 8/11 or about 73 percent. Since it is more efficient, synchronous transmission is used for high-speed devices such as card readers and magnetic tape units.

A third mode, **isochronous,** combines the elements of both asynchronous and synchronous techniques. With this approach, each character has start and stop bits so that characters may be transmitted at irregular intervals. At the same time, during data transmission the transmitter and receiver are synchronized. The advantage of this approach over asynchronous transmission is greater speed: while asynchronous is limited to about 1800 bits per second, isochronous transmission permits speeds up to 9600 bits per second. However, synchronous transmission permits even faster rates than isochronous because extra start and stop bits are not required.

The rate of data transmission in a data communication system is often stated in bits per second. This rate can be translated to characters per second by dividing by the number of bits per character. For example, if a telephone line has a rated capacity of 4800 bits per second, this is equivalent to 600 characters per second (4800 ÷ 8) for an ASCII code using synchronous transmission.

The term **baud** is sometimes used instead of bits per second. The word "baud" is derived from Baudot, who was a nineteenth-century French communications pioneer. Actually the baud is a unit of telegraph signaling speed and is not synonymous with bits per second. However, the two do coincide for certain codes. As a result, when practitioners use the term "baud" they generally mean "bits per second."

TRANSMISSION CODES

Adoption of a standard code is an important step in data communications, since it permits various devices to "talk" to each other without the need for code conversion. In 1963, the first standardized code (ASCII63) was adopted. The present version of ASCII appeared in 1968 and is widely accepted as a standard communication code. The ASCII code (both 7-bit and 8-bit versions) is described in Chapter 4.

The ASCII code is a 7-bit code, with an eighth bit added for parity checking. Thus, the ASCII code permits 2^7 or 128 valid character combinations. Table 8–1 shows the entire set of ASCII characters.

TABLE 8-1   ASCII CHARACTER SET

b_7 →	0	0	0	0	1	1	1	1
b_6 →	0	0	1	1	0	0	1	1
b_5 →	0	1	0	1	0	1	0	1

$b_4 b_3 b_2 b_1$ ↓↓↓↓	Column / Row	0	1	2	3	4	5	6	7
0 0 0 0	0	NUL	DLE	SP	0	@	P	'	p
0 0 0 1	1	SOH	DC1	!	1	A	Q	a	q
0 0 1 0	2	STX	DC2	"	2	B	R	b	r
0 0 1 1	3	ETX	DC3	#	3	C	S	c	s
0 1 0 0	4	EOT	DC4	$	4	D	T	d	t
0 1 0 1	5	ENQ	NAK	%	5	E	U	e	u
0 1 1 0	6	ACK	SYN	&	6	F	V	f	v
0 1 1 1	7	BEL	ETB	'	7	G	W	g	w
1 0 0 0	8	BS	CAN	(	8	H	X	h	x
1 0 0 1	9	HT	EM	)	9	I	Y	i	y
1 0 1 0	10	LF	SUB	*	:	J	Z	j	z
1 0 1 1	11	VT	ESC	+	;	K	[	k	{
1 1 0 0	12	FF	FS	comma ,	<	L	\	l	?
1 1 0 1	13	CR	GS	.	=	M	]	m	}
1 1 1 0	14	SO	RS	.	>	N	∩	n	—
1 1 1 1	15	SI	US	/	?	O	—	o	DEL

NUL	— Null	SI	— Shift in
SOH	— Start of heading	DLE	— Data link escape
STX	— Start of text	DC-1 to 4	— Device control
ETX	— End of text	NAK	— Negative ack.
EOT	— End of transmission	SYN	— Synchronous idle
ENQ	— Enquiry	ETB	— End of trans block
ACK	— Acknowledge	CAN	— Cancel
BEL	— Bell	EM	— End of medium
BS	— Back space	SUB	— Substitute
HT	— Horizontal tab	ESC	— Escape
LF	— Line feed	FS	— File separator
VT	— Vertical tab	GS	— Group separator
FF	— Form feed	RS	— Record separator
CR	— Carriage return	US	— Unit separator
SO	— Shift out	DEL	— Delete (rubout)

(Source: Jerry Fitzgerald & Tom Eason, *Fundamentals of Data Communications*, John Wiley & Sons, 1978)

QUESTION: Look at Table 8-1. Write the ASCII code for each of the following characters.

R _____

r _____

5 _____

ANSWER: R = 1010010, r = 1110010, 5 = 0110101

Although the ASCII code is widely used, other coding schemes are also used for data transmission. Following is a brief description of the more commonly used non-ASCII codes.

Baudot code is a 5-bit code dating back to the nineteenth century. It was used with the original Teletype equipment. By using a shift character the Baudot code is capable of representing some 62 different code combinations.

Data Interchange Code is used on newer Teletype equipment. Similar to ASCII, it is an 8-bit code that uses seven bits to represent characters plus one parity bit.

Extended Binary Coded Decimal Interchange Code (EBCDIC), used by IBM equipment, was also described in Chapter 4. This code has eight data bits plus a ninth bit for parity.

TRANSMISSION PROTOCOL

There are three basic methods of transmitting data over a communication line: simplex, half-duplex, and full duplex (see Figure 8–5).

With **simplex** transmission, data is transmitted in one direction only. One end of the link contains a transmitter and the other end, a receiver. Thus only a "one-way conversation" is permitted. This method is seldom used in data communications.

With **half-duplex** (HDX), transmission may be in both directions but in only one direction at a time; that is, one station transmits to a second station, then the second responds, and so on (corresponding to a polite telephone conversation). HDX is the most commonly used data communications method.

With **full duplex** (FDX), both stations can receive and transmit at the same time. This method is sometimes used when private telephone lines are used for data transmission.

When messages are to be transmitted between a remote terminal and a computer, a series of signals must be exchanged to set up the message. **Protocols** are predetermined signals used to control the flow of messages and synchronize their transmission. The exchange of protocols is frequently referred to as "handshaking." Following are ASCII message protocol characters.

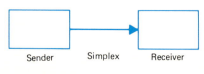
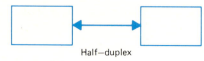
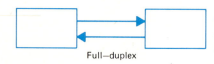

FIGURE 8–5
Basic transmission methods.

SOH — start of message.
ADD — terminal address.
ACK — acknowledge receipt of message.
STX — start of text.
ETX — end of text.

The ASCII code for each of these protocol characters is shown in Table 8–1.

MODULATION

Digital data from a computer or peripheral device is represented as a series of digital pulses corresponding to binary 0s and 1s (see Figure 8–6). Digital data cannot be directly transmitted over standard telephone lines, which are designed to transmit analog carrier signals (or sine waves). **Modulation** is the process of converting digital pulses to carrier signals, while converting these signals back to digital pulses is called **demodulation** (illustrated in Figure 8–6).

FIGURE 8–6
Modulation and demodulation of data.

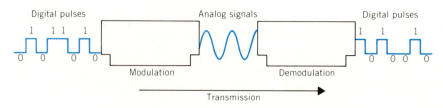

Four basic modulation techniques are used to convert digital pulses to carrier signals (Figure 8–7).

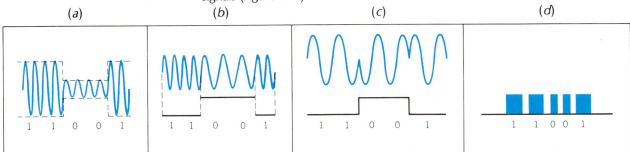

(a)   *(b)*   *(c)*   *(d)*

FIGURE 8–7
Basic modulation techniques. (*a*) Amplitude modulation. (*b*) Frequency modulation. (*c*) Phase modulation. (*d*) Pulse width modulation.

1. **Amplitude modulation** (AM)—with this technique, the amplitude (or strength) of the sine wave is varied to represent binary 0s and 1s. For example, a high peak voltage or sine wave represents a 1, a low peak voltage a 0.

2. **Frequency modulation** (FM)—with this technique, the frequency of the analog signal is varied instead of the amplitude. For example, a 1000-hertz signal may be used to represent a binary 0, while 2000 hertz represents a binary 1 (see Figure 8–7b). The term hertz (or Hz) is equivalent to cycles per second. As with radio transmission, FM is less affected by noise than AM. As a result, FM is less susceptible to error and is generally favored over AM.

3. **Phase modulation** (PM)—this technique varies the phase of the signal rather than its amplitude or frequency; that is, the phase or angular position of the signal is shifted or reversed to represent a change from binary 0 to 1 (see Figure 8–7c). Then PM is affected by noise even less than FM and is replacing FM in many applications requiring high transmission rates.

4. **Pulse code modulation** (PCM)—with this technique, data are transmitted as a train of coded pulses rather than as analog signals. Thus, PCM is a digital transmission technique. One form of PCM (pulse width modulation) is illustrated in Figure 8–7d. Finally, PCM is the most noise free of the four modulation techniques and therefore is the most error-free form of data transmission.

DATA COMMUNI- CATIONS HARDWARE

There are three basic elements of a data communications system: the source, the medium (or link), and the sink. The **source** is the sender of information, such as a person seated at a terminal. The **medium** is the communication channel, such as a telephone line. The **sink** is the receiver of information, perhaps a computer or a person seated at a terminal.

In practice, there are five basic hardware components or building blocks in most data communications systems (see Figure 8–8).

1. Computers.
2. Communications processors (or front ends).
3. Modems.

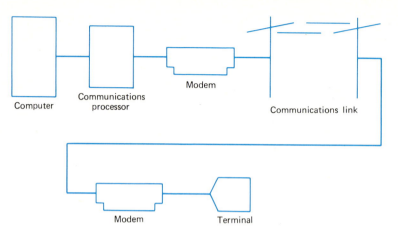

FIGURE 8-8
Basic components of a datacom system.

4. Communications links.
5. Terminals.

Each of these components is described below.

QUESTION: Examine Figure 8-8. A message sent from a remote terminal to the computer passes through the following elements (in order).

a. _____

b. _____

c. _____

d. _____

ANSWER: (a) modem, (b) communications link, (c) modem, (d) communications processor

COMPUTERS   There may be one or more computers in a data communications system. If there are several computers, some may be assigned specialized data communications functions such as message switching or local processing. Often there is a large, general-purpose computer that performs the major data processing tasks. This computer is often referred to as the **host computer.**

COMMUNICATIONS PROCESSORS   Managing a data communications network is a complex task. To service an arriving or departing message involves many short periods of activity, with intervening periods of inactivity. General-purpose computers, which are designed for data processing tasks, are relatively inefficient in performing these data communications tasks. For this reason, special devices called **communications processors** are used to manage the data communications network.

There are two types of communications processors—nonprogrammable and programmable. A nonprogrammable unit is referred to as **communications controller** or transmissions control unit. These devices are used in relatively simple communications applications.

Programmable communications processors are essentially general-purpose minicomputers programmed to perform data communications tasks. These devices are referred to as **front-end processors,** or simply as **front ends.** Front-end processors are many times more powerful than nonprogrammable units and for this reason are replacing these units in many applications.

Front-end communications processors perform the following important functions in a data communications network[1].

1. Connects the central computer (or host processor) to one or many communications lines.

2. Polls remote terminals to inquire if they have a message to send, or determines whether a terminal is ready to receive a message.

3. Accepts incoming data (or messages) in different formats and converts it into a format required by the computer. In reverse, it converts computer code into various formats required by the network.

4. Performs "**store-and-forward**" functions. Whenever one terminal is transmitting a message to another terminal that is busy or inoperable, the front end can normally store the message and later forward it to the second terminal when it is ready.

5. Provides error detection and correction for incoming messages.

6. Performs logging of all inbound and outbound messages, both for audit purposes and as a basis to restart the system should a "crash" occur.

7. Assigns priorities to inbound and outbound messages if desired.

8. Determines alternative communications links, if a given link is "busy" or "noisy."

9. Automatically places and answers calls to and from terminals in the system.

10. Maintains statistics concerning usage of the network, such as number of messages per hour and number of errors.

MODEMS   Modems are signal conversion devices that allow digital data to be transmitted over ordinary telephone lines. Digital data from a terminal or computer must be modulated before transmission, using one of the techniques described earlier. At the receiving end, the data must be demodulated. The device that performs these functions is called a **modem,** which is derived from "modulate" and "demodulate." The device must be able to perform both functions, since it both sends and receives messages. A typical modem is shown in Figure 8–9.

TYPES OF MODEMS   Modems may be classified as low-, medium-, or high-speed devices, depending on their capacity. Low-speed modems operate up to about 1800 bits per second (BPS) and generally use FM. These devices are used for teletypewriters and other low-speed printing terminals. Medium-speed modems operate from 2000 to 4800 BPS and are typically used for video display terminals and medium-speed printers. High-speed modems operate at from 4800 to 9600 BPS or faster. These devices generally employ phase modulation (PM) techniques and are used for high-speed printers, magnetic tape, and other high-speed peripheral devices.

---

[1]For a more detailed discussion of these functions and of data communications in general, see J. FitzGerald and T. S. Eason, *Fundamentals of Data Communications*, 1978, John Wiley & Sons, New York.

FIGURE 8-9
Modem (Courtesy Racal-Milgo).

One special type of low-speed modem is the **acoustic coupler.** This device is often used to connect a remote teletypewriter (or other low-speed terminal) to a computer by means of a public telephone circuit. To use the device, the user dials a number associated with the computer. When a connection is made, a special tone signal is produced and the user places the telephone handset into the cradle of the acoustic coupler (see Figure 8-10). Thus, the modem is connected acoustically rather than electrically to the telephone line.

QUESTION: An acoustic coupler is a (low-speed, high-speed) modem that requires the user

remember a _____ _____ before using a terminal.

ANSWER: low-speed, telephone number

FIGURE 8-10
Acoustic Coupler (Courtesy Racal-Vadic).

Modems, such as the one shown in Figure 8-9, are quite sophisticated devices that, in addition to converting signals, can perform some or all of the following functions.

1. Automatic dialing of remote terminals.
2. Automatic answering of calls from remote terminals.
3. Simultaneous voice and data transmission.
4. Dynamic balancing of transmission lines to minimize error rates.
5. Automatic testing of a line for proper operation ("loop-back" tests) and selection of alternate routes when a line fails.

EXERCISE 8-1

1. Which of the five types of datacom applications shown in Figure 8-1 describes each of the following?

   a. Terminal in an automobile parts store is used to access part number, description, and cost of replacement parts.

   _____

   b. Multinational company has nearly 100 computers in five countries linked by data communications.

   _____

   c. Business college has 10 terminals connected to a computer across campus, used for on-line programming.

   _____

   d. University has a large batch terminal at a branch campus, equipped with card reader and line printer.

   _____

   e. Mail order firm has 40 video display terminals for entry of sales orders directly into computer.

   _____

2. List the five basic hardware components of a datacom system.

   a. _____

   b. _____

   c. _____

   d. _____

   e. _____

COMMUNICATIONS FACILITIES

Data is transmitted between remote terminals and computers by means of a communications **channel** or **network.** Most companies use facilities provided by telephone and telegraph common carriers and by specialized common carriers for this purpose. Communications **common carriers** are companies authorized by the Federal Communications Commission (FCC) or state regulatory agencies to provide communications services to the public.

By far the largest common carrier in the United States is the American Telephone and Telegraph Company (AT&T). This company consists of some 20 interdependent operating companies, known collectively as the Bell System. Western Union, once limited to telegraph service, now offers a broad range of communications services. In addition, there are a large number of independent telephone companies, the largest of which is General Telephone. Finally, there are a large number of specialized common carriers such as Telenet, ITT, World Communications, American Satellite, and others that offer data communications services.

CLASSES OF SERVICE

The services offered by common carriers can be classified according to bandwidth: narrowband, voiceband, and broadband (or wideband). **Bandwidth** refers to the frequency range that can be accommodated by the transmission line, which in turn determines the rate at which data can be transmitted.

The three classes of service are defined as follows.

1. Narrowband. Data may be transmitted at rates up to 300 bits per second. Narrowband services are used for teletypewriters and other low-speed terminals.
2. Voiceband. Voiceband circuits are used in ordinary telephone conversations. Data rates of 4800 bits per second are commonly achieved on dialed lines, while rates up to 9600 bits per second are attainable with leased lines.
3. Broadband. Very high data rates (up to several million bits per second) can be achieved with broadband facilities, which generally use coaxial cable or microwave transmission.

QUESTION: The rate at which data can be transmitted depends on _____ . Three

categories of service are _____ , _____ , _____ .

ANSWER: bandwidth, narrowband, voiceband, broadband

LEASED VERSUS DIALED SERVICE

Communications facilities may be used in one of two basic ways. First, the user may lease a line from a common carrier on a full-time basis. The **leased** (private or dedicated) line is available 24 hours a day for the exclusive use of the user. A flat rate is charged for the service, depending on distance and size of city involved.

The second type of arrangement is **dialed** (or **switched**) service. When a message is to be transmitted, the user dials the destination number (either computer or remote terminal), just as for a telephone call. The user must compete with other users for an available line and may encounter a busy signal at any given time. The user is charged only for the time used, with rates depending on the time of day, day of the week, and distance involved.

QUESTION: The two basic types of service are _____ lines (with flat rates) and

_____ lines (with rates based on usage).

ANSWER: leased (or private), dialed (or switched)

The choice between leased and dialed lines is based on an analysis of costs, message volume, and service requirements. As a general rule, low message volume favors dialed facilities, while heavy volume favors leased facilities. Leased lines provide guaranteed access, faster response (since dialing is not necessary) and better-quality transmission than dialed service. Also, privacy is more easily maintained with leased lines. On the other hand, dialed service provides greater access to the "outside world" because extensive interconnections are available through the telephone system.

DIALED SERVICES   The major dialed (or switched) communications services are shown in Table 8-2.

All of the dialed services in Table 8-2 are billed according to usage, except for Wide Area Telephone Service, or WATS. The WATS system uses a flat monthly pricing arrangement (within monthly limits) for directly dialed station-to-station calls. The United States is divided into "bands" or service areas, and the customer can subscribe for coverage to any other band. For example, Figure 8-11 shows the WATS bands from Colorado to other areas of the country.

QUESTION: Examine Figure 8-11. According to the figure, WATS coverage to Northern California would be provided to a Colorado customer who subscribed for ser-

vice to band _____ .

ANSWER: 3 (This would also provide coverage in bands 1 and 2.)

The WATS system offers two billing plans: measured time and full business day. The measured time plan provides for 10 hours of usage per month, while the full business day allowance is for 240 hours. There is an additional charge

TABLE 8-2   DIALED DATA COMMUNICATIONS SERVICES

Class of Service	Name of Service	Description
Narrowband	Teletypewriter Exchange Service (TWX and TELEX)	Low-speed transmission (up to 150 BPS)
Voiceband	Direct Distance Dialing (DDD)	Uses dial telephone network (up to 4800 BPS)
	Wide Area Telephone Service (WATS)	Flat monthly rate, dial telephone network
Wideband	50 Kilobit	50,000 BPS, equivalent to 12 voice grade lines

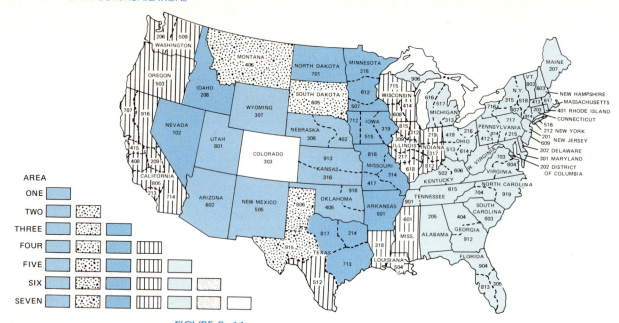

FIGURE 8-11
The WATS bands from Colorado (Courtesy AT&T).

per hour for usage exceeding these limits. Also, WATS lines provide for either inbound or outbound calls—both cannot be combined on a single line.

Generally, WATS service becomes economically attractive to the dialed-service user as the volume of voice and data traffic continues to grow.

LEASED SERVICES   The major leased (or private) data communications services are shown in Table 8-3.

One of the major advantages of leased lines over dial-up lines is that a leased (private) line can be conditioned to reduce error rates. Conditioning is the electrical balancing of a voice grade line to reduce distortion. Since error rates are reduced, private lines also permit higher transmission rates.

QUESTION: Compare Tables 8-2 and 8-3. Direct Distance Dialing permits data transmission

---

TABLE 8-3   LEASED DATA COMMUNICATIONS SERVICES

Class of Service	Name of Service	Description
Narrowband	Series 1000	Teletypewriter transmission (up to 150 BPS)
Voiceband	Series 3000	Private telephone line (up to 9600 BPS)
Wideband	TELPAK Type 5700	Group pricing arrangement, equivalent to 60 Series 3000 lines
	TELPAK Type 5800	Group pricing arrangement, equivalent to 240 Series 3000 lines
	Series 8000	50,000-BPS private line

at a rate of _____ BPS, while Series 3000 lines with conditioning permit

data rates up to _____ BPS.

ANSWER: 4800, 9600

OTHER
COMMUNICATIONS
SERVICES

There are many other communications services in addition to those shown in Tables 8-2 and 8-3. Two of the newer and more important of these services — digital data service and satellite communications — are described below.

DIGITAL DATA SERVICE   To transmit digital data on voice channels, modems must be used to modulate and demodulate the signals. The Bell System is developing a system that uses pulse code modulation, which will eliminate the need for signal modulation. This system, already available in several dozen cities, is used exclusively for data transmission. Transmission rates of 2400, 4800, and 56,000 BPS are available. The main advantages of digital data service are much lower error rates and high channel availability. The main disadvantage is that the service will be available only in 100 to 200 large metropolitan areas of the United States.

SATELLITE COMMUNICATION SERVICES   Satellite communication services are often used for long-distance data transmission. Satellite services are leased on a monthly basis and are accessed by land line facilities such as Series 3000 voice grade lines. Both voiceband and wideband facilities (up to a million bits per second) are available. For example, the cost of a single voice grade satellite channel for a distance of 1000 miles is about $500 per month.[2]

FIGURE 8-12
Westar I communications satellite. (Courtesy Western Union.)

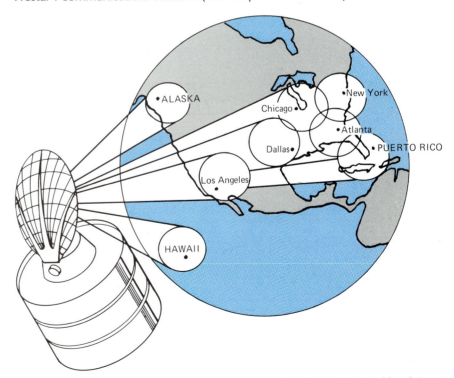

[2]For a detailed discussion of common carrier services and tariffs, see FitzGerald and Eason, op. cit.

The first domestic communications satellite—Western Union's Westar I—was launched in April 1974. This satellite orbits 22,300 miles above the equator, maintaining a stationary position with respect to the earth. Westar I covers all 50 states and Puerto Rico (see Figure 8-12) and can relay messages at a rate of more than 8 million words per second.

Since Westar, a number of domestic communications satellites have been launched. Satcom (RCA) was launched in 1975, and Comstar (AT&T) in 1976. These satellites weigh between 1000 and 2000 pounds, are powered by solar arrays, and are launched by NASA. At present there are about six U.S.-launched communications satellites in orbit and perhaps two dozen worldwide for all nations.[3]

The demand for satellite communications is expected to grow rapidly during the next decade. A number of next-generation satellites are scheduled for launch during the 1980s. New versions of Westar and Comsat will be in orbit in the early 1980s. Satellite Business Systems is planning to launch a series of domestic private line satellites beginning in 1980, with the goal of developing a private communications net for Fortune 500 corporations and large public service agencies. It is estimated that, by the year 2000, the demand for satellite communications services will be at least 10 times as great as in 1980.[4]

EXERCISE 8-2

1. Specify whether private or dialed service would be more appropriate for each of the following applications.

    a. For on-line reservations, an airline has remote terminals throughout the country, linked to a central computer.

    b. A small engineering company has two time-sharing terminals. Time is purchased from a nationwide time-sharing company to solve engineering problems that occasionally arise.

    c. A business school has six time-sharing terminals that are connected to a computer across campus. Usage is heavy throughout the day and early evening.

    d. A real estate broker subscribes to an information service that maintains a data base on homes for sale. The broker accesses the data base several times each day by means of a portable terminal.

2. Fill in the following table summarizing common carrier services.

Name of Service	Bandwidth	Dialed or Private
TWX and Telex	_____	_____
DDD	_____	_____

---

[3]Wade White and Morris Holmes, "The Future of Commercial Satellite Communications," *Datamation*, Vol. 24, No. 7, July 1978.
[4]Ibid.

WATS		
50 Kilobit		
Series 3000		
TELPAK		
Series 8000		

DATACOM TERMINALS

Five basic types of terminals are used in data communications (see Figure 8–13).

(a)

(b)

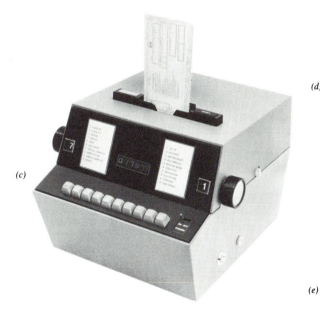
(c)

(d)

(e)

FIGURE 8-13
Types of terminals used in data communications. (a) Teletypewriter. (Courtesy Teletype Corp.) (b) Video display. (Courtesy Honeywell.) (c) Transaction terminal. (Courtesy IBM.) (d) Remote job entry terminal. (Courtesy Data 100 Corp.) (e) Intelligent terminal. (Courtesy Northern Telecom Systems.)

☐ Teletypewriter terminals.
☐ Visual display terminals.
☐ Transaction terminals.
☐ Remote job entry terminals.
☐ Intelligent terminals.

Teletypewriter terminals are typewriter-like terminals that have keyboards for data entry and printers for data output. These terminals are used primarily on low-speed leased lines or on dial-up lines where acoustic couplers are used. Teletypewriter terminals print one character at a time at speeds ranging from 10 to roughly 150 characters per second. Some of these terminals have punched paper tape readers and punches attached as auxiliary devices. Although they are tending to be replaced by visual display terminals, teletypewriter terminals continue to find widespread use in datacom systems.

Visual display terminals (VDT), sometimes called video display terminals or cathode ray tubes (CRT), have a typewriterlike keyboard and televisionlike screen. The VDTs are available in two main types, alphanumeric and graphical. These terminals are widely used for inquiry/response, transaction processing, time-sharing, and other datacom applications. Visual display terminals are described in detail in Chapter 6.

Transaction terminals are used for particular applications in industries such as retail stores, banks, supermarkets, and factories. The terminals are used for inquiry/response applications and for capturing transaction data at the point of origin. Transaction terminals often are equipped with bar code readers as well as a keyboard for manual entry of data.

A portable, hand-held transaction terminal for ordering merchandise is shown in Figure 8–14. This device is a solid state microcomputer that weighs about 26 ounces. It has a shock-mounted optical bar code reader, 16-position keyboard, LED display, and removable memory pack with 4K or 8K character capacity.

FIGURE 8–14
Portable transaction terminal. (*a*) Terminal with bar code reader. (*b*) Terminal inserted in service module. (Courtesy Bergen Brunswig.)

(a)

(b)

This terminal (called the Ultraphase) reads bar code shelf labels on drugstore or supermarket shelves (see Figure 8–14a). After the shelf label containing the product code and other descriptive information is read, the operator keys in the quantity of the item to be ordered. All entries appear on the display for visual verification.

To order merchandise, the memory pack is removed from the device and inserted into a service module that contains an acoustic coupler (see Figure 8–14b). After a connection is made, order information is transmitted to a computer processing center at 120 characters per second. Although designed for ordering merchandise, this type of terminal can obviously be used in a wide variety of applications.

Remote job entry (RJE) stations are used for transmission of large quantities of batched information between remote locations and a computer. These devices generally consist of a card reader, a line printer, and visual display, attached to a programmable control unit. Also, RJE stations may include magnetic tape or disk storage units. Minicomputers are often used as sophisticated RJE stations. These RJE stations generally transmit data over voice grade lines at 4800 or 9600 bits per second.

Intelligent terminals are terminals (often visual displays) with a small, built-in computer or microprocessor. Intelligent terminals are generally capable of doing some independent (or "stand-alone") data processing, as well as communicating with a central computer or with other intelligent terminals. In fact, some intelligent terminals are essentially minicomputers. The distinction between intelligent terminals, minicomputers, and RJE stations is rapidly disappearing since small but powerful minicomputers can perform at a low cost all of the functions previously associated with these various devices.

USING DATACOM SYSTEMS

Thus far we have described the basic functional elements or building blocks of datacom systems. In this section we will describe how datacom systems are used, including network design, data communication software, and error control and detection.

NETWORK DESIGN

A wide variety of approaches is available to the user who wishes to develop a datacom network. Several of the most important approaches are described below.

Point-to-point lines are the simplest network configuration. These lines con-

FIGURE 8–15
Point-to-point line.

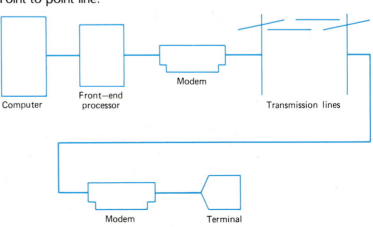

Computer   Front—end processor   Modem   Transmission lines

Modem   Terminal

nect a single terminal at one end of the communications line to a single computer at the other end. Figure 8–15 illustrates a point-to-point line connecting a computer to a remote video display terminal.

Multidrop lines have multiple terminals connected to a single communication line. Each terminal is considered a "drop point." Figure 8–16 depicts a multidrop line with three video display terminals.

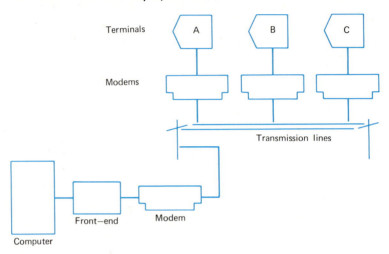

FIGURE 8–16
Multidrop line.

With multidrop lines, only one terminal can transmit at a time unless multiplexing is used (described in the next section). Each terminal has an address and must be able to recognize that a message is being sent to that address. For example, in Figure 8–16 the terminals have address A, B, and C. The computer might send a message down the line addressed to terminal C. Each terminal monitors the message addresses, so that only terminal C will receive this message.

Multidrop lines also generally have the capability of using group or broadcast addresses. In group addresses, a message is transmitted to selected terminals (for example, terminals A and C). In broadcast addresses, a message is sent to every terminal on the line.

Since only one terminal can transmit at a given time, there must be a network line control discipline to control line usage. There are two basic approaches to line control: contention and polling.

Contention is simply a first-come, first-served system; that is, if a terminal makes a request to transmit data and if the line is not in use, the message proceeds. If the line is busy, the terminal must wait until it is free. The dial telephone system is an example of a contention system.

With **polling,** the central computer controls all transmissions to and from all terminals. The computer (or communications processor) polls each terminal in sequence to determine whether it has a message to send. Referring to Figure 8–16, the computer would poll terminal A, followed by B, then C (although any polling sequence is possible). This type of polling is sometimes referred to as "roll-call" polling. Most larger datacom systems using private lines use a polling approach, rather than contention.

Loop lines are another form of multidrop lines in which several terminals are connected in a loop (see Figure 8–17). The loop line is generally short, say less than 2000 feet. Loop lines are very effective when terminals are located close together. This approach is often used for transaction terminals such as point-of-sale terminals in retail stores and factory production control terminals.

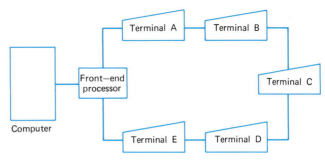

FIGURE 8-17
Loop line.

Multiplexing is the subdivision of a communications channel into two or more subchannels. With multiplexing, two or more terminals can transmit simultaneously over a multidrop line. Figure 8-18 shows a multidrop line with three video display terminals, the same configuration as was shown in Figure 8-16. However, in Figure 8-18 a **multiplexer** has been added at each end of the line. With this approach, terminals A, B, and C could communicate simultaneously with the computer.

There are two basic approaches to multiplexing. In the first approach, **frequency division** multiplexing, the channel is divided into narrow frequency bands. In the second (and newer) approach, **time division** multiplexing, the channel is assigned successively to the active users (for example, terminals A, B, and C).

Concentrators are essentially store-and-forward devices that are sometimes used instead of multiplexers. A concentrator receives messages from many different channels, stores the messages temporarily, and transmits them when the outbound line becomes available. Concentrators are generally minicomputers programmed to handle specialized datacom functions.

Packet switching is a datacom service that combines data processing and data communications. A packet switching vendor leases lines from a common carrier (such as AT&T) and "adds value" to these lines by adding minicomputers and other devices that permit packet switching. For this reason, packet switching is often referred to as a **value added network,** or VAN.

FIGURE 8-18
Multiplexing.

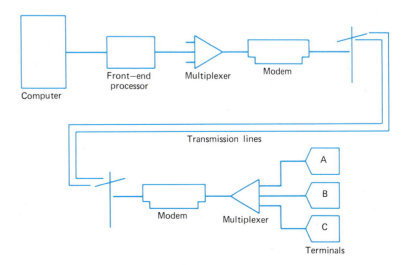

In packet switching, the user's long messages are subdivided into short blocks called **packets.** A typical packet size is 128 characters. The packets are then transmitted over the vendor's leased lines. Minicomputers are used as concentrators, to store and then forward packets and to resolve different protocols and line speeds.

A simple example of a packet-switched network is shown in Figure 8-19. The network has three minicomputers, X, Y, and Z. A user at terminal 1 wishes to transmit a 300-character message to the user at terminal 2. The message is divided into packets A and B (128 characters each) and packet C (44 characters).

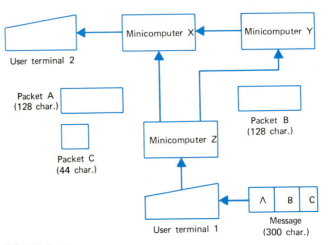

FIGURE 8-19
Example of packet switching.

QUESTION: Examine Figure 8-19. In this example, packets A and C are routed directly to

minicomputer_____ , while packet B is routed to X via minicomputer

_____

ANSWER: X, Y

The largest packet switching network vendor in the United States at this time is Telenet Communications Corporation, now a subsidiary of General Telephone. Other vendors are rapidly entering this expanding field. The main advantage of packet switching is that the user does not have to incur the expense of building his own network but leases all the required services from a single communications vendor.

DATACOM SOFTWARE   Thus far we have concentrated on the hardware elements of a datacom system. Software (or computer programs) also plays an important role in data communications. Software provides much of the human interface with the datacom system and defines how the various hardware components interact logically with each other.

Although there are many software elements, two of the most important are telecommunications access programs and network control programs.

Telecommunications access programs reside in the central computer (or host processor). These software packages form the link between user application programs and the telecommunication network. For example, when an airline reservation program in the computer requests information concerning number of passengers from a reservations clerk in a distant city, it uses the telecommunications access program to access the datacom network.

Each computer vendor furnishes its own telecommunications access programs. For example, IBM's most recent software for its 370 computers is known as Virtual Telecommunications Access Method, or VTAM.

Network control programs often reside in the front-end communications processor. These programs manage the actual functions of the communications network. Network control programs typically perform the following functions.

☐ Activation and deactivation of communication links.
☐ Queueing and routing of messages.
☐ Polling terminals.
☐ Error detection and correction.
☐ Maintaining statistics or network usage.

In the past, the development of data communications systems by different vendors proceeded in a haphazard fashion. There has been no standard terminology or master plan for developing communications software, terminal interfaces, protocols, and other important system elements. As a result, hardware or software developed by one vendor is often incompatible with that from another vendor. (Indeed, even a single vendor's products are often incompatible with each other!) The end result has been excessive operating costs, inefficient computer utilization, and postponement of the use of data communications.

Recognizing the problems resulting from lack of planning, many computer vendors have adopted master plans for developing communications-oriented products. These master plans are called **computer network architectures.**

Unfortunately, each vendor is developing its own network architecture, so that complete compatibility between vendors will not be achieved.[5] However, certain common design principles are being followed that insure at least partial compatibility.

1. Device independence, to enable different terminals to be connected to the same network.
2. To enable network functions to be moved from the host computer to other network components such as remote concentrators and intelligent terminals.
3. To make the network as transparent as possible to the end user (the user need not be a communications expert).
4. To use standard protocols throughout the network.

ERROR CONTROL Communications links (such as telephone lines) have error rates that are inherently higher than those for computers and other electronic devices. Therefore, in a datacom system it is important to use effective error detection and correction procedures; otherwise, system performance will be degraded.

SOURCES OF ERROR The principal sources of transmission error are noise, fading, and distortion.

Noise refers to random signals that interfere with the transmitted signal.

[5]For a comparison see Ralph A. Berglund, "Comparing Network Architecture," *Datamation*, Vol. 24, No. 2, February 1978.

There are two basic types of noise: **background noise** (such as one might experience in a telephone call) and impulse noise. **Impulse noise,** which is the primary source of errors in data communication, is caused by electrical storms or other disturbances that cause a burst of short-duration pulses.

Fading (temporary loss of signal) occurs primarily in microwave transmission and may be caused by atmospheric conditions, severe rainstorms, or even a bird flying between towers. **Distortion** is a form of interference within or between transmitted signals.

ERROR RATES   Two types of error rates are of concern in a data communications system—nominal rate and effective rate.

The **nominal error rate** is the rate inherent in the transmission link used. In common carrier voiceband (telephone) lines, for example, the nominal error rate at present is about 1 bit in error out of 10^5 bits transmitted. In the digital data network the rate is as low as one bit in every 10^7 bits transmitted. This rate depends on a number of factors, such as type of equipment, distance, transmission speed, and weather.

Most communications systems incorporate techniques for detecting and correcting errors. The **effective error rate** is the rate at which undetected errors occur in transmission.

QUESTION: Dialed lines tend to have higher _____ error rates than do private lines.
ANSWER: nominal

ERROR DETECTION   Errors in transmission are generally detected by some form of parity checking. A **parity check** determines whether the number of ones in a row of binary digits is odd (or even, if an even parity check is used).

As an example, recall that the ASCII code is an 8-bit code, with seven data bits and one parity bit. For example, the letter B is represented by the following data bits: 1000010. This character has two 1-bits, an even number. If odd parity checking is used, an additional 1-bit is added in the left-most position. Thus, B is represented as 11000010.

When the character is received, the parity is automatically checked. A transmission error that alters any given bit (the most common type of error) will result in a parity failure. More complex forms of parity checking (such as block parity) are also used.

CORRECTING ERRORS   When a transmission error is detected, a method for correcting the error is needed. At present, two techniques are commonly used.

1. Retransmission of the message. This is the method most frequently used today.
2. Automatic error correction. A sophisticated way to correct errors is to build enough redundancy into the code so that the receiving end not only can detect errors, but also can correct most errors that occur without retransmission.

Redundancy refers to parity bits and check characters that are added to the message, and such codes are called **error correcting codes.** Adding redundancy to the code reduces errors but also reduces transmission efficiency, since the redundant characters are not part of the message.

QUESTION: Two techniques of error correction are simple _____ of the message, and use of an _____ _____ code with redundant characters.

ANSWER: retransmission, error correcting

Human factors are an important factor in error control. Many errors that occur in data communications are caused by humans, rather than by equipment failure. Following are some of the measures that should be taken to reduce human error.

1. Provide adequate training for operators.
2. Use operator prompting and lead-through procedures, by which the operator is instructed at each step of the procedure.
3. Use computer-assisted instruction (CAI) to help train inexperienced personnel.
4. Provide adequate work areas.
5. Use edit programs to check the reasonableness of data before transmission.
6. Use graphics, color, and other techniques to reduce operator boredom.

EXAMPLES OF DATACOM USE

An example of a company with a distributed computing network, with widespread use of data communications, is Hewlett–Packard Company. Hewlett–Packard's communications network (illustrated in Figure 8–20) has some 110 nodes linking manufacturing plants and sales offices around the world to corporate headquarters in Palo Alto, California, and Geneva, Switzerland. The message volume in this network averages about 140 million characters per day for applications in manufacturing, marketing, and administration. Most lines used are switched (or dial-up) facilities, and communications line costs are nearly

FIGURE 8–20
Distributed computing network. (Courtesy Hewlett–Packard.)

● Manufacturing Facilities   ● Sales Offices

$50,000 per month. The network links together some 200 computers and over 2500 data terminals.

FUTURE DEVELOPMENTS

Research continues on improved techniques for data communications that will increase capacity and reduce costs. Two major areas of research and development are described below.

Lasers and **optical fibers** hold promise as major new transmission technologies. A laser is a very high frequency beam of light that is capable of transmitting perhaps 100,000 times as much information as today's microwave links. Optical fibers are very thin filaments of glass that provide transmission of data at the frequency of light (about 1000 times the frequency of radio waves). When coupled together, fiber optics and lasers will provide a very large communications bandwidth and will challenge satellites and other broadband media.

Advanced Communications Service (ACS) is a major new communication service proposed by AT&T. Essentially, ACS is an intelligent, switched data communications network service.[6] As proposed, it provides for the following features.

1. Sharing communications facilities, which will reduce costs and allow ACS users to share data with each other.

2. Interfacing terminals and computers having different protocols, character sets, and data rates.

3. Provision for a wide variety of communications options, from which the users can select options as needed.

4. Network management, including error detection and recovery and performance reporting.

If approved by the FCC, Advanced Communications Service will provide major new options for datacom users.

EXERCISE 8–3

1. What type of terminal would be used in data communications for each of the following applications?
   a. Slow-speed printer terminal for transmitting ASCII-coded data at 30 characters per second

   b. Terminal for use by clerks in savings and loan offices

   c. Terminal that displays either data or graphics on a screen

   d. Terminal for entry of large quantities of batched data and line printing at remote locations

   e. Terminal capable of doing stand-alone processing as well as communicating with a central computer.

---

[6]For a detailed description see Robert Rinder, "ACS Is Coming," *Datamation*, Vol. 24, No. 13, December 1978.

2. Summarize the characteristics of the datacom network shown in Figure 8-20.

   a. Number of nodes

   _____

   b. Number of computers

   _____

   c. Number of data terminals

   _____

   d. Transmission volume, characters per day

   _____

   e. Line costs, dollars per month

   _____

   _____

SUMMARY

The important characteristics of data communications (datacom) systems are described in this chapter. Such a system consists of computers, modems, multiplexers, concentrators, terminals, and transmission facilities. Also, software and network architectures are an important part of datacom systems.

Transmission facilities consist of telephone cables and microwave equipment. Both dialed and leased facilities are commonly used. A variety of network approaches, including packet switching, is available.

As you can see, a wide variety of choices is available for the prospective user of data communications. A properly designed data communications system reduces errors and delays, improves customer service, and, in some instances, permits the routine performance of services that would not otherwise be possible. Examples are the on-line reservation systems maintained by many airlines, hotel chains, and rental car agencies.

ANSWERS TO EXERCISES

EXERCISE 8-1

1. a. Inquiry/response
    b. Distributed processing
    c. Conversational time-sharing
    d. Remote job entry
    e. On-line data entry
2. a. Computer (host processor)
    b. Communications processor
    c. Modem
    d. Communications link
    e. Terminals

EXERCISE 8-2

1. a. Private
    b. Dialed
    c. Private
    d. Dialed

2.

Name of Service	Bandwidth	Dialed or Private
TWX and TELEX	Narrow	Dialed
DDD	Voice	Dialed
WATS	Voice	Dialed
50 Kilobit	Wide	Dialed
Series 3000	Voice	Private
TELPAK	Wide	Private
Series 8000	Wide	Private

EXERCISE 8-3

1. a. Teletypewriter terminal
    b. Transaction terminal
    c. Visual display terminal
    d. RJE station
    e. Intelligent terminal
2. a. 110
    b. 200
    c. 2500
    d. 140 million
    e. $50,000

CHAPTER EXAMINATION

1. Define each of the following abbreviations.

    a. Modem _____

    b. VTAM _____

    c. FCC _____

    d. WATS _____

    e. ACS _____

2. Match each of the following terms with the most appropriate definition.

    _____ Host processor   a. Random signals interfering with transmitted signal.

    _____ Modem   b. Private line.

    _____ Noise   c. Error detecting and correcting codes.

    _____ Effective error rate   d. Bandwidth greater than voiceband.

    _____ On-line   e. Many users share a central computer.

    _____ Distributed   f. Device for modulating and demodulating.

    _____ Narrowband   g. Master computer in a network.

    _____ Redundancy   h. Rate of undetected errors.

    _____ Leased   i. Processing capacity is decentralized.

    _____ Wideband   j. Transmitting by telegraph and teletypewriter.

    _____ Time-sharing   k. User has direct access to the computer.

3. Describe two common techniques of error correction.

    a. _____

    b. _____

4. Briefly describe five advantages of data communications systems.

   a. _____

   b. _____

   c. _____

   d. _____

   e. _____

5. Describe five types of data terminals, and give a typical application for each type.

   a. _____

   b. _____

   c. _____

   d. _____

   e. _____

6. What are the five basic hardware elements of a teleprocessing system?

   a. _____

   b. _____

   c. _____

   d. _____

   e. _____

7. Error correcting codes permit errors in messages to be corrected without retransmission. What is the disadvantage of using these codes?

   _____

   _____

   _____

   _____

8. Mark the following statements true or false.

   ____ a. Most data transmission is by narrowband service.

   ____ b. The principal advantage of an on-line system is that it provides near-instantaneous response to user inquiries.

_____ c.　Modems are required only when one is using leased lines.

_____ d.　WATS is a dialed service for which the user is charged a flat monthly rate.

_____ e.　The main sources of transmission error are noise, fading, and distortion.

_____ f.　Low message volumes tend to favor leased transmission service.

_____ g.　The most common method of correcting errors at present is to retransmit the message.

_____ h.　Data transmission by satellite is in the distant future.

_____ i.　With contention, the central computer controls all transmissions.

9.　What type of service (leased or dialed) would be used by each of the following?

　　a.　Small engineering firm doing occasional calculations using a terminal connected to a remote computer ___

　　_____

　　b.　Large multiplant firm transmitting sales orders to a central computer _____

10.　What is the difference between nominal and effective error rates?

　　_____

　　_____

11.　Explain briefly the difference between each of the following.

　　a.　Asynchronous versus synchronous _____

　　_____

　　_____

　　b.　Contention versus polling _____

　　_____

　　_____

　　_____

　　c.　Switched versus leased _____

　　_____

　　_____

　　_____

    d.   Multiplexers versus concentrators _____

_____

_____

_____

12.   Briefly describe three sources of error in data transmission.

    a. _____

    b. _____

    c. _____

13.   Describe briefly how packet switching works.

_____

_____

_____

14.   Write the ASCII code for each of the following characters.

    a.   H _____

    b.   7 _____

    c.   ACK _____

15.   Briefly describe three non-ASCII codes.

    a. _____

    b. _____

    c. _____

16.   Describe four modulation techniques.

    a. _____

_____

    b. _____

_____

    c. _____

_____

d. _____

_____

17. Give two examples of each of the following classes of service.

a. Narrowband _____

b. Voiceband _____

c. Wideband _____

18. What is the difference between a modem and an acoustic coupler?

_____

_____

19. List six functions of a front-end processor.

a. _____

b. _____

c. _____

d. _____

e. _____

f. _____

20. Fill in the blanks in the following statements.

a. _____ are predetermined signals used to control the flow of messages.

b. The term _____ is often used instead of bits per second, even though the terms are not synonymous.

c. _____ transmission is known as start–stop transmisssion.

d. _____ refers to the frequency range that can be accommodated by a transmission line.

e. _____ _____ is a datacom service sometimes referred to as a value added network.

f. The _____ code is an eight-bit code that is a national standard for transmission.

g. _____ is the process of converting digital pulses to carrier signals.

h. _____ lines have several terminals connected to a single line.

21.   List four features of Advanced Communications Service.

a.   _____

b.   _____

c.   _____

d.   _____

22.   Briefly describe each of the following.

a.   Fiber optics _____

_____

b.   Lasers _____

_____

23.   List five functions of network control programs.

a.   _____

b.   _____

c.   _____

d.   _____

e.   _____

24.   List four common principles of computer network architectures.

a.   _____

b.   _____

c.   _____

d.   _____

9 CONCEPTS OF DATA PROCESSING

OVERVIEW. In this chapter you will study the basic concepts and operations of data processing. These concepts follow from the nature of business operations and from the way data is stored, processed, and retrieved on computers. They have a major influence on the type of software systems that have evolved and will evolve in the future.

First, the various forms of data structures are described. Data structures represent the logical data organization—the way data are visualized by persons who use the computer. Important data structures are data items, data aggregates, records, files, arrays, and data bases. Next, the most important file organizations are discussed. File organizations are physical data organizations—the way data are physically stored in the computer. Important file organizations described in this chapter are sequential, direct, index sequential, and list organizations.

Following the description of logical and physical data organizations, we describe the basic data processing operations. These operations include capturing, classifying, sorting, calculating, and communicating. Data processing transforms data into information that is useful to the user.

DATA STRUCTURES

Data are facts concerning entities such as objects, people, places, and events. Data represent a convenient means for storing and communicating the essential attributes of such entities. For example, suppose that a manager wishes to find out how many metal tennis rackets of a particular size are in stock. It would be impractical to have to go to the warehouse each time such a need arises and count the number of units in stock. Instead, the manager refers to an inventory record that contains data for each item in stock (including the quantity currently on hand).

Data that has been organized or communicated in a form convenient for human decision making is often referred to as **information.** For example, a report containing a list of sporting good items to be ordered from a supplier would be useful information for a buyer.

To be useful, data must be organized in a logical and consistent manner. **Data structures** are techniques for logical data organization in a computer system.

DATA HIERARCHY

In a computer system, data is organized according to a hierarchy, as follows: characters, data items, data aggregates, records, files, and data bases. This hierarchy of data is illustrated in Figure 9-1 and described below.

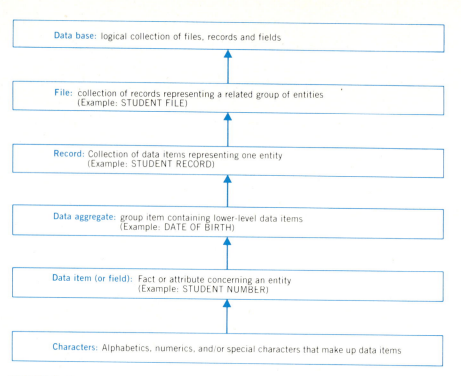

FIGURE 9-1
Hierarchy of data.

DATA ITEMS   The fundamental unit of data concerning any entity is called a **data item** (the term **field** is used interchangeably with data item). A data item is an indivisible unit of data that represents an **attribute** of some object or entity. For example, Quantity-on-hand is a data item that represents one attribute of an inventory item.

There are three essential properties of a data item: its **name,** its **value,** and its **representation.** For example, if Quantity-on-hand is a data item name, its value for a particular item might be 25. Representation specifies the maximum **length** and **type** of the data item. For example, the representation for Quantity-on-hand might be five numeric digits.

Table 9-1 shows typical data items for three entities: student, customer, and inventory item.

TABLE 9-1   EXAMPLES OF DATA ITEMS

Entity (Description)	Data Item Name	Data Item Value	Data Item Representation
Student	Student-Number	13579	5 numeric digits
	Student-Name	Ortega, Jose R.	25 alphabetics
	Address	1138 College Rd.	30 alphanumerics
	Major	Business	10 alphabetics
Customer	Customer-Name	Aardvark, John	30 alphabetics
	Balance-due	1000.00	8 digits, 2 decimal places
	Credit-limit	1200.00	8 digits, 2 decimal places
Inventory Item	Item-Number	16AX	6 alphanumerics
	Description	Tennis racquet	25 alphabetics
	Price	25.00	6 digits, 2 decimal places
	Quantity-on-hand	8	5 numeric digits

QUESTION: Examine Table 9–1. How many data items are shown for the entity Student?

_____ What is the name of the last data item for this entity?

_____ What is its current value? _____ What is its representa-

tion? _____

ANSWER: four, major, Business, 10 alphabetics. The representation of a data item (for example, 10 alphabetics) is important because it determines how the item will be stored in the computer. Chapter 4 describes how data are represented in the computer—you may wish to review that chapter at this time.

DATA AGGREGATES A data item or field may consist of two or more lower-level items. For example, the data item Date may be formed from three items: Month, Day, and Year. The structure is as follows:

Date

Year	Month	Day

When the item Date is specified, the entire date is obtained. When Year, Month, or Day is specified, only the specified portion is obtained. These three fields are referred to as **elementary items,** because they are not subdivided. The composite field (in this case Date) is referred to as a **data aggregate** or **group item.**

RECORDS The collection of data items used to describe an entity is called a **record.** A record may be visualized as a series of data items pertaining to the entity in question. For example, Figure 9–2 represents a student record using the four data items taken from Table 9–1.

Student-Number	Student-Name	Address	Major
13579	Ortega, Jose R.	1138 College Rd.	Business

FIGURE 9–2
Example of a student record.

QUESTION: Examine Figure 9–2. Name five other data items that would likely appear

in a real student record: _____ , _____ , _____ ,

_____ , _____ .

ANSWER: Typical data items would include telephone number, date of birth, class, grade point average, units taken, units remaining.

FILES There will ordinarily be one record for each entity of interest to the organization. For example, in a student information system there is one record for each student enrolled at the school. The collection of all records for a particular type of entity is called a **file** (for example, student file).

To be precise, the collection of all records of a particular type is called a **logical** file. This is in contrast to a **physical file,** which is a storage device or medium. A reel of magnetic tape and a magnetic disk module are examples of physical files. Depending on its size, a logical file may occupy only a portion of a physical file or may extend over several physical files. For example, in Figure 9-3a logical files A and B are both contained on one physical disk file. In Figure 9-3b, logical file C extends over three physical disk files.

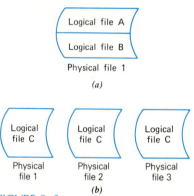

FIGURE 9-3

Comparison of logical and physical files. (a) One physical file containing two logical files. (b) One logical file extended over three physical files.

RECORD KEYS   Each record in a file is usually identified by a data item called an **identifier** or **key.** This data item is used for arranging the records in the file in sequence (if desired) and for locating records in the file. The key or identifier may be numeric (such as student number), or it may be alphabetic or alphanumeric (such as student name). Often two or more data items are used as keys for a record type.

QUESTION: Examine Table 9-1 again. What data items would likely be used as a key for each of the following record types?

Customer _____

Inventory Item _____

ANSWER: Customer – Name, Item – Number

TYPES OF FILES   A number of different types of files are used in data processing applications. The most important of these are described in Table 9-2.

QUESTION: The set of personnel records for the employees of an organization constitutes a

_____ file. Records of employee transfers or changes in the number of

dependents would appear in a _____ file. Data extracted from the personnel file to prepare a monthly personnel summary might appear in a

_____ file.

TABLE 9-2   TYPES OF DATA FILES

Type	Purpose	Examples
Master file	Set of relatively permanent records containing identifying, statistical, and historical information. Used as a source of reference for an application.	Inventory file, student file
Transaction file	Set of records resulting from transactions that affect the status of items in the master file. Used to update the master file.	Stock requisitions, registration file
History file	An obsolete master or transaction file, retained for historical use or backup.	Material receipts, grade transcripts
Report file	Set of records extracted from data in master files, used to prepare reports.	Inventory status file, enrollment report file

Thus far we have described four elements of logical data structures: data items, data aggregates, records, and files. These elements form a data hierarchy, as shown in Figure 9-1.

Until the 1970s, the top element in the data hierarchy was ordinarily the file. However, during that period the data base became the most common high-level data structure as shown in Figure 9-1. A data base is essentially a repository of data for an entire organization (a more precise definition is given in the next section).

EXERCISE 9-1   1. Using the data items in Table 9-1 for the entity Inventory Item, draw a representation of an Inventory record similar to Figure 9-2.

2. Suppose that a medical doctor wishes to create a patient file, with one record for each of her active patients. Can you identify five fields (or data items) that would appear in each record? In addition to naming the fields, give a sample value and data representation for each field.

	Data Item Name	Data Item Value	Data Item Representation
(a)	_____	_____	_____
(b)	_____	_____	_____
(c)	_____	_____	_____
(d)	_____	_____	_____
(e)	_____	_____	_____

3. Sketch an example of a data aggregate different from the Date example given in the text.

DATA BASES   A **data base** is a nonredundant collection of logically related files, organized in a manner to satisfy the information needs of an organization.

The best means of illustrating data bases and their advantages is to contrast the data base approach with the individual application approach (see Figure 9–4). In the conventional (pre-data base) application approach, separate files are used for each computer application. For example, in a bank the traditional approach is to separate banking operations into functional areas, such as demand deposit accounting (DDA), savings, and loans. As shown in Figure 9–4a, each functional area has its own file. In this example, J. Jones is a customer at the bank who has a checking account (DDA), savings account, and installment loan. Data concerning J. Jones is duplicated in the three files, and separate computer programs are used to update each file. For all practical purposes the bank's processing is handled as three distinct operations and Jones is handled as three different customers.

Although each separate application might be quite efficient in itself, there are several problems with the application approach.

1. Data are duplicated among the different files and applications (such as data concerning Jones). This duplication leads to a needless loss of valuable file space and to possible inconsistencies in the data. For example, if Jones moves to a new address, this change might be reflected in the checking and loan files but not in the savings file.

2. It is difficult to access or report data that are contained in more than one file, because the files are not interrelated. For example, if Jones

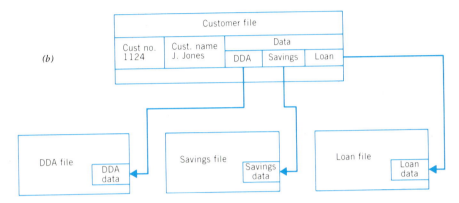

FIGURE 9-4

Comparison of application and data base approaches for banking operations. (*a*) Applications approach. (*b*) Systems approach. (Reprinted by permission from J. G. Burch, F. R. Strater, and G. Grudnitski, *Information Systems: Theory and Practice,* 2nd Edition, John Wiley & Sons, 1979.)

applied for a new loan, the loan officer would have to contact someone in Savings to determine Jones's current savings balance. Also, in the past, file updates were often not synchronized—for example, the DDA file might be updated daily, while the savings file would be updated twice a week. As a result, it would be difficult to prepare a single monthly statement for Jones showing all activity for his checking, savings, and loan accounts.

3. Data are not shared between applications. For example, when Jones moves to a new address, this change must be introduced separately in the three applications files.

4. Changes to the data structures (files) often require changing many computer programs. For example, suppose that the bank decides to include a new data item representing its customers' occupation code in each of the three files. This would likely require modifying all computer programs that manipulate the three files.

To overcome many of these disadvantages, organizations are using the data base approach. This approach for banking applications is illustrated in Figure 9-4b. A single customer file is established, with one record containing basic data for each customer such as Jones. Files are also created for each banking activity, in this case DDA, savings, and loans. In the approach shown in Figure 9-4b, each customer record contains a special field called a **pointer** that points to or associates the customer record with records in the activity files. For example, the customer record for Jones points to a record in each of three files: DDA, Savings, and Loans. The customer record thus becomes the "entry point" for processing all inquiries and transactions. Data is shared between applications, so for example it is a simple matter to transfer money between accounts (for example, from DDA to savings) or to prepare a single monthly statement.

EXERCISE 9-2 Refer to Figure 9-4, comparing the application and data base approaches. Describe how each of the following transactions would be performed with each of the two approaches.

Transaction	Application Approach	Data Base Approach
(a) Jones gets a new telephone number.		
(b) Loan officer wishes to look up Jones's average DDA balance.		
(c) Jones wishes to pay an installment on his loan from his savings account.		
(d) Jones's zip code changes from five to nine digits.		

DATA BASE DESIGN   In an actual bank or other organization the data base would be much more complex than the one illustrated in Figure 9-4. Design of data bases requires a systems approach with careful planning by various members of the organization.

There are three fundamental data base structures or models: hierarchical, network, and relational. These three models are illustrated in Figure 9-5 and described briefly below.

The **hierarchical** model is a "top-down" model. Each "parent" record at one level has one or more "offspring" records at a lower level (but each offspring has only one parent). In Figure 9-5a each Department record "points to" one or more Employee records and one or more Project records. Each Project record in turn is associated with one or more Equipment records. To process data base records, one normally enters at the highest-level parent record (in this case, Department) and progresses downward through the structure until a desired record is located. For example, to locate a particular Equipment record, one would locate a Department record, then locate a Project record for that department, and then locate an Equipment record associated with the project. This process would be repeated to locate other records.

In the **network** model, a number of records are logically related, and any one of the records can serve as an entry point. For example, Figure 9-5b shows a network structure linking Professor, Student, and Class records. Given this approach, one could locate all classes taught by a particular professor or all students taking a particular class.

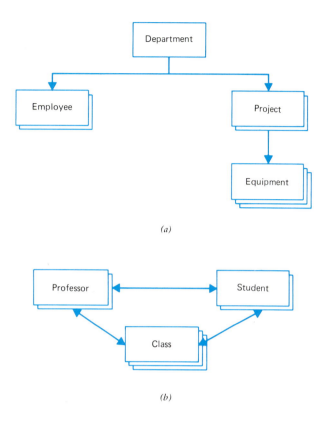

FIGURE 9-5
Three data base structures. (*a*) Hierarchical. (*b*) Network. (*c*) Relational.

In the **relational** model, all data are viewed as being stored in the form of tables. For example, Figure 9-5*c* shows one such table (or **relation**) representing student records. Other relations might represent professors, classes, and other entities. Powerful commands are used to combine data from various tables for inquiry and reporting purposes.

QUESTION: Three important data base structures are _____ (tables), _____

(top-down), and _____.

ANSWER: relational, hierarchical, network

DATA BASE ADMINISTRATION   Design of the data base is only one aspect of the data base approach. With this approach, data are viewed as a valuable resource, critical to the survival and growth of the organization. To manage the data base approach, a new function called the **data base administrator** function is often established. Some of the major functions of the data base administrator are to:

1. Coordinate data base design.

2. Load the data base.

3. Control access to the data base and insure privacy and security.

4. Establish backup and recovery procedures in the event of a failure or loss of data.

5. Control changes to the data base.

6. Select and maintain data base management software (described in Chapter 10).

7. Meet with users to resolve problems and determine changing requirements.

OTHER DATA STRUCTURES

Two special data structures that are often used in computer data processing are tables and arrays.

TABLES   The simplest table is a set of paired entries. The first entry in each pair is called the **argument,** whereas the second entry is referred to as the **function** of the argument. The table is searched until the desired argument is located; the value read out of the table is its function.

For example, consider a federal tax table (Table 9-3). Suppose an individual with four exemptions has an adjusted gross income over $11,400 but less than $11,450. From Table 9-3, the person's federal income tax is $602.

TABLE 9-3   PARTIAL FEDERAL TAX TABLE

If Form 1040, line 34, is —		And the total number of exemptions claimed on line 7 is —							
Over	But not over	2	3	4	5	6	7	8	9
		Your tax is —							
11,200	11,250	923	743	570	410	256	116	0	0
11,250	11,300	932	752	578	418	263	123	0	0
11,300	11,350	941	761	586	426	270	130	0	0
11,350	11,400	950	770	594	434	277	137	0	0
11,400	11,450	959	779	602	442	284	144	4	0
11,450	11,500	968	788	610	450	291	151	11	0
11,500	11,550	977	797	618	458	298	158	18	0
11,550	11,600	986	806	626	466	306	165	25	0
11,600	11,650	995	815	635	474	314	172	32	0
11,650	11,700	1,004	824	644	482	322	179	39	0
11,700	11,750	1,013	833	653	490	330	186	46	0
11,750	11,800	1,022	842	662	498	338	193	53	0
11,800	11,850	1,031	851	671	506	346	200	60	0
11,850	11,900	1,040	860	680	514	354	207	67	0
11,900	11,950	1,049	869	689	522	362	214	74	0
11,950	12,000	1,058	878	698	530	370	221	81	0
12,000	12,050	1,067	887	707	538	378	228	88	0
12,050	12,100	1,076	896	716	546	386	235	95	0
12,100	12,150	1,085	905	725	554	394	242	102	0
12,150	12,200	1,094	914	734	562	402	249	109	0
12,200	12,250	1,103	923	743	570	410	256	116	0
12,250	12,300	1,112	932	752	578	418	263	123	0
12,300	12,350	1,121	941	761	586	426	270	130	0
12,350	12,400	1,130	950	770	594	434	277	137	0

QUESTION: In the tax table, adjusted gross income is referred to as the _____ ; the

corresponding tax is called the _____ .

ANSWER: argument, function

An **index** (or directory) is a table that is used to locate items stored elsewhere. Indexes are often used in computer applications to locate records stored on magnetic disk or other direct access storage devices. For example, suppose that a company has personnel records for 200 employees stored on seven tracks of a magnetic disk. An internally stored table such as Table 9-4 could be used to locate records.

TABLE 9-4 INDEX TO LOCATE
PERSONNEL RECORDS

Track Number	Employee Number
1	1 to 30
2	31 to 60
3	61 to 90
4	91 to 120
5	121 to 150
6	151 to 180
7	181 to 200

QUESTION: If the record for employee 124 is desired, a search of the table would disclose

that the record was located on track _____ . In this case, the table

argument is _____ , while the function is _____ .

ANSWER: 5, employee number, track number

ARRAYS   A special form of a table is one in which the argument is simply the position of the data in the table. For example, Table 9-5 shows the gross sales for a sporting goods store during a particular week. Tables in which data are stored by position are called **arrays.** Thus an array is an ordered set of data for which the argument is one of the integers: 1, 2, 3, and so on.

TABLE 9-5   ARRAY: GROSS SALES
ORDERED BY DAY

Day	Gross Sales
1	$148.75
2	223.47
3	241.19
4	169.32
5	472.18
6	369.93

An important property of arrays is that it is not necessary to store the array argument in computer memory. Instead, the computer need store only the data itself, plus the location of the first data element. The location of any other element may then be determined by addition. For example, if sales for day 1 are stored at computer address 1001, then sales for day 4 are normally stored at address 1001 plus 3, or 1004.

In Table 9–5, gross sales appear as a single column of data. An array may also appear as a two-dimensional table, with both rows and columns. For example, the students in a particular course might be categorized by major and class, as in Table 9–6. In this array, class refers to freshman (1), sophomore (2), junior (3), and senior (4). Each entry in the table represents the number of students in the course who are in a particular class and major. For example, there are six students who are sophomores and in major 2.

TABLE 9–6　TWO-DIMENSIONAL ARRAY: NUMBER OF STUDENTS BY MAJOR AND CLASS

	Class			
Major	1	2	3	4
1	10	4	4	3
2	2	6	3	1
3	0	5	7	2

Three-dimensional (and higher) arrays are also sometimes used. For example, if the students in Table 9–6 were further classified as male or female, a three-dimensional array (for class, major, and sex) would result.

Subscripts are used to reference individual elements within an array. They are normally placed in parentheses after a name assigned to the array. For example, suppose that the student array has been given the name STUDENT. Then the element in the second row and third column is referenced as STUDENT (2,3). In Table 9–6, STUDENT (2,3) has the value 3.

EXERCISE 9–3

1. Sketch a hierarchical data base organization for the following: Each Buyer record points to several Purchase-order records and to several Supplier records. Each Purchase-order record points to several Invoice records.

2. Sketch a network diagram relating the following three record types: Buyer, Supplier, Purchase-order.

3. Sketch a two-dimensional array showing sales by day of week and by class of merchandise (there are three classes of merchandise). Enter sample data in the array.

FILE ORGANIZATIONS

The data structures you have studied thus far are logical structures—the way data appear to the user. In this section you will study how data are organized in physical files such as magnetic disk. As with manual files, there are several methods for organizing computer-based data files. The choice of method depends on the objectives of the system designer. This choice involves important trade-offs in terms of cost, processing speed, and accessibility of information. The basic objectives of a file organization are:

1. To facilitate file creation and maintenance.
2. To provide an efficient means for storing and retrieving records in the file.

To achieve these objectives, the system designer should use to advantage the characteristics of the data, the equipment (including storage), and available software systems.

The basic methods of file organization are sequential and direct; these methods were introduced in Chapter 5 and are described in more detail below. Index sequential organization and list structures are also described, since they are important to data base design.

SEQUENTIAL ORGANIZATION

In a sequential data organization, data records are placed in a file in sequence according to a particular key, called a **sort** key. For example, Figure 9-6 shows a portion of a sequential student file. In Figure 9-6a, the file is in ascending sequence according to Student Name, which is the sort key. In Figure 9-6b, the same file is in ascending sequence according to Student Number.

Student Name	Student Number	GPA
Adams	2048	2.49
Barker	1629	3.73
Crain	1073	2.05
Gribble	3167	3.89
Lawson	2086	2.76

(a)   Sort Key

Student Name	Student Number	GPA
Crain	1073	2.05
Barker	1629	3.73
Adams	2048	2.49
Lawson	2086	2.76
Gribble	3167	3.89

(b)   Sort Key

FIGURE 9-6
Sequential file organizations.

QUESTION: Examine Figure 9-6a. To locate and retrieve the record for Gribble, it is first necessary to examine how many other student records? _____

ANSWER: three

PROCESSING SEQUENTIAL FILES   The logic of processing and updating a sequential master file is shown in Figure 9-7. First, transactions that are to be used for updating are accumulated into batches and sorted into the same sequence as the master file. For example, semester grade records would be sorted into student number sequence before updating the student master file, which is also sequenced by student number.

As each transaction record is read, the master file is searched to locate the matching master file record. If a match is found, the record is updated. Master file records that have no activity (that is, no matching transaction) are merely copied from the old master to the updated master. The entire master file must

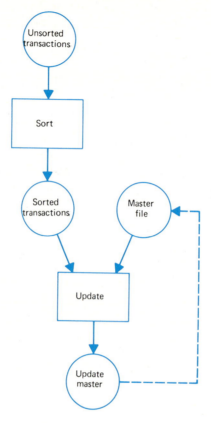

FIGURE 9–7
Sequential file updating.

be passed through the computer, even if there are only a few transactions to be processed.

QUESTION: A master file contains 1000 records. During an update run there are 80 transaction records to be processed against the file (the activity rate is 80/1000 or 8 percent).

a. How many master records are updated in this run? _____
b. How many master records are simply copied from the old master and

written on the updated master file? _____

ANSWER: a. 80
b. 920

Processing is complete when both the transaction and the master files have been read. At this time an updated master file has been created, which is then used for the next processing run. The old master file is kept intact for backup purposes.

PROCESSING INQUIRIES   It is impractical to use sequential file organizations in on-line systems, where it is necessary to determine (or update) the status of a particular record. For example, in an airline reservation system an agent at a remote terminal must frequently determine the available seating capacity for a particular flight. The agent must also post transactions such as reservations or cancellations. In a sequential file it would be necessary to search the entire file to locate a specific record. A direct access organization is required for such applications.

EVALUATION OF SEQUENTIAL FILE DESIGN   The advantages and disadvantages of sequential file organization are summarized below.

ADVANTAGES
- ☐ Low-cost file media (magnetic tape) can be used.
- ☐ Very efficient processing occurs when transactions can be batched and activity rate is relatively high.

DISADVANTAGES
- ☐ Transactions must be sorted before processing.
- ☐ Entire file must be processed, no matter how low the activity rate.
- ☐ On-line inquiries or on-line updating of records cannot be handled.

DIRECT ORGANIZATION

Unlike the case with sequential organization, with a **direct** organization–records are stored without regard to sequence. Each record is stored at a particular address on a direct access storage device (DASD) such as magnetic disk. Any record can be retrieved with a single access, without having to process other records. Sequential media such as magnetic tape cannot be used for a direct organization.

ADDRESSING RECORDS   To store a record on a direct file and subsequently retrieve it, we must assign or generate an address for that record. Two basic techniques are commonly used to address records in a direct organization.

1. Directory or index—a list of available (unused) locations on the disk file is maintained. When a new record is to be stored, it is stored at the next available location. The record key and the location where the record was stored are then placed in an index or directory for subsequent retrieval.
2. Key transformation—an algorithm (or mathematical operation) is applied to the key to transform it to a file address.

A common method of key transformation is to divide the record key by a prime number corresponding to the number of storage locations to be used. The remainder is then used as the address for the record. To illustrate, suppose there are seven records, with the following keys: 4, 13, 21, 38, 42, 55, 63. The records are to be stored in 11 locations, numbered 0 to 10.

The first record, with a key of 4, is divided by 11.

$$11\overline{)4} \\ \underline{0} \\ 4$$

Since the remainder is 4, the record is stored in location 4. Dividing the next record number (13) by 11 results in a remainder of 2, so record 13 is stored at address 2. Proceeding in this manner, we store the records as shown in Figure 9–8.

0	55
1	
2	13
3	
4	4
5	38
6	
7	
8	63
9	42
10	21

Records To Be Stored: 4, 13, 21, 38, 42, 55, 63

Number of Addresses: 11

FIGURE 9–8
Locating records using key transformation.

QUESTION: Suppose that we want to store the record whose key is 81 in the file shown in Figure 9–8. Using the above procedure, we find that the record should be

stored at address _____

ANSWER: 4, the remainder when 81 is divided by 11.

This example illustrates a problem that arises in using key transformation. Although record 81 should be stored at address 4, Figure 9–8 shows that record 4 is already stored at that address. Record keys that generate the same storage addresses are referred to as **synonyms.** One method of handling synonyms is to locate a record in the next available storage location.

QUESTION: In Figure 9–8, record 81 would be stored at address _____

ANSWER: 6, the next available address after 4.

The occurrence of synonyms creates problems when records must be retrieved. In the above example, when record 81 is to be retrieved, the computer first goes to address 4. Not finding the desired record, it must then search following records until record 81 is found — in this case, at address 6. Problems of synonyms can be kept at a minimum by using these measures.

1. Keep the file sparsely populated. As a rule of thumb, when a direct file is 50 percent full, 20 percent of the records to be retrieved will result in synonyms.
2. Use programming techniques such as chaining.

Chaining is the use of a pointer in a record to indicate the address of the next record. To illustrate, in Figure 9–9 record 81 is stored at address 6, the first available location after address 4. Address 4 contains a pointer that indicates the location of this record, so that the computer need not search intervening records to retrieve record 81.

	Record	Pointer
0	55	
1		
2	13	
3		
4	4	6
5	38	
6	81	
7		
8	63	
9	42	
10	21	

Address 4 Contains Record 4,
Plus a Pointer That "Points" to
the Location of Record 81, a Synonym.

FIGURE 9–9
Chaining is used to facilitate locating records whose keys are synonyms.

QUESTION: Suppose we want to store record 49 in the file. What changes are needed in

Figure 9–9? _____

ANSWER: The record is placed at address 7, the first available location. A pointer is placed at address 5 (the computed address), pointing to address 7.

ON-LINE PROCESSING   Direct organization permits on-line processing of transactions, referred to as **transaction processing.** With this approach, it is not necessary to accumulate transactions into batches and sort them before processing the master file. Instead, each transaction is input from a terminal as it happens, and the data base is updated immediately. Also, terminals can be used for inquiry to the data base, with immediate response. A direct (or transaction) processing system is illustrated in Figure 9–10.

FIGURE 9–10
On-line processing.

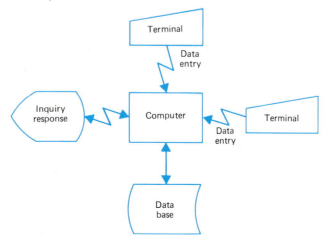

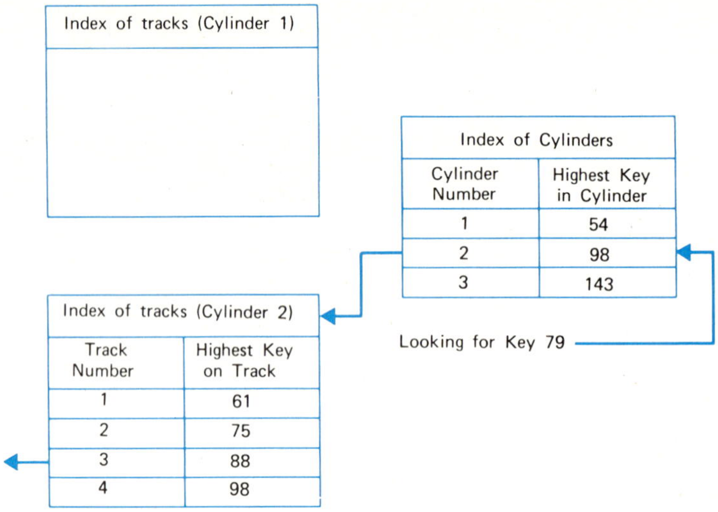

FIGURE 9-11
Searching for a record with index sequential organization.

EVALUATION OF DIRECT ORGANIZATION   The advantages and disadvantages of direct organization are summarized below.

ADVANTAGES
☐ Transactions need not be sorted.
☐ On-line inquiries and updating are easily handled.
☐ Several files can be processed or updated concurrently.

DISADVANTAGES
☐ Direct access storage devices are required.
☐ Processing is slower, less efficient than batch sequential processing for high activity rates.
☐ Special precautions are needed to safeguard direct access files.

INDEX SEQUENTIAL ORGANIZATION

In some situations it is desirable to combine the abilities of sequential and direct organizations. For example, in a payroll application the files are normally organized sequentially for the periodic payroll runs. However, sometimes the users desire to retrieve individual records from the master file, a process much more easily accomplished with a direct file.

With the index sequential technique, records are arranged sequentially on a direct access storage device. For direct access operation, tables are built into the file that permit looking up the address of an individual record. Often the tables are in hierarchical form to permit rapid location of the track containing the desired record.

An example of search under index sequential is shown in Figure 9-11. In the example, the search is for the record with key number 79. The computer first examines a table containing a master index of cylinders. The search is for the first cylinder whose highest key is greater than the desired record key. In this case, record number 79 is located on cylinder 2.

The search is then directed to an index of tracks for cylinder 2. Again the search is for the first track number with a number greater than the key. In the example, the record is located on track 3. Finally, the computer searches track 3 for the desired record. If the record is not found on this track, a pointer or reference indicates its exact location.

QUESTION: Suppose in Figure 9-11 that we want to locate record number 59. On what cylinder and track should it be located? _____

ANSWER: cylinder 2, track 1

The advantage of index sequential is that it combines the advantages of both direct and sequential organizations. The disadvantage is that extra search steps are needed to locate individual records, as compared to simple direct organization. Also, index tables require additional storage capacity and must be maintained as the file is changed.

OTHER FILE STRUCTURING METHODS

The file organizations described thus far — sequential, direct, and index sequential — are the ones most commonly used for data processing. However, with the advent of data bases, additional techniques are required to provide the linkages or associations between records. Two approaches are most often used to implement data base organizations: lists and inverted files.

LIST ORGANIZATION   A **list** is a group of logically related records, connected by means of pointers or links. A **pointer** is a field in a record that gives the address of the next record that is logically related to the first. A list may be visualized as follows.

To illustrate how a simple list structure can be used to form a data base, suppose that a company maintains a **customer file** on magnetic disk using a direct organization. Each customer record contains the customer number (which is the key or identifier), customer name and address, credit information, and other related data.

At any given time, there may be one or more outstanding invoices for a given customer. A record of each invoice is maintained on a second disk file, called the **invoice file.** A direct organization is also used for the invoice file. When an order is billed to the customer, a new invoice is added to this file; when the customer pays an invoice amount, the invoice is deleted from the file.

It is necessary for the system to be structured so that the company can determine at any time the outstanding invoices for a particular customer. To do this, a list organization as shown in Figure 9-12 would be used. Each customer record contains a pointer (or address) that "points to" the location of the first invoice for that customer in the invoice file. If there is no invoice for a customer, a special symbol is contained in the pointer field. The first invoice in turn contains a pointer that "points to" the location of the second invoice for that customer, and so on. Again, the last invoice for the customer contains a special symbol in the pointer field.

Address	Customer No.	Customer Information	Pointer	
100	1	Name, address, etc.	*	Special Symbol
101	2	,,	252	
102	3	,,		
103	4	,,		

CUSTOMER FILE

Address	Invoice No.	Invoice Information	Pointer
250	100		
251			
252	103		255
253	127		
254	116		
255	109		*
256	114		

INVOICE FILE

FIGURE 9-12
List organization.

QUESTION: Examine Figure 9-12 and answer the following questions.
a.   What invoice numbers are now outstanding for:

customer 1? _____

customer 2? _____

b.   Suppose a new invoice (number 130) is added to the invoice file for customer 2, at address 251. What will the pointer be for:

invoice 109? _____

invoice 130? _____

c.   Instead of (b), suppose that customer 2 pays the amount for invoice number 103. List two changes that will occur in Figure 9-12.

(1) _____

(2) _____

ANSWER: a.   none; 103, 109
b.   251; * (special symbol)
c.   (1)   Invoice number 103 is deleted from the invoice file.
     (2)   The pointer for customer 2 is changed to 255.

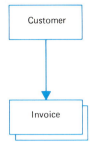

FIGURE 9-13
Customer-Invoice data base
structure.

Notice that the list structure shown in Figure 9-12 really represents a hierarchical data base structure (see Figure 9-5a). The basic structure for this data base is shown in Figure 9-13. Thus, as you can see a list organization is a physical means of implementing a data base structure.

An important type of list organization is referred to as a ring. A **ring** is a list (or chain) in which the last record "points back" to the first. This may be illustrated as follows.

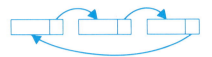

The advantage of this type of organization is that all records in the ring can be easily located, regardless of the starting point.

QUESTION: Refer to Figure 9-12 again. If the pointer for invoice 109 is changed to the

number _____, a ring will be formed.

ANSWER: 101

INVERTED FILES   Direct and index sequential organizations permit rapid retrieval of individual records, provided the record key is known. However, when using data bases we often desire to search a file for records having a particular attribute. For example, we may want to retrieve records for all employees having a particular skill, or for all students in a given major. Unless special provisions are made, it would be necessary to search the entire file to locate records with the desired fields.

Inverted file techniques facilitate searching a file on one or more fields. To illustrate, Table 9-7 shows a portion of a student record file. Each record contains the student number (key), class (1 = freshman, etc.), major (codes 1 to 4), and grade point average (GPA). It is assumed that the organization is direct, so that any record can be retrieved, given the student number.

Suppose we want to retrieve the record for each student who is a junior (class = 3). Ordinarily it would be necessary to read the entire file (in this in-

TABLE 9-7   PORTION OF STUDENT FILE

Student Number	Class	Major	GPA
105	2	2	2.87
113	1	4	3.42
129	4	3	1.93
134	3	1	2.33
147	4	4	3.63
163	2	3	2.69
171	1	2	3.08
182	3	1	2.74
190	2	2	3.16
198	3	4	2.44

stance, 10 records) to locate the desired records. However, in Table 9–8, the file has been inverted on two fields: class and major. A search of the **inverted file table** for class tells the computer it need only retrieve records with numbers 134, 182, and 198.

TABLE 9–8   INVERTED FILE TABLES FOR STUDENT FILE

Inversion by class				Inversion by major			
Class	Key	Key	Key	Major	Key	Key	Key
1	113	171		1	134	182	
2	105	163	190	2	105	171	190
3	134	182	198	3	129	163	
4	129	147		4	113	147	198

QUESTION: Suppose we want to retrieve the records for sophomores (class = 2) who are in major 2. From Table 9–8, what records should be retrieved? _____

ANSWER: Records number 105 and 190, which appear as keys for both class = 2 and major = 2.

In Table 9–8, the student file was inverted on two of the three data fields. It would also be possible to invert the file on grade point average, using a range of GPA values for each entry in the inverted file table. A file that is inverted on each field of its records is said to be **fully inverted.**

Inverted files greatly facilitate searching a particular file on multiple fields. They are also used to form logical relationships between different records in data bases.

EXERCISE 9–4

1. A file in which it is possible to access a particular record with a single access is called a _____ file.

2. Sorting transactions before file updating is characteristic of _____ file updating.

3. _____ _____ is a file organization that combines the features of sequential and direct organizations.

4. Processing transactions as they happen is referred to as _____ processing.

5. Locating records by operating on the key mathematically is referred to as

    _____

6. Refer to Figure 9–8. Where would record 23 be located? _____

7. Refer to Figure 9–11. On what cylinder should record 109 be located?

    _____

8.   Refer to Table 9-8. What record keys pertain to either seniors and/or

major 3? _____

DATA PROCESSING OPERATIONS

The previous discussion described the logical data structures and file designs that are used in data processing. This section describes the data processing operations that are used to capture data, store it in the data base, retrieve and manipulate the data, and report or communicate the data to human beings. Data processing converts raw data into useful information.

To illustrate the data processing operations we will use the example of a blood bank that uses a computer information system. The computer is used to maintain a donor file, with one record for each active blood donor. The format of this record is shown in Figure 9-14.

Donor Name	Address	Telephone	Date Last Donation	Blood Type	Other Data

FIGURE 9-14
Blood donor record.

The donor file is a direct access file maintained on magnetic disk. When a donor arrives at the blood bank for the first time, a new donor record is created in the file. On subsequent visits, the donor record is checked for accuracy and updated when changes occur (for example, new telephone number). After a donor has been inactive for a period of time, his record is eventually removed from the file.

The donor file is used to contact donors when a certain type of blood is needed. Also, the file is used to maintain statistics concerning the donor base.

DATA CAPTURE

Data capture refers to the recording of data from some event or transaction, either in human-readable or machine-readable form. The blood bank captures donor data by having each new donor fill out a donor information card. The donor enters his or her name, address, telephone number, and brief medical history on this card.

DATA ENTRY

Data entry consists of converting data to machine-readable form and reading it into the computer. In the blood bank, a new donor record is keyed into an on-line terminal in a "fill-in-the-blanks" operation, by an operator who reads the data from the donor information card (see Figure 9-15). The donor information card is then filed for historical and legal purposes.

The various devices used for input of data are described in Chapter 6.

DATA EDITING/VERIFICATION

Data editing/verification refers to various checks that are performed by people, terminals, and/or the computer to insure the completeness and accuracy of data. In the blood bank operation, when a person donates a unit of blood, a numbered tag is attached to the blood unit container. A sample of the blood is tested, the blood type is determined, and another tag indicating the blood type is then attached to the container. A technician at a terminal then accesses the donor record and visually matches the donor blood type with the type indicated on the container, to verify that the unit has been correctly labeled.

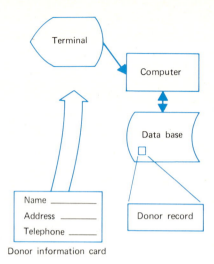

FIGURE 9–15
Entry of donor data.

STORING   In the storing operation, data contained in computer main memory is placed onto some storage device or medium such as magnetic disk, magnetic tape, or microfilm. Various devices used for storing data are described in Chapter 5.

In the blood bank, the donor master file is stored on magnetic disk using a direct organization. An index is used to record the location of each donor record in the file.

SORTING   Sorting places data items or records into a predetermined sequence. In the blood bank, each month a report is prepared providing a list of all donors whose last donation exceeds 90 days and who therefore are eligible to donate again. This report is prepared in alphabetical sequence by donor last name. These donors are then called or sent a reminder, inviting them to donate another unit.

CLASSIFYING   Classifying places data elements into categories to facilitate understanding by the user. For example, Table 9–9 gives a list of donors showing last name and blood type. In the left-hand side of the table the names are in alphabetical order. In the right-hand side the names have been classified by blood type.

TABLE 9–9   CLASSIFYING DATA

Unclassified		Classified	
Name	Blood Type	Blood Type	Name
Baker	A	A	Baker
Chavez	O		Olson
Evans	O	B	Jones
Jones	B	O	Chavez
Martinez	O		Evans
Olson	A		Martinez
Phillips	O		Phillips
Williams	O		Williams

SUMMARIZING The summarizing operation combines detail data items into aggregates or totals. For example, on a balance sheet the category "depreciation" is generally the sum or aggregate of a large number of individual depreciation accounts.

In the blood bank operation, a monthly summary is prepared that shows the number of donors by blood type, classified as new donors and previous donors (see Table 9–10).

TABLE 9–10   MONTHLY SUMMARY OF BLOOD DONORS (SEPTEMBER 198X)

Blood Type	Number of Donors		
	New	Previous	Total
O	38	112	150
A	20	40	60
B	24	30	54
AB	12	18	30
TOTAL	94	200	294

COMPUTING Computing entails the arithmetic and/or logical manipulation of data by the computer. Arithmetic operations include addition, subtraction, multiplication, division, and exponentiation. Logical operations include comparing the magnitudes of two numbers and branching (taking a different path) according to whether the first number is less than, equal to, or greater than the second.

Computing is involved in nearly all data processing operations. For example, a student grade point average is computed by dividing "quality points" earned by credit hours taken. In computing net pay for an employee, in addition to arithmetic operations, one must make a comparison between to-date FICA (social security) withholdings and the FICA maximum, to determine whether additional wages must be withheld for this purpose.

Computing is used throughout blood bank applications. For example, to determine whether a donor is eligible to donate again, it is necessary to subtract the date of the last donation from the current date to determine whether 90 days has elapsed. This procedure, which involves both an arithmetic and a logical operation, may be pictured as follows.

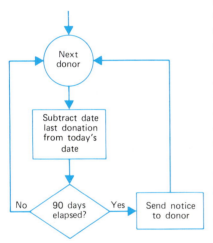

QUESTION: What computing operations are included in the above blood bank example?

Arithmetic _____

Logical _____

ANSWER: Subtraction, comparison (days elapsed with 90)

RETRIEVING Retrieving, the opposite of storing, entails locating a record on a storage medium, accessing the record, and moving it to computer main memory. Methods of accessing various storage media are described in Chapter 5.

In the blood bank, recall that each donor who has made at least one visit to the center has a donor record in the data base (the record format is shown in Figure 9–14). On repeat visits, the donor's record is simply retrieved from the data base and displayed on a terminal. This retrieving operation is shown in Figure 9–16. First, using the donor's last name, the computer searches an index that gives the storage location of each donor record. Having determined the record location, the computer accesses the record on disk file, reads it into main memory, and displays the record for a registration clerk. The clerk enters any information concerning the donor that has changed since the last visit and updates the "Date Last Donation" field. This on-line registration procedure greatly speeds up the registration process compared to previous manual procedures.

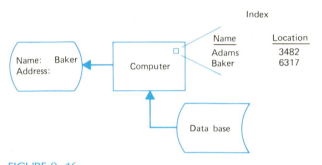

FIGURE 9–16
Retrieving a donor record.

REPRODUCING   Reproducing copies data stored on one physical file or medium onto another medium. For example, in the blood bank operation, at the end of each day the donor file is copied from the magnetic disk module and duplicated on a second magnetic disk module. The second module is stored in a safe place and is used for backup purposes in the event data is lost or destroyed in the primary file.

DISSEMINATING/   The disseminating/communicating operation transfers data from one device to
COMMUNICATING   a second device or from a device to persons who use the data. Data are disseminated to users by presenting them in the form of printed reports, screen displays, graphics, and even recorded voice. Systems for communicating data between computing devices are described in Chapter 8.

In the blood bank, data are disseminated to users in a variety of forms. Table 9–10 illustrates a typical printed report, while Figure 9–16 shows the presentation of a donor record on a video display terminal.

SUMMARY   In this chapter you have studied the basic building blocks of data processing. Data are facts concerning entities such as objects, people, places, and things. The basic unit of data is called a data item, which describes some attribute (such as name) of an entity. You have seen how data items are built up into records, files, and data bases. A data base consists of files logically connected in a manner that will satisfy the information needs of an entire organization. The advantage of the data base approach is that it reduces data duplication, facilitates access to data and sharing of data among applications, and helps introduce **data independence** – that is, data may be changed without affecting computer programs that manipulate the data.

The basic data processing operations that manipulate data and convert it into information have also been described. These operations include data capture and entry, editing, storing, retrieving, classifying, summarizing, and computing. The various types of computer programs (or software) that perform these operations are the subject of Chapter 10.

ANSWERS TO EXERCISES

EXERCISE 9-1

1.

Item-Number	Description	Price	On-hand
16AX	Tennis racquet	$25.00	8

2.

Data Item name	Data Item value	Data Item representation
(a) Patient Name	Jefferson, Thomas	25 alphabetics
(b) Address	803 Madison No. 3	25 alphanumerics
(c) Telephone	496-4628	8 alphanumerics
(d) Date last visit	July 17, 1980	20 alphanumerics
(e) Blood type	O Pos.	10 alphabetics

3. Following is an example data aggregate.

Course description

Course Number	Course Name	Units

EXERCISE 9-2

	Transaction	Application Approach	Data Base Approach
(a)	Jones gets a new telephone number.	Change phone number in three separate records and files.	Change phone number one time (in customer record).
(b)	Loan officer wishes to look up Jones's average DDA balance.	Call up DDA department — ask them to look up balance in DDA file.	Access customer file; look up DDA balance directly.
(c)	Jones wishes to pay an installment on his loan from his savings account.	Two separate file accesses — debit savings, credit installment loan.	One file access (to customer file); pointers used to reference savings, loan.
(d)	Jones's zip code changes from five to nine digits.	Change zip code field in three separate files (very likely requires change in all application programs that reference these files).	Change zip code once, in Jones's customer record (depending on data base system, may not require changes in application programs).

EXERCISE 9–3

1.

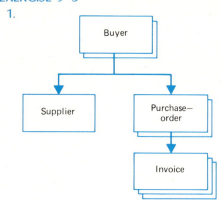

2.

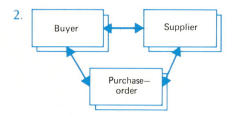

3.

Class Day	1	2	3
1	10	3	8
2	6	2	0
3	14	6	2
4	9	3	8
5	11	5	7
6	14	0	4

EXERCISE 9–4

1. direct
2. sequential
3. index sequential
4. on-line
5. key transformation
6. location 1
7. cylinder 3
8. 129, 147, 163

CHAPTER EXAMINATION

1. Define the following terms.

   a. File _____

   _____

   b. Record _____

   _____

   c. Data item _____

   _____

   d. Data base _____

   _____

   e. Key _____

   _____

2. What is the difference between a physical file and a logical file? _____

   _____

   _____

3. Give an example (not mentioned in the text) of each of the following data structures.

   a. File _____

   b. Table _____

   c. Array _____

   d. Record _____

   e. Data base _____

4. Define and give an example of each of the following.

   a. Sequential file _____

   _____

   _____

   b. Direct file _____

   _____

   _____

5. Explain the logic of sequential file updating. Why is the transaction file sorted before the update run? _____

   _____

   _____

   _____

   _____

   _____

6. For each of the following situations, state whether sequential processing or on-line processing is more appropriate. Give reasons.
   a. A customer accounts receivable file must be updated weekly, with exception reports prepared each run.

   _____

   _____

   b. A rental car agency has a central data processing system for car reservations that processes inquiries from many remote locations throughout the country.

   _____

   _____

   c. A student record file is updated three times each semester — after registration, at mid-semester, and after

   final grades. Additional inquiries must be made of student records on other occasions. _____

   _____

   d. A data processing system is used for job control in a large manufacturing facility. Job status must be updated frequently, and management desires up-to-the-minute information on the status of each job in

   the shop. _____

   _____

7. Mark the following statements true or false.

   ____ a. A common data structure is a vertical structure consisting of files, records, and fields.

_____ b. A history file is a set of records used to update a master file.

_____ c. A table consists of a set of paired entries called the argument and its function.

_____ d. An array used to store sales amount by salesman, product, and territory would be a two-dimensional array.

_____ e. In a list, logical records are connected by means of identifiers.

_____ f. The advantage of a sequential file is that it is possible to locate a specific record without examining previous records.

_____ g. On-line processing is possible with direct access files.

_____ h. Index sequential combines the advantages of sequential and direct access file organizations.

_____ i. Three types of data base structures are hierarchical, network, and index sequential.

8. List three advantages of on-line processing over sequential processing.

a. _____

b. _____

c. _____

9. Explain how an index sequential file is used for the following.

a. Sequential processing _____

_____

b. On-line processing _____

_____

10. Give an example of each of the following.

a. Summarizing _____

b. Computing _____

c. Sorting _____

d. Classifying _____

e. Retrieving _____

11. Following is a list organization for customer orders.

Address	Customer Number	Customer Information	Pointer
200	1	(Name, address, etc.)	375
201	2	(Name, address, etc.)	*
202	3	(Name, address, etc.)	*
203	4	(Name, address, etc.)	377

Address	Order Number	Pointer
375	1093	379
376	1140	*
377	1062	380
378		
379	1128	376
380	1157	*

a. What orders are now outstanding for:

customer 1? _____

customer 2? _____

customer 4? _____

b. Suppose a new order (number 1174) is added to the order file for customer 4, at address 378. What will the pointer be for:

the record at address 380? _____

the record at address 378? _____

12. Briefly describe each of the following.

a. Master file _____

_____

b. Transaction file _____

_____

c. History file _____

_____

d. Report file _____

_____

13. Sketch a network data structure showing the relationships among the following record types: Donor, Hospital, Blood-unit.

14. Sketch a hierarchical data structure for the following record types: Hospital, Department, Nurses, Patients (Nurses and Patients are both "offspring" of Department).

15. List four disadvantages of the application approach, compared to the data base approach.

   a. _____

   _____

   b. _____

   _____

   c. _____

   _____

   d. _____

   _____

16. What are three essential properties of a data item?

   a. _____

   b. _____

   c. _____

17. What is a data aggregate? Give an example. _____

   _____

   _____

18. Match each of the following terms to the most appropriate definition.

   ____ Dimension   a. Organization that permits both sequential and direct access

   ____ Pointer   b. Arranging a file into a desired sequence

   ____ Data base   c. Forming aggregates or totals

   ____ Sequential   d. Record identifier

   ____ Index sequential e. Table indexed by position

   ____ Summarizing   f. Address of a logically related record

   ____ Sorting   g. Integrated set of files for an organization

   ____ List   h. Set of paired data

   ____ Key   i. Number of subscripts in an array

   ____ Table   j. Organization with records in ascending order

   ____ Array   k. Organization using pointers to related records

19. Explain why a computerized hotel reservation system would use direct rather than sequential file organization.

_____

_____

20. What is the difference between data and information? _____

_____

_____

21. Give synonyms for each of the following terms.

   a. Key _____

   b. Data item _____

   c. Data aggregate _____

   d. Index _____

22. List six major functions of the data base administrator.

   a. _____

   b. _____

   c. _____

   d. _____

   e. _____

   f. _____

23. Identify two basic techniques commonly used to address records in a direct organization.

   a. _____

   b. _____

24. Define the following terms.

   a. Chaining _____

   b. Synonym _____

   c. Ring _____

25. What is an inverted file? How is it used? _____

_____

_____

_____

PART THREE

COMPUTER SOFTWARE

A computing system consists of hardware and software. Where hardware was the focus of Section Two, this section concentrates on software. Software is the invisible ingredient in a computing system. Although you can see the hardware, the software is not visible to the human eye because it is represented internally by bits and bytes.

An amusing definition of software was reported recently in an article in *Computerworld,* the weekly newspaper of the computer industry. A sixth grade schoolteacher asked her pupils to explain in their own words the meaning of certain computer-related terms, after viewing an introductory film on computers. Few had difficulty with the term "hardware." However, there were quite varied interpretations of the term "software." One student said it was "the underwear of programmers."

The problem in explaining software is not confined to sixth graders. We are not even sure who invented the term. The term "hardware" very nicely conveys the intended meaning—the physical elements of a computing system. The term "software" was meant to convey those portions of the system that are nonphysical. Another way of distinguishing the two elements of the computing system is by their durability—something "hard" does not deteriorate quickly whereas something "soft" has a much shorter life span. Software changes much more rapidly than hardware. If that were not true, computer manufacturers would build circuitry to perform those functions.

The French Canadians do not use the term "software" for non-hardware functions. Their term is logiciel, a more appropriate term because it focuses on the logic involved in processing data by computer. Stated another way, software comprises the instructions which direct the computer to solve problems. These sets of instructions are referred to as computer programs. Programs are input to computer memory along with the data to be processed. When a company changes its operations or when an improved solution to a problem is developed, instructions are revised accordingly. Therefore, solution logic is imbedded in a process that is more easily changed than hardware.

OPERATING SYSTEM SOFTWARE

Chapter 10 provides a detailed breakdown of the various types of software. In this introduction we will simplify the explanation by grouping software into two categories.

1. One type is typically provided by the computer manufacturer, along with the hardware. It is called an operating system and

controls the processing of programs submitted by the various computer users. It also provides services such as translating programmer language to language the machine understands, job scheduling, file management, and input/output control. A good way to visualize the operating system is to think of it as the system's "traffic cop"—it directs and controls traffic through the system.

2. The other type of software is application software. It consists of programs for solving the various problems to which the computer is applied, such as processing payroll or performing engineering calculations.

An expanded explanation of application software is provided below.

APPLICATION SOFTWARE

As described in Chapter 2, there are thousands of applications for which the computer has been utilized. Writing those instructions is called computer programming. Programming at the level the machine understands is tedious and time-consuming. Programming at this level is referred to as machine language programming. Higher-level languages have been developed to simplify the programming task. An example is the language called BASIC, an acronym for *B*eginner's *A*ll-Purpose *S*ymbolic *I*nstruction *C*ode. We will use BASIC to illustrate the concept of high-level languages. Two sample instructions in BASIC will demonstrate the reason it is called a high-level language:

```
1   C = K + L/8
2   PRINT "COST," C
```

The first instruction provides the formula for computing C, which represents cost. The second instruction calls for the value computed to be printed next to the label "Cost." These instructions are English-like and much easier to program than machine-language instructions like 5B4 201, which means "subtract the contents of storage location 201 from the contents of register 4."

A program written in a high-level language must be translated to the machine language for the specific computer being used. The computer manufacturers typically provide a program for this translation process. Such a program is called a compiler.

You may be surprised to learn that more than 100 high level languages have been developed. BASIC is only one of these languages. The illustration shown below identifies a number of those languages. It is referred to as the "Tower of Babel," based on the Biblical passage describing the confusion caused by people trying to communicate in many different languages.

You may wonder why so many programming languages have been developed. Any of these programming languages could be used to solve a given problem. However, each language was developed to specialize in certain types of problems. For example, BASIC is especially well suited for beginners. Persons with little or no experience can often write programs after a few hours of self-instruction. Also, BASIC is very efficient for solving algebraic problems.

Examples of other languages designed to specialize in a certain type of problem are GPSS (for simulation problems) and LISP (for processing alphabetic data and words rather than numbers and algebraic symbols).

COVERAGE OF SECTION THREE

Chapter 10 provides a general introduction to programming. Chapter 11 provides an overview of the programming task. Chapter 12 covers the special techniques for displaying the logic developed to solve a problem by computer.

On completion of Section Three, you will have a good understanding of the techniques for programming a computer.

FIGURE S3–1

Diversity of Programming Languages ("Tower of Babel") (Jean E. Sammet, *Programming Languages,* Copyright © 1969, Prentice-Hall, Inc., Englewood Cliffs, N.J. Reprinted by permission.)

10

INTRODUCTION TO SOFTWARE SYSTEMS

OVERVIEW. Before a user's problems can be solved on a computer, they must be stated in the form of a program, or concise set of instructions to the computer. In the early days, it was necessary for users to state their problems in machine language. This was very difficult and tedious, and the number of successful applications was quite limited.

To overcome these problems, a body of computer programs and techniques called software has been developed. Software includes programming languages and translators, as well as computer operating systems. It also includes application programs that solve problems for a particular user. Supporting documents and training programs are often considered part of software.

Software systems greatly improve the efficiency of computer use. They facilitate man–computer interaction and reduce programming time and cost. They reduce the dependence of the computer on human action and judgment, thereby increasing productivity. To a large extent, the rapid increase in data processing applications in recent years can be attributed to improved software systems.

In this chapter you will study the major languages and computer programs used in most data processing systems. A comparison of five high-level languages—COBOL, RPG, FORTRAN, BASIC, and PASCAL—is provided. Next, the important components of system software are described. These include operating systems, language translators, data base management systems, teleprocessing monitors, and service programs. Finally, the function of application programs is described and several examples of package application programs such as accounts receivable, inventory, and payroll are presented.

As a computer user you will encounter many of the terms, languages, and concepts presented in this chapter. Therefore, it is important that you study this chapter carefully and understand the concepts that are presented.

PROGRAMMING LANGUAGES

As you learned in Chapter 3, a computer performs a given task by executing a series of instructions stored in main memory. These instructions are prepared (or coded) by a programmer, who decides what instructions are required for the task and then ordinarily enters them on a coding sheet. The program is then punched into cards and loaded into the computer prior to execution. Or, when using time-sharing, the programmer keys a program directly into the computer from a terminal.

In Chapter 4 you learned how data are represented in the computer. All data and program instructions are represented by combinations of binary digits (0s and 1s). These binary digits are stored in addressable locations in main memory, which is made up of two-state devices such as magnetic cores or tiny semiconductors.

From this discussion you realize that each computer instruction must be stored in the computer as a series of binary digits. These binary instructions are called the computer's **machine language.** Do the programmers have to code their instructions in this language? In early first-generation computers this was necessary. Fortunately, in later computers more advanced languages have been developed for the programmer to use in coding instructions. In fact, it is possible to define four generations of languages: machine language (first generation), assembly language (second generation), high-level languages (third generation), and user-oriented languages (fourth generation). These language generations are not related directly to the generations of hardware. For example, both machine and assembly languages appeared during the first hardware generation.

MACHINE LANGUAGE: THE FIRST GENERATION

In the earliest first-generation computers, it was necessary for the programmer to write instructions in machine language. Often these instructions were coded in octal or hexadecimal notation. For example, in one computer the machine language hexadecimal instruction 5B4 201 means: "Subtract the contents of storage location 201 from the contents of register 4, and store the result in register 4."

QUESTION: In the above instruction, 5B is a code telling the computer to _____ two numbers. The first number is in register _____ , whereas the second number is contained in storage location _____ . The result will be stored in _____ .

ANSWER: subtract, 4, 201, register 4

Machine language programming was tedious, and the programs were very difficult to correct and modify. Consequently, only a limited number of data processing applications were coded using machine language.

ASSEMBLY LANGUAGE: THE SECOND GENERATION

Due to the shortcomings of machine language, experts in computer science quickly developed improved programming languages. The second generation of computer languages was called assembly (or symbolic) language. As stated above, assembly language was actually developed during the first generation of computers.

Using **assembly language** (as with machine language), the programmer must still normally prepare a separate instruction for each operation to be performed by the computer. However, instead of using binary digits (or their hexadecimal representation), the programmer uses more meaningful symbols. In the simplest case, each assembly language instruction specifies two things.

1. The **operation** to be performed.
2. The **operand,** which is the symbolic name for the data to be used in the operation.

For example, an instruction to write a total amount on a printed report might appear as follows.

WRITE TOTAL

In this instruction, the verb WRITE specifies the operation to be performed. The noun TOTAL is the operand, the symbolic name for the data to be printed out.

QUESTION: A simple assembly language instruction contains an _____ (specifying the action to be performed) and an _____ (symbolic name of the data to be used).

ANSWER: operation, operand

An operand (such as TOTAL in the above example) is both a **variable name** and a **symbolic address.** To programmers, an operand is the name of a variable to which they can refer anywhere in the program. For example, they can add to, subtract from, and print out the quantity they have called TOTAL. To the computer, the operand is a symbolic address or location where this quantity is stored. Before the computer can execute this program it will assign a specific storage location (such as address 0100) to contain the quantity called TOTAL. All references by the programmer to TOTAL will then cause the computer to refer to the quantity stored at location 0100.

Two important features of assembly language programming are the following.

1. The operations (or commands) are verbs or mnemonics that are easily understood by human beings.
2. Operands are meaningful data names that are used to stand for computer addresses.

Assembly language instructions are best illustrated by an example. Suppose that a new inventory balance is to be calculated by subtracting sales from the old balance. Assume that the programmer has assigned the variable names OLDBAL, SALES, and NEWBAL to these quantities. The old balance (1500 units) and sales (250 units) have been read into the computer so that the storage locations containing these quantities appear as follows.

1500	250	?
OLDBAL	SALES	NEWBAL

The results of arithmetic operations in a computer are developed in a special storage device called an **accumulator** or **register.** These devices are part of the arithmetic/logical unit. In this example, assume that register 4 has been arbitrarily selected as the accumulator.

Step 1.

> L   4,OLDBAL

This instruction loads (L) the contents of OLDBAL into the accumulator (register 4). The contents of the memory locations are now as follows.

1500	250	?		1500
OLDBAL	SALES	NEWBAL		Register #4

QUESTION: The operation in the above instruction is _____ , specified by the letter

_____ . The operand is _____ .

ANSWER: load, L, OLDBAL

Step 2.

> S   4,SALES

This instruction subtracts (S) SALES from the contents of register 4, giving the new balance. The memory locations are now as follows.

1500	250	?		1250
OLDBAL	SALES	NEWBAL		Register #4

Step 3.

> ST   4,NEWBAL

This instruction stores (ST) the contents of register 4 in the location called NEWBAL, replacing whatever quantity was previously stored at that location. The computation is now completed, and the memory locations are as follows.

1500	250	1250		1250
OLDBAL	SALES	NEWBAL		Register #4

QUESTION: Summarize the contents of the four memory locations after the store instruction

is executed. OLDBAL _____ SALES _____ NEWBAL _____

Register 4 _____

ANSWER: 1500, 250, 1250, 1250

The instructions for the inventory calculation are summarized in Figure 10-1.

```
L    4,OLDBAL      load the old balance into register #4
S    4,SALES       subtract sales from the old balance
ST   4,NEWBAL      store the result into NEWBAL
```

FIGURE 10-1
Assembly language instructions for inventory calculations.

DISADVANTAGES OF ASSEMBLY LANGUAGE   Programming in assembly language is clearly easier than using binary machine language. However, assembly language still has a number of disadvantages.

1. Assembly language is difficult to learn and understand.
2. Coding in assembly language is still slow and tedious.
3. It is difficult to modify programs and to detect and correct program errors.
4. Assembly language programs can be run only on the specific computer for which they were developed.

For these reasons, assembly language is not widely used today for data processing applications.

HIGH-LEVEL LANGUAGES: THE THIRD GENERATION

Assembly languages are oriented to the computer rather than to the problem to be solved. They do allow expert programmers to write efficient computer code. However, programmers are limited by the rate at which they can code assembly language programs.

To improve the efficiency of writing computer programs, a number of high-level languages have been developed. Several hundred such languages have been developed during the past 20 years. Many of these are no longer used or are used only for limited applications. There are about 10 high-level languages in widespread use today for most applications.

High-level languages are more "people oriented" than earlier languages and permit programmers to write computer instructions in procedural form or in the language of the problem to be solved. Generally, each statement in the language is equivalent to several machine or assembly language instructions — perhaps as many as 10 or 20 or more. This condensing greatly increases the productivity of the programmer and also makes programs easier to read, correct, and interpret.

Some of these languages are "universal" languages; that is, they are standard languages that can be processed with only slight modifications on any of the computers of the major manufacturers. Machine and assembly languages are not universal; they can be used only on one manufacturer's equipment. For example, programs written in CDC assembly language cannot be processed by Honeywell computers. In fact, the machine and assembly languages for one line of equipment are generally not transferable to a second line of the same manufacturer.

To give you an appreciation for high-level languages, we will provide a brief comparison of five of the most commonly used of these languages: BASIC, COBOL, FORTRAN, RPG, and PASCAL. For this comparison, we will use the simple example of reading a student record containing student name, number, units taken this semester, and total units taken prior to this semester (see Figure 10-2).

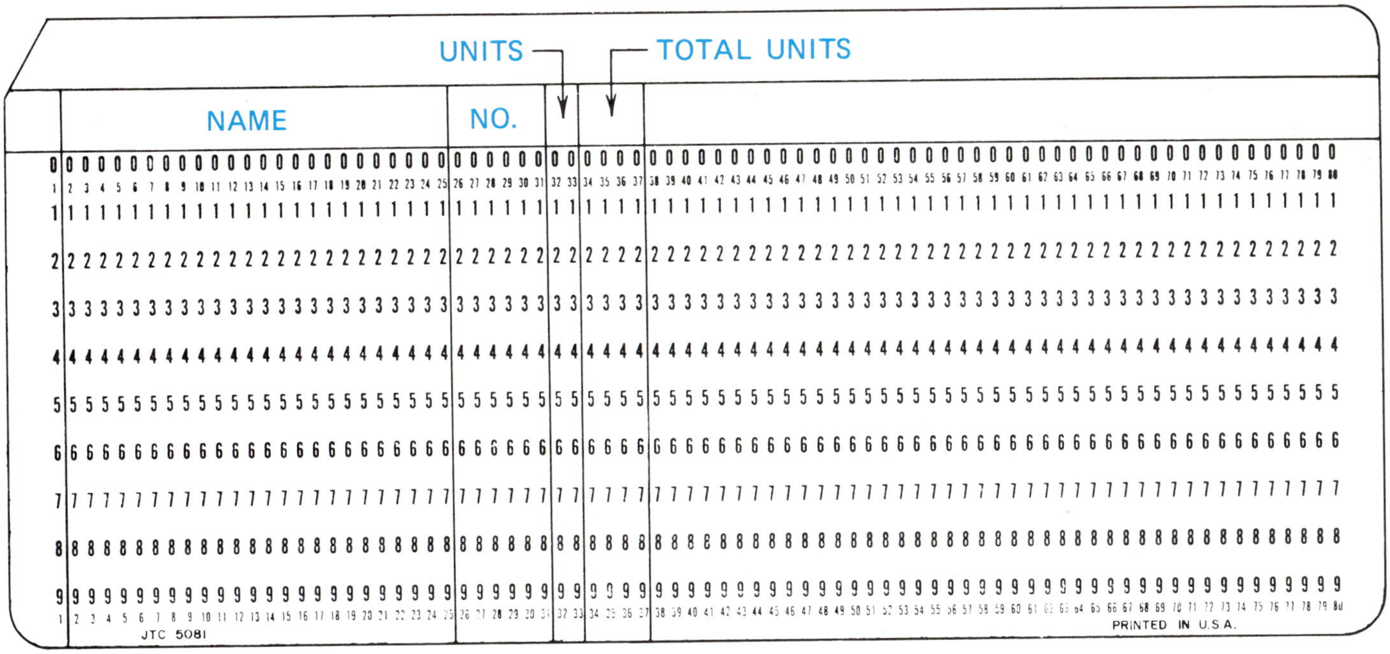

FIGURE 10-2
Input student record.

One card or input record such as the one shown in Figure 10-2 will be read for each student. The amount representing units taken by the student this semester is to be added to the previous total, and the new information is to be printed. Also, the figure for total units taken by all students this semester is to be accumulated and printed out at the end of the report.

The last student record to be read will have the fictitious student number of all zeros, which is to signify end of processing.

BASIC   BASIC is an acronym for Beginner's All-purpose Symbolic Instruction Code. It was developed by Professors John Kemeny and Thomas Kurtz at Dartmouth College in the 1960s. BASIC was developed as an instructional language and therefore is relatively simple and easy to use. It is an interactive language that is used with time-sharing systems.

A BASIC program for the student records example is shown in Figure 10-3.

```
00100 REM     PROGRAM TO READ STUDENT NUMBER, CURRENT UNITS,
00110 REM     AND TOTAL UNITS.  A CUMULATIVE TOTAL OF CURRENT
00120 REM     UNITS IS KEPT.
00130 REM     THE TERMINATING CONDITION IS A STUDENT NUMBER OF 0.
00140 REM       N$= STUDENT NAME
00150 REM       N= STUDENT NUMBER
00160 REM       U= CURRENT UNITS
00170 REM       U1= TOTAL UNITS FOR A STUDENT
00180 REM       C= CUMULATIVE CURRENT UNITS
00190 REM
00200 LET C= 0
00210 PRINT "STUDENT NAME"," ","NUMBER","UNITS","TOTAL"
00220 PRINT "============"," ","======","=====","====="
00230 READ N$,N,U,U1
```

```
00240 IF N= 0 THEN 00290
00250 LET U1= U1+U
00260 LET C= C+U
00270 PRINT N$,N,U,U1
00280 GO TO 00230
00290 PRINT
00300 PRINT "           TOTAL UNITS"," ",C
00310 REM   N$ MUST BE AT LEAST 16 CHARACTERS LONG.
00320 DATA "ADAMS, PETER R.       ",13978,9,104
00330 DATA "GOODMAN, HAROLD R.",20875,16,0
00340 DATA "JOHNSON, SHARON C.",24432,15,74
00350 DATA "LARSON, JAMES I.",47739,6,48
00360 DATA "LEWIS, BARBARA C.",1339,18,107
00370 DATA "ROTHCHILD, CHARLES K.",80336,10,100
00380 DATA "THOMPSON, LAURA W.",59325,7,88
00390 DATA " ",0,0,0
00400 END
```

RUN

STUDENT NAME	NUMBER	UNITS	TOTAL
============	======	=====	=====
ADAMS, PETER R.	13978	9	113
GOODMAN, HAROLD R.	20875	16	16
JOHNSON, SHARON C.	24432	15	89
LARSON, JAMES I.	47739	6	54
LEWIS, BARBARA C.	1339	18	125
ROTHCHILD, CHARLES K.	80336	10	110
THOMPSON, LAURA W.	59325	7	95
TOTAL UNITS		81	

FIGURE 10-3
BASIC program.

Following are the important types of statements included in most BASIC programs, such as the one in Figure 10-3.

1. REM (remark) statements, which provide explanatory comments at any point in the program. In Figure 10-3, notice that the variables used in the program are defined in an introductory REMARK section.

2. READ statements, which cause input data to be read into the computer from a DATA statement contained in the BASIC program. The READ statement includes the names of the variables to be input to the computer.

3. Arithmetic statements, which define variables to be computed. In Figure 10-3, the statement U1 = U1 + U computes a new value for total units by adding the previous total units to units taken this semester.

4. PRINT statements, which cause the literals (in quotation marks) and the named variables to be printed.

5. IF statements, which compare two quantities and cause the program to branch. In Figure 10-3, the statement:

IF N = 0   THEN 00290

causes the program to branch to statement 00290 if the input student number (variable N) is equal to 0.

6. DATA statements, that contain the actual data to be read into the program. For example, in the program shown in Figure 10–3, the first time the READ statement is executed it will cause the data in the first DATA statement (line no. 00320) to be read by the program.

7. END statement, which terminates the program.

Although BASIC is primarily an instructional language, it is often used for data processing applications. In fact, some small business computers use BASIC as the primary language. In such cases, additional instructions are often added to the BASIC set, the results being called "Extended BASIC."

The main advantages of BASIC are the following.

1. It is extremely simple and easy to use. A programmer can begin to write BASIC programs after only a few hours of instruction.

2. BASIC is available for a majority of computers.

3. With an expanded instruction set, it can be used for business applications.

The main disadvantages of BASIC are:

1. A national standard does not exist, so that some differences exist in the different versions.

2. Commands for structured programming are not available in most versions (structured programming is described in Chapter 12).

EXERCISE 10–1 Refer to Figure 10–3 to answer the following questions.

1. What is the name given to each of the following variables in the program?

   a. student name _____

   b. student number _____

   c. units taken this semester _____

   d. total units for student _____

2. What is the name given to the variable that accumulates total units for all

   students? _____

3. What is the student number specified in the last DATA statement? _____

COBOL   COBOL stands for COmmon Business-Oriented Language. As the name implies, this language was designed expressly for business applications. In fact, COBOL is by far the most widely used language for such applications.

Surveys consistently show that COBOL is the programming language used in over half of all business applications.

The development of COBOL was initiated in the late 1950s when representatives of several large users and computer manufacturers formed a committee called the Conference on Data Systems Languages, or CODASYL. The first version of COBOL appeared in 1959. Subsequent versions have occurred since then; the most recent version appeared in 1974. The CODASYL group remains active and is continually reviewing and updating COBOL. The next version of COBOL is scheduled to be published in the early 1980s. The major feature of this version will be additional commands and features for structured programming.

COBOL is available on most computers, including minis and even some microcomputers. The American National Standards Institute (or ANSI) enforces standards for COBOL. These standards insure that COBOL is truly a common language and that the same version (or a common subset) is available on most computers. As a result, a COBOL program written for one computer can ordinarily be transferred to another computer with only relatively minor modifications required.

Procedural statements in COBOL have an English-like format. For example, a COBOL statement to subtract sales from current balance to obtain a new balance would appear as follows.

SUBTRACT SALES FROM OLD-BALANCE GIVING NEW-BALANCE

QUESTION: Compare the above COBOL statement with the assembly language statements it replaces (see Figure 10–1). This COBOL statement is equivalent to

_____ assembly language statements.

ANSWER: three

A COBOL program for the student record example is shown in Figure 10–4.

IDENTIFICATION DIVISION.

PROGRAM-ID.   PROB2.
DATE-WRITTEN.   9/12/79.
DATE-COMPILED.   10/21/79.
REMARKS.
    PROB2 ADDS CURRENT UNITS TO STUDENT*S TOTAL UNITS AND KEEPS A CUMULATIVE TOTAL OF CURRENT UNITS FOR ALL STUDENTS.

ENVIRONMENT DIVISION.

CONFIGURATION SECTION.
    SOURCE-COMPUTER.   IBM 360/370.
INPUT-OUTPUT SECTION.
FILE-CONTROL.
    SELECT STUDENT-FILE   ASSIGN TO INPUT.
    SELECT PRINT-FILE   ASSIGN TO OUTPUT.
DATA DIVISION.

```
FILE SECTION.
FD  STUDENT-FILE
    LABEL RECORDS ARE OMITTED
    DATA RECORD IS STUDENT-REC.
01  STUDENT-REC.
    05  FILLER                    PICTURE X.
    05  STUDENT-NAME-IN           PICTURE X(24).
    05  STUDENT-NUMBER-IN         PICTURE 9(6).
    05  UNITS-IN                  PICTURE 99.
    05  TOTAL-UNITS-IN            PICTURE 999.
    05  FILLER                    PICTURE X(44).


FD  PRINT-FILE
    LABEL RECORDS ARE OMITTED
    DATA RECORD IS PRINT-REC.
01  PRINT-REC.
    05  FILLER                    PICTURE X(133).


WORKING-STORAGE SECTION.
01  MISC-VARIABLES.
    05  CUM-TOTAL                 PICTURE 9(5)     VALUE IS ZERO.
    05  EOF                       PICTURE X        VALUE IS 'N'.


01  PRINT-LINE.
    05  FILLER                    PICTURE X(15)    VALUE IS SPACES.
    05  NAME-OUT                  PICTURE X(24).
    05  FILLER                    PICTURE X(5)     VALUE IS SPACES.
    05  NUMBER-OUT                PICTURE Z(5)9.
    05  FILLER                    PICTURE X(8)     VALUE IS SPACES.
    05  UNITS-OUT                 PICTURE Z9.
    05  FILLER                    PICTURE X(7)     VALUE IS SPACES.
    05  TOTAL-OUT                 PICTURE ZZ9.
    05  FILLER                    PICTURE X(63)    VALUE IS SPACES.


01  HEADER
    05  FILLER                    PICTURE X(22)    VALUE IS SPACES.
    05  FILLER                    PICTURE X(12)    VALUE IS 'STUDENT NAME'.
    05  FILLER                    PICTURE X(11)    VALUE IS SPACES.
    05  FILLER                    PICTURE X(6)     VALUE IS 'NUMBER'.
    05  FILLER                    PICTURE X(5)     VALUE IS SPACES.
    05  FILLER                    PICTURE X(5)     VALUE IS 'UNITS'.
    05  FILLER                    PICTURE X(5)     VALUE IS SPACES.
    05  FILLER                    PICTURE X(5)     VALUE IS 'TOTAL'.
    05  FILLER                    PICTURE X(62)    VALUE IS SPACES.


01  TOTAL-LINE.
    05  FILLER                    PICTURE X(38)    VALUE IS SPACES.
    05  FILLER                    PICTURE X(11)    VALUE IS 'TOTAL UNITS'.
    05  FILLER                    PICTURE X(6)     VALUE IS SPACES.
    05  CUM-TOTAL-OUT             PICTURE Z(4)9.
    05  FILLER                    PICTURE X(73)    VALUE IS SPACES.
```

```
PROCEDURE DIVISION.
000-MAINLINE-CONTROL.
    PERFORM 100-INITIALIZE THRU 100-EXIT.
    PERFORM 200-PROCESS THRU 200-EXIT
        UNTIL EOF = 'Y'.
    PERFORM 300-END THRU 300-EXIT.
    STOP RUN.
000-EXIT.   EXIT.


100-INITIALIZE.
    OPEN INPUT STUDENT-FILE.
    OPEN OUTPUT PRINT-FILE.
    WRITE PRINT-REC FROM HEADER
        AFTER ADVANCING 2 LINES.
    READ STUDENT-FILE
        AT END STOP RUN.
100-EXIT.   EXIT.


200-PROCESS.
    ADD UNITS-IN TO TOTAL-UNITS-IN.
    ADD UNITS-IN TO CUM-TOTAL.
    MOVE STUDENT-NAME-IN TO NAME-OUT.
    MOVE STUDENT-NUMBER-IN TO NUMBER-OUT.
    MOVE UNITS-IN TO UNITS-OUT.
    MOVE TOTAL-UNITS-IN TO TOTAL-OUT.
    WRITE PRINT-REC FROM PRINT-LINE
        AFTER ADVANCING 1 LINE.
    READ STUDENT-FILE
        AT END MOVE 'Y' TO EOF.
200-EXIT.   EXIT.


300-END.
    MOVE CUM-TOTAL TO CUM-TOTAL-OUT.
    WRITE PRINT-REC FROM TOTAL-LINE
        AFTER ADVANCING 2 LINES.
    CLOSE STUDENT-FILE
        PRINT-FILE.
300-EXIT.   EXIT.


999-END-OF-PROGRAM.
```

STUDENT NAME	NUMBER	UNITS	TOTAL
ADAMS, PETER R.	13978	9	113
GOODMAN, HAROLD R.	20875	16	16
JOHNSON, SHARON C.	24432	15	89
LARSON, JAMES I.	47739	6	54
LEWIS, BARBARA C.	1339	18	125
ROTHCHILD, CHARLES K.	80336	10	110
THOMPSON, LAURA W.	59325	7	95
TOTAL UNITS		81	

FIGURE 10-4
COBOL program.

As shown in Figure 10-4, a COBOL program is divided into four divisions, as follows.

1. An **Identification Division,** which simply assigns the program a name and may contain additional miscellaneous comments. In Figure 10-4, the Identification Division includes a REMARKS clause that briefly describes the purpose of the program.

2. An **Environment Division,** which identifies the computer to be used (Configuration Section) and assigns names to input and output files (Input-Output Section).

3. A **Data Division,** which identifies the files, records, and data items or fields used in the program. The Data Division normally consists of two sections: File Section and Working-Storage Section.

    (a)   The **File Section** identifies input and output files and records and also the name and representation of each data item within these records.

    (b)   The **Working-Storage Section** contains a description of all constants, intermediate totals, and work areas that are not a part of input or output.

4. A **Procedure Division,** which contains the statements that read and manipulate data and print out information.

The Procedure Division in turn is divided into **Paragraphs.** Each paragraph is given an identifying name and performs a specific function. The paragraphs in Figure 10-4 are the following.

1. 000-MAINLINE-CONTROL: executes the remaining paragraphs in the correct order, using PERFORM statements.

2. 100-INITIALIZE: Opens input and output files, prints a report header, and reads the first student record.

3. 200-PROCESS: Computes the new "total units" for each student and "cumulative units" for all students, moves the student data to an output area, and prints the student record.

4. 300-END: When an "end of file" condition is encountered (last student record has been processed), this paragraph prints the cumulative units for all students and closes the files.

5. 999-END-OF-PROGRAM.

The major advantages of COBOL are the following.

1. It is designed specifically for business applications.

2. It is a universal language, available on most computers.

3. It has an ANSI standard, so that versions for different computers are highly compatible.

4. Most data base systems have a standard interface (are compatible) with COBOL.

5. COBOL procedure statements are easy to read, even by nonprogrammers.

6. The language is continually being evaluated for improvements by the CODASYL committee.

7. There is a large supply of programmers with COBOL experience.

8. Structured programming commands are available in most COBOL versions.

The main disadvantages of COBOL are the following.

1. Even simple programs tend to be quite long (compare the COBOL program of Figure 10-4 with the equivalent BASIC program of Figure 10-3).

2. COBOL is not intended for applications requiring extensive mathematical computations.

EXERCISE 10-2   Refer to Figure 10-4 to answer the following questions.

1. What is the name given to the input and output files in the COBOL program?

   a. INPUT _____

   b. OUTPUT _____

2. What is the name given to the Student Name data item in the record called STUDENT-REC?

   _____

3. PICTURE clauses are used to identify the representation of a data item. X stands for an alphanumeric field, whereas 9 stands for a numeric field. The length of a field is stated within parentheses. For example, X(10) indicates a 10-character alphanumeric field, while 9(10) indicates a 10-digit numeric field.

   From the PICTURE clauses in Figure 10-4, describe the representation for each of the following fields.

   a. STUDENT-NAME-IN _____

   b. STUDENT-NUMBER-IN _____

4. In the PROCEDURE division, write down the statement that does each of the following.
   a. Computes the new total units for each student

   _____

   b. Computes the new total units for all students

   _____

   c. Prints out the detail information for each student

   _____

FORTRAN   Most of the early applications of computers were for mathematical computations in science, engineering, and the military. Thus, the programming languages that were developed were designed to express a mathematical notation and procedures. In 1954, IBM began work on FORTRAN, which stands for FORmula TRANslator. The goal was to develop a language that would enable the programmer to solve problems using a concise notation similar to mathematics. For example, the formula to compute a compound amount after N years at interest rate R, and the corresponding FORTRAN statement, are given below.

Formula: $\qquad\qquad A = S \times (1 + R)^N$
FORTRAN statement: $\quad$ A = S * (1. + R)**N

Just as COBOL has become the most widely used business language, FORTRAN is the most widely used language for scientific applications. A FORTRAN program for the student record application is shown in Figure 10–5.

```
      INTEGER NUMB,UNITS,TUNITS,TOTAL
      DIMENSION NAME (6)
      WRITE (6,10)
10    FORMAT (1H1,21X,'STUDENT NAME               NUMBER      UNITS      TOTAL')
      TOTAL = 0
20    READ (5,30) NAME,NUMB,UNITS,TUNITS
30    FORMAT (1X,6A4,I6,I2,I3)
      IF (NUMB.EQ.0) GO TO 50
          TUNITS = TUNITS + UNITS
          TOTAL = TOTAL + UNITS
          WRITE (6,40) NAME,NUMB,UNITS,TUNITS
40        FORMAT (1H ,14X,6A4,5X,I6,8X,I2,7X,I3)
      GO TO 20
50    WRITE (6,60) TOTAL
60    FORMAT (1H ,38X,≠TOTAL UNITS≠,5X,I5)
      STOP
      END
```

STUDENT NAME	NUMBER	UNITS	TOTAL
ADAMS, PETER R.	13978	9	113
GOODMAN, HAROLD R.	20875	16	16
JOHNSON, SHARON C.	24432	15	89
LARSON, JAMES I.	47739	6	54
LEWIS, BARBARA C.	1339	18	125
ROTHCHILD, CHARLES K.	80336	10	110
THOMPSON, LAURA W.	59325	7	95
TOTAL UNITS		81	

FIGURE 10–5
FORTRAN program.

The most important statements found in most FORTRAN programs are the following.

1. DIMENSION statements, which name and dimension an array. In Figure 10–5, NAME is an array with six positions or subscripts.

2. FORMAT statements, which define the type, length and location of each data item or field to be input or output by the computer. For example, in Figure 10–5 the first FORMAT statement defines the format of the header for the output report.

3. READ statements, which cause a record to be input to the computer. The READ statement in Figure 10–5 causes a student record to be read according to the second FORMAT statement (statement number 30). The list of variables to be read in is included in the READ statement.

4. WRITE statements, which cause a record to be transmitted to an output device. In Figure 10–5, the second WRITE statement causes a student record to be printed (the FORMAT for this WRITE is given in statement number 40).

5. Arithmetic statements, which cause arithmetic operations to be performed on the data. For example, in Figure 10–5 the statement TUNITS = TUNITS + UNITS causes the student's previous total units to be added to the units for this semester, to form a new total.

6. Logical statements, which cause two numbers to be compared and the program to branch, depending on the result of the comparison. For Figure 10–5, the statement:

    IF (NUMB.EQ.0) GO TO 50

    causes the program to branch to statement 50 if the input student number is equal to 0 (otherwise the program continues to the next statement).

7. STOP and END statements, which terminate the program.

FORTRAN is not designed for business applications, although it is sometimes used for that purpose. The main advantages of FORTRAN are the following.

1. A national standard (ANSI) exists for the language.
2. FORTRAN compilers are available on a majority of computers.
3. It is a powerful language for scientific applications.
4. A large number of programmers have FORTRAN backgrounds or expertise.
5. Structured programming commands are available in some FORTRAN versions (structured programming is described in Chapter 12).

EXERCISE 10–3   Refer to Figure 10–5 to answer the following questions.

1. What is the name given to each of the following variables in the first READ statement?

    a.   Student name _____

    b.   Student number _____

    c.   Units taken this semester _____

    d.   Total units taken to date _____

2. In the second FORMAT statement the term I6 appears in parentheses. This defines the field "student number," which is an integer field six digits in

length. In the same FORMAT statement, the term I2 defines the "units"

field, which is an _____ field _____ digits in length.

3. The name of the field used to accumulate total units for all students is

_____

RPG   RPG (for Report Program Generator) is a high-level, problem-oriented language developed for simple data processing tasks. RPG was developed by IBM for its small business computers but is now available on computers from other vendors as well. Although not as widely used as COBOL, RPG is nevertheless a popular language for business applications.

In writing an RPG program, the user starts with a desired format for a report and writes a set of specifications for the report and the input file to be used. Simple computations can also be defined.

An RPG program for the student record program is shown in Figure 10-6.

FIGURE 10-6
RPG program.

```
FSTUDFL  IP  F   80   80              READ40 SYSRDR
FPRINTFL O   F  132  132      OF      PRINTERSYSLST
ISTUDFL  AA  05   01 CS
I                                        2   25 NAME
I                                       26   310STNO
I                                       32   330UNITS
I                                       34   360TOTAL
C    05        UNITS    ADD   TOTAL     TOTAL
C    05        UNITS    ADD   FTOTAL    FTOTAL    50
OPRINTFL H  201      1P
O       OR         OF
O                                       33 'STUDENT NAME'
O                                       49 'NUMBER'
O                                       59 'UNITS'
O                                       70 'TOTAL'
O         D   1      05
O                              NAME     39
O                              STNO  Z  49
O                              UNITS Z  59
O                              TOTAL Z  69
O         T   2      LR
O                                       49 'TOTAL UNITS'
O                              FTOTALZ  59
```

STUDENT NAME	NUMBER	UNITS	TOTAL
ADAMS, PETER R.	13978	9	113
GOODMAN, HAROLD R.	20875	16	16
JOHNSON, SHARON C.	24432	15	89
LARSON, JAMES I.	47739	5	54
LEWIS, BARBARA C.	1339	18	125
ROTHSCHILD, CHARLES K.	80336	10	110
THOMPSON, LAURA W.	59325	7	95

| | TOTAL UNITS | 81 | |

RPG programs are defined by filling out a set of **specification forms.** Four types of specification forms are used in most RPG programs: file specifications, input specifications, calculation specifications, and output specifications. The statements in the RPG program in Figure 10-6 were developed from these specifications, as follows.

1. File specifications, designated by an F in column 1 of the statement. The first two statements are file specifications. The first assigns the name STUDFL to the input student file, whereas the second assigns the name PRINTFL to the output print file.

2. Input specifications (letter I in column 1), given in the next five statements. These statements assign names to the input fields and indicate where they are contained on the data card (Figure 10-2). For example, the second input statement indicates that the field NAME (for student name) appears in card columns 2 through 25.

3. Calculation specifications (letter C in column 1). The first of these two statements causes UNITS to be added to TOTAL, giving a new total. The second causes UNITS to be added to FTOTAL, the cumulative total for all students.

4. Output specifications (letter O in column 1). The first series of output statements causes header information to be printed. For example, the literal STUDENT NAME is printed on the output report, ending in column 33. The next series of output statements defines the output record for each student, whereas the last two statements print out TOTAL UNITS for all students.

The main advantages of RPG are the following.

1. It is a simple language, relatively easy to learn and use.
2. Programs to produce reports from files can be written quickly and easily.
3. Although there is no national (ANSI) standard, there is a de facto IBM standard.

The main disadvantages of RPG are the following.

1. RPG cannot be used to define complex file structures or data bases.
2. RPG is suitable only for simple arithmetic calculations.
3. RPG does not have an interface with most of the major data base management systems (an exception is the DBMS for the IBM System/38 series).

PASCAL   PASCAL is the newest of the languages compared in this chapter, having been first introduced in 1970. It was developed by Swiss computer scientist Nicklaus Wirth. PASCAL is named after the French mathematician and philosopher Blaise Pascal.

PASCAL was the first major language to be developed after the concepts of structured programming became popular and therefore incorporates many of its commands and features. For example, all variables and constants must be clearly defined at the **front** of a program. Top-down programming style is provided by the use of procedures and functions that are invoked just by using them in a main-line routine. The principles and advantages of structured programming are described in Chapter 12.

PASCAL is a general-purpose language, adaptable to a wide variety of applications. In the past its primary uses have been as an instructional language (to teach structured programming) and as a language for writing systems programs. However, it is also becoming increasingly popular for business and scientific applications. PASCAL uses a natural English language style and allows free-form coding (that is, the programmer need not follow a rigid coding format). The PASCAL language is available on all types of computers from micros to supercomputers.

A PASCAL program for the student records problem is shown in Figure 10-7.

```
0   1    PROGRAM PROB2 (INPUT, OUTPUT);
0   2    TYPE
0   3
0   4        STUDENTREC =
0   5          RECORD
1   6            NAME: ARRAY (1..20) OF CHAR;
1   7            NUMBER,
1   8            UNITS,
1   9            TOTALUNITS: INTEGER;
1  10          END;
0  11
0  12    VAR
0  13        STUDENTFILE: STUDENTREC;
0  14        INDEX,
0  15        FINALTOTAL: INTEGER;
0  16
0  17    BEGIN (* PROB2 *)
1  18        WRITELN (≡      STUDENT NAME          NUMBER          UNITS          TOTAL≡);
1  19        FINALTOTAL   := 0;
1  20        WITH STUDENTFILE DO
1  21          BEGIN
2  22          WHILE NOT EOF DO
2  23          BEGIN
3  24            WRITE (≡    ≡);
3  25            FOR INDEX := 1 TO 20 DO
3  26            BEGIN
4  27              READ (NAME [INDEX]);
4  28              WRITE (NAME [INDEX]);
4  29            END;
3  30            READLN (NUMBER,UNITS,TOTALUNITS);
3  31            FINALTOTAL := FINALTOTAL + UNITS;
3  32            TOTALUNITS := TOTALUNITS + UNITS;
3  33            WRITELN (NUMBER,UNITS,TOTALUNITS);
3  34          END;
2  35          WRITELN (≡0      TOTAL UNITS      ≡,FINALTOTAL);
2  36        END;
1  37    END. (* PROB 2 *)
```

STUDENT NAME	NUMBER	UNITS	TOTAL
ADAMS, PETER R.	13978	9	113
GOODMAN, HAROLD R.	20875	16	16
JOHNSON, SHARON C.	24432	15	89
LARSON, JAMES I.	47739	6	54
LEWIS, BARBARA C.	1339	18	125
ROTHSCHILD, CHARLES	80336	10	110
THOMPSON, LAURA W.	59325	7	95
TOTAL UNITS		81	

FIGURE 10–7
PASCAL program.

Following are the main features of this program.

1. All records and variables are declared and defined in opening sections, as follows.
   (a) STUDENTREC is defined as a record.
   (b) NAME is declared as an array containing up to 20 characters (student name).
   (c) NUMBER, UNITS, TOTALUNITS, INDEX, and FINALTOTAL are declared as integers.

2. Terms enclosed in asterisks (such as *STUDENT NAME*) are explanatory comments.

3. The body of the program follows a block structure: a BEGIN statement opens each block; a matching END statement closes the block. For example, the statement BEGIN (*PROB2*) introduces the main body of the program.

4. Nested blocks are indented. For example, in Figure 10–7 there are two nested blocks in the body of the program.

5. Arithmetic statements are similar to those in FORTRAN. For example, the statement:

FINALTOTAL: = FINALTOTAL + UNITS

computes the new total of units for each student. However, unlike the case in FORTRAN, a variable name can be any length.

The main advantages of PASCAL are the following.

1. It is ideally suited to the structured programming approach.

2. It is a general-purpose language, suited to both business and scientific applications.

3. It is available on a wide variety of computers.

4. Although there is no standard at present, there is widespread agreement on what should constitute PASCAL. An international standard for PASCAL is in the review process.

The only disadvantage of PASCAL is that it is somewhat complex and more difficult to learn than simple languages such as BASIC and RPG.

SUMMARY   A summary comparison of the five high-level languages is presented in Table 10-1.

TABLE 10-1   COMPARISON OF HIGH-LEVEL LANGUAGES

Language	Type of Application	Major Advantages	Major Disadvantages
BASIC	Instructional	1. Simplicity	1. Non-ANSI standard 2. Not business oriented 3. Moderately structured
COBOL	Business	1. ANSI standard 2. Widespread usage 3. Data base compatible	1. Wordy (length) 2. Not structured 3. Business only
RPG	Business	1. Simplicity 2. Define reports quickly	1. Non-ANSI standard 2. Simple file structures only
FORTRAN	Scientific	1. ANSI standard 2. Partially structured 3. Widespread use	1. Not suited to business
PASCAL	General	1. Highly structured 2. All applications	1. Somewhat complex

Although the languages shown in Table 10-1 are the ones that are most frequently used today, a number of other high-level languages are also commonly used. Three of the more important of these languages are described briefly below.

ALGOL (for ALGOrithmic Language) is a scientific language that was first introduced in 1958. ALGOL uses a block structure and in many respects resembles PASCAL. It has gained wider acceptance in some European countries than in the United States.

APL (A Programming Language) was developed by Kenneth Iverson of IBM. It is a user-oriented time-sharing language with powerful commands for data structuring and manipulation. Although intended mainly for mathematical applications, APL is also used for certain business applications such as financial modeling.

PL/1 (Programming Language One) was developed by IBM. Like PASCAL, PL/1 is a general-purpose language suitable for both scientific and business applications. However, PASCAL seems more suited to structured programming applications, and PASCAL is available on a much wider range of computers.

EXERCISE 10-4   1. Refer to Figure 10-6. What is the RPG field name for each of the following?

a.   Units taken this semester _____

b.   Total units taken to date by a student

    c. Cumulative units taken by all students

_____

2. Refer to Figure 10-7.
   a. What is the function of the innermost block (BEGIN statement, followed by READ and WRITE statements, END statement)?

   _____

   _____

   b. What is the function of the variable whose name is INDEX? _____

   _____

3. Refer to Table 10-1. What language is most appropriate for each of the following applications?

   a. Specifying the format for a new report _____

   b. Solving an engineering design problem _____
   c. Teaching programming to college freshmen

   _____

   d. Processing data base applications _____

   e. Teaching structured programming _____

USER-ORIENTED LANGUAGES: THE FOURTH GENERATION

The high-level languages described above provide a powerful means for solving user problems. However, each language is procedurally oriented and requires a trained programmer to use it effectively. With the advent of data bases and the increased need for up-to-date information, it is increasingly important for nonprogramming personnel to be able to access data. For example, a marketing manager wishes to access the marketing data base, or a registrar to access the student data base, both without having to write programs.

Fourth-generation languages, often called **user-oriented languages,** permit nonprogrammer personnel to access data with only minimal training in the language. For example, suppose a personnel manager has the following request: "Produce a list of the names and numbers of all employees in department 10 whose salaries are greater than $20,000 or whose commissions are greater than their salaries." A typical user-oriented query language request for this data is shown in Figure 10-8.

```
SELECT ENAME, EMPNO
   FROM EMPDATA
  WHERE DEPTNO = 10
    AND SALARY > 20000
     OR COMM > SALARY;
```

FIGURE 10-8
Query language request for employee data.

Query languages such as this, used on an interactive terminal, allow the user great flexibility in accessing or "browsing" a data base. At the same time, they increase the risk that unauthorized users will gain access to data. Increased safeguards such as passwords and control of access to terminals are required when query languages are used.

SYSTEM SOFTWARE

When an organization acquires a computer, it purchases not merely hardware but also abundant software for satisfying its information processing needs. A number of programs, called **system software,** are generally furnished by the vendor to assist the user in solving his problems. System software is designed to satisfy three important (and sometimes conflicting) objectives.

1. To utilize the computer resources (hardware and software) as efficiently as possible.
2. To provide such standard, commonly used functions as language translation, sorting, and report generation.
3. To provide simple user interfaces so that the users need not be overly concerned about internal computer operations.

The important types of system software include operating systems, language translators, data base management systems, teleprocessing monitors, and service programs. These components are described below.

OPERATING SYSTEM

The most important type of system software is the computer operating system. An **operating system** is an integrated set of programs that coordinates and controls the operation of the computer. Some of the important functions performed by operating systems are the following.

1. Job scheduling—selects jobs waiting in an input queue and schedules them for processing.
2. Memory management—assigns jobs (programs) to specific locations in main memory and frees main memory when the jobs are completed or inactive.
3. Input/output control—directs input/output activities and handles interrupt conditions, attempting to efficiently utilize channels and input/output devices.
4. Multiprogramming—schedules and controls the concurrent execution of several programs or jobs.

SUPERVISOR   The central component of an operating system is referred to as the supervisor, or the monitor or executive. The **supervisor** schedules and controls the various operations of the computer. A typical supervisor performs the following functions.

1. Loads processing programs (for example, payroll or sales analysis programs) into main memory from magnetic disk, as required.
2. Schedules the sequence of jobs to be run for maximum efficiency.
3. Schedules and controls input/output operations and handles interrupts, or signals to the CPU when an exceptional condition exists in the system.

The actual tasks performed by the supervisor depend on whether batch processing or on-line processing methods are being used.

BATCH PROCESSING   In batch processing, jobs to be run on the computer are typically stacked in a card reader (or on magnetic tape or disk). At the beginning of each job (such as a payroll program to be run) is a set of **job control cards.** These cards provide the name of the program to be executed, together with information such as which magnetic disk cartridges to mount in disk drives that will be used by the program. For example, Figure 10-9 shows the job deck for a program written in COBOL for IBM's Disk Operating System, or DOS (other operating systems would use different job control cards).

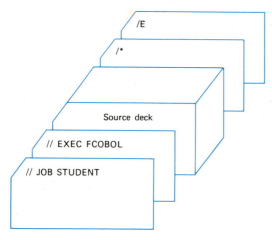

FIGURE 10-9

Example of job control cards.

The cards shown in Figure 10-9 are the following.

1. //JOB (job card). Assigns a name to the source program (in this case, STUDENT).
2. //EXEC FCOBOL. Causes the COBOL compiler to be loaded from magnetic disk and executed. FCOBOL is the name given to the COBOL compiler stored in the library for this system.
3. Source deck. The program written in COBOL language, which is to be compiled and executed.
4. /* (end-of-file card). Indicates end of source deck.
5. /E (end-of-job card). Indicates that the job is completed.

QUESTION: The above cards are an example of the _____ _____ cards for a particular operating system.

ANSWER: job control

ON-LINE PROCESSING   In on-line processing, various users are accessing the computer from local or remote terminals. The operating system must identify the terminal communicating a message, check to see whether the operator is an authorized user, accept the transmitted message, and load any programs required by the user. Following processing, the supervisor initiates a return message or response to the user. The supervisor operates in conjunction with a telecommunications monitor (described below).

Many computers use batch and on-line processing at the same time, so the supervisor must be able to coordinate and control both types of operations.

An operating system is a series of programs, too large to be stored in central memory at any one time. Generally, only that portion of the operating system that loads other programs is stored permanently in memory. Remaining portions of the operating system are stored on direct access devices such as magnetic disk. These portions, called **segments** or **overlays,** are read into main memory as needed.

MULTIPROGRAMMING   Consider a simple computer in which programs must be executed serially, one program or job at a time. For example, there might be three jobs (X, Y, and Z) waiting to be processed. The computer might be assigned to execute job X first; this job must be completed before job Y is started, and so on.

Serial execution of jobs in this manner is very inefficient and results in excessive idle time for the central processing unit (CPU), since the CPU would spend much of its time waiting for much slower input/output devices. A simple example of serial execution with idle time is shown in Figure 10-10.

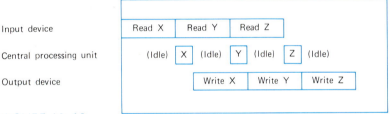

FIGURE 10-10
Serial execution of computer programs.

In Figure 10-10, computations are overlapped with input/output operations. For example, data is being read for job Y at the same time as the CPU is processing job X. This is made possible by input/output channels, which were described in Chapter 6. However, since the jobs are processed sequentially, job Y cannot start until the input operations have been completed for both jobs X and Y. As a result, the CPU is frequently idle while waiting for input and output operations to be completed. Throughput (number of jobs processed per hour) is limited to a large extent by input/output speeds.

To overcome this limitation, most computers today use a technique called multiprogramming. With **multiprogramming,** several programs are loaded into main memory and are executed concurrently.[1] The supervisor schedules jobs to be executed so as to minimize delays. For example, if program Y is interrupted while data is being read from a disk device, the supervisor may assign the CPU to job Z until the input operation for job Y is completed.

An example of the multiprogrammed execution of jobs X, Y, and Z is shown in Figure 10-11. It is assumed that all three programs are in the main memory, and that separate input and output devices are available for the three programs. Notice that the three read operations are performed simultaneously, and as soon as execution begins on program X the CPU proceeds without interruption.

[1]A human analogy to multiprogramming is watching a football game and working on a term paper simultaneously. We'll leave it to you to decide whether humans or computers excel at such operations!

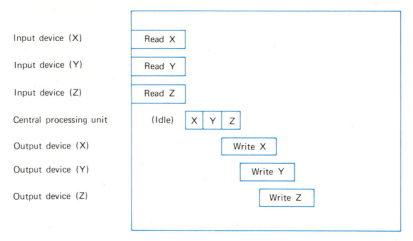

FIGURE 10-11
Multiprogrammed execution of computer programs.

QUESTION: Compare Figures 10-10 and 10-11. The CPU is idle a much (larger, smaller) fraction of the time with multiprogramming.

ANSWER: smaller

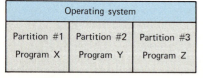

FIGURE 10-12
Use of partitions
in multiprogramming.

One approach to multiprogramming is to subdivide main memory units into areas called **partitions.** For example, Figure 10-12 shows main memory divided into three partitions for programs X, Y, and Z. These partitions may be all the same size (**fixed-size** partitions) or of different sizes (**variable-size** partitions). Also, one of the programs (say program Y) may be assigned a higher priority than the other programs. By means of a procedure called an **interrupt** the program with higher priority can preempt the use of a needed resource such as the CPU or a channel or input/output device.

QUESTION: In Figure 10-12, program Z is in partition _____ . If this program was of higher priority, it could seize the use of the CPU from program X by means of

an _____

ANSWER: 3, interrupt

In a multiprogramming environment, several programs in various partitions often must share the use of a common input/output device such as a line printer. To resolve contention for the use of such a device, output data from a given program is first diverted to magnetic disk and then printed when the printer becomes available. The diversion of output to magnetic disk is called **output spooling.** In a similar manner, **input spooling** is used to create a queue of waiting jobs on magnetic disk for jobs read from the card reader or other input device.

The number of partitions that can exist in a computer with multiprogramming depends on the size of main memory and on the operating system. A microcomputer may have two partitions, whereas a large computer may permit the concurrent execution of several dozen programs. The advantages of multi-programming are better use of computer resources and faster throughput of user jobs.

LANGUAGE TRANSLATORS

In the previous section you studied five high-level languages that are the most commonly used for programming actual applications. Before programs written in such languages can be executed by the computer, they must be translated into machine language — binary patterns of zeros and ones.

A program written in any language other than machine language is called a **source program.** Source programs are translated into machine language by system programs called **translators.** If the source program is written in assembly language, the translator program is called an **assembler.** If the source program is written in a high-level language, the translator program is called a **compiler.** The output of the language translation process (in machine language) is called an **object** program. In another approach (used in the BASIC language), each instruction is decoded and executed a step at a time by a program called an **interpreter.**

There are four basic steps in language translation. These steps (shown in Figure 10-13) are the following.

1. The assembler or compiler program is read into computer memory. The translating program is commonly stored on magnetic disk. When a program is to be translated, the translating program is loaded into main memory.

2. The set of instructions written by the programmer (or source program) is then read into main memory.

3. The translator then translates the source program into machine language instructions. This step may require one or more computer passes or runs. The resulting machine language instructions are referred to as the object program. The object program may be punched into cards to form an **object deck.** However, the object program is often stored on magnetic tape or disk, or it may be loaded directly into main memory for processing.

4. The object program deck (if any) and data are then read into memory, and program execution begins.

Compilers and assemblers provide a number of supporting functions that assist the programmer in correcting and documenting his program. For example, in the translation process common errors in use of the language are detected and messages are printed. Since the computer is "diagnosing" errors, these messages are called **diagnostics.** Diagnostics are useful in correcting errors in a source program. The process of correcting errors, referred to as **debugging** the program, is described in Chapter 11.

DATA BASE MANAGEMENT SYSTEMS

In Chapter 9 a data base was defined as a collection of files, logically structured to meet the information needs of an organization. You learned that there are a number of advantages to the data base approach, including sharing of data between applications and eliminating the duplication of data.

Establishing, maintaining, and protecting a data base is a complex process. It requires the use of a number of computer programs and techniques, especially for maintaining the logical relationships among records. Very few users would

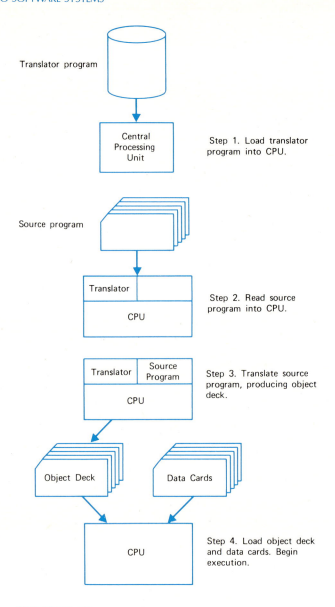

Translator program

Step 1. Load translator program into CPU.

Central Processing Unit

Source program

Step 2. Read source program into CPU.

Translator

CPU

Translator | Source Program

Step 3. Translate source program, producing object deck.

CPU

Object Deck

Data Cards

Step 4. Load object deck and data cards. Begin execution.

CPU

FIGURE 10-13
Steps in language translation.

be able to justify writing these programs, so the benefits of the data base approach would not be realized.

Fortunately, package programs are available from vendors for this purpose. A **data base management system** (or DBMS) is a set of generalized programs for managing a data base. A DBMS is used to assist the user in performing the following functions.

1. Designing and describing the data base.
2. Loading the data base.
3. Accessing and manipulating the data base.
4. Protecting and maintaining the integrity of the data base.

Data base management systems are available both from computer manufacturers and from independent software vendors. Some of the more popular DBMSs are shown in Table 10-2.

TABLE 10-2   POPULAR DATA BASE MANAGEMENT SYSTEMS

DBMS	Vendor	Data Structure
IMS	IBM	Hierarchical
IDMS	Cullinane	Network (CODASYL)
ADABAS	Software AG	Network (inverted)
System 2000	MRI	Hierarchical (inverted)
TOTAL	Cincom	Network

Table 10-2 indicates the data structures for each of these systems. The basic logical structures (hierarchical, network, and relational) are described in Chapter 9. The term CODASYL in Table 10-2 stands for Conference on Data Systems Languages. Recall from an earlier section that this committee has developed the COBOL language. A subcommittee of this group, called the Data Base Task Group, has developed a proposed standard for DBMSs called the CODASYL model. IDMS is an example of a CODASYL system.

QUESTION: Examine Table 10-2. Four of the DBMSs shown are non-CODASYL systems. Name two systems for each of the following types of data structures.

Hierarchical _____ _____

Network _____ _____

ANSWER: hierarchical — IMS, System 2000; network — ADABAS, TOTAL

Part of the CODASYL specifications defines a set of common data base languages. There are two basic languages: a data description language (or DDL) for describing a data base, and a data manipulation language (or DML), which, when associated with a "host" language like COBOL, allows the user to manipulate the data base.

In accessing a data base, a DBMS serves as an interface between the user and the data base. As shown in Figure 10-14, a user application program makes a request for a logical record from the DBMS. The DBMS determines the physical record (or records) that are required to satisfy this request and passes this information to the operating system. The operating system accesses the requested data and loads it into a user work area for use by the application program. With a DBMS, the user need not be concerned with the physical details of how the data are stored.

TELEPROCESSING MONITORS

In many applications, users access a data base from on-line terminals. These might be inquiry/response applications (such as credit checking), or on-line updating (such as sales order entry or inventory applications). A type of system software called a teleprocessing monitor is used for many on-line applications.

A **teleprocessing monitor** is a system program that forms an interface between remote, on-line users and the computer data base (see Figure 10-15). The teleprocessing monitor performs such functions as polling terminals, checking incoming messages, handling priorities, and formatting outgoing messages. The components and functions of a telecommunications system are described in Chapter 8. In some computers, the teleprocessing monitor is an integral part of the operating system.

As shown in Figure 10-15, the teleprocessing monitor accepts messages

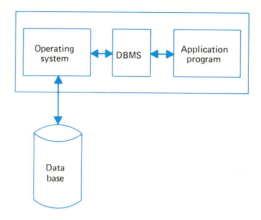

FIGURE 10-14
Function of a data base management system.

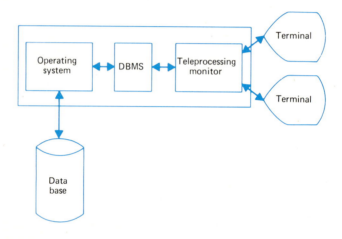

FIGURE 10-15
Function of a teleprocessing monitor.

from users at terminals. These messages are then routed to the DBMS, which calls on the operating system to access requested records in the data base.

QUESTION: Examine Figure 10-15. Suppose that a user at a terminal requests a customer record in the data base for a credit check. Indicate the path followed by the data base record:

data base — _____ — _____ — _____ — _____ .

ANSWER: operating system, DBMS, teleprocessing monitor, terminal.

SERVICE PROGRAMS   **Service programs** are system software packages that are used to perform specialized data processing functions. Following are the more commonly used of these service programs.

Librarian programs are used to catalog, control, and maintain a directory of the various programs used by the computer system. These programs are generally maintained on magnetic disk (or other direct access device) and transferred to main memory as needed.

Subroutines are sets of instructions that perform a specific task, such as a particular mathematical computation. Most high-level languages such as FORTRAN have a library of subroutines that can be called in by a program as needed.

Utility programs are used to perform common housekeeping functions such as sorts, merges, and file copies and dumps.

System aids are miscellaneous programs such as performance evaluation tools, debugging aids, and simulators and emulators that are used to measure and improve the performance of the computer system.

APPLICATION PROGRAMS

Application or **user** programs are programs that are written to solve specific problems such as those in business and engineering. An application program might range from a 10-statement BASIC program written by a student to compute and print out a standard deviation, to a program consisting of thousands of statements to process insurance policies.

There are two basic types of application programs.

1. **Custom** programs are written to solve problems or process applications that are peculiar to a particular user. For example, a mail-order company might write a program to analyze sales by product and region. There are two basic sources of custom programs: they may be developed internally by the user, or they may be developed under contract by an outside software company.

2. **Package** programs are prewritten programs for common applications that can be used by a wide variety of users with little or no modification. Package programs are available both from computer vendors and from independent software vendors.

Package programs are generally much less expensive than custom application programs, because they are marketed to a large number of users. Typical package application programs are the following: payroll, accounts receivable, accounts payable, inventory, and general ledger. A brief description of each type of program, together with typical reports, is given below.

Payroll is one of the earlier business applications to be computerized. A typical payroll system calculates earnings for hourly, salaried, and commissioned employees, including deductions for taxes, medical insurance, and other appropriate categories. Typical documents and reports produced by a payroll system include payroll checks, W-2 forms, and payroll registers (see Figure 10-16).

Accounts receivable programs support the billing and accounts receivable functions of the organization. The billing function includes the selection and extension of prices and the application of discounts, freight charges, and taxes. Accounts receivable maintains the amounts owed by customers according to due date. Typical outputs of accounts receivable programs are customer invoices, invoice registers, aged accounts receivable reports (see Figure 10-17), and past due letters.

Accounts payable programs maintain data and produce documents concerning amounts owed by an organization to outside vendors. These systems provide for making payments on invoices, taking advantage of early payment discounts, estimating cash requirements, and maintaining cost center disbursements. Typical outputs include vendor checks and check registers, outstanding invoices report, cost center disbursements, and cash requirements reports (see Figure 10-18).

PAYROLL REGISTER
PERIOD ENDING 07/05/--

DATE 7/27/--
PAGE 5

PAY PERIOD 27

EMPL NO.	EMPLOYEE NAME / ITEM DESCRIPTION	PER.	GROSS EARNINGS	FEDERAL W/TAX	FICA TAX	STATE TAX	DESCRIPTION ACCT CD HOURS RATE	AMOUNTS
33104	D. GORDON							
	PREV YTD	26	5,325.68	1,065.14	234.33	53.27		
	SALARY	27					0314954	223.00
	ALLOWANCE	27					0314964	2.50
	SUMMARY	27	225.50	42.00	9.90	4.46	TOTAL TAX	56.36—
	HOSP INS	27					0314200	11.21—
	UNITED FND	27					0314210	1.00—
286-09-4549	NEW YTD	27	5,551.18	1,107.14	244.23	57.73	NET PAY	156.93
	DEPS. 03							
33126	J. GOSSELIN							
	PREV YTD	26	5,850.00	1,462.50	257.40	58.50		
	EARNINGS	27					0314854 40.0 5.72	228.80
	OVERTIME	27					0314874 2.0 5.72	22.88
	SUMMARY	27	251.68	62.97	11.08	2.52	TOTAL TAX	76.57—
	HOSP INS	27					0314200	5.80—
	CRED UNION	27					0314205	10.00—
	UNITED FND	27					0314210	4.00—
453-07-8877	NEW YTD	27	6,101.68	1,525.47	268.48	61.02	NET PAY	155.31
	DEPS. 01							
33148	G. GRAHAM							
	PREV YTD	26	6,219.96	1,243.99	273.68	62.20		
	EARNINGS	27					0314874 40.0 5.03	201.20
	SUMMARY	27	201.20	40.24	8.85	2.01	TOTAL TAX	51.10—
	HOSP INS	27					0314200	2.90—
	UNION DUES	27					0314215	5.00—
139-01-4113	NEW YTD	27	6,421.16	1,284.23	282.53	64.21	NET PAY	142.20
	DEPS. 02							

FINAL TOTALS CURRENT   61,931.85
FIT   11,012.71
FICA   2,420.68
STATE   6,193.19
OTHER   4,214.91
NET PAY   38,090.36

FIGURE 10-16
Outputs from a payroll system.

AGED ACCOUNTS RECEIVABLE REPORT
APRIL 15,198–

CUSTOMER NAME	INVOICE NUMBER	TOTAL OUT	< = 30 DAYS	31–60 DAYS	61–90 DAYS	> 90 DAYS
AMAX TOOL SUPPLY	608	806.00	806.00	0.00	0.00	0.00
	623	3203.27	3203.27	0.00	0.00	0.00
CUSTOMER TOTAL		4009.27	4009.27	0.00	0.00	0.00
BRANDON MILLING COMPANY	506	5601.63	0.00	0.00	5601.63	0.00
	610	1060.50	1060.50	0.00	0.00	0.00
CUSTOMER TOTAL		6662.13	1060.50	0.00	5601.63	0.00
BETTER TOOL SUPPLY COMPANY	475	2770.18	0.00	0.00	0.00	2770.18
	635	3567.75	3567.75	0.00	0.00	0.00
CUSTOMER TOTAL		6337.93	3567.75	0.00	0.00	2770.18
COLORADO TOOL & JIG	534	576.52	0.00	0.00	576.52	0.00
	591	8749.75	8749.75	0.00	0.00	0.00
CUSTOMER TOTAL		9326.27	8749.75	0.00	576.52	0.00
DENVER PATTERN MAKING	489	2291.36	0.00	0.00	0.00	2291.36
	495	2930.89	0.00	0.00	0.00	2930.89
CUSTOMER TOTAL		5222.25	0.00	0.00	0.00	5222.25

FIGURE 10-17
Outputs of an accounts receivable system.

CASH REQUIREMENTS REPORT
DEPARTMENT 1
APRIL 15, 198–

DUE DATE	VENDOR NO.	INVOICE NO.	TOTAL AMT.	DISCOUNT	PARTIAL PAYMENT	NET AMT.
4/30/8–	2	2005	8954.69	0.00	0.00	8954.69
3/01/8–	5	1032	423.72	0.00	0.00	423.72
2/12/8–	7	1015	894.56	0.00	0.00	894.56
			10272.97	0.00	0.00	10272.97

FIGURE 10-18
Outputs of an accounts payable system.

Inventory program packages maintain information required to control inventory levels and reorder inventory items. Inventory programs maintain stock status, year-to-date usage, on-order status, and inventory turnover figures. Output reports include inventory status reports (see Figure 10–19), distribution-by-value reports, and turnover reports.

INVENTORY STATUS REPORT

ITEM NO. DESCRIPTION	QUAN. ON HAND	QUAN. ON ORDER	TRANS-ACTION QUAN.	QUAN. B/O	AVG. UNIT COST	EX-TENDED COST	LAST RECEIPT	LAST ISSUE	MIN. BAL.	MAX. BAL.
411116 B500 TWINLITE SOCKET BLUE	458	500			.35	160.30			800	1600
ADJUSTMENT			42		.35	14.70				
RECEIPT			500		.37	185.00				
ISSUE			50—		.36	18.00—	2/11/--	2/14/--		
	950*				.36	342.00				
411122 B506 SOCKET ADAPTER BROWN	325				.19	61.75			300	800
ISSUE			20—		.19	3.80—				
ISSUE			38—		.19	7.22—				
ISSUE			10—		.19	1.90—	12/19/--	2/11/-- UNDER		
	257*				.19	48.83				
411173 C151C SILENT SWITCH IVORY	50	150			1.16	58.00			100	200
RECEIPT			150		1.20	180.00	2/10/--	2/03/--		
	200*				1.19	238.00				
411254 A210 PULL CORD GOLD	62	75			2.25	139.50			80	165
ISSUE			16		2.25	36.00				
ISSUE			30		2.25	67.50	11/17/--	2/10/--		
	16*	75			2.25	36.00				

FINAL TOTALS   BEG. INV 48295.26
CHANGE 700.08
NEW VALUE 48995.34

FIGURE 10–19
Outputs of an inventory system.

General ledger packages maintain a data base of financial information for a company. Typical documents and reports generated by the general ledger programs are journal listings, trial balances, income statements, and balance sheets (see Figure 10–20).

LAKE MACHINE TOOL COMPANY
BALANCE SHEET

APRIL 15
198–

ASSETS

CURRENT ASSETS
CASH	36840.34
ACCOUNTS RECEIVABLE	80600.00
INVENTORY	311888.30
MARKETABLE SECURITIES	50325.00
PREPAID EXPENSES	1100.00
TOTAL CURRENT ASSETS	480753.64

FIXED ASSETS
LAND	1128643.00
EQUIPMENT	145646.70
BUILDINGS	418787.84
TOTAL FIXED ASSETS	1693077.54

OTHER ASSETS
CASH VALUE INSURANCE	118093.00
INTANGIBLES	115953.00
TOTAL OTHER ASSETS	234046.00

TOTAL ASSETS   2407877.18

LIABILITIES & STKHLDR'S EQUITY

LIABILITIES

CURRENT LIABILITIES
BANK NOTE PAYABLE	9000.00
ACCOUNTS PAYABLE	17335.84
ACCRUED PAYROLL TAXES	97290.00
ACCRD PAYROLL DEDUCTIONS	9700.00
ACCRUED STATE & FED TAX	195273.00
ACCRUED OTHER EXPENSE	5100.00
CURRENT PORTION LTD	40000.00
TOTAL CURRENT LIABILITIES	373698.84

LONG TERM LIABILITIES
FIRST MORTGAGE BONDS	870000.00
TOTAL LONG TERM LIABILITIES	870000.00

TOTAL LIABILITIES	1243698.84
STOCKHOLDER'S EQUITY	
CAPITAL STOCK	175000.00
PAID IN CAPITAL	500000.00
RETAINED EARNINGS	489178.34
TOTAL STOCKHOLDER'S EQUITY	1164178.34
TOTAL LIABILITIES & STKHLDR'S EQUITY	2407877.18

FIGURE 10-20
Outputs of a general ledger system.

SUMMARY

Software is what makes a computer useful to an organization. Without software, a computer is a useless chunk of hardware. With improper or inefficient software, the best computer will fail to meet an organization's need for information.

As you have learned, a variety of high-level programming languages is available for developing application programs. The most important languages for business applications today are COBOL and RPG. Extended forms of BASIC are also used for these applications, and PASCAL (a structured programming language) is rapidly growing in popularity.

The selection of a programming language is an important decision for an organization. There are two reasons: application programs represent a large investment, and, once a language is chosen, it is generally impractical (or at least very expensive) to switch to another language.

There are two sources of application programs. They can be custom made, or they can be obtained as preprogrammed packages from vendors. Package programs are available for such common business applications as payroll, accounts receivable, inventory, and general ledger.

System software provides indispensable services for the user. The operating system coordinates and controls the operation of the computer. It schedules jobs, manages memory, and supervises multiprogramming operations, where the computer processes several jobs concurrently.

Data base management systems (DBMS) are important, relatively new types of system software that are used to establish, maintain, and protect data bases. Other important elements of system software are teleprocessing monitors and service programs.

ANSWERS TO EXERCISES

EXERCISE 10-1
1. a. N$
   b. N
   c. U
   d. U1
2. C
3. 0 (zero)

EXERCISE 10-2
1. a. STUDENT-FILE
   b. PRINT-FILE
2. STUDENT-NAME-IN
3. a. 24 alphanumeric characters
   b. 6 numeric characters
4. a. ADD UNITS-IN TO TOTAL-UNITS-IN.
   b. ADD UNITS-IN TO CUM-TOTAL.
   c. WRITE PRINT-REC FROM PRINT-LINE AFTER ADVANCING 1 LINE.

EXERCISE 10-3
1. a. NAME
   b. NUMB
   c. UNITS
   d. TUNITS
2. integer, 2
3. TOTAL

EXERCISE 10-4
1. a. UNITS
   b. TOTAL
   c. FTOTAL
2. a. Read the student name into the array called NAME, then write (or print out) the name
   b. Serves as a counter or index while reading up to 20 characters into the NAME array
3. a. RPG
   b. FORTRAN
   c. BASIC (PASCAL adherents may object!)
   d. COBOL
   e. PASCAL

CHAPTER EXAMINATION

1. Match each of the following terms to the most appropriate definition.

   ____ Compiler   a. Several programs executed concurrently

   ____ Operand   b. Translator for assembly language

   ____ Supervisor   c. Diversion of output to magnetic disk

   ____ Job control card   d. Software that controls flow of work

   ____ Multiprogramming   e. Translator for high-order languages

   ____ Assembler   f. Symbolic address

   ____ Spooling   g. Used to instruct the operating system

   ____ Operating system   h. Control programs in an operating system

2. Describe four disadvantages of programming in assembly language.

   a. _____

   b. _____

   c. _____

   d. _____

3. Identify the four generations of computer languages.

   a. _____

   b. _____

   c. _____

   d. _____

4. What programming language would be most appropriate for each of the following applications?

   a. Personnel data base applications _____

b. Statistical regression analysis _____

c. Variety of applications, structured programming environment _____

d. Generating simple financial reports on a small computer, including balance sheets and sources and

applications of funds _____

e. Introducing beginning students to time-sharing _____

5. What are the advantages of multiprogramming? _____

_____

_____

_____

6. Describe the three major functions performed by an operating system.

a. _____

b. _____

c. _____

7. What are the four steps in translating a source program?

a. _____

b. _____

c. _____

d. _____

8. Describe three objectives of systems programs.

a. _____

b. _____

c. _____

9. Briefly describe the functions of the supervisor in an on-line processing system. _____

_____

_____

_____

10. The data management languages proposed by the CODASYL Data Base Task Group consist of two separate languages. Describe each briefly.

a. _____

b. _____

11. Mark the following statements true or false.

____ a. A single assembly language instruction is generally equivalent to one machine language instruction.

____ b. An assembly language program is easier to read and interpret than one written in a high-level language.

____ c. Assembly language is a low-level language in which mnemonic symbols are used rather than binary-based notation.

____ d. A balance sheet is one output of an accounts payable system.

____ e. COBOL and RPG are high-order languages designed primarily for scientific applications.

____ f. PASCAL is highly suited to structured programming applications.

12. Give two examples of each of the following.

a. Business-oriented languages _____

_____

b. Scientific and engineering languages _____

_____

c. Time-sharing languages _____

_____

d. General-purpose languages _____

_____

13. Describe the function of each of the following.

a. Job card _____

_____

b. End-of-file card _____

_____

c. End-of-job card _____

_____

14. Describe two types of partitions in multiprogramming.

a. _____

_____

b. _____

_____

15. Describe four functions of a DBMS.

a. _____

b. _____

c. _____

d. _____

16. What is the purpose of a query language? _____

_____

_____

17. Describe the two basic types of applications programs.

a. _____

b. _____

18. List five typical package application programs. For each, list a typical output or report other than those illustrated in the chapter.

a. _____

b. _____

c. _____

d. _____

e. _____

19. List six advantages of the COBOL language.

a. _____

b. _____

c. _____

d. _____

e. _____

f. _____

20. List the four major types of specifications that appear in most RPG programs.

   a. _____

   b. _____

   c. _____

   d. _____

21. List one major disadvantage of each of the following languages.

   a. FORTRAN _____

   b. COBOL _____

   c. RPG _____

   d. PASCAL _____

   e. BASIC _____

22. Distinguish between the following terms.

   a. Input spooling versus output spooling

   _____

   _____

   b. Source program versus object program

   _____

   _____

   c. Assembler versus compiler

   _____

   _____

   d. Custom programs versus package programs

   _____

   _____

23. Briefly describe each of the following languages. For what type of application is each intended?

a. PL/1 _____

_____

b. APL _____

_____

c. ALGOL _____

_____

24. The number of partitions that can exist in a multiprogrammed computer depends on what factors?

a. _____

b. _____

25. List five data base management systems and the data structures each supports.

a. _____

b. _____

c. _____

d. _____

e. _____

11 THE PROGRAMMING TASK

OVERVIEW. Writing instructions in the code of a particular programming language is only part of the programming task. The programmer must first develop programmer-oriented flowcharts or decision tables depicting the logic of the system. After coding come debugging and testing. The total task is an exacting one.

Special techniques have been developed to facilitate the job of programming. *First,* the system designer documents system specifications in a format to expedite programming. System documentation consists of narrative description, data base layout, processing procedures, and input and output formats. *Second,* the task of program design is facilitated by use of standard programming concepts. *Third,* the tasks of coding and testing are facilitated by use of a high-level language in which syntax errors (errors in use of the language) are identified by the system during compilation. Other special software, such as trace routines, enables the programmer to isolate errors in coding.

In this chapter you will study these programmer aids and their role in the preparation of the complete programming package (program documentation): problem description, program abstract, program description, operating instructions, program controls, and test plan.

PLANNING THE PROGRAM

The documentation prepared by the system designer provides a general set of specifications for a computer program. Before the program is coded, the programmer must plan the program in detail and prepare detailed processing logic. The following steps are generally required.

1. Design the program. A structure chart is prepared, dividing the program into a series of logical subunits or modules.

2. Develop program logic charts showing the processing logic. For some programs the programmer may prepare several levels of logic charts—macro logic charts showing the overall logic and micro logic charts showing the detailed logic of each problem module.

3. Decide on the use of library functions, subroutines, subprograms, and other programming aids.

4. Plan for testing the program. This planning includes deciding on the test data and procedures to be used. There should be a test plan for each program module, as well as a system test for the entire program.

OUTPUT OF THE PROGRAMMING TASK

In addition to developing the program, the programmer is responsible for preparing the procedure for processing the program. An important part of this procedure is program documentation, a description of program contents and logic, to facilitate revision of the program. Revisions are not caused by poor program design but by inevitable changes in company circumstances. Also, once the users of a system become familiar with its operation they think of ways to improve it. Therefore, detailed program documentation is crucial for effective processing and efficient revision. The following sections are generally included in program documentation.

Section	Description
Problem description	A description of the problem to be solved by the program.
Program abstract	A brief description of the various tasks a program performs, the files used, and other miscellaneous information.
Program description	Detailed description of the program, including structure and logic charts and program listing. The listing should include a **data dictionary** showing the meaning of each variable (or data name) used in the program.
Operating instructions	Instructions to the computer operator on running the program.
Program controls	Summary of error controls built into the program.
Test plan	Documentation of the test plan and data used to test the program, record of changes made, and record of approvals.

STRUCTURED PROGRAM DESIGN

In recent years a major innovation has occurred in program design. Traditionally programs were designed using the **bottom-up** approach. Detailed **modules** were designed and programmed, then linked to other modules. Problems often occurred during the linking and testing phase because integration of modules was held off until late in the program development.

The new emphasis is the **top-down approach.** Program design begins by the planner's developing a chart showing overall structure of the system, with each level in the chart depicting progressively more detail. As each module is coded it is added to all other modules and tested. This method assures that the modules are integrated as development progresses.

IMPROVEMENTS PRODUCED BY STRUCTURED TECHNIQUES

Figure 11-1 shows the effect of top-down/structured programming on programming cost. Labor cost continues to accelerate while technological innovation reduces the cost of hardware. The accelerating cost of labor forced the industry to concentrate on ways to improve programming efficiency. Top-down/structured programming reversed the trend in programming cost. The downward swing in the curve began in the latter part of the 1970s and continues in the 1980s.

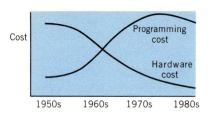

FIGURE 11-1
Reversal in the trend of programming cost resulting from top-down, structured programming and other new programming approaches. (The curve excludes inflationary effects.)

Examples of the improvement in efficiency are as follows.[1]

1. IBM Federal Systems Division: 40 percent average improvement over 20 projects.
2. McDonnell–Douglas Automaton Company: 36 percent improvement on first three projects.
3. Hughes Aircraft Company: 50 percent improvement on first two projects.

The principal benefit is simplification of the program so errors are easily detected and corrected. Traditionally, one bug per 200 lines of code is not detected until the system is put into operation. Use of structured methodology has reduced that error rate to one per 3000 lines of code.[2]

QUESTION: The average improvement in programming due to top-down/structured techniques experienced by these firms was _____ percent. (Compute the average for the three firms rather than the average for all projects.)

ANSWER: 42 percent

DEVELOPING STRUCTURE CHARTS   Figure 11-2 illustrates the first step in program design, developing an overall structure for the program. The program is separated into modules—one for each major function to be performed by the program. Modules are coded and tested, starting with the top and moving down the hierarchy.

Upon completion of the structure charts, the programmer begins conversion of system logic to detailed programming logic.

How does one go about developing a structure chart? Examine Figure 11-2 as we describe how a structure chart is developed.

[1]Ware Myers, "The Need for Software Engineering," *Tutorial: Software Management*, edited by D. J. Riefer, 1979, IEEE Computer Society, Long Beach, CA, pp. 273–286.
[2]F. Bauer, "Software and Software Engineering," *SIAM Review*, April, 1973, pp. 469–480.

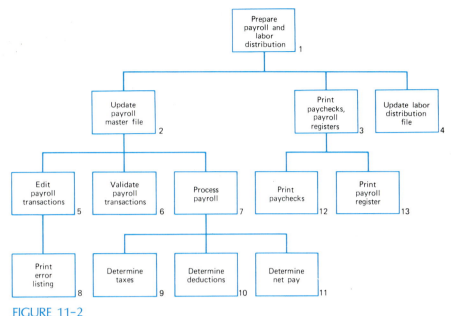

FIGURE 11–2
Structure chart, prepared as first step in program design.

MODULE 1:   The top module identifies the overall function performed by the system — to prepare payroll and use those data to validate labor costs in the cost accounting system. The second level of the structure chart (modules 2, 3, 4) separates the major functions of the payroll system.

MODULE 2:   UPDATE PAYROLL MASTER FILE   At the end of each pay period, all the payroll transactions are accumulated, entered into the system, and checked for accuracy. The payroll is processed. Upon completion of these activities, the master file for payroll is updated.

MODULE 3:   PRINT PAYCHECKS AND PAYROLL REGISTERS   After pay has been calculated for each employee, paychecks are printed. In addition, a payroll register is prepared. It serves as a record for the payroll department, in case questions arise, and for auditing purposes.

MODULE 4:   UPDATE LABOR DISTRIBUTION FILE   The results of payroll processing are also used as input to the labor distribution subsystem. Here, labor costs are allocated to various departments and/or products.

MODULES 5-13:   Subfunctions within the master file updating function are identified next. The editing subfunction consists of checking all transactions to make sure they are in the correct format, that is, entered in the right columns. The next subfunction is validation. This is a check to insure the data adhere to prescribed conditions or reasonableness limits. Examples are: checking to make sure a month is not numbered higher than a 12 or that regular pay hours are not greater than 40. Editing and validating of data may be broken down into other levels of detail, depending on the complexity of the system. For example, examining input to an atomic energy control system would have many more checks than that of a payroll system would.

MODULES 14-20: The number of modules in Figure 11-2 stops at 13. In actuality, the structure chart would be broken into many lower levels of detail. For example, module 10 (determine deductions) could be very complicated for some organizations. The company might allow employees to charge purchases at the company store, to borrow money from the credit union, to deduct for insurance premiums, and so on.

QUESTION: Every module on a structure chart includes the functions of input, processing, and output. Prove this to yourself by identifying those functions for module 12, print paychecks.

Input: _____

_____

Processing: _____

_____

Output: _____

_____

ANSWER: *Input:* The payroll file serves as input.
Processing: Printing paychecks is the processing activity.
Output: Paychecks are the output.

Upon completion of the structure charts, the programmer begins conversion of system logic to detailed programming logic. Flowcharts or decision tables, described in Chapter 12, are typically used to display detailed programming logic.

ASSIGNMENT OF RESPONSIBILITIES For a large program such as the payroll program in Figure 11-2, a team of programmers headed by a chief programmer is often assigned to the project. The **chief programmer** prepares the structure chart, deciding on the program modules to be used and the relationships between modules. The chief programmer then creates program specifications for the individual modules. Each module specification must be self-contained, describing fully the data to be used, the processing to be done, and module output. The quality of work done at this planning and design stage determines whether or not the system will be effective.

After the program planning is completed, the chief programmer designs each module. Program modules are then assigned to individual programmers for coding. The chief programmer may code the modules in the top of the hierarchy before assigning the remaining modules. He or she assists the programmers with any specification inconsistencies and provides technical support. The approach facilitates project scheduling and control. Figure 11-3 shows a simple schedule chart for the early modules in the payroll program.

Examine Figure 11-3. Note that, during the development process, as each module is debugged it is tested with the previously completed modules. This is called the **system test;** the system consists of all the program modules. The chief programmer is responsible for insuring that each of these ongoing system tests is successfully completed.

Week	1	2	3	4	5	6	7	8
Chief Programmer	Design, Code Module 1	Design, Code Module 2	Design Modules 3, 4	Design Modules 5, 6	Design Modules 7, 8		Design Modules 9, 10	
	Test Module 1	Test Module 2	Systems Test 1-2			Systems Test 1-4		Systems Test 1-6
Programmer A	Complete Work On Previous System			Code Module 3	Code Module 5		Code Module 7	
				Test Module 3	Systems Test 1-4		Test Module 5	Systems Test 1-6
Programmer B	Complete Work On Previous System			Code Module 4	Code Module 6		Code Module 8	
				Test Module 4	Systems Test 1-4		Test Module 6	Systems Test 1-6

FIGURE 11-3
Programming team schedule, with system test performed as each module is completed.

EXERCISE 11-1 Compare the schedule chart (Figure 11-3) to the structure chart (Figure 11-2). Answer the following questions.

1. The chief programmer is responsible for the following activities.

    a. _____

    _____

    b. _____

    _____

    c. _____

    _____

    d. _____

    _____

    e. _____

    _____

f.   _____

_____

2. Figure 11-3 was simplified by showing all modules completed successfully. By examining Figure 11-2, you can see that it might be more appropriate to assign module 8 to Programmer A rather than to Programmer B. Why?

_____

_____

3. Following the same logic as question 2, to whom would modules 9 to 11

be assigned for coding? _____

_____

4. Programmers are module testing and coding in parallel, because they can be coding the next module while the previous one is at the computer center for testing. The system tests are not performed in parallel with coding. Figure 11-3 shows that all other work stops while each system test is performed. Although the reason was not stated specifically in the text,

you can probably deduce the reason. Why? _____

_____

_____

STRUCTURED PROGRAMMING PROCEDURES
The principal contribution of structured programming is the concept that any program can be written using only three logical structures. By simplifying the structure of programs, we make them easier to code and to test. And, because of their simplicity of structure, these programs are easier to modify when revision is necessary. The three structures are as follows.

1. **Simple sequence:** The program structure consists of execution of functions in sequence, as illustrated below.

2. **Selection:** The program execution branches in either of two directions, based on results of testing a condition, as illustrated below.

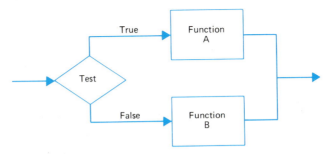

3. **Repetition:** The program continues to cycle through one or more functions until a condition is met, illustrated as follows.

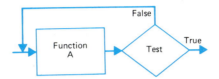

EXAMPLES   An example will be provided to illustrate each of the three logical structures. Assume an investor has $5000 to invest. She is considering several investment alternatives. She has decided that she wants her initial capital to double in at least five years and is trying to determine what interest rate will produce that result.

The compounding formula is

$$c = p(1 + r)^n$$

where

c = compounded principal
p = starting principal
r = rate of interest
n = number of years

We could rewrite the formula to solve for r in one computation. However, we will use a different solution approach to illustrate the three programming structures. The sample program contains all three structures, which is typical. Figure 11-4 shows the programming steps to produce the solution. The three types of structures are identified by dotted lines.

The first two functions are performed in sequence, therefore representing sequence structure. Processing the next set of logic involves cycling through the two functions and the test. If the starting rate of interest (arbitrarily set at 9 percent) does not produce $10,000 in five years, the rate is incremented by one-tenth of one percent. The compounding is reaccomplished at the higher rate. This repetition goes on until the test shows that c has reached $10,000 and the processing moves into the third structure, selection. In that block of logic, the computed interest rate is compared to the maximum rate that the market would provide at the time of investment. The investor would then choose an investment alternative.

QUESTION: Use of only three programming structures facilitated both the development and testing of programs because they _____ the structures used in programming.

ANSWER: simplified

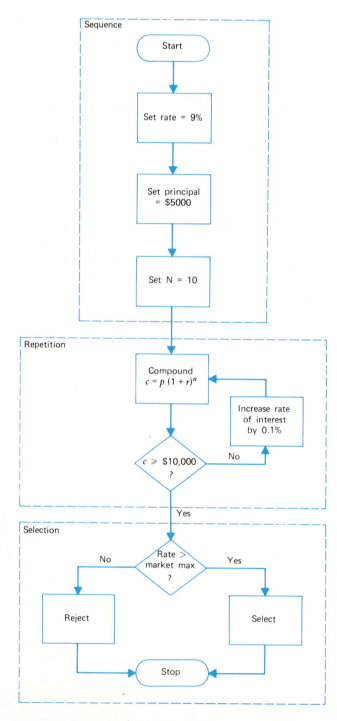

FIGURE 11-4
Examples of the three programming structures applied to a compounding principal problem.

Two other rules were established for developing structured programs.

1. Each module is designed to accomplish a single, well-defined task — for example, edit data from an input record, or format an error message.
2. Only one entry and only one exit are permitted per module.

These rules limit both the size and complexity of modules. Therefore, development and testing are simplified.

QUESTION: The three principal rules of structured programming are:

1) Use of _____

2) A single _____

3) Only one _____

ANSWER: only 3 logical structures, well-defined task, entry and exit per module

---

CODING THE PROGRAM

After program planning has been completed, the computer program is ready to be coded. **Coding** is the process of writing a sequence of computer instructions to accomplish a desired task. As described in Chapter 10, a program may be coded in a low-level language. Most business applications are programmed in a higher-level language such as COBOL, FORTRAN, or PL/1.

Instructions are generally entered on preprinted coding paper, which assists the programmer in following the correct format for the language being used. For example, Figure 11–5 shows a program coded on a FORTRAN coding sheet. This program, which locates and prints out the largest of five numbers, will be used as an illustration in the remainder of this chapter. Don't try to comprehend the program at this point — you need further explanation. However, without further explanation you can see that the program contains all the elements of a complete module: input, processing, and output.

QUESTION: Observe Figure 11–5. The FORTRAN statements for input and output begin with what words?

1) Input = _____

2) Output = _____

ANSWER: READ, WRITE

IMPROVING PROGRAM DOCUMENTATION

When the program coding is completed, the program is translated (assembled or compiled) into machine language instructions by the computer. The computer translator produces a listing of the program coded by the programmer. This program listing is one of the best (and most frequently used) sources of program documentation.

Higher-level languages produce better documentation than low-level languages, since the high-level languages are problem- or procedure-oriented,

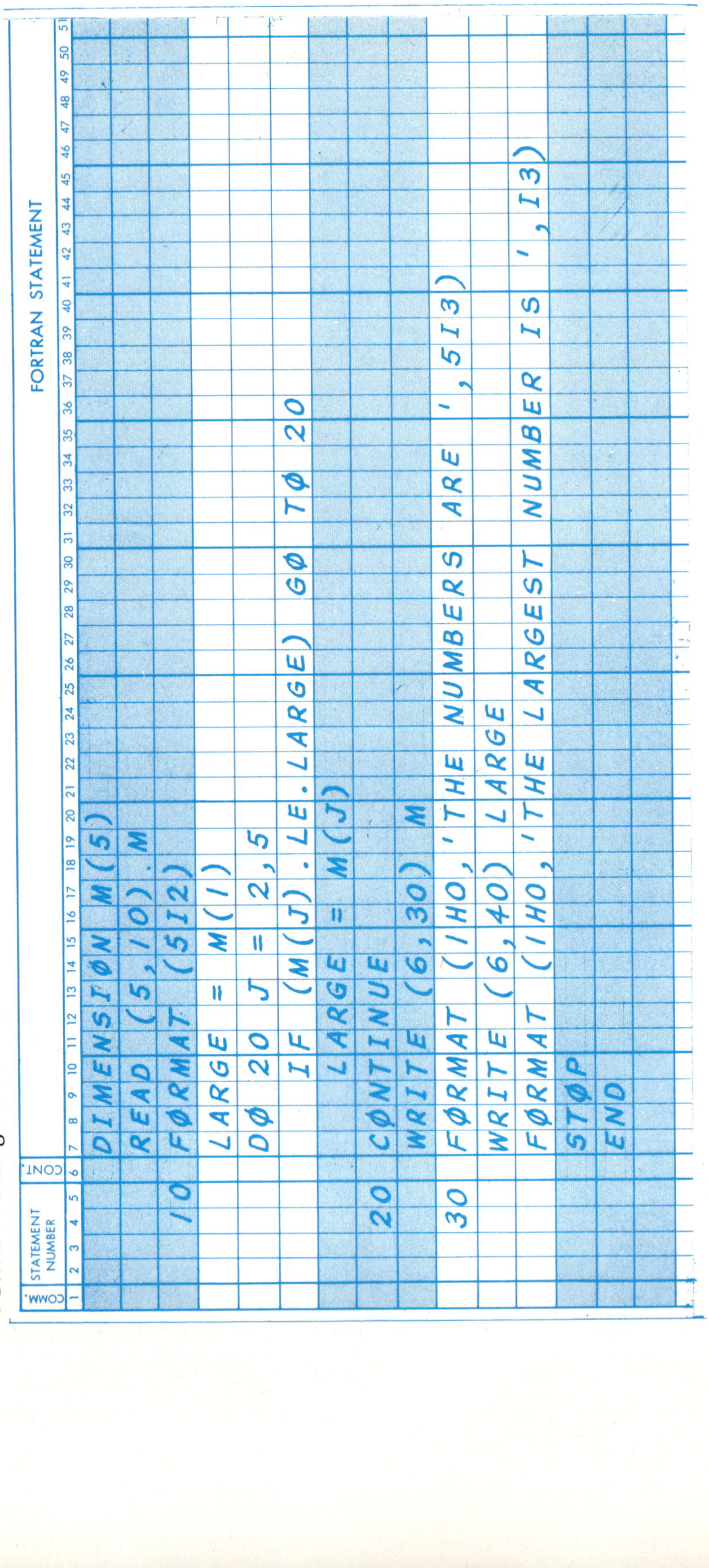

FIGURE 11-5
FORTRAN coding sheet.

COMM.	STATEMENT NUMBER	CONT.	FORTRAN STATEMENT
			DIMENSION M(5)
			READ (5,10) M
	10		FORMAT (5I2)
			LARGE = M(1)
			DO 20 J = 2,5
			IF (M(J).LE.LARGE) GO TO 20
			LARGE = M(J)
	20		CONTINUE
			WRITE (6,30) M
	30		FORMAT (1HO,'THE NUMBERS ARE ',5I3)
			WRITE (6,40) LARGE
			FORMAT (1HO,'THE LARGEST NUMBER IS ',I3)
			STOP
			END

rather than computer-oriented. COBOL programs are particularly easy to read, since COBOL is an English-like language.

The programmer can improve program documentation by following good coding practice. For example, most programming languages permit the insertion of notes or comments at any point in a program, to explain the purpose of a given segment of coding. Such comments are a valuable aid when the programmer (or someone else) must read the program several weeks or months after it was coded.

The use of comments in a program is illustrated in Figure 11-6. This FORTRAN program (introduced in Figure 11-5) computes and prints out the largest of five numbers. Even the reader who is not familiar with FORTRAN can follow the logic of the program, aided by the comment statements (which begin with the letter C in the first column).

QUESTION: Examine Figure 11-6 and answer the following questions.

a. Briefly state the purpose of the program _____

_____

_____

b. Complete the data dictionary.

M _____

LARGE _____

c. Look at the output. Did the program identify the largest number? _____

ANSWER: a. Compares numbers and prints largest.
b. M — the array in which the numbers are stored
     LARGE — the largest number in the array.
c. Yes; it identified the number 9.

USING LIBRARY ROUTINES

Programming may be considerably simplified by the use of precoded **library routines.** Many programming language systems include a library of routines for solving common computational problems, such as inverting a matrix or obtaining the square root of a number. Some of these routines are included in the manufacturer-supplied software systems, whereas others are coded by the customer.

Two types of library routines are commonly used: open subroutines and closed subroutines. An **open subroutine** is copied into the main program whenever it is referenced by the programmer. For example, if the programmer references a particular subroutine at three different points in a program, the same section of coding is inserted in the program at three different locations. The open subroutine format is generally used for relatively short sections of coding.

In contrast, a **closed subroutine** is stored once as a separate program in computer memory. Each time the programmer references a closed subroutine, information is "passed" to the subroutine for computation, and results are "passed" back to the main program. This is accomplished by means of **linkages** between the two programs. Closed subroutines are used for more extensive computations and are extremely important in programming.

The distinction between open and closed subroutines is illustrated in Figure 11-7.

FIGURE 11-6
FORTRAN program with comments.

```
            PROGRAM LARGEST(INPUT,OUTPUT,TAPE5=INPUT,TAPE6=OUTPUT)
      C******************************************************************
      C***THIS ROUTINE READS FIVE NUMBERS FROM A CARD               ***
      C***THE FIRST NUMBER IS IN COLUMNS 1 AND 2. THE SECOND IN COLUMNS 3 AND
      C***4,AND SO ON.                                              ***
      C***IT THEN COMPUTES AND PRINTS OUT THE LARGEST OF THE FIVE NUMBERS. ***
      C******************************************************************
      C***VARIABLE NAMES ARE THE FOLLOWING                          ***
      C***M--ARRAY IN WHICH THE FIVE NUMBERS ARE STORED            ***
      C***LARGE--LARGEST VALUE ENCOUNTERED IN THE ARRAY M          ***
      C******************************************************************
      C***DIMENSION THE ARRAY M
            DIMENSION M(5)
      C***READ THE NUMBERS INTO M
            READ (5,10) M
000003    10 FORMAT (5I2)
000003
000011
      C***SET LARGE EQUAL TO THE FIRST NUMBER. THEN EXAMINE THE REMAINING
      C***NUMBERS, SETTING LARGE EQUAL TO ANY NUMBER WHICH IS GREATER THAN
      C***THE CURRENT VALUE.
000011       LARGE = M(1)
000013       DO 20 J = 2,5
000014          IF (M(J).LE.LARGE) GO TO 20
000017             LARGE = M(J)
000020    20 CONTINUE
      C***PRINT OUT THE FIVE NUMBERS.
000022       WRITE (6,30) M
000030    30 FORMAT (1H0,*THE NUMBERS ARE *,5I3)
      C***PRINT OUT THE LARGEST NUMBER. THEN TERMINATE THE PROGRAM.
000030       WRITE (6,40) LARGE
000036    40 FORMAT (1H0,*THE LARGEST NUMBER IS *,I3)
000036       STOP
000040       END


THE NUMBERS ARE   8   5   1   9   3

THE LARGEST NUMBER IS   9
```

The left side shows how open subroutines are handled. The program is "opened" and a copy of the subroutine is inserted into the program each place where it is used (that is, after each "call" for its use). The right side illustrates a closed subroutine. Instead of a copy of the subroutine being inserted, a linkage is set up to branch to the subroutine and then return to the main program after the subroutine function has been executed.

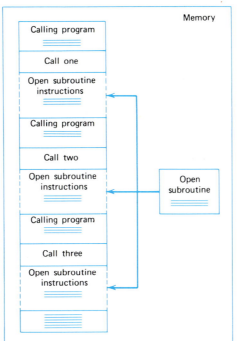

FIGURE 11-7
Comparison of open and closed subroutines.

QUESTION: Examine Figure 11-7. After a closed subroutine is executed, control is returned

to what point in the main program? _____

ANSWER: the instruction immediately following the subroutine call

EXERCISE 11-2   1.   Explain whether each of the following is an open or closed subroutine.
a.   The FORTRAN function subprogram SQRT (for square root), which is inserted into a FORTRAN program each time it is referenced by a programmer

b.   A programmer-coded FORTRAN subroutine subprogram called MATINV (for matrix inversion), which is stored in memory as a separate program

2. Examine Figure 11-6 again. From the comments included in the program, explain the function of each of the following statements.

a. READ (5,10) M _____

b. LARGE = M(1) _____

c. IF (M(J).LE.LARGE) GO TO 20 _____

d. LARGE = M(J) _____

TESTING AND DEBUGGING THE PROGRAM

Programming is an exacting task. Even the smallest error in coding a program will usually cause the program either to produce incorrect results or not to run at all. Careful planning and coding will reduce errors; however, a program rarely runs perfectly the first time it is tried. The program must be tested and errors (bugs) removed. The process of removing errors is called **debugging.** Figure 11-8 identifies some of the problems associated with debugging a program. This somewhat humorous set of "laws" was developed to depict the problems and effects of bugs on a program.

Debugging is both perplexing and time consuming. If you ever become involved in debugging a nontrivial program, you will be convinced of the value of spending more time on program design for your next program. Nevertheless, the typical programmer writes a program that has a few errors. There are two principal types of errors that occur in coding computer programs.

1. Syntax errors—errors in usage of the programming language.
2. Logical errors—errors in programming logic.

SYNTAX ERRORS

Every programming language has a set of rules concerning format, spelling, punctuation, naming of variables, and other conventions that must be observed by the programmer. An error in usage of the language (similar to a spelling or punctuation error) is often referred to as a **syntax error.**

An example of a syntax error in a computer program is shown in Figure 11-9. This program is identical to the one shown in Figure 11-6 except for a syntax error in the statement at line 000014.

QUESTION: Compare Figures 11-6 and 11-9 and identify the syntax error in the statement at line 000014.

Incorrect statement _____

Correct statement _____

ANSWER: Incorrect: IF (M(J) LE LARGE) GO TO 20
Correct: IF (M(J).LE.LARGE) GO TO 20

(FORTRAN syntax requires that a logical comparison be separated from variables by periods.)

Definition	A "working" program is one that has only unobserved bugs.
Law I	Every nontrivial program has at least one bug.
Corollary I	A sufficient condition for program triviality is that it have no bugs.
Corollary II	At least one bug will be observed after the author leaves the organization
Law II	The subtlest bugs cause the greatest damage or problems.
Corollary I	A subtle bug will modify storage, thereby masquerading as some other problem.
Law III	Bugs will appear in one part of a working program when another "unrelated" part is modified.
Law IV	(Lulled-into-Security Law). A "debugged" program that crashed will wipe out source files on storage devices when there is the least available backup.
Law V	A hardware failure will cause system software to crash, and the CE (computer company's customer engineer) will blame the programmers.
Law VI	A system software crash will cause hardware to act strangely, and the programmers will blame the CE.
Law VII	The documented interfaces between standard software modules will have undocumented quirks.
Law VIII	The probability of a hardware failure's disappearing is inversely proportional to the distance between the computer and the CE.
Law IX	Murphy designed the computer in your organization.
Law X	(O'Shea's Law) Murphy was an optimist.

(NOTE: For those who may be in doubt, Murphy's Law states that if anything can go wrong, it will — and always at the most inconvenient time).

FIGURE 11–8
The Laws of Programming (author unknown).

Errors in usage are normally detected during translation by the assembler or compiler. The program generally will not run, but instead an error message called a **diagnostic** will be printed for each error that is detected. The diagnostic will indicate the nature of the error and the location (line number) in the program where it was detected.

QUESTION: Examine Figure 11–9 again. The FORTRAN diagnostic that was printed is the following:

Diagnostic _____

Line Number _____

ANSWER: IMPROPER LOGICAL EXP. WITHIN LOGICAL IF STMT (line 000014)

LOGICAL ERRORS   Although the compiler (or assembler) will detect syntax errors, it will *not* detect errors in programming logic. Thus a program with an error-free listing may still

```
          PROGRAM LARGEST(INPUT,OUTPUT,TAPE5=INPUT,TAPE6=OUTPUT)
      C*********************************************************************
      C***THIS ROUTINE READS FIVE NUMBERS FROM A CARD
      C***THE FIRST NUMBER IS IN COLUMNS 1 AND 2. THE SECOND IN COLUMNS 3 AND
      C***4,AND SO ON.
      C***IT THEN COMPUTES AND PRINTS OUT THE LARGEST OF THE FIVE NUMBERS.
      C*********************************************************************
      C***VARIABLE NAMES ARE THE FOLLOWING
      C*****M--ARRAY IN WHICH THE FIVE NUMBERS ARE STORED
      C*****LARGE--LARGEST VALUE ENCOUNTERED IN THE ARRAY M
      C*********************************************************************
      C***DIMENSION THE ARRAY M
000003          DIMENSION M(5)
      C***READ THE NUMBERS INTO M
000003          READ (5,10) M
000011       10 FORMAT (5I2)
      C***SET LARGE EQUAL TO THE FIRST NUMBER. THEN EXAMINE THE REMAINING
      C***NUMBERS, SETTING LARGE EQUAL TO ANY NUMBER WHICH IS GREATER THAN
      C***THE CURRENT VALUE.
000011          LARGE = M(1)
000013          DO 20 J = 2,5
000014          IF (M(J) LE LARGE) GO TO 20
***LXF**********
000015          LARGE = M(J)
000017       20 CONTINUE
      C***PRINT OUT THE FIVE NUMBERS.
000021          WRITE (6,30) M
000026       30 FORMAT (1H0,*THE NUMBERS ARE *,5I3)
      C***PRINT OUT THE LARGEST NUMBER, THEN TERMINATE THE PROGRAM.
000026          WRITE (6,40) LARGE
000034       40 FORMAT (1H0,*THE LARGEST NUMBER IS *,I3)
000034          STOP
000036          END


LX********IMPROPER LOGICAL EXP. WITHIN LOGICAL IF STMT
     000014
```

FIGURE 11-9
FORTRAN program with syntax error.

contain logical errors that produce incorrect results or cause the program to be aborted during execution.

An example of a logical program error is shown in Figure 11-10. This program is the same program (to compare and print out the largest of five numbers) as that of Figures 11-6 and 11-9. However, the logical IF statement at line 000014 has been reversed.

Correct Statement Figure 11-6	*Statement in Figure 11-10*
IF (M(J).LE.LARGE) GO TO 20	IF (LARGE.LE.M(J)) GO TO 20

As a result of this logical error, the program compares the five numbers and prints out the *smallest* instead of the largest as intended. Notice that the program listing contains no diagnostic message to warn the programmer of this error and that the program runs and produces output. Only by careful testing (using methods discussed in the next section) can this type of error be detected.

A logical program error will lead to one of two results.

1. The program will produce incorrect results but terminate normally, as in Figure 11-10.

```
        PROGRAM LARGEST(INPUT,OUTPUT,TAPE5=INPUT,TAPE6=OUTPUT)
C************************************************************************
C***THIS ROUTINE READS FIVE NUMBERS FROM A CARD
C***THE FIRST NUMBER IS IN COLUMNS 1 AND 2. THE SECOND IN COLUMNS 3 AND
C***4,AND SO ON.
C***IT THEN COMPUTES AND PRINTS OUT THE LARGEST OF THE FIVE NUMBERS.
C************************************************************************
C***VARIABLE NAMES ARE THE FOLLOWING
C*****M--ARRAY IN WHICH THE FIVE NUMBERS ARE STORED
C*****LARGE--LARGEST VALUE ENCOUNTERED IN THE ARRAY M
C************************************************************************
            C***DIMENSION THE ARRAY M
000003           DIMENSION M(5)
            C***READ THE NUMBERS INTO M
000003           READ (5,10) M
000011        10 FORMAT (5I2)
            C***SET LARGE EQUAL TO THE FIRST NUMBER. THEN EXAMINE THE REMAINING
            C***NUMBERS, SETTING LARGE EQUAL TO ANY NUMBER WHICH IS GREATER THAN
            C***THE CURRENT VALUE.
000011           LARGE = M(1)
000013           DO 20 J = 2,5
000014           IF (LARGE.LE.M(J)) GO TO 20
000017              LARGE = M(J)
000020        20 CONTINUE
            C***PRINT OUT THE FIVE NUMBERS.
000022           WRITE (6,30) M
000030        30 FORMAT (1H0,*THE NUMBERS ARE *,5I3)
            C***PRINT OUT THE LARGEST NUMBER, THEN TERMINATE THE PROGRAM.
000030           WRITE (6,40) LARGE
000036        40 FORMAT (1H0,*THE LARGEST NUMBER IS *,I3)
000036           STOP
000040           END

THE NUMBERS ARE   8  5  1  9  3

THE LARGEST NUMBER IS    1
```

FIGURE 11-10
FORTRAN program with logic error.

2. An unusual condition will be encountered that leads to early termination of the program, as in Figure 11-9. Other conditions that can be diagnosed during compilation are as follows.
   a. The program may contain an endless loop, in which case the operating system should terminate the program after a prescribed time has elapsed.
   b. The program (and data used by the program) may lead to an impossible or unacceptable operation, such as division by zero. In such cases, the operating system generally prints out an error message and terminates the program. Such messages are termed **execution-time** (or **run-time**) **error** messages, in contrast to the diagnostics printed out by the compiler during **compile time.**

PROGRAM TESTING

There are several stages in testing a program.

1. Desk checking.
2. Compiler or assembler system checking.
3. Program run with hypothetical data.

4. Diagnostic procedures, if needed.

5. Full-scale test with actual data.

DESK CHECKING

The programmer should carefully check each step in coding a program. When the program is completed, the programmer should manually step through the program using sample data, to insure that the logic is correct. The program should also be reviewed by another programmer or by the programming supervisor before it is released for keypunching.

Careful **desk checking** is an often neglected aspect of program testing. Too often the programmer follows the faulty maxim, "Let the compiler do the checking." Unfortunately the compiler is unable to detect logical errors, and such errors may be missed in subsequent testing stages.

QUESTION: Manual checking of a program before it is keypunched or entered into the computer is called _____

ANSWER: desk checking

COMPILER SYSTEM CHECKING

After the program has been desk checked, it is keyentered and submitted for compilation (or assembly, if an assembly language has been used). As indicated earlier, syntax errors are detected during this stage and indicated by diagnostics. The programmer corrects these errors and resubmits the program, until an error-free listing is obtained.

RUN WITH HYPOTHETICAL TEST DATA

When the steps above are completed, the programmer should conduct several trial runs of the program using hypothetical test data. The results to be expected from each set of test data should be known. For example, in the program of Figure 11–6 the test data consisted of the numbers 8, 5, 1, 9, 3; it was known in advance that the correct output would be 9, the largest of these numbers.

The test data should include all important variations in input data, including data with errors. This will test the handling of error conditions by the program. Also, all of the paths in the processing logic should be tested. There are "checked-out" programs that have produced correct output for months or even years, only to produce erroneous output when a previously unused condition or path is encountered.

QUESTION: Is the input data used in the program of Figure 11–6 adequate for a comprehensive test of this program? State your reason why or why not. _____

ANSWER: No; the data does not test all possible conditions. For example, what happens if one of the numbers is zero or negative?

DIAGNOSTIC PROCEDURES

Sometimes a program does not run correctly, but the logical errors in the program are difficult to find. This often happens in complex programs. In such cases various diagnostic procedures may be used, depending on the programming language and compiler being used.

A common diagnostic procedure makes use of a program called a **trace routine.** Such a routine prints out the results of key processing steps in the program being tested, such as the value of selected variables and indication of various paths taken in the program. If a trace routine is not available, the programmer may insert temporary instructions in the program to print out results at critical points.

It is a good programming practice where possible to print out information read into a program, to insure that the program is reading data as intended. More errors occur on data input than at any other processing phase. In the program shown in Figure 11-6 the numbers read into the computer are printed out as part of the output, even though only the largest of these numbers is required.

TEST WITH ACTUAL DATA

Programs for data processing are typically run in parallel with the existing system for a short time to insure acceptable system performance. This test is made using actual input data, for example, payroll data. The parallel test is part of the implementation phase of the system development cycle and is discussed in greater detail in Part Four.

EXERCISE 11-3

1. In desk checking a program, the programmer manually "steps through" his program using sample data. Refer to Figure 11-6. Assume the following data have been correctly read into the array M.

Position (J)	Value M(J)
1	8
2	5
3	1
4	9
5	3

Step through the program in Figure 11-6 and complete the following.

a. LARGE $= M(1) = $ _____
   $J = 2$

b. Is M(J) less than or equal to LARGE? _____

c. GO TO _____
   $J = 3$

d. Is M(J) less than or equal to LARGE? _____

e. GO TO _____
   $J = 4$

f. Is M(J) less than or equal to LARGE? _____

g. LARGE $= M($_____$) = $ _____
   $J = 5$

h. Is M(J) less than or equal to LARGE? _____

i. GO TO _____
   Print out results and terminate the program.

2. Run the program of Figure 11-6 to determine if it will produce correct
   results when one of the numbers is negative. To do this, keypunch the
   program (to simplify the keypunching, all comment cards my be omitted).
   You'll need a set of control cards to precede your FORTRAN program.
   Ask your instructor about job cards for your school's computer system.
   Use the following input test data: 8, −5, 1, 9, 3.

   Does the program produce the correct output for these data? _____

SUMMARY

Program preparation is the second major phase in the system development
cycle, which includes system analysis and design, programming, and implementation. System documentation provides the specifications for each computer
program. The major steps in program preparation are program planning, coding, testing and debugging, and documentation. Documentation is the preparation of a program description, so it can be modified when changes occur in
the system. The overall flow of events in program preparation is shown in Figure 11-11.

FIGURE 11-11
Steps in program preparation.

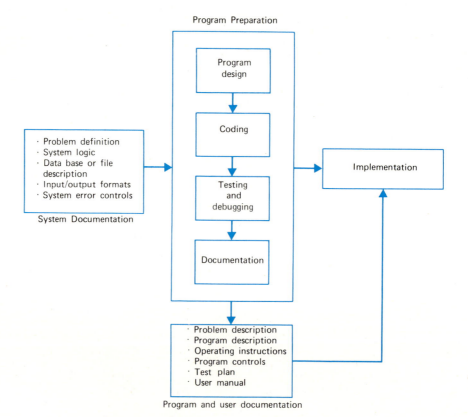

ANSWERS TO EXERCISES

EXERCISE 11-1

1. a. Developing the structure chart
   b. Creating program specifications for each module
   c. Designing all program modules
   d. Coding modules at the top of the hierarchy (typically done, but sometimes assigned to other programmers)
   e. Supervising ongoing system tests
   f. Assisting other programmers

2. Programmer A coded the module for editing payroll transactions. Printing the error listing as a result of editing (update 8) is a function closely related to module 3.

3. Programmer A, because that programmer was assigned the coding of the next higher module to which these three modules are most directly related.

4. All modules are tested simultaneously so all programmers who coded them are involved. Also, the complexity of the system test is such that all programmers are typically needed to insure that the test is complete and valid.

EXERCISE 11-2

1. a. open   b. closed

2. a. Read five numbers into the array M.
   b. Set the variable LARGE equal to the first number stored in the array M.
   c. If the number stored in position J of the array M is less than or equal to the number stored in LARGE, go to statement number 20.
   d. Set LARGE equal to M(J).

EXERCISE 11-3

1. a. 8   d. yes   g. M(4), 9
   b. yes   e. 20   h. yes
   c. 20   f. no   i. 20

2. Yes. The program is shown below.

```
          PROGRAM LARGEST(INPUT,OUTPUT,TAPE5=INPUT,TAPE6=OUTPUT)
       C*****************************************************************
       C***THIS ROUTINE READS FIVE NUMBERS FROM A CARD
       C***THE FIRST NUMBER IS IN COLUMNS 1 AND 2, THE SECOND IN COLUMNS 3 AND
       C***4,AND SO ON.
       C***IT THEN COMPUTES AND PRINTS OUT THE LARGEST OF THE FIVE NUMBERS.
       C*****************************************************************
       C***VARIABLE NAMES ARE THE FOLLOWING
       C*****M--ARRAY IN WHICH THE FIVE NUMBERS ARE STORED
       C*****LARGE--LARGEST VALUE ENCOUNTERED IN THE ARRAY M
       C*****************************************************************
       C***DIMENSION THE ARRAY M
000003         DIMENSION M(5)
       C***READ THE NUMBERS INTO M
000003         READ (5,10) M
000011      10 FORMAT (5I2)
       C***SET LARGE EQUAL TO THE FIRST NUMBER. THEN EXAMINE THE REMAINING
       C***NUMBERS, SETTING LARGE EQUAL TO ANY NUMBER WHICH IS GREATER THAN
       C***THE CURRENT VALUE.
000011         LARGE = M(1)
000013         DO 20 J = 2,5
000014            IF (M(J).LE.LARGE) GO TO 20
000017            LARGE = M(J)
000020      20 CONTINUE
       C***PRINT OUT THE FIVE NUMBERS.
000022         WRITE (6,30) M
000030      30 FORMAT (1H0,*THE NUMBERS ARE *,5I3)
       C***PRINT OUT THE LARGEST NUMBER. THEN TERMINATE THE PROGRAM.
000030         WRITE (6,40) LARGE
000036      40 FORMAT (1H0,*THE LARGEST NUMBER IS *,I3)
000036         STOP
000040         END

THE NUMBERS ARE    8  -5   1   9   3

THE LARGEST NUMBER IS    9
```

CHAPTER EXAMINATION

1. Match each of the following terms to the most appropriate definition.

   ____ Program abstract   a.   Depict overall structure of program

   ____ Data dictionary   b.   Used for diagnosing errors

   ____ Chief programmer   c.   Compiled as a separate program

   ____ Open subroutine   d.   Brief description of program

   ____ Closed subroutine   e.   Program produces incorrect results

   ____ Syntax error   f.   Simplifies coding and testing

   ____ Debugging   g.   Description of variables used

   ____ Logical error   h.   Inserted in program whenever referenced

   ____ Diagnostic   i.   Error in usage of langauge

   ____ Trace routine   j.   Designs each program module

   ____ Structure charts   k.   Error message during compilation

   ____ Top-down program design   l.   Removing program errors

   ____ Coding   m.   Writing computer instructions

2. List four steps in planning a computer program.

   a. _____

   b. _____

   c. _____

   d. _____

3. Identify the programming structure used to accomplish the following logic.

   a. _____ structure   Step 1. $A = B + C$
                                           Step 2. $E = B - 7$
                                           Step 3. $F = A \div E$

b. _____ structure   Step 1. X = Y + Z
                              Step 2. If X is negative, multiply it by 2; otherwise, divide it by 4

c. _____ structure   Step 1. C = B + 2
                              Step 2. Repeat step 1 until C = 12; then add F to C, producing G.

4. What are two rules for developing structured programs?

   a. _____
      _____
      _____

   b. _____
      _____

5. Suppose that a FORTRAN program has been keypunched and is ready for compilation and trial run with test data. Indicate whether the following program errors are most likely to result in (1) compiler diagnostic, (2) abnormal termination with run-time error message, or (3) normal termination with incorrect results produced.

   ____ a. Programmer uses variable name GROSSPROFIT, which exceeds the allowable length for a FORTRAN variable name.

   ____ b. Program attempts to divide by zero.

   ____ c. Program computes the area of a rectangle by adding length to width, instead of multiplying.

   ____ d. Programmer fails to include a program check to determine whether the amount of a payroll check is reasonable, in case erroneous payroll data is read into the computer.

   ____ e. Multiplication leads to a number that exceeds the computer word size.

   ____ f. Programmer omits a right parentheses in a FORMAT statement.

6. Explain why a structured program (compared to a nonstructured program).

   a. Generally reduces coding time. _____
      _____

   b. Is easier to test and debug. _____
      _____

   c. Is less complex. _____
      _____

   d. Is easier to maintain and modify. _____
      _____

7. Explain the difference between the following.

    a. Syntax errors versus logical errors _____

    _____

    _____

    _____

    b. Open subroutines versus closed subroutines _____

    _____

    _____

    _____

    c. Compile time versus execution time _____

    _____

8. List six advantages of structured programming.

    a. _____

    b. _____

    c. _____

    d. _____

    e. _____

    f. _____

9. List five functions of a chief programmer in developing a large structured program.

    a. _____

    b. _____

    c. _____

    d. _____

    e. _____

10. Mark the following statements true or false.

    ____ a. Documentation is generally prepared after programming has been completed.

    ____ b. Structured programming involves dividing large programs into a number of small self-contained units, or modules.

____ c. Although structured programming tends to reduce errors and simplify testing, it generally requires more planning time than conventional programming.

____ d. Liberal use of comment statements can improve program documentation.

____ e. Closed subroutines are copied into the main program each time they are called in the program.

____ f. The process of removing program errors is called tracing.

____ g. The compiler will generally detect logical program errors during translation.

____ h. A program with a logical error may terminate normally.

11. Indicate whether each of the following would be found in (1) program abstract, (2) program description, (3) program controls, or (4) test plan.

____ a. Structure and logic charts   ____ d. File descriptions

____ b. Program listing   ____ e. Data for testing the program

____ c. Data dictionary   ____ f. Description of controls built into the system

12. List four techniques that help the programmer prepare a computer program.

a. _____

b. _____

c. _____

d. _____

13. List five steps in testing a program.

a. _____

b. _____

c. _____

d. _____

e. _____

14. Describe two possible results when a logical program error is encountered.

a. _____

_____

b. _____

_____

15. List four steps in preparing a computer program (see Figure 11–11).

    a. _____

    b. _____

    c. _____

    d. _____

16. A syntax error _____
    a. if present will prevent the program from being run.
    b. will cause an error message called a diagnostic to be printed.
    c. is an error in the use of a programming language.
    d. all of the above.

17. Define the following terms.

    a. Coding _____

    b. Calling program _____

    c. Desk checking _____

    d. Documentation _____

    e. Murphy's Law _____

    f. Structured programming _____

18. How has system testing changed with the introduction of the top-down-structured approach? _____

    _____

    _____

19. In the three representative companies,
    a. What was the least amount of improvement on efficiency through the change to top-down-structured

       techniques? _____
    b. Traditionally one bug in 200 lines of code was not detected until the system was put into operation.

       Structured techniques reduced the error rate to one per _____ lines of code.

20. Examine the structure chart (Figure 11–2) and answer the following questions.

    a. Why was module 3 (print) not placed under module 2 (update payroll master file)? _____

       _____

    b. Why was labor distribution (distributing labor list to the appropriate accounting journals) not included under

       module 2? _____

       _____

c. Could labor distribution (module 4) be programmed before module 3? _____ Explain. _____

_____

d. Must module 5 precede module 6

(1) in programming? _____ Explain. _____

_____

(2) in operation of the system? _____ Explain. _____

_____

21. Prepare a fifth level of detail for the structure chart in Figure 11-2. Provide further detail for the following blocks. (Record your answer on the following flowcharting worksheet.)
a. Module 9 — Determine Taxes
b. Module 10 — Determine Deductions
c. Module 11 — Determine Net Pay

12

DISPLAYING SOLUTION LOGIC IN FLOWCHARTS AND DECISION TABLES

OVERVIEW. In Chapter 3, computer programming was defined as the process of preparing the instructions required to solve a problem by means of a computer. Computer programming is accomplished in four steps.

1. Developing the logic to solve the problem.
2. Coding the solution in a language acceptable to the computer.
3. Testing or debugging the program to insure its validity.
4. Documenting the program to facilitate modification.

Deriving the logic to solve a problem, step 1, can be facilitated by using a logic flowchart or decision table. A flowchart is a schematic or graphic representation of the logic required to solve a problem. It's called a flowchart because it depicts the flow, or sequence, of processing steps to solve a problem. A decision table also displays logic for solving a problem. However, it is more useful when the solution contains many possible actions depending on a variety of conditions.

It is usually easier to analyze logic on paper rather than to try to visualize it mentally. Flowcharts and decision tables aid in developing logic. Flowchart techniques will be explained first.

FLOWCHARTS

As the name implies, **flowcharts** depict the flow (sequence) of computer processing to solve a problem. Special symbols aid in developing solution logic and also make it easy to explain the logic to the person for whom the system is designed. In Chapter 2, a system was defined as consisting of input, processing, and output. Therefore, a flowchart portraying a system would have at least three **blocks,** one for each function. In Figure 12–1 logic is flowcharted for solution of a compounded interest problem. Note two things: (1) that the same symbol (parallelogram) is used for input and output and (2) that another symbol is added to indicate starting and terminating activities.

In Figure 12–1 you also see that the shape of the symbol represents the type of function to be performed.

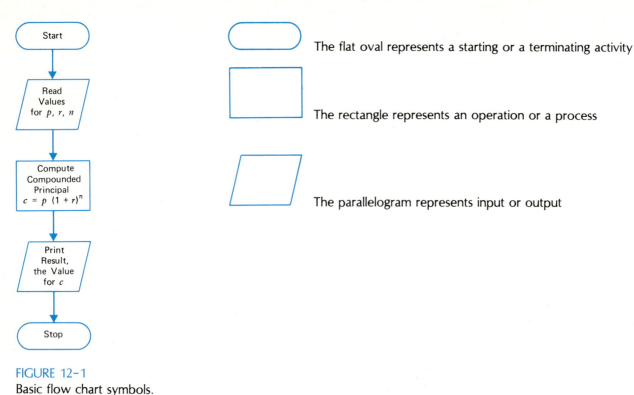

FIGURE 12-1
Basic flow chart symbols.

QUESTION: Figure 12-1 illustrates two characteristics of flowcharts.
1.   The minimum number of flowchart **blocks** to represent program logic is

_____ .

2.   The minimum number of **symbols** to represent program logic is

_____ .

ANSWER: 5, 3

The logic required to solve the elementary problem shown in Figure 12-1 could be visualized without the aid of a flowchart. However, most problems to be computer processed are complex enough to require flowcharting.

Analyze the following flowchart (Figure 12-2). The resulting program causes the computer to read, process, and write one record. Such a program would be uneconomical for computer use. So would the program for compounding interest (Figure 12-1). It would be easier and quicker to solve the problem by hand. The computer becomes economical when many successive computations must be made or when many records must be processed, such as all the inventory transactions for a company with many different products. For the latter case, the flowchart is revised, as shown in Figure 12-3. An inventory transaction is read, inventory is updated, and the results are recorded. The line drawn from the Write block to the Read block shows that the logic is repeated continuously. In a situation where many cycles of processing are required, computer processing is more economical than manual processing.

The titles under Figures 12-2 and 12-3 refer to iterative versus noniterative processing. To **iterate** is to execute successively a series of operations. Two other terms are used synonymously in computing: **cycling** and **looping.** The

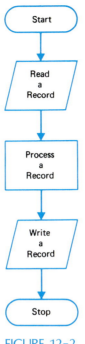

FIGURE 12-2
Noniterative processing.

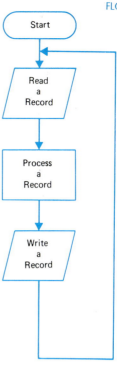

FIGURE 12-3
Iterative processing.

process of cycling repetitively through a series of steps or computer instructions is referred to as **looping.**

QUESTION: The term "loop" is synonymous with the terms "cycle" or "iterate." An iteration is one _____ through a set of logical steps.

ANSWER: loop or cycle

Use of the looping process is a key to solving a problem efficiently with a computer. By cycling back through the same set of instructions, we can use the same logic for an almost infinite set of data. For example, the logic of the flowchart in Figure 12-3 causes hundreds or thousands of records to be processed. In fact, if a program were written to implement the logic in Figure 12-3, processing would never stop. This is called an endless loop. We will discuss methods for halting processing shortly.

QUESTION: Let's illustrate the looping concept another way. Review Figure 12-1. To enable this flowchart to serve for compounding many different sets of data, a line should be drawn between which blocks?

ANSWER: From the Print to the Read block

DECISION LOGIC   In the previous flowcharts, each step was performed in sequence. Use of the **decision function** permits alternative actions. Computer processing will branch to one of several alternatives, depending on the outcome of the decision depicted in the block, as shown below.

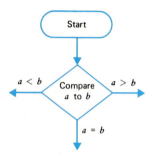

To illustrate the use of the decision symbol, the logic for maintaining inventory will be flowcharted. The procedure is as follows: In processing an inventory record, reorder when the quantity of electric toasters in inventory falls below 75.

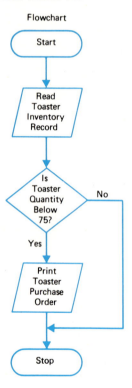

QUESTION: Is the following terminology equally acceptable for the decision block: Quantity $\leq$ 75? If not, change it to produce the same result as that shown above.

ANSWER: No. The rule stated earlier said reorder when the quantity fell *below*. It should be stated: Quantity < 75.

GENERALIZED FLOWCHARTS   The preceding inventory flowchart was a **special-purpose flowchart,** designed specifically for maintaining an inventory level for toasters. A **general-purpose flowchart** permits the same logic to be used to maintain inventory for all products.

QUESTION: Revise the wording in the blocks to make the flowchart general purpose, appropriate for maintaining specified levels for *any* item in inventory, not just toasters.

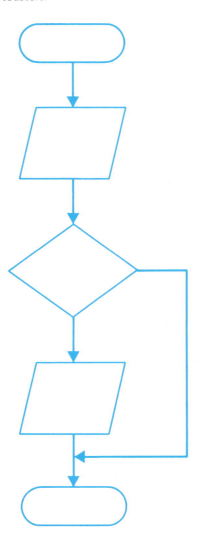

ANSWER: The logic would be identical to that shown previously, with the removal of the word "toaster" from the input/output blocks and the rewording of the decision block to "Quantity below the reorder point?"

The primary purpose of flowcharting, indicated by the question above, is to develop a generalized logic that will represent all the conditions of the problem.

LOGIC FOR TERMINATING LOOPS Loops are terminated according to conditions provided in the programmer's solution logic. In the inventory problem, it would be logical to establish the terminating condition as follows: When all records have been read, halt processing.

Assume we have a "transaction file" containing a daily record of activity in inventory, such as additions or withdrawals from inventory. The transaction file is processed each evening to update the inventory master file. When transactions have been punched in cards, the programmer often arranges for a "trailer" card to be inserted at the end of the **deck** (the set of cards). The trailer card typically is punched with some large value in a field, such as 9999 in the product number field (for inventory) or in the employee number field (for payroll). Therefore the end-of-processing test would be as follows.

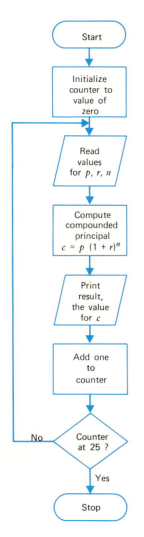

FIGURE 12-4
Illustration of counter concept.

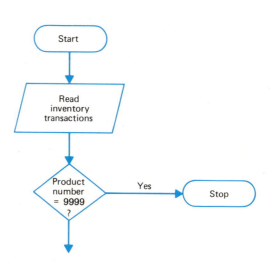

When using magnetic tape or magnetic disk media for the transaction file, one may use an **end-of-file** (EOF) symbol. The logic shown above would be the same, with only a change in the value being tested.

The above example showed the logic for terminating processing after all transactions had been read. Another set of logic is required when the objective is termination after a certain number of processing cycles. An example is the problem of compounding interest, illustrated in Figure 12-1. Assume that you are asked to develop a flowchart to compute compounded interest over a period of 25 years, for mortgage payments on a home. Assume also that you are asked to print the results for each year. During each cycle through the program, interest for one year would be computed and added to the principal. At the end of each cycle the termination test would be, "Have 25 years been completed?" To keep track of cycles a counter function is required. A **counter** is a location in computer memory that the programmer sets up to keep track of the number of cycles. After each cycle, the value of one is added to the counter. The value of the counter is tested each cycle to see if processing is complete. In our example, the test would be made to see if the counter contained a value of 25. Figure 12-4 depicts the flowchart with the counter.

QUESTION: Sometimes, instead of the above approach, a programmer includes logic to **decrement** (subtract from) rather than **increment** the counter. Reword the logic in the selected blocks to represent **de**crementing instead of **in**crementing the counter for 25 cycles.

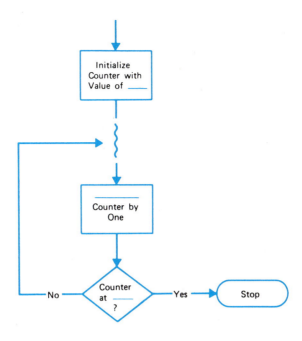

ANSWER: 25, decrement, 0

FLOWCHARTING MULTIPLE ALTERNATIVES

When more than three alternatives are possible, several decision blocks are used in conjunction. As shown in the preceding illustrations, the decision functions are the key ones in most programs. The programmer has considerable flexibility in recording decision logic. Figure 12-5 shows three ways of displaying identical logic. The experience of a prospective employee is to be compared to the amount of experience required by a job.

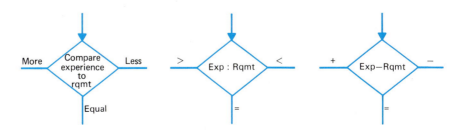

FIGURE 12-5
Variations for displaying decision alternatives.

EXERCISE 12-1 The flowchart in Figure 12-6 was prepared by a student of the authors. It incorrectly portrays the logic in the following procedure. In the space next to the flowchart, draw a flowchart that correctly portrays the logic of the following procedure.

Procedure. An organization has a "talent bank" system that contains key information for determining promotable employees: birth date, sex, address, Social Security number, education, experience in a maximum of three jobs (for example, three years summer work as a chauffeur, two years as a bank teller, and four years as a computer programmer).

Insert the changes necessary to process records to read the employee file and list all persons who meet the following criteria: sex (male, heavy lifting required), at least one year of college education, five years experience in construction, and one year experience in supervision. Also, report the total number of persons who met the criteria.

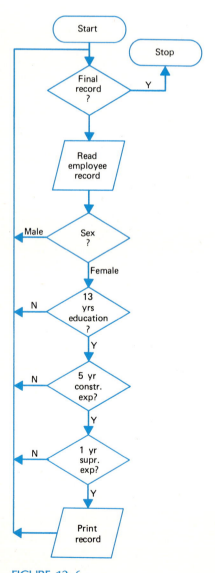

FIGURE 12-6

Flowchart for talent bank procedure.

CONNECTORS The circle symbol provides a way to connect segments of a flowchart. Few solutions can be shown on a single page. **Connectors** may also be used on a single page to avoid intersecting lines that might be confusing.

To illustrate the function of a connector, assume the inventory procedure for reordering varies according to the price of the item. Not all of the solution logic can be provided on one sheet. Figure 12-7 shows the continuation of the flowchart on another page and how connector circles are used to keep track of the flow of logic.

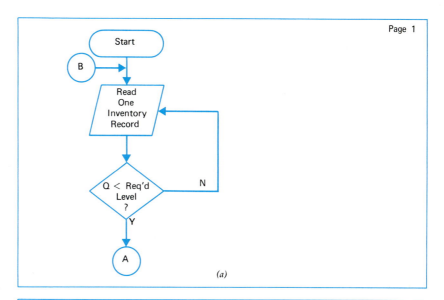

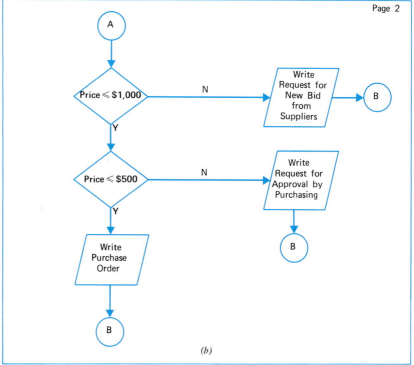

FIGURE 12-7
Connecting flowchart logic. (a) Page 1 of two pages of logic. (b) Page 2 of two pages of logic.

QUESTION: Circle the letter designating the appropriate connector for the two pages of logic in Figure 12-7*a* and 12-7*b*.

   a.   Reenter original loop to read another record.   Connector A or B?

   b.   When reorder is necessary, use a procedure determined by the price of the item.   Connector A or B?

ANSWER: (a) B, (b) A

EXERCISE 12-2   Review the logic in Figure 12-7 and answer the following questions.

1.   What action is taken when the inventory quantity is less than the required level? _____

   _____

   _____

2.   What action is taken when the quantity in inventory is exactly equal to the required level? _____

   _____

   _____

3.   What action is taken when the price of the inventory item is $1500?

   _____

   _____

4.   What action is taken when the price of the inventory item is $999?

   _____

   _____

5.   What action is taken when the price of the inventory item is $1?

   _____

   _____

STRUCTURED FLOWCHARTS   Chapter 11 introduced the three programming structures used to simplify program development and testing: sequence, selection, and repetition. Figure 12–8 contains the flowchart for those three structures. The logic of any problem, regardless of its complexity, can be portrayed by combinations of these three structures.

Flowchart of the programming structures.

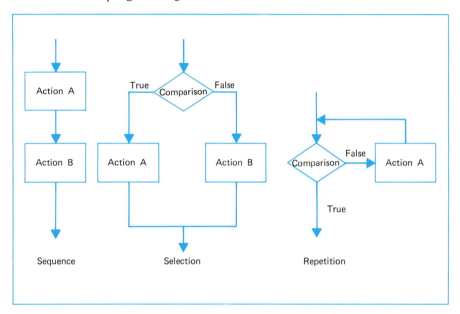

Sequence   Selection   Repetition

Let's illustrate those structures on a real-life problem. The decision criteria in a typical college admissions procedure are as follows.

Procedure.   Persons who score 23 or better on the ACT (American College Test) and who are in the upper 50 percent of their high school graduating classes will be admitted. Persons whose class rank is between 25 percent and 50 percent must have an ACT score of 28 or better to be admitted. Persons whose ACT is less than 23 but greater than 18 may be admitted if they rank in the upper two-thirds of their graduating class.

Figure 12–9 is the flowchart depicting the logic of this procedure.

QUESTION: Examine Figure 12–9. If the procedure were changed as follows, what changes would be needed on the flowchart: The college substitutes the SAT (Scholastic Aptitude Test) for the ACT. Persons who score 1000 or better and are in the upper 50 percent of their class are admitted. Persons whose class standing is between 25 and 50 percent and who score 1200 or better on the SAT will be admitted. Persons who rank in the top two-thirds of their class may be admitted with a SAT score of 800 or better.

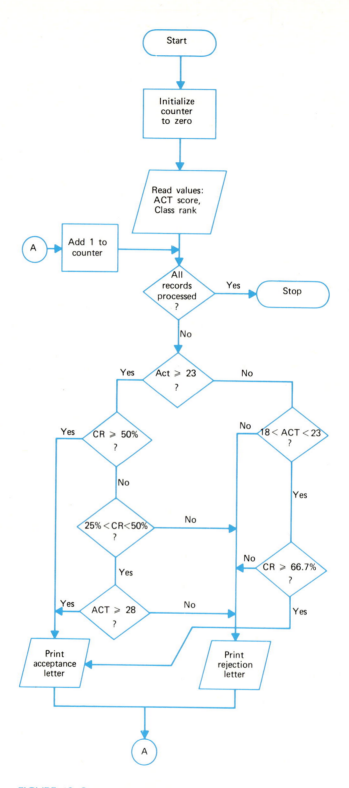

FIGURE 12-9
College admissions procedure.

ANSWER: The three blocks dealing with ACT are changed, as follows: SAT $\geq$ 1000, 800 $\leq$ SAT $<$ 1000, SAT $\geq$ 1200. Also the Read block must be changed to read SAT scores.

ILLUSTRATING SEVERAL   The flowchart of the admissions procedure illustrates a number of the points in
FLOWCHARTING PRINCIPLES   this chapter.

1. Use of the three control structures.
    Sequence is illustrated by the top three blocks.
    Selection is illustrated by the lower half of the flowchart.
    Repetition is illustrated by the first decision block and all the remaining blocks; that is, the action part of the repetition cycle is to perform all those comparisons, update the counter, and then check again to see if all records have been processed.

2. Converting to a generalized flowchart.
    The way the flowchart presently reads requires a change each time one of the admissions criteria change. For example, if the new cutoff for ACT score becomes 24, both the flowchart and the computer program would have to be changed. If we had used variables instead of specific data, the flowchart and program would remain unchanged. Only the data fed into the program would need revision. A great deal of programming time would be saved by such an approach. To make sure you understand the conversion from a special-purpose to a generalized flowchart, we will convert the admissions flowchart.
    The new variables are:

A = Target ACT score

B = Minimally acceptable ACT score

C = ACT score requirement for class rank less than target

D = Target class rank

E = Minimally acceptable class rank

F = Class rank for ACT score less than target

We have converted the top half of the admissions procedure flowchart to a generalized version in the figure below.

EXERCISE 12-3   A. Complete the conversion of the admissions procedure flowchart from a special-purpose to a general-purpose flowchart.
    B. Draw dotted lines around the sections of the flowchart that illustrate sequence, selection, and repetition (an example is Figure 11-4 in Chapter 11).

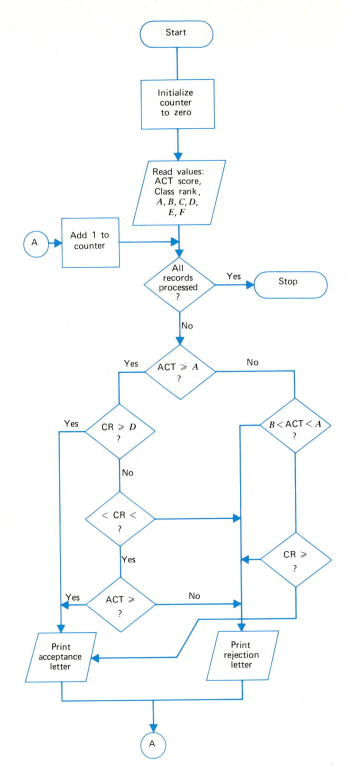

Revised college admissions procedure. (To be completed by student.)

PSEUDOCODE Some organizations are using pseudocode as a substitute for flowcharts. **Pseudocode** is an English-like description of the processing steps in a program. The approach is to use a language that represents the logical steps in a structured program and to avoid the details of an actual programming language. Pseudocode is especially useful for expressing complex logic. It implements the top-down-structured approach. Also, the pseudocode can be easily converted to actual programming language instructions since it closely corresponds to a programming language.

There are few rules in writing pseudocode. To put in effect the three control structures, terms like IF, THEN and ELSE are used. For example, the following pseudocode implements the procedure for college admissions (Figure 12–9).

```
DOWHILE there are more records
    IF ACT score is ≥ 28 AND class rank ≥ 25%
    ELSE IF ACT score is ≥ 23 AND class rank ≥ 50%
    ELSE IF ACT score is > 18 AND class rank ≥ 66.7%
        THEN print acceptance letter
    ELSE print rejection letter
    ENDIF
ENDDO
```

QUESTION: As the above example shows, pseudocode gets its name from the fact that it resembles _____ without requiring all the rules of a particular programming language.

ANSWER: actual programming language

STANDARD FLOWCHART SYMBOLS The key symbols in portraying solution logic have now been covered. However, professional programmers use, in addition, specialized symbols to provide for the specific circumstances of their computer environment. They may be using a system limited to magnetic tape for input; they may be in a disk-only environment; or they may have a tape and disk environment. They may output results on paper or on a cathode ray tube (CRT).

The American National Standards Institute (ANSI) provides for all possibilities in its array of logic symbols. Figure 12–10 gives the ANSI set of symbols. Use of the standard symbols facilitates sharing of programs. For example, the University of Colorado uses programs developed at Dartmouth, Stanford, Texas, and many other schools. Because standardized flowcharts for programs are available, programs from many sources can be easily understood and used. The flowcharts also permit students to follow the logic embedded in programs before using them.

Some of the symbols in Figure 12–10 are not used in programming but are used for system analysis and design. They will be explained in Section Four.

QUESTION: Use of ANSI symbols facilitates _____

ANSWER: understanding another person's program and sharing programs.

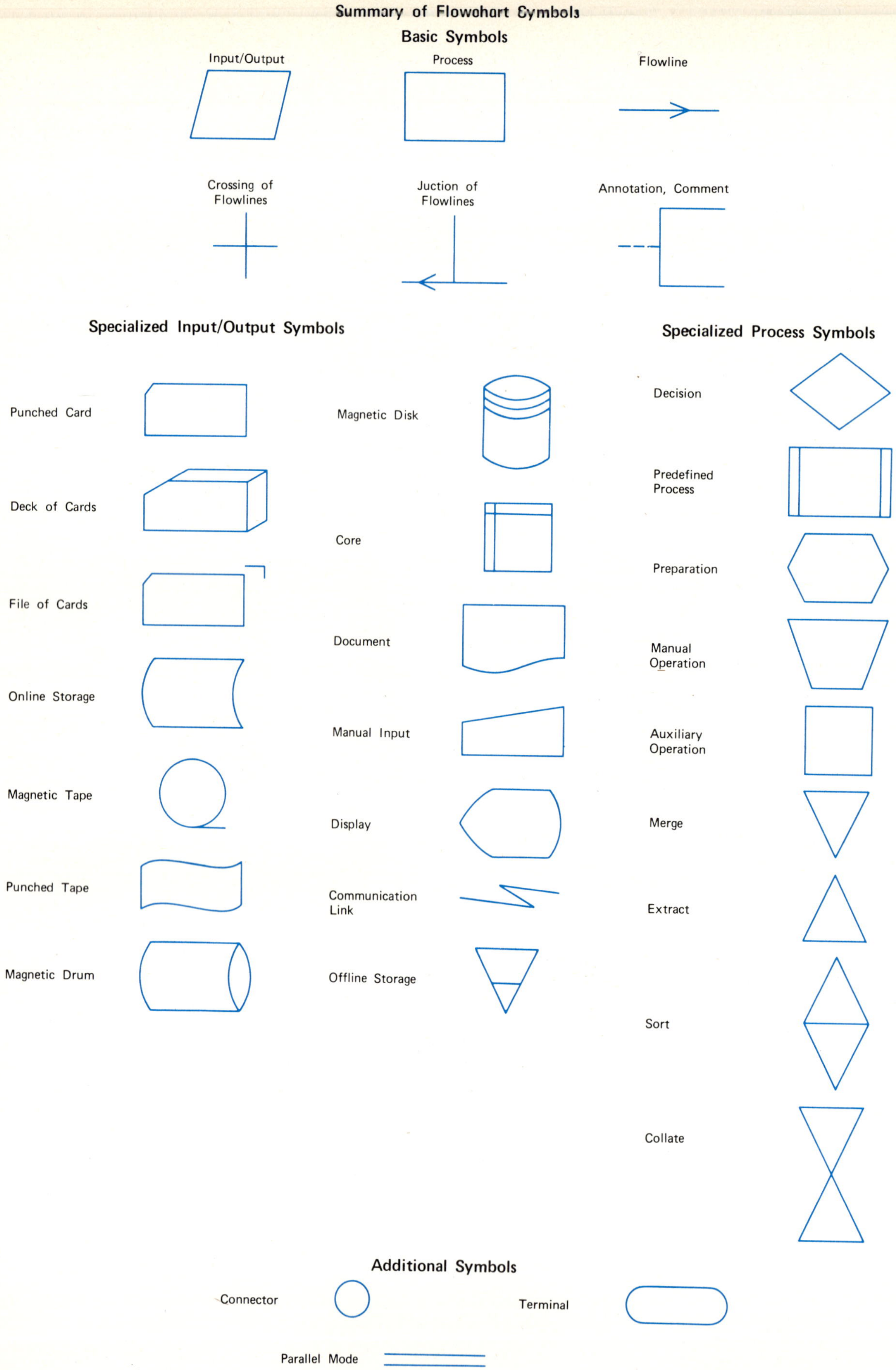

Summary of Flowchart Symbols
Basic Symbols

Input/Output   Process   Flowline

Crossing of Flowlines   Juction of Flowlines   Annotation, Comment

Specialized Input/Output Symbols

Punched Card

Deck of Cards

File of Cards

Online Storage

Magnetic Tape

Punched Tape

Magnetic Drum

Magnetic Disk

Core

Document

Manual Input

Display

Communication Link

Offline Storage

Specialized Process Symbols

Decision

Predefined Process

Preparation

Manual Operation

Auxiliary Operation

Merge

Extract

Sort

Collate

Additional Symbols

Connector   Terminal

Parallel Mode

FIGURE 12-10

American National Standards Institute (ANSI) flowchart symbols.

GUIDELINES FOR DEVELOPING FLOWCHARTS In addition to standard flowchart symbols, there are generally accepted guidelines for preparing flowcharts. These guidelines are listed in Figure 12–11.

---

1. Use standard flowcharting symbols.
2. Develop machine-independent flowcharts and evaluate logic before reducing to machine-dependent flowcharts.
3. Try to keep flow of logic from top to bottom and from left to right.
4. Avoid intersecting of lines used to depict flow of logic.
5. Use connectors to reduce the number of flow lines.

FIGURE 12–11
Guidelines for flowchart development.

Adherence to the guidelines facilitates the review of logic in a flowchart. A person may need to revise a program several months after original development. Use of the guidelines makes it easy to reorient before incorporating changes. Also, when several programmers are preparing modules to be integrated, use of the guidelines is mandatory to insure compatibility. Finally, when organizations share programs, use of nationally recognized guidelines facilitates communication and understanding of the program logic.

EXERCISE 12–4

1. Three reasons for using flowcharts are:

   a. _____

   b. _____

   c. _____

2. Why is it important to use ANSI flowcharting symbols?

   _____

   _____

   _____

3. General-purpose flowcharts are useful for _____

   _____

   _____

4. Special-purpose flowcharts are more appropriate for _____

   _____

   _____

5. Item 3 in Figure 12–11 indicates that the flow of logic should be "southeasterly" on a sheet. In your opinion, what is the reason for this rule?

   _____

DECISION LOGIC TABLES

The flow (sequence) in computer processing to solve a problem may also be portrayed in a **decision logic table.** When a large number of conditions are being evaluated in the program, decision tables are more efficient than flowcharts.

The components of a decision logic table are: conditions, condition entries, actions, and action entries (see Figure 12–12). Conditions and actions have an "if . . . then" relationship (**if** a set of conditions exists, **then** the following actions are to be taken). The following decision logic table portrays a simplified payroll procedure. The first condition identifies the category of pay. The condition tested is, "Is the person a salaried employee?" Decision rule 1 applies when the answer is "yes." The action under decision rule 1 is, "Go to the salary pay table." In other words, Figure 12–13 applies only to hourly paid employees. Another table is used to portray the logic for paying salaried employees. Rule 2 applies when the employee is an hourly employee.

FIGURE 12–12
Components of a decision logic table.

Conditions	Conditions Entries			
Actions	Actions Entries			

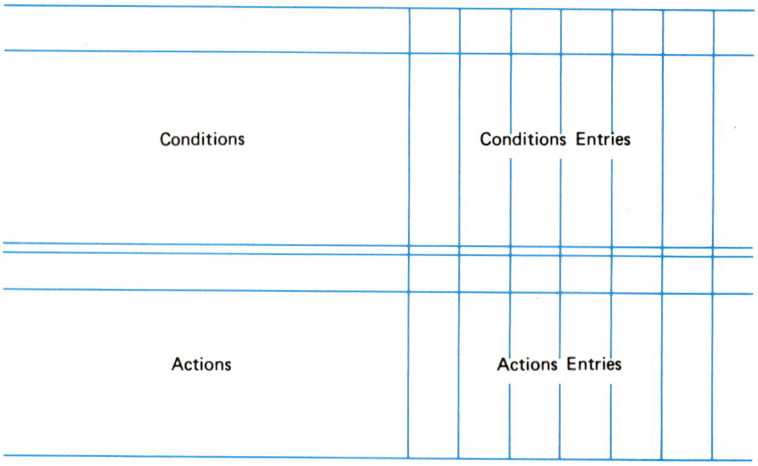

FIGURE 12–13
Decision logic table for portion of payroll procedure.

	Payroll Table	Decision Rules			
		1	2	3	4
Conditions	1. Salaried Employee	Y	N	N	N
	2. Hours Worked $\leq$ 40		Y	N	N
	3. Deductions			Y	N
Actions	1. Go to Salary Pay Table	X			
	2. Hours Worked $\times$ Hourly Rate		X	X	X
	3. (Hours Worked $-$ 40) $\times$ (1.5 $\times$ Rate)			X	X
	4. Go to Deductions Table			X	
	5. Go to Tax Table				X

The next condition tested is the amount of hours worked. If the amount is 40 hours or less, the action under Rule 2 applies (hours worked are multiplied by the hourly rate). If the hours worked are more than 40, Rule 3 applies. Action 2 is repeated (pay for the first 40 hours is computed). Action 3 also applies. Overtime hours are computed and paid at a rate of $1\frac{1}{2}$ times the hourly rate. Condition 3 tests to determine if the employee has deductions to be made. If so, action 4 causes the procedure to transfer to another table, the deductions table. If not, processing continues with the next decision logic table, the tax table. (Incidentally, the last step in the deductions table would also route processing to the tax table. The final step in that table would be computing net pay.)

With the explanation of the operation of a decision logic table, you are ready to follow the development of a table. Figure 12–14 provides a step-by-step description of development of a decision table from a narrative procedure. Read this procedure carefully — you will use it to complete Exercise 12-5 and several problems in the Chapter Examination.

QUESTION: Figure 12–14 shows that duplication may not be obvious from reading a narrative procedure. The conditions in the narrative were reduced from

_____ to three in the decision logic table, whereas the actions were

reduced from _____ to four.

ANSWER: eight, five

An important advantage of decision logic tables is that they can be translated directly into COBOL or FORTRAN language. Special translators, called **interpreters,** were developed for this process. Data-entry personnel punch cards for each line in the table. The resulting deck of cards is read into the computer and translated into COBOL statements, bypassing the coding function for this portion of the system.

QUESTION: Not only is the decision logic table advantageous for recording complex decision criteria, it can be keypunched and processed to automatically produce

COBOL statements, by means of a _____

ANSWER: Translator or interpreter. The decision logic table then becomes a part of the documentation package.

PROCEDURE FOR DEVELOPING DECISION TABLES   Use of the following procedure will facilitate preparation of a decision table.

1. Separate conditions from actions.

2. Record each condition above the double line and each action below the double line.

3. Identify rules by drawing vertical lines (columns) next to the conditions and actions. For each rule, ask yourself, "If this condition is true, which action should be taken?" Record a "Y" (yes) next to the condition and an "X" next to the appropriate action. This column is labeled as Rule 1 in the table.

The procedure the systems analyst follows in preparing a decision table may be simply to identify conditions and actions of the problem statement as he encounters them. Conditions are placed on the top half of the form; actions on the bottom half.

Consider the following problem narrative:

When the quantity ordered for a particular item does not exceed the order limit and the credit approval is "OK", move the quantity-ordered amount to the quantity-shipped field; then go to a table to prepare a shipment release. Of course, there must be a sufficient quantity on hand to fill the order.

When the quantity ordered exceeds the order limit, go to a table named "Order Reject". Do the same if the credit approval is not "OK".

Occasionally, the quantity ordered does not exceed the order limit, credit approval is "OK", but there is insufficient quantity on hand to fill the order. In this case, go to a table named "Back Order".

Note that this is not written with all conditions first, prefixed by "if", and with all actions following, prefixed by "then". The narrative was written casually with conditions and actions scrambled, much like the original baseball problem. Words like "when" and "occasionally" are used instead of the more precise "if". Such ambiguity is typical of most narratives. For illustrative purposes the problem is restated below with a solid line under conditions and a broken line under actions.

When the quantity ordered for a particular item does not exceed the order limit and the credit approval is "OK", move the quantity-ordered amount to the quantity-shipped field, then go to a table to prepare a shipment release. Of course, there must be a sufficient quantity on hand to fill the order.

When the quantity ordered exceeds the order limit, go to a table named "Order Reject". Do the same if the credit approval is not "OK".

Occasionally, the quantity ordered does not exceed the order limit, credit approval is "OK", but there is insufficient quantity on hand to fill the order. In this case, go to a table named "Back Order".

A count shows eight conditions and five actions for the problem.

C1 QTY ORDERED IS LESS THAN OR EQUAL TO ORDER LIMIT
C2 CREDIT APPROVAL IS "OK"
C3 QTY ON HAND IS GREATER THAN OR EQUAL TO QTY ORDERED
C4 QTY ORDERED IS GREATER THAN ORDER LIMIT
C5 CREDIT APPROVAL IS NOT "OK"
C6 QTY ORDERED IS LESS THAN OR EQUAL TO ORDER LIMIT
C7 CREDIT APPROVAL IS "OK"
C8 QTY ON HAND IS LESS THAN QTY ORDERED

A1 MOVE QTY ORDERED TO QTY SHIP
A2 GO TO SHIP RELEASE
A3 GO TO ORDER REJECT
A4 GO TO ORDER REJECT
A5 GO TO BACK ORDER

Notice that C1 and C2 are identical to C6 and C7, and that A3 is identical to A4. This occurs because a narrative describes rules one after another (serially). Thus two sets of two conditions common to two rules, appear in the narrative. On the other hand, a decision table aligns rules side by side (parallel). Thus a condition or action common to several rules need appear only once. Furthermore, C5 is not necessary since it is the negative of C2. Similarly C4 and C8 are the negatives of C1 and C3. Negative entries after the positive statements of C1, C2 and C3 cover the other cases.

The next step in preparing the table might be to identify and consolidate similar rows. C1, C6 and C4 are combined. C2, C5 and C7 are combined. Finally, C3 and C8 are combined.

In the action half of the decision table form, A3 and A4 are combined. After consolidation there are only three condition rows and four action rows.

Condition Stub

QTY ORDERED IS LESS THAN OR EQUAL TO ORDER LIMIT
CREDIT APPROVAL IS "OK"
QTY ON HAND IS GREATER THAN OR EQUAL TO QTY ORDERED

Action Stub

MOVE QTY ORDERED TO QTY SHIP
GO TO PREPARE SHIP RELEASE
GO TO ORDER REJECT
GO TO BACK ORDER

The stub portion of the table is now completed. In order to fill out the entry portions, the analyst must determine the rules expressed in the narrative. In this example, the first paragraph describes a single rule. The analyst enters the appropriate Y, N or X in the entry portions for rule 1. The second paragraph contains two rules. The analyst enters the appropriate Y, N, or X in the entry portion for rules 2 and 3. Finally, the last paragraph becomes rule 4 of the decision table. The final result is shown below:

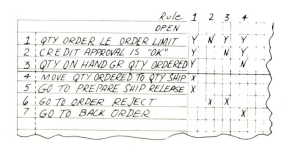

FIGURE 12-14

Development of decision logic table.

4. Then ask, "If this condition is not true, which action should be taken?" Record an "N" (no) next to the condition in the second column. However, an action may not be required if the condition is false. If one is required, place an "X" next to the appropriate action, in column two. The second column is then labeled as Rule 2.

5. Continue this procedure until all conditions and actions have been identified.

   Test your understanding of this procedure on the following exercise. Otherwise you will have difficulty completing the problems in the chapter exam.

EXERCISE 12–5 Develop a decision logic table for the following set of decision logic.

1. Read employees' cards with the following information.
   a. Employee clock number
   b. Gross pay

2. Use the following table to compute the tax and find the net pay where net is equal to gross pay, less tax.

Gross Earnings	Tax
Less than $2000	0
$2000 or more, but less than $5,000	2 percent of the excess over $2000
$5000 or more	$60, plus 5 percent of the excess over $5000

3. Terminate when the employee's clock number is zero.

4. Print the clock number, gross pay, tax, and net pay for each employee.

   We have demonstrated the value of logic charts in developing and evaluating the solution to a problem. Coding a program from a logic chart decreases programming time and effort. An error in logic would be more difficult to trace without such a chart. Most computer installations require logic charts for this reason.

PROGRAM DOCUMENTATION Logic charts, both decision tables and flowcharts, are valuable for another reason. They serve as **documentation** of a program, facilitating revision of the program when procedures change. Documentation is particularly important in organizations where personnel turnover is high. Analyzing another person's computer program is quite difficult if one must work solely with the code. Reviewing the logic of the program makes incorporating changes much easier.

QUESTION: The completed package of both logic and instructions is referred to as _____

ANSWER: documentation

SUMMARY

For some unexplainable reason, it is difficult to convince students of the value in preparing flowcharts or decision tables prior to programming. The "Tiger" cartoon below illustrates the approach of many students. Developing a graphic representation of logic in either flowchart or decision table form is an important part of the programming task.

TIGER

ANSWERS TO EXERCISES

EXERCISE 12–1

The flowchart has the following errors:

1. The procedure did not call for a person with 13 years of education but for a person with one year of college. Also, the male/female arrows are reversed.
2. A counter is needed to tally the number of persons meeting the criteria. The flowchart below causes the number to be printed each time a person's record is printed. To print the final total only, another Print block is needed, just before the Stop block. (See flowchart on following page.)

EXERCISE 12–2

1. Program branches to further decision functions to determine various actions based on the price.
2. No action taken. The next inventory record is read and analyzed.
3. Program branches to output function, printing a request for a new bid from the suppliers.
4. Program branches to another decision function, with a price of $500 as the determinant for further action.
5. Program branches to output function, printing a purchase order to procure the reorder quantity.

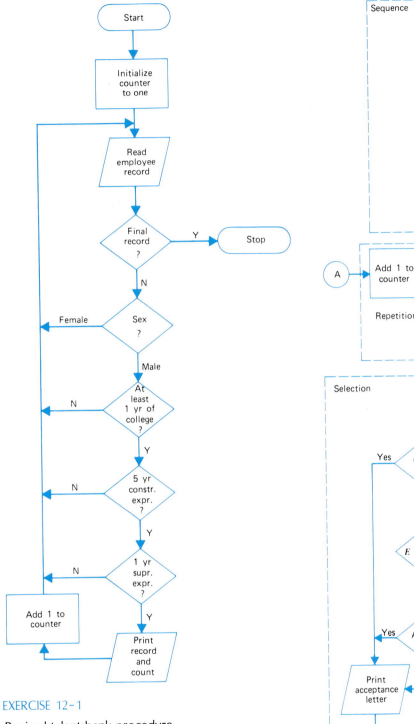

EXERCISE 12-1

Revised talent bank procedure

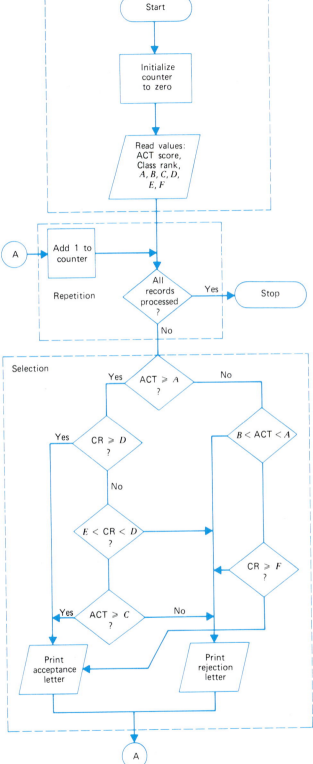

EXERCISE 12-3

Revised college admissions procedure—completed.

EXERCISE 12-4

1. a. To aid in developing and evaluating solution logic
   b. To reduce coding and debugging time
   c. To provide documentation for subsequent revision
2. Use of standard symbols simplifies revision of programs when a change in the application occurs. It also facilitates sharing of programs between organizations (or passing on programs to next year's students!).
3. General-purpose flowcharts express the logic for a general class of problems (for example, maintain inventory for all products).
4. Special-purpose flowcharts express the logic for a specific problem (for example, maintain inventory for toasters).
5. Why record the flow of logic southeasterly on a sheet? This simplifies interpretation of a flowchart by another person.

EXERCISE 12-5

PROCEDURE TO COMPUTE PAYROLL

Conditions	Rules			
	1	2	3	4
Clock number zero?	Y	N	N	N
Earnings				
Less than $2000		Y	N	N
$\geq 2000 < 5000$			Y	N
≥ 5000				Y
Compute tax				
Zero Tax		X		
2% of excess > $2000			X	
$60 plus 5% of excess > $5000				X
Calculate net pay		X	X	X
Print clock number, gross pay, tax, net pay		X	X	X
Terminate program	X			

CHAPTER EXAMINATION

1. Match each of the following terms to the appropriate definition.

   ___ Programmer

   ___ Loop

   ___ Counter

   ___ Initialize

   ___ Decision function

   ___ Documentation

   ___ Decision logic tables

   ___ General-purpose flowcharts

   ___ Special-purpose flowcharts

   ___ Systems analyst/designer

   ___ Pseudocode

   a. A series of instructions used repeatedly

   b. A physical location in the CPU that keeps track of the number of cycles of processing

   c. Flowcharts and computer programs for a computerized activity

   d. Process of evaluating criteria and selecting alternatives

   e. Person who develops problem-oriented flowcharts

   f. Person who develops programmer-oriented flowcharts

   g. Express generalized logic

   h. Express specialized logic

   i. Used to display logic for decisions involving many conditions

   j. To establish an initial value for a counter

   k. English-like programming approach to express detailed logic

2. What are the four steps in computer programming?

   a. _____

   b. _____

   c. _____

   d. _____

3. What are the three principal symbols used to depict logic in a flowchart? Explain the use of each.

   a. _____

   _____

b. _____

_____

c. _____

_____

_____

4. Another, less important symbol, is the small circle, used to _____

_____

5. A loop is a key programming technique. Define and explain a loop. _____

_____

_____

6. In Chapter 11, the three structures used in structured programming were explained. Identify the structure and draw a flowchart depicting the logic for each of the three structures below:

a. _____ structure   Flowchart A
   Step 1. $A = B + C$
   Step 2. $E = B - 7$
   Step 3. $F = A \div E$

b. _____ structure   Flowchart B
   Step 1. $X = Y + Z$
   Step 2. If X is negative, multiply it by 2; otherwise, divide it
            by 4

c. _____ structure   Flowchart C
   Step 1. $C = B + 2$
   Step 2. Repeat step 1 until $C = 12$, then add F to C,
            producing G

7. Counters are also important in solution logic. Explain the concept of a counter. _____

_____

_____

8. Describe the differences between Special-purpose flowcharts and General-purpose flowcharts.

_____

_____

_____

_____

9. What is pseudocode? How is it used? _____

_____

_____

10. What is the purpose behind standardizing flowchart symbols?

_____

_____

_____

11. Prepare a flowchart to depict the logic for computer solution for computing expected time for an event on a PERT network (see Figure 5 and accompanying explanation in the final chapter of the book, Feasibility Analysis and System Implementation).

12. Develop a flowchart to depict the logic for computing cost of a CPM network activity. Develop an average time/cost figure from the three points on the curve in Figure 6 in the final chapter of the book, Feasibility Analysis and System Implementation. Explanation of that curve is provided alongside the figure.

13. Develop a flowchart to revise the logic in Figure 12-5 to the following: (Use a form at the end of the chapter exam.)

    The talent bank is revised to include data on promotion potential of employees. The supervisor's evaluation is entered on the file every six months. The ratings are numerical, from 1 (lowest rating) to 10 (highest rating). Once per year all employees with ratings averaging 7.5 or better on the last three evaluations are sorted out to be considered for promotion. The output is sorted in three ways, (1) a listing by job experience category, (2) a listing by rank in supervisor's evaluations, and (3) a listing by years of education.

14. Prepare a flowchart to depict the logic for computer solution for determining payback (explained in Table 3 of the final chapter of the book, Feasibility Analysis and System Implementation).

15. Prepare a flowchart for problem 7 for the Introduction to BASIC chapter examination.

16. Prepare a flowchart for problem 8 for the Introduction to BASIC chapter examination.

17. Prepare a flowchart for problem 10 for the Introduction to BASIC chapter examination.

18. Prepare a flowchart for problem 11 for the Introduction to BASIC chapter examination.

19. Prepare a flowchart for problem 12 for the Introduction to BASIC chapter examination.

20. Problem 26 asks you to develop a decision table to depict the logic of the problem. Develop a flowchart instead.

21. Problem 27 asks you to develop a decision table to depict the logic of the problem. Develop a flowchart instead.

22. Problem 28 asks you to develop a decision table to depict the logic of the problem. Develop a flowchart instead.

23.   Problem 29 asks you to develop a decision table to depict the logic of the problem. Develop a flow-chart instead.

24.   Problem 30 asks you to develop a decision table to depict the logic of the problem. Develop a flow-chart instead.

25.   Prepare a flowchart for the following problem: Develop the logic for end-of-the-semester processing of the student record file. Student records are set up as follows:

Field 1.   Name — last name, first name, middle name
Field 2.   Class — freshman, sophomore, junior, senior, graduate
Field 3.   Course record — course number, semester hours, grade
Field 4.   Grade point average — total grade points divided by total semester hours (A = 4, B = 3, C = 2, D = 1, F = 0)
Field 5.   Remaining requirements — courses completed this term deducted from degree program

The end-of-semester processing should accomplish the following:

a.   Update each student record.
b.   Prepare the following reports:
   (1)   A class report arranged alphabetically within each class. (The report should list total hours, total points, and GPA.)
   (2)   A dean's list arranged according to GPA. (Only students with GPA higher than 3.0 are eligible.)
   (3)   A course report listing all students by course, arranged in GPA order.
c.   Include logic to accomplish the following:
   (1)   Compute GPA for entire class on the class report.
   (2)   Print the number of students in each class at the end of the class report.
   (3)   Print the number of students in each course at the end of the course report.

26.   Develop a decision logic table to portray the following set of logic:
A small oil dealer uses the following decision criteria for shipping orders:
   1.   If the order is for 10 barrels or less, and if the customer's credit is good, and if the quantity on hand is greater than or equal to the order size, ship the order.
   2.   If the order is for more than 10 barrels, obtain approval from the credit department head even if the customer's past credit performance is good. If the quantity on hand is greater than or equal to the order size, ship the order.
   3.   If the quantity on hand is not sufficient to fill the order, put on "back order."

27.   Develop a decision logic table to portray the following set of logic for personnel selection.
Given:

Field names:
   Employee name
   Department number
   Hourly rate
   Hours worked
   Deduction code (A,B,C,D)
   Sex (M = male, F = female)

Obtain:
a.   Select all females who satisfy the following conditions:
   (1)   They must work in department 8, 9, or 10.
   (2)   Weekly hours not over 40.
   (3)   Must have a deduction under code "A" or hourly rate must be more than $4.

    b. Select all males who satisfy the following conditions:

      (1)   They must work in Department 4.

      (2)   Weekly hours not over 40.

      (3)   Must have a deduction code "B" or code "C".

    c. If logic in section a is satisfied — go to routine 1.

      If logic in section b is satisfied — go to routine 2.

      If neither a nor b is satisfied — go to routine 3.

28. Develop a decision table to portray the following set of logic:

Classification of Capital Gains and Losses. The phrase "short-term" applies to gains and losses from the sale or exchange of capital assets held for six months or less; the phrase "long-term" applies to capital assets held for more than six months.

Treatment of capital gains and losses: Short-term capital gains and losses will be merged to obtain the net short-term capital gain or loss. Long-term capital gains and losses (taken into account at 100 percent) will be merged to obtain the net long-term capital gain or loss.

Given: Purchase date

          Sales date

          Net sales price

          Net cost

Obtain: Total long-term result

          Total short-term result

          Type of long-term result (gain, loss)

          Type of short-term result (gain, loss)

          Net result

29. Develop a decision table to portray the following set of logic:

Stockholder Reports. From a file of stockholder records, we wish to extract the records of stockholders other than individuals and the records of individuals who hold more than 20,000 shares.

With this information produce a detail listing containing the name of each stockholder, the type of stockholder (decoded), and number of shares owned. Also produce a final total of the number of stockholders and number of shares owned listed in this report.

For each stockholder we have:

a.   Stockholder name

b.   Stockholder type (individual, 01; bank, 02; trust, 03; broker, 04)

c.   Number of shares owned

30. Develop a decision table to portray the following set of logic:

There are two input files. A master file is in sequence by identification number (I.O.). Each I.O. number has an associated on hand (O.H.) amount. The other file is a detail transaction file also in sequence by identification number (I.O.). Each I.O. number in this file has associated types of transactions — receipt, issue, recount and their amounts, sequenced respectively. There can be multiple receipts and issues, but only a single recount. Duplicate recounts have been checked.

The output is one file, a new master, which contains I.O. number and on hand amount.

The processing procedure should:

Provide for writing old masters with no activity on the new master, provide for start and end of job, provide for an error routine in the case of a transaction occurring for which there is no master, not provide for additions or deletions to the master file, and provide for computing the new on hand amount (receipt = add, issues = subtract, recount = replace).

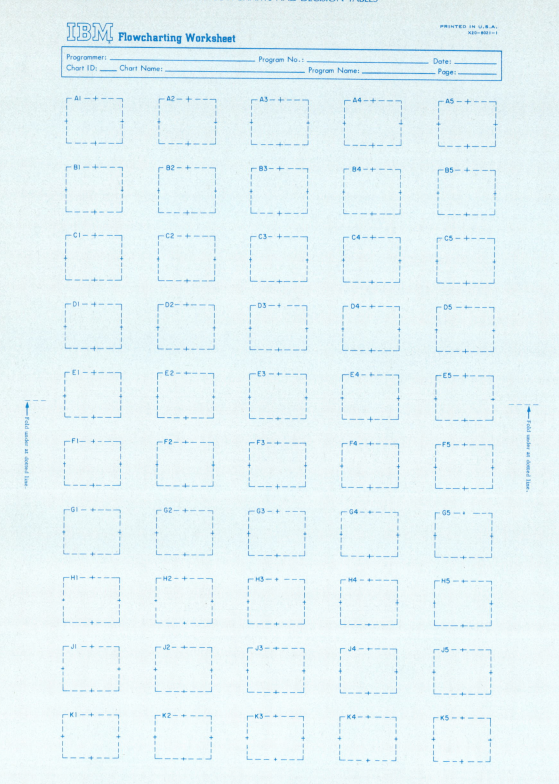

13

INTRODUCTION TO BASIC

OVERVIEW. BASIC stands for Beginner's All-purpose Symbolic Instruction Code. BASIC was developed by Professors John Kemeny and Thomas Kurtz at Dartmouth College. It is a high-level, time-sharing language that was developed largely for instructional purposes. Since its development BASIC has been extended by many users and is often used for data processing applications as well as for instructing students in computer programming.

To illustrate the concepts of BASIC programming, three examples will be introduced. These examples are all based on processing student records.

EXAMPLE 1: SIMPLE INPUT/OUTPUT OPERATIONS

Suppose that the following data is maintained for each student.

Student name (alphanumeric).

Student number (numeric).

Current units (numeric).

Total units (numeric).

A BASIC program is required to read the above data for each student. The same data is to be listed (one line per student), with spacing provided between fields in the output.

A BASIC program to read and list student data, together with sample output, is shown in Figure 13-1.

```
00100 REM *************************************************************************
00110 REM
00120 REM PROGRAM PROB1
00130 REM     PROGRAM TO PRINT A REPORT CONTAINING STUDENT
00140 REM     NAME, NUMBER, CURRENT UNITS, AND TOTAL UNITS
00150 REM     VARIABLES USED ARE;
00160 REM          N$ = STUDENT NAME
00170 REM          N  = STUDENT NUMBER
00180 REM          U  = CURRENT UNITS
00190 REM          U1 = TOTAL UNITS
00200 REM
00210 REM *************************************************************************
00220 READ N$,N,U,U1
00230 IF N = 0 THEN 00340
00240     PRINT N$,N,U,U1
```

```
00250    GO TO 00220
00260 DATA "ADAMS, PETER R.           ",13978,09,104
00270 DATA "GOODMAN, HAROLD R.        ",20875,16,000
00280 DATA "JOHNSON, SHARON C.        ",24432,15,074
00290 DATA "LARSON, JAMES I.          ",47739,06,048
00300 DATA "LEWIS, BARBARA C.         ",01339,18,107
00310 DATA "ROTHCHILD, CHARLES K. ",80336,10,100
00320 DATA "THOMPSON, LAURA W.    ",59325,07,088
00330 DATA "                          ",00000,00,000
00340 END

RUN
```

ADAMS, PETER R.	13978	9	104
GOODMAN, HAROLD R.	20875	16	0
JOHNSON, SHARON C.	24432	15	74
LARSON, JAMES I.	47739	6	48
LEWIS, BARBARA C.	1339	18	107
ROTHCHILD, CHARLES K.	80336	10	100
THOMPSON, LAURA W.	59325	7	88

FIGURE 13-1
BASIC Program for Example 1.

Seven types of BASIC statements are included in the program shown in Figure 13-1.

1. The annotation statement with the key word REM.
2. The read statement with the key word READ.
3. The decision statement with the key words IF and THEN.
4. The output statement with the key word PRINT.
5. The unconditional transfer statement with the key word GO TO.
6. The data statement with the key word DATA.
7. The termination statement with the key word END.

LINE NUMBERS Each BASIC statement is preceded by a line number. In Figure 13-1, the line numbers are 00100, 00110, 00120, ... Leaving gaps in the number sequence in this manner allows one to add statements to the program if required without renumbering. After the BASIC statement has been entered, the programmer depresses the RETURN key on the terminal and proceeds to the next statement.

REM STATEMENT The annotation statement REM (for remark) is used to describe or explain the operation of a BASIC program or some portion of the program. Notice that in Figure 13-1 there are 12 REM statements, which are used to name the program (PROB1), briefly describe the purpose of this program, and list the variables that are used in the program.

QUESTION: List the variable names for each variable in the program.

student name _____

student number _____

current units _____

total units _____

ANSWER: N$, N, U, U1.

The REM statement is a nonexecutable statement. When a REM statement is encountered in a BASIC program, control passes automatically to the next executable statement.

CONSTANTS A constant is a quantity whose value remains fixed throughout the execution of a program. Two types of constants are used in BASIC: numeric constants and character strings (or literal strings).

Numeric Constants may be expressed with or without decimal points and may be either positive or negative. Examples of valid numeric constants are:

3.1416, −621, 100, −1.027

Character strings consist of alphanumeric (or alphabetic) information. Examples of character strings are names, addresses, and Social Security numbers. In BASIC, character strings are always enclosed in quotes. Following are examples of character strings.

"ANN", "A + B =", "861–73–2191", "1984"

VARIABLES A variable is a name given to a quantity that can assume different values during execution of a program. There are two types of variables in a BASIC program: numeric variables and character string variables.

Numeric variable names are limited to a single letter, or a letter followed by a single digit.

Following are valid BASIC variable names: X, X1, A, D9.

The following variable names are not valid.

2C   (does not start with a letter).

NAME   (too long).

X/   (second character is not a digit).

Character string variables consist of a letter followed by a dollar sign ($). For example, A$, N$ are valid character string variable names.

QUESTION: Examine the BASIC program in Figure 13–1 again. Write down the variable names for each of the following.

numeric variables _____

string variable _____

ANSWER: N, U, U1 are numeric variables; N$ is a string variable.

DATA STATEMENTS One method of introducing data into a BASIC program is by means of the DATA statement. As shown in Figure 13–1, a separate DATA statement contains the data for each student.

The general form of the DATA statement is:

statement-number DATA constant-list

The constant-list consists of numeric constants and/or character strings. In Example 1, the first item in each DATA statement is the student's name. This item is enclosed in quotes, since it is a character string. The next three items are numeric constants: student number, current units, and total units taken to date. Notice that items in the constant-list are separated by commas.

The DATA statement informs the BASIC system that the items contained in the constant-list are to be stored in memory in an area called the DATA block. DATA statements are nonexecutable and may be placed anywhere in the program before the END statement.

READ STATEMENT The READ statement causes values to be fetched from the DATA block (as specified in the DATA statements) and assigned to variables in the READ statement. The general form of this statement is:

statement-number READ variable-list

The variable-list consists of variable names (numeric and character string) separated by commas. When the READ statement is executed, values are assigned to these variables in the order in which they are specified in the DATA statement.

QUESTION: Examine Figure 13–1. When the READ statement (statement number 00220) is executed the first time, indicate the values that are assigned to each of the following variables.

N$ _____

N _____

U _____

U1 _____

ANSWER: N$ ADAMS, PETER R.

N 13978

U 9

U1 104

IF/THEN STATEMENT The IF/THEN decision statement affords the ability to test whether a certain condition exists. If the condition exists, the program transfers (or branches) to a nonsequential program instruction. If the condition does not exist, the program goes to the next instruction in sequence.

The general form of the decision statement is

statement-   IF   relational-   THEN   transfer
number   expression   statement-
                                              number

The relational-expression allows the programmer to compare two arithmetic expressions. The relational-expressions (and operators) that are used in BASIC are shown in Table 13–1.

TABLE 13-1   RELATIONAL OPERATORS IN BASIC

Relational Operator	Meaning
=	Equal to
<	Less than
>	Greater than
<=	Less than or equal to
>=	Greater than or equal to
<>	Not equal to

In Example 1, after the last valid student record, a record for a fictitious student with student number equal to zero is inserted in the DATA statement (see statement number 00330). After each student record is READ, the following statement is executed.

00230 IF N = 0 THEN 00340

When the last record is READ with student number equal to 0, this statement causes the program to branch to statement number 00340 which terminates the program.

QUESTION: When the *first* student record is read, the student number is N =

_____ When statement number 00230 is executed, instead of branching to statement number 00340 the program will next go to statement number

_____

ANSWER: 13978, 00240 (the next statement in sequence)

PRINT STATEMENT   The PRINT statement causes a line of output to be printed (or displayed). This statement has the following format.

statement-number PRINT expression-list

The expression-list consists of the following.

1.   Variable names (numeric or character string).
2.   String literals (enclosed in quotes).
3.   Arithmetic expressions.
4.   Combinations of the above.

The items in the expression-list are separated either by commas or by semicolons. Items separated by semicolons in the expression-list will be separated in the output line by a single blank. A comma between items in the expression list will cause items to be separated and printed in columnar fashion in the output line.

In Example 1, the output PRINT statement is the following.

00240 PRINT N$, N, U, U1

This statement causes the four data items (name, number, current units, total units) to be printed for each student. Since the items in the expression-list are separated by commas, the output is arranged in columns in the output (see Figure 13-1).

THE GO TO STATEMENT

The general form of the GO TO statement is

statement-   GO TO   transfer-
    number   statement-number

This statement causes an unconditional transfer to the statement-number following the key words GO TO.

In Example 1, after each student record has been PRINTED, the following statement is executed.

00250   GO TO 00220

This statement causes the program to transfer to statement-number 00220 to READ the next student record.

END STATEMENT

The END statement causes termination of the BASIC program. It must be the highest-numbered statement in the program (statement number 00340 in Figure 13-1).

EXECUTING A BASIC PROGRAM

To execute a BASIC program, the operator enters the command RUN, followed by a carriage return. The RUN command is called a **system command.** It is not a BASIC statement and therefore does not have a line number.

The result of executing the BASIC program for Example 1 is repeated in Figure 13-2. You should review this program and make sure you understand each of the BASIC statements contained in this program.

```
00100 REM ****************************************************************************
00110 REM
00120 REM PROGRAM PROB1
00130 REM      PROGRAM TO PRINT A REPORT CONTAINING STUDENT
00140 REM      NAME, NUMBER, CURRENT UNITS AND TOTAL UNITS
00150 REM      VARIABLES USED ARE:
00160 REM           N$ = STUDENT NAME
00170 REM           N  = STUDENT NUMBER
00180 REM           U  = CURRENT UNITS
00190 REM           U1 = TOTAL UNITS
00200 REM
00210 REM ****************************************************************************
00220 READ N$,N,U,U1
00230 IF N = 0 THEN 00340
00240     PRINT N$,N,U,U1
00250   GO TO 00220
00260 DATA "ADAMS, PETER R.        ",13978,09,104
00270 DATA "GOODMAN, HAROLD R.     ",20875,16,000
00280 DATA "JOHNSON, SHARON C.     ",24432,15,074
00290 DATA "LARSON, JAMES I.       ",47739,06,048
00300 DATA "LEWIS, BARBARA C.      ",01339,18,107
00310 DATA "ROTHCHILD, CHARLES K. ",80336,10,100
00320 DATA "THOMPSON, LAURA W.     ",59325,07,088
00330 DATA "                       ",00000,00,000
00340 END
```

RUN

ADAMS, PETER R.	13978	9	104
GOODMAN, HAROLD R.	20875	16	0
JOHNSON, SHARON C.	24432	15	74
LARSON, JAMES I.	47739	6	48
LEWIS, BARBARA C.	1339	18	107
ROTHCHILD, CHARLES K.	80336	10	100
THOMPSON, LAURA W.	59325	7	88

FIGURE 13-2
BASIC program and output for Example 1.

In addition to RUN, a number of other BASIC system commands are often used. These commands vary somewhat from one BASIC system to another. However, the system commands shown in Table 13-2 are available on most systems.

TABLE 13-2   COMMON BASIC SYSTEM COMMANDS

Command	Meaning or Purpose
RUN	Executes current BASIC program
LIST	Creates a clean listing of a current program
NEW	Clears memory (used before typing in a new BASIC program)
SAVE	Stores a copy of current program on systems auxiliary memory
OLD	Recalls a SAVED program
BYE	Ends a terminal session

EXERCISE 13-1   1. Identify each of the following as valid or invalid BASIC names.

a. A1 _____   f. A12 _____

b. 1A _____   g. Y3 _____

c. AB _____   h. Y- _____

d. TEMP _____   i. Y$ _____

e. K _____   j. Y0 _____

2. Suppose that the following brief BASIC program is executed.

```
00010 READ N$, A, S$
00020 PRINT N$, A, S$
00030 DATA "TOM SMITH", 23, "968-20-0458"
0040  END
```

Indicate below the output from this program.

_____   _____   _____

3. Suppose the following statement is executed.

00010 IF X $>=$ 10 THEN 00300
00120 . . .

Indicate below the statement number that will be executed next if X is equal to:

a. 3 _____

b. 10 _____

c. 28 _____

EXAMPLE 2: SIMPLE CALCULATIONS

This example introduces simple arithmetic operations and the replacement (or LET) statement in BASIC. As in Example 1, input data is to be read for each student. "Current units" is to be added to "previous units" to obtain an updated "total units" for each student.

A listing is to be prepared with the following column headings: STUDENT NAME, NUMBER, UNITS, TOTAL. One line of output is to be printed for each student under these column headings. Also, "current units" is to be totaled for all students and printed at the end of the listing.

A BASIC program for Example 2, together with sample output, is shown in Figure 13-3. The main features of this program are described below.

```
00100 REM      PROGRAM TO READ STUDENT NUMBER, CURRENT UNITS,
00110 REM      AND TOTAL UNITS.  A CUMULATIVE TOTAL OF CURRENT
00120 REM      UNITS IS KEPT.
00130 REM      THE TERMINATING CONDITION IS A STUDENT NUMBER OF 0.
00140 REM        N$= STUDENT NAME
00150 REM        N= STUDENT NUMBER
00160 REM        U= CURRENT UNITS
00170 REM        U1= TOTAL UNITS FOR A STUDENT
00180 REM        C= CUMULATIVE CURRENT UNITS
00190 REM
00200 LET C= 0
00210 PRINT "STUDENT NAME"," ","NUMBER","UNITS","TOTAL"
00220 PRINT "=============="," ","======","=====","====="
00230 READ N$,N,U,U1
00240 IF N= 0 THEN 00290
00250 LET U1= U1+U
00260 LET C= C+U
00270 PRINT N$,N,U,U1
00280 GOTO 00230
00290 PRINT
00300 PRINT "            TOTAL UNITS"," ",C
00310 REM    N$ MUST BE AT LEAST 16 CHARACTERS LONG.
00320 DATA "ADAMS, PETER R.     ",13978,9,104
00330 DATA "GOODMAN, HAROLD R.",20875,16,0
00340 DATA "JOHNSON, SHARON C.",24432,15,74
00350 DATA "LARSON, JAMES I.",47739,6,48
```

```
00360 DATA "LEWIS, BARBARA C.",1339,18,107
00370 DATA "ROTHCHILD, CHARLES K.",80336,10,100
00380 DATA "THOMPSON, LAURA W.",59325,7,88
00390 DATA " ",0,0,0
00400 END
```

RUN

STUDENT NAME	NUMBER	UNITS	TOTAL
============	======	=====	=====
ADAMS, PETER R.	13978	9	113
GOODMAN, HAROLD R.	20875	16	16
JOHNSON, SHARON C.	24432	15	89
LARSON, JAMES I.	47739	6	54
LEWIS, BARBARA C.	1339	18	125
ROTHCHILD, CHARLES K.	80336	10	110
THOMPSON, LAURA W.	59325	7	95
TOTAL UNITS		81	

FIGURE 13-3
BASIC program and output for Example 2.

ARITHMETIC STATEMENTS Arithmetic operations in BASIC are performed by replacement statements. The general form of a BASIC replacement statement is:

statement-number LET variable = expression

The value of the expression is computed and then assigned to the variable whose name appears to the left of the equals sign.
Examples of valid BASIC replacement statements are shown below.

	Comment
10 LET S = 0	Assign the value zero to S
20 LET X = (A1 + A2)/D	Compute A1 + A2, divide by D, call the result X
30 LET Y = (R − S)↑2	Subtract S from R, square the difference, result is Y

There are three replacement statements in Example 2 (see Figure 13-3). The first (statement number 00200) initializes (or assigns an initial value) of zero to the variable C. This variable is used to accumulate the total units taken by all students during the current semester.
The second replacement statement is the following.

00250 LET U1 = U1 + U

This statement causes the current units (U) to be added to previous units (U1) for each student. The result, which is the new total units, is assigned to U1.

QUESTION: Examine the DATA statement for the first student (statement number 00320) in Figure 13-3. The amount of current units (U) for this student is equal to

_____ , whereas the amount of previous units (U1) is equal to

_____ . When statement number 00250 is executed, U1 will be set

equal to _____

ANSWER: 9, 104, 113

The third replacement statement in Figure 13–3 is the following.

00260 LET C = C + U

This statement causes the current units for a student (U) to be added to the total for all students (C), forming a new total.

In an arithmetic expression, arithmetic operators are used to indicate the arithmetic operations to be performed. The five basic arithmetic operations are add, subtract, multiply, divide, and exponentiate. The arithmetic operators in BASIC, together with examples, are shown in Table 13–3.

TABLE 13–3   BASIC ARITHMETIC OPERATORS

Operation	Symbol	Example
Add	+	X + Y
Subtract	−	R − 8.3
Multiply	*	A * C
Divide	/	M/5
Exponentiate	↑	X↑2

COLUMN HEADINGS Two PRINT statements (numbers 00210 and 00220) in Figure 13–3 are used to create the column headings for Example 2. In the first of these statements, the column headings are contained in the PRINT expression-list. Since the column headings consist of alphanumeric characters, they are represented as character strings and are enclosed in quotes in the PRINT statement.

The second of these PRINT statements (number 00220) contains a series of equal signs enclosed in quotes. These character strings are used to underline the column headings (see the sample output in Figure 13–3).

EXERCISE 13–2 1. Write BASIC expressions for each of the following.

a. R divided by M3 _____

b. A plus B minus C _____

c. 100 times Z _____

d. M to the fourth power _____

2. Write BASIC statements for each of the following (include statement numbers).

a. Y equals R divided by M3 _____

b.   F equals A plus B minus C _____

c.   V equals 100 times Z _____

d.   N equals M to the fourth power _____

EXAMPLE 3: SIMPLE LOGICAL OPERATIONS

This example introduces additional BASIC logical operations. As in the previous examples, student data are to be read by means of DATA statements. Student tuition is to be computed by means of the following formula.

If units taken is less than 12, tuition is units taken times $35. If units taken is 12 or more, tuition is $420.

Total student fees consist of tuition plus an incidental fee of $12.50. This total is to be printed for each student along with student name, number, and units taken. Also, the total of fees for all students is to be computed and printed at the end of the listing.

A BASIC program for this example, together with sample output, is shown in Figure 13-4. The main features of this program are described below.

```
00100 REM *************************************************************************************
00110 REM
00120 REM      PROGRAM PROB3 READS STUDENT NAME, NUMBER, CURRENT
00130 REM      UNITS AND CALCULATES FEES BASED ON CURRENT NUMBER OF
00140 REM      UNITS AS FOLLOWS.
00150 REM      IF THE STUDENT HAS 12 UNITS OR LESS THE FEES ARE
00160 REM      $35.00 TIMES THE TOTAL NUMBER OF CURRENT UNITS.
00170 REM      IF THE STUDENT HAS MORE THAN 12 UNITS THE FEES ARE
00180 REM      SIMPLY $420.00.  AN ADDITIONAL FEE OF $12.50 IS THEN
00190 REM      ADDED TO THE FEES.
00200 REM      N$ = STUDENT NAME
00210 REM      N  = STUDENT NUMBER
00220 REM      U  = STUDENT'S CURRENT NUMBER OF UNITS
00230 REM      F  = FEES
00240 REM      F1 = CUMULATIVE TOTAL OF ALL FEES FOR PERIOD
00250 REM
00260 REM *************************************************************************************
00270 F1 = 0
00280 PRINT "STUDENT NAME"," ","NUMBER","UNITS","FEES"
00290 PRINT "=============="," ","======","=====","===="
00300 PRINT
00310 READ N$,N,U
00320 IF N = 0 THEN 00410
00330     IF U > 12 THEN 00360
00340         F = 35.00 * U
00350       GO TO 00370
00360         F = 420.00
00370     F = F + 12.50
00380     PRINT N$,N,U,F
00390     F1 = F1 + F
00400   GO TO 00310
00410 PRINT
```

```
00420 PRINT " "," ","    TOTAL FEES   $"," ", F1
00430 DATA "ADAMS, PETER R.         ",13978,09
00440 DATA "GOODMAN, HAROLD R.      ",20875,16
00450 DATA "JOHNSON, SHARON C.      ",24432,15
00460 DATA "LARSON, JAMES I.        ",47739,06
00470 DATA "LEWIS, BARBARA C.       ",01339,18
00480 DATA "ROTHCHILD, CHARLES K. ",80336,10
00490 DATA "THOMPSON, LAURA W.      ",59325,07
00500 DATA "                        ",00000,00
00510 END
```

RUN

STUDENT NAME	NUMBER	UNITS	FEES
============	======	=====	====
ADAMS, PETER R.	13978	9	327.5
GOODMAN, HAROLD R.	20875	16	432.5
JOHNSON, SHARON C.	24432	15	432.5
LARSON, JAMES I.	47739	6	222.5
LEWIS, BARBARA C.	1339	18	432.5
ROTHCHILD, CHARLES K.	80336	10	362.5
THOMPSON, LAURA W.	59325	7	257.5

TOTAL FEES $ 2467.5

FIGURE 13-4
BASIC program and output for Example 3.

REMARKS SECTION   The initial statements of this program describe the program briefly and list the variable names that are used.

QUESTION: Examine Figure 13-4. What variable name is used for each of the following.

fees for each student _____

cumulative fees for all students _____

ANSWER: F, F1

The first executable statement in this program (statement number 00270) initializes the variable F1 to zero.

COLUMN HEADINGS   Two print statements (00280 and 00290) are used to print the column headings. As in Example 2, the character strings (or string literals) are enclosed in quotes in the PRINT expression-list. The PRINT statement with the blank expression-list (statement 00300) creates a line spacing between the column heading and the first line of output (see the sample output).

TUITION LOGIC   The main feature of this program is the logic of the tuition calculation. This logic is shown in flowchart form in Figure 13-5. The statement numbers from the BASIC program are included in the flowchart.

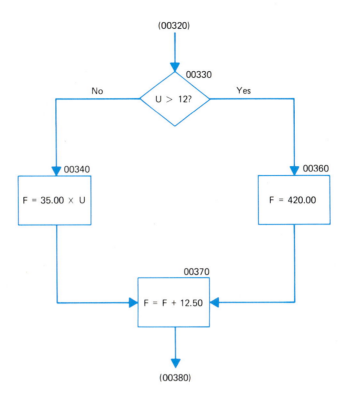

FIGURE 13-5
Logic of tuition calculation.

QUESTION: Examine Figure 13-5. Statement number 00330 compares units (U) with 12. What statement is executed next if:

a. U = 9? _____

b. U = 12? _____

c. U = 18? _____

ANSWER: (a)   00340   (b)   00340   (c)   00360

After tuition is calculated, the incidental fee is added to obtain total fees (statement number 00370). After a line of information is printed for each student (statement number 00380), the student's fees are added to cumulative fees (00390). The program then transfers to statement number 00310 to READ the data for the next student.

End of student data is indicated when the program encounters a student number equal to zero. Statement 00320 then causes the program to branch to statement 00410, which creates a blank line after the last line of student information. The next statement (00420) then prints the total fees accumulated for all students, after which the program terminates.

LOOPS IN BASIC   In many programs the programmer wishes to cause the program to execute the same instruction (or more than one instruction) several times. A **loop** is a set of program instructions that is executed repeatedly.

To illustrate loops in BASIC, suppose that a program is to be written to compute the average of student examination grades. Ten grades are to be read by the program, and the average is to be computed. If the average grade is greater than 75, it is to be printed out and then the program is to terminate. If the average grade is 75 or less, the program is to terminate without printing the average.

A flowchart for this program, which will be referred to as the GRADES program, is shown in Figure 13–6. This figure also shows the BASIC program statements corresponding to each flowchart symbol.

The program for computing the average of 10 grades contains four numeric variables. In the flowchart of Figure 13–6 these variables have been given the following names.

X—individual grade.

S—running sum of grades.

A—average of 10 grades.

J—loop variable that controls reading and summing the numbers.

In the flowchart for the GRADES program, the third symbol represents the beginning of the loop to read the data and form the sum.

The BASIC instruction corresponding to this symbol is the following.

20 FOR J=1 TO 10

The FOR statement indicates the beginning of a loop. The loop is terminated by a NEXT statement (statement number 50). Thus the loop consists of program statements number 30 and 40.

The variable J is the loop counter. It is set initially to 1. Each time the loop is executed, the value of J is incremented by 1 (other increments can also be used, as we will explain below). The looping process continues until the loop counter exceeds the limit following TO, in this case 10. Thus in the GRADES program the loop may be summarized as follows.

Execute 10 times as J is incremented from 1 to 10
$\left\{ \begin{array}{l} \text{20 FOR J} = \text{1 TO 10} \\ \text{30 READ X} \\ \text{40 LET S} = \text{S} + \text{X} \\ \text{50 NEXT J} \end{array} \right.$

Other values may be used for the beginning and ending values in a FOR statement. Also, a STEP clause can be used to increment by values other than 1. For example, the following statement causes a loop to be executed five times, as the loop counter C takes on the values 2, 4, 6, 8, 10.

15 FOR C = 2 TO 10 STEP 2

The loop counter can also be decremented, as in the following example.

25 FOR M = 9 TO 1 STEP −2

This statement causes a loop to be executed five times, as the loop counter M takes on the values 9, 7, 5, 3, 1.

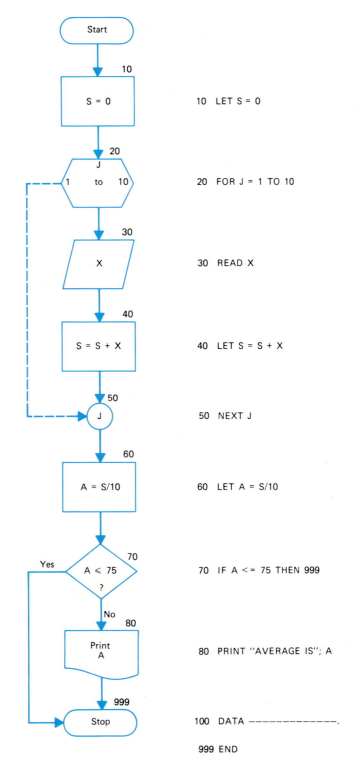

Flowchart	BASIC program
10 S = 0	10 LET S = 0
20 J 1 to 10	20 FOR J = 1 TO 10
30 X	30 READ X
40 S = S + X	40 LET S = S + X
50 J	50 NEXT J
60 A = S/10	60 LET A = S/10
70 A ≤ 75 ?	70 IF A <= 75 THEN 999
80 Print A	80 PRINT "AVERAGE IS"; A
999 Stop	100 DATA --------------.
	999 END

FIGURE 13-6
Flowchart and BASIC program for computing average grade.

QUESTION: Consider the following statement.

9 FOR T = 3 TO 15 STEP 4

This statement causes a loop to be executed _____ times as T is as-

signed the values _____

ANSWER: four; 3, 7, 11, 15

After the FOR statement in the GRADES program, statement number 30 causes the program to READ the next student grade. Statement number 40 then adds this grade to the previous sum to form a new sum. The following NEXT statement is then used to terminate the loop.

50 NEXT J

Notice that, in the NEXT statement, the word NEXT is followed by the variable name for the loop counter. This statement causes the loop counter (in this case J) to be incremented and tested. If the loop counter now exceeds its final value (10 in this program) the loop is terminated and control passes to the statement immediately following NEXT. Otherwise, the loop is executed another cycle.

A listing of the GRADES program, together with sample input and output, is shown in Figure 13-7.

EXERCISE 13-3   1.   Write FOR statements for each of the following.

a.   Loop variable I is to take on the values 1, 4, 7, 10 _____

FIGURE 13-7
Program listing and sample output of grades program.

```
PROGRAM    GRADES

00010 LET  S=0
00020 FOR  J=1 TO 10
00030    READ  X
00040    LET  S=S+X
00050 NEXT J
00060 LET  A=S/10
00070 IF  A<=75 THEN 00999
00080 PRINT "AVERAGE IS";A
00100 DATA  90,85,63,74,87,69,79,95,84,74
00999 END
READY.

RUN

AVERAGE IS 80
```

b. Loop variable L is to take on the values 10, 7, 4, 1 _____

c. Loop variable R is to take on the values 5, 10, 15,. . ., 100 _____

2. Write IF statements for each of the following.
    a. If the variable M1 is not equal to 10, then the program is to branch to

        statement number 100. _____

    b. If the variable M2 is greater than or equal to 100, then the program is

        to branch to statement number 200. _____

    c. If the variable M3 is less than 1000, the program is to go to the next
        statement after the IF statement; otherwise it is to branch to statement

        number 300 (be careful!). _____

ADDITIONAL BASIC STATEMENTS AND FEATURES

A number of statements and features are available in BASIC, in addition to those described above. Some of the more important of these are described below.

INPUT STATEMENT

In the programs described thus far, data is read by a combination of the READ and DATA statements. With the DATA statement, the actual data to be used must be entered along with the other program statements before the program is RUN. If the program is to be run a second time with new data, the DATA statement would have to be changed.

An alternative approach to entering data is to use the INPUT statement. With this statement, the input data is not defined when the program is coded. Instead, when the program is executed and an INPUT statement is encountered, the program prompts the user to enter the required data.

In the GRADES program, the following statement could be used to enter each data value.

```
30 INPUT X
```

When the program is run, each time the program encounters this INPUT statement it will respond with a question mark (?) to prompt the terminal operator to enter a data value. If the INPUT statement is contained within the program loop it will be executed 10 times, prompting the operator to enter 10 data values.

Several variables may be contained in an INPUT statement list. For example, the following statement requires that the operator enter four data values corresponding to the variables X1, X2, X3, and X4.

37 INPUT X1, X2, X3, X4

When this statement is encountered in a program as it is being executed, it will prompt the operator with a question mark. The operator must enter four values, separated by commas. Following is an example response.

? 6.2, 1.9, 7.8, 0

In this example, X1 is assigned the value 6.2, X2 the value 1.9, X3 the value 7.8, and X4 the value 0.

ARRAYS In the GRADES program, as each data value X is read it replaces the previous value. For example, in Figure 13-7 when the first data value (90) is READ, it is assigned to the variable X. When the second value (85) is read, it is also assigned to the variable X and replaces the previous value.

Suppose one desired in this program to calculate and print out the difference between each grade and the average grade. To accomplish this, all 10 data values must be stored simultaneously in computer memory. The simplest method to store the 10 grades is to use an array.

An **array** is a sequence of memory locations used to store related data. Each data item in the array is referenced by specifying the array name and a **subscript** indicating the position of the item in the array. For example, suppose the array of grades is given the name X. Then X(1) would indicate the first grade in the array, X(2) the second grade, and so on.

When using arrays in a BASIC program, we must declare each array by using a dimension (DIM) statement. The upper limit on the subscript to be used with an array is enclosed in parentheses after the array name. For example, in the GRADES program the following dimension statement might be used.

5 DIM X(10)

DIM statements are normally inserted at the beginning of a BASIC program.

A revised GRADES program, using the INPUT statement and an array called X, is shown in Figure 13-8. Notice that statement number 00140 causes the program to print out the value of X(J) that is to be INPUT to the program. Since the print-list ends with a semicolon, the following INPUT statement (number 00150) causes a question mark to be printed on the same line. The programmer then responds by entering the value for X(J). You should compare Figures 13-7 and 13-8 and make sure you understand how these new statements are used.

QUESTION: In Figure _____, only one data value is stored in memory at a given

time. In Figure _____, after the average grade is computed, all 10 of the data values are stored in memory.

ANSWER: 13-7, 13-8.

NESTED LOOPS In the GRADES program a single loop is used to read data items and form a sum. In many BASIC programs it is necessary to use two (or more) loops. Often the

PROGRAM   ARRAY

```
00100 REM        GRADES PROGRAM USING ARRAY AND INPUT STATEMENT
00110 DIM  X(10)
00120 LET  S=0
00130 FOR  J=1 TO 10
00140     PRINT "VALUE OF  X(";J;")IS";
00150     INPUT X(J)
00160     LET  S=S+X(J)
00170 NEXT J
00180 LET  A=S/10
00190 PRINT
00200 PRINT "AVERAGE IS:";A
00210 END
```

RUN

```
VALUE  OF  X( 1 )IS ? 90
VALUE  OF  X( 2 )IS ? 85
VALUE  OF  X( 3 )IS ? 63
VALUE  OF  X( 4 )IS ? 74
VALUE  OF  X( 5 )IS ? 87
VALUE  OF  X( 6 )IS ? 69
VALUE  OF  X( 7 )IS ? 79
VALUE  OF  X( 8 )IS ? 95
VALUE  OF  X( 9 )IS ? 84
VALUE  OF  X( 10 )IS? 74

AVERAGE IS: 80
```

FIGURE 13-8
Revised GRADES program.

second loop is contained within the body of the first loop, thus forming **nested** loops.

As an example, consider the following compound interest problem. It is desired to compute and print out the compound amount for $100 compounded annually each year for five years. The compound amounts are to be computed for interest rates of 5, 10, 15, and 20 percent.

The compound amount (S) for a principal P, at interest rate I, after N years is given by the following formula.

$$S = P (1 + I)^N$$

A flowchart for this problem is shown in Figure 13-9. The "outer" loop in this flowchart causes the number of years (N) to vary from one to five. The "inner" (or nested) loop causes the interest rate to take on the values 0.05, 0.10, 0.15, and 0.20. These values are repeated for each number of years and the compound amount is computed and printed out.

The BASIC program for the compound interest problem, together with program output, is shown in Figure 13-10.

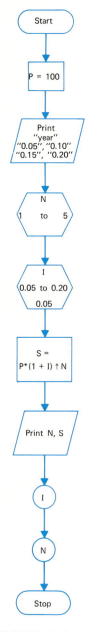

FIGURE 13-9
Compound interest problems with nested loops.

```
00100  REM COMPOUND INTEREST
00110  LET P = 100
00120  PRINT "YEAR",".05",".10",".15",".20"
00130  PRINT "====","===","===","===","==="
00140  FOR N = 1 TO 5
00150      PRINT
00160      PRINT N,
00170      FOR I = .05 TO .20 STEP .05
00180          LET S = P * (1 + I) ↑N
00190          PRINT S,
00200      NEXT I
00210  NEXT N
00220  END
```

RUN

YEAR	.05	.10	.15	.20
====	===	===	===	===
1	105.	110.	115.	120.
2	110.25	121.	132.25	144.
3	115.762	133.1	152.087	172.8
4	121.551	146.41	174.901	207.36
5	127.628	161.051	201.136	248.832

FIGURE 13-10
BASIC program for compound interest problem.

QUESTION: In the BASIC program, the inner loop is terminated by the statement _____
ANSWER: 00200 NEXT I

In Figure 13-10, the statement that computes the compound amount is the following.

00180 LET S = P * (1 + I) ↑N

The expression to the right of the equals sign is evaluated as follows. First, the expression in parentheses (1+I) is computed. Next, the resulting value is raised to the power N. Finally, this result is multiplied by P.

In BASIC, arithmetic operations are performed in the following order.

1. First, expressions in parentheses ( ) are evaluated.
2. Next, exponentiation (↑) operations are performed.
3. Next, multiplications (*) and divisions (/) are performed.
4. Finally, additions (+) and subtractions (−) are performed.

EXERCISE 13-4   1. Explain in words how each of the following BASIC expressions is evaluated.

    a. C+D*E _____

_____

    b. A*B↑4 _____

_____

    c. X−(A/B)↑2 _____

_____

2. Suppose that A = 2, B = 4, and C = 6. Write down the result of evaluating each of the following BASIC expressions.

    a. C+B/A _____

    b. (A+B)*C _____

    c. (C+B↑2)↑A _____

ANSWERS TO EXERCISES

EXERCISE 13-1

1. a. Valid
   b. Invalid (first character not a letter)
   c. Invalid (second character not a digit)
   d. Invalid (too long)
   e. Valid
   f. Invalid (too long)
   g. Valid
   h. Invalid (second character not a digit)
   i. Valid (designates a character string)
   j. Valid (second character is a zero, not letter "O")

2. TOM SMITH   23   968-20-0458

3. a. 00120
   b. 00300
   c. 00300

EXERCISE 13-2

1. a. R/M3
    b. A + B − C
    c. 100*Z
    d. M↑4
2. a. 10 LET Y = R/M3
    b. 20 LET F = A + B − C
    c. 30 LET V = 100*Z
    d. 40 LET N = M↑4

EXERCISE 13-3

1. a. FOR I = 1 TO 10 STEP 3
    b. FOR L = 10 TO 1 STEP −3
    c. FOR R = 5 TO 100 STEP 5
2. a. IF M1 <> 10 THEN 100
    b. IF M2 >= 100 THEN 200
    c. IF M3 >= 1000 THEN 300

EXERCISE 13-4

1. a. First, D is multiplied by E. The result is then added to C.
    b. First, B is raised to the fourth power. The result is then multiplied by A.
    c. First, A is divided by B. The result is then squared. Finally, this result is subtracted from X.
2. a. 8
    b. 36
    c. 484

CHAPTER EXAMINATION

1. Write BASIC LET statements for each of the following formulas (ignore statement numbers).

   a. $A = PR^2$ _____

   b. $Y = AX^2 + BX + C$ _____

   c. $P = S(1 + I)$ _____

   d. $\dfrac{A + B}{C \times D}$ _____

   e. $\dfrac{X}{Y + Z}$ _____

2. Write BASIC statements corresponding to each of the following flowchart symbols.

   a. _____

   b. _____

c.

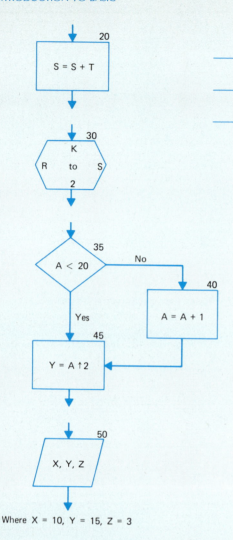

Where X = 10, Y = 15, Z = 3

_____

_____

_____

d.   _____

_____

3. Write a BASIC program to compute and print out the average of 10 grades and the deviation of each grade from the average.

4. Write a BASIC program to compute and print out the average of 10 grades and the standard deviation of the grades. The standard deviation is given by the following formula.

$$s = \left(\frac{\Sigma (X - \overline{X})^2}{n} \right)^{\frac{1}{2}}$$

5. Write a BASIC program to print out two columns of temperatures. One column is to show Fahrenheit (F) temperatures for F = 0, 5, 10, 15,..., 100. The second column is to show the Celsius (C) equivalent for each Fahrenheit temperature. The conversion is given by the following formula.

$$C = \tfrac{5}{9}(F - 32)$$

6. Write a BASIC program to compute and print out the present value of one dollar for years 1 through 10. Use the INPUT statement to input the interest rate (I). Test your program for $I = 0.10$. The present value (P) of an

amount (S) for N years at interest rate I is given by the following formula.

$$P = \frac{S}{(1 + I)^N}$$

7. Write a program that will accept from the terminal 10 integer numbers, one at a time. If the number is greater than 50, go to the next number. If the number is less than or equal to 50, print the number and its squared value.

8. Write a program to compute a simple payroll. The program is to read Employee Number, Hours Worked, and Pay Rate for each employee. The program is to compute and print out Gross Pay and Overtime Pay for each employee. Overtime Pay (for hours exceeding 40) is at 1.5 times the regular pay rate.

   The following headings are to be printed.

   EMPLOYEE NUMBER   GROSS PAY   OVERTIME PAY

   Test your program with the following data.

Employee Number	Hours Worked	Pay Rate
100	30	7
101	48	6
102	40	8

9. Write a program to compute and print out the length of the hypotenuse of any right triangle, given its two legs L1 and L2. The program is to accept L1 and L2 from the terminal. Test your program using L1 = 16 and L2 = 9.

10. A salesman is paid a commission on the following basis.

Sale	Commission
Up through $100	Zero
Over $100 through $1000	2%
Over $1000	3%

    Write a program to input a sale amount and compute and print out the commission.

11. The Brownout Electric Company charges its customers for electricity according to the following schedule.

Kilowatt-Hours	Cost ($)
0 to 500	10.00
501 to 1000	10.00 + 0.05 for each kwh above 500
over 1000	35.00 + 0.03 for each kwh above 1000

    Write a BASIC program to accept as input the old and new meter reading for a customer, and calculate and print out the amount of the customer's bill.

12. The Amazing Toy Company (ATC) manufactures a wide line of children's toys. Total fixed costs (FC) for ATC during the coming year are expected to be $100,000. Variable costs as a percent of dollar sales (P) are expected to range between 60 and 80 percent. Write a BASIC program to compute and print out the break-even point (BEP) for P = 0.60, 0.65, 0.70, 0.75, and 0.80. The BEP (in dollars) is given by the following formula.

$$BEP = \frac{FC}{1 - P}$$

13. The 1960 U.S. Population Census shows that five central cities (CC) had populations of over 1 million. The following table shows the populations and areas in square miles of the five central cities and their standard metropolitan statistical areas (SMSAs), which include the central cities.

	Population		Area (sq. miles)	
	CC	SMSA	CC	SMSA
New York	7,781,984	10,694,633	315	2149
Chicago	3,550,404	6,220,913	224	3714
Philadelphia	3,002,512	4,342,897	127	3549
Detroit	1,670,144	3,762,360	140	1965
San Francisco	1,104,035	2,783,359	98	3313

Write a program to read the above data and compute and print out the following.
a. Population density (population per square mile) for each CC, SMSA, and SMSA ring (SMSA excluding the CC)
b. Area of each CC as a percent of the area of the SMSA

14

INTRODUCTION TO FORTRAN

OVERVIEW. FORTRAN is a high-level language especially suited for describing mathematical and procedural problems for computer solution. FORTRAN (acronym for FORmula TRANslator) is largely machine independent and is the most widely used algebraic-oriented programming language. FORTRAN is often used for quantitative business applications such as statistical analysis.

FORTRAN was originally developed by IBM in the mid-1950s. The American National Standards Institute (ANSI) has set uniform standards for the FORTRAN language. Today most computer manufacturers provide FORTRAN compilers as part of their software systems. This chapter describes the basic features of FORTRAN IV, which is the most common version in use today.

FORTRAN CODING FORM

A FORTRAN program is a series of statements designed to solve a specific problem. The program may also include comments or explanatory information inserted to make the program easier to read.

FORTRAN statements and comments must be keypunched in program cards in a specific format. In preparation for keypunching, the program is first written on a coding form that has the same format as the program card. A sample FORTRAN coding form is shown is Figure 14-1. The form contains a sample program based on a compound amount calculation.

FIGURE 14-1
Sample FORTRAN program.

```
IBM                                              FORTRAN Coding Form
PROGRAM  COMPOUND AMOUNT                          PUNCHING        GRAPHIC
PROGRAMMER  FRM                      DATE 7/24     INSTRUCTIONS    PUNCH

CØMMENT  P IS PRINCIPAL, R IS INTEREST, N IS YEARS, S IS AMØUNT
         P = 1000.
         R = .10
         N = 10
         S = P * (1.+R) **N
         WRITE (6,10) S
    10   FØRMAT(1H0,'CØMPØUND AMØUNT IS',F8.2)
         STØP
         END
```

QUESTION: Examine Figure 14-1. The program will compute and print out the amount in

$N =$ _____ years for a principal of $P =$ _____ dollars at an

interest rate of $R =$ _____ percent compounded annually.

ANSWER: 10, 1000, 0.10

STATEMENT FIELD
FORTRAN statements are entered in the **statement field,** which extends from columns 7 through 72. A statement need not start in column 7 but must be confined to this field. If a statement cannot be completed at column 72, it must be continued on the following card in the statement field. No more than one statement may be written in the field.

STATEMENT NUMBER FIELD
Some statements in a FORTRAN program must be numbered because they are referenced by other statements in the same program. **Statement numbers** are entered (right justified) in columns 1 through 5. Any integer not exceeding the field width may be used as a statement number. All numbers must be unique; that is, two or more statements may not be assigned the same number.

In Figure 14-1, only one statement is numbered—a **format** statement, which is arbitrarily assigned the number 10. This statement must be numbered because it is referenced by the **write** statement that immediately precedes it. This combination of statements will be explained in subsequent sections.

CONTINUATION FIELD
The first card of a FORTRAN statement must contain a blank (or zero) in column 6. If the statement extends beyond column 72, it must be continued on a following card. In this case, the following statement is a **continuation statement** and must have a continuation character punched in column 6. A **continuation character** is any valid FORTRAN character other than zero or blank. Continuation statements will be illustrated later in the chapter.

IDENTIFICATION FIELD
Columns 73 through 80 may be left blank or used for sequence numbers or other identifying information. This field is ignored by the FORTRAN compiler.

COMMENTS
FORTRAN permits the insertion of comments at any point to improve the readability of the program. Comments are printed on the program listing but do not affect the program. Column 1 is punched with the letter C to indicate that a card contains a comment rather than a program statement. Notice that the first line of coding in Figure 14-1 is a comment.

To illustrate the basic concepts of FORTRAN programming, three sample problems will be introduced. These examples are all based on processing a student record file.

EXAMPLE 1: BASIC INPUT/OUTPUT OPERATIONS

A student file is maintained on punched cards, one card per student. The format of the record is shown in Figure 14-2. Each card contains student name (columns 2 to 25), number (26 to 31), units taken this semester (32 to 33), and total units prior to this semester (34 to 37). Column 1 and columns 38 to 80 are not used.

The last card in the data deck is a **trailer card,** with the number 999999 punched in columns 26-31.

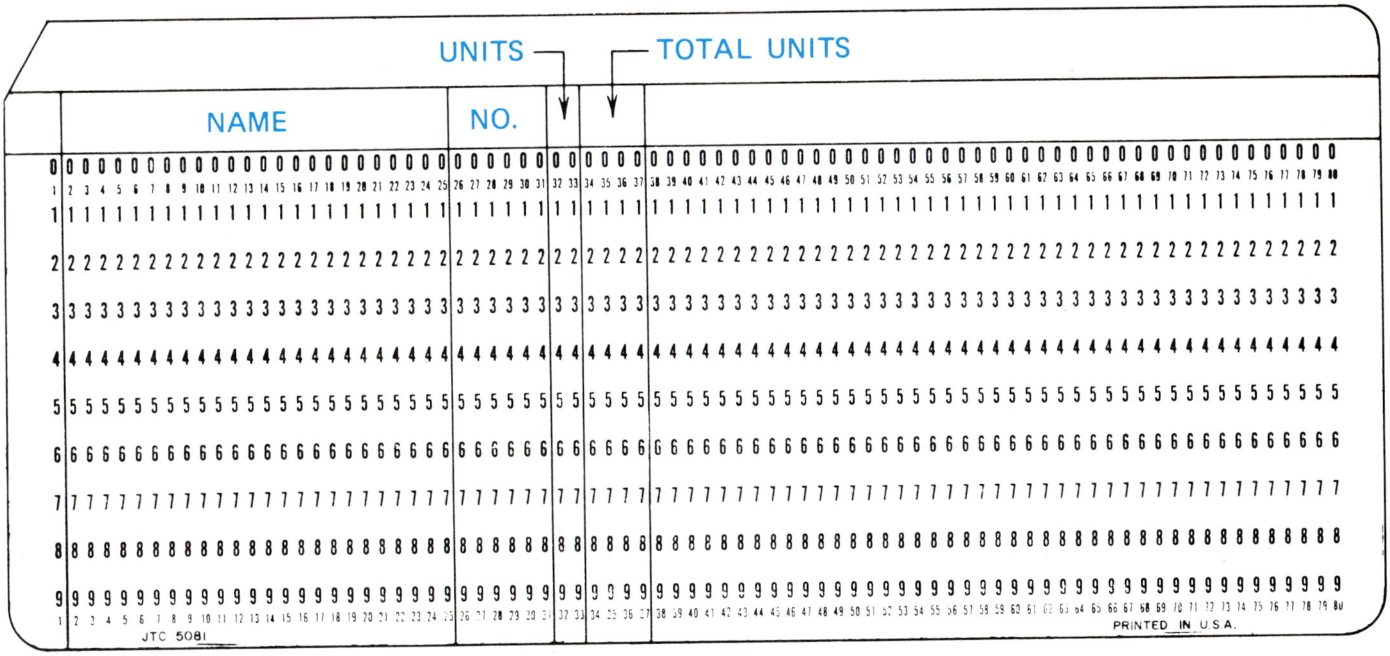

FIGURE 14-2
Input student record for Example 1.

An output listing is to be prepared from the cards. Each card field is to be printed, with blank spaces between fields. A printer spacing chart of the desired output format is shown in Figure 14-3.

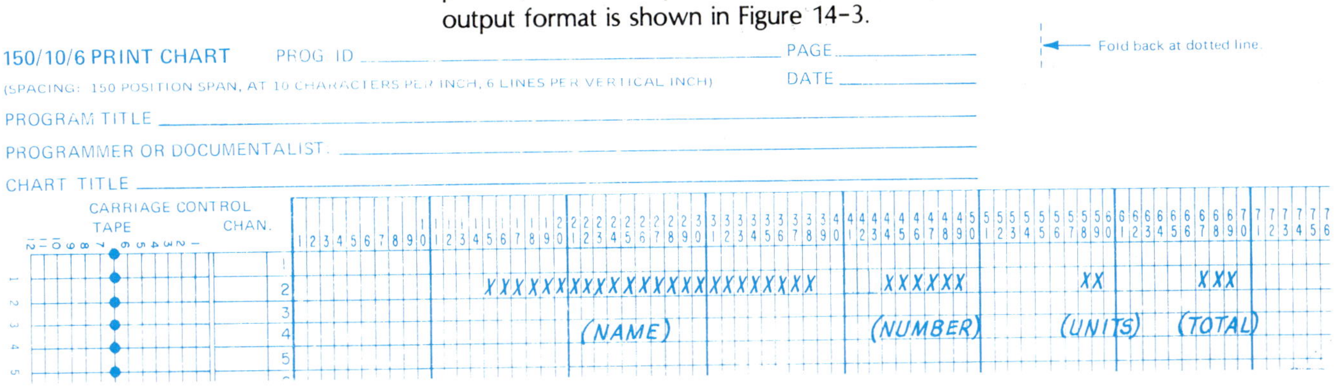

FIGURE 14-3
Printer spacing chart for Example 1.

PROGRAM The FORTRAN program to prepare the printed report is shown in Figure 14-4.

TYPE DECLARATION.   Each variable in a FORTRAN program is assigned a variable name that may consist of from one to six characters, the first of which must be a letter. In the program shown in Figure 14-4 there are four FORTRAN variables, as follows.

NAME (for student name).

```
IBM                                    FORTRAN Coding Form                                              GX28-7327-
                                                                                                         Printe
PROGRAM                                              PUNCHING      GRAPHIC                    PAGE    OF
PROGRAMMER                              DATE         INSTRUCTIONS  PUNCH                      CARD ELECTRO NUMBER*

         INTEGER NUMB,UNITS,TUNITS
         DIMENSION NAME(6)
   20    READ(5,30)NAME,NUMB,UNITS,TUNITS
   30    FORMAT(1X,6A4,I6,I2,I3)
         IF (NUMB.EQ.0) GO TO 50
             WRITE(6,40)NAME,NUMB,UNITS,TUNITS
   40        FORMAT(1H ,14X,6A4,5X,I6,8X,I2,7X,I3)
         GO TO 20
   50    STOP
         END
```

FIGURE 14-4
FORTRAN program for Example 1.

NUMB (for student number).

UNITS (for units taken).

TUNITS (for total units).

The first statement in Figure 14-4 is a **type** declaration. It designates the variables NUMB, UNITS, and TUNITS as integer variables (whole numbers, or numbers that do not contain decimal points). A number of type declarations are available in FORTRAN, for example, INTEGER, REAL, and COMPLEX. Type declarations such as the one in Figure 14-4 must appear at the beginning of a FORTRAN program.

If type declarations are not incuded, the FORTRAN compiler assigns type to variables by default. Variables whose names begin with the letters I, J, K, L, M, or N are designated integer variables, whereas variables that begin with the letters A through H or O through Z are designated real (or decimal) variables. For example, in the absence of a TYPE declaration the variable NUMB is treated as integer, while the variable TEMP is treated as decimal.

QUESTION: In Figure 14-4, the variable NUMB (for student number) is an integer variable. It (is, is not) necessary to include this variable in the INTEGER type declaration.

ANSWER: is not. FORTRAN will treat NUMB as an integer variable by default.

DIMENSION STATEMENT.   The next statement in the FORTRAN program is a **DIMENSION statement,** as shown in Figure 14-5.

The field NAME in the FORTRAN program is an alphanumeric field—that is, it may consist of a combination of letters, numbers, and special characters. In Chapter 4 you learned that alphanumeric data is stored in the computer in coded form—generally either seven or eight bits per character. If the computer uses a fixed word length, the number of characters that can be stored depends on the word length and the type of code used. For example, an IBM 370 computer stores four alphanumeric characters in each 32-bit word.

The student name field in Example 1 (called NAME) is 24 characters long. It is

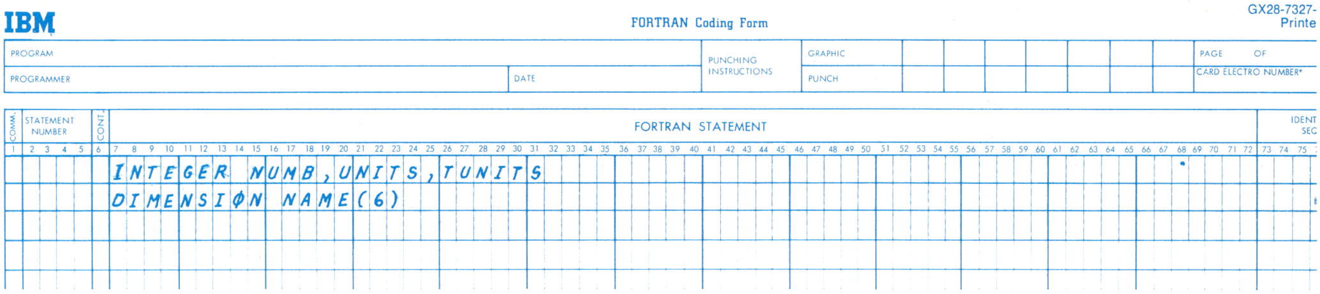

FORTRAN Coding Form

```
INTEGER  NUMB,UNITS,TUNITS
DIMENSIØN  NAME(6)
```

FIGURE 14-5
FORTRAN TYPE and DIMENSION statements.

assumed that data are stored four characters per word, so that 24 ÷ by 4 or 6 words are required. To illustrate, the name JOHNSTON, STANLEY R. would be stored as follows.

Word 1 |J |O |H |N |

Word 2 |S |T |O |N |

Word 3 |, | |S |T |

Word 4 |A |N |L |E |

Word 5 |Y | |R |. |

Word 6 | | | | |

In FORTRAN, a table such as the one above is called an **array.** Each array used in a program must be identified by a DIMENSION statement that reserves the necessary memory positions. In Figure 14-5 the statement DIMENSION NAME (6) indicates that the variable NAME will require six words or positions. DIMENSION statements must appear near the beginning of a program.

In addition to storing alphanumeric data, arrays are widely used in FORTRAN for storing tables of numbers. For example, a table showing number of students by class and major could be represented as a two-dimensional array in FORTRAN. (See Chapter 9 for discussion of arrays and other data structures.)

THE READ STATEMENT.   The FORTRAN READ statement causes an input record to be read into storage. The READ statement for Example 1 is shown in Figure 14-6.

The statement is numbered 20, since it is referenced by another statement in the program. The entry after READ is (5,30). The 5 is a device number that indicates to the computer the input device to be used. In many installations, the number 5 designates the card reader; however, FORTRAN users should check with their installation to determine the correct number.

The 30 in the entry (5,30) references the FORMAT statement that follows the READ statement. The FORMAT statement is described below.

The input variable names appear in the READ statement immediately following the parentheses. These names appear in the same order as do the corresponding fields on the punched cards to be read by the program.

INPUT FORMAT STATEMENT.   Every command to read or print information in FORTRAN must be accompanied by a FORMAT statement. This statement describes the type, size, and location of each data field. The input FORMAT statement for Example 1 is shown in Figure 14-7.

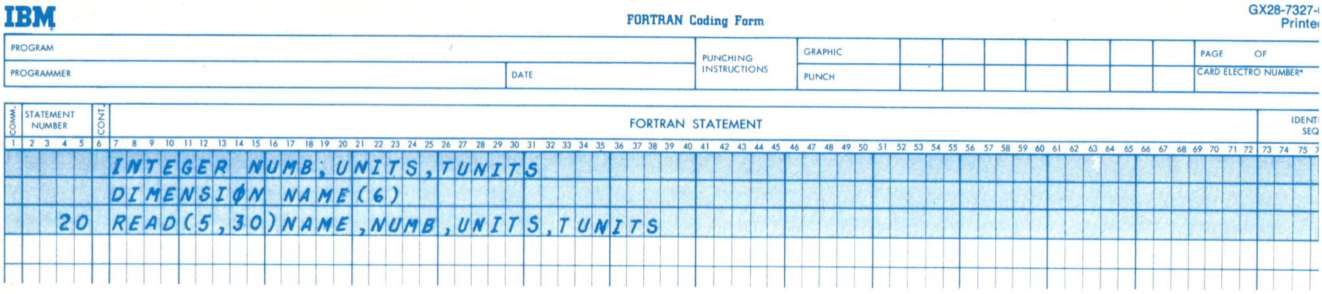

FIGURE 14-6
FORTRAN READ statement.

Each FORMAT statement must be numbered, since it is referenced by a READ or WRITE statement. The input FORMAT statement in FIGURE 14-7 is identified by a 30 in the statement number field. The word FORMAT then identifies the statement as a FORMAT statement.

The entries in parentheses describe the data fields in the input cards. Entries are separated by commas and appear in the same order as the data items on the punched card input. Three types of format codes appear in the example.

X   designates spaces or unused card columns.

A   designates alphanumeric data.

I   designates integer data.

The number *preceding* the X code designates the number of spaces or unused card columns. In Example 1, card column 1 is unused (see Figure 14-2); therefore 1X is the correct specification.

The number *following* an A or I code indicates the number of card columns for an alphanumeric or integer field. In Figure 14-7, A4 means a four-position alphanumeric field, whereas I6 means a six-position integer field.

The number *preceding* an A or I code is a repeat specification, indicating the number of times the particular format is repeated. In Figure 14-7, the entry 6A4 is used. This indicates the format 6A4 is required for the name field — recall that the student name is to be stored in an array of six words, each four characters long.

QUESTION: To summarize the input format specifications, the first column on the input card

FIGURE 14-7
FORTRAN FORMAT statement.

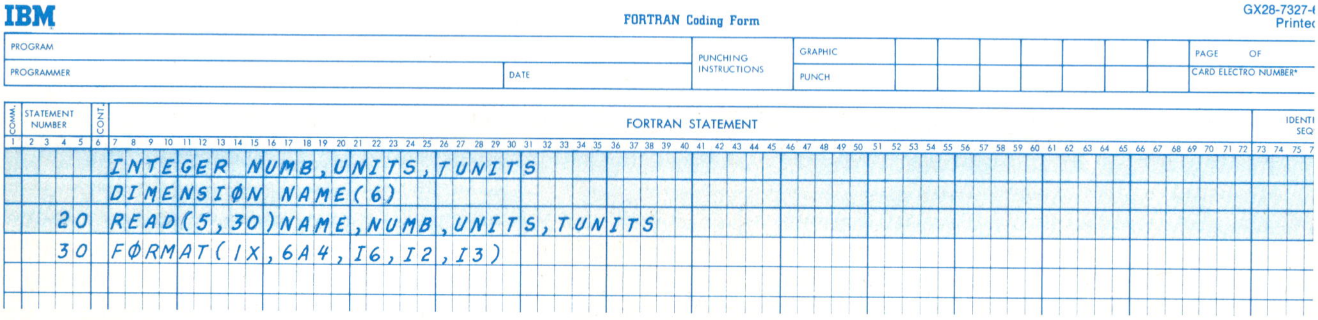

is a _____. The first data item (student name) is to be read as 6 _____-position alphanumeric items. The last three items (student number, units, total units) are, respectively, _____-position, _____-position, and _____-position integers.

ANSWER: space, four, six, two, three

LOGICAL IF STATEMENT.

A convenient method to detect the end of data cards to be processed in a FORTRAN program is to place a trailer card at the end of the data deck. The trailer card normally contains some distinguishing value in a data field, such as blanks or all nines. In the program logic, a test is made when each card is read. If the card contains the distinguishing value, the program branches to an end-of-file routine, otherwise normal processing takes place.

In the program for Example 1, the last card in the student input deck is to be left blank. In FORTRAN, fields that are left blank are read as zeros. As a result, the student number field (NUMB) is set equal to zero when the last card is read.

A FORTRAN logical IF statement is used to test whether NUMB is equal (EQ) to zero. This statement (shown in Figure 14-8) appears as follows.

IF (NUMB.EQ.0) GO TO 50

With this statement, when the condition is satisfied (NUMB equals zero) the program branches to statement number 50, which terminates the program. Otherwise, the program continues to the statement following the logical IF statement.

The term EQ in the logical IF statement is called a relational operator. The relational operations that are used in FORTRAN are shown in Table 14-1.

THE WRITE STATEMENT.

The WRITE statement causes a record to be transmitted to an output device. In the example, the output device is the line printer. The WRITE statement for the example is shown in Figure 14-9.

The entry (6,40) in the WRITE statement specifies the device number (6) and

FIGURE 14-8
FORTRAN logical IF statement.

```
INTEGER NUMB,UNITS TUNITS
DIMENSION NAME(6)
20 READ(5,30)NAME,NUMB,UNITS,TUNITS
30 FORMAT(1X,6A4,I6,I2,I3)
IF(NUMB.EQ.0)GO TO 50
```

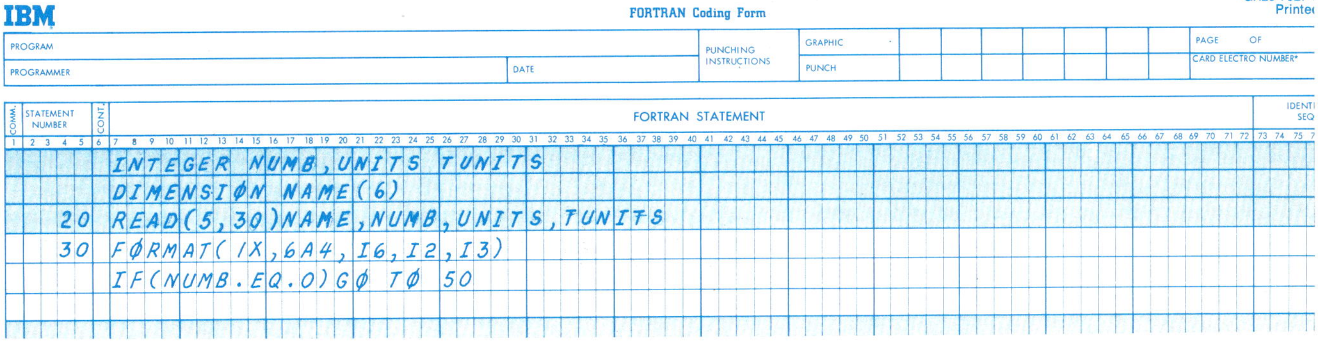

TABLE 14-1 FORTRAN RELATIONAL OPERATORS

Relational Operation Symbol	Meaning
.LT.	Less than
.LE.	Less than or equal to
.EQ.	Equal to
.NE.	Not equal to
.GE.	Greater than or equal to
.GT.	Greater than

IBM

FORTRAN Coding Form

GX28-7327-6
Printed

| PROGRAM | | PUNCHING INSTRUCTIONS | GRAPHIC | | | | | | PAGE OF |
| PROGRAMMER | DATE | | PUNCH | | | | | | CARD ELECTRO NUMBER* |

```
      INTEGER NUMB,UNITS,TUNITS
      DIMENSION NAME(6)
   20 READ(5,30)NAME,NUMB,UNITS,TUNITS
   30 FORMAT(1X,6A4,I6,I2,I3)
      IF(NUMB.EQ.0) GO TO 50
         WRITE(6,40)NAME,NUMB,UNITS,TUNITS
```

FIGURE 14-9
FORTRAN WRITE statement.

the output FORMAT statement number (40). In many installations, the device number 6 is used to specify the line printer.

The symbolic names following the parentheses specify the variables to be printed. The names are associated with format specifications in the output FORMAT statement (statement 40), as shown in Figure 14-10.

FIGURE 14-10
Correspondence between variable names and format applications.

OUTPUT FORMAT STATEMENT.   Similar to the input FORMAT statement, the output FORMAT statement describes the data items to appear in the printed report. The output FORMAT statement for Example 1 is shown in Figure 14-11.

When output is for the line printer, the first entry in an output FORMAT statement is for carriage control. The acceptable entries in FORTRAN are as follows.

1H   (1H followed by a blank) designates single spacing before printing.

1H0   designates double spacing before printing.

1H1   designates advance to top of next page before printing.

In other words, a blank, 0, or 1 following the entry 1H specifies (respectively) single spacing, double spacing, and skip to top of next page. In the example, the entry 1H is used for a single-spaced report.

```
IBM                                    FORTRAN Coding Form                                        GX28-7327-(
                                                                                                 Printe(
PROGRAM                                              PUNCHING      GRAPHIC                    PAGE    OF
                                                     INSTRUCTIONS
PROGRAMMER                               DATE                      PUNCH                      CARD ELECTRO NUMBER*

        INTEGER NUMB,UNITS,TUNITS
        DIMENSION NAME(6)
   20   READ(5,30)NAME,NUMB,UNITS,TUNITS
   30   FORMAT(1X,6A4,I6,I2,I3)
        IF (NUMB.EQ.0) GO TO 50
          WRITE(6,40)NAME,NUMB,UNITS,TUNITS
   40     FORMAT(1H ,14X,6A4,5X,I6,8X,I2,7X,I3)
```

FIGURE 14-11
Output FORMAT statement for Example 1.

THE GO TO STATEMENT.   A FORTRAN GO TO statement causes the program to branch to the statement number following the GO TO. In the example, after a line is printed, control must be transferred to the READ statement to read another record. The effect of the GO TO statement shown in Figure 14-12 is to transfer control to statement 20, which reads the next student record.

```
IBM                                    FORTRAN Coding Form                                        GX28-7327-(
                                                                                                 Printe(
PROGRAM                                              PUNCHING      GRAPHIC                    PAGE    OF
                                                     INSTRUCTIONS
PROGRAMMER                               DATE                      PUNCH                      CARD ELECTRO NUMBER*

        INTEGER NUMB,UNITS,TUNITS
        DIMENSION NAME(6)
   20   READ(5,30)NAME,NUMB,UNITS,TUNITS
   30   FORMAT(1X,6A4,I6,I2,I3)
        IF (NUMB.EQ.0) GO TO 50
          WRITE(6,40)NAME,NUMB,UNITS,TUNITS
   40     FORMAT(1H ,14X,6A4,5X,I6,8X,I2,7X,I3)
        GO TO 20
```

FIGURE 14-12
FORTRAN GO TO statement.

THE STOP STATEMENT.   The STOP instruction in a FORTRAN program terminates execution of the object program. In the example, when the trailer card is read, the IF statement transfers control to statement 50 to terminate the program.

END STATEMENT.   The END statement is always the last statement in a FORTRAN program. The statement defines the end of the source program for the FORTRAN compiler. A listing of the FORTRAN program for Example 1, together with sample output, is shown in Figure 14-13.

EXERCISE 14-1   1. Indicate whether the following variable names specify integer or decimal data items.

SUM _____   J _____

```
        INTEGER  NUMB,UNITS,TUNITS
        DIMENSION  NAME(6)
20      READ(5,30)NAME,NUMB,UNITS,TUNITS
30      FORMAT(1X,6A4,I6,I2,I3)
        IF (NUMB.EQ.0)  GO  TO  50
            WRITE(6,40)NAME,NUMB,UNITS,TUNITS
40          FORMAT(1H ,14X,6A4,5X,I6,8X,I2,7X,I3)
        GO  TO  20
50      STOP
        END
```

ADAMS, PETER R.	13978	9	104
GOODMAN, HAROLD R.	20875	16	0
JOHNSON, SHARON C.	24432	15	74
LARSON, JAMES I.	47739	6	48
LEWIS, BARBARA C.	1339	18	107
ROTHCHILD, CHARLES K.	80336	10	100
THOMPSON, LAURA W.	59325	7	88

FIGURE 14-13
FORTRAN program and output for Example 1.

GROSS _____   X _____

COUNT _____   MEAN _____

KOUNT _____   AVE _____

CODE _____   KSTNO _____

STNO _____   LARGE _____

2. An address field contains 20 alphanumeric characters. The item is to be stored in a computer that contains 4 bytes per word. Write a DIMENSION statement to define an array called KADDR for storing the data item.

    _____

    _____

3. Write an input FORMAT statement to define punched card input as follows.

Card Columns	Content
1-2	unused
3-10	integer
11-14	unused
15-19	integer
20-25	integer
26-30	unused

4. Write a logical IF statement to test the value of the variable NBR. If NBR is not equal (NE) to zero, the program is to branch to statement number 100.

EXAMPLE 2: SIMPLE CALCULATIONS

Example 2 introduces simple FORTRAN calculations. The card record for each student is to be read, and "units taken this semester" is to be added to "total units to date" to obtain an updated total. The record is then to be printed, with the updated total replacing the previous total.

In addition to updating each record, we are to total "units taken this semester" for all students and print it at the end of the listing. Header information is also to be printed at the top of the listing.

The input format for Example 2 is the same as for Example 1 (see Figure 14-2). The output format is shown on the printer spacing chart, Figure 14-14.

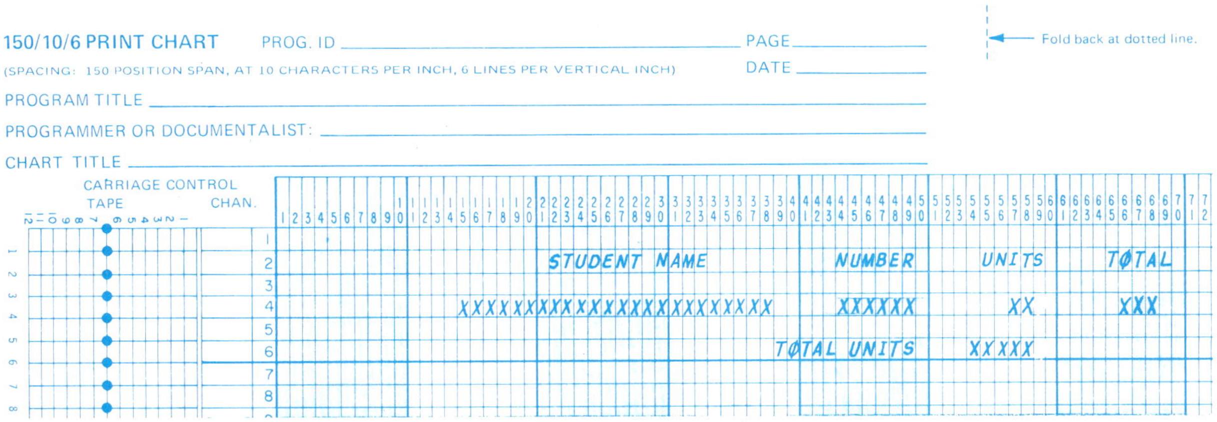

FIGURE 14-14
Printer spacing chart for Example 2.

TYPE DECLARATION

In Example 2, the variables NAME, NUMB, UNITS, and TUNITS have the same meaning as in Example 1. The variable TOTAL is used to accumulate units taken for all students. All of these variables are declared as type INTEGER in the program.

COLUMN HEADINGS

Column headings for Example 2 are printed out by the WRITE and FORMAT statements shown in Figure 14-15. The FORMAT statement (statement number 10) contains **literals,** or strings of characters to be printed as they appear in the statement. Literals are specified by enclosing the characters within special characters such as single quotes (') or asterisks (*).

FIGURE 14-15
WRITE and FORMAT statements for printing column headings.

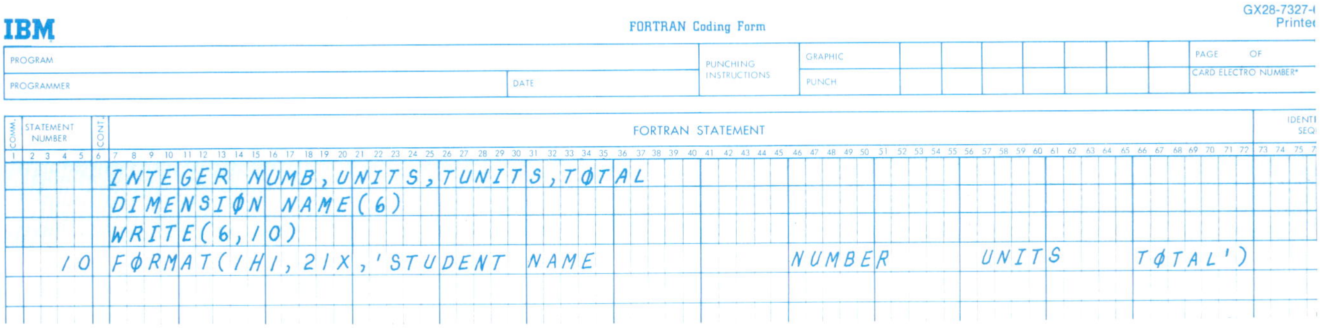

```
      INTEGER NUMB,UNITS,TUNITS,TOTAL
      DIMENSION NAME(6)
      WRITE(6,10)
   10 FORMAT(1H1,21X,'STUDENT NAME          NUMBER      UNITS     TOTAL')
```

PROGRAM LOGIC The computational steps for Example 2 are shown in Figure 14-16.

```
      INTEGER NUMB,UNITS,TUNITS,TOTAL
      DIMENSION NAME(6)
      WRITE(6,10)
   10 FORMAT(1H1,'STUDENT NAME             NUMBER     UNITS    TOTAL')
      TOTAL = 0
   20 READ(5,30)NAME,NUMB,UNITS,TUNITS
   30 FORMAT(1X,6A4,I6,I2,I3)
      IF(NUMB.EQ.0) GO TO 50
          TUNITS = TUNITS + UNITS
          TOTAL = TOTAL + UNITS
          WRITE(6,40)NAME,NUMB,UNITS,TUNITS
   40     FORMAT(1H ,14X,6A4,5X,I6,8X,I2,7X,I3)
      GO TO 20
   50 WRITE(6,60)TOTAL
   60 FORMAT(1H ,38X,'TOTAL UNITS',5X,I5)
      STOP
      END
```

FIGURE 14-16
Computational steps for Example 2.

First, the program executes a WRITE statement to print the header defined in statement 10. The cumulative units taken (called TOTAL) is then initialized by setting the variable equal to zero. These two steps are performed only once by the program.

In statement 20, the next student record is read. A logical IF statement is then used to test whether the last (or trailer) card has been read. If not, the total units taken by the student is updated by addition, as is the cumulative units taken by all students. The program then prints the record and returns to statement 20 to read the next card.

When the last card has been encountered, the program branches to statement 50 to print the cumulative total and then terminates execution.

A listing of the program for Example 2, together with sample output, is shown in Figure 14-17.

ARITHMETIC STATEMENTS

The main purpose of most computer programs is to perform computations and manipulate data for a desired result. These functions are accomplished in FORTRAN largely by arithmetic statements.

An **arithmetic statement** assigns a specific value to a FORTRAN variable. In Example 2, total units taken was updated by the following statement.

TUNITS = TUNITS + UNITS

This statement causes the variable UNITS to be added to TUNITS (the sum for all students). The new sum is called TUNITS, while the value of UNITS remains unchanged as a result of the addition.

The general form of an arithmetic statement is:

```
       INTEGER  NUMB,UNITS,TUNITS,TOTAL
       DIMENSION  NAME(6)
       WRITE(6,10)
10     FORMAT(1H1,21X,'STUDENT NAME       NUMBER       UNITS       TOTAL')
       TOTAL = 0
20     READ(5,30)NAME,NUMB,UNITS,TUNITS
30     FORMAT(1X,6A4,I6,I2,I3)
       IF (NUMB.EQ.0) GO TO 50
           TUNITS = TUNITS + UNITS
           TOTAL = TOTAL + UNITS
           WRITE(6,40)NAME,NUMB,UNITS,TUNITS
40         FORMAT(1H ,14X,6A4,5X,I6,8X,I2,7X,I3)
       GO TO 20
50     WRITE(6,60)TOTAL
60     FORMAT(1H ,38X,'TOTAL UNITS',5X,I5)
       STOP
       END
```

STUDENT NAME	NUMBER	UNITS	TOTAL
ADAMS, PETER R.	13978	9	113
GOODMAN, HAROLD R.	20875	16	16
JOHNSON, SHARON C.	24432	15	89
LARSON, JAMES I.	47739	6	54
LEWIS, BARBARA C.	1339	18	125
ROTHCHILD, CHARLES K.	80336	10	110
THOMPSON, LAURA W.	59325	7	95
	TOTAL UNITS	81	

FIGURE 14-17
FORTRAN program and output for Example 2.

variable name = arithmetic expression

A single variable name must appear to the left of the equals sign.
There are five arithmetic operations in FORTRAN. They are:

**	Exponentiate	A ** B means A raised to the B power
*	Multiply	A * B means A times B
/	Divide	A / B means A divided by B
+	Add	A + B means A plus B
—	Subtract	A — B means A minus B

Parentheses may (and often must) be used in arithmetic expressions to group constants and/or variables so that operations will be performed in the correct order. For example, to multiply the sum A plus B by 8.5, the correct expression is 8.5 * (A + B).

RULES FOR WRITING EXPRESSIONS The following rules must be followed in writing arithmetic expressions that contain two or more constants and variable names.

1. Each constant and/or variable name must be separated by an arithmetic operator. Arithmetic operators are never implied in

FORTRAN. For example, in algebra, the expression XY is often used to indicate "X times Y." In FORTRAN, XY would be interpreted as a variable name. Similarly, to indicate 4 times the quantity J plus K, the correct FORTRAN expression is 4 * (J + K), not 4(J + K).

2. Two or more arithmetic operators must not appear in sequence in an arithmetic expression. For example, in FORTRAN the quantity "X times minus 4.2" cannot be written X * −4.2. However, it is permissible to use parentheses to separate arithmetic operators, so that the above expression may be written X * (−4.2).

QUESTION: Two of the following three expressions are incorrect FORTRAN expressions. Which are incorrect, and for what reason?

a. WAGES = (40 + OTIME) RATE _____

b. SALARY = 1.2 * BASE + COMISH _____

c. SALARY = BASE * + 1.2 + COMISH _____

ANSWER: a. Multiplication symbol omitted
c. Two operators in sequence.

EVALUATING ARITHMETIC EXPRESSIONS The order of computation in a FORTRAN expression is very similar to that in algebra. There is a hierarchy of operations, as follows.

First: Quantities within parentheses are computed. If there are parentheses within parentheses (nested parentheses) the innermost pair is evaluated first.

Second: Exponentiation operations are performed.

Third: Multiplication and division operations are done. Neither takes precedence over the other.

Fourth: Addition and subtraction operations are done. Neither takes precedence over the other.

Fifth: If two or more operations of the same precedence occur in the same expression, they are performed *from left to right*.

The use of the above rules in evaluating a FORTRAN expression can be illustrated with the following example.

A * (B + C) − D / E ** 2 * G

The computer would first scan from left to right and evaluate the parenthetical expression B + C. If the result of this calculation is called "S," the expression now appears as:

A * S − D / E ** 2 * G

The computer next scans from left to right looking for exponentiation operations, and evaluates E ** 2. Calling this result "T," the expression now becomes:

A * S − D / T * G

The computer now performs all multiplications and divisions from left to right. Let "X" stand for the result A * S and "Y" stand for the result D / T * G; the result becomes X — Y. Finally, the computer subtracts Y from X to complete the evaluation of the expression.

In the above sequence, Y represents the result D / T * G. A word of caution is in order in writing such expressions. Since evaluation proceeds from left to right, D / T is performed first; the result is then multiplied by G. Thus, the result corresponds to the algebraic expression

$$\frac{D \cdot G}{T}$$

and not

$$\frac{D}{T \cdot G}$$

If the latter result is desired, it may be expressed in FORTRAN as:

D / (T * G)

or as

D / T / G

QUESTION: Five FORTRAN variables have been assigned the following values: A = 2, B = 5, C = 3, D = 18, E = 3, F = 4. Using the rules for evaluating FORTRAN expressions, what is the resulting value of Y in the statement Y = A * (B — C) + D / E ** 2 * F?

ANSWER: 12.

Blanks separating constants, variable names, or arithmetic operators are ignored by the compiler. Thus, the following two statements would be interpreted the same.

Y=A*X**2—B
Y = A * X ** 2 — B

MIXED MODE EXPRESSIONS

Recall that two types of numbers are defined in FORTRAN: integer and decimal. Decimal numbers are often termed **real numbers.** Variable names beginning with the letters I through N always represent integer numbers; names beginning with any other letter represent integer numbers; names beginning with any other letter represent decimal or real numbers.

If all of the constants and variable names in an arithmetic expression are real numbers, the expression is said to be in the **real mode.** Similarly, an expression is in the **integer mode** if all constants and variable names are integer. If an expression contains a combination of integer and real constants and/or variable names, it is called **mixed mode.**

Following are examples of expressions in each of the three modes.

Real	*Integer*	*Mixed*
X / Y	M / N	X / N
6. * UNITS	6 * NUNITS	6 * UNITS
XJ * XK + XL/3.	J + K + L/3	XJ + K + ZL/3.

An exception to this definition of a mixed mode expression is that an integer exponent may be used in a real expression. For example, the expressions X ** 2 and Y ** K are real, not mixed mode. If a number is to be raised to a whole number power, it is computationally faster to express the exponent as an integer or variable.

QUESTION: Except for the case of an integer exponent, when an expression contains a combination of integer and real constants and/or variable names, it is said to be

in _____ mode.

ANSWER: mixed

INTEGER MODE DIVISION

When division is performed in an integer mode expression in FORTRAN, the result is in integer mode. Thus any fractional part of the quotient is lost. Following are several examples.

J	K	J/K
1	2	0
2	2	1
3	2	1
4	2	2
5	2	2

If the fractional part of a division operation is to be retained, the division must be performed in real mode.

QUESTION: Last semester Stephen Billiard took 15 units and earned 55 total points. If 55 is

divided by 15 in integer mode, what is his grade point average? _____

ANSWER: 3. The actual result is 3.67, but the fractional part is lost in integer mode division.

MIXED MODE STATEMENTS

A **mixed mode statement** is one in which the variable name to the left of the equals sign and the arithmetic expression to the right are not in the same mode. For example:

NET = GROSS − DEDUCT

In this example, the variable NET is integer while the expression GROSS − DEDUCT is real.

In a mixed mode statement, the result of evaluating the arithmetic expression will be stored as integer or real, depending on whether the variable name to the left of the equals sign is integer or real. If the expression is real and the variable name is integer, any fractional part of the result is **truncated** (dropped without rounding) and lost. For example, if the statement M = 10.35 is executed, the value stored at the symbolic address M is 10.

Use of an integer variable name can lead to undesired results if truncation is not wanted. For example, consider the following sequence of statements in a payroll program.

GROSS = 135.40

DEDUCT = 29.75

NET = GROSS − DEDUCT

When deductions are subtracted from gross pay, the result is 105.65. However, since the variable name NET is integer mode, the result will be stored as 105. The fractional part may be retained simply by assigning the variable NET a real name, such as ZNET.

EXERCISE 14–2   1. Write an output FORMAT statement to print a header line. The header should appear at the top of a new page. The output format is as follows.

Print Positions	Content
1–10	unused
11–23	EMPLOYEE NAME (literal)
24–29	unused
30–36	ADDRESS (literal)

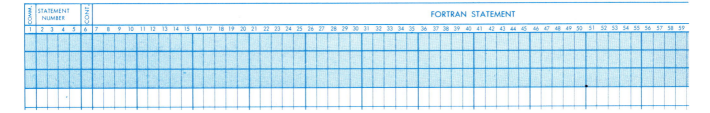

2. Write an output FORMAT statement to print a total line. The printer should double-space before printing this line. The output format is as follows.

Print Positions	Content
1–35	unused
36–40	TOTAL (literal)
41–44	unused
45–50	six-position integer

3. Which of the following arithmetic statements are invalid in FORTRAN? Explain why.

    a. $Y = AX^2 + BX + C$ _____

    b. AREA = PI * R ** 2 _____

    c. X + 3.2 = 10.4 * Y _____

    d. NET = GROSS $\div$ DEDUCT _____

    e. AVE = SUM − NUMB _____

    f. YTD = YTD + AMT _____

4. Evaluate each of the following FORTRAN expressions. Assume the following values: A = 9.0, B = 2.0, C = 10.0, D = 5.0.

    a. Y = A / B _____

    b. N = A / B _____

    c. X = A * B ** 2 _____

    d. X = A * B ** 2 + C − D _____

    e. X = C / D * B _____

    f. X = C / (D * B) _____

EXAMPLE 3: SIMPLE LOGICAL OPERATIONS

Example 3 introduces additional FORTRAN logical operations. The student record cards are to be read, and tuition is to be computed according to the following formula.

If units is less than 12, tuition is units time $35; if units is 12 or more, tuition is $420.

Total student fees consist of tuition plus an incidental fee of $12.50. This total is to be printed along with student name, number, and units taken. Also, total fees for all students is to be computed and printed at the end of the listing.

The input format for Example 3 is the same as for Examples 1 and 2 (see Figure 14-2). The desired output format is shown in Figure 14-18.

PROGRAM   The FORTRAN program for Example 3 is shown in Figure 14-19.

TYPE DECLARATION   In Example 3, the variables NUMB and UNITS are declared as type INTEGER, as before. Two variables are declared as type REAL (or decimal). They are FEES (fees for each student) and CUMFEE (cumulative fees for all students).

PROGRAM LOGIC   The following logical IF statement is used to test for number of units taken by a student.

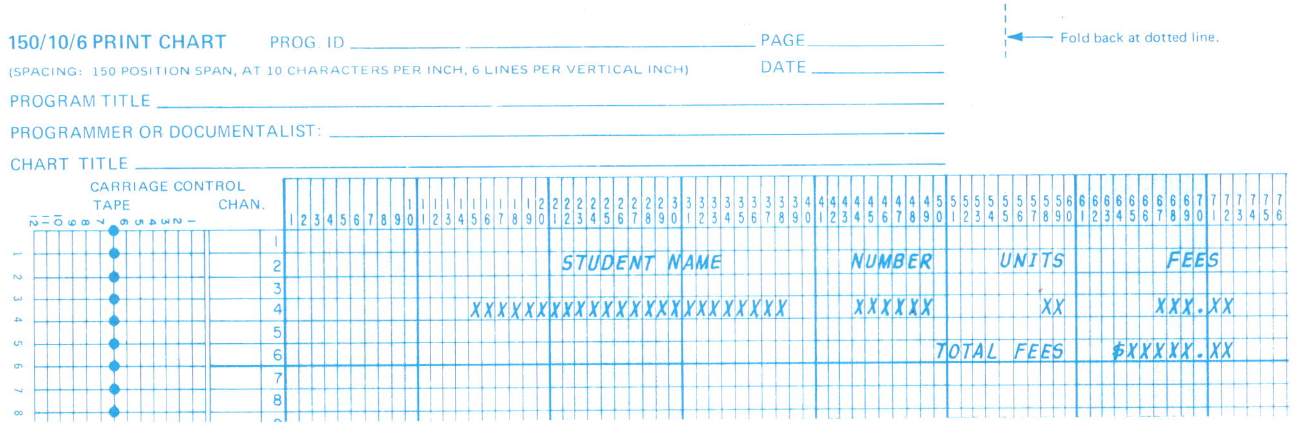

150/10/6 PRINT CHART   PROG. ID _____ _____ PAGE_____   ←— Fold back at dotted line.
(SPACING: 150 POSITION SPAN, AT 10 CHARACTERS PER INCH, 6 LINES PER VERTICAL INCH)   DATE _____

PROGRAM TITLE _____ _____

PROGRAMMER OR DOCUMENTALIST: _____

CHART TITLE _____ _____

	STUDENT NAME	NUMBER	UNITS	FEES
	XXXXXXXXXXXXXXXXXXXXXXXXXX	XXXXXX	XX	XXX.XX
			TOTAL FEES	$XXXXX.XX

FIGURE 14-18
Printer spacing chart for Example 2.

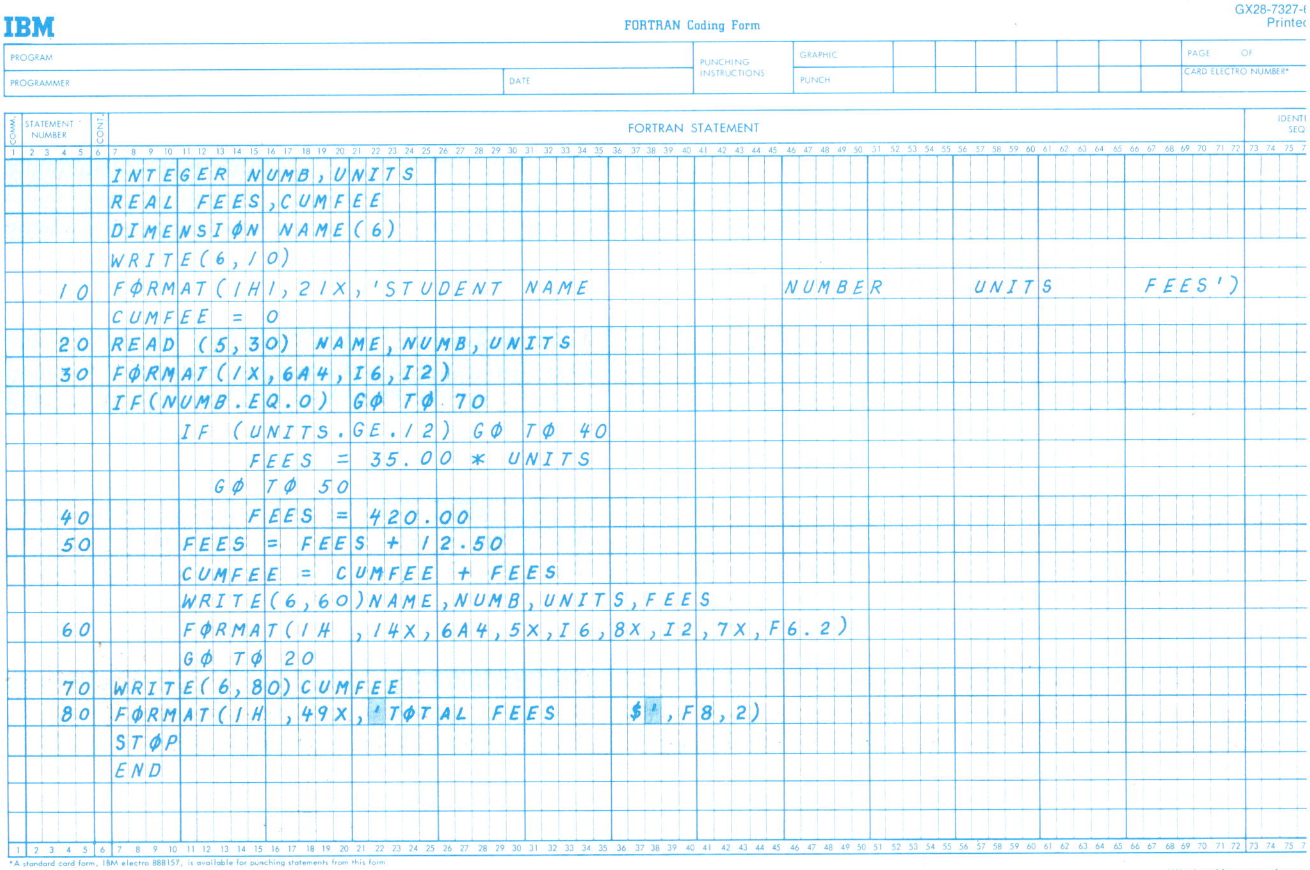

IBM   FORTRAN Coding Form   GX28-7327-(
                                                     Printed

| PROGRAM | | | PUNCHING INSTRUCTIONS | GRAPHIC | | | | | | PAGE   OF |
| PROGRAMMER | | DATE | | PUNCH | | | | | | CARD ELECTRO NUMBER* |

```
      INTEGER NUMB,UNITS
      REAL FEES,CUMFEE
      DIMENSION NAME(6)
      WRITE(6,10)
   10 FORMAT(1H1,21X,'STUDENT NAME         NUMBER     UNITS      FEES')
      CUMFEE = 0
   20 READ (5,30) NAME,NUMB,UNITS
   30 FORMAT(1X,6A4,I6,I2)
      IF(NUMB.EQ.0) GO TO 70
         IF (UNITS.GE.12) GO TO 40
            FEES = 35.00 * UNITS
         GO TO 50
   40       FEES = 420.00
   50    FEES = FEES + 12.50
         CUMFEE = CUMFEE + FEES
         WRITE(6,60)NAME,NUMB,UNITS,FEES
   60    FORMAT(1H ,14X,6A4,5X,I6,8X,I2,7X,F6.2)
         GO TO 20
   70 WRITE(6,80)CUMFEE
   80 FORMAT(1H ,49X,'TOTAL FEES     $',F8.2)
      STOP
      END
```

*A standard card form, IBM electro 888157, is available for punching statements from this form.   **Number of forms per pad may vi

FIGURE 14-19
FORTRAN program for Example 3.

IF (UNITS. GE.12) GO TO 40

If the number of units taken is 12 or greater, the program branches to statement number 40 to compute tuition. Otherwise, the program goes to the next statement in sequence to compute tuition.

After tuition is computed, the incidental fee of $12.50 is added to obtain total fees. The amount for cumulative fees for all students is then updated, the student record is printed, and the program branches to read another record.

The data items to be printed for each student are name, number, units, and fees. The last data item (fees) is a real number, representing dollars and cents. From the printer spacing chart, Figure 14–18, the format for this item is XXX.XX.

The FORMAT statement 60 specifies the format for output student records. In Figure 14–19, the format specification for the student fee item is F6.2. The letter F in a format specification designates a real (or decimal) number. The numbers following F designate the total number of positions (including decimal point) and the number of positions to the right of the decimal point. Thus, F6.2 specifies a real number with six positions, two positions to the right of the decimal.

QUESTION: Examine FORMAT statement 80. What is the meaning of the format specification for CUMFEE?

ANSWER: F8.2 specifies an eight-position field with two decimal positions. This is equivalent to the format XXXXX.XX.

The program and output listing for Example 3 are shown in Figure 14–20.

THE DO STATEMENT

One of the most powerful features of the FORTRAN language is the DO statement. This statement makes it possible to loop or perform a section of a program repeatedly, while incrementing the value of an integer variable at each repetition. Suppose we want to execute the following program segment 10 times and then exit from the loop and continue further processing.

```
READ (5,1)X
SUM = SUM + X
```

This segment repeated 10 times would read and form the sum of 10 numbers. A loop could be set up by initializing a counter, incrementing the counter each time a card is read, and testing the counter value with an IF statement. The instructions would appear as follows.

```
    K = 0
4   READ (5,1)X
    K = K + 1
    SUM = SUM + X
    IF (K − 10)4,5,5
5   (next instruction)
```

The loop can be controlled with a DO statement as follows.

```
    DO 4 I = 1, 10, 1
    READ (5,1)X
```

```
        INTEGER NUMB,UNITS
        REAL FEES,CUMFEE
        DIMENSION NAME(6)
        WRITE (6,10)
10      FORMAT(1H1,21X,'STUDENT NAME        NUMBER        UNITS        FEES')
        CUMFEE = 0
20      READ (5,30) NAME,NUMB,UNITS
30      FORMAT (1X,6A4,I6,I2)
        IF (NUMB.EQ.0) GO TO 70
            IF (UNITS.GE.12) GO TO 40
                FEES = 35.00 * UNITS
            GO TO 50
40              FEES = 420.00
50          FEES = FEES + 12.50
            CUMFEE = CUMFEE + FEES
            WRITE(6,60)NAME,NUMB,UNITS,FEES
60          FORMAT(1H ,14X,6A4,5X,I6,8X,I2,7X,F6.2)
            GO TO 20
70      WRITE(6,80)CUMFEE
80      FORMAT(1H ,49X,'TOTAL FEES     $',F8.2)
        STOP
        END
```

STUDENT NAME	NUMBER	UNITS	FEES
ADAMS, PETER R.	13978	9	327.50
GOODMAN, HAROLD R.	20875	16	432.50
JOHNSON, SHARON C.	24432	15	432.50
LARSON, JAMES I.	47739	6	222.50
LEWIS, BARBARA C.	1339	18	432.50
ROTHCHILD, CHARLES K.	80336	10	362.50
THOMPSON, LAURA W.	59325	7	257.50
		TOTAL FEES	$ 2467.50

FIGURE 14-20
FORTRAN program and output for Example 3.

```
4  SUM = SUM + X
5  (next instruction)
```

In the DO statement, the first number indicates the loop range — in this case, all statements up to and including number 4 are to be executed each cycle. The counter is given the integer variable name I. The three numbers after the equals sign are, respectively, the initial counter value, the test value, and the value used to increment the counter each cycle.

The counter is initially set to 1. Since this is less than 10 the segment is executed. The counter is now incremented by 1; since its value (I = 2) is still less than 10, the cycle is repeated, and so on. When the counter has been incremented to I = 11, it exceeds the test value; the cycle is terminated, and the program proceeds to the statement following the last one in the range of the DO statement (in this case, statement 5).

The counter in a DO statement must have an integer variable name. The three numbers following the equals sign may be either constants or integer variable names.

The value used to increment the counter in a DO statement need not be 1. In fact, when this number is 1, it may be omitted. Thus the following two statements are equivalent.

DO 25 I = 1, 10, 1
DO 25 I = 1, 10

QUESTION: Explain the meaning of the following statement.

DO 10 J = 1, 11, 2

ANSWER: Execute all statements through statement 10 for J = 1, 3, 5, 7, 9, 11 (the program segment is executed six times).

FORTRAN SUBPROGRAMS

The concept — and importance — of subroutines was discussed in Chapter 12. Recall that a subroutine is a precoded program segment designed to accomplish a specific computational task. When the programmer requires a particular subroutine, he writes a macro-instruction (or subroutine "call") that causes the subroutine to be inserted into his program. There are two basic types of subroutines: **open subroutines** (spliced into the user's program each time they are called) and **closed subroutines** (inserted only one time, regardless of the number of calls).

FORTRAN provides considerable flexibility in the use of subroutines (or subprograms). There are two basic types of FORTRAN subprograms.

1. Library (or built-in) functions, stored in the FORTRAN library.
2. User-written subprograms (these may be added to the library, if they are to be used by several different programs).

LIBRARY FUNCTIONS

A number of functions are so commonly used that they are included in most FORTRAN IV system libraries. These include functions to compute square roots, find the minimum or maximum of a set of numbers, and so on. When the programmer needs a particular function, he simply inserts the function name and its arguments in his program. A few of the most commonly used library functions are listed in Table 14-2.

TABLE 14-2   COMMON FORTRAN LIBRARY FUNCTIONS.

Function Name	Explanation	Example of Use
SQRT	Computes the square root of the argument	Y = SQRT(X)
ABS	Computes the absolute value of the argument	Y = ABS(X)
AMAX0	Computes the maximum of a set of integer arguments	S = AMAX0(J,K,L)
AMAX1	Computes the maximum of a set of real arguments	S = AMAX1(X,Y,Z)
AMIN0	Computes the minimum of a set of integer arguments	S = AMIN0(J,K,L)
AMIN1	Computes the minimum of a set of real arguments	S = AMIN1(X,Y,Z)

QUESTION: Suppose four variables currently have the following values: A = 23.4, B = 38.2, C = −15.7, D = 0.0.

a. If the following instruction is executed, what is the resulting value of Y?

   Y = AMAX1(A,B,C,D) _____

b. If the following instruction is executed, what is the resulting value of Y?

   Y = AMIN1(A,B,C,D) _____

ANSWER: (a) 38.2, (b) -15.7

Most FORTRAN libraries contain some 30 or 40 functions similar to those shown in Table 14–2. Users add new functions to the library as needed.

USER-WRITTEN SUBPROGRAMS

FORTRAN programmers often require subprograms that are not part of the present FORTRAN library. In such instances they may write their own subprograms and either include them in their own programs or add them to the system library.

There are three basic types of user-written subprograms: statement functions, function subprograms, and subroutine subprograms. The differences among these types are the following.

1. **Statement functions** must consist of only a single FORTRAN statement.
2. **Function subprograms** may consist of a large number of FORTRAN statements but may return only a single result.
3. **Subroutine subprograms** may consist of a large number of FORTRAN statements and may return as many results as desired.

User-supplied FORTRAN subprograms will be illustrated by a simple function subprogram. Suppose a programmer wishes to write a subprogram to compute the compound amount at a given interest rate (a FORTRAN program for this calculation is shown in Figure 14–1). The formula for compound amount is

$$S = P(1 + R)^N$$

where P is the principal, R the interest rate per period, N the number of periods, and S the compound amount.

The following FORTRAN function (called AMOUNT) will perform this calculation.

```
FUNCTION AMOUNT (P,R,N)
AMOUNT = P * (1. + R) ** N
RETURN
END
```

This subprogram is very simple; however, it has the essential features of any function subprogram.

1. The word FUNCTION, which identifies the type of subprogram.
2. The function name (in this case, AMOUNT), followed by the argument list in parentheses.
3. The program steps defining the calculation (in this case there is only one step). In a function subprogram, at least one instruction must

contain the function name on the left-hand side of an assignment statement.

4. A RETURN statement, which returns control to the main program.

5. An END statement, identifying the end of the subprogram.

A subprogram is used by referencing its name in the main program, together with the actual arguments to be used in the calculation. For example, the function AMOUNT might be used in a program (similar to the one in Figure 14–1) as follows.

```
     S = AMOUNT (1000.,0.10,10)
     WRITE (6,10) S
10   FORMAT (1HO, 'COMPOUND AMOUNT IS',F8.2)
     STOP
     END
```

The first statement in this program "calls" the function AMOUNT. The quantities in parentheses are assigned to the arguments in the same order they appear in the function definition. Therefore the values used are the following: $P = 1000., R = 0.10, N = 10$.

It is not necessary to use constants in the argument list (within parentheses) when calling the function. Instead, other variable names (or even simple expressions) may be used. In the above program, for example, the following statement could be used.

```
S = AMOUNT (PRIN,X,10)
```

With this statement the function would compute the compound amount using as principal the current value of PRIN, as interest the current value of X, and 10 as the number of periods.

SUMMARY

FORTRAN is designed primarily for mathematical and scientific applications. It has several shortcomings that limit its usefulness in a business data processing environment. First, the language is not designed to describe and manipulate complex file structures and data bases. Secondly, the ability to edit output data is limited in FORTRAN. Finally, the language is not easily read or understood by a manager who is not a trained programmer.

FORTRAN is used in statistical analysis and other quantitative business applications. Also, it is widely used in business schools to introduce students to computer programming.

In Chapter 15, you will study COBOL language, which is the most widely used language for business data processing applications.

ANSWERS TO EXERCISES

EXERCISE 14–1

1. Integer: KOUNT, J, MEAN, KSTNO, LARGE
    Decimal: SUM, GROSS, COUNT, CODE, STNO, X, AVE
2. DIMENSION KADDR (5)
3. FORMAT (2X, I8, 4X, I5, I6, 55X)
4. IF (NBR.NE.0) GO TO 100

EXERCISE 14-2

1.

COMM.	STATEMENT NUMBER				CONT.	FORTRAN STATEMENT
1	2	3	4	5	6	7 8 9 10 11 12 13 14 15 16 17 18 19 20 21 22 23 24 25 26 27 28 29 30 31 32 33 34 35 36 37 38 39 40 41 42 43 44 45 46 47 48 49 50 51 52 53 54 55 5
						FØRMAT (1H1,10X,'EMPLØYEE NAME',6X,'ADDRESS')

2.

COMM.	STATEMENT NUMBER				CONT.	FORTRAN STATEMENT
1	2	3	4	5	6	7 8 9 10 11 12 13 14 15 16 17 18 19 20 21 22 23 24 25 26 27 28 29 30 31 32 33 34 35 36 37 38 39 40 41 42 43 44
						FØRMAT (1H0,35X,'TØTAL',4X,I6)

3. a. Arithmetic operators for multiplication (*) and exponentiation (**) are missing.
   c. Only a single variable (not an arithmetic expression) may appear to the left of the equals sign.
   d. Divide operator is /, not ÷.

4. a. 4.5
   b. 4
   c. 36.
   d. 41.
   e. 4.
   f. 1.

CHAPTER EXAMINATION

1. Assign valid FORTRAN variable names to each of the following quantities.

    a. Principal (real) _____

    b. Temperature (real) _____

    c. Student number (integer) _____

    d. Zip code (integer) _____

    e. Acceleration (real) _____

2. Compute and record the results of each of the following statements, given these variables and their values: A = −5., B = 1., C = 8., I = 3, K = 4.

    a. Y = I / K _____

    b. Z = K / I _____

    c. N = A + C − B _____

    d. M = C * A − B _____

    e. Y = B * C − I / K _____

3. Three FORTRAN variables have the following current values: COST = 10.98, PRICE = 14.95, NUMBER = 50. Specify the output, giving the exact spacing, for each of the following WRITE statements.
    a.   WRITE (6,5) COST, PRICE, NUMBER
        5   FORMAT (1H0, 2F6.2, 3X, I3)
    b.   WRITE (6,5) COST, PRICE, NUMBER
        5   FORMAT (1H0, 'COST', F6.2, 2X, 'PRICE', F6.2, 2X, 'NUMBER', I3)

4. Cards are punched with data as follows.

Columns	Contents
1–5	Unused
6–11	COST (XXX.XX)
12–15	Unused
16–21	PRICE (XXX.XX)
22–25	Unused
26–28	NUMBER (XXX)

Write FORTRAN READ and FORMAT statements to read data from the cards.

5. In a FORTRAN program, the variable PAY is to be compared to $10,000. If PAY is less than $10,000, the program is to branch to statement number 200. Otherwise, the program is to go to the next statement in

   sequence. Write a FORTRAN logical IF statement for this step. _____

6. What is the resulting value of the variable J after one executes the following FORTRAN segment? _____

   ```
   J = 1
   DO 10 I = 1,5
   10 J = J * I
   ```

7. Find the errors in each of the following pairs of statements.

```
      WRITE (6,10) I,J,K
(a) 10 FORMAT (1H ,2I4,F8.2)

      WRITE (6,11) A,B
(b)    FORMAT (1H0,F4.2,F6.2)

      WRITE (6,12) A,T
(c) 12 FORMAT (2F6.2)

      READ (6,13) M,X,Y
(d) 13 FORMAT (4X,I3,5X,F7.2)
```

8. List the rules for evaluating FORTRAN arithmetic expressions.

   a. First: _____

   _____

b.   Second: _____

_____

c.   Third: _____

_____

d.   Fourth: _____

_____

e.   Fifth: _____

_____

9.   Write a FORTRAN function subprogram called KFACT that for any integer K will calculate K! (K factorial). Hint: See problem 6.

IBM   FORTRAN Coding Form

PROGRAM								PUNCHING INSTRUCTIONS	GRAPHIC					
PROGRAMMER					DATE				PUNCH					

COMM.	STATEMENT NUMBER	CONT.	FORTRAN STATEMENT

10.   Fifty students took an examination. The grade for each student is punched on a card in columns 2 through 4 (grades range from 0 to 100). Write a FORTRAN program to do the following.
a.   Compute and print out the average grade for the 50 students.
b.   Determine and print out the number of students who received a grade higher than the average. (Hint: Read and store the data as an array called GRADE. For example, GRADE (6) is the grade received by the sixth student.)

IBM   FORTRAN Coding Form

PROGRAM			PUNCHING INSTRUCTIONS	GRAPHIC					
PROGRAMMER		DATE		PUNCH					

FORTRAN STATEMENT coding form (blank grid)

11. The 1960 U.S. Population Census shows that five central cities (CC) had populations of over 1 million. The following table shows the populations and areas in square miles of the five central cities and their standard metropolitan statistical areas (SMSAs), which include the central cities.

	Population		Area (sq. miles)	
	CC	SMSA	CC	SMSA
New York	7,781,984	10,694,633	315	2149
Chicago	3,550,404	6,220,913	224	3714
Philadelphia	3,002,512	4,342,897	127	3549
Detroit	1,670,144	3,762,360	140	1965
San Francisco	1,104,035	2,783,359	98	3313

Write a program to read the above data and compute and print out the following.
a. Population density (population per square mile) for each CC, SMSA, and SMSA ring (SMSA excluding the CC)
b. Area of each CC as a percent of the area of the SMSA

12. Write a program to condense some statistics on the students in a class. One data card is punched for each student, as follows.

Item	Columns	
Age	1 and 2	
Sex	5	(1 = male, 2 = female)
Class standing	7	(1 = freshman, 2 = sophomore, 3 = junior, 4 = senior)

The required output is the following.
a. Average age of the students
b. Percent males, percent females
c. Percent freshmen, sophomores, juniors, seniors

Use the following data.

20	1	2
18	2	1
26	2	4
21	1	3
23	1	2
19	2	1
21	1	4
20	2	2
23	1	4
17	2	1

The cards are not counted, so use a blank card to indicate the end of the data deck.

13. Write a FORTRAN program to compute the mean, variance, and standard deviation of a sample. Use the following formulas.

$$\text{Mean} = \overline{X} = \frac{\Sigma X}{N}$$

$$\text{Variance} = S^2 = \frac{\Sigma X^2 - (\Sigma X)^2/N}{N - 1}$$

$$\text{Standard deviation} = S = \sqrt{S^2}$$

The sample size, N, is contained in columns 1 through 3 of the first card in the data deck. Values of X_i are punched one per card in the form XXX.X, beginning in column 1 of the data card.

Print as output the value of N and the sample mean, variance, and the standard deviation.

Use the following values to test your program.

i	X_i
1	134.7
2	68.9
3	761.0
4	54.2
5	165.5
6	512.8
7	48.9
8	326.0
9	261.3
10	420.7

$$N = 10$$

14. Write a program to compute employee net pay. This program should do the following.
    a. Read employee cards with the following information.

    Clock number, columns 1 to 5 (integer).
    Gross pay, columns 6 to 15, format XXXXXXX.XX.

    b. Use the following table to compute the tax and find the net pay, where net pay is equal to gross pay less tax.

Gross Pay	Tax
Less than $2000	0
$2000 or more, but less than $5000	5% of excess over $2000
$5000	$150, plus 10% of excess over $5000

    c. Print the clock number, gross pay, tax, and net pay for each employee.
    d. Terminate when the employee's clock number is zero.

    Test your program with the following data.

Employee Clock Number	Gross Pay
01000	1420.68
01001	2000.00
01002	2538.49
01003	5000.00
01004	25389.50
00000	

15. The sales slips on merchandise sold in a department contain the amount of the sale and the salesperson's ID number. At the end of the day, these are punched into cards with the salesperson's ID number in columns 1 through 3 and the amount of the sale in F format in columns 4 through 13. The cards are neither counted nor ordered in any particular way.

    Prepare a FORTRAN program to (1) calculate the total sales of each salesperson, (2) calculate the percent of total sales represented by each salesperson total, and (3) calculate his or her commission for the day (3 percent of the sales above $50). The program output should be columns containing ID number, total sales for the day, percent of the total, and his or her commission. Use the following data.

Employee Number	Sales Amount
4	25.00
5	300.00
4	75.00
2	50.00
5	200.00
1	15.00
3	25.00
5	500.00
3	25.00
3	25.00

16. Write a FORTRAN program to locate and print out the largest number in an array of numbers. The program should print out both the largest number and its location in the array. In case there are two or more such numbers, arbitrarily print out the location of the first one.

IBM — FORTRAN Coding Form — GX28-7327-6 U/M 050** — Printed in U.S.A.

PROGRAM
PROGRAMMER — DATE — PUNCHING INSTRUCTIONS — GRAPHIC — PUNCH — PAGE — OF — CARD ELECTRO NUMBER*

COMM. | STATEMENT NUMBER | CONT. | FORTRAN STATEMENT | IDENTIFICATION SEQUENCE

*A standard card form, IBM electro 888157, is available for punching statements from this form

**Number of forms per pad may vary slightly

IBM — FORTRAN Coding Form — GX28-7327-6 U/M 050** — Printed in U.S.A.

PROGRAM
PROGRAMMER — DATE — PUNCHING INSTRUCTIONS — GRAPHIC — PUNCH — PAGE — OF — CARD ELECTRO NUMBER*

COMM. | STATEMENT NUMBER | CONT. | FORTRAN STATEMENT | IDENTIFICATION SEQUENCE

*A standard card form, IBM electro 888157, is available for punching statements from this form

**Number of forms per pad may vary slightly

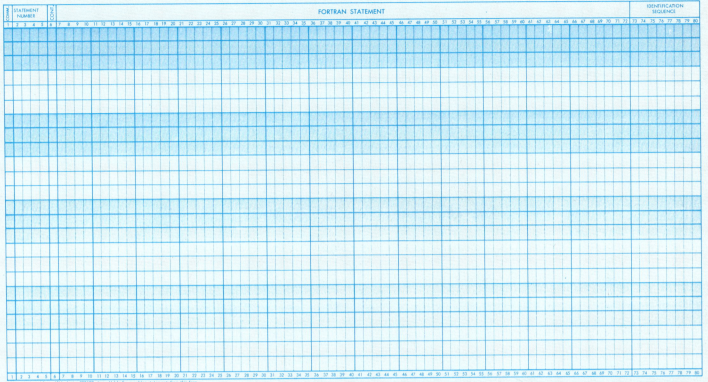

IBM

FORTRAN Coding Form

| PROGRAM | | PUNCHING INSTRUCTIONS | GRAPHIC | | | | | | | PAGE | OF |
| PROGRAMMER | DATE | | PUNCH | | | | | | | CARD ELECTRO NUMBER* | |

*A standard card form, IBM electro 888157, is available for punching statements from this form

**Number of forms per pad may vary slightly

15

INTRODUCTION TO COBOL

OVERVIEW. COBOL stands for COmmon Business-Oriented Language. It is the most widely used programming language for business data processing applications today.

COBOL was conceived in May 1959 in a meeting called by the Department of Defense to initiate development of a common language for business applications. Representatives of major computer manufacturers, computer users, and the government were present and formed a committee called the Conference on Data Systems Languages, or CODASYL. This committee is active today and is responsible for initiating and reviewing changes to COBOL and keeping the language up to date.

COBOL is a standard business programming language that is well suited to file handling, report generation, data manipulation, and data base management. The present version is referred to as American National Standard (or ANSI) COBOL. COBOL is an English-like language that is largely self-documenting; that is, a person who knows little about computers or programming languages can check much of the logic in a COBOL program.

COBOL PROGRAM ORGANIZATION

COBOL programs are often written on COBOL coding forms such as that shown in Figure 15–1. They facilitate proper positioning of the program statements.

The significant columns on the coding form and their usage are as follows.

Line sequence number (columns 1 to 6) is used to number the statments in ascending order. The first line is often assigned serial number 010, the second 020, and so on. Lines are numbered by tens in this manner so that insertions can easily be made.

Continuation column (column 7) is used to indicate the continuation of a statement from the previous line. A hyphen in this column indicates that the content of this line starting in column 12 is a continuation from column 72 of the previous line.

Program statements are entered in columns 8 to 72. Column 8 is called the A margin; certain COBOL entries (such as paragraph names) must begin in the A margin. Column 12 is the B margin; the majority of COBOL statements begin in this margin or, at the programmer's option, may be indented to column 13, 14, and so on.

Identification characters (columns 73 to 80) are optional in a COBOL program. They are printed on the compiler listing but do not affect the computer

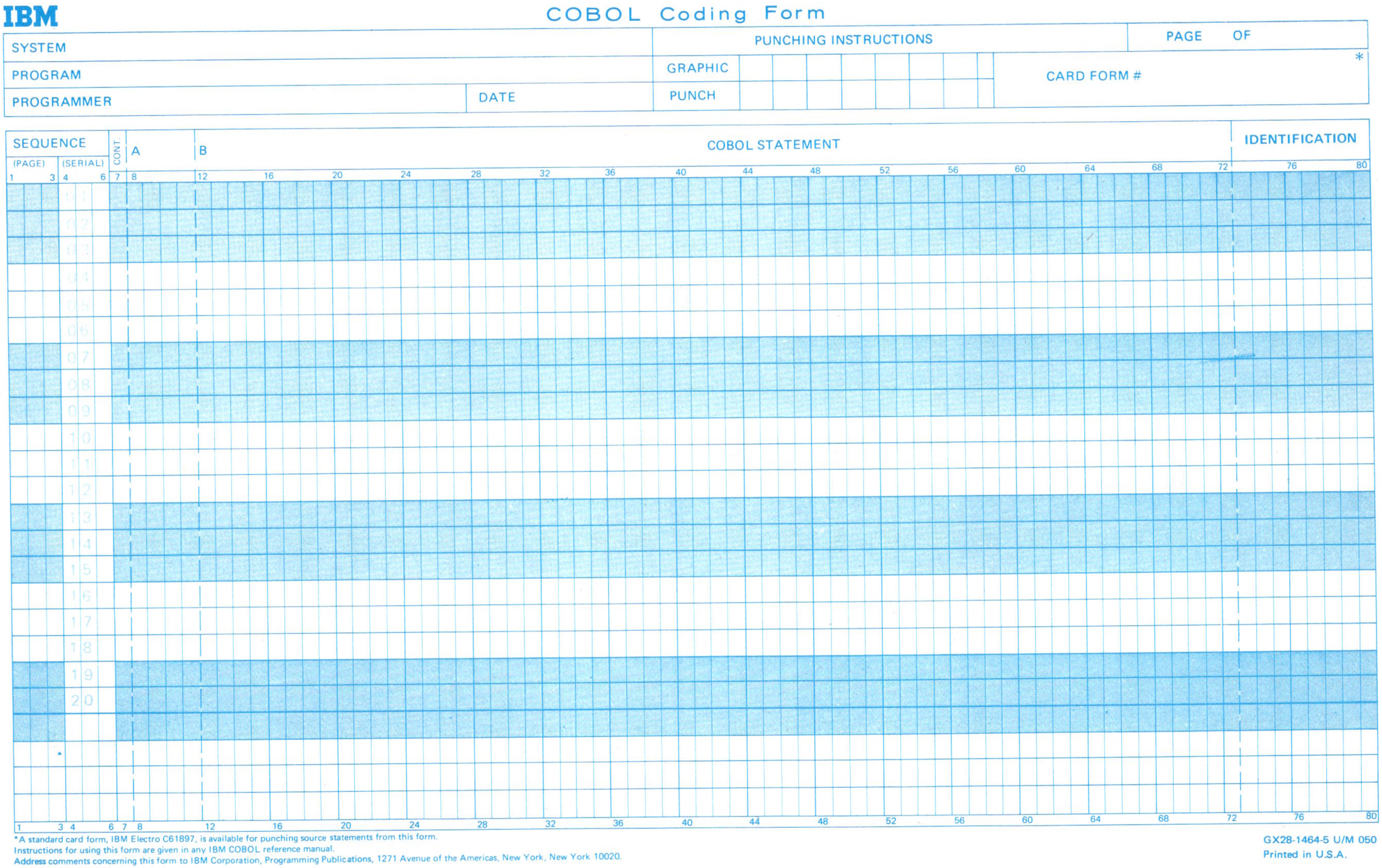
IBM
COBOL Coding Form
SYSTEM
PUNCHING INSTRUCTIONS
PAGE OF
PROGRAM
GRAPHIC
CARD FORM #
*
PROGRAMMER
DATE
PUNCH
SEQUENCE
(PAGE) (SERIAL)
CONT.
A
B
COBOL STATEMENT
IDENTIFICATION
1 3 4 6 7 8 12 16 20 24 28 32 36 40 44 48 52 56 60 64 68 72 76 80
01 02 03 04 05 06 07 08 09 10 11 12 13 14 15 16 17 18 19 20
*A standard card form, IBM Electro C61897, is available for punching source statements from this form.
Instructions for using this form are given in any IBM COBOL reference manual.
Address comments concerning this form to IBM Corporation, Programming Publications, 1271 Avenue of the Americas, New York, New York 10020.
GX28-1464-5 U/M 050
Printed in U.S.A.

FIGURE 15–1
COBOL coding form.

program. The program name is sometimes punched in these columns for identification purposes.

COBOL DIVISIONS

Every COBOL program is divided into four divisions. Each division provides a unique and essential portion of the information required by the COBOL compiler. The four COBOL divisions are:

1. *Identification division.* Identifies the program to the computer and/or user.
2. *Environment division.* Specifies the computer equipment (or hardware) to be used by the program.
3. *Data division.* Defines the files, record layouts, and storage areas used.
4. *Procedure division.* Contains the program logic or instructions to be executed by the computer.

Each COBOL division is identified by a division header, for example, DATA DIVISION. Division headers are coded in margin A.

QUESTION: To summarize, every COBOL program must contain four division headers.

These headers must appear in the following order: _____

DIVISION, _____ DIVISION, _____ DIVISION,

_____ DIVISION. Each division header starts in column

_____.

ANSWER: IDENTIFICATION, ENVIRONMENT, DATA, PROCEDURE, 8.

Coding a COBOL program consists of writing entries for the four divisions. The divisions in turn consist of sections, paragraphs, and entries. To illustrate the basic concepts of COBOL programming, three examples will be introduced. These example problems are all based on processing a student record file.

EXAMPLE 1: BASIC INPUT/OUTPUT OPERATIONS

A student file is maintained on punched cards, one card record per student. The format of the records is shown in Figure 15-2. Each card contains student name (columns 2 to 25), number (26 to 31), units taken this semester (32 to 33), and total units prior to this semester (34 to 36).

An output listing is to be prepared from the cards. Each card field is to be printed, with blank spaces between fields. Leading zeros (if any) are to be suppressed for numeric fields. A printer spacing chart of the output format together with a sample listing is shown in Figure 15-3.

IDENTIFICATION DIVISION

The **identification division** supplies the name of the program, together with several optional entries to improve program documentation. The identification division for Example 1 is shown in Figure 15-4.

Every COBOL program identification division must contain a PROGRAM-ID paragraph, with a program name supplied by the programmer. The program

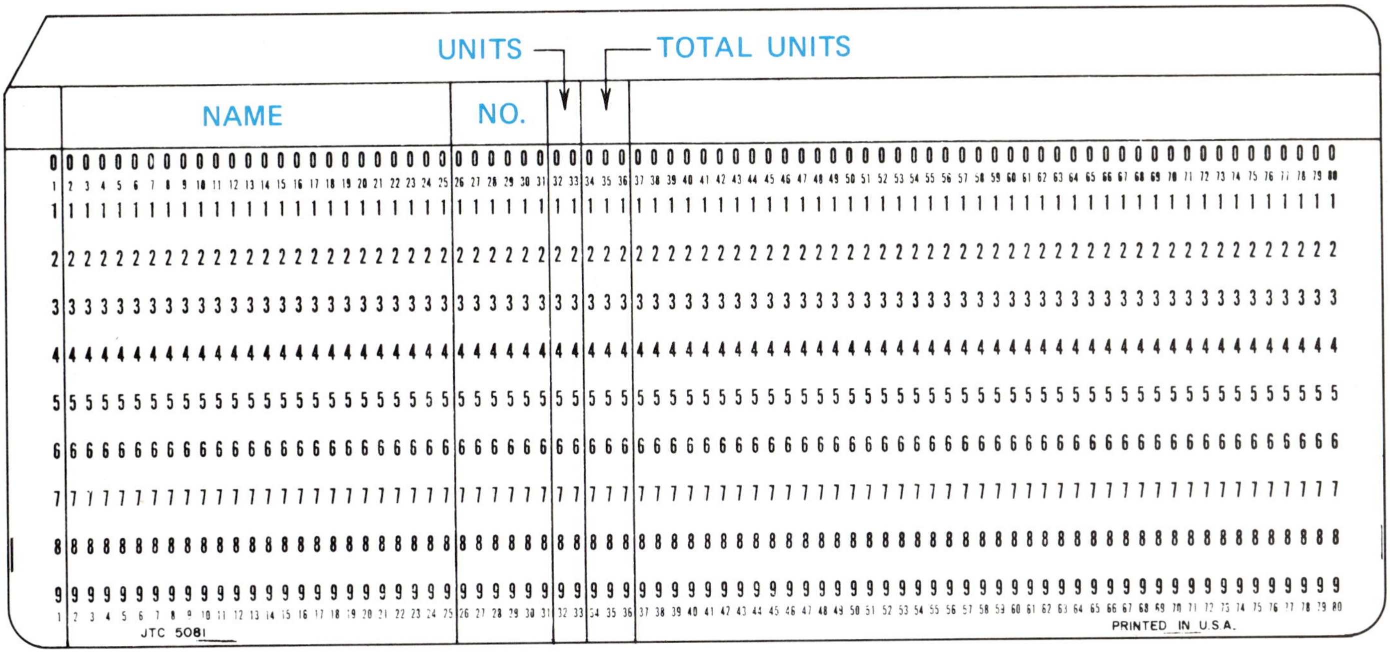

FIGURE 15-2
Student input record card.

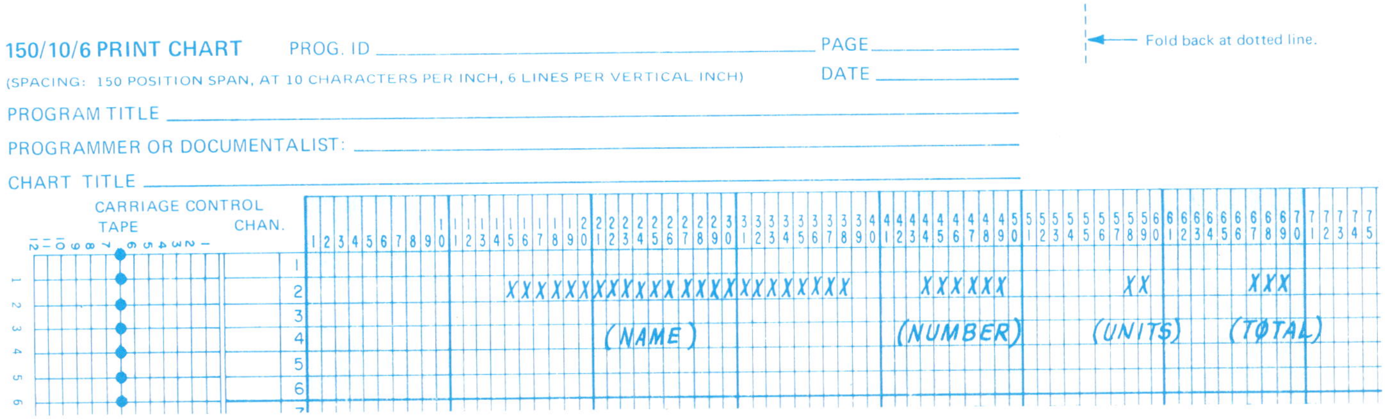

FIGURE 15-3
Printer spacing chart for Example 1.

name must begin with a letter, must be composed of letters and/or digits only, and must not exceed 30 characters in length.

The general format of COBOL identification division is as follows.

IDENTIFICATION DIVISION.
PROGRAM-ID. program name
[AUTHOR. entry]
[INSTALLATION. entry]
[DATE-WRITTEN. entry]
[DATE-COMPILED. entry]
[SECURITY. entry]
[REMARKS. entry]

IBM COBOL Coding Form GX28-146

SYSTEM			PUNCHING INSTRUCTIONS		PAGE	OF
PROGRAM			GRAPHIC			
PROGRAMMER		DATE	PUNCH		CARD FORM #	

```
IDENTIFICATION DIVISION.
PROGRAM-ID. PROB1.
DATE-WRITTEN. 8/20/8X.
DATE-COMPILED.        10/21/8X.
REMARKS.
     PROB1 READS STUDENT RECORDS AND GENERATES A REPORT
     CONTAINING THE STUDENT*S NAME, NUMBER, UNITS AND TOTAL UNITS.
```

FIGURE 15-4
Identification division for Example 1.

In the above format, required reserved words are capitalized. These include the division header and following paragraph names. Bracketed names [ ] are optional and may be left out of the program. However, if the user elects to use a bracketed name, the capitalized reserve word in that name must be used. Lowercase words indicate names or entries to be supplied by the programmer.

QUESTION: The minimum entries in the indentification division for a COBOL program con-

sist of the division header, _____,

and the paragraph entry, _____.

ANSWER: IDENTIFICATION DIVISION, PROGRAM-ID

ENVIRONMENT DIVISION The second division of a COBOL program is the **environment division.** It specifies the computer to be used in compiling and processing the object program. It also assigns data files to input/output devices. The environment division for Example 1 is shown in Figure 15-5.

FIGURE 15-5
Environment division for Example 1.

IBM COBOL Coding Form GX28-146

```
ENVIRONMENT DIVISION.
CONFIGURATION SECTION.
   SOURCE COMPUTER. IBM 360/370
INPUT-OUTPUT SECTION.
   FILE-CONTROL.
      SELECT STUDENT-FILE ASSIGN TO INPUT.
      SELECT PRINT-FILE ASSIGN TO OUTPUT.
```

Two sections are required in a COBOL environment division: a configuration section and an input/output section. The **configuration section** specifies the computer type on which the COBOL program will be compiled and executed. The sample program is compiled and run on an IBM 360 or 370 series computer. COBOL users should check with their own installations to complete this section correctly.

The **input/output section** identifies input and output files used in the program. The only required paragraph in this section is called **file control.** This paragraph associates each file used in the program with an input or output device.

The actual assignment of files to devices is accomplished with a SELECT statement, as follows.

SELECT (file name) ASSIGN TO (design).

In Example 1, the input file is given the name STUDENT-FILE; the device is the card reader that has the symbolic device name INPUT.

QUESTION: Examine Figure 15–5. What are the names given to the output file and device for Example 1?

ANSWER: PRINT-FILE, OUTPUT

File names (such as STUDENT-FILE and PRINT-FILE) are specified by the programmer, and there are a number of such **programmer-defined words** in a COBOL program. The programmer has considerable flexibility in defining words, but must follow these rules.

1. A programmer-defined word must not exceed 30 characters.
2. A programmer-defined word may contain alphabetic and numeric characters and embedded hyphens. However, it may not contain any other special characters, including spaces.
3. COBOL reserved words may not be used. COBOL **reserved words** are those that have special significance to the compiler. Examples of reserved words are SELECT, ASSIGN, FILE, ADD, and REPORT. These words must be used without alteration in meaning or definition. There are well over 200 COBOL reserved words, with some variation among compiling systems.

QUESTION: Two types of COBOL words are _____ words and _____ words.

ANSWER: programmer-defined, reserved

DATA DIVISION The data division in a COBOL program consists of two sections.

1. The FILE SECTION, where input and output files are defined.
2. The WORKING-STORAGE SECTION, where constants and intermediate results used in the program are defined.

The data division for Example 1 is shown in Figure 15–6.

| | COBOL Coding Form | | GX28-146 |

IBM

SYSTEM		PUNCHING INSTRUCTIONS	PAGE	OF
PROGRAM		GRAPHIC		
PROGRAMMER	DATE	PUNCH	CARD FORM #	

```
DATA DIVISION.
FILE SECTION.
FD  STUDENT-FILE
    LABEL RECORDS ARE OMITTED
    DATA RECORD IS STUDENT-REC.
01  STUDENT-REC.
    05 FILLER                   PICTURE X.
    05 STUDENT-NAME-IN          PICTURE X(24).
    05 STUDENT-NUMBER-IN        PICTURE 9(6).
    05 UNITS-IN                 PICTURE 9(2).
    05 TOTAL-UNITS-IN           PICTURE 9(3).
    05 FILLER                   PICTURE X(44).
FD  PRINT-FILE
    LABEL RECORDS ARE OMITTED
    DATA RECORD IS PRINT-LINE.
01  PRINT-LINE.
    05 FILLER                   PICTURE X(15).
    05 STUDENT-NAME-OUT         PICTURE X(24).
    05 FILLER                   PICTURE X(5).
    05 STUDENT-NUMBER-OUT       PICTURE Z(5)9.
    05 FILLER                   PICTURE X(8).
    05 UNITS-OUT                PICTURE Z9.
    05 FILLER                   PICTURE X(7).
    05 TOTAL-UNITS-OUT          PICTURE ZZ9.
    05 FILLER                   PICTURE X(63).
WORKING-STORAGE SECTION.
01  EOF                         PICTURE X    VALUE 'N'.
```

FIGURE 15-6
Data division for Example 1.

Following the FILE SECTION header (coded in margin A), there is a complete description of each file named in the SELECT clauses of the environment division. There are two files in this program: STUDENT-FILE (input) and PRINT-FILE (output). Each file description begins with an FD in margin A followed by the file name in margin B. The entry following the FD header for the input file in Figure 15-6 is as follows.

FD STUDENT-FILE LABEL RECORDS ARE OMITTED
    DATA RECORD IS STUDENT-REC.

In this entry, the file name (STUDENT-FILE) is given first. A clause concerning label records is then presented. Label records are used in many data processing applications, to insure that the correct file is being accessed. In the examples in this chapter, label records are not used. The above clause must be used to indicate this condition.

The last clause in the entry identifies the data record within the file. STUDENT-FILE contains only one type of record, which has been given the programmer-assigned name STUDENT-REC.

QUESTION: Examine the FD for the output file in Figure 15-6. What can be said regarding (a) label records, (b) record name?

a. _____

b. _____

ANSWER: (a) Label records are omitted; (b) record name is PRINT-LINE.

RECORD DESCRIPTION   After a given data file has been described, each different record contained in the file must be described. This description consists of a record header, followed by entries that describe each data item in the record.

In the example (Figure 15-6), the input file contains only one record, which has been named STUDENT-REC. The description header is as follows:

01   STUDENT-REC

The number 01 is called a COBOL **level number.** Level number 01 is always used to introduce a record, which is the highest level of data structure contained in a file.

ITEM DESCRIPTION   A separate entry is made under the record header for each data item (or field) contained in the record. This entry specifies the level number, data name (or the reserved word FILLER), and a clause indicating the length and type of field.

Refer back to Figure 15-2, which shows the format for the input student record cards. Each card contains a blank (column 1), student name (columns 2 to 25), student number (columns 26 to 31), units taken (columns 32 to 33), and total units (columns 34 to 37). Now refer to the item descriptions (Figure 15-6), which describe these same fields.

Each item in STUDENT-REC is coded at the 02 level. This indicates that the items are subordinate to the 01-level entry (the record itself), but are independent of each other—that is, they are separate fields, to be treated equally.

In many instances a data field may be further subdivided into dependent fields. For example, the field EMPLOYEE-NAME might be subdivided as follows.

EMPLOYEE - NAME		
LAST	FIRST	MI
1 10	11 19	20

In this case, the level structure might be coded as follows.

02   EMPLOYEE-NAME
    03   LAST (entry)
    03   FIRST (entry)
    03   MI (entry)

An item that is further subdivided (such as EMPLOYEE-NAME above) is referred to as a **group item,** whereas an item that is not further subdivided is called an **elementary item.**

QUESTION: A field called DATE might be subdivided into MONTH, DAY, YEAR. In this case,

DATE is called a _____ item, while MONTH, DAY, and YEAR are called

_____ items.

ANSWER: group, elementary

The word FILLER is used to designate unused portions of the record. In Example 1, the first column and the last 44 columns are unused and so are designated FILLER.

The final entry in each item description is a **picture clause,** which indicates the length and type of data field. The **type** of data field is designated by one of three characters, as follows.

Character	Type of Field
9	Numeric
A	Alphabetic
X	Alphanumeric

The **length** of each data field is specified by repeating the above characters, or by specifying the field length in parentheses following the type character. For example, 999 means a 3-digit numeric field, whereas XXXX is the picture for a four-character alphanumeric field. These pictures could also have been written as 9(3) and X(4), respectively.

A decimal field is specified by using the decimal indicator (V) in the picture clause. For example 99V99 specifies a four-digit decimal field with two digits to the right of the decimal point.

QUESTION: The field STUDENT-NAME-OUT in the output record PRINT-LINE (Figure 15–6)

has the picture _____ This means that the field type is

_____ and is of length _____

ANSWER: X(24), alphanumeric, 24.

Zero suppression is specified for a numeric field in COBOL by the programmer's using the letter Z (repeated as necessary) before the type character 9. For example, in Figure 15–6 the output field TOTAL-UNITS-OUT has the picture clause ZZ9. This means that TOTAL-UNITS-OUT is a 3-digit numeric field and that, if the first two digits are leading zeros, they are to be suppressed on printout.

QUESTION: The output field UNITS-OUT has the picture clause _____ This means

that UNITS-OUT is a _____-digit numeric field and that the leading zero is to be _____ on printout.

ANSWER: Z9, 2, suppressed.

The **working-storage section** follows immediately after the file section. This section is used to define constants and intermediate totals and record layouts. The rules for levels, data names, and picture clauses are the same as for the file section.

In the program for Example 1, there is only one entry in the working-storage section, as follows.

01   EOF   PICTURE X   VALUE 'N'

This entry defines a variable named EOF (for End-of-File). EOF is a single-character alphanumeric field (PICTURE X). The VALUE clause assigns EOF an initial value of N (for No). The value of this variable will be tested by a statement in the procedure division to determine whether an end-of-file condition has been encountered (that is, there are no more student data cards to be read).

PROCEDURE DIVISION   The **procedure division** of a COBOL program defines the program logic or instruction to be executed by the computer. The procedure division for Example 1 is shown in Figure 15–7.

The procedure division for this program of processing a student record file follows the principles of structured programming (introduced in Chapter 12). The overall logic is broken down into a series of modules, each of which performs a specific function. Each module (or paragraph) has a single entry and a single exit. One mainline module controls the execution of program logic.

The procedure division for the program in Figure 15–7 contains the following modules or paragraphs.

1. 000-CONTROL-ROUTINE: mainline module that causes the remaining modules to be executed, using PERFORM statements.
2. 100-INITIALIZE: opens input and output files, initializes the first student input record.
3. 200-READ-AND-LIST: moves input data items to the output area, writes the output record, and reads the next student input record. Moves Y (for Yes) to EOF field when an end-of-file condition is encountered.
4. 300-END: Closes input and output files.
5. 999-END-OF-PROGRAM.

THE PERFORM STATEMENT   The basic form of the PERFORM statement is as follows.

PERFORM (paragraph name)

This statement causes the program to transfer to the first statement in the named paragraph, the program returns to the statement immediately following the PERFORM statement.

In the program shown in Figure 15–7, an extended form of the PERFORM statement is used that includes the use of a THRU clause. The form of this statement is as follows:

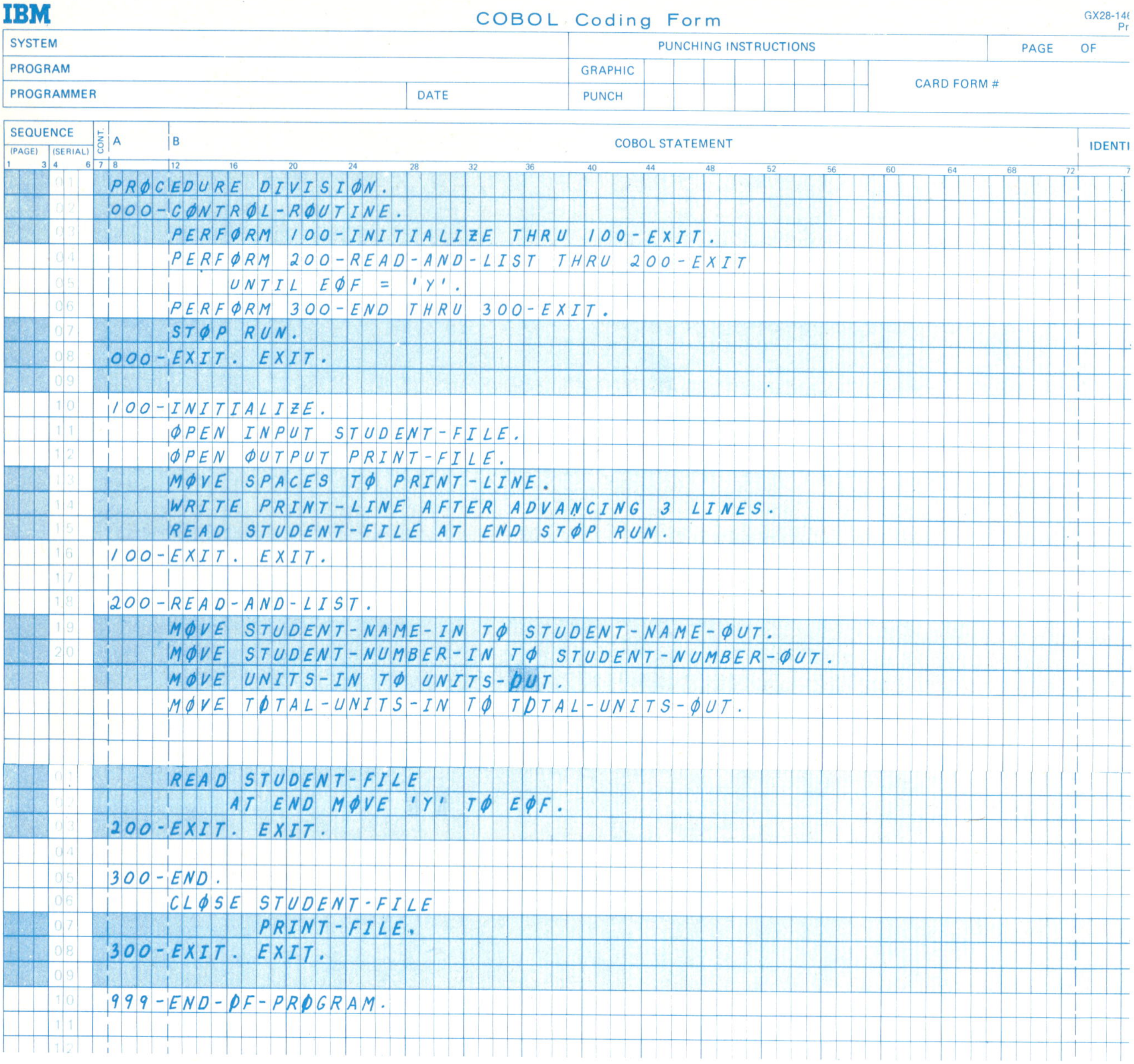

IBM COBOL Coding Form GX28-14(

SYSTEM		PUNCHING INSTRUCTIONS		PAGE OF
PROGRAM		GRAPHIC		CARD FORM #
PROGRAMMER	DATE	PUNCH		

```
PROCEDURE DIVISION.
000-CONTROL-ROUTINE.
    PERFORM 100-INITIALIZE THRU 100-EXIT.
    PERFORM 200-READ-AND-LIST THRU 200-EXIT
        UNTIL EOF = 'Y'.
    PERFORM 300-END THRU 300-EXIT.
    STOP RUN.
000-EXIT. EXIT.

100-INITIALIZE.
    OPEN INPUT STUDENT-FILE.
    OPEN OUTPUT PRINT-FILE.
    MOVE SPACES TO PRINT-LINE.
    WRITE PRINT-LINE AFTER ADVANCING 3 LINES.
    READ STUDENT-FILE AT END STOP RUN.
100-EXIT. EXIT.

200-READ-AND-LIST.
    MOVE STUDENT-NAME-IN TO STUDENT-NAME-OUT.
    MOVE STUDENT-NUMBER-IN TO STUDENT-NUMBER-OUT.
    MOVE UNITS-IN TO UNITS-OUT.
    MOVE TOTAL-UNITS-IN TO TOTAL-UNITS-OUT.

    READ STUDENT-FILE
        AT END MOVE 'Y' TO EOF.
200-EXIT. EXIT.

300-END.
    CLOSE STUDENT-FILE
          PRINT-FILE.
300-EXIT. EXIT.

999-END-OF-PROGRAM.
```

FIGURE 15-7
Procedure division for Example 1.

PERFORM (paragraph-name-1) THRU (paragraph-name-2)

This form of the PERFORM statement causes the program to transfer to the first statement in paragraph-name-1. After executing the last statement in paragraph-name-2, the program automatically returns to the statement following the PERFORM statement. Paragraph-name-2 normally contains the single verb EXIT.

An example of the use of the PERFORM statement with the THRU option is the following.

PERFORM 100-INITIALIZE THRU 100-EXIT.

This statement causes the initializing module to be executed, after which control is transferred to the next PERFORM statement.

A further extension to the PERFORM statement includes an UNTIL clause and has the following format.

PERFORM (paragraph-name-1) THRU (paragraph-name-2)
  UNTIL (condition)

The PERFORM-UNTIL statement will test for the condition following the UNTIL clause prior to transferring to paragraph-name-1. If the condition is not satisfied, transfer will be made to paragraph-name-1 and the module will be executed. If the stated condition is satisfied, control passes to the statement following the PERFORM-UNTIL statement.

In Figure 15–7, the following PERFORM-UNTIL statement appears in the procedure division.

PERFORM 200-READ-AND-LIST THRU 200-EXIT
  UNTIL EOF = 'Y'.

This statement causes the "read-and-list" module to be performed as long as an end-of-file condition has not been encountered (EOF = $\neq$N$\neq$). However, when the EOF condition is encountered, EOF is set to the value Y and control is transferred to the next statement in the program.

INPUT/OUTPUT   Input/output statements process data into and out of the computer. The statements most often used are OPEN, CLOSE, READ, and WRITE. All of these statements are used in Example 1.

The OPEN statement performs two basic functions: (1) It indicates which files are used for input and which will serve as output; and (2) it makes files available for processing by accessing specific devices, checking labels (input files), and writing label records (output files). The general format of an OPEN statement is as follows.

$$\text{OPEN} \begin{bmatrix} \text{INPUT} \\ \text{or} \\ \text{OUTPUT} \end{bmatrix} \text{(file name)}.$$

QUESTION: In Example 1, what file is used for input? _____. For

output? _____
ANSWER: STUDENT-FILE, PRINT-FILE

A READ statement transmits data from an input device to an input storage area defined in the file section of the data division. In sequential files, it provides for branching on an end-of-file condition. The general form of the READ statement is:

READ (file name) AT END (statement).

A WRITE statement transmits data from an output area (defined in the file section of the data division) to an output device. The general format of a WRITE statement is:

WRITE (record name) AFTER ADVANCING (N) LINES.

The number of lines advanced, called N, must be either 1, 2, or 3 lines. This provides single, double, or triple spacing between lines of printed output.

QUESTION: Compare the formats for READ and WRITE statements. The verb READ is followed by a _____ name, while WRITE must be followed by a _____ name.

ANSWER: file, record

When processing has terminated, all files used in the program must be closed. The general form of the CLOSE statement is:

CLOSE (file name(s)).

DATA MOVEMENT   An important operation in data processing is moving data from one storage location to another. For example, an output record is often assembled by moving data from input and working storage areas to the output storage area. The editing of data is often an important part of this operation.

Movement of data is accomplished by the MOVE statement. The general format is:

MOVE (data-name-1) TO (data-name-2).

Data-name-1 is the sending field, data-name-2 is the receiving field. Both fields must be defined by a picture clause in the data division.

There are two important rules for use of the MOVE statement.

An alphabetic item must not be moved to a numeric item (as defined in the picture clause), or vice-versa.

Data transferred from a numeric sending area to a numeric receiving area are positioned according to the decimal point in the receiving area, with excess characters truncated. If no decimal point is specified, data received will be right-justified.

The use of the MOVE statement is illustrated in Table 15–1.

TABLE 15–1   USE OF A MOVE STATEMENT*

Sending Field		Receiving Field		Comment
Picture	Contents	Picture	Contents (after MOVE)	
999	328	999	328	Whole number 328 moved
99V99	41$_\wedge$25	99V99	41$_\wedge$25	Implied decimal point after first 2 digits
A(5)	JONES	9(5)		Illegal (alphabetic to numeric)
99V99	41$_\wedge$25	99V9	41$_\wedge$2	Excess digit truncated

*Caret ($_\wedge$) indicates implied decimal point.

The MOVE statement has a second format that permits transmitting literals.

MOVE (literal) TO (data-name).

Examples are given in Table 15-2.

TABLE 15-2   USING THE MOVE STATEMENT TO TRANSMIT LITERALS

MOVE Statement	Comment
MOVE 175 TO WEIGHT-LIMIT.	175 moved to receiving field
MOVE 'AUG 1, 1985' TO DATE.	Aug. 1, 1985 moved to receiving field
MOVE ZEROS TO GROSS-PAY.	Receiving field filled with zeros
MOVE SPACES TO PRINT-LINE.	Receiving field filled with spaces

QUESTION: Examine the procedure division (Figure 15-7). Which statement causes a literal to be transmitted to a receiving field? _____

ANSWER: MOVE SPACES TO PRINT-LINE. In this case, the receiving field is the entire record called PRINT-LINE.

Thus the description of the COBOL program for Example 1 is finished. The complete program for this example is shown in Figure 15-8.

```
IDENTIFICATION DIVISION.

PROGRAM-ID.   PROB 1.
DATE-WRITTEN.  8/20/79.
DATE-COMPILED.          10/21/79.
REMARKS.
    PROB 1 READS STUDENT RECORDS AND GENERATES A REPORT
    CONTAINING THE STUDENT'S NAME, NUMBER, UNITS, AND TOTAL UNITS.
ENVIRONMENT DIVISION.

CONFIGURATION SECTION.
  SOURCE-COMPUTER.   IBM 360/370.
INPUT-OUTPUT SECTION.
  FILE-CONTROL.
    SELECT STUDENT-FILE ASSIGN TO INPUT.
    SELECT PRINT-FILE    ASSIGN TO OUTPUT.

DATA DIVISION.

FILE SECTION.
FD  STUDENT-FILE
    LABEL RECORDS ARE OMITTED
    DATA RECORD IS STUDENT-REC.
01  STUDENT-REC.
    05  FILLER                 PICTURE X.
    05  STUDENT-NAME-OUT        PICTURE X(24).
    05  STUDENT-NUMBER-IN       PICTURE 9(6).
    05  UNITS-IN                PICTURE 9(2).
```

```
    05  TOTAL-UNITS-IN                 PICTURE 9(3).
    05  FILLER                         PICTURE X(44).


FD  PRINT-FILE
    LABEL RECORDS ARE OMITTED
    DATA RECORD IS PRINT-LINE.
01  PRINT-LINE.
    05  FILLER                         PICTURE X(15).
    05  STUDENT-NAME-OUT               PICTURE X(24).
    05  FILLER                         PICTURE X(5).
    05  STUDENT-NUMBER-OUT             PICTURE Z(5)9.
    05  FILLER                         PICTURE X(8).
    05  UNITS-OUT                      PICTURE Z9.
    05  FILLER                         PICTURE X(7).
    05  TOTAL-UNITS-OUT                PICTURE ZZ9.
    05  FILLER                         PICTURE X(63).


WORKING-STORAGE SECTION.
01  EOF                                PICTURE X     VALUE 'N'.


PROCEDURE DIVISION.


000-CONTROL-ROUTINE.
    PERFORM 100-INITIALIZE THRU 100-EXIT.
    PERFORM 200-READ-AND-LIST THRU 200-EXIT
        UNTIL EOF = 'Y'.
    PERFORM 300-END THRU 300-EXIT.
    STOP RUN.
000-EXIT.  EXIT.


100-INITIALIZE.
    OPEN INPUT STUDENT-FILE.
    OPEN OUTPUT PRINT-FILE.
    MOVE SPACES TO PRINT-LINE.
    WRITE PRINT-LINE AFTER ADVANCING 3 LINES.
    READ STUDENT-FILE AT END STOP RUN.
100-EXIT.  EXIT.


200-READ-AND-LIST.
    MOVE STUDENT-NAME-IN TO STUDENT-NAME-OUT.
    MOVE STUDENT-NUMBER-IN TO STUDENT-NUMBER OUT.
    MOVE UNITS-IN TO UNITS-OUT.
    MOVE TOTAL-UNITS-IN TO TOTAL-UNITS-OUT.
    WRITE PRINT-LINE AFTER ADVANCING 1 LINE.
    READ STUDENT-FILE
        AT END MOVE 'Y' TO EOF.
200-EXIT.  EXIT.


300-END.
    CLOSE STUDENT-FILE
          PRINT-FILE.
300-EXIT.  EXIT.


999-END-OF-PROGRAM.
```

ADAMS, PETER R.	13978	9	104
GOODMAN, HAROLD R.	20875	16	0
JOHNSON, SHARON C.	24432	15	74
LARSON, JAMES I.	47739	6	48
LEWIS, BARBARA C.	1339	18	107
ROTHCHILD, CHARLES K.	80336	10	100
THOMPSON, LAURA W.	59325	7	88

FIGURE 15-8
COBOL program and output for Example 1.

EXERCISE 15-1

1. All COBOL programs are composed of four divisions. The names of these divisions, in the order that they appear in a program, are _____, _____, _____, and _____.

2. Which of the following program names are not valid?
RECEIVABLES   2RUN
PAY-ROLL   SORT
INVENTORY   RUN2

3. If a COBOL program is to run on a different computer from the one indicated by the program, the only division that would change significantly is the _____ division.

4. The first time a file name appears in a COBOL program is in a _____ clause of the _____ division.

5. The file section of the data division consists of a hierarchy of entries for each file. First, there is a _____ description, then a _____ description, and finally a _____ description.

6. The length and type of data field is defined by a _____ clause.

7. An item that is further subdivided is referred to as a _____ item, whereas an item that is not further subdivided is called a _____ item.

8. State the result of each of the following MOVE operations.

Sending Field		Receiving Field	
Picture	Contents	Picture	Contents (after MOVE)
99V99	94ᴧ67	99V99	_____

99V99	94ˬ67	99V9	_____
99V99	94ˬ67	9V99	_____
A(4)	JOHN	A(4)	_____
	SPACES	A(8)	_____

9.   The environment division contains two sections, the _____ section

and the _____ section.

10.   The data division contains two sections, the _____ section and the

_____ section.

EXAMPLE 2: SIMPLE CALCULATIONS

Example 2 introduces the use of calculations in a COBOL program. The card for each student is to be read, and "units taken this semester" is to be added to "total units to date" to obtain an updated total. The record is then to be printed, with the updated total replacing the previous total.

In addition to updating each record, we must total "units taken this semester" for all students and print it at the end of the listing. Header information is also to be printed at the top of the listing.

The input format for Example 2 is the same as for Example 1 (see Figure 15–2). Figure 15–9 shows the output format on a printer spacing chart, together with a sample listing.

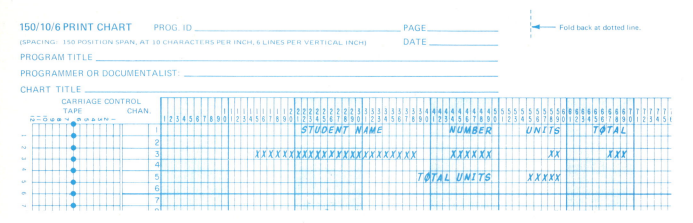

FIGURE 15–9
Printer spacing chart for Example 2.

DATA DIVISION

The principal changes in Example 2 are in the data and procedure divisions. The data division for this example is shown in Figure 15–10.

In Example 2, the working storage section is expanded considerably compared to Example 1. A group item called MISC-VARIABLES is defined at the 01 level. This item contains two elementary items: CUM-TOTAL and EOF. The CUM-TOTAL field is used to accumulate total units taken for all students.

The remaining entries in the working storage section are used to define three different print lines, as follows.

IBM   COBOL Coding Form   GX28-146
Pri

SYSTEM		PUNCHING INSTRUCTIONS			PAGE	OF
PROGRAM		GRAPHIC		CARD FORM #		
PROGRAMMER	DATE	PUNCH				

```
DATA DIVISION.
FILE-SECTION.
FD  STUDENT-FILE
    LABEL RECORDS ARE OMITTED
    DATA RECORD IS STUDENT-REC.
01  STUDENT-REC.
    05 FILLER                 PICTURE X.
    05 STUDENT-NAME-IN        PICTURE X(24).
    05 STUDENT-NUMBER-IN      PICTURE 9(6).
    05 UNITS-IN               PICTURE 99.
    05 TOTAL-UNITS-IN         PICTURE 999.
    05 FILLER                 PICTURE X(44).
FD  PRINT-FILE
    LABEL RECORDS ARE OMITTED
    DATA RECORD IS PRINT-REC.
01  PRINT-REC.
    05  FILLER                PICTURE X(133).

WORKING-STORAGE SECTION.
01  MISC-VARIABLES.
    05  CUM-TOTAL             PICTURE 9(5)      VALUE IS ZERO.
    05  EOF                   PICTURE X         VALUE IS 'N'.
01  PRINT-LINE.
    05  FILLER                PICTURE X(15)     VALUE IS SPACES.
    05  NAME-OUT              PICTURE X(24).
    05  FILLER                PICTURE X(5)      VALUE IS SPACES.
    05  NUMBER-OUT            PICTURE Z(5)9.
    05  FILLER                PICTURE X(8)      VALUE IS SPACES.
    05  UNITS-OUT             PICTURE Z9.
    05  FILLER                PICTURE X(7)      VALUE IS SPACES.
    05  TOTAL-OUT             PICTURE ZZ9.
    05  FILLER                PICTURE X(63)     VALUE IS SPACES.
01  HEADER.
    05  FILLER                PICTURE X(22)     VALUE IS SPACES.
    05  FILLER                PICTURE X(12)
                                  VALUE IS 'STUDENT NAME'.
    05  FILLER                PICTURE X(11)     VALUE IS SPACES.
    05  FILLER                PICTURE X(6)      VALUE IS 'NUMBER'.
    05  FILLER                PICTURE X(5)      VALUE IS SPACES.
    05  FILLER                PICTURE X(5)      VALUE IS 'UNITS'.
    05  FILLER                PICTURE X(5)      VALUE IS SPACES.
    05  FILLER                PICTURE X(5)      VALUE IS 'TOTAL'.
    05  FILLER                PICTURE X(62)     VALUE IS SPACES.
01  TOTAL-LINE.
    05  FILLER                PICTURE X(38)     VALUE IS SPACES.
    05  FILLER                PICTURE X(11)
                                  VALUE IS 'TOTAL UNITS'.
    05  FILLER                PICTURE X(6)      VALUE IS SPACES.
    05  CUM-TOTAL-OUT         PICTURE Z(4)9.
    05  FILLER                PICTURE X(73)     VALUE IS SPACES.
```

FIGURE 15-10
Data division for Example 2.

01 PRINT–LINE: used to print detail data for each student.

01 HEADER: used to print column headings.

01 TOTAL–LINE: used to print the cumulative total for all students.

Notice that the individual fields for each of these print lines are defined in working storage using the PICTURE clause. Also, initial values are assigned to the data items using the VALUE clause.

QUESTION: Examine Figure 15–10. The second data item in the HEADER record appears as follows.

05 FILLER PICTURE X(12) VALUE IS 'STUDENT-NAME'.

This indicates that the field is a _____-character alphanumeric field and

that the field is initialized with the characters _____

ANSWER: 12, STUDENT-NAME.

PROCEDURE DIVISION The procedure division for Example 2 is shown in Figure 15–11.

The procedure division for this example contains two new features compared to Example 1.

1. ADD statements, which add "units" to "total units" to obtain an updated total for each student and to accumulate "total units" for all students.
2. WRITE-FROM statements, which cause a record to be printed from a named area in working storage.

The complete COBOL program for Example 2 is shown in Figure 15–12.

```
IDENTIFICATION DIVISION.

PROGRAM-ID.   PROB2.
DATE-WRITTEN.      9/12/79.
DATE-COMPILED.          10/21/79.
REMARKS.
     PROB2 ADDS CURRENT UNITS TO STUDENT'S TOTAL UNITS AND KEEPS
     A CUMULATIVE TOTAL OF CURRENT UNITS FOR ALL STUDENTS.

ENVIRONMENT DIVISION.

CONFIGURATION SECTION.
   SOURCE-COMPUTER.   IBM 360/370.
INPUT-OUTPUT SECTION.
FILE-CONTROL.
     SELECT STUDENT-FILE ASSIGN TO INPUT.
     SELECT PRINT-FILE      ASSIGN TO OUTPUT.
DATA DIVISION.
```

IBM   COBOL Coding Form   GX28-14(Pr

SYSTEM				PUNCHING INSTRUCTIONS					PAGE	OF
PROGRAM				GRAPHIC				CARD FORM #		
PROGRAMMER		DATE		PUNCH						

```
PROCEDURE DIVISION.
000-MAINLINE-CONTROL.
    PERFORM 100-INITIALIZE THRU 100-EXIT.
    PERFORM 200-PROCESS THRU 200-EXIT
        UNTIL EOF = 'Y'.
    PERFORM 300-END THRU 300-EXIT.
    STOP RUN.
000-EXIT. EXIT.

100-INITIALIZE.
    OPEN INPUT STUDENT-FILE.
    OPEN OUTPUT PRINT-FILE.
    WRITE PRINT-REC FROM HEADER
        AFTER ADVANCING 2 LINES.
    READ STUDENT-FILE
        AT END STOP RUN.
100-EXIT. EXIT.

200-PROCESS.
    ADD UNITS-IN TO TOTAL-UNITS-IN.
    ADD UNITS-IN TO CUM-TOTAL.
    MOVE STUDENT-NAME-IN TO NAME-OUT
    MOVE STUDENT-NUMBER-IN TO NUMBER-OUT.
    MOVE UNITS-IN TO UNITS-OUT.
    MOVE TOTAL-UNITS-IN TO TOTAL-OUT.
    WRITE PRINT-REC FROM PRINT-LINE
        AFTER ADVANCING 1 LINE.
    READ STUDENT-FILE
        AT END MOVE 'Y' TO EOF.
200-EXIT. EXIT.

300-END
    MOVE CUM-TOTAL TO CUM-TOTAL-OUT.
    WRITE PRINT-REC FROM TOTAL-LINE
        AFTER ADVANCING 2 LINES.
    CLOSE STUDENT-FILE
        PRINT-FILE.
300-EXIT. EXIT.

999-END-OF-PROGRAM.
```

FIGURE 15-11
Procedure division for Example 2.

```
FILE SECTION.
FD  STUDENT-FILE
    LABEL RECORDS ARE OMITTED
    DATA RECORD IS STUDENT-REC.
01  STUDENT-REC.
    05 FILLER                       PICTURE X.
    05 STUDENT-NAME-IN              PICTURE X(24).
    05 STUDENT-NUMBER-IN            PICTURE 9(6).
    05 UNITS-IN                     PICTURE 99.
    05 TOTAL-UNITS-IN               PICTURE 999.
    05 FILLER                       PICTURE X(44).

FD  PRINT-FILE
    LABEL RECORDS ARE OMITTED
    DATA RECORD IS PRINT-REC.
01  PRINT-REC.
    05 FILLER                       PICTURE X(133).

WORKING-STORAGE SECTION.
01  MISC-VARIABLES.
    05 CUM-TOTAL                    PICTURE 9(5)      VALUE IS ZERO.
    05 EOF                          PICTURE X         VALUE IS 'N'.

01  PRINT-LINE.
    05 FILLER                       PICTURE X(15)     VALUE IS SPACES.
    05 NAME-OUT                     PICTURE X(24).
    05 FILLER                       PICTURE X(5)      VALUE IS SPACES.
    05 NUMBER-OUT                   PICTURE Z(5)9.
    05 FILLER                       PICTURE X(8)      VALUE IS SPACES.
    05 UNITS-OUT                    PICTURE Z9.
    05 FILLER                       PICTURE X(7)      VALUE IS SPACES.
    05 TOTAL-OUT                    PICTURE ZZ9.
    05 FILLER                       PICTURE X(63)     VALUE IS SPACES.

01  HEADER.
    05 FILLER                       PICTURE X(22)     VALUE IS SPACES.
    05 FILLER                       PICTURE X(12)     VALUE IS 'STUDENT NAME'.
    05 FILLER                       PICTURE X(11)     VALUE IS SPACES.
    05 FILLER                       PICTURE X(6)      VALUE IS 'NUMBER'.
    05 FILLER                       PICTURE X(5)      VALUE IS SPACES.
    05 FILLER                       PICTURE X(5)      VALUE IS 'UNITS'.
    05 FILLER                       PICTURE X(5)      VALUE IS SPACES.
    05 FILLER                       PICTURE X(5)      VALUE 'TOTAL'.
    05 FILLER                       PICTURE X(62)     VALUE IS SPACES.

01  TOTAL-LINE.
    05 FILLER                       PICTURE X(38)     VALUE IS SPACES.
    05 FILLER                       PICTURE X(11)     VALUE IS 'TOTAL UNITS'.
    05 FILLER                       PICTURE X(6)      VALUE IS SPACES.
    05 CUM-TOTAL-OUT                PICTURE Z(4)9.
    05 FILLER                       PICTURE X(73)     VALUE IS SPACES.
```

```
PROCEDURE DIVISION.

000-MAINLINE-CONTROL.
    PERFORM 100-INITIALIZE THRU 100-EXIT.
    PERFORM 200-PROCESS THRU 200-EXIT
        UNTIL EOF = 'Y'.
    PERFORM 300-END THRU 300-EXIT.
    STOP RUN.
000-EXIT.  EXIT.

100-INITIALIZE.
    OPEN INPUT STUDENT-FILE.
    OPEN OUTPUT PRINT-FILE.
    WRITE PRINT-REC FROM HEADER
        AFTER ADVANCING 2 LINES.
    READ STUDENT-FILE
        AT END STOP RUN.
100-EXIT.  EXIT.

200-PROCESS.
    ADD UNITS-IN TO TOTAL-UNITS-IN.
    ADD UNITS-IN TO CUM-TOTAL.
    MOVE STUDENT-NAME-IN TO NAME-OUT.
    MOVE STUDENT-NUMBER-IN TO NUMBER-OUT.
    MOVE UNITS-IN TO UNITS-OUT.
    MOVE TOTAL-UNITS-IN TO TOTAL-OUT.
    WRITE PRINT-REC FROM PRINT-LINE
        AFTER ADVANCING 1 LINE.
    READ STUDENT-FILE
        AT END MOVE 'Y' TO EOF.
200-EXIT.  EXIT.

300-END.
    MOVE CUM-TOTAL TO CUM-TOTAL-OUT.
    WRITE PRINT-REC FROM TOTAL-LINE
        AFTER ADVANCING 2 LINES.
    CLOSE STUDENT-FILE
        PRINT-FILE.
300-EXIT.  EXIT.

999-END-OF-PROGRAM.
```

STUDENT NAME	NUMBER	UNITS	TOTAL
ADAMS, PETER R.	13978	9	113
GOODMAN, HAROLD R.	20875	16	16
JOHNSON, SHARON C.	24432	15	89
LARSON, JAMES I.	47739	6	54
LEWIS, BARBARA C.	1339	18	125
ROTHCHILD, CHARLES K.	80336	10	110
THOMPSON, LAURA W.	59325	7	95
	TOTAL UNITS	81	

FIGURE 15-12
COBOL program and output for Example 2.

ARITHMETIC STATEMENTS

Arithmetic statements are at the core of many programs. Only the simple ADD statement is used in Example 2. This section discusses the COBOL statements ADD, SUBTRACT, MULTIPLY, DIVIDE, and COMPUTE.

ADD

A simple ADD statement has two possible formats.

$$\text{Format 1} \quad \text{ADD} \begin{bmatrix} \text{data-name-1} \\ \text{(or)} \\ \text{literal} \end{bmatrix} \text{TO (data-name-2)}.$$

Examples are:

ADD A TO B.
ADD 40 TO HOURS.

In each example, the sum is stored in the second field, whereas the first field remains unchanged.

$$\text{Format 2} \qquad \text{ADD} \begin{bmatrix} \text{data-name-1} \\ \text{(or)} \\ \text{literal-1} \end{bmatrix}, \begin{bmatrix} \text{data-name-2} \\ \text{(or)} \\ \text{literal-2} \end{bmatrix}$$

ADD A, B GIVING C.
ADD A, 39.40 GIVING C.

In each example, the sum is stored in the third field (field C). The other fields remain unchanged.

The choice of format for the ADD statement depends on the result desired. If the contents of all operands are to be retained, format 2 (the GIVING format) should be used. Otherwise, the TO format may be used.

QUESTION: Suppose the three fields A, B, and C contain the following numbers: A = 5, B = 7, and C = 6. Indicate the contents of each of the fields after the following operations.

a. ADD A TO B: A ____, B ____, C ____

b. ADD A, B, GIVING C: A ____, B ____, C ____

ANSWER: (a) 5, 12, 6; (b) 5, 7, 12

Care must be taken to use arithmetic statement formats without alteration. For example, the following statement is *invalid*.

ADD A TO B GIVING C.

It is illegal to use TO with the GIVING option. Instead, the expression ADD A, B GIVING C should be used.

Both formats may be expanded to include an arbitrary number of operands. For example, the following statements are valid.

ADD A, B, C, 109 TO D.

ADD INSURANCE, TAX, RETIREMENT GIVING DEDUCTIONS.

SUBTRACT   The SUBTRACT statement also has two formats. Some examples will illustrate its usage.

SUBTRACT A FROM B.
SUBTRACT A FROM B GIVING C.
SUBTRACT A, B, 25 FROM D GIVING E.

QUESTION: Suppose the three fields A, B, and C contain the following numbers: A = 5, B = 7, and C = 6. Indicate the contents of each of the fields after the following operations.

a. SUBTRACT A FROM B: A ___, B ___, C ___

b. SUBTRACT A FROM B GIVING C: A ___, B ___, C ___

ANSWER: (a) 5, 2, 6; (b) 5, 7, 2

MULTIPLY   The MULTIPLY statement multiplies two quantities and stores the result in the second item, or if desired, in a third field. The following examples illustrate its usage.

MULTIPLY A BY B. (product in B)
MULTIPLY A BY B GIVING C. (product in C)
MULTIPLY HOURLY-RATE BY HOURS GIVING GROSS-PAY.

QUESTION: Suppose the three fields A, B, and C contain the following numbers: A = 5, B = 7, and C = 6. Indicate the contents of each of the fields after the following operations:

a. MULTIPLY A BY B: A ___, B ___, C ___

b. MULTIPLY A BY B GIVING C: A ___, B ___, C ___

ANSWER: (a) 5, 35, 6; (b) 5, 7, 35

DIVIDE   The DIVIDE statement also permits storing the quotient of two numbers in the second field or, by using a GIVING clause, in a third field.
Examples are:

DIVIDE A INTO B. (quotient in B)
DIVIDE A INTO B GIVING C. (quotient in C)
DIVIDE 12 INTO SALES GIVING MONTHLY-SALES.

COMPUTE   Although COBOL is not used for scientific applications, it is sometimes necessary to evaluate more complicated algebraic expressions. Such expressions could be evaluated by using several simple COBOL arithmetic statements. However, it is often easier to use the COMPUTE statement, which also permits exponentiation to be performed.
The general form of this statement is:

COMPUTE (data name) = (expression).

In the expression after the equals sign, arithmetic symbols are used rather than COBOL reserved words such as ADD and MULTIPLY.

As an example, the compound amount in an interest calculation is computed using the formula AMOUNT = PRINCIPAL * (1 + RATE) ** PERIODS where ** means exponentiation. This would be expressed in COBOL as follows.

COMPUTE AMOUNT = PRINCIPAL * (1 + RATE) ** PERIODS.

EXERCISE 15-2

1. Descriptions of constants, intermediate totals, and work areas used in a COBOL program are entered in the _____ section of the _____ division.

2. Initial values may be assigned to items in working storage by means of _____ clauses.

3. Indicate the content of FLDA in each of the following examples.

   a. FLDA PICTURE 9(4) VALUE 329. _____

   b. FLDA PICTURE 99V99 VALUE 3.29. _____

   c. FLDA PICTURE 99V99 VALUE 623.294. _____

   d. FLDA PICTURE A(10) VALUE 'LOIS MOREY'. _____

   e. FLDA PICTURE X(5) VALUE SPACES. _____

4. Three fields, FLDA, FLDB, and FLDC, are defined as follows.

	FLDA	FLDB	FLDC
Picture	99V99	99V99	99V99
Present contents	4ᴧ50	17ᴧ75	56ᴧ25

   Indicate the contents of each of the three fields after the following operations.
   a. ADD FLDA TO FLDB.
   b. ADD FLDA, FLDB TO FLDC.
   c. ADD FLDA, FLDB GIVING FLDC.
   d. ADD FLDA TO FLDB GIVING FLDC.
   e. SUBTRACT FLDA FROM FLDB.
   f. SUBTRACT FLDA FROM FLDB GIVING FLDC.
   g. SUBTRACT FLDA, FLDB FROM FLDC.

FLDA	FLDB	FLDC
a. _____	_____	_____
b. _____	_____	_____

c. _____   _____   _____

d. _____   _____   _____

e. _____   _____   _____

f. _____   _____   _____

g. _____   _____   _____

5. Three fields, FLDA, FLDB, and FLDC, are defined as follows.

	FLDA	FLDB	FLDC
Picture	9	9V99	99V99
Present contents	4	9$_\wedge$60	20$_\wedge$37

Indicate the contents of each of the three fields after the following operations.
a. MULTIPLY FLDA BY FLDB.
b. DIVIDE FLDA INTO FLDB.
c. DIVIDE FLDA INTO FLDB GIVING FLDC.
d. MULTIPLY FLDA BY FLDB GIVING FLDC.

FLDA   *FLDB*   *FLDC*

a. _____   _____   _____

b. _____   _____   _____

c. _____   _____   _____

d. _____   _____   _____

6. Write COBOL COMPUTE statements for each of the following expressions.
a. $Y = AX^2 + BX + C$
b. HOURS = 1.5 (HOURS-WORKED − 40) + 40

a. _____

b. _____

EXAMPLE 3: SIMPLE LOGICAL OPERATIONS

Example 3 introduces the use of simple comparisons or logical operations in COBOL. The student record is to be read, and tuition is to be computed according to the following formula.

If units is less than 12, tuition is units times $35; if units is 12 or more, tuition is $420.

Total student fees consist of tuition plus an incidental fee of $12.50. This total is to be printed along with student name, number, and units taken. Also, the amount of total fees for all students is to be computed and printed at the end of the listing.

The input format for Example 3 is the same as for Examples 1 and 2 (see Figure 15–2). The desired output formula together with a sample listing is shown in Figure 15–13.

150/10/6 PRINT CHART   PROG. ID _____   PAGE _____   ◄── Fold back at dotted line.

(SPACING: 150 POSITION SPAN, AT 10 CHARACTERS PER INCH, 6 LINES PER VERTICAL INCH)   DATE _____

PROGRAM TITLE _____

PROGRAMMER OR DOCUMENTALIST: _____

CHART TITLE _____

```
          STUDENT NAME              NUMBER      UNITS          FEES

    XXXXXXXXXXXXXXXXXXXXXXXXXXX     XXXXXX        XX          XXX.XX

                                            TOTAL FEES    $XX,XXX.XX
```

FIGURE 15–13
Printer spacing chart for Example 3.

PROCEDURE DIVISION

The identification, environment, and data divisions for Example 3 are substantially the same as those for Example 2. Therefore, only the procedure division (shown in Figure 15–14) will be described in detail.

The main feature of this example is the conditional statement used to compute tuition. The determination of tuition is represented in flowchart form in Figure 15–15.

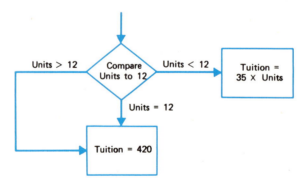

FIGURE 15–15
Flowchart of tuition logic.

The comparison and resulting computation of tuition is expressed by the following COBOL statement, contained in the paragraph 200–PROCESS.

IF UNITS–IN IS LESS THAN 12 MULTIPLY UNITS–IN BY 35.00 GIVING TUITION ELSE MOVE 420.00 TO TUITION.

After tuition is computed, the $12.50 incidental fee is added to it to determine the total student fee, called FEES in Figure 15–14. FEES is then added to TOTAL-FEES, which is the cumulative sum of fees for all students. At the end of

IBM COBOL Coding Form GX28-146

SYSTEM	PUNCHING INSTRUCTIONS	PAGE OF
PROGRAM	GRAPHIC	CARD FORM #
PROGRAMMER / DATE	PUNCH	

SEQUENCE (PAGE) (SERIAL) CONT. A B COBOL STATEMENT IDENTIFICATION

```
       PROCEDURE DIVISION.
       000-MAINLINE-CONTROL.
           PERFORM 100-INITIALIZE THRU 100-EXIT.
           PERFORM 200-PROCESS THRU 200-EXIT
               UNTIL EOF = 'Y'.
           PERFORM 300-END THRU 300-EXIT.
           STOP RUN.
       000-EXIT. EXIT.

       100-INITIALIZE.
           OPEN INPUT STUDENT-FILE.
           OPEN OUTPUT PRINT-FILE.
           WRITE PRINT-REC FROM HEADER
               AFTER ADVANCING 2 LINES.
           READ STUDENT-FILE
               AT END STOP RUN.
       100-EXIT. EXIT.

       200-PROCESS.
           IF UNITS-IN IS LESS THAN 12
               MULTIPLY UNITS-IN BY 35.00 GIVING TUITION
           ELSE
               MOVE 420.00 TO TUITION.

           ADD 12.50 TO TUITION GIVING FEES.
           ADD FEES TO TOTAL-FEES.
           MOVE SPACES TO PRINT-LINE.
           MOVE STUDENT-NAME-IN TO NAME-OUT.
           MOVE STUDENT-NUMBER-IN TO NUMBER-OUT.
           MOVE UNITS-IN TO UNITS-OUT.
           MOVE FEES TO FEES-OUT.
           WRITE PRINT-REC FROM PRINT-LINE
               AFTER ADVANCING 1 LINE.
           READ STUDENT-FILE
               AT END MOVE 'Y' TO EOF.
       200-EXIT. EXIT.

       300-END.
           MOVE TOTAL-FEES TO TOTAL-FEES-OUT.
           WRITE PRINT-REC FROM TOTAL-LINE
               AFTER ADVANCING 3 LINES.
           CLOSE STUDENT-FILE
                 PRINT FILE.
       300-EXIT. EXIT.

       999-END-OF-PROGRAM.
```

*A standard card form, IBM Electro C61897, is available for punching source statements from this form.
Instructions for using this form are given in any IBM COBOL reference manual.
Address comments concerning this form to IBM Corporation, Programming Publications, 1271 Avenue of the Americas, New York, New York 10020.

*No. of sheets per pad

FIGURE 15-14
Procedure division for Example 3.

the program, TOTAL-FEES is printed from the working-storage record called TOTAL-LINE.

The complete COBOL program for Example 3, together with sample output, is shown in Figure 15-16.

```
IDENTIFICATION DIVISION.

PROGRAM-ID.  PROB3.
DATE-WRITTEN.    9/22/79.
DATE-COMPILED.

ENVIRONMENT DIVISION.

CONFIGURATION SECTION.
SOURCE-COMPUTER.  IBM 360/370.
INPUT-OUTPUT SECTION.
FILE-CONTROL.
    SELECT STUDENT-FILE ASSIGN TO INPUT.
    SELECT PRINT-FILE      ASSIGN TO OUTPUT.

DATA DIVISION.

FILE SECTION.
FD STUDENT-FILE
    LABEL RECORDS ARE OMITTED
    DATA RECORD IS STUDENT-REC.
01  STUDENT-REC.
    05 FILLER                      PICTURE X.
    05 STUDENT-NAME-IN             PICTURE X(24).
    05 STUDENT-NUMBER-IN           PICTURE 9(6).
    05 UNITS-IN                    PICTURE 99.
    05 TOTAL-UNITS-IN              PICTURE 999.
    05 FILLER                      PICTURE X(44).

FD  PRINT-FILE
    LABEL RECORDS ARE OMITTED
    DATA RECORD IS PRINT-REC.
01  PRINT-REC.
    05 FILLER                      PICTURE X(133).

WORKING-STORAGE SECTION.
01  MISC-VARIABLES.
    05 TUITION                     PICTURE 999V99.
    05 TOTAL-FEES                  PICTURE 9(6)V99      VALUE IS ZERO.
    05 FEES                        PICTURE 999V99.
    05 EOF                         PICTURE X            VALUE IS 'N'.

01  PRINT-LINE.
    05 FILLER                      PICTURE X(14).
    05 NAME-OUT                    PICTURE X(23).
    05 FILLER                      PICTURE X(6).
    05 NUMBER-OUT                  PICTURE 9(6).
    05 FILLER                      PICTURE X(8).
    05 UNITS-OUT                   PICTURE 9(2).
```

```
        05 FILLER                      PICTURE X(7).
        05 FEES-OUT                    PICTURE ZZ9.99.
        05 FILLER                      PICTURE X(61).


    01  HEADER.
        05 FILLER                      PICTURE X(22)    VALUE IS SPACES.
        05 FILLER                      PICTURE X(12)    VALUE IS 'STUDENT NAME'.
        05 FILLER                      PICTURE X(9)     VALUE IS SPACES.
        05 FILLER                      PICTURE X(16)    VALUE IS 'NUMBER     UNITS'.
        05 FILLER                      PICTURE X(7)     VALUE IS SPACES.
        05 FILLER                      PICTURE X(4)     VALUE IS 'FEES'.
        05 FILLER                      PICTURE X(63)    VALUE IS SPACES.


    01  TOTAL-LINE.
        05 FILLER                      PICTURE X(50)    VALUE IS SPACES.
        05 FILLER                      PICTURE X(10)    VALUE IS 'TOTAL FEES'.
        05 FILLER                      PICTURE X(2)     VALUE IS SPACES.
        05 TOTAL-FEES-OUT              PICTURE $$$,$$9.99.
        05 FILLER                      PICTURE X(61)    VALUE IS SPACES.

PROCEDURE DIVISION.

000-MAINLINE-CONTROL.
    PERFORM 100-INITIALIZE THRU 100-EXIT.
    PERFORM 200-PROCESS THRU 200-EXIT
        UNTIL EOF = 'Y'.
    PERFORM 300-END THRU 300-EXIT.
    STOP RUN.
000-EXIT.  EXIT.


100-INITIALIZE.
    OPEN INPUT STUDENT-FILE.
    OPEN OUTPUT PRINT-FILE.
    WRITE PRINT-REC FROM HEADER
        AFTER ADVANCING 2 LINES.
    READ STUDENT-FILE
        AT END STOP RUN.
100-EXIT.  EXIT.
200-PROCESS.
    IF UNITS-IN IS LESS THAN 12
        MULTIPLY UNITS-IN BY 35.00 GIVING TUITION
        ELSE MOVE 420.00 TO TUITION.
    ADD 12.50 TO TUITION GIVING FEES.
    ADD FEES TO TOTAL-FEES.
    MOVE SPACES TO PRINT-LINE.
    MOVE STUDENT-NAME-IN TO NAME-OUT.
    MOVE STUDENT-NUMBER-IN TO NUMBER-OUT.
    MOVE UNITS-IN TO UNITS-OUT.
    MOVE FEES TO FEES-OUT.
    WRITE PRINT-REC FROM PRINT-LINE
        AFTER ADVANCING 1 LINE.
    READ STUDENT-FILE
        AT END MOVE 'Y' TO EOF.
200-EXIT.  EXIT.
```

```
300-END.
    MOVE TOTAL-FEES TO TOTAL-FEES-OUT.
    WRITE PRINT-REC FROM TOTAL-LINE
        AFTER ADVANCING 3 LINES.
    CLOSE STUDENT-FILE
            PRINT-FILE.
300-EXIT.  EXIT.

999-END-OF-PROGRAM.
```

STUDENT NAME	NUMBER	UNITS	FEES
ADAMS, PETER R.	013978	09	327.50
GOODMAN, HAROLD R.	020875	16	432.50
JOHNSON, SHARON C.	024432	15	432.50
LARSON, JAMES I.	047739	06	222.50
LEWIS, BARBARA C.	001339	18	432.50
ROTHCHILD, CHARLES K.	080336	10	362.50
THOMPSON, LAURA W.	059325	07	257.50
		TOTAL FEES	$2,467.50

FIGURE 15-16
COBOL program and output for Example 3.

THE IF STATEMENT The path to be taken in a program often depends on the result of comparing two quantities. In Example 3, the calculation of student tuition depended on the number of units taken. The testing of a condition and branching, depending on the result, are accomplished with a COBOL IF statement. In Example 3, the statement was as follows.

IF UNITS-IN IS LESS THAN 12 MULTIPLY UNITS-IN BY 35.00 GIVING TUITION ELSE MOVE 420.00 TO TUITION.

The general form of the IF statement is:

IF (test condition) (statement-1) ELSE (statement-2)

The **test condition** generally specifies a relation between two quantities. The general form is:

$$\begin{bmatrix} \text{data-name-1} \\ \text{(or)} \\ \text{literal} \end{bmatrix} \text{(relational operator)} \begin{bmatrix} \text{data-name-2} \\ \text{(or)} \\ \text{literal} \end{bmatrix}$$

The **relational operator** specifies the type of comparison. It may be any one of the following.

IS EQUAL TO (or =)
IS GREATER THAN (or >)
IS LESS THAN (or <)
IS NOT EQUAL TO
IS NOT GREATER THAN
IS NOT LESS THAN

Following are several examples of the use of the IF statement.

Example	Comment
IF A IS GREATER THAN B GO TO START	If A is less than or equal to B, the program goes to the next sequential instruction.
IF A IS GREATER THAN B GO TO NEXT ELSE GO TO START.	The program branches to either NEXT or START, depending on the relation between A and B.
IF PAYMENT IS GREATER THAN BALANCE GO TO ADJUST ELSE SUBTRACT PAY MENT FROM BALANCE.	If PAYMENT is less than or equal to BALANCE, it is subtracted from BALANCE and the program goes to the next sequential instruction.
IF A < B ADD C TO D GO TO FIRST ELSE MULTIPLY A BY C GIVING E GO TO START.	Several COBOL statements may be executed for each test condition.

QUESTION: Suppose six fields contain the following data: FLDA = 12, FLDB = 7, A = 14, B = 3, C = 6, and D = 9. What are the contents of each field after the following instruction is executed?

IF FLDA IS NOT EQUAL TO FLDB ADD A TO B
ELSE SUBTRACT C FROM D.

FLDA ____, FLDB ____, A ____, B ____, C ____, D ____

ANSWER: FLDA = 12, FLDB = 7, A = 14, B = 17, C = 6, D = 9

STOP   The STOP statement causes either a temporary or a permanent halt in program execution. The following statement will cause a permanent halt.

STOP RUN.

A temporary halt will result if a literal is used in place of RUN.

STOP (literal).

An example of this option is:

STOP 'ERROR'.

The computer will stop and print the literal on the console typewriter. When the start button is pushed, continuation of the run begins with the next sequential statement.

SUMMARY

In this chapter, you have studied COBOL, the major language used today in data processing applications. The main advantage of COBOL is that it is an English-like language that is relatively easy to learn and understand. Also, COBOL has extensive features for handling different file structures and for manipulating and editing data. COBOL is available for use on most computers (including some minicomputers) used in data processing applications.

Another language that is often used in business data processing is called Report Program Generator, or RPG. You will study this programming technique in Chapter 16.

ANSWERS TO EXERCISES

EXERCISE 15–1

1. Identification, environment, data, procedure
2. PAY-ROLL (special character)
   2RUN (first character not a letter)
3. Environment
4. SELECT, environment
5. File, record, item
6. Picture
7. Group, elementary
8.

Sending Field		Receiving Field	
Picture	Contents	Picture	Contents
99V99	94‸67	99V99	94‸67
99V99	94‸67	99V9	94‸6
99V99	94‸67	9V99	4‸67
A(4)	JOHN	A(4)	JOHN
	SPACES	A(8)	bbbbbbbb

9. Configuration, input/output
10. File, working-storage

EXERCISE 15–2

1. Working-storage, data
2. Value
3. (a) 0329, (b) 03‸29, (c) 23‸29, (d) LOIS MOREY, (e) bbbbb
4.

	FLDA	FLDB	FLDC
a.	4‸50	22‸25	56‸25
b.	4‸50	17‸75	78‸50
c.	4‸50	17‸75	22‸25
d.	Illegal		
e.	4‸50	13‸25	56‸25
f.	4‸50	17‸75	13‸25
g.	4‸50	17‸75	34‸00

5.

	FLDA	FLDB	FLDC
a.	4	38‸40	20‸37
b.	4	2‸40	20‸37
c.	4	9‸60	02‸40
d.	4	9‸60	38‸40

6. a. COMPUTE Y = A * X ** 2 + B * X + C.
   b. COMPUTE HOURS = 1.5 * (HOURS-WORKED − 40) + 40.

CHAPTER EXAMINATION

1. Each of the following statements contains one error. Identify each error.

   a. ADD A,B TO C GIVING D. _____

   b. DIVIDE A BY B GIVING C. _____

   c. MULTIPLY X TIMES Y. _____

   d. MOVE A INTO B. _____

   e. DIVIDE A INTO 20. _____

2. Fill in the "After" line in each of the following statement:

   a. MOVE A TO B.

	A	B
Before	139	620
After	___	___

   b. ADD A,B, TO C.

	A	B	C
Before	9	5	18
After	___	___	___

   c. SUBTRACT A FROM D GIVING F.

	A	D	F
Before	9	42	91
After	___	___	___

   d. MULTIPLY A BY B GIVING S.

	A	B	S
Before	11	4	50
After	___	___	___

   c. DIVIDE A INTO B.

	A	B
Before	4	20
After	___	___

3. Write COBOL statements to do each of the following.
   a. There are two data items called QUANTITY and AMOUNT in storage. Write a statement to make the value AMOUNT the same as the value of QUANTITY, leaving the latter unchanged.

   _____

b.   Write a statement to make the value of QUANTITY equal to zero.

_____

c.   Move the literal JOHN DOE to a field called NAME.

_____

d.   Determine whether the value of BALANCE is greater than 50; if so, transfer to a paragraph called NEXT; if not, subtract AMOUNT from BALANCE.

_____

4.   A salesman's commission is calculated based on the type of product, as follows.

PRODUCT-CODE	COMMISSION
1	$(0.15) \times (SALES\text{-}PRICE)$
2	$(0.30) \times (SALES\text{-}PRICE)$
3	$\$50 + (.10) \times (SALES\text{-}PRICE)$
4	$\$100$

Given values for PRODUCT-CODE and SALES-PRICE, write COBOL statements to compute COMMISSION.

_____

_____

_____

_____

_____

_____

_____

_____

5.   Identify the errors in each of the following.

a.   WORKING STORAGE SECTION. _____

b.   02 BALANCE PICTURE 9(5) VALUE '50'. _____

c.   FILE-SECTION _____

d.   02 BALANCE PICTURE 9(5). VALUE ZERO. _____

e.   03 NAME PICTURE X(6) VALUE 'HOSTETTLER'. _____

6. Following is a student record layout.

STUDENT-REC						
NAME	MATRIC-DATE			NUMBER	ADDRESS	GP-AVE
	MONTH	DAY	YEAR			

Each item is as follows.

NAME	20 letters
MONTH	2 digits
DAY	2 digits
YEAR	2 digits
NUMBER	6 digits
ADDRESS	20 alphanumeric
GP-AVE	3 digits, 2 decimal places

Write a complete COBOL record description.

SEQUENCE		CONT.	A	B										
(PAGE) 1 3	(SERIAL) 4 6	7	8	12	16	20	24	28	32	36	40	44	48
	0 1												
	0 2												
	0 3												
	0 4												
	0 5												
	0 6												
	0 7												
	0 8												
	0 9												
	1 0												

7. Fill in the "Edited Result" column in each of the following.

Source Area		Receiving Area	
Picture	Sample Data	Picture	Edited Result
9(5)	00345	ZZZ,999	_____
999V99	02345	Z,ZZ9.99	_____
999V99	02345	$,$$9.99	_____
9(5)	00003	ZZ,999	_____

8. The 1960 U.S. Population Census shows that five central cities (CC) had populations of over 1 million. The following table shows the populations and areas in square miles of the five central cities and their standard metropolitan statistical areas (SMSAs), which include the central cities.

	Population		Area (sq. miles)	
	CC	SMSA	CC	SMSA
New York	7,781,984	10,694,633	315	2149
Chicago	3,550,404	6,220,913	224	3714
Philadelphia	3,002,512	4,342,897	127	3549
Detroit	1,670,144	3,762,360	140	1965
San Francisco	1,104,035	2,783,359	98	3313

Write a program to read the above data and compute and print out the following.
a. Population density (population per square mile) for each CC, SMSA, and SMSA ring (SMSA excluding the CC)
b. Area of each CC as a percent of the area of the SMSA

9. Write a program to condense some statistics on the students in a class. One data card is punched for each student as follows.

Item	Columns	
Age	1 and 2	
Sex	5	(1 = male, 2 = female)
Class standing	7	(1 = freshman, 2 = sophomore, 3 = junior, 4 = senior)

The required output is the following.
a. Average age of the students
b. Percent males, percent females
c. Percent freshmen, sophomores, juniors, seniors

Use the following data.

Age	Sex	Class Standing
20	1	2
18	2	1
26	2	4
21	1	3
23	1	2
19	2	1
21	1	4
20	2	2
23	1	4
17	2	1

10. Write a COBOL program for problem 14 in the Chapter 14 exam.

11. Write a COBOL program for problem 15 in the Chapter 14 exam.

IBM

COBOL Coding Form

SYSTEM

PROGRAM

PROGRAMMER

PUNCHING INSTRUCTIONS

GRAPHIC			
PUNCH			

DATE

CARD FORM #

PAGE ___ OF ___

*

SEQUENCE (PAGE) (SERIAL) CONT A B COBOL STATEMENT

IDENTIFICATION

GX28-1464-5 U/M 050
Printed in U.S.A.

IBM

COBOL Coding Form

SYSTEM				PUNCHING INSTRUCTIONS		PAGE	OF	
PROGRAM								*
PROGRAMMER		DATE		GRAPHIC		CARD FORM #		
				PUNCH				

COBOL STATEMENT

*A standard card form, IBM Electro C61897, is available for punching source statements from this form.
Instructions for using this form are given in any IBM COBOL reference manual.
Address comments concerning this form to IBM Corporation, Programming Publications, 1271 Avenue of the Americas, New York, New York 10020.

GX28-1464-5 U/M 050
Printed in U.S.A.

16

INTRODUCTION TO RPG

OVERVIEW. Report Program Generator, or RPG, provides an efficient method for writing computer instructions for many simple data processing jobs. RPG is particularly useful for the generation of routine business reports in situations where file structures and computational procedures are relatively simple. This language is widely used in many small business computers and is also gaining wide acceptance in medium- and large-scale computer installations, where it is often used in addition to COBOL or other languages.

RPG is a high-order, problem-oriented language. The user starts with a desired format for a listing or report and writes a set of specifications for the report and the input file to be used. The language is particularly easy to learn and use and does not require knowledge of machine instructions or lengthy training and experience.

RPG SPECIFICATION FORMS

RPG programs are recorded on a series of specification forms. The forms required for most programs are the following.

1. *File description specifications*. Entries describe the files to be used by the program.
2. *Input specifications*. Entries describe input records.
3. *Calculation specifications*. Entries describe calculation and data manipulation.
4. *Output-format specifications*. Entries describe output record formats.

Some programs require the use of tables, such as tax tables or frequency distributions. For such programs, the format and size of the tables are described on an additional form, the *file extension specifications*. This form will not be used in this chapter.

The RPG specification forms (except file extension) are shown in Figure 16–1. After the forms have been completed for a given program, they are ready to be keypunched to obtain the source deck.

QUESTION: What specification forms are required for most RPG programs? _____

ANSWER: file description, input, calculation, output-format

IBM

International Business Machines Corporation

RPG   INPUT SPECIFICATIONS

GX21-9094-1 U/M 050*
Printed in U.S.A

Date _____

Program _____

Programmer _____

Punching Instruction	Graphic					
	Punch					

Page [1] [2]

Program Identification [75] [76] [77] [78] [79] [80]

			ng Indicator	Record Identification Codes			Binary	Field Location			L9)	or	dation	Field Indicators
			*	1	2	3								

IBM

International Business Machines Corporation

RPG   CALCULATION SPECIFICATIONS

GX21-9093-1 U/M 050*
Printed in U.S.A.
*No. of forms per pad may vary slightly

Date _____

Program _____

Programmer _____

Punching Instruction	Graphic					
	Punch					

Page [1] [2]

Program Identification [75] [76] [77] [78] [79] [80]

Line	Type	ol Level 8, LR, SR)	Indicators And	Indicators And	Factor 1	Operation	Factor 2	Result Field	Field Length	nal Positions	Adjust (H)	Resulting Indicators Plus	Arithmetic Minus	Zero	Comments
											High 1>2	Low 1<2	Equal 1=2	

Resulting Indicators — Compare

IBM

International Business Machines Corporation

RPG   CONTROL CARD AND FILE DESCRIPTION SPECIFICATIONS

GX21-9092-2 UM/050*
Printed in U.S.A.

Date _____

Program _____

Programmer _____

Punching Instruction	Graphic					
	Punch					

Page [1] [2]

Program Identification [75] [76] [77] [78] [79] [80]

Control Card Specifications

				Sequence	Sterling gs ngs	ffer	g Sequence	Model 20	Model 20	nput t	n	ros ters	Dump	Conversion

---

IBM

International Business Machines Corporation

RPG   OUTPUT - FORMAT SPECIFICATIONS

GX21-9090-1 U/M 050*
Printed in U.S.A.

Date _____

Program _____

Programmer _____

Punching Instruction	Graphic					
	Punch					

Page [1] [2]

Program Identification [75] [76] [77] [78] [79] [80]

Line	Form Type	Filename	Type (H/D/T/E)	Stacker Select/Fetch Overflow (F)	Space Before	Space After	Skip Before	Skip After	Output Indicators Not	And Not	And Not	Field Name	Edit Codes	Blank After (B)	End Position in Output Record	P = Packed/B = Binary	Edit Codes				Sterling Sign Position

Edit Codes				
Commas	Zero Balances to Print	No Sign	CR	-
Yes	Yes	1	A	J
Yes	No	2	B	K
No	Yes	3	C	L
No	No	4	D	M

X = Remove Plus Sign
Y = Date Field Edit
Z = Zero Suppress

Constant or Edit Word

3	4	5	6	7	8	9	10	11	12	13	14	15	16	17	18	19	20	21	22	23	24	25	26	27	28	29	30	31	32	33	34	35	36	37	38	39	40	41	42	43	44	45	46	47	48	49	50	51	52	53	54	55	56	57	58	59	60	61	62	63	64	65	66	67	68	69	70	71	72	73	74
0	1		0																																																																					

FIGURE 16-1
RPG specification forms.

At the top of each specification form, space is provided for general information about the program. Entries include program name, programmer, date, and punching instructions. These entries are not punched on the RPG program cards.

Program specifications are recorded in positions 1 through 80 of the RPG specification forms. There are four basic entries that are common to all of the forms. These are: page number, line number, form type, and program identification.

PAGE NUMBER (POSITIONS 1 TO 2) The pages of each specification form may be numbered for reference. The pages are numbered beginning with the file description specifications, in ascending order as follows.

File description page(s).

Input specification page(s).

Calculation specification page (s).

Output-format page(s).

LINE NUMBER (POSITIONS 3 TO 5) Each specification line is normally identified by a line number. The first two digits are preprinted on the specification form; position 5 is normally left blank, so that lines are numbered 010, 020, 030, and so on. Then if it is necessary to add an entry between two lines, the entry may be given a subnumber such as 015 or 026.

FORM TYPE (POSITION 6) Each specification form has a type code preprinted in column 6. This code must be punched into the specification cards. The codes are as follows.

F—File description specifications.

I—Input specifications.

C—Calculation specifications.

O—Output-format specifications.

PROGRAM IDENTIFICATION (POSITIONS 75 TO 80) An entry identifying the program may be placed in positions 75 through 80. Entries in these positions are not punched into the source deck but into columns 75 through 80 of a control card that precedes the source deck. The program identification entry appears on the program listing but does not affect the object program.

QUESTION: What are the four entries common to all of the RPG specification forms?

_____

_____

Which of the entries are _required_ to be punched into the source deck?

_____

_____

ANSWER: Page number, line number, form type, and program identification. Of these, only form type is required. However, the others are recommended.

In addition to the above entries, comment lines may be inserted on any of the RPG specification forms to improve documentation. An asterisk (*) in position 7 specifies that a comment follows. Comments appear on the program listing but do not affect the program.

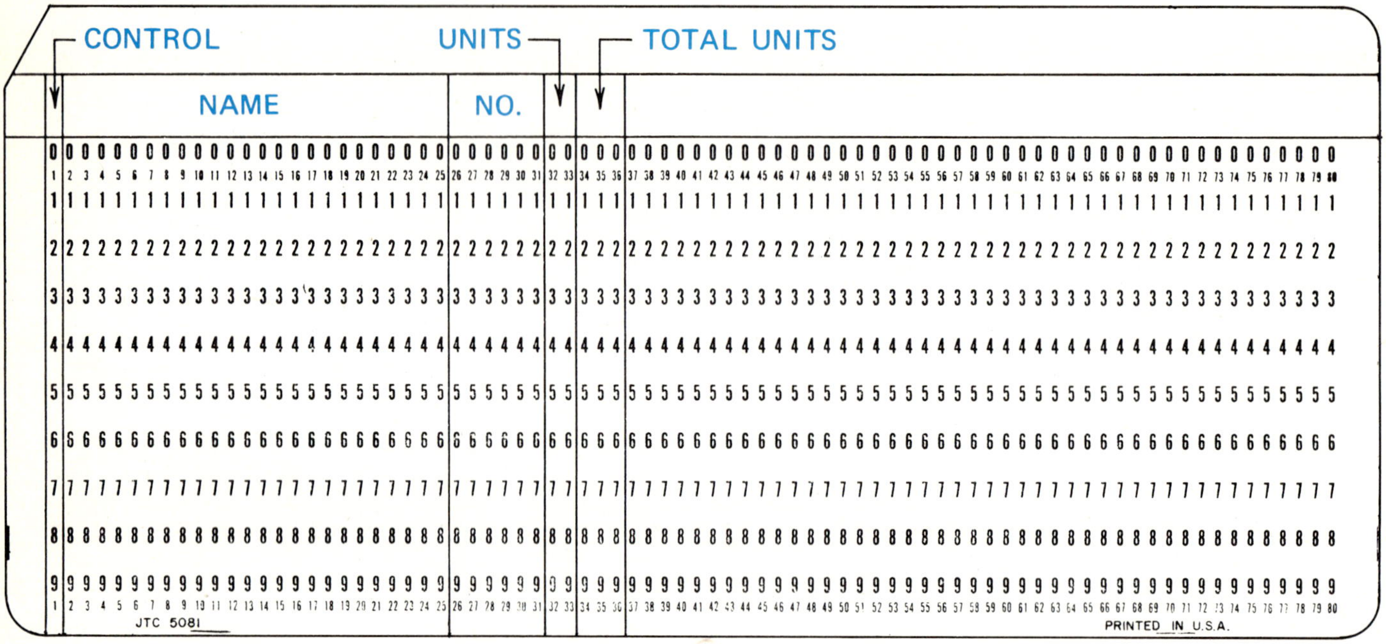

FIGURE 16-2
Input student record card.

To illustrate the basic concepts of RPG programming, three example problems will be introduced. These examples are all based on processing a student record file.

EXAMPLE 1: BASIC INPUT/OUTPUT OPERATIONS

A student file is maintained on punched cards, one card record per student. The format of the records is shown in Figure 16-2. Each card contains student name (columns 2 to 25), number (26 to 31), units taken this semester (32 to 33), and total units prior to this semester (34 to 36). In addition, column 1, contains an S control punch.

An output listing is to be prepared from the cards. Each card field is to be printed, with blank spaces between fields. Leading zeros (if any) are to be suppressed for numeric fields. A printer spacing chart of the output format is shown in Figure 16-3.

FILE DESCRIPTION SPECIFICATIONS

The first step in writing an RPG program for this example is to describe the input and output files. This information is recorded on the file description specifications form. The entries for the example are shown in Figure 16-4.

File name (positions 7 to 14) is used to assign symbolic names to input and output files. In the example, the input file was called STUDFL, the output file PRINTFL. File names must start with a letter, may be up to seven characters long, and are left-justified in the field. File names are referenced by the programmer at other points in the RPG program.

QUESTION: The names STUDFL and PRINTFL are mnemonics. What terms do they stand

for? _____

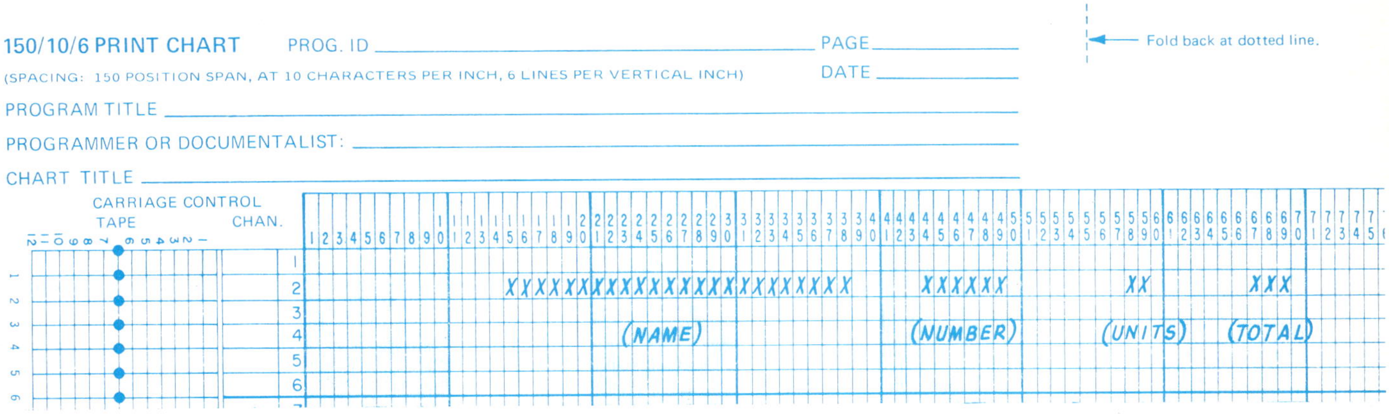

150/10/6 PRINT CHART   PROG. ID _____   PAGE _____   ← Fold back at dotted line.

(SPACING: 150 POSITION SPAN, AT 10 CHARACTERS PER INCH, 6 LINES PER VERTICAL INCH)   DATE _____

PROGRAM TITLE _____

PROGRAMMER OR DOCUMENTALIST: _____

CHART TITLE _____

FIGURE 16-3
Printer spacing chart for Example 1.

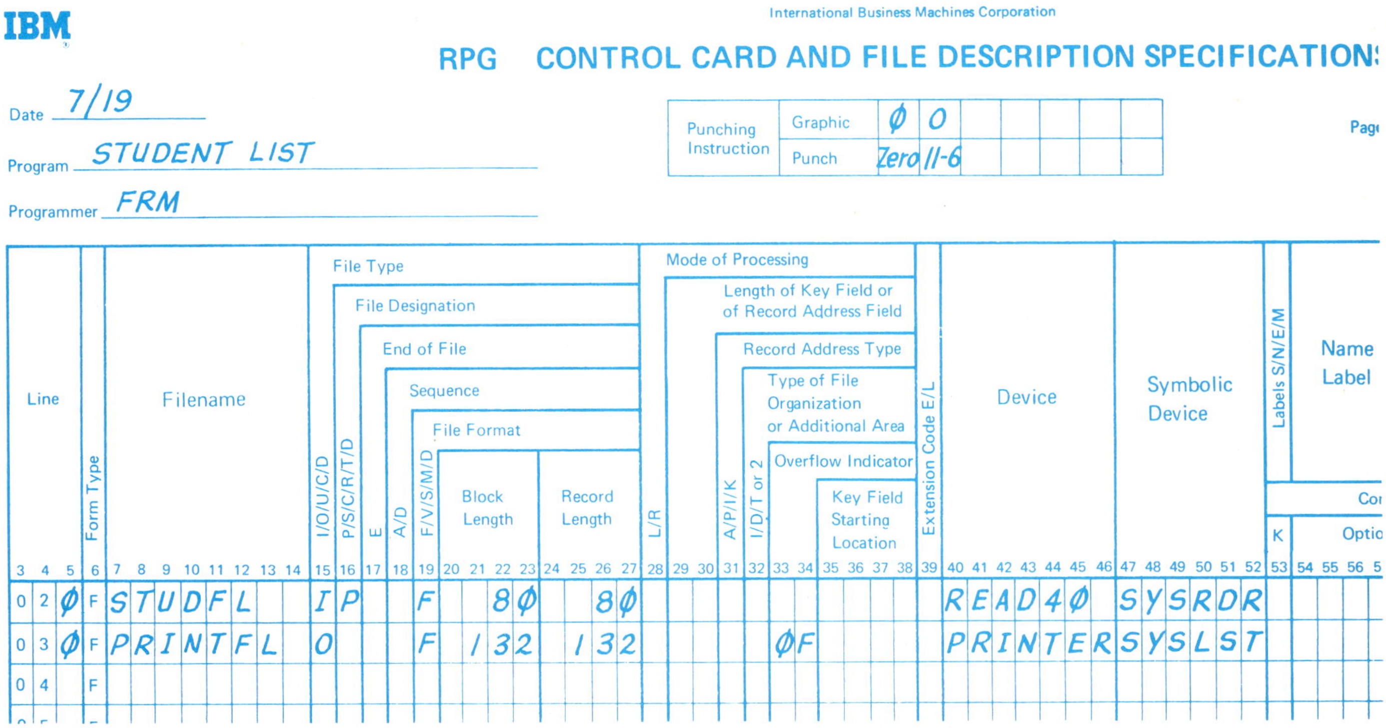

FIGURE 16-4
File description specifications for Example 1.

ANSWER: student file, print file

File type (position 15) is used to designate whether the file is input (I), output (O), or some other type. In Figure 16-4, STUDFL is designated I; PRINTFL is designated O.

File format (position 19) specifies whether the input records are fixed length (F) or variable length (V). In the example, both files are designated F.

Record length (positions 24 to 27) specifies the length of input and output records. For STUDFL the record length is 80 (corresponding to card columns); for PRINTFL the record length is 132 (corresponding to print positions).

Block length (positions 20 to 23) specifies the length of blocked data. For the example, block length is the same as record length.

Overflow indicator (positions 33 to 34 in the output file description) is used to control the printing of header information on the second and subsequent pages when the volume of output information is large.

Device (positions 40 to 46) is used to specify the name of the input or output unit. The appropriate entry depends on the device being used. In the example, cards are read from an IBM 2501 card reader, whose device name is READ40. The output unit is an IBM 2203 printer, which has device designation PRINTER.

Symbolic device (positions 47 to 52) requires the entry SYSRDR for the 2501 card reader and SYSLST for the 2203 printer.

QUESTION: Of the above entries on the file description specifications, which are at the

programmer's option? _____

ANSWER: Only file name (STUDFL and PRINTFL). The remaining entries are determined by file characteristics and devices used.

INPUT SPECIFICATIONS

Now that the files to be used have been described, the next step is to complete the input format specifications. The entries in Figure 16–5 provide the specifications for Example 1.

File name (positions 7 to 14) repeats the symbolic name of the input file, in this case STUDFL. Each input file named on the file specifications form must be described on input specifications.

Sequence (positions 15 to 16) allows for checking the sequence of records within a control group. This feature is not used in Example 1. When sequence checking is not used, RPG requires the entry of any two alphabetic characters. In Figure 16–5, the letters AA are used arbitrarily to meet this requirement.

Resulting indicator (positions 19 to 20) represents an important feature of the RPG language. With RPG every input card must contain a control punch. If the control punch is present when the card is read, an indicator (called the "resulting indicator") is turned on, and the card is processed. If the control punch is not present, the card is not processed, and the next card is read.

The resulting indicator is referenced by a two-digit number from 01 to 99 recorded in positions 19 and 20. In Example 1, the resulting indicator is arbitrarily assigned the number 01.

Position (columns 21 to 24) indicates the card column that contains the control punch. In Example 1, the control punch is contained in column 1 of the student cards.

C/Z/D (position 26) indicates the type of control punch used. The punch may be a character (or letter), designated by C; a zone punch (Z), or a digit (D). In Example 1, the control punch is the letter S, so the correct entry in position 26 is C.

Character (position 27) indicates the actual control code character used. In this example, the letter S is entered in position 27.

QUESTION: To summarize, the above entries will cause the program to check for the character _____ in card column _____ of each student record. If the

IBM

International Business Machines Corporation

RPG   INPUT SPECIFICATIONS

Date _7/19_

Program _STUDENT LIST_

Programmer _FRM_

Punching Instruction	Graphic	O	Ø			
	Punch	11-6 Zero				

Page: 1 2 — `0 3`

Line	Form Type	Filename	Sequence	Number (1-N)	Option (O)	Record Identifying Indicator or **	Record Identification Codes 1 Position	Not (N)	C/Z/D	Character	2 Position	Not (N)	C/Z/D	Character	3 Position	Not (N)	C/Z/D	Character	Stacker Select	P = Packed/B = Binary	Field Location From	To	Decimal Positions	Field Name	Control Level (L1-L9)	Matching Fields or Chaining Fields
0 1	Ø I	STUDFL	A	A		Ø1	Ø1		C	S																
0 2	Ø I																				2	25		NAME		
0 3	Ø I																				26	31	Ø	STNO		
0 4	Ø I																				32	33	Ø	UNITS		
0 5	Ø I																				34	36	Ø	TOTAL		
0 6	I																									

FIGURE 16-5
Input specifications for Example 1.

character is present, record identifying indicator _____ is turned on, and

the card is _____

ANSWER: S, 1; 01, processed

Field name (positions 53 to 58) is used to assign a symbolic name to fields (or data items) contained in the file whose names appear in positions 7 through 14. All fields to be processed must be described. Field name must begin with a letter and may contain up to six characters.

QUESTION: In Example 1 (Figure 16-5), the field names are _____, _____,

_____, and _____.

ANSWER: NAME, STNO, UNITS, TOTAL

Field location (positions 44 to 51) specifies the card columns containing the fields named above. **From** (positions 44 to 47) indicates the beginning card column of each field, and **To** (positions 48 to 51) the ending card columns. For example, STNO begins in column 27 and ends in column 31.

Decimal position (position 52) indicates the number of decimal positions in a numeric field. Whenever a numeric field is to be zero-suppressed or edited on output, or involved in a calculation, an entry must appear in the decimal position. Since the fields STNO, UNITS, and TOTAL are to be zero-suppressed when listed, an entry is required in position 52. Since the fields are integer numbers, the entry 0 (zero) is recorded for each field.

OUTPUT-FORMAT SPECIFICATIONS The RPG output-format specifications form is used to describe output records, and is similar to the input specification form. The output-format specifications for Example 1 are shown in Figure 16–6.

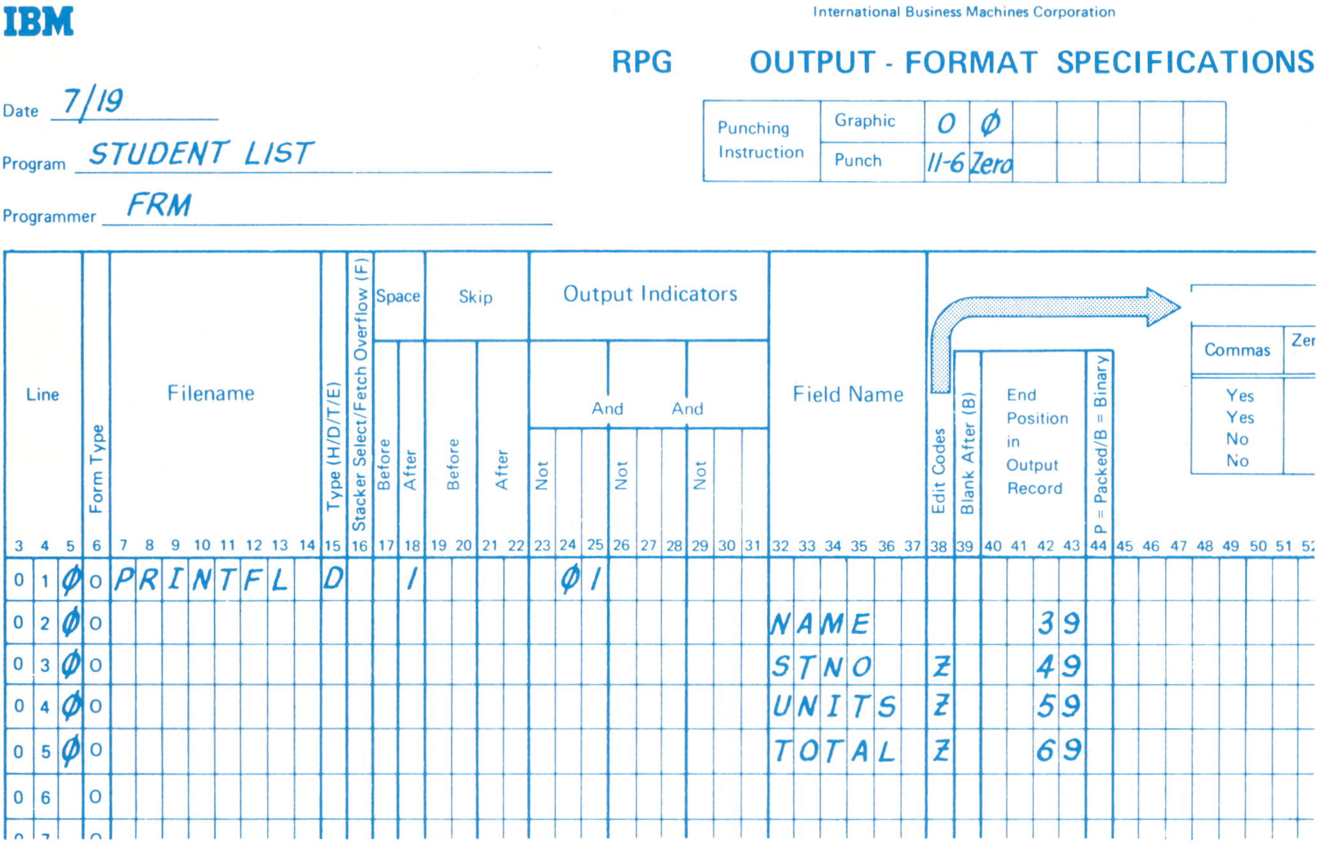

FIGURE 16–6
Output-format specifications for Example 1.

File name (positions 7 to 14) is used to record the name of the output file, in this case PRINTFL.

Type (position 15) indicates when the output is to occur. An output may be a header (H), detail (D), or total (T). The listing of Example 1 is to occur at detail time (D).

Output indicators (positions 24 to 25) control the printing of output. On the input specifications, the indicator 01 was designed to be turned on when a valid student record was read. The effect of entering indicator number 01 in positions 24 and 25 is to cause a line to be printed only when this same indicator is on, as desired.

Field name (positions 32 to 37) is used to record the symbolic name of data items to be listed. These are the same names as were recorded on the input specifications.

Zero suppression (position 38) is used to indicate numerical fields that are to be zero-suppressed when printed. In Figure 16–6, the symbol Z is recorded in this position for STNO, UNITS, and TOTAL.

End position (positions 40 to 43) records the last position of each printed field, as specified on the printer spacing chart (Figure 16–3).

This completes the RPG program specifications for Example 1. Since no calculations are required, the calculation specifications form is omitted. The complete program for this example, together with sample output, is shown in Figure 16–7.

```
FSTUDFL   IP  F   80  80            READ40 SYSRDR
FPRINTFL  O   F  132 132     OF     PRINTERSYSLST
ISTUDFL   AA  01   01  CS
I                                        2  26 NAME
I                                       27  31OSTNO
I                                       32  33OUNITS
I                                       34  36OTOTAL
OPRINTFL D 1      01
O                            NAME      39
O                            STNO  Z   49
O                            UNITS Z   59
O                            TOTAL Z   69

END OF SOURCE

    ADAMS, PETER R.          0   13978      9      104
    GOODMAN, HAROLD R.       0   20875     16
    JOHNSON, SHARON C.       0   24432     15       74
    LARSON, JAMES I.         0   47739      6       48
    LEWIS,BARBARA C.         0    1339     18      107
    ROTHSCHILD, CHARLES K.   0   80336     10      100
    THOMPSON, LAURA W.       0   59325      7       88
```

FIGURE 16–7
RPG program and output for Example 1.

EXERCISE 16–1

1. What forms are required for most RPG programs? List the forms in the order in which they are used in a program.

   a. _____

   b. _____

   c. _____

   d. _____

2. In Example 1, suppose that the student record cards (see Figure 16–2) contained the control code 2 in column 79. What changes would be required in the input specifications form (Figure 16–5)?

   a. _____

   _____

   b. _____

   c. _____

   _____

3. What entries in the completed program (Figure 16–7) would probably

need to be changed if the program were to be run on a different computer? _____

_____

_____

_____

_____

4. Explain the significance of the zero entries in position 52 of the input specifications (Figure 16–5) for Example 1. How are entries related to the

Z entry of the output-format specifications (Figure 16–6)? _____

_____

_____

_____

_____

EXAMPLE 2: SIMPLE CALCULATIONS

Example 2 introduces the use of the calculation specifications forms. The card record for each student is to be read, and "units taken this semester" is to be added to "total units to date" to obtain an updated total. The record is then to be printed, with the updated total replacing the previous total.

In addition to updating each record, we are to total "units taken this semester" for all students and print the total at the end of the listing. Header information is also to be printed at the top of the listing.

The input format for Example 2 is the same as for Example 1 (see Figure 16–2). The output format is shown on the printer spacing chart, Figure 16–8.

FIGURE 16–8
Printer spacing chart for Example 2.

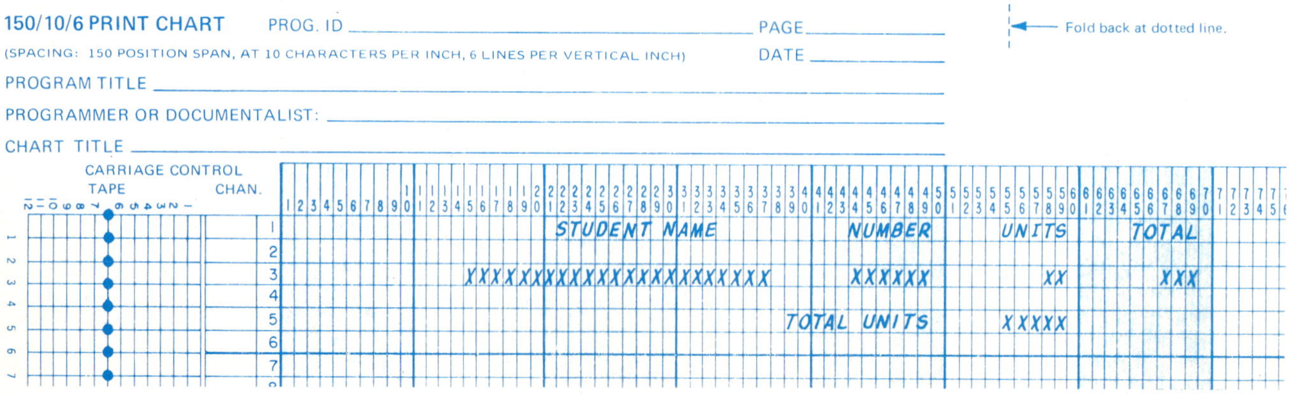

FILE SPECIFICATIONS The file specifications for Example 2 are identical to those for Example 1 (see Figure 16-4), and are not repeated here.

INPUT SPECIFICATIONS The input specifications for Example 2 are also the same as for Example 1. However, the record identifying indicator (positions 19 to 20) has arbitrarily been assigned the number 05. Thus, when a card with the control punch S in column 1 is read, indicator number 05 is turned on. The input specifications for Example 2 are shown in Figure 16-9.

IBM

International Business Machines Corporation

RPG   INPUT SPECIFICATIONS

Date 7/19

Program STUDENT TOTAL

Programmer FRM

| Punching Instruction | Graphic | Ø | O | | |
| | Punch | Zero II-6 | | | |

Page 02

Line	Form Type	Filename	Sequence	Number (1-N)	Option (O)	Record Identifying Indicator or **	Record Identification Codes 1 Position	Not (N)	C/Z/D	Character	2 Position	Not (N)	C/Z/D	Character	3 Position	Not (N)	C/Z/D	Character	Stacker Select	P = Packed/B = Binary	Field Location From	To	Decimal Positions	Field Name	Control Level (L1-L9)	Matching Fields or Chaining Fields
0 1	Ø I	STUDFL		A	A	Ø5	Ø1		C	S																
0 2	Ø I																				2	25		NAME		
0 3	Ø I																				26	31 Ø		STNO		
0 4	Ø I																				32	33 Ø		UNITS		
0 5	Ø I																				34	36 Ø		TOTAL		
0 6	I																									

FIGURE 16-9
Input specifications for Example 2.

CALCULATION SPECIFICATIONS In most programs, calculations and logical operations are required. These operations are described on the RPG calculation specifications form. The specifications for Example 2 are shown in Figure 16-10.

Indicator (positions 10 to 11) permits the desired calculations to occur when a valid control punch is present. In Example 2, indicator 05 is used.

In RPG, calculations are specified by four entries: factor 1, factor 2, operation, and result field. Also, the field length of result field is specified.

In Example 2, the first operation is to add UNITS to TOTAL for each student. The result field is the updated total, also called TOTAL. Next, UNITS is added to a field called FTOTAL, resulting in FTOTAL. FTOTAL is a running total of the number of units taken this semester by students.

QUESTION: Suppose that a student has taken 15 units this semester and had a total of 74 units at the beginning of the semester. When the student's record is read, the

IBM

International Business Machines Corporation

RPG   CALCULATION SPECIFICATIONS

Date __7/19__

Program __STUDENT TOTAL__

Programmer __FRM__

Punching Instruction	Graphic	Ø	0				
	Punch	Zero II-6					

Line	Form Type	Control Level (L0-L9, LR, SR)	Indicators						Factor 1	Operation	Factor 2	Result Field	Field Length	Decimal Positions	Half Adjust (H)	Resulting Indicators
			And		And											
0 1 Ø	C		Ø5						UNITS	ADD	TOTAL	TOTAL	3 Ø			
0 2 Ø	C		Ø5						UNITS	ADD	FTOTAL	FTOTAL	5 Ø			
0 3	C															

FIGURE 16-10
Calculation specifications for Example 2.

running total of units for all students is 1680. What are the values for each of the fields shown in Figure 16-10? _____

ANSWER: UNITS = 15, TOTAL = 74 (factor 2), TOTAL = 89 (result field), FTOTAL = 1680 (factor 2), FTOTAL = 1695 (result field).

Field length (positions 49 to 51) specifies the length of the result field. Since TOTAL and FTOTAL are to be zero-suppressed when printed, the entry 0 is placed in decimal positions (position 52).

Although addition is the only arithmetic calculation required in Example 2, other operations may also be specified. The format for basic arithmetic operations is the following.

Factor 1	Operation	Factor 2	Comment
A	ADD	B	Add A to B, sum in result field
A	SUB	B	Subtract B from A, difference in result field
A	MULT	B	Multiply B by A, product in result field
A	DIV	B	Divide A by B, quotient in result field

OUTPUT-FORMAT SPECIFICATIONS The output format must be expanded for Example 2 to provide header information as well as the final total of student hours. The output-format specifications for this example are shown in Figure 16-11.

IBM

International Business Machines Corporation

RPG   OUTPUT - FORMAT SPECIFICATIONS

Date **7/19**

Program **STUDENT TOTAL**

Programmer **FRM**

Punching Instruction			
Graphic	Ø	O	
Punch	Zero II-6		

1 2

Page **0 4**

Line	Form Type	Filename	Type (H/D/T/E)	Stacker Select/Fetch Overflow (F)	Space Before	Space After	Skip Before	Skip After	Not	And	Not	And	Not	Field Name	Edit Codes	Blank After (B)	End Position in Output Record	P = Packed/B = Binary	Constant or Edit Word
0 1	0	O	PRINTFL	H			2	0 1					1 P						
0 2	0	O		OR									O F						
0 3	0	O															3 3		'STUDENT NAME'
0 4	0	O															4 9		'NUMBER'
0 5	0	O															5 9		'UNITS'
0 6	0	O															7 0		'TOTAL'
0 7	0	O		D		1							0 5						
0 8	0	O												NAME			3 9		
0 9	0	O												STNO	Z		4 9		
1 0	0	O												UNITS	Z		5 9		
1 1	0	O												TOTAL	Z		6 9		
1 2	0	O		T		2							L R						
1 3	0	O															4 9		'TOTAL UNITS'
1 4	0	O												FTOTAL	Z		5 9		
1 5		O																	

Edit Codes

Commas	Zero Balances to Print	No Sign	CR	-
Yes	Yes	1	A	J
Yes	No	2	B	K
No	Yes	3	C	L
No	No	4	D	M

FIGURE 16-11

Output-format specifications for Example 2.

The entry "H" in position 15 (Type) specifies that header information is to follow. The entry "01" in SKIP BEFORE causes the printer to be positioned at the first printing line when the header is printed. The entry "2" in SPACE AFTER causes the printer to double-space after the header is printed.

There are two output indicators that will cause a header to be printed. These are 1P (for first page) and OF (for overflow). These indicators are coupled with the entry OR in positions 14 and 15. The effect of these entries is that a header will be printed on the first page OR at the top of succeeding pages.

The header data to be printed is recorded under Constant or Edit Word. In the example, the headings STUDENT NAME, NUMBER, UNITS, and TOTAL are to be printed. Constants or literals must be enclosed in single quotes. The printed location of each heading is specified under end position (positions 40 to 43).

The entries for the student records are the same as for Example 1. The entry D under Type indicates "detail."

The last entries on the output-format specifications specify the printing of total hours. The entry T indicates "total." After the last record has been processed, the indicator LR (for "last record") is turned on. This indicator permits the total information to be printed.

QUESTION: From Figure 16-11, what entries will appear at the end of the listing?

ANSWER: the notation TOTAL UNITS, followed by the cumulative total, whose symbolic name is FTOTAL

Thus we finish the RPG program specifications for Example 2. The complete program, together with sample output, is shown in Figure 16-12.

```
FSTUDFL  IP  F  80  80              READ40 SYSRDR
FPRINTFL O   F 132 132      OF      PRINTERSYSLST
ISTUDFL  AA   05   01 CS
I                                        2    25 NAME
I                                       26   310STNO
I                                       32   330UNITS
I                                       34   360TOTAL
C     05         UNITS     ADD  TOTAL      TOTAL
C     05         UNITS     ADD  FTOTAL     FTOTAL   50
OPRINTFL H  201     1P
O         OR        OF
O                                       33 'STUDENT NAME'
O                                       49 'NUMBER'
O                                       59 'UNITS'
O                                       70 'TOTAL'
O         D  1      05
O                            NAME       39
O                            STNO  Z    49
O                            UNITS Z    59
O                            TOTAL Z    69
O         T  2      LR
O                                       49 'TOTAL UNITS'
O                            FTOTALZ  . 59
```

STUDENT NAME	NUMBER	UNITS	TOTAL
ADAMS, PETER R.	13978	9	113
GOODMAN, HAROLD R.	20875	16	16
JOHNSON, SHARON C.	24432	15	89
LARSON, JAMES I.	47739	6	54
LEWIS,BARBARA C.	1339	18	125
ROTHSCHILD, CHARLES K.	80336	10	110
THOMPSON, LAURA W.	59325	7	95
TOTAL UNITS		81	

FIGURE 16-12
RPG program and output for Example 2.

EXAMPLE 3: SIMPLE LOGICAL OPERATIONS

The use of simple comparisons in RPG is shown in Example 3. The student record cards are to be read, and tuition is to be computed according to the following formula.

If UNITS is less than 12, tuition is UNITS times $35; if UNITS is 12 or more, tuition is $420.00

Total student fees consist of tuition plus an incidental fee of $12.50. This total is to be printed along with student name, number, and hours taken. Also, the total of fees for all students is to be computed and printed at the end of the listing.

The input format for Example 3 is the same as for Examples 1 and 2 (see Figure 16-2). The desired output format is shown in Figure 16-13.

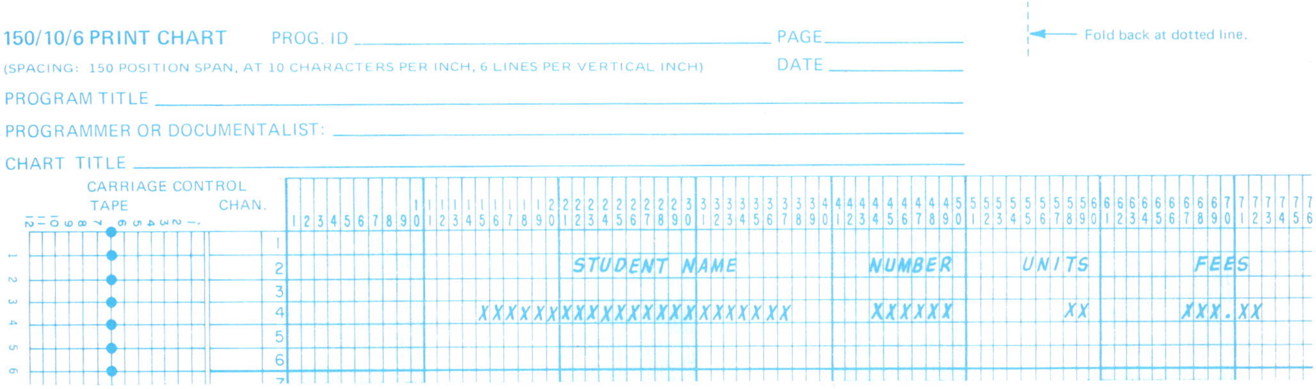

FIGURE 16-13
Printer spacing chart for Example 3.

CALCULATION SPECIFICATIONS

The main feature of this example is the introduction of the comparison operation. In RPG, comparisons are specified on the calculation specifications form. The specifications for Example 3 are shown in Figure 16-14.

In computing tuition, we must compare student UNITS with 12 to select the formula to be used. This comparison is shown on line 01 of the specification form. UNITS (factor 1) is compared (COMP) with 12 (factor 2). In a comparison, the result field is not used.

The result of a comparison is shown in **compare** (positions 54 to 59). If factor 1 is greater than factor 2 (high), the resulting indicator in positions 54 and 55 is turned on. If factor 1 is less than factor 2 (low), the resulting indicator in positions 56 and 57 is turned on. Finally, if the factors are equal, the resulting indicator in positions 58 and 59 is turned on.

QUESTION: In Figure 16-14, what resulting indicator will be turned on for a student who has taken 9 units, 15 units, 12 units? _____ , _____ , _____

ANSWER: 03, 02, 02

After the comparison is made, the calculations performed by the computer depend on the indicators that have been turned on. If indicator 03 is on (indicating UNITS is less than 12), UNITS is multiplied by 35, giving the result field called

IBM

International Business Machines Corporation

RPG   CALCULATION SPECIFICATIONS

Date _7/19_

Program _STUDENT FEES_

Programmer _FRM_

Punching Instruction	Graphic	Ø	O			
	Punch	Zero	11-6			

Page _03_

Line	Form Type	Control Level (L0-L9, LR, SR)	Indicators						Factor 1	Operation	Factor 2	Result Field	Field Length	Decimal Positions	Half Adjust (H)	Resulting Indicators		
				And		And										Arithmetic / Compare / Lookup		
			Not		Not		Not									High 1>2 / 54 55	Low 1<2 / 56 57	Equal 1=2 / 58 59
0 1	Ø C		Ø 1					U N I T S	C O M P	1 2					Ø 2	Ø 3	Ø 2
0 2	Ø C		Ø 2						M O V E	4 2 Ø . Ø Ø	F E E S	5 2					
0 3	Ø C		Ø 3					U N I T S	M U L T	3 5	F E E S	5 2					
0 4	Ø C		Ø 1					F E E S	A D D	1 2 . 5 Ø	F E E S	5 2					
0 5	Ø C		Ø 1					F E E S	A D D	T F E E S	T F E E S	7 2					
0 6	C																

FIGURE 16-14

Calculation specifications for Example 3.

FEES. If indicator 02 is turned on, the constant 420.00 is moved to FEES. Since either indicator 02 or 03 (but not both) is on, only one of the above operations is performed.

Indicator 01 is used in Example 3 as the input indicator for the card control punch. After tuition is computed, the result (called FEES) is added to the incidental fee of $12.50, yielding total fees (also called FEES). This quantity is then added to the running total of student fees, called TFEES. Each of these quantities has two decimal positions, as indicated in position 52.

QUESTION: A student has taken 10 units during the previous semester. The running total of student fees (before his card is processed) is $8439.00. What should be the values of each of the variables in Figure 16-14 as the student's card is processed?

ANSWER: UNITS = 10; FEES = 350.00 (tuition); FEES = 362.50 (with incidental fee); TFEES = 8801.50

The MOVE entry in Figure 16-14 causes factor 2 to be moved to the result field. Factor 2 may be a literal (as in this example) or a field name. It may be a numeric or alphanumeric quantity. The move is from the right-most positions of factor 2 to the right-most positions of the result field, with the shorter field terminating the move.

The use of the MOVE operation in RPG may be illustrated by three examples.

Example Number	Operation	Factor 2	Result Field	Field Length
1	MOVE	DATA	RSLT	6
2	MOVE	'DATA'	RSLT	6
3	MOVE	25	RSLT	6

Assume that the field DATA contains the quantity 1234 and that RSLT contains ABCDEF. The result of the above MOVES is as follows.

Example Number	Contents of Result Field	Comment
1	AB1234	Content of DATA moved to RSLT
2	ABDATA	Literal 'DATA' moved to RSLT
3	ABCD25	Literal 25 moved to RSLT

QUESTION: In Example 2 above, suppose that the field RSLT had field length 3 and contained ABC. What is the result of the MOVE? _____

ANSWER: ATA. Since the field RSLT is only 3 positions, it cannot contain the entire literal 'DATA.' Since movement is from right to left, the D is truncated.

OUTPUT-FORMAT SPECIFICATIONS

The output-format specifications for Example 3 are shown in Figure 16–15. The format provides for listings of header, detail, and total information, similar to Example 2.

The only feature in Figure 16–15 not previously discussed is the use of edit words (lines 11 and 14). Editing symbols (such as blanks, commas, decimals, and dollar signs) are enclosed in single quotes, in the relative positions they are to appear in the output listing. A zero in an edit word indicates that zero suppression of a numeric field is to occur up to and including the zero symbol. When an edit word is used, position 38 of the output-format specifications form should be left blank.

In Figure 16–15, the field FEES is to be zero-suppressed, and a decimal point is to be inserted in the output field to indicate dollars and cents. The field TFEES is also to be zero-suppressed, with a dollar sign, comma, and decimal point inserted in the indicated positions.

QUESTION: How will the quantity TFEES appear on the output listing if TFEES is $8,640.50; $125.00? _____   _____

ANSWER: $ 8,640.00; $ 125.00

The complete RPG program for Example 3, together with sample output, is shown in Figure 16–16.

IBM

International Business Machines Corporation

RPG   OUTPUT - FORMAT SPECIFICATIONS

Punching Instruction	Graphic	Ø	0				
	Punch	Zero	11-6				

Page ☐ ☐ (1 2)

Date _7/19_

Program _STUDENT FEES_

Programmer _FRM_

Line	Form Type	Filename	Type (H/D/T/E)	Stacker Select/Fetch Overflow (F)	Space Before	Space After	Skip Before	Skip After	Output Indicators Not	And Not	And Not	Field Name	Edit Codes	Blank After (B)	End Position in Output Record	P = Packed/B = Binary	Constant or Edit Word
0 1	Ø	O	P R I N T F L	H		2	Ø 1			I P								
0 2	Ø	O		O R						O F							
0 3	Ø	O													3 3		' S T U D E N T N A M E '
0 4	Ø	O													4 9		' N U M B E R '
0 5	Ø	O													5 9		' U N I T S '
0 6	Ø	O													7 1		' F E E S '
0 7	Ø	O		D		1				Ø 1								
0 8	Ø	O											N A M E			3 9		
0 9	Ø	O											S T N O	Z		4 9		
1 0	Ø	O											U N I T S	Z		5 9		
1 1	Ø	O											F E E S			7 2		' Ø . '
1 2	Ø	O		T	2					L R								
1 3	Ø	O													5 5		' T O T A L F E E S '
1 4	Ø	O											T F E E S			7 2		' $, Ø . '
1 5		O																

Edit Codes

	Commas	Zero Balances to Print	No Sign	CR	-
	Yes	Yes	1	A	J
	Yes	No	2	B	K
	No	Yes	3	C	L
	No	No	4	D	M

FIGURE 16-15
Output-format specifications for Example 3.

EXERCISE 16-2

1. FLDA contains the number 100; FLDB contains 25. The result field RSLT as field length 6, with zero decimal positions. Indicate the contents of RSLT for each of the following arithmetic operations.

	Factor 1	Operation	Factor 2	Contents of RSLT
a.	FLDA	SUB	FLDB	_____
b.	FLDA	ADD	FLDB	_____
c.	FLDA	MULT	FLDB	_____
d.	FLDA	DIV	FLDB	_____
e.	FLDA	DIV	100	_____

```
FSTUDFL   IP  F   80   80                READ40 SYSRDR
FPRINTFL  O   F  132  132       OF       PRINTERSYSLST
ISTUDFL   AA  01   01 CS
I                                               2   25 NAME
I                                              26   310STNO
I                                              32   330UNITS
C    01        UNITS       COMP 12                        020302
C    02                    MOVE 420.00     FEES       52
C    03        UNITS       MULT 35          FEES       52
C    01        FEES        ADD  12.50       FEES       52
C    01        FEES        ADD  TFEES       TFEES      72
OPRINTFL H   201    1P
O         OR              OF
O                                              33 'STUDENT NAME'
O                                              49 'NUMBER'
O                                              59 'UNITS'
O                                              71 'FEES'
O          D  1      01
O                          NAME        39
O                          STNO  Z     49
O                          UNITS Z     59
O                          FEES        72 '   0.  '
O          T  2      LR
O                                              55 'TOTAL FEES'
O                          TFEES       72 '$   ,   0.  '
```

```
       STUDENT NAME                NUMBER      UNITS        FEES

ADAMS, PETER R.                    13978         9         327.50
GOODMAN, HAROLD R.                 20875        16         432.50
JOHNSON, SHARON C.                 24432        15         432.50
LARSON, JAMES I.                   47739         6         222.50
LEWIS,BARBARA C.                    1339        18         432.50
ROTHSCHILD, CHARLES K.            80336        10         362.50
THOMPSON, LAURA W.                 59325         7         257.50


                                 TOTAL FEES           $ 2,467.50
```

FIGURE 16-16
RPG program and output for Example 3.

2. Explain the operations performed by the following segment of an RPG calculation.

Indicator	Factor 1	Operation	Factor 2	Result Field	Compare High	Low	Equal
a. 01	AMT	COMP	25		02	03	04
b. 02	AMT	SUB	15	AMT			
c. 03	AMT	SUB	5	AMT			
d. 04	AMT	SUB	10	AMT			

a. _____

_____

b. _____

c. _____

_____

_____

d. _____

_____

3. FLDC contains the quantity 1000, and RSLT contains 000185. RSLT has field length 6. Indicate the content of RSLT after each of the following operations.

	Operation	*Factor 2*	*Contents of RSLT*
a.	MOVE	FLDC	_____
b.	MOVE	'FLDC'	_____
c.	MOVE	35	_____

4. The edit word for an output report appears as follows.

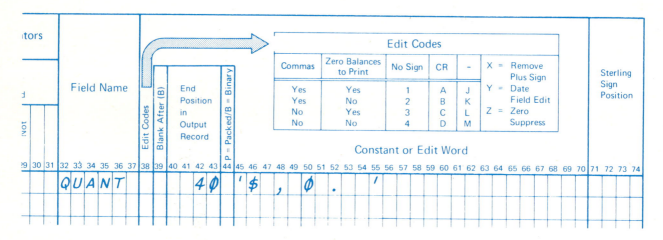

Indicate how QUANT will be printed out for each of the following values.

	QUANT	*Format*
a.	1,643.38	_____
b.	519.31	_____
c.	6.72	_____
d.	.47	_____

SUMMARY   This chapter has provided an introduction to RPG programming. The language contains many additional capabilities, including the ability to process magnetic tape and disk files. Also, a number of additional computational features are available.

The principal advantages of RPG are its simplicity and the ease of learning and using the language. Smaller installations that do not have skilled programmers can train their people in a relatively short time to use RPG. On the other hand, the language is quite flexible, and a surprising number of data processing tasks can be successfully programmed in RPG.

The principal disadvantage of RPG is its limited ability to handle calculations and more complicated data structures. Also, since it is a general-purpose language, RPG tends to be somewhat inefficient in terms of computational speed and use of storage. However, when used in applications for which it is suited, RPG often results in considerable savings in programming time and effort.

ANSWERS TO EXERCISES

EXERCISE 16-1

1. a. File description specifications
    b. Input specifications
    c. Calculation specifications
    d. Output-format specifications
2. The record identification codes would be changed as follows.
    a. Position (columns 23 to 24) would contain the entry 79, which is the location of the control code.
    b. Column 26 would contain the entry D, to indicate that the control code is a digit.
    c. Column 27 would contain 2, the actual digit used.
3. The file description specifications, which are the first two lines of the program.
4. When a numeric field is to be edited or zero-suppressed on output, an entry must appear in the decimal position field (column 52). Since the fields are integer, the entry 0 is used to indicate zero decimal positions.

EXERCISE 16-2

1. a. 75
    b. 125
    c. 2500
    d. 4
    e. 1
2. a. Compare AMT with 25, and turn on an indicator as follows: If AMT is greater than 25, turn on indicator 02; if AMT is less than 25, turn on indicator 03; if AMT equals 25, turn on indicator 04.
    b. If indicator 02 is on, subtract 15 from AMT and store the result in AMT.
    c. If indicator 03 is on, subtract 5 from AMT and store the result in AMT.
    d. If indicator 04 is on, subtract 10 from AMT and store the result in AMT.
3. a. 001000
    b. 00FLDC
    c. 000135
4. a. $1,643.38
    b. $ 519.31
    c. $ 6.72
    d. $ 0.47

CHAPTER EXAMINATION

1. The following is a segment of an RPG calculation.

Indicator	Factor 1	Operation	Factor 2	Result Field	Compare		
					High	Low	Equal
01	QTY	COMP	38		03	07	05
03	QTY	SUB	38	AMT			
07	QTY	ADD	15	AMT			
05	QTY	DIV	2	AMT			

What is the content of the field AMT after the above instructions are executed if the present content of QTY is:

a.   38 _____

b.   54 _____

c.   7 _____

2. The field RSLT has field length 5, with current contents 00139. The field AMT contains the quantity 016. Indicate the contents of RSLT after each of the following operations.

Operation	Factor 2	Contents of RSLT
MOVE	AMT	
MOVE	6240	
MOVE	'AMT'	

3. The edit word for an output report appears as follows.

tors		Field Name	Edit Codes	Blank After (B)	End Position in Output Record	P = Packed/B = Binary	Edit Codes							Sterling Sign Position
							Commas	Zero Balances to Print	No Sign	CR	–	X = Remove Plus Sign		
							Yes	Yes	1	A	J	Y = Date		
							Yes	No	2	B	K	Field Edit		
							No	Yes	3	C	L	Z = Zero		
							No	No	4	D	M	Suppress		
									Constant or Edit Word					
9 30 31	32 33 34 35 36 37	38	39	40 41 42 43	44	45 46 47 48 49 50 51 52 53 54 55 56 57 58 59 60 61 62 63 64 65 66 67 68 69 70								71 72 73 74
	QUANT			60		'$, 0 . '								

Indicate how QUANT will be printed out for each of the following values.

	QUANT	Format
a.	13,238.65	
b.	6,921.08	
c.	846.29	
d.	24.79	
e.	6.12	
f.	.98	

4. The 1960 U.S. Population Census shows that five central cities (CC) had populations of over 1 million. The following table shows the population and areas in square miles of the five central cities and their standard metropolitan statistical areas (SMSAs), which include the central cities.

	Population		Area (sq. miles)	
	CC	SMSA	CC	SMSA
New York	7,781,984	10,694,633	315	2149
Chicago	3,550,404	6,220,913	224	3714
Philadelphia	3,002,512	4,342,897	127	3549
Detroit	1,670,144	3,762,360	140	1965
San Francisco	1,104,035	2,783,359	98	3313

Write a program to read the above data and compute and print out the following.
a. Population density (population per square mile) for each CC, SMSA, and SMSA ring (SMSA excluding the CC)
b. Area of each CC as a percent of the area of the SMSA

5. Write a program to condense some statistics on the students in a class. One data card is punched for each student, as follows.

Item	Columns	
Age	1 and 2	
Sex	5	(1 = male, 2 = female)
Class standing	7	(1 = freshman, 2 = sophomore, 3 = junior, 4 = senior)

The required output is the following.
a. Average age of the students
b. Percent males, percent females
c. Percent freshmen, sophomores, juniors, seniors
Use the following data.

20	1	2	19	2	1
18	2	1	21	1	4
26	2	4	20	2	2
21	1	3	23	1	4
23	1	2	17	2	1

6. Write a RPG II program for problem 14 of the Chapter 14 exam.

7. Write a RPG II program for problem 15 of the Chapter 14 exam.

REPORT PROGRAM GENERATOR FILE DESCRIPTION SPECIFICATIONS

IBM System/360

Date _____
Program _____
Programmer _____

Punching Instruction — Graphic — Punch

Page 1 2

Program Identification 75 76 77 78 79 80

Line — Form Type — Filename — File Type — I/O/U/C — File Designation — P/S/C/R/T — End of File — E — Sequence — A/D — File Format — F/V — Block Length — Record Length — Mode of Processing — L/R — Length of Record Address Field — K/I — Record Address Type — Type of File Organization — I/D/T — Overflow Indicator — Key Field Starting Location — Extension Code E/L — Device — Symbolic Device — Labels (S, N, or E) — Name of Label Exit — Extent Exit for DAM — Comments

Card Electro Number

REPORT PROGRAM GENERATOR INPUT SPECIFICATIONS
IBM System/360

REPORT PROGRAM GENERATOR   CALCULATION SPECIFICATIONS

IBM System/360

Date _____

Program _____

Programmer _____

Punching Instruction

Graphic

Punch

Page [ ] 1 2

Program Identification 75 76 77 78 79 80

Line	Form Type	Control Level (10-19, LR)	Indicators						Factor 1	Operation	Factor 2	Result Field	Field Length	Decimal Positions	Half Adjust (H)	Resulting Indicators				Comments

Indicators: And (Not 9 10 11), And (Not 12 13 14), (Not 15 16 17)

Resulting Indicators — Plus, Minus, Zero or Blank

Compare — High 1>2 54 55, Low 1<2 56 57, Equal 1=2 58 59

Factor 1: 18 19 20 21 22 23 24 25 26 27

Operation: 28 29 30 31 32

Factor 2: 33 34 35 36 37 38 39 40 41 42

Result Field: 43 44 45 46 47 48

Field Length: 49 50 51

Decimal Positions: 52

Half Adjust (H): 53

Comments: 60 61 62 63 64 65 66 67 68 69 70 71 72 73 74

Line: 3 4 5 6 7 8

01 02 03 04 05 06 07 08 09 10 11 12 13 14 15

Card Electro Number _____

REPORT PROGRAM GENERATOR OUTPUT-FORMAT SPECIFICATIONS
IBM System/360

Program Identification — 75 76 77 78 79 80

Page — 1 2

Punching Instruction — Graphic / Punch

Card Electro Number

PART FOUR

SYSTEM ANALYSIS, DESIGN AND IMPLEMENTATION

Section Four covers system analysis, design, and implementation. The following illustration shows the relationship of those activities, both in sequence and cost. The two cost curves represent the difference in cost in the 1980s versus the 1970s. Costs are high today—which may seem surprising in light of the improved efficiency of computers. However, the costs shown in the illustration are labor costs, not hardware costs. Moreover, the increased costs of the 1980s are not the result of inflation—the cost curve is adjusted to exclude the effects of inflation.

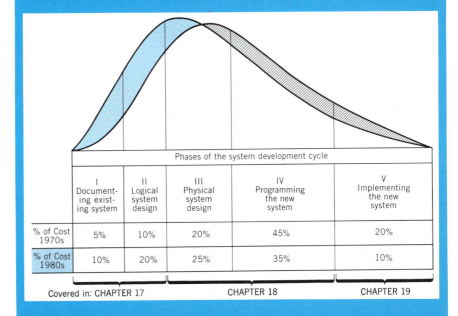

	Phases of the system development cycle				
	I Documenting existing system	II Logical system design	III Physical system design	IV Programming the new system	V Implementing the new system
% of Cost 1970s	5%	10%	20%	45%	20%
% of Cost 1980s	10%	20%	25%	35%	10%
Covered in:	CHAPTER 17		CHAPTER 18		CHAPTER 19

INCREASED SCOPE OF SYSTEM

In the early days of computers, phase I (documenting the existing system) was simple, compared to the other phases. In those days, only subsystems were analyzed—such as the payroll system. Today, in the era of integrated systems, the scope of the system is many times enlarged. The payroll subsystem is only one part of the accounting system, which is only one part of the finance system.

The present-day approach to system analysis emphasizes the interrelationships of systems. First, the company is viewed as a system—consisting of major subsystems. However, the company is also a subsystem of the industry.

Designing a decision support system requires analysis of the environment in which decisions are made. The environment includes areas external to the company as well as internal. Earlier system approaches concentrated on internal systems. Today system approach includes all areas of managerial information needs—external as well as internal.

INCREASE IN SHARED DATA

Costs are higher today—at the front end of the system development cycle—because more analysis is occurring. To design data bases useful for several computer applications, more preliminary analysis is necessary. Analysts must search out and define data elements to be used by related applications. For example, part number and inventory status would be used in both the purchasing and the production systems. Employee data would be used in both the payroll and the employee information systems. Also, more emphasis is being placed on the logical design phase. The design is more detailed, increasing the cost of that phase. However, these efforts reduce costs in the program testing and implementation phases—fewer errors arise because of better system definition.

INCREASED COMPLEXITY OF SYSTEMS

Today's systems are also more difficult to develop. The computer was applied to relatively simple systems in the 1960s and 1970s. Much more of the computer's potential is used today in a broad range of applications. In earlier years, the most common business application at that time, payroll, was designed independently. However, the payroll subsystem is a part of both the accounting system and the personnel system of the firm. When converted from an earlier computerized version, the payroll subsystems of today are redesigned to feed both these major systems.

Not only are development costs higher, but operations costs are higher. Systems include more activities than their predecessors. For example, in a division of a major U.S. oil company, 6500 of 35,000 employees are involved in development and operation of computerized information systems. However, even though computing activities now utilize one-sixth of all employees, the division's total cost of operation has decreased as a result of converting many operations to the computer.

SYSTEM DEVELOPMENT CYCLE

Looking at the bottom portion of the figure, you see that Chapter 17 concentrates on phases I and II of the system development cycle. In phase I information about the present system is gathered and organized. In phase II (logical design) information is analyzed to determine if the system can be improved. Logical design is machine independent—it identifies what information the manager needs for decision making. Phase III, physical system design, is covered in Chapter 18. This phase is machine dependent. It determines specific computer requirements to implement the logical design.

Only an overview of phase IV, programming the new system, is included in this section of the textbook. Programming is covered in depth in Chapters 9 through 11. After coverage of programming materials, students have a better understanding of the system design task. They recognize the need for systems to be precisely defined for the programming task. Chapter 19 covers system implementation. It also covers feasibility analysis and computer justification. The latter subjects are placed in Chapter 19 to keep each chapter a workable size.

The term "cycle" is used in the above figure because system development is rarely done once. Organizational environment and procedures change frequently in the typical company or governmental agency. Systems must be revised accordingly. Thus, system development starts a new cycle.

Section Four begins with coverage of phase I, system documentation.

17

SYSTEM DOCUMENTATION AND LOGICAL DESIGN

OVERVIEW. A system is an activity consisting of input, processing, and output. A change must occur in the intermediate step—the processing—if the activity is to be classified as a system. For example, the activity of a secretary in receiving a letter from the mail carrier and passing it on to the boss is not a system. This activity is just a step in the input phase of a system. Opening the envelope to enable the letter to be read is still a part of input. Reading and taking action on the letter is the process step; conveying the results of that action is the output step.

The complete set of systems for an organization is its management information system (MIS). Every manager has an information system, whether computerized or not. Augustus Caesar was famous for his organized set of managerial systems for waging war. A major subsystem within this set was his logistics subsystem, a remarkable system for that era. The range of materials, both weapons and foodstuffs, to support 50,000 soldiers was enormous. Yet the highly organized system functioned smoothly. Lack of a system of comparable quality caused the defeat of Alexander the Great.

A system that has been converted to computer processing is referred to as a computer application. The integrated set of computerized systems that undergird the management process is a computer-based management information system (CBMIS). Development of a CBMIS is a complex process. First, the existing management information system must be documented and analyzed. System analysis determines which of the subsystems within the MIS are feasible for computer processing. However, the system analyst seeks to improve all subsystems—not just those that can be computerized.

Analysis of complex systems is simplified by use of special techniques for gathering and displaying information about the system. The goal is documentation of information about the company and the environment in which it operates. The system analyst's task is to identify sources and processes for producing the information needed for decision making.

The result is the design of one or more data bases that will

be utilized by all computer applications. This chapter explains the special techniques used to analyze the existing management process and the steps in designing an improved system—logical system design.

OVERVIEW OF A COMPUTER-BASED MIS

Progressive companies treat information as a principal resource, along with people, materials, and equipment. One reason is its cost. In Chapter 1, we cited a recent national study that showed more than 50 percent of the U.S. labor force is involved in information handling and processing.

An even more important reason exists for treating information as a major company resource. Huge resources of people, materials, and equipment do not insure a successful company. Valid and up-to-date information is essential to proper allocation of resources—being in the right business at the right time, with the right amount of resources.

Producing such a result is the objective of management; a system to provide information and support decisions is essential in meeting this objective. As a consequence some organizations are relabeling their CBMIS, calling it a **Decision Support System** (DSS). Identifying such systems as a DSS places emphasis on the principal goal of the system—improving the decision process. However, the choice of a title (MIS, CBMIS or DSS) is not important. The important objective is to undergird the decision process. We will use the term CBMIS.

Figure 17–1 pictures a CBMIS with the two essential ingredients: (1) data capture and processing subsystems (the lower half of Figure 17–1) and (2) data analysis and decision support subsystems (the upper half of the figure). Figure 17–1 shows that output may consist of: (1) transactions sorted into some desired sequence, (2) results of computations, or (3) logical comparisons. Output may be in the form of a computer printout or a video display; it may be a listing of results or a graphical presentation.

In Figure 17–1, a major system of a firm is used to illustrate each level of output—the order-processing subsystem of the marketing decision support system. From the transaction processing (of orders), customer invoices and order-filling requisitions are produced (nonsupervisory output). In addition, data are captured that affect three of the four major sections of the data base for internal information: (1) order data are entered to the customer data base, (2) the quantity ordered is deducted from the inventory portion of the product data base, and (3) invoice amounts are entered to the financial data base.

These same data are entered into the analytical models of the decision support systems. For example, the sales manager (first-line supervisor) would receive statistical reports on salesperson performance: (1) comparing performance this period to that of prior periods and (2) comparing performance to goals for each individual. The sales manager would also receive output that results primarily from transaction processing, that is, computing and listing sales commissions.

Analytical models for decision support of middle and executive management normally are more complex. In Figure 17–1, a sales statistics report illustrates middle management output. Rather than dealing with salesperson performance, management at this level is more concerned with sales by region or by product type. Additional concerns are: (1) total sales versus target and (2) comparisons to previous periods. In addition, middle managers want an analysis of cost versus revenue.

Executive-level management is also concerned with performance. However, a longer time horizon is involved. Forecasting models are important to decision making at this level. Emphasis is placed on external data: economic conditions,

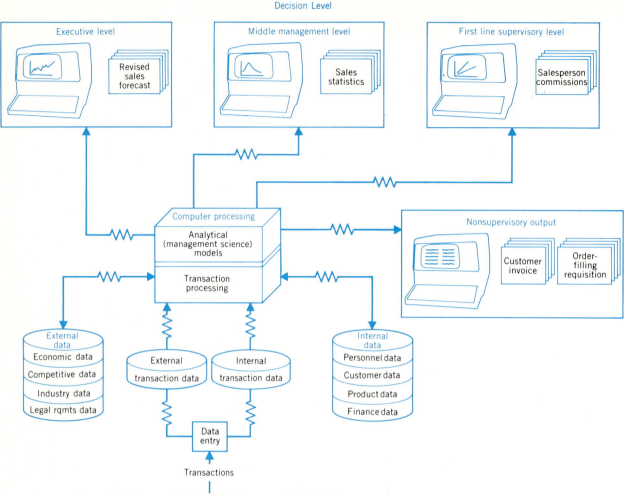

FIGURE 17-1

Major ingredients in a computer-based management information system output, illustrated on an order-processing and marketing decision support system.

competitive considerations, and impending legislative requirements that impact business. Data from both external and internal sources are required as input to forecasting models.

Not only does the CBMIS provide this information more quickly, it performs analysis (through models) that improves the quality of information.

When data are transformed into information, we have a true decision support system.

EXERCISE 17-1 Examine Figure 17-1 and answer the following questions.

1. Transactions are entered and stored in either of two data bases. One data base consists of data originating from _____ sources and the other consists of data originating from _____ sources.

2. An analytical model may simply compute invoice totals or salesperson commissions. At the other extreme it may analyze hundreds of variables to produce a sales forecast. The latter system requires access to which data bases?

_____

_____

3. The models produce information from data, transforming data to a form that supports the _____ process.

OBJECTIVES OF A COMPUTER-BASED MANAGEMENT INFORMATION SYSTEM

How is a decision support system achieved? First, it is essential that designers of each major system area are working on the same set of objectives. The objectives in designing a CBMIS are:

1. To capture or generate all data pertinent to the firm's operations.
2. To process data in the most efficient and economical manner, utilizing management science techniques to the fullest extent feasible.
3. To produce concise and timely information, as required by each level of management.

OBJECTIVE 1: CAPTURE OR GENERATE ALL PERTINENT DATA

There are key phrases in each objective. In the first objective, the key phrase is "all pertinent data." Too often the system designer develops a system that floods the manager with computer output. This point was illustrated in a chemical company where one of the authors served as a consultant. A manager was describing the output of the first system designed for his use: "I was excited about the prospect of a comprehensive set of reports," he said. "On Monday of the first week the reports were produced, I told my secretary to try to avoid scheduling any meetings that I could put off until the following week. I wanted to devote full attention to the output of my new system. However, by Friday I was only a little over halfway through the reports. So, when I arrived at work the next Monday and found a new set of reports awaiting me, I was somewhat overwhelmed!" His system designers had not met objective 1; they had designed the system to produce *all* data, instead of data *pertinent* to the manager.

Contrast this example with another one. A new general manager told his system designers: "I don't know a lot about the electronics business, coming from the wholesale distribution business. Therefore, details are not of much value to me at this point. I want a system that produces reports only when there are problems I should know about." He then proceeded to identify the criteria for such reports. For example, he wanted to be informed when any department was ±5 percent from its budgeted performance. He wanted to know about any customer order that was delinquent more than 10 days. He set up a full list of criteria, insuring that the system designed for his use provided only data pertinent to his decision-making process.

The **management-by-exception** principle is illustrated by the latter manager. He devoted his scarce resource, time, to only those "exceptional" conditions that required his attention. System designers must design a management-by-exception reporting system for the CBMIS. This approach insures that the firm's executive talents are utilized properly.

QUESTION: The system analysts, therefore, meet with the managers for whom the system is being designed. In addition to standard reports, managers specify those

_____ that are to be identified and reported by the system.

ANSWER: exceptions

QUESTION: The first objective in design of a computer-based management information

system insures that the system captures or generates all data _____ to the firm's operations. Under what circumstances would the admissions officer of a college require that all data on each student's high school transcript be

captured and entered into the student file? _____

_____

_____

_____

_____

_____

_____

ANSWER: Pertinent. The admissions officer is concerned only that all requirements have been fulfilled. However, the dean of students might want each student's college performance compared to high school performance. Identifying problems early in a student's college career might reduce the chance that the student would drop out. Therefore, the admissions officer would be asked to capture those data at the same time the transcript was processed for admission.

The fact that an organization has converted a number of systems to the computer does not necessarily mean it has a CBMIS. The key concept in design of computer-based management information systems is **integration.** Figure 17–1 illustrates major systems and subsystems that are integrated; that is, there is sharing of information among systems. Data are captured as close as possible to the point of origin, then shared with all systems that use the data.

OBJECTIVE 2:
UTILIZE MANAGEMENT
SCIENCE TECHNIQUES
In the second objective in designing a CBMIS, the key phrase is "utilizing management science techniques." What are management science techniques? Figure 17–2 lists some of these techniques and shows areas of application within each of the major subsystems of a firm.

QUESTION: Break-even analysis, a technique covered in your introductory economics

course, is applicable to what major systems? _____

ANSWER: marketing and planning, finance and accounting

MANAGEMENT SCIENCE TECHNIQUES \ FUNCTIONAL AREAS	Marketing and Planning	R and D and Engineering	Manufacturing and Q C	Purchasing, Inventory and Distribution	Labor and Industrial Relations	Finance and Accounting	Total Firm
DETERMINISTIC							
Linear Programming	**********	**********	**********	**********	**********	**********	
Economic Order Quantity				**********			
Economic Lot Quantity			**********				
Breakeven Analysis	**********					**********	
Improvement Curve	**********	**********	**********		**********	**********	
CPM Network Analysis	**********	**********	**********	**********	**********	**********	**********
Time Series Analysis	**********				**********	**********	
Dynamic Programming	**********		**********			**********	
Dimensional Analysis	**********	**********					
Symbolic Logic		**********			**********		
STOCHASTIC							
Heuristic Modeling	**********						
Sensitivity Analysis	**********						
Decision Theory	**********			**********			**********
Competitive Modeling	**********						**********
Queuing Theory	**********		**********	**********	**********		
Statistical Quality Control			**********	**********			
PERT Network Analysis	**********	**********	**********	**********	**********	**********	**********
Monte Carlo Theory	**********	**********	**********	**********			
Behavioral Modeling	**********				**********	**********	
Markov Process	**********	**********			**********	**********	
Simulation	**********	**********	**********	**********	**********	**********	**********

FIGURE 17-2
Application of management science techniques to major systems within the CBMIS.

22 / INTRODUCTION TO CBMIS

Computers are sometimes justified for only one reason—to process data faster. Orders and invoices are produced more quickly and management reports are more up to date. Computers are doing what people formerly did—but at much higher rates of speed. However, the main advantage of computers is to perform tasks that are very difficult for humans.

Using the computer for complex analyses produces much higher return on investment than just processing data more quickly.

It is possible to computerize systems without utilizing management science techniques. However, it is rarely possible to optimize these systems without use of such techniques. For example, consider the linear programming technique, which applies to every area of the firm. **Linear programming** is a technique for optimizing, or making the best assignment of resources. It could be used in the marketing system to analyze brand preferences, in the manufacturing system for machine loading, and in the distribution system to determine warehouse location.

QUESTION: Management science techniques are embedded in the system in order to

_____ the system.

ANSWER: optimize

OBJECTIVE 3: PRODUCE INFORMATION FOR EACH LEVEL OF MANAGEMENT

The key phrase in objective 3 is "each level of management." The previous examples illustrate that the other phrase in this objective is also very important: "to produce concise and timely information." The manager in the chemical firm was provided timely information that was *not* concise. His report was too large to be useful. The manager in the electronics firm wanted exceptions to be reported from his system. As a result, he received concise and timely information.

Some systems have met half of objective 3, providing concise and timely information—but only for one level of management. A business application is not necessarily a management application. The payroll application is a clerical rather than a managerial system. The computerized grade report system in the college is also a clerical system rather than a managerial system. These systems are referred to as **operational level systems.** Both were designed to replace or improve clerical operations.

However, the payroll system can be designed to produce managerial information as well as perform a clerical operation. The designer can provide for sharing payroll information with other systems of the company. Examples of other subsystems that use this information are the accounting and personnel subsystems.

In addition to a horizontal integration, or sharing of data, there should be a vertical integration. In some cases this is a summary process; for example, payroll costs are summarized to be included in budget performance reports (a middle-level management report) and in the balance sheet (a top-level management report). Figure 17–3 illustrates the vertical and horizontal sharing of information. **Strategic-level systems** support executive-level decision making, whereas **tactical-level systems** support middle management.

In other cases, management needs information that is not merely a summary. For example, top management needs a planning simulation model. Static reports on past performance, such as income statements and balance sheets, are insufficient for managing the firm. Management also needs income statements and

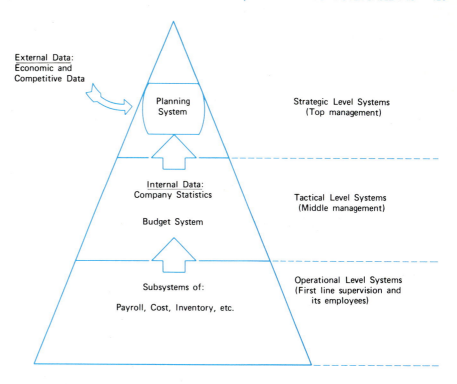

External Data:
Economic and
Competitive Data

Planning
System

Strategic Level Systems
(Top management)

Internal Data:
Company Statistics

Budget System

Tactical Level Systems
(Middle management)

Subsystems of:

Payroll, Cost, Inventory, etc.

Operational Level Systems
(First line supervision and
its employees)

FIGURE 17-3
Vertical versus horizontal processing of management information.

balance sheets projected for future years under varying economic conditions. A **computer simulation** provides such information. It allows management to vary factors in order to forecast the effect on the enterprise—for example, the effects of new product lines or new plants. Simulation is one of the tools of management science (see Figure 17-2).

Modern-day system design gives priority to computerization of **lifestream activities** of the firm—activities that are key to the life and growth of the organization. System analysts concentrate on the lifestream systems of planning, marketing, production, and distribution. To design such systems, the analysis team must understand the goals of the firm. Phase I provides the background for designing the CBMIS, relating system objectives to the objectives of the company.

QUESTION: The above description may appear to suggest that planning models are separate systems, unrelated to the integrated set of systems and subsystems. How are top-level management systems related to the other systems within the CBMIS?

Use Figure 17-3 for assistance in answering this question. _____

_____

_____

_____

ANSWER: Some data for the planning system must come from external sources (for example, economic and industry data). However, a large amount of the input is derived from the data base of existing systems. Therefore the planning system is integrated with the operational and middle-level management systems within the CBMIS.

PHASE I: DOCUMENTING THE EXISTING SYSTEM

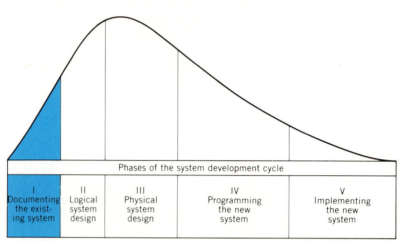

Phase I of the system development cycle is documentation of the existing management system. Findings are organized into the following categories (see Figure 17–4) for detailed breakdown).

1. Company history.
2. External environment.
3. Objectives.
4. Master plan.

GATHERING DATA ON COMPANY HISTORY   A summary of significant events in the organization's history is important for system analysis. The objective is to provide a basis for projecting the future of the business.

Included in the history are:

1. Growth statistics (personnel, sales, profit, plant capacity).
2. Evolution of products or services (types, quantities, product names).
3. Management pattern (organizational structure, decentralized or centralized decision making).
4. Expansion characteristics (mergers, spinoffs, acquisitions).

QUESTION: All four elements of the history are important in understanding the company situation. However, element 3 perhaps has the greatest impact on the design of

the CBMIS. Why? _____

ANSWER: The CBMIS must be designed to support the decision process. For example, decentralized companies may have data bases at each location.

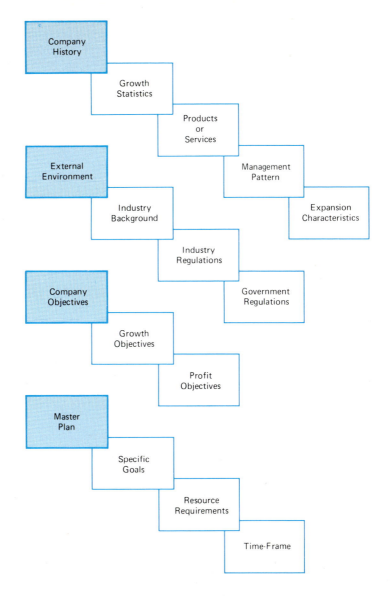

FIGURE 17-4
Documents produced in phase I of system development cycle.

GATHERING DATA ON THE EXTERNAL ENVIRONMENT

The growth of a firm is constrained by the environment in which it operates. The firm may be competing in regional, national, or international markets. It may be a nonprofit organization or an agency of local, state, or federal government. It may produce a product or may be a service organization.

Data on the external environment are recorded from the perspective of the management of the enterprise. Included are:

1. Industry background (total volume, constituency, share of market, demand curves, technological characteristics).

2. Industry regulations (trade agreements, labor practices).

3. Government regulations (monopoly and antitrust laws, labor laws, fair-employment laws).

QUESTION: Referring to item 3 in the list, give an example of how a government regulation on record keeping might affect a company. (Hint: Some utility companies are required to keep records on each customer for 50 years.)

_____

_____

_____

ANSWER: Large resources might be required to store and maintain records; for example, a Texas-based gas utility buries its customer meter reading records to avoid building warehouses. Storage costs are low; however, access costs are rather high!

GATHERING INFORMATION ON COMPANY OBJECTIVES

Understanding the historical perspective and the external environment enables the system team to have a better feel for the managerial task of the organization. Integration of systems is quite difficult without identifying the objectives of the organization. In earlier years, when analysts were working solely on subsystems, relating subsystem objectives to the firm's objectives was rarely done.

Company objectives are translated into system design requirements for each of the major systems. For example, the marketing system has a subsystem (sales statistics) that is designed to provide information on performance against sales objectives. However, that subsystem would also supply sales information to the financial reporting subsystem, to produce the income statement.

The organization's growth objective, for example, might be stated as follows: "Expand sales at a compounded rate of 10 percent annually" or "Maintain the existing share of the market." An approach to implement such objectives might be: "Expand the product line." A very different policy for meeting those objectives would be: "Grow by acquisition of other companies."

The difference in these two approaches has significant effects on the design of an information system. A company that plans growth by merger may be united with a firm that has its own computer and CBMIS. Special data processing needs arise from such situations. For example, the account number systems are usually different. System designers who are aware of their company's merger objectives can design an account numbering system with greater flexibility. Otherwise, they must design a translator that converts the two accounting systems before preparing financial reports.

Such a situation is more complicated than that of a company that plans growth by expansion of sales. For the latter, the accounting system is merely designed to handle new products — a less complex design than one that must coordinate with another firm's accounting system.

The system approach of the 1980s translates company objectives into system objectives. Subsystems are then designed to correspond to major system objectives.

QUESTION: Using the 1980s system approach, system objectives are developed within the

framework of _____.

ANSWER: company objectives

GATHERING INFORMATION
ABOUT THE MASTER PLAN

The objectives of the organization are quantified in the master plan. The master plan identifies the means by which the firm will achieve its objectives. The firm may seek to become much more capital intensive, affecting the priority of development of subsystems. The financial subsystem would take priority over many of the labor-control subsystems for such an organization.

The master plan identifies: (1) specific goals, (2) the resources required to attain those goals, and (3) a time frame for use of resources.

How would the information in the master plan aid the system analyst? The master plan shows where the majority of resources are applied; therefore, it identifies possible areas for savings through computerization. It also shows which activities are constraints — in terms of the time available to perform them.

In the 1970s documentation covered goals and resources but did not put them into the perspective of specific product lines and levels of resource allocation by time period. Only the master plan provides such perspective.

QUESTION: The master plan helps the system analyst determine _____

ANSWER: possible areas for savings

EXERCISE 17-2

1. Phase I documents four major areas concerning the organization.

   a. _____

   b. _____

   c. _____

   d. _____

2. Why is the term "documentation" used for phase I of the system development cycle?

3. Another widely used textbook does not identify the master plan as one of the documents to be included in a system survey. Give two reasons for including the master plan.

   a. _____

   b. _____

The information shown in Figure 17–4 is gathered to determine where the computer will be most beneficial for the organization as a whole. With this information, priority of systems can be identified and a three-year system development plan prepared.

However, for system design more detailed information is necessary. The information is gathered and organized as shown in Figure 17–5. This package of information is prepared for each system on the three-year system development plan.

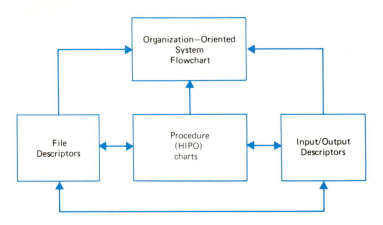

FIGURE 17–5
Information needed for system analysis.

ORGANIZATION-ORIENTED SYSTEM FLOWCHART

Since the emphasis in the 1980s is upon integration of systems, a technique has been developed to facilitate such analysis — the **organization-oriented system flowchart** (abbreviated **O²S flowchart**).

As shown in Figure 17–7, the organization-oriented system flowchart has three characteristics: (1) identification of organization responsibility, (2) display of information flow, and (3) identification of resource levels.

At the bottom of each O²S flowchart the resources utilized in each organization involved in the system are shown. The figures are not the total expenditures of the organization, but only that portion of expenditures involved in the system under study. Resources are identified in three categories: personnel, materials, and equipment.

With the information from such a chart, the analyst has a good basis for developing an improved system. The existing system is analyzed to determine what improvements might be made before any analysis to determine if the system will be computerized.

QUESTION: What information is shown on the O²S flowchart that was not produced as a part of phase I documentation? _____

_____

ANSWER: flow of information across organization lines and resource requirements by system

The chapter examination contains two problems in which you are asked to examine O²S flowcharts and to develop an improved method. In preparation for that assignment we will perform the same kind of analysis on the system shown in Figure 17–7, which is the purchasing activity for a mail order firm.

First, we need to explain some additional flowcharting symbols for organization-oriented flowcharts. The symbols shown in Figure 17–6 are added to the set established in Chapter 12. They are used in system flowcharts as opposed to programming flowcharts.

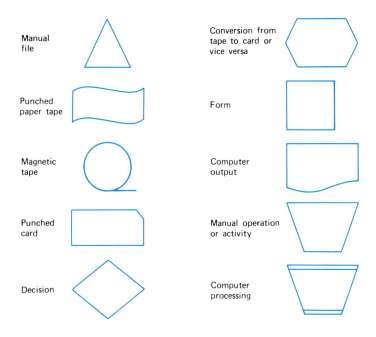

FIGURE 17–6
Additional flowchart symbols for organization-oriented flowcharts.

To understand the use of the O²S flowchart, examine the operations of the receiving department in Figure 17–7. Note that copy 4 of the purchase order (PO) is filed there, awaiting receipt of the goods ordered. When the goods arrive, the bill of lading supplied by the vendor is compared to the PO, to insure that all items ordered were delivered and in the correct quantities. A receiving report is prepared to notify all affected departments. The original is filed in the receiving department along with copy 4 of the purchase order.

However, copy 2 of the receiving report is sent to the buyer, where it is matched against copy 3 of the PO filed there. So we now have copies of the PO attached to copies of the receiver, filed in two locations. The system analyst should question the need for duplicate files.

QUESTION: Which of the two files could be eliminated, in your opinion? Explain. _____

ANSWER: Wouldn't the buyer's file be sufficient? Most questions would be directed there. Why not eliminate the file in the receiving department and have those personnel call the buyer's secretary when any question arises concerning a completed order?

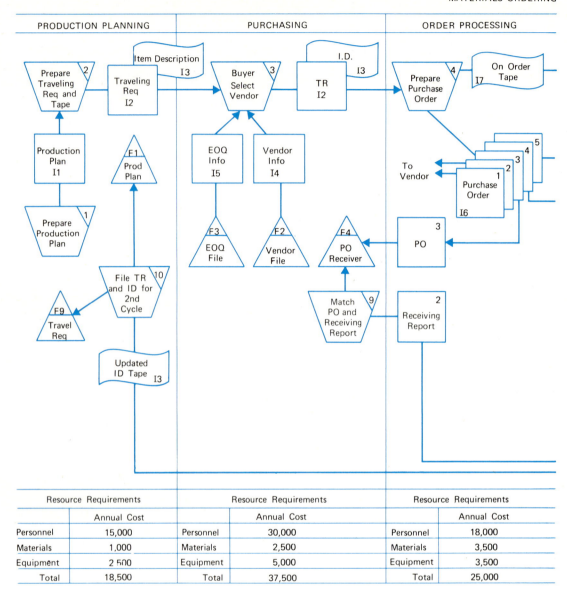

FIGURE 17–7
Organization-oriented system flowchart.

This example shows the advantages of the O²S flowchart in analyzing information flows.

INPUT/OUTPUT DESCRIPTOR
All information entering the system under study is identified on the **input/output (I/O) descriptor.** The same form is used to identify all information leaving the system. Input is usually received on a form of some type. However, it may be entered by some other media, such as by telephone or from an individual who drops by to provide some verbal input.

If the system is to be computerized, all input must be identified and described. Likewise, the information produced by an operation, whether verbal or

SYSTEM

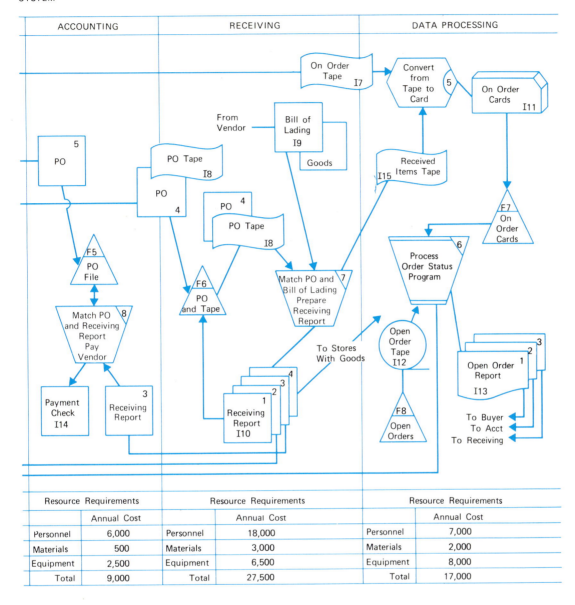

Resource Requirements		Resource Requirements		Resource Requirements	
	Annual Cost		Annual Cost		Annual Cost
Personnel	6,000	Personnel	18,000	Personnel	7,000
Materials	500	Materials	3,000	Materials	2,000
Equipment	2,500	Equipment	6,500	Equipment	8,000
Total	9,000	Total	27,500	Total	17,000

written, must be quantified. The input/output descriptor is the device used to record such information. A sample I/O descriptor is shown in Figure 17–8.

QUESTION: Examine the I/O descriptor in Figure 17–8. It describes an output of the manual production control system. Read the description section and suggest why this system has good potential for computer processing.

ANSWER: A large amount of data must be processed and a number of calculations must be made in producing this weekly report.

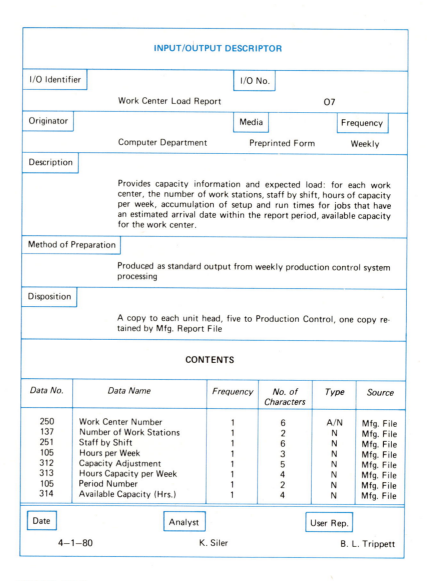

<table>
<tr><th colspan="6">INPUT/OUTPUT DESCRIPTOR</th></tr>
</table>

INPUT/OUTPUT DESCRIPTOR

I/O Identifier   I/O No.

Work Center Load Report   O7

Originator   Media   Frequency

Computer Department   Preprinted Form   Weekly

Description

Provides capacity information and expected load: for each work center, the number of work stations, staff by shift, hours of capacity per week, accumulation of setup and run times for jobs that have an estimated arrival date within the report period, available capacity for the work center.

Method of Preparation

Produced as standard output from weekly production control system processing

Disposition

A copy to each unit head, five to Production Control, one copy retained by Mfg. Report File

CONTENTS

Data No.	Data Name	Frequency	No. of Characters	Type	Source
250	Work Center Number	1	6	A/N	Mfg. File
137	Number of Work Stations	1	2	N	Mfg. File
251	Staff by Shift	1	6	N	Mfg. File
105	Hours per Week	1	3	N	Mfg. File
312	Capacity Adjustment	1	5	N	Mfg. File
313	Hours Capacity per Week	1	4	N	Mfg. File
105	Period Number	1	2	N	Mfg. File
314	Available Capacity (Hrs.)	1	4	N	Mfg. File

Date   Analyst   User Rep.

4–1–80   K. Siler   B. L. Trippett

FIGURE 17–8
Output specification using I/O descriptor form.

FILE DESCRIPTOR In the precomputer era, systems and procedures specialists concentrated on simplification of operations. They also sought to reduce the number of copies of documents, to cut down on filing space and equipment. Computer system analysts also seek to reduce file space. However, the need is much more important in the computer era, due to the high cost of storage media. Computer files are maintained on media that can communicate directly with a computer and are many times more expensive than filing cabinets.

The system analyst searches for ways to combine files. To facilitate such analysis, a **file descriptor** is prepared. Each file is keyed to the organization-oriented system flowchart for continuity in analysis. An example of a file descriptor is shown in Figure 17–9.

FILE DESCRIPTOR

File Identifier		File No.	
	Purchase Order/Receiver		F 4

Location		Media	
	Buying Department		Preprinted Forms

Description

Copy of P.O. filed in open order file until receiver arrives. The two are then stapled, placed in a folder, and transferred to the inactive section of the same file.

Access Requirements

Within 1 minute when Buyer is called concerning status of order

Sequence

By Purchase Order Number

Retention Requirements

Until product is discontinued; then transferred to historical records file

Frequency of Updating

Within 2 hours of arrival of P.O. and Receiver in department

CONTENTS

Data No.	Data Name	Quantity in File	Characters Per Input	Characters per file Average	Peak
	File contains copy of each P.O. and each Receiver.				
12	Open Orders	230	760	175,000	250,000
13	Inactive Orders	6500	760	46,000,000	60,000,000

Date	Analyst	User Rep
5–12–80	R. Sprague	H. Morgan

FIGURE 17–9

File descriptor, used to provide detailed information for each file in the system, whether or not computerized.

QUESTION: Examine the file descriptor in Figure 17- 9. The section on access requirements

shows that the demand for access must be met in _____ minute(s) because the buyer (or his secretary) must respond while the inquirer is on the phone.

ANSWER: One. Therefore, if computerized, the system will have to be on-line to respond this quickly.

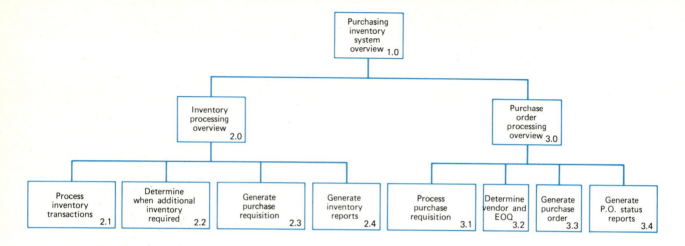

FIGURE 17-10
HIPO structure chart for purchasing/inventory systems.

PROCEDURE (HIPO) CHARTS

As defined earlier, a system exists if the following occur: input, processing, and output. The O²S flowcharts show the major systems of the company. There may be a dozen or more of these charts to cover the major systems of the firm. For example, in a typical bank these systems would include the checking account system, savings system, installment loan system, and commercial loan system.

To provide the complete set of information needed for a system, the O²S charts are further refined into procedure charts. The **HIPO technique** is one of the most commonly used approaches to display procedures. HIPO is an acronym for Hierarchy plus Input-Process-Output. It was developed by IBM to delineate the functions of a system. The term "hierarchy" is used because the procedure is to start with a high-level chart to show the overall system functions and then to provide increasing amounts of detail with each lower level in the hierarchy. The number of levels depends on the degree of complexity in the particular system being studied.

The first step is to develop a structure chart, which identifies major functions performed by the system. Figure 17-10 illustrates a **structure chart** for the purchasing/inventory system we have been using as an example.

The second step is to prepare **HIPO diagrams** for each block on the structure chart. The top charts will not be illustrated because of their very general nature. They are the three overview blocks (numbered 1.0, 2.0 and 3.0). Block 3.2 will be diagrammed to illustrate HIPO methodology. Figure 17-11 shows the HIPO diagram for a third level in the hierarchy, for determining economic order quantity and selecting a vendor.

The HIPO diagram shows inputs, processing steps, and outputs. It also identifies the preceding diagram (input) and following diagram (output).

With the information in the O²S charts, input/output descriptors, file descriptors, and HIPO diagrams, the system designer has a basis for designing an improved system.

QUESTION: What information is provided in HIPO charts that is not available in I/O and file descriptors?

ANSWER: The procedure for processing and the specific input and output associated with each step of processing

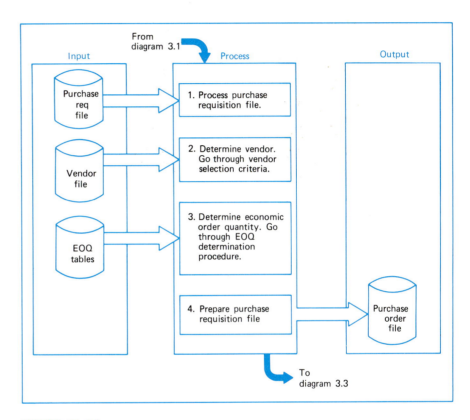

FIGURE 17-11

HIPO diagram (3.2) for block at the third level of the structure chart.

SUMMARY OF PHASE I

The goal in system analysis is to determine how a system can be improved. The analyst works with the users of the system to identify what improvements are needed. Then, the present system is examined in depth to determine how it can be improved.

The resulting information is organized for efficient analysis, into the phase I documentation package: O^2S flowcharts, input descriptors, procedure (HIPO) diagrams, file descriptors, and output descriptors.

Often, the analysts who conducted the phase I study also perform phase II, logical design. However, complexity of modern systems requires a number of persons to be involved. Accurate and detailed documentation of the present system insures that all these persons have a common set of information with which to design an improved system.

However, if only one analyst were performing both phase I and phase II activities, the information would still need to be organized in this manner; this organization is the most efficient approach in determining how to improve the system.

PHASE II: LOGICAL SYSTEM DESIGN

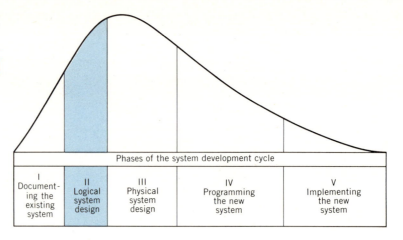

Phases of the system development cycle				
I Documenting the existing system	II Logical system design	III Physical system design	IV Programming the new system	V Implementing the new system

LOGICAL DESIGN COMPONENTS

The logical system design consists of five components: output specifications, processing rules, decision logic, file specifications, and input specifications. Figure 17–12 shows the relationship of the documents produced in phases I and II. An overview of each of these tasks will be presented before each is described in detail.

Phases in system development cycle

I Documenting existing system	II Logical system design	III Physical system design
Documentation package	Logical design package	Physical design package
O^{2}S flowcharts	Input specifications	
Input descriptors	Processing procedures	
Procedure (HIPO) diagrams	Decision logic tables	
Output descriptors	File specifications	
File descriptors	Output specifications	

FIGURE 17–12
Packages produced in phases I and II.

OUTPUT SPECIFICATIONS

Through in-depth discussions with users of the system, the system analyst identifies the output required of the system. Both content and media are described.

In describing **content,** the analyst identifies precisely what the system should provide the user. For example, reports to various levels of management may differ in the degree of detail. The chief executive may be interested only in total value of inventory, while the controller must know cost of the raw material, work-in-process (WIP), and finished goods inventory. The first-line supervisor (of raw material) maintains raw material records and needs to have detailed reports for each item in stock: receipts, results of incoming inspection, and issues.

In identifying **media,** the analyst determines the most appropriate form of output. For the chief executive, this may be a printed exception report, providing information on activities *not* meeting the executive's criteria for performance. For example, a report would not be produced unless inventory levels exceeded an amount prescribed by the executive. For the controller, both printed reports and on-line visual display may be appropriate. When the exception report reveals a problem, the visual display unit may be used to trace the cause of the inventory overage. The dock clerk may need the visual display unit for both input and output. Receipts and issues could be entered into the system by a keyboard and visually verified on the display unit. Inquiries about specific stock items could be entered through the keyboard and status displayed on the screen.

PROCESSING PROCEDURES   Decision criteria and processing procedures are developed at the same time. Processing procedures show the relationship of the various decision modules and the flow of processing.

DECISION LOGIC   Each decision is identified, along with the conditions that necessitate the decision and the possible actions. As an example, from the inventory system explained above, the analyst would record the decision logic as specified by the chief executive for exception reports.

FILE SPECIFICATIONS   After output and processing specifications have been established, the analyst determines the files necessary to support these activities. File specifications include file size (characters), frequency of update, peak and average message volume, access requirements, and retention requirements.

INPUT SPECIFICATIONS   When output requirements, processing rules, decision criteria, and file requirements have been specified, the analyst determines input requirements. As in the case of output, both content and media are specified.

QUESTION: Which of the five logical design components would be used to show how the manager prefers his computer printout to be formatted?

ANSWER: output specifications

IMPROVEMENT ANALYSIS The first step in logical design is analysis of the existing system to determine areas for improvement. Phase I documentation is the basis of this analysis. To understand clearly the tasks of the user of the system, analysts should try to visualize themselves performing that role. Since it is not possible to exchange roles, the analyst often gains knowledge about the needs of the system through step-by-step review of existing reports. Using the output descriptors prepared in the data gathering phase, the analyst can evaluate the output requirements of the present system. Referencing output descriptors, the analyst discusses with the users possible changes in output that would enable users to do their jobs more easily and more effectively. The questioning technique common to all types of analysis is utilized: the five Ws and H—who, where, why, when, how, and with what resources.

The analyst examines the O²S flowchart to isolate the following.

1. Bottlenecks or unnecessary delays in processing.
2. Ways to reduce the amount of paperwork.
3. Approaches to simplifying each activity.
4. High-cost activities.

These areas have high priority for further analysis. The following exercise will give you an opportunity to use this analytical approach.

EXERCISE 17–3

1. Develop an organization-oriented system flowchart from the narrative description of the procedure below. (Omit the resources section of the flowchart.)

   Order Processing for a Mail-Order Firm. A clerk opens each envelope and dumps the contents on the work table. Checks and cash are compared to the order, to see if the amount agrees with the customer's figure. Cash and checks are sent to accounts receivable. If payment is not received for an order, two copies of the order are reproduced. One copy is sent to customer service and filed in case complaints arise. The other copy goes to accounts receivable, where an invoice is typed and mailed. One copy of the invoice is filed for follow-up and another is sent to customer service.

   The original order is forwarded to a second clerk, who types a mailing label with a carbon and paper clips them to the order. Orders are batched in groups of 25 and forwarded to order processing.

   The order is filled and packed in a carton. The order form is placed on top of the merchandise with a mailing label and blank order. The other label is removed, moistened, and attached to the carton. Paper is stuffed around the merchandise to keep it tightly packed. The carton is then sealed and placed on a skid. The skid is transported to the mail department, where packages are weighed, postage is attached, and the packages are placed in a truck for shipment.

   When a customer complaint is received, it is sent to customer service. The company takes the word of the customer and sends the requested items. If the complaint concerns the invoice, a copy is pulled from the file and compared to the customer's tally. A letter is sent to the customer with a refund or an explanation of the invoice if the original invoice is determined to be correct.

2. Now review your flowchart to determine what activities appear unnecessary. You should be able to identify at least two unnecessary activities.

   a. _____

   _____

   b. _____

   _____

3. What activities might be reassigned to other departments, to improve the system? At least one reassignment is feasible. Compare your ideas with the list provided in the Answers to Exercises.

PREPARING THE LOGICAL DESIGN   With the completion of improvement analysis, the analyst is ready to develop the logical design of the new system. Logical system design is essentially hardware independent. The result of logical system design is a set of specifications for physical system design. Physical system design determines the specific computer configuration necessary to implement the system.

PREPARING OUTPUT SPECIFICATIONS   The *content* of input cannot be specified until output requirements have been established. For the chief executive, work-in-process inventory may be calculated as the difference between starting and ending inventory. The controller often needs a more detailed breakdown, such as WIP by product type or by physical location. The analyst must determine how WIP input is to be made — for example, by each manufacturing organization, or at points in production that facilitate measurement, or by random audits.

As a consequence, input *media* are also suggested by the analyst. However, determination of media must wait until the physical design has been completed. The analysis of input media and output media is not considered separately, as illustrated by the dock clerk who used the same visual display terminal for input and output.

The document for preparing I/O specifications is the same as that used to record information on inputs and outputs of the old system, the I/O descriptor.

QUESTION: Using the output descriptors prepared in phase II, the system analyst works with

the _____ to determine what improvements in reports would aid the decision-making process.

ANSWER: user

PREPARING PROCESSING PROCEDURES   A good technique for depicting processing procedures is a HIPO diagram. These diagrams provide the whole picture of the procedure required in processing the system.

To delineate the processing rules, the analyst further defines the HIPO diagrams developed in phase I. For example, the three-level structure chart in Figure 17-10 is broken down further, as shown below in Figure 17-13.

Figure 17-14 shows the HIPO diagram for the fourth level, corresponding to the structure chart of Figure 17-13. This level of detail is still insufficient to serve as a system specification for the physical design phase. For example, look at box 3. A further level of detail would be necessary to identify the criteria for measuring quality.

QUESTION: Examine Figure 17-13. What might be an example of the detailed procedure needed at the fifth level to determine if vendor quality performance is acceptable (box 3)?

ANSWER: Determine if inspection revealed that 95 percent of the items supplied by the vendor met quality requirements.

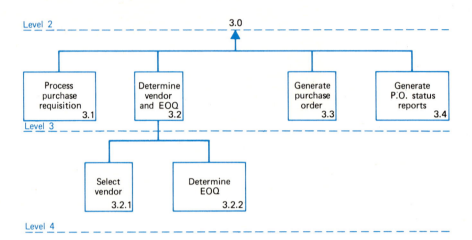

FIGURE 17–13

HIPO structure chart further defined to fourth level.

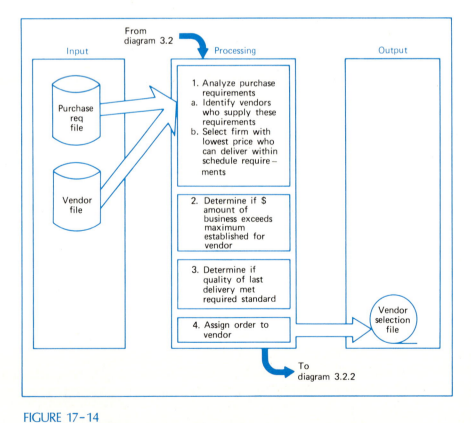

FIGURE 17–14

HIPO diagram (3.2.1) for block at the fourth level of the structure chart.

PREPARING DECISION LOGIC SPECIFICATIONS   While HIPO diagrams provide information on system flow and procedure, further detail is needed for some portions of the system. HIPO diagrams are unwieldy in portraying decision logic. Instead, decision logic tables are used. Such tables are designed to show the conditions requiring a decision and the actions to be taken. An explanation of the use of decision tables was provided in Chapter 12 and will not be repeated here. In analyzing the fourth level of the HIPO diagram (Figure 17–14), we see that further detail is necessary. For example, the logic in vendor selection would be more appropriately displayed in a decision table than by successively more detailed levels of the HIPO diagram.

PREPARING FILE SPECIFICATIONS   A file descriptor form was used to record the data in the manual files. Using this information and the newly developed specifications for processing, the analyst can determine the files needed to support the system. Response requirements determine the file media; however, final determination of media occurs in physical design. Logical design identifies file contents, frequency of update, peak and average message volume, access requirements, and retention requirements. A file descriptor form is used to record file specifications.

PREPARING INPUT SPECIFICATIONS   The final task in logical system design is definition of input. When specifications for output, processing, and design logic have been prepared, input specifications are easily determined.

QUESTION: Phase I provided material recorded on descriptor charts. Phase II produced specifications for an improved system. Why was the term "descriptor" used for Phase I documents? _____

ANSWER: Phase I *describes* what is being done; hence the term **descriptor.** Phase II specifies what should be done; hence the term **specification.**

DESIGNING THE DATA BASE   When a logical design is completed for each of the lifestream systems, a data base is designed to serve these systems.

Theoretically, the logical design process should begin with data base design. A data dictionary would be developed. All data items would be captured and stored in the common data base — available for all applications. In practice, the reverse occurs, for the following reasons.

Benefits of a common data base are difficult to quantify. The cost effectiveness of an individual application is much easier to assess. In the past, applications have been justified individually, based on capturing only those data essential to that application.

For example, the payroll system captured and stored in a file those data needed to generate paychecks, payroll records, and W2 forms for income tax reporting. The closely related personnel system is typically installed at a much later date, perhaps several years later — primarily because the savings are more difficult to quantify. Much of the personnel and payroll data are in common (name, job classification, pay grade, years with company, etc.). However, the cost of capturing and storing data for future uses was uneconomical in earlier years. Therefore, as a company continued to expand its computer applications, redundancy occurred. Costs began to mount for both the cost of capturing the data multiple times and the cost of storing it in multiple files. Also, managers became frustrated in trying to compare reports. Files were not updated at the same time, so information on the same data elements was often inconsistent.

Eventually, the company "bites the bullet" and converts to a common data base for each major category.

Slowly, the industry is building its own data base on costs versus benefits of data base use. A company considering a computer for the first time can use this information to justify moving to a data base with its initial computer installation. It is ironic that companies who are longtime users of computers find it more difficult to install a data base than companies considering their first computer. The early computer users must justify the cost of converting all their data and their programs to the data base mode.

While a small percentage of firms in the 1970s utilized the data base approach, a large number of firms utilize data bases today. The next chapter will explain how a logical data base is implemented on specific physical devices.

SUMMARY

The term for the set of computer applications designed for management's use is a "computer-based management information system."

The CBMIS is suboptimal if it merely produces reports; it should also be designed as a decision support system (DSS).

Another part of the CBMIS approach is the provision for horizontally oriented systems and vertically oriented systems. Horizontally oriented systems are operational-level systems because they handle the basic operations of the organization, for example, a checking account system in a bank. Vertically oriented systems provide information needed by each level of management, for example, a market forecasting system for the bank's executive committee.

The CBMIS approach provides for integration of both horizontal and vertical systems. For example, a customer profile can be automatically produced from the checking account system as an input to the higher-level market forecasting system. The checking account system also shares data horizontally with subsystems such as the basic accounting system of the bank.

Phase I of the system development cycle consolidates information about the company and the environment in which it operates. A CBMIS cannot produce optimal results unless its design supports the objectives of the organization.

Using the information gathered in phase I, the analyst determines how the system can be improved. The analysis is computer independent; that is, the analyst looks for ways to improve the system irrespective of whether the system is to be computerized. Information about the system is portrayed so that improvement analysis of all types is possible: manual improvement, semiautomated improvement, and automated improvement. The major systems, such as the manufacturing system, are subdivided into subsystems (such as the production planning subsystem, the final assembly subsystem, and the shipping subsystem).

In phase II, new logical designs are prepared for each subsystem. Here is the place where integration of data into a common data base is emphasized. For example, one set of input is used for financial inventory and another for physical inventory. Design of these inputs is coordinated to insure compatibility, or the two inventories will never agree. Likewise, if data input to one system can also serve another system, entry costs are reduced.

The resulting logical design consists of five major components, prepared in the following sequence: output specifications, processing rules, decision logic, file specifications, and input specifications.

Upon completion of logical system design, phase III, physical system design, is begun. Physical system design is the subject of Chapter 18.

ANSWERS TO EXERCISES

EXERCISE 17-1
1. External, internal
2. Both internal (product, customer, personnel) and external (economic, competitive, industry, and legal)
3. Decision

EXERCISE 17-2
1. a. Company history
   b. External environment: industry background, government regulations
   c. Objectives
   d. Master plan
2. The system team gathers documents and information about the organization. It "documents" the system as it presently exists.
3. a. The master plan identifies the means by which the firm plans to achieve its objectives. The way those objectives are implemented affects the approach to system design.
   b. The master plan identifies specific goals, resources required to attain those goals, and a time frame for use of resources. Prior documentation included goals and resources but did not put them into the perspective of specific product lines by time period.

EXERCISE 17-3
1.

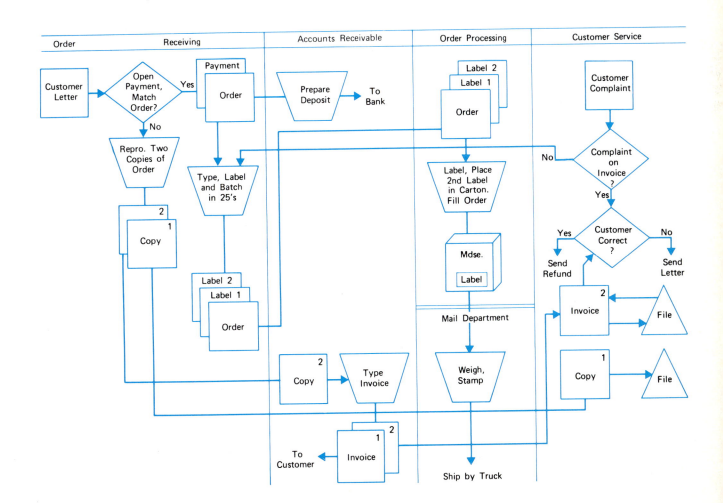

2. Unnecessary activities:
   a. *Reproducing 2 copies of order.* Customer service can use its copy only to verify quantity of items ordered against customer complaint. There is no assurance that order filling sent all the items or that the Post Office got the package to the customer.
   b. *Sending customer complaints on invoices to customer service.* When a customer complaint concerns the invoice, it should be routed to accounts receivable, where records of payments are maintained. Therefore, customer service does not need a copy of the invoice, eliminating one file.
   c. *Typing two labels.* Although the second label comes at no cost except for materials, it must be handled in shipping. A study should be made to determine the percentage of these labels that are actually used by customers. Many will be discarded or lost, or addresses will be changed.
3. Suggested reassignment of responsibilities:
   a. Item 2*b* shows how customer complaints on invoices could be more effectively handled by accounts receivable.
   b. Sending customers all items reported to be missing is a company policy. However, the company could afford to add a checker in shipping if there is a large number of such complaints.

CHAPTER EXAMINATION

1. Match the following.

   ____ DSS

   ____ CBMIS

   ____ Optimization

   ____ Independent of hardware

   ____ HIPO charts

   ____ Integration

   ____ Computer application

   ____ External environment

   ____ O²S flowchart

   ____ Lifestream activities

   ____ Master plan

   ____ Phase I

   ____ Projected income statement

   a. System converted to computer processing

   b. Organization-oriented system flowchart

   c. Specific goals, responses, time frame

   d. Example of strategic level system

   e. Logical system design

   f. Documenting existing systems

   g. Industry background, industry regulations, government regulations

   h. Best results for entire organization

   i. Computer-based management information system

   j. Key to staying in business

   k. Hierarchy plus input-process-output

   l. Sharing information among systems

   m. System to support management decisions

2. Place the following five phases in the system development cycle in the proper sequence.

   ____ a. Implementation

   ____ b. Documentation of existing system

   ____ c. Logical system design

   ____ d. Physical system design

   ____ e. Programming

3. Why is reason for the term "cycle" to be used with system development? _____

_____

4. Explain how CBMIS supports the concept of management by exception. _____

_____

5. Explain the difference between an MIS and a CBMIS. _____

_____

_____

6. Explain the difference between a CBMIS and a DSS. _____

_____

_____

7. Figure 17–1 pictures the two essential ingredients of a CBMIS. Explain each.

    a. _____

    _____

    b. _____

    _____

8. Which of the following are objectives of a computer-based management information system?

    ____ a.   Gathering information on company objectives

    ____ b.   Gathering information about the master plan

    ____ c.   Producing concise and timely information

    ____ d.   Gathering information on company history

    ____ e.   Capturing or generating all data pertinent to the firm's operations

    What objective is missing from the list? _____

    _____

9. Explain the purpose of each of the documents produced in phase I of the system development cycle.

    a. _____

    b. _____

    c. _____

d. _____

e. _____

f. _____

g. _____

h. _____

i. _____

j. _____

k. _____

l. _____

10. Twice as much budget is allocated to phase I in the 1980s as was allocated in the 1970s. Give three reasons for this difference.

a. _____

b. _____

c. _____

11. What information does the O^2S flowchart provide that was not provided in the phase I documentation?

_____

_____

_____

12. What are the four factors to isolate in examining systems for possible improvement?

a. _____

b. _____

c. _____

d. _____

13. The key phrase in CBMIS objective 1 is _____.
Think of an illustration other than the one provided in the book. Use a college president's system to illustrate the key phrase in objective 1.

_____

_____

_____

14. The key phrase in CBMIS objective 2 is _____.

Use a college president's system to illustrate this one also. _____

_____

_____

_____

15. The key phrase in CBMIS objective 3 is _____.
Use a college president's system to illustrate this one, also.

_____

_____

_____

16. What information is provided in the input/output descriptor that is not available on the O^2S flowchart? _____

_____

_____

_____

17. What information is provided in the file descriptor that is not available on the O^2S flowchart? _____

_____

_____

_____

18. What is shown in the O^2S flowchart that cannot be shown on the I/O descriptors and file descriptors? _____

_____

_____

_____

19. Distinguish logical design from physical design.

Logical design is _____

_____

Physical design is _____

_____

20. How does the I/O descriptor aid the analyst in deciding whether an operation should be computerized? ____

_____

_____

_____

21. How does the file descriptor aid the analyst in deciding whether an operation could be computerized? _____

_____

_____

_____

22. Explain the procedure to prepare a HIPO diagram.

Step 1. _____

_____

Step 2. _____

_____

23. Phase I is a costly and time-consuming activity. Give three reasons for not bypassing it and going directly to phase II of the system development cycle.

a. _____

_____

b. _____

_____

c. _____

_____

24. Match the following.

____Strategic-level systems   a.   Support top management

____Operational-level systems   b.   Support first-line supervision

____Tactical-level systems   c.   Support middle management

25. Prepare an O²S flowchart for the following system, to analyze for improvements (as you did in Exercise 17–3). Be thorough because you will be working with this same problem in Chapter 18, developing the physical system design.

Student Records System.   Applicant sends two copies of his transcript, along with his application, to the admissions office. There high school and/or prior college grades are compared to the admission standard. The results of the College Board exams are also analyzed against the admission standard. Rejected applicants are notified by letter, as are those accepted. One copy of each transcript and the application are retained in admissions, in the permanent student file. A second copy of each is forwarded to the department in which the applicant plans to major. There a degree plan is prepared, showing credits earned toward degree requirements. One copy is sent to the student; one is retained in the permanent file for that department. A third copy is sent to the student adviser, who makes an appointment with the student each semester to prepare class schedules. The adviser updates his copy of the degree plan each semester when grades are received. Faculty prepare grade slips in triplicate: (1) to admissions, (2) to department, and (3) to adviser. The student learns his grade from a list posted on the doors of faculty offices. In the final semester the student completes an application for degree. The application is sent to the head of the department, who approves it and forwards it to his secretary. Copies go to admissions, the department file, and the adviser. Admissions prepares the degree when the final grade slips are received.

26.   Prepare an O^2S flowchart for the following system, to analyze for improvements (as you did in Exercise 17–3). Be thorough because you will be working with this same problem in Chapter 18, developing the physical system design.

Checking Account System.   The customer applies for an account and is issued checks and an account number. Checks are forwarded to the bank by the payee. A bookkeeping department clerk posts the withdrawal to the customer account sheet. Deposits are entered on the same record. Once per month the account sheet is reproduced; one copy is sent to the customer unless it is a joint account—for these a copy is made for each party. Monthly summaries for all accounts are forwarded to the president, who compares checking account totals to balances in other systems (such as personal loan, savings, commercial loan). He requests funds from the Federal Reserve system as needed and is provided funds in proportion to his deposit level and reserves.

27. Prepare a HIPO diagram for the following accounting system.

All receipts of payments are key-entered each night and processed to update a master file maintained on magnetic disk. Adjustments to the file are processed at night. All transactions have been key-entered on magnetic tape. New purchases are processed on-line from each sales department. Output consists of the following: error listing, listing of past due accounts, and report on value of outstanding accounts.

28. Prepare a HIPO diagram for the following system.
    a. Edit and process inventory transactions
    b. Update inventory file for the following transactions:
       (1) Additions to inventory
       (2) Withdrawals from inventory
    c. Reorder if inventory below reorder point
    d. Provide following output:
       (1) Order for inventory replenishment
       (2) Inventory usage report
       (3) Inventory order report
       (4) Inventory value report
    e. Update related files:
       (1) Back order file
       (2) Cost file

29. Prepare an O²S flowchart for the following system, to analyze for improvements (as you did in Exercise 17–3). Be thorough because you will be working on this same problem in Chapter 18, developing a physical system design.

Mail Order System.   An order is received by the company and sent to the credit department for approval. If satisfactory, the order is sent to the order department; if not satisfactory, the order is returned to the customer with a letter requesting advance payment. Orders received by the order department are written in triplicate with copy 1 sent to the accounting department, copy 2 to the stock or order-filling department, and copy 3, an acknowledgement, sent to the customer. The order-filling department picks the requested merchandise from the shelves, prepares it for shipment, adds transportation charges to its copy 2, marks it "shipped," adds date of shipment, and sends this copy to the accounting department. Here copy 2 is matched with copy 1. On copy 1 the transportation charges are recorded, and copy 2 is mailed to the customer. This constitutes the bill for the goods shipped. The order-filling department types the shipping label, which is affixed to the package. In the case selected, the customer receives the merchandise satisfactorily but notes that the freight charges on the invoice are incorrect. The customer then returns the invoice to the company along with a letter of explanation. The complaint is referred to the stock-filling department for a recheck. Information is sent to the accounting department where an employee writes the customer a letter of explanation, and, if necessary, a revised invoice is also sent. Upon receipt by customer, the latest information is checked. Payment and invoice are then sent to the company by the customer. The accounting department endorses check, deposits, marks both its copy and customer's copy of invoice "paid," retains its copy for future reference, and returns customer's copy.

18 PHYSICAL SYSTEM DESIGN

OVERVIEW. Phase II of the system development cycle produced the logical design of the new system: the specifications for input, output, and files of the system along with the decision criteria and processing rules. Phase III, the physical design phase, determines the organization of files and the devices to be used.

Physical system design is concerned with converting the logical system design into a form that can be processed by the computer economically and effectively. The process of physical system design includes: (1) selecting a data organization and processing scheme, (2) designing the physical data base, (3) incorporating controls to insure processing reliability, and (4) formatting or layout of input and output.

Actually logical and physical design are interactive rather than sequential as implied above. Logical design prescribes the processing and decision rules by which input is converted to output. The physical design process determines the necessary hardware/software configuration to implement the logical design. A feasibility analysis is then prepared for the target system. The company may not have the resources to implement the target system. Therefore the design team devises a plan for developing and implementing the system in stages, within the resource constraints of the organization. Savings from each stage underwrite the increased level of sophistication of the next stage.

The physical system design package also includes specifications for computer programming and file conversion and procedures for data control and computer processing.

Phase IV of the system development cycle deals with computer programming. The programmers convert the physical design into a machine-processable form. Use of the top-down-structured technique simplifies program development and testing. It also facilitates the inevitable changes that occur in an environment as dynamic as that of U.S. business.

This chapter covers design and programming, both of which are involved in converting a logical design into something capable of computer processing.

PHASE III: PHYSICAL DESIGN

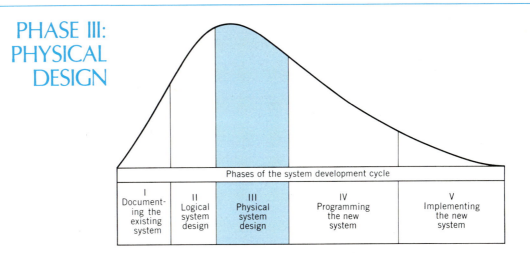

Phases of the system development cycle				
I Document- ing the existing system	II Logical system design	III Physical system design	IV Programming the new system	V Implementing the new system

The task of the system designer is to develop file layouts, file processing procedures, input and output formats, and a file conversion plan. Figure 18–1 shows the input and output of the physical design process. In the first half of this chapter we will concentrate on explaining what is done in the central function — the physical design process.

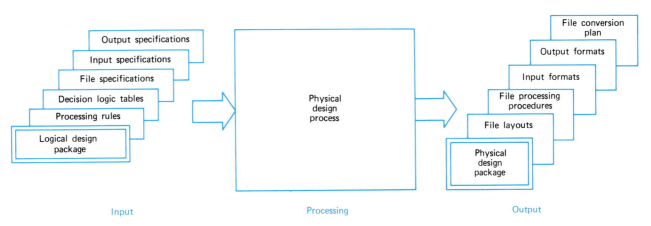

Input   Processing   Output

FIGURE 18–1

Information input to and output from the physical design activity.

DETERMINING THE LEVEL OF SOPHISTICATION

In developing a physical system design, the system designer has two principal options.

1. Optimizing the system *within* the constraints of the existing computer configuration.

2. Optimizing the system *without* considering the constraints of the existing computer configuration.

The firm may be considering its first computer or may be adding applications to a computer already installed. Or, it may be using a service bureau's computer or may be sharing a computer with another organization.

The logical design phase converted the "wish list" of the user into computer specifics. Yet, the company may not have the resources to accomplish all the desired improvements at one time.

Frequently a company will identify a target expenditure level for its computing activities. Management may feel uncomfortable in targeting a budget any higher than the average for its industry (e.g., a common guideline is a certain percent of gross sales, such as 2 percent in the manufacturing industry). A progressive management may discard guidelines and determine its expenditure by the return-on-investment (ROI) that is expected from its computer use. Even when the latter approach is used, the firm often implements its systems in stages—not only for economic reasons but because of organizational impact. People within the organization need to develop an understanding of the advantages of computer use. A revolutionary change in the organization's system may have detrimental rather than positive effects on employees. An effective interaction between workers and the computer depends partly on the employees' capacity for change and partly on how the computerized system is introduced. Research has shown that careful training and planning are necessary so that the system will meet the job satisfaction needs of individual employees. Designing a system to be implemented in stages reduces the impact on the individual.

Four levels of sophistication in system design will be considered.

Level 1.   Basic mechanization of subsystems.

Level 2.   Combining subsystems.

Level 3.   Utilizing management science techniques.

Level 4.   Integrating and optimizing systems.

Figure 18–2 provides a graphic illustration of developing a system in stages. In this example, one level of sophistication was achieved in each stage. In reality, several levels of sophistication might be designed into one stage. However, such an approach would lengthen the design process considerably or would require a large amount of resources. As mentioned above, the impact on the organization would be significant. However, the firm may be in a competitive situation that requires telescoping levels of sophistication. For example, an airline may find it necessary to combine all four levels of sophistication into one stage—in order to meet competition of other airlines that began computer use much earlier. However, there is a risk in telescoping levels of sophistication. When systems are implemented in stages, employees gain experience with each successive stage. They are able to contribute more to the design of each succeeding level of sophistication.

The level of sophistication of each design stage will depend on the firm's resources. Many months may elapse before the stream of benefits begins to emerge. If a firm has several design teams working on systems concurrently, the resource problem is greater.

QUESTION: The principal reason for designing and implementing systems in stages is to stay within the resource constraints of the firm, that is, hold costs down until

ANSWER: benefits of the installed systems provide funds for further sophistication of these systems.

Stages of System Development

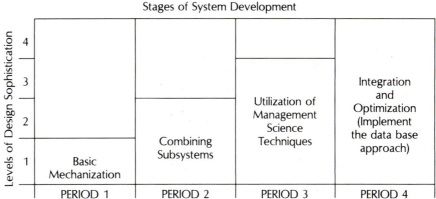

FIGURE 18-2
Designing four levels of sophistication in successive stages of development.

A plan for implementation is developed cooperatively by the design teams. The common objective is to move to the fourth level of sophistication for each of the major systems as soon as possible within the resource constraints of the organization. However, the priority of development is determined by the impact of the systems on the lifestream activities of the firm. You will probably understand the differences in levels of sophistication better after considering the following example.

LEVELS OF SOPHISTICATION IN RETAIL STORE OPERATION

LEVEL 1. BASIC MECHANIZATION   Tags are keypunched and attached to each item to be sold. When an item is sold, the tag is removed. All tags are batched and processed each night. The next day, reports are available for the manager to determine when additional inventory should be obtained. The sales summary system operates similarly. As an item is rung up on the cash register, the amount is punched into a paper tape. Tapes for all cash registers are batched and processed each night to enable the manager to know each day's sales.

LEVEL 2. COMBINING SUBSYSTEMS   The sales and inventory systems could be combined by entering the item number at the time the sale is made. Therefore, keypunching of tags is eliminated. The cash register must be modified to permit item numbers to be entered, since the item number often consists of alphabetic as well as numeric characters. Each night the reports are prepared from only one input instead of two, simplifying processing.

LEVEL 3. UTILIZING MANAGEMENT SCIENCE TECHNIQUES   With the data from each sales transaction, statistical analyses could be made. Instead of merely reporting amount of sales and inventory, the system could compute statistical trends on sales and inventory use. It could also make statistical projections of sales for future periods.

LEVEL 4. INTEGRATION AND OPTIMIZATION   The system could be redesigned to use point-of-sale devices with on-line capability. This system responds within seconds, enabling a credit check system to be combined with the other two systems. When a purchase is made, the record of the transaction is electronically input to the inventory, accounts receivable, and sales statistics systems. If the salesperson enters an employee number with each transaction, the sales commission system is also updated with the same transaction. This approach results in a common data base of information for all major systems.

Typically a firm cannot afford to produce the fourth level of sophistication in the first system design. Figure 18–3 illustrates a firm that has the resource limitation of developing only two major systems concurrently. During the first 18 months of the CBMIS implementation schedule, level 1 of sophistication is implemented for each of six major systems. Thereafter, the benefits derived from these systems justify design of level 2, which is accomplished for three systems simultaneously (in year 2, the sales, inventory, and accounts receivable systems are combined).

The third level of sophistication would be achieved in year 2 if management science techniques were incorporated into the design (an inventory model, for example).

Systems	Year 1	Year 2	Year 3
Sales Processing	I	II	
Inventory	I	II	
Accounts Receivable	I	II	
Payroll	I		II
Accounts Payable		I	II
General Ledger		I	II

FIGURE 18–3
Implementing systems in levels consistent with the firm's resource limitations.

QUESTION: Observe Figure 18–3. Level 1 for all six systems is implemented over an

18-month period to keep design costs consistent with the firm's _____.

ANSWER: constraints.

DATA BASE DESIGN

A data base is a repository of data so structured that appropriate applications access and update it but do not constrain its design or contents. While it is not necessary that all data be on the same physical device, it is essential that all data items are logically related. Otherwise, the system is file oriented rather than data base oriented.

Special software, referred to as a **data base management system** (DBMS), allows the data base to be independent of application programs. If programs are revised, the data base is unaffected (unless new data are required by the application program). Conversely, if the data base is restructured, application programs are unaffected. For the first time there is true separation of logical and physical design.

DESIGNING A DATA BASE

The three fundamental data base structures are hierarchical, network, and relational. They are explained in detail in Chapter 9. The procedure by which records are accessed is also explained in that chapter. An understanding of the distinction between program logic and data handling was necessary before the reader began the programming portion of the book. Therefore, the detailed explanation of data and data manipulation was covered at that point in the book. If you have difficulty answering the questions on the following exercise, a review of Chapter 9 would be appropriate.

EXERCISE 18-1   1. What is a data aggregate, or group item? _____

_____

2. What are the elements on the data hierarchy? (Hint: see Figure 9-1.)

a. _____

b. _____

c. _____

d. _____

e. _____

f. _____

3. Distinguish the three data base structures.

a. Hierarchical: _____

_____

b. Network: _____

_____

c. Relational: _____

_____

4. The above structures refer to logical structures. Data are organized into physical files according to the following structures (explain each).

a. Sequential organization: _____

_____

_____

b. Direct organization: _____

_____

_____

c. Index sequential organization: _____

_____

5. The three file organizations in question 4 are the ones most commonly used. However, with the advent of data bases, additional techniques were developed to provide linkages between records. Explain each.

a. List organization: _____

_____

_____

b. Inverted organization: _____

_____

_____

DATA BASE VERSUS TRADITIONAL APPROACH

Must a company have several years experience in computer use before it implements the data base approach? The answer is no. However, start-up costs are higher for a firm that begins its computer use with the data base approach. In the long run, costs are less if the data base approach is adopted from the beginning. If a company carefully plans and budgets its computer activities, it can successfully move into the data base era with its first computer installation.

Let's compare the data base approach with the traditional, file-oriented approach. The file-oriented approach was a natural extension of the manual system. Each department had its own set of files — typically copies of documents stored in five-drawer file cabinets. A second type of file was a ledger, where transactions were recorded. Sometimes, ledger cards were used instead of a ledger. For example, the old inventory systems kept track of the supply of a given part or item by posting withdrawals and additions to inventory on a ledger card for each item. An example of use of another type of file, the five-drawer version, was the purchasing system. Copies of purchase orders were filed by vendor or by part number. The file was accessed when a request for status was received. Pieces of paper were added to the file when (1) stock was withdrawn from the warehouse for use in production, or (2) stock was received from the dock.

Until recently computer systems were patterned after the old manual system. Each transaction was punched into a card and was used to update a magnetic tape file. Reports on stock status were produced by processing and printing data from the magnetic tape.

Computer processing permitted the file to be updated more quickly and a wide variety of reports to be prepared. For example, managers would get reports sorted by item number or dollar value of the item, by vendor or by product type. To have such a variety of reports under a manual file approach would require a great deal of time and effort.

Unfortunately, as each new computer application was developed, a new computer file resulted. Data were often the same or very similar to those on another file. The resulting redundancy was similar to that of the old manual systems (e.g., copies of the purchase order might be in six departments). After several years the cost of such redundancy was significant. Also, reports were inconsistent. The inventory file might be updated daily while the purchase-order file was updated twice a week. "Amount on inventory" shown on the inventory file reflected daily usage. The same item in the purchasing file reflected usage several days previous — at the time of the last processing of that file.

QUESTION: Redundancy was the major **cost** inefficiency of file-oriented systems. The major

use inefficiency resulted from files' being updated _____ , making reports inconsistent.

ANSWER: at different times.

EXAMPLE OF THE DATA BASE APPROACH

To better understand the data base approach, we need to distinguish logical from physical records. In the magnetic tape era many logical records were combined into one physical record. Record "gaps" enabled a computer to distinguish one record from another. The interrecord gap was lengthy, compared to one logical record — therefore space consuming and time consuming to detect. Combining several logical records cut processing time. The records were separated when needed by an application, then recombined when they were written on magnetic tape.

Present technology permits true separation of logical and physical records, to make processing more efficient.

Figure 18–4 illustrates the difference between logical and physical data bases. The analysts responsible for the company's personnel system work with users to identify the reports needed for proper management of the personnel resource. The analysts also determine the data necessary to produce these reports.

FIGURE 18–4

In the data base approach, the logical structure is independent of the physical structure. Software enables the physical records to be combined to meet the logical requirements. The employee number is the key to linking these records in each data base.

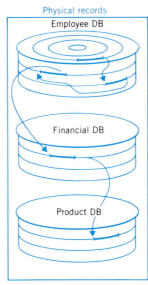

The data base design team earlier had organized the company's data into four major data bases: (1) employee data base, (2) financial data bases, (3) product data base, and (4) customer data base. The first three data bases contain information about employees, as shown on the left side of Figure 18–4.

Assume that one of the planned reports will provide information on employee performance, for the employees reporting to each first-line supervisor. One element reported is labor cost per unit produced. The data necessary to produce this report are identified on the left, the logical records. The files involved in producing the report are shown on the right, the physical records.

QUESTION: Examine Figure 18–4. In which data base would the data for the following employee-related logical records be found?
a. Number of dependents

b. Machines the person is qualified to operate

ANSWER: (a) Financial data base (payroll record)
(b) Employee record (experience)

It is not economical to reserve large spaces at the end of each physical record for data to be added to a file (e.g., an employee's completing a training course or receiving a bachelor's degree). When data are added, the software (DBMS) provides a pointer to the new record. In the example, the three data fields on the employee record are linked (chained) by pointers. To simplify the diagram only one file location is shown for the payroll record (financial data base) and for the productivity record (product data base). The software takes care of the linkages necessary to pull the data together for the employee performance report. The key that ties these records together is the employee number, the only data item repeated in each record. In a file-oriented approach, however, another programmer who needed the data for another application would restructure the data and create a new file. It is easy to see that, after several years, massive duplication would exist.

Using a data base approach, each programmer may have his/her own logical data structure without affecting the way the data is actually (physically) stored. **Logical structure,** therefore, refers to the way the analysts and programmers view the data. The way the data is stored on tapes, disks, or other media is the **physical structure.**

QUESTION: The purpose of a DBMS is _____

ANSWER: to store and retrieve data in the data base

ADVANTAGES OF IMPLEMENTING THE DATA BASE CONCEPT

Designing and implementing a data base has a number of advantages over using independently processed systems.

1. Reduction of input cost through sharing of data.
2. Elimination of duplicate records.

3. Common definition of a data element among all systems.

4. Reduction in computer processing time.

5. Validation of data because they are entered once and shared thereafter.

6. Reduction in sorting of records because of fewer duplicates.

7. Reduction in the number of computer programs to be written since data will be retrieved using a standard procedure.

EXERCISE 18-2 Look at the seven advantages of the data base. Which produce savings in computer cost and which in labor cost?

1. Computer cost reduction: _____

_____

2. Labor cost reduction: _____

_____

PROVIDING FOR DATA COMMUNICATIONS An added complexity in the physical system design process for many present-day systems is the data communication specification. A background on data communication is provided in Chapter 8. The system designer usually calls on a specialist to assist in designing the data communications portion of the system. One or more specialists are employed full time in large companies; however, the small firm usually relies on outside expertise. The telephone company, or other organizations that provide communications, will also provide consulting aid in designing the communications portion of the system.

The key part played by the system designer is specifying data communications requirements for the system.

DESIGNING DATA COMMUNICATIONS Although detailed information is provided in Chapter 8, the important aspect to remember here is that such systems are rarely justified for one application alone. Design teams of the various major systems cooperatively determine the level of sophistication required to offset the cost of communication. For example, the system may only provide transmission of input data from remote locations. Or, it may be designed for two-way transmission with interactive capability. The selection of facilities is based on the factors listed below.

SELECTION OF FACILITIES   The class of facilities selected by a particular user depends on the volume of messages to be transmitted and their priority or urgency. A cost/benefit analysis is required to select an optimum configuration of terminals and lines. The American Telephone and Telegraph Company suggests the following criteria be used in planning a telecommunications system.

1. *Function.* The type of information to be transmitted and the operations to be performed.

2. *Distribution.* The number of locations involved in the transmission and receipt of information.

3. *Volume.* The total amount of information that must be transmitted over a given period of time.

4. *Urgency.* The speed with which messages must be delivered.

5. *Language.* The form in which data are received and the code in which data are transmitted.

6. *Accuracy.* The greater accuracy achieved using error detection and correction techniques; however, such systems are more costly.

7. *Cost.* Total systems costs of hardware, software, and personnel.

QUESTION: Which criterion would be least important in designing a time-sharing system for

college student use? _____

Why? _____

ANSWER: Urgency. Although the student prefers immediate response, fast response would be more crucial for a system like an airline reservation system.

DISTRIBUTED SYSTEMS

With the significant reduction in the cost of terminals, plus the slow-but-sure reduction in the cost of data communications, distributed systems are becoming advantageous. Any or all of the following functions can be distributed: (1) input, (2) output, (3) processing, and (4) data bases.

Although one of these functions may be distributed to a remote site, it is still on-line to the central computer.

DISTRIBUTED INPUT

According to a recent survey, data entry accounts for 10 to 25 percent of the DP department budget. A survey report (by Frost and Sullivan of New York City) shows that keypunches still predominate, with 230,000 installed in the United States alone. However, the extinction of the 96-column keypunch is certain, and a similar fate awaits the 80-column keypunch.

The new emphasis in data entry is placement of entry devices at the source of the data. As an example, accounting personnel would enter data directly through on-line terminals in their department, into accounting applications processed at the central computer. This approach has three advantages.

1. Entry personnel know more about the area of application and can recognize errors more readily.

2. This plan eliminates preparation of special input documents to send to a central key-entry area.

3. The computer can be programmed to look for typical errors in key-entry so they can be corrected on the spot, such as transposing numbers and letters in a street address.

Even though labor costs are rising, input costs are being reduced by simplifying input procedures. For example, the distributed input system of St. Francis Hospital (Blue Island, Illinois) recognizes the fact that most health-care professionals do not type. Almost all communications, orders, and other information are entered into the system simply by the user's touching one of the 20 metal "selection contacts" in a vertical row on the terminal display screen. The user calls up a series of information displays he or she needs by touching the appropriate contact as each display appears. Then, when an order is complete, the user displays it in full on the screen and scans it for accuracy before touching the contact opposite "enter order."

The 394-bed hospital has 60 special video display terminals linked to dual Sperry Univac V77-400 minicomputers. The terminals communicate with the minicomputers in "real time" and they, in turn, communicate periodically each day and evening with a Sperry Univac 1100/11 maxicomputer in the data center.

The terminals are located at nursing stations, emergency room, operating rooms, admitting office, lab, pharmacy, central supply, and so forth.

"Through increased productivity, most of which can be attributed to the computer/communications system, we have eliminated at least one payroll hour per patient day, at $6 per hour," explained Robert R. Renken, associate executive director at St. Francis' Health Center. Last year, for example, St. Francis' had 186,621 patient days, which works out to a saving of $1,119,726.

QUESTION: Two of the three advantages of distributing input deal with improving

_____

ANSWER: accuracy (reducing errors)

DISTRIBUTED DATA BASES

The move to decentralized data bases is even more recent. Previously, the hardware and software cost of processing an item in the data base was less on large-scale equipment. Also, data base management, until recently, required a rather sophisticated hardware/software system. Minicomputers are now powerful enough to handle these functions—and at a cost per transaction no greater than that of large-scale computers.

However, many items of data are useful only to the local organization. It makes more sense to localize the data base and to send forward only those data that are needed by other organizations.

A good example of how data is distributed is provided by the U.S. airlines. One system common to all airlines is the reservation system; a centralized data base is shared among all airlines. However, other systems are peculiar to each airline. For example, each company has its own cost accounting and financial reporting system. That information would reside in the local company data base.

Another example, Ford Motor Company, has both centralized computers and minicomputers, tied into a network. Each region has its own warehouse and minicomputer. One minicomputer application is high-bay warehousing, in which the mini controls the loading of materials into bins located from floor level to bins 30 to 50 feet in height. Data on inventory levels are transmitted back to a central computer. Data concerning storage location are maintained solely in the local minicomputer data base.

In the Ford example, the distributed data peculiar to the local organization are the bin locations. Other local data are employee (payroll) records and cost accounting records for local management reports.

QUESTION: The principal advantage of distributing a data base is _____

ANSWER: keeping locally the data needed by those employees and forwarding only that needed by others

DISTRIBUTED PROCESSING

Until recently, processing was centralized — for economical reasons. The cost per computation was much less on a large-scale computer. Technological breakthroughs have made processing on micros and minis just as economical. Data can be processed locally, with only that needed by other organizations sent forward.

Travelers Insurance Company is an example of a company that distributes computer processing to remote locations. The Travelers claims processing system is implemented nationwide. Installed in 200 claims offices, computers process 40,000 claims and 75,000 checks per day. A total of 200 minicomputers (IBM 3790 Communication Systems/8100 Information Systems) and three maxicomputers (IBM 3033 processors) support the effort.

Distributed processing improves the capabilities of Travelers' field offices and 20,000 field people by providing them with a more effective communications system for claims processing, rating, policy issuance, preparation of quotations for producers, and administrative office functions. "Installation of intelligent devices in field offices also enables users to tailor business applications to the peculiar needs of the state, region, office, customer or producer served," says Mr. Joseph T. Brophy, vice-president of data processing. "A one-second delay in average computer response time costs us $1 million a year in productivity. By distributing computing power to the field offices, we improve response time, and achieve higher availability and better timeliness, which support higher operator productivity." Travelers has 4500 terminal devices in remote locations.

The Travelers claims processing system "prompts" the claim processor in a conversational (interactive) manner to enter required data. The system edits data as necessary and displays the results of processing. It automatically assigns claim numbers, verifies coverage, and issues claim payments or installments on such lines as group health, life, pensions, disability, dental, automobile, homeowners, and workers compensation. Where appropriate, it performs benefit calculations using the master schedule for benefits and maintains claim data for subsequent retrieval, update, and inquiry.

In this example of distributed processing, the minicomputers (IBM 8100s) perform local processing yet are tied to the corporate computers (IBM 3033s). Information needed for corporate management, such as statistics on sales, number of claims processed, and so on, is forwarded through the network to the corporate system. Likewise, information needed locally is sent back from the corporate system (e.g., price changes).

QUESTION: Distributed processing permitted Travelers to improve _____, saving $1 million per year.

ANSWER: response time

DISTRIBUTED OUTPUT

By locating printers or output terminals near the ultimate user, one can access information more readily. The other advantage is reduction in the amount of printed reports. People can search a computer file for a specific item and have the results displayed on video output.

An example is the United Missouri Bank in Kansas City. "Traditionally, a bank gets some 80 percent of its balance inquiry calls from the 20 percent of its customers with the lowest deposits — those most concerned about being overdrawn," says Dan S. Spencer, Jr., executive vice-president of operations. "Consequently, a reliable on-line network which allows the customer to inquire about his own balance is a real factor in the quality of service we offer and allows more personal attention to our customers who provide the most profitable relationships."

Another form of distributed output is the **electronic mail system.** As the cost of postage and the delay in mail increase, electronic mail systems are becoming economical. Most of these systems use computers and, therefore, can be considered as distributed systems.

There are four major groups into which the various alternate electronic mail systems, services, and products can be classified: (1) facsimile, (2) computer-based message systems, (3) communicating word processors, and (4) hybrid systems. On the horizon is verbal electronic mail, but it is a computer-based system that fits into the message system category.

1. **Facsimile,** or fax, is the most widely used type of electronic mail. One version, the Rapifax System 50 is programmable; transmits a page in 35 seconds; can automatically dial up to 50 telephone numbers stored in memory and can transmit to each one or to as many as required and programmed in advance by the user; can transmit documents to satellite units; and can poll a single terminal or groups of satellite terminals to receive documents from them.

2. The second major form of electronic mail is the **computer-based message system** (CBMS). A CBMS is a computer network, either self-contained or part of another communications network, that uses a computer and special software for store-and-forward message handling. Users have CRT terminals, some with hardcopy output. The software is written specifically for message handling, using familiar English words as commands, and a typical "office memo" format on the CRT screen. Such a system holds messages and "mail" in a sender's electronic mailbox or specific area within the computer and sends mail on command to the recipient's mailbox or to multiple mailboxes if carbon copies are needed, or if more than a single other user is a recipient.

   In a study done by Citibank in New York City, it was estimated that a $10 million CBMS servicing 4000 executives resulted in a cost avoidance of $15 million. The basis for the savings is a 28 percent increase in the "span of control" for those executives.

3. **Communicating word processors** (CWPs) offer several distinct advantages over facsimile machines for low-cost electronic mail: they have superior transmission speed, such as full page sent in six to eight seconds versus 35 seconds on fax; they produce far superior output or print quality; they eliminate the need to create a hard copy (the text can be sent as it appears on a CRT screen); cost of communications option on a word processing unit is less than the cost of a fax machine; and a CWP can communicate with other terminals or computers, while fax can only talk to fax.

4. The fourth major group of electronic mail devices can be called **hybrid,** the group of all those that do not fit into the three previous categories. In this category are TWX/Telex service provided by Western Union (WU); the Mailgram service also provided by TDX Telecommunications from its Chicago office; and the ECOM (electronic com-

puter-originated mail) system, a joint project by the U.S. Postal Service and Western Union.

Mailgram allows various methods of input, including telephoning a CRT operator who types and sends the message. ECOM provides high-volume users with two-day delivery of messages, partly via electronic transmission using Western Union's store-and-forward computerized message switching centers, which route the messages to the post offices for delivery.

QUESTION: Distributed output takes many forms. Two principal reasons exist for distributing output:

a. _____

b. _____

ANSWER: (a) speeding output to the ultimate user
(b) reducing the number of printed reports

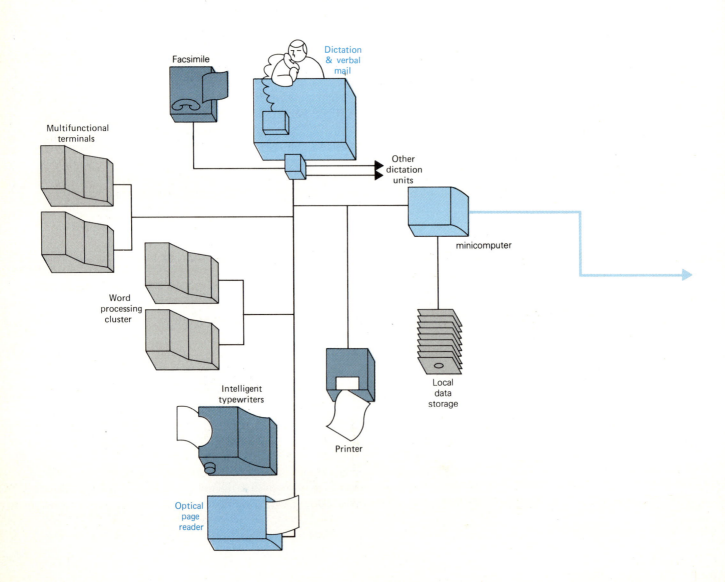

Figure 18–5 illustrates how all the information functions of a firm are being linked through a distributed system network. The figure identifies two units that have not been discussed: intelligent typewriters/terminals and word processing clusters. An **intelligent terminal** or typewriter is capable of performing calculations and processing data. A nonintelligent unit is capable only of entering data or producing output. **Word processing** is the preparation and dissemination of letters, memoranda, reports, and articles. Rather than performing calculations, word processing concentrates on text units — words, sentences, paragraphs, and finally, documents.

It is inappropriate at this time to go into the details of the communication network. A number of concepts need to be covered before networking can be thoroughly understood. Chapter 8 provides that material.

QUESTION: The distributed network in Figure 18–5 contains examples of all four distributed functions. Identify one example in each category.

FIGURE 18–5
Example of a distributed system network, linking all the information functions of an organization.

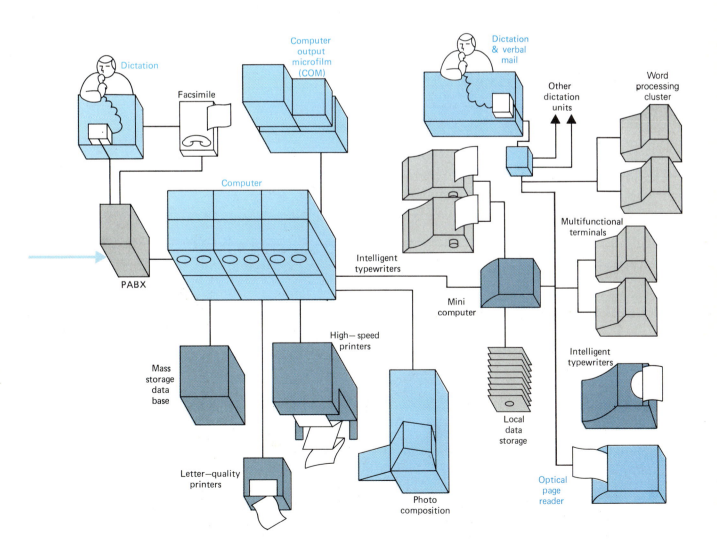

  a. Input: _____

  b. Processing: _____

  c. Data base: _____

  d. Output: _____

ANSWER: (a) Input: dictation, terminal, typewriter, optical page reader, facsimile, photo composition
         (b) Processing: word processing cluster, intelligent terminals
         (c) Data base: local data storage
         (d) Output: high-speed printer, terminal, typewriter, facsimile, letter-quality printer

---

EXERCISE 18–3 1. Any of the following computing functions can be distributed:

  (a) _____ , (b) _____ , (c) _____ ,

  (d) _____ _____ .

2. Distributing input has the following advantages.

  (a) _____

  (b) _____

  (c) _____

3. The principal advantage of distributing the processing function is to _____
  _____ .

4. Distributing a data base and distributing the processing of that data base have one benefit in common. What is it? _____
  _____ .

5. Electronic mail is considered as a category of distributed output because
  _____ .

6. Technically, facsimile could be considered as a form of word processing. Why? _____ .

7. The term "intelligent" is applied to a device when it is capable of _____
  _____ .

DESIGNING INPUT

With the reduction in the cost of terminals and data communication, on-line entry is replacing the keypunch machine. Not only does this approach speed up input, it improves accuracy. Logical edits can be performed by the computer system, to catch irregularities at the point of entry. For example, assume the figure 80 was key-entered for the amount of hours worked for last week. The system could flag this apparent discrepancy to the attention of the operator, indicating that the amount was unusually high. The operator then could change it, if a wrong key had been hit in entering the data.

With the advent of on-line data entry, the location of the data entry function is being shifted, from the computer department to the user department. This approach has two principal advantages.

1. The responsibility for accurate input rests with the organization most concerned with the data (e.g., the payroll department inputting labor data).
2. Personnel are more knowledgeable about the application and can detect and correct irregularities in data.

Figure 18-6 illustrates on-line data entry approach. The screen (CRT) at top illustrates a **menu.** This is a listing of transaction types from which the appropriate type is selected. The second screen illustrates the data entry format produced by selecting transaction type 1, "ENTER EDIT/JOURNAL TRANSACTIONS." The operator now enters the data in the appropriate columns. The entries are shown in color.

QUESTION: In designing input for on-line entry, the system designer prepares a set of input

formats, referred to as a —————.

ANSWER: menu

DESIGNING FILE LAYOUTS/ PROCESSING

Not all computer applications are data base oriented. For example, a department may acquire its own mini or microcomputer for which a DBMS is not available. For applications of this type, **file layouts** would be prepared for the physical device being used. The file layout would specify all the record types associated with that application.

An appropriate file processing technique would then be selected: sequential, direct, or index sequential. The HIPO diagrams and decision tables developed in the logical design phase would provide the **processing procedure.**

In addition a **file conversion** plan would be developed, for converting existing files to the format needed for the new application. Conversion of files that are already in some machine-processable medium (cards, tape, etc.) is quite easy compared to the time and cost to convert a manual file. A special computer program is often required when several computer-media files are being merged.

QUESTION: What is the counterpart of the file layout for a data base-oriented system?

ANSWER: Layout of records in the data base.

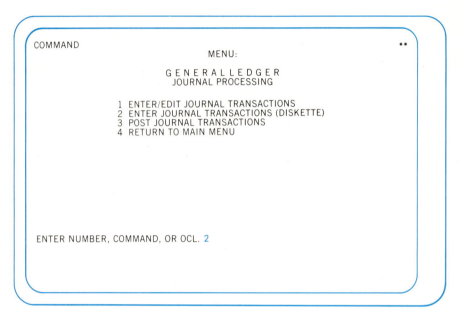

FIGURE 18–6
On-line input. The first screen provides a "menu" of transaction categories. When one is selected the screen displays a format for entering data. Data entered is shown in color (or boldface), to identify data from a screen format.

DESIGNING OUTPUT

With the variety of output media available today, the task of preparing output formats has increased in scope. For example, a bank may provide audio output in response to a customer's inquiry entered through a touchtone telephone device in the lobby of the bank or at another location. Many brokers' offices have visual output devices in customer lounges and at the brokers' desks. Microfiche output is becoming much less expensive. Even the granddaddy of output, the printed report, has a variety of forms: from simple printing on blank stock to elaborate reports on preprinted forms. Examples of the various output media are provided in Chapter 6.

The physical system design includes output formats for each of the media utilized. Figure 18-7 shows the designer's output layout for a report to be printed on standard output paper.

```
    0        1        2        3        4        5        6        7        8        9        10       11       12

                                          LOOART  PRESS  INC.
          OPEN ITEM SUMMARY               RETAIL  ACCOUNTS  RECEIVABLE
                                          AUGUST  30,  1981

          ACCOUNT      CUSTOMER NAME       ADDRESS                      **** INVOICE ****        TOTAL
          NUMBER                           CITY/STATE                   DATE    NUMBER   AMOUNT   AMOUNT

          981052495  WASHINGTON BOOKSTORE INC.   4315 UNIVERSITY WAY N E   12/01/80  XX99999  999.99   999.99
                                                 SEATTLE, WASH

          981252133  NORTHGATE CARD SHOP         527 NORTHGATE MALL        01/16/80  W 27321   46.50
                                                 SEATTLE, WASH            05/17/80  W 63777   35.62    82.12

          984990414  PIONEER PRINTING            10111 D GRAVELLY LANE DRIVE  05/01/80  P 36272  40.15
                                                 TACOMA, WASH             05/10/80  W 64716   46.26
                                                                         06/15/80  W 68269   35.61
                                                                         08/21/80  W 70707   34.21   156.23
```

FIGURE 18-7

Example of format specification for computer printout where printing is on plain output paper.

As terminals become more cost-effective, the system designer is spending an increasing amount of time in designing CRT screen formats for output.

Similar to input, a menu is designed for each output type. The user keys-in the type of report desired, as shown in Figure 18-8. The menu for General Ledger (G.L.) reports is shown here. However, the report shown to illustrate CRT output is the Aged Open Payables (A.O.P.) Inquiry. The variety of reports from the G.L. system is larger than that of the Accounts Payable system and we wanted to illustrate a large menu selection. However, the A.O.P. report illustrates a system design feature that we wanted to stress—management by exception. Rather than produce a lengthy printed report on all accounts, the on-line system permits inquiries on specific accounts to be processed. A similar format would be used for the Accounts Receivable (A.R.) system. Assume that a customer habitually owed large amounts. The A.R. manager asks for a status on that customer to determine if further action is necessary. Also, the A.R. manager may be preparing a follow-up letter, "strongly" urging the customer to settle the account. Before the letter is typed, the data base is accessed via the CRT to make sure a payment hasn't been received.

The move to on-line, data base environment has generated more demand for inquiries and reports of this type. The system designer will be devoting more time to design of CRT output than output provided on printers.

EXERCISE 18-4   1.   The system designer determines both the type of output device and the
_____ of the output.

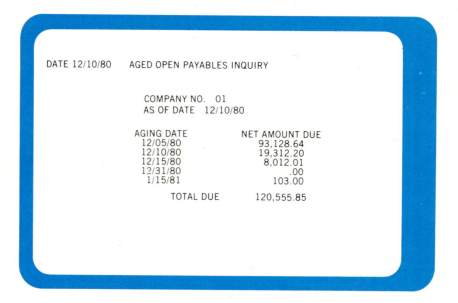

```
COMMAND                                                    **
                        MENU: AMGM20

                     G E N E R A L L E D G E R
                        DEMAND REPORTS

               1 FINANCIAL WORKSHEET
               2 AGED OPEN PAYABLES
               3 DETAIL AUDIT GENERAL LEDGER
               4 SUMMARY AUDIT GENERAL LEDGER
               5 PRELIMINARY GENERAL LEDGER
               6 COMPARATIVE GENERAL LEDGER
               7 INCOME STATEMENT
               8 FISCAL PERIOD CLOSE STATEMENTS
               9 RETURN TO MAIN MENU




ENTER NUMBER, COMMAND, OR OCL. 2


                                              <- READY
```

```
DATE 12/10/80     AGED OPEN PAYABLES INQUIRY


                      COMPANY NO.  01
                      AS OF DATE  12/10/80

                  AGING DATE          NET AMOUNT DUE
                  12/05/80               93,128.64
                  12/10/80               19,312.20
                  12/15/80                8,012.01
                  12/31/80                     .00
                   1/15/81                  103.00

                      TOTAL DUE         120,555.85
```

FIGURE 18-8

On-line output. The first screen provides a "menu" of report types and the second screen displays one report type.

2. Output formats are prepared to facilitate the next phase in the system development process, that of _____.

3. Although this section did not state it precisely, would you expect that the same kind of output format would be used for printed output and for a

CRT-oriented system? _____ What differences would there be?

_____

_____

DESIGNING CONTROLS FOR I/O AND PROCESSING

The last part of the system design task is to develop controls to insure that the system accomplishes what it is designed to do. Controls are designed to insure:

1. Validity and completeness of data entry.
2. Proper data flow.
3. Reliability of computer processing.

CONTROLS ON DATA ENTRY

Computerized systems must have completeness of input. For example, if a transaction on withdrawal of inventory is not entered into the system, the inventory is no longer accurate. Or, if a bank deposit slip is misplaced, the customer's balance is incorrect. User procedures establish controls to insure that all transactions are routed to the appropriate person for the data entry operation.

The input procedure also provides checks and balances to insure that all transactions enter the system. Numbering forms is one approach. Another is consolidating documents into groups or batches. At each handling station, the batch total is compared to the number of documents to insure that no documents have been lost.

Using the new disk-oriented or tape-oriented data entry systems, we couple multiple data entry devices to a minicomputer. Editing of data is programmed into the minicomputer so the data can be checked for logical errors as well as keying errors. Previously, editing was accomplished in the main computer, requiring recycling through the manual operations to correct the detected errors. Now, a great deal of editing is completed in the key-entry system. For example, the common key-entry error of transposition can be logically edited if the part numbering system is designed for certain positions to be only alphabetic or numeric. Tables can be referenced, such as zip code tables, to compare a zip code against city and state to insure its validity. The system flags errors to the key-entry operator for immediate correction.

A similar editing function is designed for systems where data are entered directly into the system by a user. Detection of errors occurs and is signaled back to the CRT at the entry terminal so correction can be made immediately. It is the system designer's task to determine which entry approach is feasible and to design control procedures.

CONTROLS ON DATA FLOW

With the large volume of data flowing into and out of the computer organization, a data control function is usually established. The system designer incorporates two kinds of controls in this operation.

1. Schedule control.
2. Completeness of input and validity of output.

Schedule control consists of monitoring flow of input to make sure it is entered on time to the proper processing run. It also insures that output is distributed on time to the various users.

Insuring completeness of input requires procedures for handling input. Just as input may be batched prior to the preparation of data transmittals, the transmittals must be controlled to insure that all data are converted to machine-readable media. Numbering is the common control for data transmittals. When key-entry occurs directly from a form, such as a customer order form, counting into batches (for example, 25 or 50) is the common control, with dollar totals and/or hash totals also included in the batch control. The **dollar total** might be total sales dollars for orders, or total purchase commitment for purchase orders.

The **hash total** is a tally of items in certain fields, which has no value except as a control. When a bank processes deposit slips, the number of items per deposit slip might be totalled to compare with the number of checks associated with the deposit, as a double control that all input was included. That total has significance and thus is not a hash total. An example of a hash total would be the sum of all account numbers, which has no physical significance, hence the term "hash."

The data control function is also responsible for gathering the materials necessary to process the job: the cards, magnetic tapes or disk packs containing input, and the computer program. On completion of processing, the data control group refiles these materials. Therefore, media labeling and storage are included in the control procedures for this function.

The data control procedure specifies routing of printed output from the computer; therefore, this group is responsible for getting output to the specified persons on schedule.

The data control procedure also specifies checks on the validity of output. For example a computer system malfunction may have been undetected during processing. A **reasonableness** check by data control personnel controls against such malfunctions. Such controls consist of two parts. The first is a random check of transactions (for example, is the total for randomly selected invoices correct for items ordered?) The second check is on control totals (for example, is the payroll total consistent with predetermined maximums?)

QUESTION: For input, data control operators check to insure _____.

For output the check is on _____.

ANSWER: completeness, validity

CONTROLS ON COMPUTER PROCESSING

Although controls will be designed into the output analysis function, the desirable place to catch processing errors is as close as possible to the point where they occur. Therefore, the system designer builds checkpoints into the processing cycle. One approach is to interrupt processing to print control totals on the console typewriter. The operator compares these totals to predetermined ranges for reasonableness before proceeding with the processing. For example, the total payroll might be compared to a predetermined amount to insure processing validity before payroll checks are printed. However, this interruption approach is no longer used. It is costly and time-consuming to halt processing for an operator action. The check is built into the logic of the application. That way, processing proceeds without interruption unless the check is negative. A negative result **aborts** the job; that is, the job is discontinued. The computer continues to process other jobs while the data control group determines the cause of the problem. The system designer and programmer determine **checkpoints** for the system to evaluate progress toward completing a job. Rather than finding at the end of the job that several hours of processing were wasted, users rely on checkpoints that are provided throughout processing.

QUESTION: It is costly to interrupt processing to print out messages to be interpreted by

operators. The system logic specifies interruption only when the _____ check is negative.

ANSWER: reasonableness

TOP-DOWN PROGRAM DEVELOPMENT

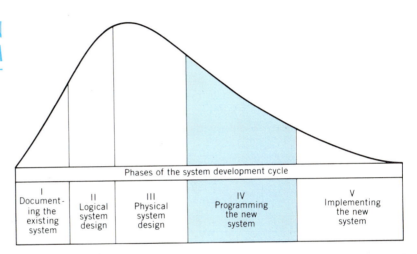

Phases of the system development cycle				
I Document- ing the existing system	II Logical system design	III Physical system design	IV Programming the new system	V Implementing the new system

With the information prepared in the physical design phase, programming can begin. Traditional program development consists of a **bottom-up** procedure where the lowest-level units were programmed, tested, and combined with other modules for the system test. If the test failed, it was difficult to determine which unit (or units) caused the problem. Each programmer determined his/her own definitions, structure, and sequence. Inconsistency between units resulted, in terms of quality and degree of detail. To reduce problems of this type, the programming sequence has been reversed. A **top-down programming** approach is used. A structure chart is prepared, similar to the HIPO structure chart, where the top module is first identified. Then the system is partitioned into lower levels of detail, as shown in Figure 18–9. Programming begins with the top module and proceeds down the hierarchy. The modules at each level are designed, coded, and tested before the next lower level is accomplished. This approach assures that each module is completely debugged before it is consolidated with other modules. Since some modules use data generated by — or pass control to or from — lower-level modules, dummy modules are created for testing purposes. The dummy modules do not normally perform meaningful computations but produce messages during testing to indicate that a specific function has been executed. In other words, the high-level modules can be tested by simulating the work of lower-level modules.

The main advantages of top-down structure are:

1. Programming begins sooner, overlapping the program design of subsequent modules. High-level functions are coded and tested before detailed specifications are developed for lower-level functions.

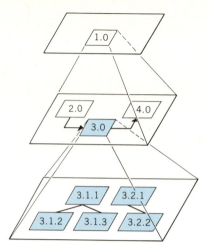

FIGURE 18–9
Partitioning program modules in a top-down sequence.

2. Testing is improved, because each time a new module, or small group of modules, is added to the system an integration test is run.

3. Computer test time is distributed more evenly and is more accurately predicted. Since coding and testing is occurring for upper-level modules while program design is underway for lower-level modules, computer use in debugging is leveled throughout the development process. In the traditional approach huge blocks of computer time were required when the system tests were performed.

QUESTION: Use of the top-down structure reduces the time span for program development and testing over the bottom-up approach because the objectives of the project are clear and

a. _____

b. _____

ANSWER: (a) programming begins sooner, overlapping program design of subsequent modules.
(b) high-level functions are coded and tested before further programming.

STRUCTURED PROGRAMMING An integral part of the top-down methodology is the structured programming (S.P.) technique. Modules are structured to simplify coding and to expedite testing. One rule of S.P. is that each module should have only one entry point and one exit point. This rule simplifies flow of control; modules are partitioned so that control flows from the top down to lower-level modules. A second rule is that each module should perform only one principal function. Examples are, as shown in Level 2 of Figure 18–10: the coding of transactions, updating of master records, and printing of results. A third rule is a limit on the number of program instructions per module. Many organizations select one page of program code, or 50 lines. This practice keeps the module small and easy to debug. A fourth rule provides for indentation of code, so all of the instructions within one block of logic were easily identified.

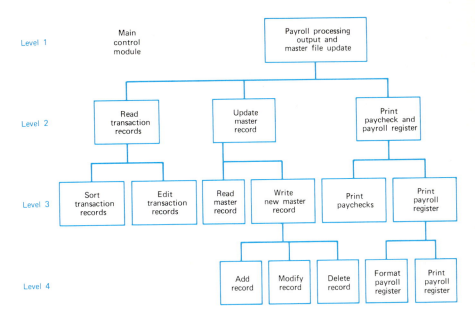

FIGURE 18–10
Top-down structure chart for program design and coding.

Other rules, dealing with the constructs in structured programming, were explained in Chapter 11.

The benefits of the top-down program design/structured programming methodology are as follows.

1. The cost per debugged instruction has decreased, because programming is simplified and errors are more easily detected. With the accelerating cost of labor and the increasing scope of systems, such an improvement is imperative to keep pace with demand for computer services.

2. Program modification is facilitated, because programs are less complex and are written using a uniform procedure. Many organizations spend more than 50 percent of the annual budget on modifying existing systems. Simplifying the modification of programs permits more of scarce programming resources to be applied to new systems.

QUESTION: Standardization of programming procedures is one of the major objectives in

---

ANSWER: structured programming

OUTPUT OF THE PROGRAMMING FUNCTION Figure 18–11 shows the output of the programming function: top-down structure charts, debugged code (the computer program), the program documentation. Program documentation consists of flowcharts, HIPO diagrams, decision tables and, when additional explanation is required, narrative description. Some organizations have discontinued the use of flowcharts and narrative description by including lines of explanation within each program module. These lines are given a special symbol that causes the compiler to ignore them as commands and merely repeat them when the list of programming instructions is printed.

Therefore, another programmer can more easily understand the purpose of each block of logic when it is necessary to modify the program.

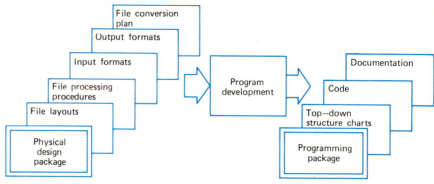

FIGURE 18-11

Inputs and outputs for program development activity.

The whole purpose of program documentation is to facilitate system testing and subsequent modification. Since organizations change procedures frequently and users often change their minds on program output, modification is a "way of life" in almost all organizations. Without adequate documentation, changes are costly and time consuming.

QUESTION: The three principal ingredients of the program package are top-down structure charts, code, and documentation. Documentation consists of:

a. —————, —————, —————;

b. when additional explanation is required, ————— —————.

ANSWER: (a) flowcharts, HIPO diagrams, decision tables
(b) narrative description

SUMMARY The two phases of the system development cycle directly associated with the computer are physical system design and programming. The physical design phase converts the logical design into all the information required by the programming team. When the data base approach is used, the physical design activity concentrates on determining storage media organization and accessing methods. When the "individual application" approach is used, file layouts and file processing procedures are prepared.

In both cases, the remaining portion of the physical design package consists of: HIPO diagrams and decision tables, input formats, and output formats. An integral part of this activity is the design of controls to insure system reliability.

With the reduction in communication costs, most companies that are geographically dispersed are designing distributed information systems. In this case, the physical design includes specifications for a communications network.

During the physical design phase, the level of system sophistication is determined. Although the goal is complete integration and optimization of all systems (the fourth level of sophistication), the company may not have the resources to accomplish this goal in the near term. Typically a three-year plan is developed to enable the company to evolve its systems to the fourth level of sophistication.

Upon completion of physical design, phase IV begins. Top-down programming structure has replaced the traditional bottom-up approach. Modules are designed, coded, and tested, starting from the top of the structure. The approach enables programming to be "telescoped" — that is, reduced in span of time. Testing time is reduced and reliability improved because, each time a module is added, an integration test is run.

Use of the structured programming methodology also expedites phase IV. The resulting standardization of programming practices removes it from the realm of a "black art." Instead of being personal creations, unintelligible to all but the developer, programs that are structured have standard features that facilitate testing and integration with other programs. Standardization also simplifies the inevitable modification of programs.

The next phase of the system development cycle concentrates on implementation of the system.

ANSWERS TO EXERCISES

EXERCISE 18-1

1. A composite field of several data items.
2. a. data items
   b. data aggregates
   c. records
   d. files
   e. data base
3. a. Hierarchical: a top-down approach where each "parent" record has one or more "offspring" records at a lower level.
   b. Network: records are logically related and any one of the records can serve as an entry point.
   c. Relational: data are viewed as being stored in the form of various tables and are combined for inquiry and reporting purposes.
4. a. Sequential: data are placed in a file in sequence, according to a particular key, called a sort key.
   b. Direct: data are stored without regard to sequence and are accessed by a specific address on a physical file. Records are chained through use of a pointer.
   c. Index sequential: records are arranged sequentially on a direct access storage device; records are accessed by referring to an index or table containing addresses of individual records.
5. a. List organization: a group of logically related records, connected by pointers or links.
   b. Inverted organization: a structure that permits searching a file for records with a particular attribute.

EXERCISE 18-2

1. 2, 4, 6
2. 1, 3, 5, 7

EXERCISE 18-3

1. Input, output, processing, data bases
2. a. Reduces errors because entry personnel familiar with application
   b. Eliminates input documents to be transferred to central key-entry area
   c. Detects and flags errors so they can be corrected on the spot
3. Improve response time
4. Only the data needed by other organizations is sent forward. Data unique to local needs is processed locally and is retained in the local data base.

5. Most of these systems use computers.
6. Included in the definition of word processing is the dissemination of letters and reports, the function of a facsimile system.
7. Processing data and performing calculations

EXERCISE 18–4
1. Format
2. Computer programming
3. Yes; the manufacturer specifies how many data can be displayed, so an output format would show the precise positions on the CRT screen where the output is to be displayed.

CHAPTER EXAMINATION

1. The four levels of sophistication in system design are:

   Level 1 _____

   Level 2 _____

   Level 3 _____

   Level 4 _____

2. What are the major components of the system design package?

   Logical Design   *Physical Design*

   a. _____

   b. _____

   c. _____

   d. _____

   e. _____

3. What factors are considered in selecting data communication facilities?

   a. _____

   b. _____

   c. _____

   d. _____

   e. _____

   f. _____

   g. _____

4. What is a data base? _____

_____

_____

5. Match the following terms.

     ____ Intelligent terminal   a.   Levels of sophistication in design

     ____ Stages of system sophistication   b.   Seven steps in computerizing a system

     ____ Phases of system development   c.   Phase III in the system development cycle

     ____ Basic mechanization   d.   Key to staying in business

     ____ Physical system design   e.   Concentrates on text rather than data

     ____ Logical system design   f.   Capable of computations

     ____ Lifestream system   g.   A level of design sophistication

     ____ Independent systems   h.   Phase II in the system development cycle

     ____ Word processing   i.   Non–data base orientation

6. The advantages of implementing the data base concept are:

     a. _____

     b. _____

     c. _____

     d. _____

     e. _____

     f. _____

     g. _____

7. Although an organization may achieve the fourth level of sophistication in the first implementation, this is rare. Why?

_____

_____

_____

8. Explain the difference between the data base approach and traditional file design. _____

_____
_____
_____
_____

9. Explain the differences between the three data base structures.

   a. _____
     _____

   b. _____
     _____

   c. _____
     _____

10. Can data bases be distributed? _____ Explain.

_____
_____
_____
_____
_____

11. Explain the four categories of distributed systems.

   a. Input: _____
     _____

   b. Output: _____
     _____

   c. Processing: _____
     _____
     _____

   d. Data bases: _____
     _____

12.   What are the advantages of distributed systems?

a.   _____

_____

b.   _____

_____

c.   _____

_____

13.   Explain the four alternatives for electronic mail systems:

a.   _____

_____

b.   _____

_____

c.   _____

_____

d.   _____

_____

14.   Explain how logical and physical design are actually done interactively rather than sequentially.

_____

_____

_____

_____

15.   What are the advantages of designing several levels of sophistication instead of moving directly to the fourth level of sophistication for the initial implementation?

_____

_____

_____

16.   What are the advantages of the "menu" approach to input and output?

_____

17. The main advantages of top-down programming structure are:

    a. _____

    _____

    b. _____

    _____

    c. _____

    _____

18. The principal benefits of top-down program design/structured programming methodology are:

    a. _____

    b. _____

19. What are the four types of controls that designers build into their system?

    a. _____

    b. _____

    c. _____

    d. _____

20. What are the two reasons for locating data entry in the user department?

    a. _____

    _____

    _____

    b. _____

    _____

    _____

21. Define and explain a DBMS.

_____

_____

_____

_____

_____

_____

22. Which of the controls listed in the section on controls should be included in every system? Explain.

_____

_____

23. Prepare a record layout for the manufacturing file, detailed on the file descriptor form in Figure 17-8. Don't worry about the fields' being proportional; just record the layout in the space below, identifying positions and field names. The first field is filled in for you.

File Positions	
1–6	
Work Center	

24. Prepare a report layout for the output descriptor in Figure 17-8, using the form provided at the end of the chapter exam. (Use Figure 18-7 as a guide.)

25. Explain the four categories of electronic mail.

a. _____

_____

b. _____

_____

c. _____

_____

d. _____

_____

26. Examine Figure 18-5. Identify a device used in each of the four types of distributed systems.

a. Input: _____

b. Processing: _____

c. Data base: _____

d. Output: _____

27. Develop a top-down program structure for problem 4 of the Chapter 12 examination.

28. Develop a top-down program structure for problem 30 of the Chapter 12 examination.

29. Using Figure 18-4 as a guideline, set up a common data base for the Student Record System described in problem 25 of the Chapter 17 examination.

30. Using Figure 18-4 as a guideline, set up a common data base for the Checking Account System described in problem 26 of the Chapter 17 examination.

31. Using Figure 18-4 as a guideline, set up a common data base for the Mail Order System described in problem 29 of the Chapter 13 examination.

PRINTER LAYOUT WORKSHEET

19 FEASIBILITY ANALYSIS AND SYSTEM IMPLEMENTATION

OVERVIEW. The term system feasibility analysis **refers to the process of evaluating the advantages versus the costs of converting a manual operation to the computer.** Computer justification **refers to the process of evaluating the pros and cons of acquiring a computer.**

Justification of a computer installation normally requires feasibility analysis for several applications. Rarely is a computer justified by one application. An exception would be a computer for an airline reservation system or for control of an oil refinery process. Another exception would be a micro or minicomputer dedicated to one application, typically for one department in a company. Normally, an organization first evaluates the advantages of computerization of individual systems, such as the inventory system or the sales analysis system. Then the combined benefits of computerization of several systems are considered to determine if computer installation is justified.

On the other hand, it is usually suboptimal to evaluate each system independently. Some systems may be marginally feasible when evaluated alone and yet be quite economical when using data captured by another system. For example, the market analysis system relies heavily on data generated by the sales order processing system.

Therefore, the feasibility analysis should concentrate on the information needs of the entire operation. Then it is easier to identify the major systems where feasibility should be analyzed. This is the reason that the organization study outlined in Chapter 17 is so important.

Feasibility analysis is actually a continual process rather than a one-time activity. It begins in phase II during the logical system design and concludes in phase III during the physical system design. The system designer usually has some general computer configuration in mind in preparing the physical system design. The system may ultimately be designed for on-line processing but may be limited initially to the batch processing mode, due to resource constraints. Therefore, the designer considers several possibilities.

Likewise, the benefits must be estimated for several system

alternatives. For example, the on-line system may produce 50 percent higher saving than a batch-processing system yet not justify the cost of on-line computing at this stage of the company's growth.

Typically, a sizable investment is involved in development of a CBMIS. Management needs to compare this investment with other investment opportunities. A priority is established for development of the data base and conversion of manual systems to computer processing. Usually a three- to five-year implementation plan is prepared. Lifestream systems are given highest priority since they will provide the greatest return to the organization.

The implementation plan is broken into schedules for each major system and subsystem to insure proper control. Implementation is phase V of the system development cycle. The tasks of system implementation include: (1) testing the system, (2) development of procedures, (3) training personnel to operate the system, (4) running it in parallel with the old system to insure proper operation, and (5) cut-over to the new system.

Since many activities are involved (and the phasing of these activities is critical), careful planning is necessary. The Gantt and PERT planning techniques have proven applicable to implementation of computer systems, particularly when combining systems into a data base.

You will also cover in this chapter phases VI and VII of the system development cycle: operation of the system and maintenance of the system. Operation consists of the repetitive tasks of data preparation, data entry, data control, computer processing, and distribution of results. Maintenance consists of making minor changes in the system, that is, maintaining it to correspond to changes in the company's procedures.

BENEFITS OF COMPUTER USE

In the early days of computer use, operations were converted to the computer primarily to reduce clerical costs. For some organizations, such as insurance companies and banks, reduction of clerical costs remains a principal reason for computerizing an activity. One expert estimated that by 1985, 50 percent of the U.S. population between the ages of 18 and 36 would be needed to work in banking activities if the computer had not been introduced before that date.

However, reduction of clerical costs is not the only reason for using a computer. Speed of response is a more important benefit from computer use for some organizations. For example, few of us would be content with airline reservation systems as slow and inaccurate as those in operation in the early 1950s. Today, a major airline would not be able to compete without a computerized reservation system.

Speed of response is equally important in other types of business. In a seasonal business, such as providing products for Christmas gifts, the order processing cycle is crucial to success. Not only is quick response important for competitive reasons, it can result in a higher level of reorders. A mail-order company found that reducing the order-processing time from four weeks to less than a week resulted in an increase of 15 percent in reorders. The customer received the merchandise, liked it, and had time to make another catalog purchase before Christmas.

Accuracy is another important reason for converting to computer operations. Computerizing complicated procedures, such as insurance policy preparation, results in far fewer errors. A fourth major category of benefits from computer processing is improved information for managerial decision making.

In summary, varied benefits are possible from computer use. Table 19–1 provides a listing of 23 benefits.

TABLE 19–1   ADVANTAGES OF DATA PROCESSING APPLICATIONS

1. Lower costs
   a. Reduction in clerical operations
   b. Savings in space required for personnel, desks, and files
   c. Reduction in redundant files
   d. Reduction in duplication of operations
   e. Detection of problems before they become costly
   f. Reduction in the routine, clerical elements in high-caliber jobs
   g. Reduction in amount of paperwork by utilizing exception principle
   h. Reduction in inventory
   i. Combination of like functions in several departments

2. Faster reaction
   a. Improved ability to react to changing external conditions
   b. Larger reservoir of information for producing realistic operating plans and forecasting market conditions
   c. Closer monitoring of operations and utilization of feedback principle to produce corrective actions
   d. Assessing impact of problems of one area on the other activities of the firm
   e. Faster turnaround time for processing jobs due to less clerical activity
   f. Ability to compare alternative courses of action more comprehensively and rapidly

3. Improved accuracy
   a. Mechanization of operations, permitting more checks and fewer error possibilities
   b. Sharing of information between files, reducing the errors resulting from manual intervention
   c. Ability to raise confidence limits on activities due to more information for measuring performance and more information to permit more accurate forecasts
   d. Integrity of information maintained through improved validation techniques

4. Improved information for management
   a. Higher-quality information through employment of management science techniques
   b. Capability of utilizing management-by-exception principle to a greater extent
   c. Capability of developing simulation models for inclusion of all factors in forecasting and developing alternative management plans
   d. Improved performance indicators through more quantitative data and faster response on performance of all functions

EXERCISE 19-1 Which advantages of data processing listed in Table 19-1 would *not* apply to the following applications. Explain your answers.

1. Airline reservation system _____

_____

_____

2. Utility company billing system _____

_____

_____

3. University student records system _____

_____

_____

DETERMINING BENEFITS Determining the benefits of the proposed system is done jointly by designers and the users of the system. However, the manager of the area where the computer is applied is ultimately responsible for both the cost and productivity. This person has the major role in estimating the benefits of the system. The system designer supports the manager in data gathering and analysis to determine benefits.

For example, marketing management might calculate benefits of adopting a sales order processing system as follows.

1. Reduction in clerical costs: $7950
   ($.53 per order × 15,000 orders/year).
2. Increase in reorders due to faster order turnaround: $23,625
   (15 percent × 15,000 orders/year × $105 revenue/order × 10 percent before tax profit).
3. Competitive advantage of capturing sales data for marketing data base: $63,000
   (4 percent improvement in annual sales × $105 revenue/order × 15,000 orders).

SAVINGS FROM COMPUTERIZING LIFESTREAM SYSTEMS The designers of the 1980s place emphasis on systems that are lifestream activities of the firm (for example, the sales order processing system, the inventory system, the production system, and the distribution system). Designers of the 1970s placed emphasis on administrative systems, such as payroll or sales statistics. Whereas the payroll application might replace several clerks, the sales order processing application could speed up the order cycle enough to gain new customers and obtain more reorders, as well as reduce clerical costs.

Also, the computer's capacity makes the sales order processing operation more flexible and able to handle wide swings in volume, instead of the company's having to hire and lay off order-processing personnel. At the same time, by capturing sales information as a by-product, we establish the marketing data base. Marketing analysis using these data gives the company a competitive advantage that may produce more savings than any of the previously cited savings potentials (as shown in the above example). Modern design approach is to determine feasibility based on computerization of several interrelated systems.

QUESTION: Using the feasibility approach of the data base era places emphasis on computerizing _____ operations instead of _____ operations.

ANSWER: lifestream, administrative

EXERCISE 19-2

1. Ms. Clair E. Cull, manager of operations at the Littlefield Valley Bank, estimates a cost of 12 cents per check in clerical processing costs if the system is converted from manual to computer processing. A bank across town will computer process checks for Littlefield Valley for 10.5 cents each. However, it charges $5 per trip to pick up and deliver the checks each evening. The bank has a volume of 2000 checks for each day. Is it feasible for Ms. Cull to utilize the computer service? _____

_____

_____

2. Ms. Cull would like her own computer next year. A minicomputer appropriate for this operation rents for only $300 per month. What volume of check processing will be necessary next year to justify the minicomputer, assuming she can process as cheaply as the bank across town?

_____

_____

3. By expanding the system to handle all transactions, both deposits and withdrawals, Ms. Cull calculates that she can reduce clerical costs by $250 per month. She has also determined that an in-house computer would enable her department to process all transactions within one hour of receipt. Ms. Cull has asked Mr. Monte Bags (the bank president) to estimate the probable increase in accounts if a depositor could have an up-to-date balance within the hour. Mr. Bags estimates a 5 percent increase in customers. The bank now has 2000 accounts with an average monthly income of 75 cents per customer for demand deposit accounting alone. Can Ms. Cull justify the computer on the one-hour turnaround principle, or must she find other areas of application?

_____

_____

_____

_____

4. Ever persistent, Ms. Cull asks the loan department manager, Mr. Tye T. Wad, what benefits would accrue by using the computer for his department. He can't think of any. Can you? (Refer to Table 19–1.)

5. How might the checking account data base be used by the loan department?

COST OF COMPUTER USE

The three components of the cost of computerization are: (1) development cost, (2) implementation cost, and (3) operating cost.

Development costs are *one-time* costs, consisting of:

1. Documenting the existing system.
2. Analyzing the system to determine how improvements can be made.
3. Designing a new system.
4. Programming and debugging the system.

Implementation costs are *one-time* costs, consisting of:

1. Training the users of the system.
2. Training the computer department personnel to operate the system.
3. Installing and testing system.

Operating costs are *recurring* costs, consisting of:

1. Preparing data for entry to the system
2. Performing control checks on input and output.
3. Computer processing.

QUESTION: Data entry costs also occur in the development phase but usually are not large enough to list under that heading. Why?

ANSWER: Only the test data are entered.

DEVELOPMENT COSTS   Comparison of system costs of the 1970s versus the 1980s is provided in the introduction to Part Four. The illustration shows that costs are higher today because more emphasis is placed on phases I through III of the development cycle. The sophisticated systems of today require more effort in the early phases of the development cycle. On the other hand, returns are higher because the computer is applied to lifestream systems.

The resource levels required to support the development effort for a given system might appear as illustrated in Figure 19-1.

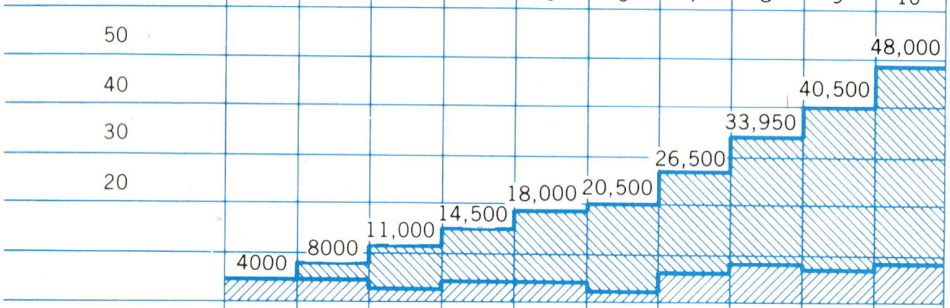

System Cost in K Dollars	Time Periods										Total
	1	2	3	4	5	6	7	8	9	10	
PHASES	I	II	III			III	IV		IV	V	
Cost Element											
PERSONNEL											
User Representatives	2000	2000	1000	500	500	500	500	500	500	2000	
Analysts/Designers	2000	2000	2000	3000	3000	2000	1000	1000	1000	1000	
Programmers							4000	5000	4000	500	
Data Entry							100	200	300	2500	
Computer Operators							50	100	100	200	
COMPUTER							300	600	600	1200	
SUPPLIES							50	50	50	100	
Total	4000	4000	3000	3500	3500	2500	6000	7450	6550	7500	48,000

Chart values: 4000, 8000, 11,000, 14,500, 18,000, 20,500, 26,500, 33,950, 40,500, 48,000

FIGURE 19-1
Resource levels for typical system development.

QUESTION: Why would the cost of user representatives jump so drastically in phase V?

ANSWER: The system has been installed and needs close attention during the first month of operation to work out all the kinks.

IMPLEMENTATION COSTS   Training costs are a large part of the cost of implementing today's systems. In earlier system design approaches, systems were converted to the computer with little change in operating procedure. The computer was used merely to perform operations more quickly. Today's systems are designed to take full advantage of the computer's capabilities—to perform analysis as well as increase processing speed.

For example, in processing insurance applications the computer program can compare the applicant's medical examination results with a wide variety of criteria to determine if he or she is an acceptable risk. Similar analysis can be made on the financial qualifications of the applicant. The manual system of processing applications is replaced to permit more thorough analysis of the insurance application.

As a consequence of these increases in system complexity and changes in system emphasis, training of personnel to utilize the system becomes more complicated. Training was often quite informal prior to the data base era.

An operating procedure needs to be developed both for users of the system (for example, the insurance application review department in the above-cited instance) and the data processing department personnel who run the system. The training activity is designed to review this procedure in depth and to give everyone involved an understanding of the system objectives.

The other part of implementation cost is the actual installation and testing of the system. The system logic has been thoroughly tested, using both hypothetical and actual data. However, the test is not concluded until the person responsible for its operation is satisfied with its performance. In the above case, the person responsible would be the head of the insurance application review department.

Typically, the new system is run in parallel with the old system for a short time to insure correct results. However, since the systems of the 1980s are usually very different from the previous system, it is rarely practical to run the two in parallel for more than a few days. Is it practical to expect the staff to work 16 hours per day, operating the old system during the first shift and the new system during the second shift? The more common practice is to test the new system on last month's data, that is, to run last month's input through the new system to compare results.

The emphasis on shorter parallel testing periods requires more careful planning of the tests. Therefore, the users and system analyst/designers are developing operating procedures, training programs, implementation plans, and test procedures while the system is being programmed.

QUESTION: Observe Figure 19-1. Documentation of the existing system requires ＿＿ periods; logical design requires ＿＿ periods; physical design requires ＿＿ periods; programming and testing require ＿＿ periods; while implementation requires ＿＿ periods.

ANSWER: 1, 1, 4, 3, 1

OPERATING COSTS   Operating costs occur once the system is implemented. The major categories of operating costs are data entry costs, data control costs, and computer processing costs.

While development and implementation costs are one-time costs, operating costs are recurring. The typical cycle is shown in Figure 19-2.

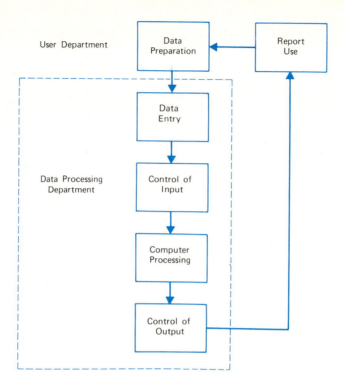

FIGURE 19-2
System operating cycle.

QUESTION: Which of these costs also occur during system development?

_____

_____

ANSWER: The control function on I/O is not needed until the system is installed. Data entry and computer operators are involved in the testing phases.

DATA ENTRY COSTS The user department prepares data in a format that can be used by data entry personnel. In some cases, data are transcribed from a document to a form designed to facilitate data entry. In other cases, the user document itself is redesigned to permit data entry directly from the document.

QUESTION: The dotted line in Figure 19-2 refers to activities within the data processing department. Based on the discussion of design of input, in Chapter 17, how might that border be redrawn to reflect the direction of data entry in the

1980s? _____

_____

ANSWER: Move dotted line below data entry because trend is to perform it on-line, in the user department.

DATA CONTROL COSTS As shown in Figure 19-2, the typical system input is batched before and checked after processing to insure that all data were processed. Also, many systems are designed to include an editing operation to search for data entry errors before processing. The edit program is a separate computer program prepared to analyze input and search for errors before the processing of the main program begins. Examples of errors that may be detected through the editing program are: (1) incorrect part numbers or account numbers, (2) omission of data that should have been entered, (3) illogical entries, such as an invoice total inconsistent with quantity ordered multiplied by prices of items, or a zip code inconsistent with address.

The data control function has the following responsibilities: (1) control of input to insure all data are entered into the system, (2) providing data, programs, and processing procedures to computer operations for each job run, and (3) checking output to insure correct processing of the job. Printed output is distributed by data control.

QUESTION: Data control functions did not exist for many first-generation applications. What do you think may have caused this function to be developed? _____

_____

_____

ANSWER: Input was lost or output misplaced as systems became more complex with a wider variety of input and larger numbers of users. Also, more control was needed to reduce errors in input data.

COMPUTER PROCESSING COSTS Since the editing function is accomplished by a computer program, the typical application has at least two passes through the computer: (1) processing of the editing program and (2) processing of the main program.

However, the main processing may also be separated into several phases. For example, data may be input to the system daily with some processing occurring, such as updating the inventory. However, other processing steps may occur weekly, monthly, or quarterly — such as preparation of reports.

The computer operator is provided data, operating instructions, and the computer programs. Typically, the input is recorded on magnetic tape, and these tapes must be mounted on the tape drives. However, the computer programs may be on magnetic disk. The operator loads the program into the computer. A variety of media may be involved since the master file may also be on magnetic disk or tape. The job is then processed according to the operating instructions. In preparing output, multiple media may again be involved. A printed report may be produced, or some special output documents, such as paychecks or invoices, may be produced. Increasingly, the operator's task is being programmed into the operating system, not so much to reduce labor cost as to reduce the opportunity for error. Some systems have reduced the operator's task to mere loading and unloading of magnetic tapes.

QUESTION: Figure 19-1 shows operator costs are quite low, because _____

ANSWER: Many functions are now performed by the operating system.

EXERCISE 19-3   To better understand the characteristics of development costs, answer these questions concerning the example in Figure 19-1.

1.   The three major components of development costs are:

   a.   _____

   b.   _____

   c.   _____

2.   Total the costs.
   a.   Personnel

      User representatives   _____

      Analyst/designers   _____

      Programmers   _____

      Data entry   _____

      Operators   _____   _____

   b.   Computer   _____

   c.   Supplies   =============
                                                              48,000

3.   Determine the percentage of total cost allocated to each cost area.

   a.   User representatives   _____

   b.   Analyst/designers   _____

   c.   Programmers   _____

   d.   Data entry   _____

   e.   Operators   _____

   f.   Computer   _____

   g.   Supplies   =============
                                            100.0%

FEASIBILITY ANALYSIS   When estimated benefits exceed costs of the proposed system, it still may not be feasible to proceed with development. The resources required to develop the system are always scarce and must be evaluated for use on a variety of company projects.

The $48,000 system (Figure 19–1) may provide rapid payback. However, assume that manufacturing management wants to purchase an expensive machine and the marketing management division is recommending addition of a market research function. Both organizations have completed cost/benefit analyses to show that their recommendations are economically justified, just as the computer-project is.

Company management must choose among these three alternatives. Financial analysis techniques are utilized in determining feasibility of a project, whether it is a computer project, a manufacturing project, or a marketing project.

For example, assume the cost/benefit analysis of computerizing the inventory system is summarized in Table 19–2. The system will pay for itself in 4.4 years and save $10,800 per year until it is obsolete, as shown in Table 19–3.

TABLE 19–2   COST/BENEFIT COMPARISON FOR INVENTORY SYSTEM

Cost		Benefits	
One-time		Annual	
Development cost	$48,000	Inventory reduction	$19,200
Annual		Purchase-order preparation simplification	7,200
Operating cost	$24,000		
		Revenue from back order reduction	8,400
			$34,800

TABLE 19–3   PAYBACK PERIOD FOR INVENTORY SYSTEM

Gross annual savings	$34,800
Less operating cost	24,000
Net annual savings	$10,800

$$\text{Payback period} = \frac{\text{Development cost}}{\text{Net savings}} = \frac{\$48,000}{\$10,800} = 4.4 \text{ years}$$

QUESTION: Is the period of 4.4 years a reasonable time for payback? _____ Explain.

ANSWER: This depends on the company's policy toward investment opportunity and its cash flow position. Other investment opportunities may require less development cost or may produce a larger return on investment (ROI).

The inventory project appears to be a reasonable investment, if the system has a life of at least 4.4 years. However, the company must acquire the resources to cover the years of cash drain until benefits exceed cost. Or, management may decide to break the project into phases to reduce the initial cash outlay. The feasibility study enables the financial officer to plan for the availability of funds to underwrite the system.

Management typically will not rely on payback analysis alone. The techniques of cash flow analysis, return on investment analysis, and present value analysis will also be utilized.

FEASIBILITY DECISION The key to success for the system designer is preparation of a comprehensive package for the feasibility determination. If both quantitative and qualitative considerations are included in the package, management has an excellent basis for determining system feasibility. The decision is rarely based on financial factors alone. Other important considerations are involved.

1. The system may be necessary because of a shortage of skilled labor in the locality.

2. The system may be necessary to handle variations in product demand that would be difficult to meet with existing facilities and labor force.

3. The system may be essential to meet competition that provides better customer service due to computerization of operations.

4. The system may provide a data base necessary for other functions in the firm.

However, benefit projections could be developed for each of the above considerations. Each has a probability of occurrence and a tangible cost/benefit. Management evaluates the feasibility of the proposed system in light of the cost/benefits and the effect on the firm's operations.

EXERCISE 19-4

1. Perform a payback analysis for the following system.

Development Cost	$20,000

Annual Figures	
Operating cost	$3,000
Clerical savings	12,200
Floor space saving	500
Equipment savings	1,800

2. Assume the above system represented computerization of the checking account system of a bank. You are the bank officer deciding whether to approve the system.

   a. If the system must be replaced after two years, is it feasible? Explain your answer. _____

   _____

   _____

   _____

   b. What other factors would enter into your feasibility decision?

   (1) _____

   _____

(2) _____

_____

_____

(3) _____

_____

(4) _____

_____

_____

IMPLEMENTATION

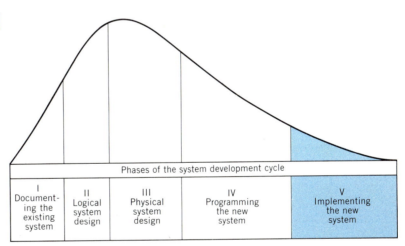

Phases of the system development cycle

| I Document-ing the existing system | II Logical system design | III Physical system design | IV Programming the new system | V Implementing the new system |

Even though cost of implementation is much less than that of the other phases, this phase in the development cycle consists of a number of activities crucial to the success of the system. These activities are: testing the system, procedure development, training personnel, parallel processing, file conversion, and cutover to the new system.

Insuring system reliability involves the following series of tests: (1) module test, (2) system test, and (3) parallel processing test.

Procedures are developed for two groups, the user group and the data processing group. Within the latter group are the data control function, data entry function, and computer operations function. These groups require training in application of procedures.

File conversion planning is very important because a variety of files are involved in implementing lifestream systems. The time and cost to convert manual files to computer-oriented media are significant. Time and cost are especially significant when one is converting a number of files to a common data base.

Integrating systems into a complex computer-based management information system requires use of special planning techniques. The Gantt chart technique is appropriate for planning the activities for individuals. A network technique is required for the complicated task of interrelating all activities in a major system implementation. Either the PERT or CPM network methods are used for this purpose.

TESTING THE SYSTEM

Testing of a system is separated into three parts: (1) module tests, (2) system tests, and (3) parallel processing tests.

MODULE TESTS

During preparation of programs, programmers develop test data to prove the validity of logic in each module. However, these are usually hypothetical data. For example, in testing a payroll system, the programmer will enter data for several hypothetical employees whose pay will be calculated using all types of deductions. This approach insures proper logic for handling each payroll variation.

Prior to such testing, programmers have utilized **structured walk-throughs** to reduce the possibility of programming errors. The procedure works as follows: (1) When a module has been programmed, copies of the code are distributed to a group of programmers. (2) They analyze the code for errors that the programmer might have overlooked. (3) Then the group meets and "walks through" the code, line by line, providing the developer suggestions and comments to improve the program. This walk-through procedure has reduced test time significantly.

SYSTEM TESTS

When all programming modules are finished, the final system test is conducted. Using the payroll example again, we see that one programmer may be assigned the module that handles input to the system: (1) establishing the file of employee records, with information supplied by the personnel department; (2) input on deductions; and (3) weekly input concerning hours worked, and so on. Another programmer may be assigned the module that calculates payroll and prepares payroll checks.

As explained in the section on top-down design (Chapter 17), system tests are run repeatedly, as each module on the hierarchy is completed. This procedure prevents lengthy error-detection situations that occurred previously when the system tests were not begun until all modules were completed.

Hypothetical data may be used for the first series of tests. It is the responsibility of the system designer to prepare system test data, working with the user to design test data representative of actual data that will be handled by the system after implementation.

Conversion to a data base requires even more thorough system testing. Typically a company will implement a small data base (e.g., the product data base) to gain experience before tackling the large applications such as the customer data base.

PARALLEL PROCESSING TESTS

The third in the series of tests before cutover to the new system is the parallel processing of old and new systems. This three-test procedure may appear to be excessive testing. However, experience has proved the necessity of a thorough testing approach. When companies are computerizing lifestream systems, vital to the continuing success of the firm, careful testing is essential.

The length of parallel processing depends upon the type of system. A payroll system would not require lengthy parallel processing. The system designer could use the input for the prior month's payroll as data for the system test. The parallel processing of the entire payroll for one period should be sufficient testing of the typical payroll system.

QUESTION: Would the same approach, using last month's transactions, be appropriate for

testing a checking account system for a bank? Explain your answer. _____

_____

_____

ANSWER: Yes; the approach should prove the system logic unless the system were changed so much that a direct comparison was difficult to make.

Testing of other systems may be much more complicated than testing the payroll system. For example, the new inventory system may be very different from the old one. The new system undoubtedly includes new logic, such as economic order quantity determination and reorder point calculation. Or, a new system may integrate two systems, such as the inventory and purchasing systems. Therefore, system implementation may be very complicated, requiring six weeks to two months of parallel processing.

On the other hand, lengthy parallel processing is constrained by practical considerations, such as the availability of personnel to operate both the old and new systems.

A manager cannot expect the staff to operate the old system on the first shift and the new system on the second shift. Although the new system should require far fewer activities in the user department, the two systems will be different enough to complicate parallel processing.

QUESTION: What do you think would be a satisfactory approach to parallel processing for

testing a student records system? _____

_____

_____

ANSWER: To test it over a vacation period, or a period during the term when the least difficulty could arise. The start and end of terms would be the least appropriate times.

A typical industrial testing approach is to operate the old system during the week and to parallel the new system over the weekend. Since less manual activity is required with the new system, the full crew would not be needed each weekend. Most employees would be willing to receive overtime pay to work every other weekend for one month, to enable a full month's parallel processing.

In summary, for more sophisticated systems, the system test rather than parallel processing is the key to determining system reliabiliy. However, other steps can be taken to lessen the risk associated with short-term parallel processing: (1) detailed user procedures, (2) detailed data processing procedures, (3) file conversion, and (4) thorough training. These activities will be covered in the following sections.

DEVELOPMENT OF PROCEDURES

USER PROCEDURES   User procedures include both narrative and graphic materials. Understanding the procedure is easier if the narrative portion is supported by flowcharts, logic charts, and/or decision tables. In-depth, comprehensive user procedures have a major impact on ease of conversion to the new computerized system. They also aid in training of personnel.

QUESTION: One of the authors worked with a firm where the data entry employees worked on a team with the systems designer to develop input procedures.

What are the advantages of this approach? _____

_____

ANSWER: Whether data entry personnel are involved in the preparation of procedures or in debugging them, the views of these employees are needed before the procedures are prepared in final form. This approach insures that the input procedure is workable. It also enhances data entry employees' morale through participation in the process.

DATA PROCESSING PROCEDURES   Just as user personnel need procedures, personnel in the data processing operation must have procedures. Part of the design task is preparation of these procedures.

1. *Data entry procedures.* Data entry procedures identify precisely where each field of data is to be recorded. If the input document is a form, such as an order, the procedure must also specify where on the document each data element is found.

2. *Computer operator procedures.* Computer operator procedures identify the media to be used and the operator actions during processing.

3. *Data control procedures.* Input sheets may be lost or misplaced. The data control function assures that all data are entered into the system. Usually input is batched to make sure no items are lost during processing. For example, sales orders may be batched in groups of 50. Or, input may be logged to insure that all transactions enter the system. For on-line systems, the data control activities are accomplished by the department in which the terminals reside.

In a company with a small computer operation, each department may have its own data control activity. When a large volume of material is passing through the computer center, a data control group is usually established in that department. This group insures that all items entering the data entry area complete that activity and that all items entering the computer operations are processed. It also audits the computer output to insure that the information is reasonable and complete. For example, assume the computer operator loaded a wrong magnetic tape. Instead of Tuesday's tape of transactions being used, Monday's tape was reused. The data control personnel could compare output and isolate such errors.

QUESTION: In the example above, why would the magnetic tape record of Monday's transactions be retained? _____

_____

ANSWER: Standard operating procedure requires that several days' data are retained. A machine malfunction might occur and "clobber" the Tuesday tape. The operator then must reconstruct the master tape by reprocessing transactions against the Monday tape before moving on to Tuesday's transactions.

EXERCISE 19-5   1. Why would several months of parallel processing be infeasible for a highly integrated system? _____

_____

2. What approach would be used? _____

_____

3. In what respects are procedures for data processing similar to user procedures? _____

_____

FILE CONVERSION   A major activity in system implementation is file conversion—both manual and computer-media files. A company for which one of the authors serves as consultant was forced to shelve a bill-of-materials system when the cost of converting manual to computer files was determined to be more than $40,000. The system design was already completed; however, the feasibility study had not considered conversion of manual to machine-processable records.

Conversion of a file that is already on some machine-processable medium, such as punched cards or magnetic tape, is not nearly so difficult. Nevertheless, this activity requires careful planning and control. Often it occupies the computer for an extended period and must be performed over a weekend—perhaps seven shifts (Friday night third shift, and three shifts each on Saturday and Sunday).

An example of complexity in file conversion is the integration of two major systems. The material requirements system may be combined with the inventory system. A special computer program usually is required to consolidate several files into a common data base. Although the computer program is rarely large or complicated, the sheer volume of the files may make the conversion time-consuming. If a manual system must be converted to machine-processable media, the cost can be large—depending on the volume of records.

QUESTION: Assume a bank is implementing a banking system in which all records for each customer are consolidated. A combined monthly statement is produced for the customer instead of separate statements for checking account, savings account, loans, trust funds, and so on. A computer program is written to merge these records. Would you expect the bank to implement this new system for a few customers at a time to reduce the impact of file conversion or to cut over all at

one time? Why? _____

_____

ANSWER: The answer would depend on the volume and media involved. Some activities, such as the loan department, may not be computerized and data may have to be key-entered before any consolidation is done. The consolidated statement system could be implemented over several days or weeks because it is primarily a reporting system. The other systems feeding this one are unchanged except for providing input to this system as a by-product of their output. If the bank were combining all the systems into one major system, a complete cut-over would be the only feasible approach.

TRAINING   When all procedures (user and data processing) have been completed, the user/system designer team can begin training personnel concerning the new system.

   The entire user group is brought together to explain user input procedures for the system as a whole. The overall objectives of the system are reviewed; then the detailed operation of the system is discussed, with ample opportunity for questions.

   Then, each person is instructed on his or her specific duties associated with the system. If this task is done thoroughly, it can serve as the final "debugging" activity prior to publication of the procedures.

QUESTION: To what extent should supervisory personnel be involved in user training?

_____

_____

ANSWER: If the user/designer team has done its job properly, supervisory personnel have been involved throughout the system analysis, design, and implementation activities. Otherwise, the user is tempted to regard the system as belonging to "that computer group." Obviously, the system remains the responsibility of the user. To assume responsibility, the user must have the opportunity to assess and evaluate the system *throughout* development.

EXERCISE 19-6   1. Is the user representative or the system designer primarily responsible for developing the following types of procedures? Explain your reasoning.

      a.   User procedures _____

          _____

      b.   Operations procedures _____

          _____

      c.   Data control procedures _____

          _____

2.   The explanation about training should enable you to suggest who should conduct the training session. Explain your choices.

      a.   User department training _____

          _____

      b.   Data processing department training _____

          _____

IMPLEMENTATION PLANNING TECHNIQUES

Effective implementation planning and control use the same techniques as other activities of the firm. The Gantt chart technique is appropriate for the planning of an individual's efforts in system development, as shown in Figure 19-3. The number of activities is small enough that the Gantt chart easily portrays the schedule for each activity.

When we consider the multitude of activities for an entire system, the Gantt chart approach is not adequate. Too many interrelationships are involved to be

FIGURE 19-3
Gantt chart of programmer activities.

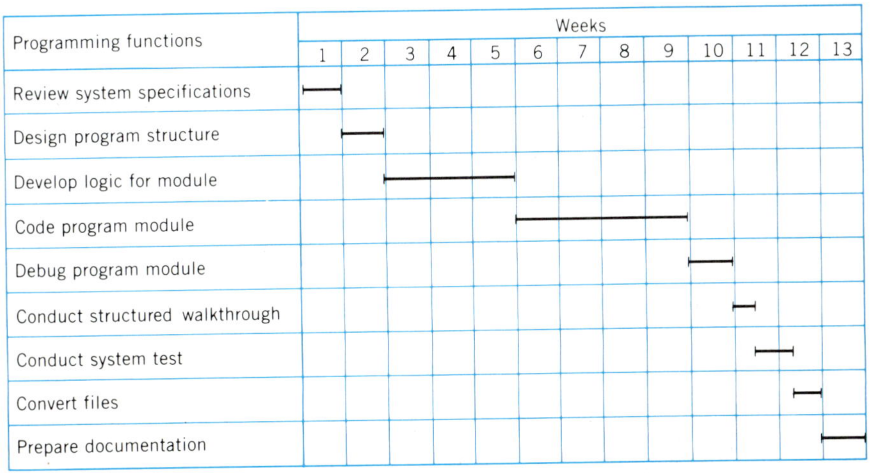

Programming functions	Weeks												
	1	2	3	4	5	6	7	8	9	10	11	12	13
Review system specifications	⊢—⊣												
Design program structure		⊢—⊣											
Develop logic for module				⊢——⊣									
Code program module						⊢——⊣							
Debug program module										⊢—⊣			
Conduct structured walkthrough											⊢—⊣		
Conduct system test											⊢—⊣		
Convert files												⊢—⊣	
Prepare documentation													⊢—⊣

handled by a Gantt chart. Network techniques such as PERT and CPM charts[1] are more appropriate for planning and controlling development of complex information systems. Figure 19–4 illustrates the use of a PERT chart for planning and control of a major system. The network technique is needed to show the interrelationships of all the activities.

Both PERT and CPM techniques are based on similar logic: (1) activities required for system development and implementation are arranged according to sequence of occurrence; (2) estimates are made for the time to accomplish each activity; (3) a critical path is determined along with alternate paths progressively less critical.

Figure 19–4 illustrates the complexity in planning and control of a major system develoment. Many interrelated activities are involved, and the network technique is a good approach to identify these relationships. Computer manufacturers provide computerized network packages to simplify use of this technique in system development. Either PERT or CPM may be appropriate. The main distinction between the two techniques is that PERT provides for three time estimates for each activity, as shown in Figure 19–5: (1) the optimistic estimate, (2) the most likely estimate, and (3) the pessimistic estimate. Looking at the estimate for programming (Figure 19–5), we see the three time estimates as follows.

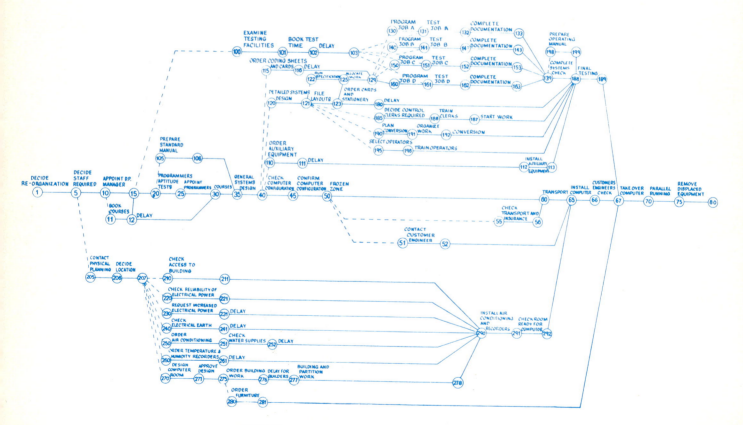

FIGURE 19–4

Hardware/software implementation plan, using network technique. (Courtesy IBM.)

---

[1]PERT is an acronym for Program Evaluation and Review Technique. CPM stands for Critical Path Method.

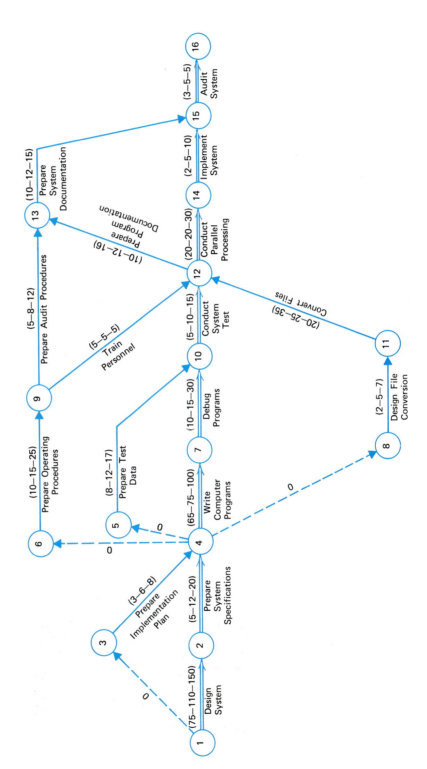

FIGURE 19-5
Use of a PERT network for system development and implementation plan.

$$\left(65 \ - \ 75 \ - \ 100\right)$$

④────────────────⑦

Write Computer Programs

QUESTION: Observe Figure 19-5. List the numbers that define the activities of system personnel as distinguished from those involved in programming (the paths converge at event 15).

System activities _____

Programming activities _____

ANSWER: System activities: 1-2-4-5-10-12-14-15; Programming activities: 4-7-10-12-14-15. Activities 6-9-12-13-15 are also system designer responsibilities. Observe the advantage over the Gantt chart — interdependent activities are linked in a PERT chart.

QUESTION: What other differences do you see between the Gantt chart and PERT network?

a. _____

b. _____

c. _____

ANSWER: a. Three times are shown for each PERT activity instead of one for Gantt.
b. Lengths of lines on PERT chart do not correspond to amount of time required.
c. Parallel activities are more easily identified with PERT.

Using CPM, the designer develops a cost/time curve for each activity, as shown in Figure 19-6. Three points define the curve. Observing the curve, you can see that the time for completing the activity of programming, T, can be shortened by increasing the level of resources applied, C.

FIGURE 19-6
CPM cost/time curve.

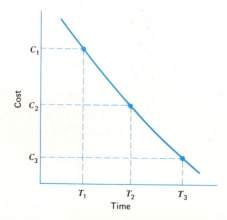

The CPM method provides cost as well as time estimates for completing a job. However, PERT cost packages have been developed that enable budgets to be established for each activity.

The advantage of CPM is the ability to vary the time along the critical path to determine its effect on cost, and vice versa. The advantage of PERT is the ability to develop probability estimates for each activity, and for the critical path.

CPM is used for situations where good historical data exist, such as installation of a computer. PERT is more appropriate where the activity is done for the first time, like development of a CBMIS or conversion to a data base.

POSTIMPLEMENTATION AUDIT

A recent addition to the implementation process is a **postimplementation audit.** Within three months of cut-over to the new system, an audit is performed. System performance is compared to the original system objectives to insure that the system is accomplishing what it was designed to accomplish.

Since it is a violation of the concept of control to have a group audit itself, the audit is performed by a group other than the original system development team. Some companies assign the responsibility to the internal audit department within the controller's division. Others set up a group within the computer department to perform such audits.

OTHER PHASES

Phase VI of the system development cycle is the operational phase. Once installed, the operation consists of the repetitive tasks of data preparation, data entry, data control, computer processing, and distribution of results. If procedures are detailed and if all personnel are properly trained, operation should run smoothly.

Phase VII is the maintenance phase. Two types of changes are made to installed systems: (1) changes resulting from revision in the function that was computerized (for example, the company sets up a new chart of accounts) and (2) changes to improve the efficiency of the system (for example, reprogramming as a result of acquiring new peripheral equipment for the computer). The maintenance phase is not to be interpreted as the next stage of development. Systems are planned to be implemented in several stages, to achieve increasing levels of sophistication. However, it is inevitable that minor changes will need to be made within each stage. Such activities are referred to as maintenance of the system.

SYSTEM DOCUMENTATION

There is an axiom in the computer field called Murphy's law: Anything that can go wrong, will go wrong. Murphy's view was that today's systems are so complex that problems are bound to occur.

However, problems can be minimized by proper system documentation. Also, the next stage of design is greatly facilitated if each stage is properly documented. System documentation consists of the materials shown in Figure 19-7.

SUMMARY

Feasibility analysis provides management with the information to determine if a system should be approved. However, in system design practice of the 1980s, systems are not designed independently. Nor are they analyzed independently for feasibility. Integrated systems have some common input data and share common files. Therefore, the teams designing the various systems for the firm coordinate feasibility studies. The set of systems may justify the first computer for the organization. Or, perhaps a more powerful computer may be justified for a firm that already has a computer. Some systems may be processed on external computers, shared with other organizations. In any event, the pro-

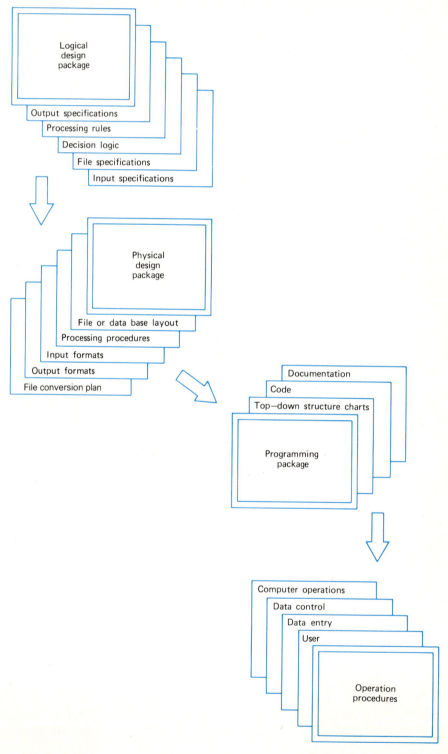

FIGURE 19-7

System documentation package.

cedure for determining feasibility does not vary—only the cost and benefit factors vary.

Application of the computer to lifestream operations (such as sales order processing, production, inventory, and distribution) produces more benefit than administrative and clerical applications. On the other hand, costs for lifestream systems may be higher than for administrative applications because backup must be provided for a lifestream operation in the event the computer goes down. As is the case throughout system development, the analyst/designer works with the user to determine costs and benefits. Such cooperation insures that the system meets the need of users within cost constraints of the firm.

Once a firm decides the CBMIS is feasible, the CBMIS is divided into stages according to priorities. Few companies have the resources to implement all systems simultaneously. An implementation plan, using a network technique such as PERT, is developed for each system to be installed. Network planning techniques are needed because the move to a data base requires integration of many files. Implementation includes: testing, procedure development, training, parallel processing, file conversion, and cut-over to the new system.

Postimplementation audits are required once the system is operational to insure that the system is meeting design criteria. Some revisions might be necessary, and this activity is referred to as the maintenance phase. Maintenance is facilitated if the system is documented properly. Also, the next stage of sophistication is more readily designed and implemented when the documentation package includes the items identified in Figure 19–7.

Computerizing lifestream operations of the firm can produce significant benefits. Likewise, considerable risk is associated with computerizing such systems since they are vital to the firm's continued success. Careful planning for implementation, with use of the procedures and techniques described in this chapter, can reduce that risk.

It is a dual responsibility—of the user representative and the system analyst/designers—to insure that these tasks are properly planned and implemented.

ANSWERS TO EXERCISES

EXERCISE 19–1

1. *Airline reservation system:* 1-f, computerized airline reservations would not reduce routine in high-caliber jobs, but would definitely improve all other phases, for example, reduction in number of flights, better forecasting, and response to changing situations.
2. *Utility company billing system:* 1-h, no reduction in inventory.
3. *University student records system:* 1-f, for reasons given in (1) above; 1-h, no inventory; 2-f, no alternative courses available.

EXERCISE 19–2

1. Ms. Cull should utilize the computer service.

	Littlefield Bank	Computer Service
Check processing charge[a]	$240	$210
Pick-up cost	0	5
Delivery cost	0	5
Total cost	$240	$220

[a]$.12 \times 2000 = 240$
$.105 \times 2000 = 210$

2. X = volume of checks necessary to justify minicomputer

$$X = \frac{\text{Monthly cost}}{\text{Cost per check}} = \frac{\$300}{\$.105} = 2857 \text{ checks per month}$$

3. Ms. Cull can justify the computer on the one-hour turnaround principle.

Benefit	Possible Monthly Saving
Reduced clerical costs	= $250
Increase in no. of accounts (2000 customers × 5%) = 100 × $.75 =	75
Savings to bank per month	$325
Rental cost per month	−300
	$ 25

4. a. The computer could provide a fast, accurate update on the status of loans his department is responsible for.
   b. Paperwork would be reduced.
   c. Since data on loans would now be entered and stored on magnetic tape or disc, there would be a savings in the amount of space required for files.
   d. Information on different types of loans could be processed faster.
   e. There would be fewer errors, due to mechanization of operations.
   f. The computer could provide an analysis of the market structure of people taking out loans.
   g. Information could be shared between files of different departments.
   h. The impact of different managerial decisions on the loan department could be assessed.

5. To show cash reserve requirements due to turnover in demand deposits and thus prevent overloaning. Also, to calculate how much interest to charge for loans based on demand deposit data and interest payments.

EXERCISE 19-3

1. The three major components of development costs are:
   a. Personnel costs
   b. Computer costs
   c. Supply costs

2. Total costs.
   a. Personnel

User representatives	$10,000	
Analyst/designers	18,000	
Programmers	13,500	
Data entry	3,100	
Operators	450	$45,050

   b. Computer — 2,700
   c. Supplies — 250

   $48,000

3. Determine the percentage of total cost allocated to each cost area.
   a. User representatives — 20.8%
   b. Analyst/designers — 37.5
   c. Programmers — 28.1
   d. Data entry — 6.5
   e. Operators — 1.0
   f. Computer — 5.6
   g. Supplies — .5

   100.0%

EXERCISE 19-4

1. Payback period $= \dfrac{\text{Development cost}}{\text{Net savings}}$

   Net savings $= \$14{,}500 - \$3{,}000 = \$11{,}500/\text{yr.}$

   Payback period $= \dfrac{20{,}000}{11{,}500} = 1.7$ yr.

2. a. If the system has a life cycle of only two years or more, it is feasible. It must be compared to other investment alternatives in the company, which may have a higher return in investment.
   b. Other factors in the feasibility decision:
      (1) the system may provide a data base necessary for other functions in the firm.
      (2) There may be a shortage of clerical help.
      (3) The system may be necessary to handle large volumes of data that would be infeasible with existing facilities.
      (4) The system may be essential to meet competition that provides fast response due to computerization of its operations.

EXERCISE 19-5

1. When major systems are integrated, the activities change so much that the new system would not be similar enough to parallel the old.
2. Run the old system during the week and parallel on the weekend. More care is taken in planning fourth-level sophistication system to insure reliability. The system test must prove the reliability of the system.
3. Instructions must be explicit to insure that input is accurately prepared and processed.

EXERCISE 19-6

1. a. System designer, in cooperation with the user representative. The user representative is most knowledgeable about the area of application, and the user is ultimately responsible for the system. However, the system designer is responsible for *all* procedures related to the system.
   b. System designer. These are technical procedures in which the user is not expected to be knowledgeable.
   c. System designer and user representative. User personnel interact with data control personnel in handling input and output.
2. a. User personnel. Operation of the system is a user responsibility. Training by the user representative will reinforce that concept. Also, the user representative will be able to understand better the user perspective to insure that all aspects are covered in the training sessions.
   b. System designer. Same reasoning as above, applied to the data processing functions and personnel.

CHAPTER EXAMINATION

1. What four principal categories of benefits result from computerizing systems?

    a. _____

    b. _____

    c. _____

    d. _____

2. Match each of the following with the proper category of cost of computerization. Development cost = 1, Implementation cost = 2, Operating cost = 3

    a. Documenting the existing system ____

    b. Designing a new system ____

    c. Training the computer department personnel to operate the system ____

    d. Installing and testing the system ____

    e. Training the users of the system ____

    f. Analyzing the system to determine how improvement can be made ____

    g. Computer processing ____

    h. Performing control checks on input and output ____

    i. Preparing data for entry to the system ____

    j. Programming and debugging the system ____

3. Match the following terms.

    ____ Implementation   a. Conducted after phase V

    ____ Postimplementation audit   b. Evaluating a system for computerization

    ____ Feasibility analysis   c. Crucial for firm to stay in business

____ Lifestream system d. Phase VI of system life cycle

____ Operation e. Evaluating acquiring a computer

____ Justification f. Phase VII of system life cycle

____ Maintenance g. Phase V of system development cycle

4. In which of the four categories of advantages of data processing do the following fall?

Category   *Benefit*

_____ a. Capability of developing simulation models for inclusion of all factors in forecasting and developing alternative management plans

_____ b. Reduction in the routine, clerical elements in high-caliber jobs

_____ c. Sharing information between files, reducing the errors resulting from manual intervention

_____ d. Reduction in redundant files

_____ e. Reduction in clerical operations

_____ f. Faster turnaround time for processing jobs due to less clerical activity

_____ g. Capability of utilizing management-by-exception principle to a greater extent

5. Why do lifestream operations produce greater savings than the kinds of applications computerized in the 1960s and 1970s? _____

_____

6. Analyze the costs in Figure 19–1 and mark the following statements true or false.

____ a. User representatives and system analyst/designers are involved during the entire development cycle.

____ b. Computer cost is twice as high during implementation, compared to the previous phase, programming/testing.

____ c. Since key-entry costs balloon when phase V begins, it appears that only sample transactions are keypunched during the programming/testing phase.

____ d. The cost of computer operators is approximately one-sixth of the cost of computer processing.

____ e. Labor costs constitute over 80 percent of total system development cost.

____ f. Phase III is the most costly phase of system development.

7. Examine Figure 19-1. Costs are shown only for the five phases of system development. Which cost elements continue after the system is implemented? (Hint — review material near end of chapter, on other phases.)

_____

_____

8. What would be the lifestream applications for a bank? What benefits would result from computerizing these

systems? _____

_____

_____

9. What would be the lifestream applications for a college? What benefits would result from computerizing these

systems? _____

_____

_____

10. Assume a new cost/benefit analysis has been conducted for the system illustrated in Figure 19-1 and Table 19-2. By increasing both analyst/designer and programming personnel, we make the system more sophisticated. A 25 percent increase in these personnel costs will produce an increase of 35 percent in annual benefits

for inventory reduction. Recalculate payback. _____

_____

11. What would your advice be to management after your feasibility analysis for problem 10? _____

_____

_____

12. Analyze the expected benefits for a college preregistration system. The admissions officer estimates that he will receive advance tuition payments. Total average tuition per semester = $575,000. The college can invest the tuition at a return of 12 percent per annum and will expect to have use of the money two months earlier than it would have it under the present system.

13. What recommendations would you make to the admissions officer, based on the analysis performed in completing problem 12? Should he/she proceed to implement the system? Explain.

_____

_____

_____

14. Explain the tests involved in validation of a computerized system.

    a. _____

b. _____

c. _____

15. What determines the length of parallel processing?

a. _____

b. _____

c. _____

16. Examine Figure 19-1. Assume programmers earn $1500 per month and analyst/designers earn $2000 per month. Total man-months of effort are as follows.

Analyst/designers _____

Programmers _____

17. Examine Figure 19-1.
    a. What are the user representatives doing in phase IV?

    _____

    b. What are the analyst/designers doing in phase IV?

    _____

18. Examine the network depicted in Figure 19-4, the hardware/software implementation plan, and answer the following questions.
    a. Jobs A, B, C, D are being programmed in parallel. Are they merely modules of the same system? Explain.

    _____

    b. Activity 101-102, entitled "Book Test Time" means arranging for programming test time on someone else's computer since ours will not arrive until the first set of programs is completed. Unless the computer is a local one, the cost of transporting programmers is significant. What programming procedures could be

    introduced to keep transportation costs down? _____

19. With the information obtained by developing a PERT network, management control functions are possible. Examine Figure 19–5 and answer the following questions.

    a. Which activity is most time consuming? _____

    b. What might be done to reduce this constraint on system development? _____

        _____

    c. What is the next most time-consuming activity? _____

    d. What might be done to reduce this time constraint? (Several possibilities are the same as with the system design constraint. However, additional possibilities exist for the programming constraint. Whereas design could have begun sooner, programming must wait until the specifications are prepared.)

        _____

        _____

        _____

    e. Designers are preparing test data, operating procedures, and file conversion while programming is going on. However, both programmers and designers are involved in system tests and parallel processing. What might a manager do regarding computer availability to speed up these two activities (other than overtime or additional manpower)?

        _____

        _____

        _____

20. As a project manager, when would you use the Gantt technique instead of PERT?

    _____

    _____

    _____

21. Why not use CPM instead of PERT? Certainly the project manager needs to control costs as well as schedule.

    _____

    _____

    _____

22. The postimplementation audit is designed to accomplish what function? _____

    _____

23. Which group should perform such an audit? Explain. _____

    _____

24. What are the distinctions between input specifications (logical design package), input formats (physical design package), and data entry procedures (operations procedures package)?

25. What is the distinction between processing rules (logical design) and processing procedures (physical system design)?

26. Compare Figures 19-3 and 19-5. Is the length of the line proportional to the time estimate? Explain.

   a. Gantt chart _____

   _____

   b. PERT chart _____

   _____

27. Differentiate between feasibility analysis and computer justification.

28. What is the payback period for a system where the following costs and benefits apply?

Development cost	$75,000
Monthly operating cost	1,100
Monthly benefits	2,900

   Payback period = _____ years.

29. What determines whether the company should proceed with the system where payback was computed in

   problem 28? _____

30. Examine Figure 19-1. What difference on the payback calculation (Table 19-3) would result if the time periods were quarters instead of months? Explain.

_____

_____

_____

31. Recalculate the payback in Table 19-3 if a more advanced computer were acquired, reducing cost per calculation such that computer cost in Figure 19-1 was reduced 25 percent.

_____

_____

_____

32. Examine Table 19-1. The benefits in category four are more easily produced if a company implements a data base. Why? (Review the material on data base, in Chapter 17.)

_____

_____

33. Review the descriptions of the Kroger grocery system in the section on Computers in Business (Chapter 2) and list the system benefits. Then identify in which of the four benefit categories (Table 19-1) this benefit falls.

	Benefit	Category
a.	_____	_____
b.	_____	_____
c.	_____	_____
d.	_____	_____
e.	_____	_____
f.	_____	_____
g.	_____	_____
h.	_____	_____
i.	_____	_____
j.	_____	_____
k.	_____	_____

GLOSSARY

Abend Abnormal ending of a computer program.

Absolute value An integer or whole number, represented by a symbol such as 0, 1, 2, 3, etc. For example, the decimal number system has ten absolute values, viz 0 thru 9; the octal number system has eight absolute values, viz 0 thru 7.

Access mechanism In magnetic disk units, a group of access arms that move together as a unit.

Access method A technique for moving data between main memory and peripheral devices.

Access motion time In accessing a disk, it is that time necessary for the access arm to move in or out to the correct track location.

Accumulator A register which is used to accumulate the results of arithmetic operations. In some computers the accumulator cannot be referenced directly while in others several addressable accumulators are available.

Adder A set of logical circuitry that receives data from two sources, performs addition, and stores the result.

Address A label, name, or number identifying a register, location, or unit where information is stored. Also, the operand part of an instruction.

Addressable register A register which may be specifically referenced by the programmer.

ALGOL ALGOrithmic Language. A general-purpose programming language used to express problem-solving formulas for machine solution.

Algorithm A procedure for solution of a problem in a finite number of steps.

Alphanumeric A character set that includes letters, numeric digits, and usually other special characters.

Amplitude modulation (AM) Coding of information by varying the strength (or amplitude) of a carrier signal.

Analog computer A device which operates on continuous data. An electronic analog computer solves problems by translating physical conditions, such as temperature, pressure, speed, or voltage into related electrical quantities and used electrical-equivalent circuits as an analog for the physical phenomenon being investigated.

Analyst See System analyst.

APL A Programming Language. A programming language designed primarily for mathematical applications.

Application See Computer application.

Application program a computer program written for or by a user, to solve a particular problem or application.

Argument The known reference factor necessary to find the desired item (function) in a table.

Arithmetic/logic unit A major component of the CPU which performs all arithmetic and logical operations under the direction of the control unit.

Arithmetic overflow That condition which exists when the outcome of an arithmetic operation exceeds the storage space made available for the results. When this condition occurs, core is generally dumped (contents printed) and processing is terminated.

Array An ordered collection of data elements.

ASCII American Standard Code for Information Interchange. A standard code for interchange of information among data processing and data communications systems. The standard ASCII code consists of 7-bit coded characters plus one parity bit.

Assembler A computer program that directs a computer to operate upon a symbolic language program and produce a machine language program which then may be directly executed by the machine. The assembler thus serves as a translating routine, which accepts or selects required subroutines, assembles parts of a routine, and usually makes the necessary adjustments required for cross-referencing.

Assembly language A machine-oriented language designed to be used to write or express statements of an assembly program. The instruction code written in an assembly language is often a mnemonic code for assembling machine language computer instructions.

Asynchronous data transmission In this type of data transmission, additional bits are included with each character to indicate the beginning and end of the character.

Auxiliary storage See Secondary storage.

Bandwidth In data transmission, it refers to the frequency range that can be accommodated by a transmission line, which in turn determines the rate at which data can be transmitted.

Base In a number system, the base is the value which indicates how many absolute values are used in the system, e.g., the binary number system has base 2, octal has base 8, hexadecimal has base 16.

BASIC Beginner's All-purpose Symbolic Instruction Code. A data processing language developed at Dartmouth College as an instructional tool for the teaching of fundamental programming concepts. It has since gained wide acceptance as a time-sharing language and is considered to be perhaps the easiest programming language to learn.

Batch processing system Data processing mode in which a number of similar input data items are grouped together before they are processed. Used extensively in applications with high input volume, where there is no great need for fast response times.

Batch terminal A terminal oriented to high input volume and relatively low response time. A batch terminal often includes high speed card readers, line printers, and magnetic tape units.

Baud In data transmission, it is a unit of measurement often used to specify transmission speeds. A baud, or a bit can be numerically the same (in the case of narrowband transmission), or may be numerically different (as in broadband transmission). That is, in narrowband transmission, a baud is equivalent to one bit per second. In broadband transmission, a baud is equivalent to a "bit set" per second. Therefore, if a "bit set" consists of eight bits, one baud is equivalent to eight bits per second.

Binary coded decimal representation (BCD) A system of representing decimal numbers, in which each decimal digit is represented by a combination of four digits (bits). For example, the decimal value 6 is represented by 0110 in BCD, the decimal value 15 is represented by 0001 0101.

Binary digit (bit) A numeral in the binary scale of notation. This digit may be zero (0), or one (1), which is equivalent to an off or on position, respectively. Often abbreviated to "bit".

Binary number system The number system which has base 2, and uses the binary digits 0 and 1.

Bit A single character in a binary number. Often used as an abbreviation for binary digit.

Block One or more records considered or transferred as a unit, particularly with reference to input and output.

Block parity check In data transmission, it is an error detection technique, which is used in addition to parity checks.

Branching A computer operation where a selection is made between two or more possible courses of action depending upon some related fact or condition.

Branch instruction A computer instruction that enables the programmer to instruct the computer to choose between alternative subprograms depending upon the condition and outcome of some arithmetic or logic operation, or on the state of some indicator.

Broadband In data transmission, it is used to denote facilities capable of transmitting ultra-high data rates (up to several million bits per second). Broadband facilities generally use coaxial cable or microwave transmission.

Buffer A temporary storage device used to compensate for a difference in rate of flow of data, or time of occurrence of events when transmitting data from one device to another.

Business application Computer application that pertains to the functions of a business, such as invoicing, accounting, payroll, and scheduling.

Byte A group of binary digits usually operated on as a unit.

Card punch A device that will make holes in cards in certain patterns so as to represent data. The holes are punched at specific locations in accordance with signals received by the punch. Usually, provisions are made to automatically remove a card from a feeder hopper, move the card along a track as a pattern of holes are punched to represent characters, in accordance with coded signals received, and then place the card in a stacking hopper.

Card reader A device that reads, or senses, holes in cards, transforming the data from patterns of holes to patterns of electrical pulses. Usually, a card reader has facilities for holding a deck of cards, feeding the cards past sensing stations, generating pulse patterns corresponding to the data on the cards, and stacking the cards that have been read.

Cashless-checkless society Where electronic transfer of funds will eliminate the need for cash and checks.

Cathode-ray tube (CRT) A vacuum tube (similar to a television picture tube), with a screen and a controlled beam of electrons, that may be used as a display or a storage device, or both.

CBMIS See Computer-based management information system.

Centralized processing A system that consists of a central computer facility interconnected to a system of remote data terminals. All data is transmitted to the central computer, which maintains and updates the data base. Results of processing data and inquiries are transmitted to the remote locations.

Central processing unit (CPU) Controlling center of a digital computer system which processes data, supervises and coordinates the various functional units of the computer system, and provides primary storage capacity. Major components of the CPU are: a control unit, an arithmetic/logic unit, and a storage unit.

Chaining The use of a pointer in a record to indicate the address of another record that is logically related to the first.

Character One symbol of a set of elementary symbols. The symbols include the decimal digits 0 to 9, the letters A to Z, punctuation marks, operation symbols, and any other single symbols that a computer may read, store, or write.

Character printer A printer in which a single character at a time is selected, or composed, and determined within the device prior to its being printed.

Character set A defined set of characters that can be used in a given application or computer system.

Check digit A means of verifying data through the assignment of an extra digit to coded numbers, enabling the computer to perform the arithmetic needed to establish the probable correctness of the number.

Civisor A movable, visible mark used to indicate a position on a video display screen.

Classifying The grouping of data into categories or classes.

Closed subroutine A subroutine that is not stored in the main path of the routine. Such a subroutine is entered by a jump operation, and provision is made to return control to the main routine at the end of the operation.

COBOL Common Business Oriented Language. A business data-processing language developed by CODASYL, designed to express data manipulation and processing problems in English narrative form, in a precise and standard manner.

CODASYL A committee organized and sponsored by the United States Department of Defense and responsible for COBOL.

Coding The act of writing a sequence of computer instructions to accomplish a desired task.

Coding check A means of verifying data to insure that it conforms with established codes.

Combination check A means of verifying relationships between two fields of coded information to insure that an acceptable relation exists.

Communications control unit (CCU) In a data communications system, the CCU is the means by which the central CPU communicates with various input-output devices. The CCU is connected to the CPU by means of data channels that coordinate the flow of information into and out of the computer.

Communication link The physical equipment used to connect one location to another for the purpose of transmitting and receiving information.

Communicating word processors (CWPS) Word processors that can be linked through a communication network.

Compiler A computer program that prepares a machine-language program from instructions or subroutines written in a high-level language. A compiler usually generates more than one machine instruction for each symbolic instruction.

Composition check A means of verifying data to insure that appropriate characters are in the appropriate fields or that hash totals are correct.

Computer A device capable of solving problems by accepting data, performing prescribed operations on the data under the direction of a stored program, and supplying the results of these operations.

Computer application The specific problem or job to be solved or accomplished by automatic data-processing devices.

Computer assisted instruction (CAI) Use of computers to present drills, practice exercises, tutorial sequences to students.

Computer-based management information system (CBMIS) The set of computerized systems that undergird the management process. In CBMIS, data is captured as close as possible to the point of origin, then is shared with all those systems where it is used.

Computer-based message system (CBMS) A computer network that uses the computer for store-and-forward message handling.

Computer justification The process of evaluating the pros and cons of acquiring a computer.

Computer literacy Understanding enough about computers to interact successfully with computer based systems.

Computer managed instruction (CMI) Use of computer as an aid to teachers in testing, diagnosing, grading, record keeping.

Computer network Two or more interconnected computers that individually perform local processing tasks as well as transmitting messages to a central computer for updating central files or processing inquiries.

Computer output microfilm (COM) Microfilm that is produced by the use of a COM device. That is, a COM device displays data on a CRT screen, and the data is exposed to microfilm. Output is a microfilm copy of the data, either in roll or microfiche form. The computer then produces an index to locate the proper roll and frame for a given output. The device may display data on-line from the computer, or off-line from magnetic tape.

Computer simulation The simulation of physical systems or real-world phenomena through the use of a computer by means of mathematical or physical models that are designed to represent the particular phenomenon being investigated.

Computer system An organized collection of hardware and software, whose interaction is designed to accomplish specific functions, such as process computer applications.

Computing Consists of arithmetic operations performed on data and logical operations necessary for program control.

Concentrator A device designed to improve the efficiency of data transmission by allowing devices to share communications channels.

Conditional branch instruction An instruction that is taken only if a specific condition or set of conditions is satisfied. If the condition is not satisfied, the computer performs the next instruction in sequence.

Console The part of a computer that is used for communications between the operators or service personnel and the system. The console contains lights, keys, switches, and related circuits for man-machine communication. The console may be used to control the machine manually, correct errors, determine the status of machine circuits, registers, and counters, determine the contents of storage, and manually revise the contents of storage.

Constant The quantity or message that will be present in the computer and available as data for the program, and which usually are not subject to change with time.

Control unit A major component of the CPU that directs the activities of the computer by interpreting a set of instructions, called a program.

Core See Magnetic core.

Counter A device for storing a number and allowing the number to be increased or decreased as directed by the computer instructions.

CPM See Critical path method.

Critical path method A graphical management tool for defining and interrelating on a time scale the jobs and events that must take place to accomplish desired objectives. The interdependency of tasks establishes a network in which the longest path through the network is the critical path that determines the duration of the overall project. In contrast to PERT, CPM has the ability to vary the time along the critical path to determine its effect on cost, and vice versa.

Cross-footing check A means of verifying data to insure that arithmetical accuracy of individual records and/or a group of records is attained.

Cryogenic memory A storage device that uses the superconductive properties of certain materials at temperatures near absolute zero.

Cybernetic The scientific study of those methods of control and communication that are common to living organisms and machines. For example, the comparative study of complex electronic calculating machines and the human nervous system to explain the nature of the brain.

Cycle One iteration or loop through a set of logical steps.

Cycle time Interval between the call for and delivery to, information from a storage device.

Cylinder In a disk pack, the set of all tracks that can be accessed without repositioning the access mechanism.

Data A representation of facts, concepts or instructions in a form suitable for communication or processing by humans and/or machines.

Data base An organized collection of data, designed to serve the needs of an organization.

Data base concept A concept in data-processing that emphasizes integration of data, information, and files. Data elements are captured at the earliest possible source and are made available to all systems and subsystems.

Data base management system (DBMS) Software that accomplishes the tasks of creating, accessing and maintaining the data base.

Data channel A physical path along which data may be transferred or transmitted. A channel is essentially a minicomputer, contained near or in the CPU, which permits input-output operations to be controlled independently of the central processing unit (CPU).

Data communication system A system of terminals, communications equipment and channels, and software that links together the various elements of data-processing systems.

Data control Those procedures necessary to control the flow of data or information.

Data item A named unit of recorded information; a field.

Data management system A comprehensive software system to store, retrieve, and update data. It provides for the definition and creation of files or databases or both, the maintenance of indexes, and for file security.

Data set In a data communications system, it is the device that modulates (dc signal to tones) and demodulates (tones back to dc signals) data between two or more input-output devices and a data transmission link.

Data structure A systematic method of organizing or visualizing data.

Data throughput The rate in messages per minute at which data is transmitted from source to destination.

Debugging The process of identifying and correcting mistakes in a computer program.

Decision criteria Identified conditions or actions that are necessary before a decision is made.

Decision function The process of evaluating criteria and selecting alternatives.

Decision logic table A table of possible courses of action, alternatives, or contingencies to be considered in the description of a problem, with the actions to be taken. Decision tables are often used in place of flowcharts for problem description, analysis, and accompanying documentation.

Decision support systems (DSS) Systems designed to facilitate the managerial decision making process.

Demodulation The process of converting tones to a direct current signal. The conversion process is performed by a data set.

Design logic The set of logic used in developing an improved system

Desk checking Manual checking of a program before it is keypunched.

Development costs One-time costs of system development, consisting of: analyzing and documenting the existing system, designing, programming, debugging, and implementing a new system.

Diagnostics Computer output designed to provide the programmer with information of maximum utility and convenience in checking out programs.

Dialed service In data transmission, dialed service is the intermittent use of communication facilities. When a message is to be transmitted, the user dials the destination number (either computer or remote terminal), just as for a telephone call. With dialed service, the user must compete with other users for an available line, and he may encounter a busy signal at any given time. The user is charged only for the time used, with rates depending on the time of day, day of the week, and distance involved.

Digit A graphic character used to represent an integer.

Digital computer Basically, a counting device that operates on discrete or discontinuous data or numbers. More specifically, it is a device for performing sequences of arithmetical and logical operations, not only on data but also on its own program.

Direct access Type of access in which data may be referenced or accessed directly, without reference to data previously accessed.

Direct access storage device A device in which the access time is independent of the location of the data.

Direct-entry system System oriented to direct entry of data from a keyboard. The system typically includes a disk storage unit for mass storage of data files. Output may be by means of a line printer or a visual display device or both.

Directory A table or index, consisting of identifiers and references to the corresponding data items or records.

Disk pack A removable assembly of magnetic disks.

Diskette A small magnetic disk (resembles a 45-rpm record),

which is sealed in a plastic jacket about 8 inches square and weighs less than 2 ounces.

Distributed data base A system where data bases reside at the location which has primary use or responsibility for those data but where sharing of data is possible through a network.

Distributed data entry Data entry from several locations, handled through a communications network.

Distributed network Networks with alternative routings between nodes.

Distributed output Locating output devices for the ultimate users.

Distributed processing A system in which the processing workload is spread out through the teleprocessing network.

Documentation Organization and communication or recorded knowledge to maintain a complete record to facilitate changes in conditions.

Echo checking See Loop checking.

Edit To prepare or transform data. Editing operations include rearranging data, deletion of unwanted data, zero suppression, and code conversion.

Effective error rate In data transmission, it is the rate at which undetected errors occur in transmission. Effective error rates depend on the nominal error rates, quality of transmission facilities used, and on the sophistication of the error detection and correction techniques used.

Elementary item A data item or field containing no subordinate items. In other words, elementary items are data items or fields that are not subdivided.

Error correction codes In data transmission, it is a code containing redundant data to assist in error correction and detection.

Execution time (E-time) The time necessary for the computer to execute an instruction. Several machine cycles are often required for execution time, depending on the instruction.

Extended binary coded decimal interchange code (EBCDIC) A system of representing data (alphabetic, numeric, and special characters), in which each character is represented by a combination of eight bit positions (excluding parity bit position). The eight positions consist of four zone bits and four numeric bits.

External storage A storage device or medium outside the computer that can store information in a form acceptable to the computer. External storage devices usually have larger capacities and lower access speeds than internal and secondary storage. External storage consists of punched cards, magnetic tape, and documents encoded with magnetic ink characters, or optical characters.

Fading In data transmission, fading refers to temporary loss of signal that occurs primarily in microwave transmission and may be caused by atmospheric conditions, severe rain-storms, or even a bird flying between towers.

Facsimile A version of electronic mail where a page is transmitted to a remote location.

File descriptor A document used to describe and provide detailed information for each file in the system, whether or not computerized.

File maintenance The activity of keeping a file up to date by adding, changing, or deleting data.

Firmware Intermediate between hardware and software; logic circuits in read-only memory that may be altered by the software under certain circumstances.

First generation system design approach A systems development approach that placed emphasis on adminis-trative functions and concentrated on individual systems rather than integrated systems.

Fixed word length A computer word in which each storage address references a fixed number of bit positions.

Floating point (FORTRAN) The mode that utilizes decimal numbers and/or variable names beginning with the letters A to H, and O to Z. These variables are called floating point or real mode variables, because the computer "floats" numbers into proper decimal alignment before computing.

Flowchart A schematic or graphic presentation of the logic required to solve a problem.

Flying spot scanner In optical character recognition (OCR), a device employing a moving spot of light to scan a sample space, the intensity of the transmitted or reflected light being sensed by a photoelectric transducer.

Forms flowchart A chart that depicts the flow of paperwork and forms.

FORTRAN FORmula TRANslator. A compiler language developed by the IBM Corporation, originally conceived for use on scientific problems but sometimes adapted for commercial problems as well.

Freeform area In terminal data entry, where operator may enter coded information in any order.

Front-end processor In distributed computer networks, the front-end processor is a computer (typically a minicom-puter) that is attached to and facilitates the host processor. When a front-end processor is used, all communications control functions are removed from the host (central) processor to the front-end processor.

Full duplex In data transmission, full duplex is a transmission mode that permits transmission of data in both directions simultaneously.

Future shock Impact of rapidly accelerating technological advances upon persons who do not keep pace.

Gantt chart The predecessor to network analysis, in which the representation of tasks and their relationship is shown via time scale.

General-purpose flowchart A flowchart designed for a general purpose. That is, the terminology utilized is of a general nature and is not oriented toward any specific pro-gramming language.

Graphics Pertaining to visual display in which three-dimensional objects may be displayed via a CRT device. Some graphic units use a light pen or other device that permits an operator to input data in graphical form.

Graph plotter A device capable of representing data in graphic form, such as two-dimensional curves or line draw-ings, either as direct computer output or from magnetic tape. Graph plotters are often used as a computer output device to display the results of computation.

Group item An item that is further subdivided.

Half duplex In data transmission, half duplex is a transmis-sion mode that permits transmission of data in both direc-tions, but only one direction at a time.

Halographic memory A reusable storage medium that is a high-resolution photographic plate embedded in a heat sensitive plastic.

Hardware Physical equipment, such as the mechanical, electronic, and magnetic units in a computer.

Hash total An account, total, or tally of items in certain fields, used for control of input, processing, and output operations.

Hexadecimal number system The number system that has base 16, that is 16^0, 16^1, 16^2, 16^3, etc., and uses characters representing the absolute values 0 to 15.

High-order languages The programming languages that tend toward being independent of the limitations of a specific computer, such as COBOL, FORTRAN, PL/1, and PASCAL.

HIPO (Hierarchy plus Input-Process-Output) A documen-tation technique that depicts inputs, processing and out-puts for modules on the structure chart.

History file An obsolete master or transaction file, retained for historical use or reference.

Hollerith code An alpha-numeric punched-card code in-vented by Dr. Herman Hollerith in 1889, in which the top three positions in a column are called "zone" punches (12, 11, and 0, from the top downward), and are combined with the remaining punches, or digit punches (1 to 9) to repre-sent alphabetic, numeric, and special characters.

Horizontally-oriented systems Operational systems that handle the basic operations of the organization, for exam-ple, a checking account system, and a demand deposit account system.

Host processor In a data communications system, there may be several computers, some of which may be assigned specialized functions such as message switching and local processing. In such a system, there is generally a large central computer that performs the major data-processing tasks. This computer is often referred to as the "host processor."

Hybrid computer A combination analog and digital computer.

Hybrid electronic mail system Mixture of devices on an electronic communication system for handling messages.

Identifier One or more characters utilized in the identification or location of an item or record.

Impact printer A printer that forms characters by the use of print hammers that press the paper and ribbon against selected type characters as they pass in front of the paper. Type characters are commonly mounted on a moving chain or are engraved on the face of a rotating drum.

Implementation costs In system development, they are one-time costs that consist of: training personnel to operate the system, plus the cost of installing and testing the system.

Index sequential organization A file organization combining the efficiency of sequential organization with the ability to rapidly access records out of sequence. It may be used only on direct-access devices.

Information analyst The person who serves as the link or liaison between the user department and the computer department. These persons determine the information needs of the organization based on a knowledge of its functions and upon interaction with the various managers of the organization.

Information system The network of all communication methods within an organization.

Initialize The establishment of an initial value for a counter.

Input-output descriptor A document used to describe and provide detailed information for each system input and output.

Input specification A document, prepared by the system analyst, that delineates the appropriate input, content, and media required for the system.

Inquiry A request for information.

Instruction A coded program step that tells the computer what to do and where to find or store data for a single operation in a program. Basically, an instruction consists of two parts: operation code and operand.

Instruction counter A special purpose register that contains the address of the next instruction to be executed.

Instruction register Temporary storage location which contains the instruction to be processed.

Instruction time (I-time) The time necessary for a computer to move an instruction from main memory to the storage register. During this time the operation code is routed to the operation-code register, and the address portion to the address register. Total instruction time generally requires one machine cycle.

Integer mode (FORTRAN) The mode that utilizes integer numbers or variable names or both beginning with the letters I to N.

Integration The sharing of data or information among subsystems and systems.

Intelligent terminal Essentially, a minicomputer with an input keyboard and often a CRT display. An intelligent terminal can perform checking, editing, and formatting on input data; error control; message routing and switching; and stand alone computing, that is, performing small-scale processing tasks.

Interactive A mode of operation in which each entry calls forth a response from the system.

Interblock gap An interval of space between recorded portions of data or physical records that permits tape stop-start operations.

Interface A common boundary between automatic data-processing systems or parts of a single system. For example, the connection between a data channel and the control unit.

Internal storage See Primary storage.

Interrecord gap See Interblock gap.

Interrupt To temporarily suspend the execution of a computer program, in such a way that execution can be resumed.

Inverted files A method of file organization in which a data item, field, or keyword identifies a record instead of the original identifier or key.

Iteration One loop or cycle through a set of logical steps.

I-time See Instruction time.

Job control cards Cards that contain program names, parameters, or special instructions for a specific application. The data on the control cards usually represent information for executing a computer program other than the actual input data or the actual program to be run.

Job control language The specific data processing language used for a particular set of job control cards.

Job deck See Job control cards.

Key See Identifier.

Keyboard printer A device that permits a versatile means of transmitting messages and data between a remote user and the computer at speeds related to the common-carrier service available.

Key-disk system A system in which data is entered from a keyboard device (similar to a typewriter) and is recorded directly onto a magnetic disk. Often, this approach is facilitated through the use of a minicomputer. That is, data is entered through keyboards, is processed by the systems-shared computer and then is stored on a magnetic disk.

Keypunch machine A special device to record information in cards or tape to represent letters, digits, and special characters.

Key-tape system A system in which data is entered from a keyboard device (similar to a typewriter) and is recorded directly on magnetic tape. Generally, the data being keyed is stored in a buffer (or small memory device) and is displayed on a CRT, so that the operator can see what is being recorded. In the event of an error, the operator merely backspaces and retypes the data. When the record is completed, it is then released to the magnetic tape.

Key transformation A scheme, usually mathematical, which is utilized to determine a number that is used as the address of a record.

Large-scale integrated (LSI) circuitry An ultra-high speed storage device that uses miniature semiconductors (such as transistors) to form very small, compact memory arrays.

Latency See Rotational delay time.

Leased service In data transmission systems, leased service refers to the use of communication facilities through a lease arrangement. The user may lease a line from a common carrier on a fulltime basis, permitting 24-hours-a-day availability. A flat rate is charged for the service, depending on the distance.

Libraries An organized collection of standard, checked-out routines that may be incorporated into larger routines as the need arises.

Lifestream activities Those activities that are key to the life of an organization.

Linear programming The analysis of problems in which a linear function of a number of variables is to be maximized (or minimized) when those variables are subject to a number of linear constraints.

Line printer A printer in which an entire line of characters is composed and determined within the device prior to printing.

Links See Pointer.

List A data structure in which logical records are connected by means of pointers.

Location In a computer, it is an addressable area in main memory or auxiliary storage where a unit of data may be stored or retrieved.

Logic The science that deals with the principles of correct or reliable inferences.

Logical data base design Designing the interactions between data, independent of physical devices which will house the data.

Logical design Phase II of the system development process that is essentially hardware-independent. In this phase, the system analyst works with the users, or their representatives, to define precisely what the system is intended to perform.

Logical errors Errors in the logic of a particular program.

Logical file A complete set of related records for a specific area or purpose that may occupy a fraction or all of a physical file, or may require more than one physical file, for example, an inventory master file that may require one or more reels of magnetic tape (i.e., physical files).

Logical operation The examination of data to determine relationships, such as comparing, selecting, referencing, matching, sorting, merging, and the like.

Logical record A collection or an association of data items, fields, or records on the basis of their content instead of on their physical location. For example, all data relating to a given person forms a logical record regardless of where or how the data may be located, dispersed, or distributed.

Loop An iteration or cycle through a set of logical steps.

Loop checking An error detection and correction technique used in data transmission. In loop checking, when an operator strikes a key on the typewriter terminal, it is transmitted to the computer where it is received and checked. The character is then transmitted back to the terminal and printed. If the character that is printed is the same as the key that was struck, the operator is insured that the message has been properly received by the computer.

Low-order language Those programming languages that most closely resemble machine language. Generally, each instruction is equivalent to one machine instruction.

Machine language A programming language or instruction code used directly by the computer. The code (binary-based notation) is in a form directly acceptable to a computer and requires no translation.

Machine-readable Pertaining to the characteristic of being able to be sensed or read by a device, usually by a device that has been designed and built specifically to perform the reading or sensing function. Thus data on tapes, cards, drums, disks, and similar media are machine readable.

Macro-instruction An instruction that programmers can write in a source program to call for special or library routines that perform wanted functions as open, seek, close, and the like. Macro-instructions result in one-for-many instructions and are extensively used.

Magnetic core A tiny doughnut-shaped element about the size of a grain of salt, which is capable of being polarized in one of two directions (i.e., ON or OFF).

Magnetic disk A storage device of magnetically coated disks, on the surface of which information is stored in the form of magnetic spots arranged in a manner to represent binary data. These data are arranged in circular tracks around the disks and are accessible to reading and writing heads on an arm that can be moved mechanically to the desired disk, and then to the desired track on that disk. Data from a given track is read or written sequentially as the disk rotates.

Magnetic drum A cylinder with a magnetic surface on which data can be stored by selective magnetization of portions of the curved surface. Data is written and sensed by a set of read-write heads positioned close to the surface of the drum while it is rotating at high speed.

Magnetic ink character recognition (MICR) A technique in which characters are inscribed on documents with magnetic ink containing particles of iron oxide. The document reader senses the magnetic pattern, permitting sorting, summing, and control. Only 14 characters are used in MICR (the 10 digits 0 to 9, plus 4 special characters). MICR was pioneered, developed, and is currently in widespread use among American banks.

Magnetic tape An external storage medium in the form of a ferrous oxide coating on a reel of metallic or plastic tape on which bits may be recorded magnetically as a means of retaining data.

Main storage See Primary storage.

Maintenance Incorporating changes and enhancements in a system.

Management-by-exception The management principle that is concerned with exceptional conditions, that is, when actual results differ from planned results. When results occur within a normal range they are not reported.

Management information system (MIS) The complete set of business techniques designed and operated to assist in decision making at various levels of management. A management information system may or may not be computerized.

Mass cartridge storage Mass data storage medium in which data are stored on short strips of magnetic tape contained in a cartridge. The cartridges are stored in cells in a storage unit or facility. To access the data, cartridges are transported to a read/write station and the strip of tape is automatically unwound into a vacuum column.

Master file A set of relatively permanent records containing identifying, statistical, and historical information, used as a source of reference for an application.

Matching checks A means of verifying data through the matching of identifiers or coded transaction numbers.

Merging The combining of two or more files into a single file in the same sequence.

Menu A listing of items on a CRT from which the user can make a selection for a next-level-of-detail reporting on the screen.

Message A coded communication of information from a source to one or more destinations.

MICR See Magnetic ink character recognition.

Microcomputer Relatively small but powerful computer mounted on a single semiconductor chip or printed circuit board.

Microprocessor The CPU for a microcomputer.

Microprogram A machine-language instruction causes a single functional step to be performed. Each instruction is actually a composite of a number of still more elementary steps, called micro-instructions. Each micro-instruction is coded as several bits, one bit for each functional unit or data path in the computer hardware. The program that transforms each machine language instruction into a series of micro-instructions is called "microprogram."

Microprogramming Machine language coding in which the coder builds instructions from primitive basic instructions built into the hardware.

Microsecond One-millionth of a second.

Millisecond One-thousandth of a second.

Minicomputer A small, general-purpose computer.

Mixed mode (FORTRAN) An expression that contains a combination of integer and real constants and/or variable names. In evaluating a mixed mode expression the FORTRAN compiler usually converts integer quantities to floating-point quantities and performs the arithmetic in floating-point mode.

Modem See Data set.

Modular programming The segmentation of a large program into a number of small, self-contained subprograms or subroutines.

Modulation The process of converting a direct current (dc) signal to tones for transmission via a communications link. The conversion process is performed by a data set.

Module A separate and distinct (yet, integral) part of a computer program that can be compiled independently.

Module tests Those individual tests performed on the separate programs, subroutines, or parts of a system, for purposes of assuring accuracy, capability, and adequacy of each unit.

Monitor See Supervisor.

Multidrop A communications line that interconnects several terminals or other devices.

Multiformat Many formats for key entry.

Multiplexor channel A channel that permits the transmission of two or more messages on a single channel by use of an interleaving process. That is, the multiplexor channel receives a message from an input unit one character at a time in its usual operation. In between these characters the multiplexor channel sandwiches a character from each of the other units that also want to communicate with the processing unit.

Multiprocessing A mode of operation that provides for parallel processing by two or more computer processors.

Multiprogramming A mode of operation that provides for the concurrent (or interleaved) execution of two or more computer programs by a single computer processor.

Nanosecond One-billionth of a second.

Narrowband Facilities capable of transmitting data at rates from 45 to 300 bits per second. Narrowband facilities are typically limited to applications with low volumes.

Network An interconnection of computers, terminals, and communications equipment.

Noise In data transmission, noise refers to random signals that interfere with the transmitted signal. There are two basic types of noise: background noise and impulse noise. Impulse noise, which is the greater source of error, is caused by electrical storms (or other disturbances) that cause a burst of short-duration pulses.

Nominal error rate In data transmission, nominal error rate is the rate which is inherent in the transmission link that is used. This rate depends on a number of factors such as type of equipment, distance, transmission speed, and weather.

Nondestructive read A reading process that does not destroy or change the data in the source.

Nonimpact printer A printer that forms characters by transferring electrical charges to the paper.

Nonoverlapped processing A process in which the typical cycle, that is, read, process, and write, is performed serially (i.e., in sequence). Thus the total cycle time is the sum of the read time, plus the process time, plus the write time.

Object computer The computer that accepts the object program to thus execute the instructions, as contrasted to a computer that might be used to merely compile the object program from the source program.

Octal number system The number system that has base 8, and uses characters representing the absolute values 0 to 7.

OEM Original equipment manufacturer. Term for equipment sold by one manufacturer to another for use in products, as opposed to the end user.

Off-line communication system A system in which data is recorded on a machine-readable medium, instead of being transmitted directly to or from the computer.

On-line batch system A system in which data is accumulated in batches and transmitted directly to the computer for processing.

On-line processing system The operation of terminals, files, and other auxiliary equipment under direct control of the central processor to eliminate the need for human intervention at any stage between initial input and computer output.

On-line real-time system An on-line system that provides near-instantaneous responses to inquiries from a terminal. Typically, such a system has immediate access to all necessary data, which often permits a response within seconds.

Open subroutine A subroutine inserted directly into the linear operational sequence rather than by a jump. Such a subroutine must be recopied at each point that it is needed in a routine.

Operand The second part of an instruction that tells the computer "where" to find or to store data to be processed, or the location of the next instruction. It is the address of a storage location where the desired data or instruction is found.

Operating costs Recurring costs, consisting of (1) entering data on machine processible media, (2) performing control checks on input, and output, and (3) computer processing.

Operating system An integrated set of programs and subroutines that controls the execution of programs and provides services such as language translation, input-output control, and job scheduling.

Operation code The first part of an instruction that tells the computer "what" operation to perform, such as add, multiply, compare, and read.

Optical character recognition (OCR) The identification of graphic characters, directly from a printer or handwritten document, by use of photosensitive devices. Thus, OCR eliminates the need for data conversion.

Optical character reader A device that reads hand or machine printed symbols from documents, and inputs the data into a computing system.

Organization-oriented system flowchart (O²S flowchart) A flowchart in which organizational responsibility is identified for each activity performed, each major system within the organization has a flowchart, and the resources required in each organization in the system are delineated.

Output specifications Those documents produced through in-depth discussions with users of the system. Output specifications identify precisely what the system should provide the user.

Overlapped processing A process in which the typical cycle, that is, read, process, and write, is performed simultaneously. The total cycle time is determined by that event which takes the most time to perform (either read time, or write time, or processing time).

Packed decimal A decimal format in EBCDIC in which the

zone portions of numerical digits are removed and two decimal digits are packed into each eight-bit set. The sign of the number is stored in the rightmost portion of the character string.

Page In a virtual storage system, a block of instructions and/or data that can be located either in main storage or in secondary storage.

Paging memory High-speed secondary storage device used for storing pages of data and/or instructions.

Page swapping Exchanging of pages between main storage and secondary storage.

Parallel processing tests The processing of the new system and the old system with the same input and time period to verify that the new system satisfactorily meets design criteria.

Parity checking A summation check in which the binary digits, in a character or word, are added, and the sum is checked against a single, previously computed parity digit. The check tests whether the number of ones (bits in "on" position) in a word is odd or even, depending on the particular parity check.

PASCAL A high level, general purpose structured programming language.

Payback analysis An analysis to determine the period of time necessary to recover the costs of an investment or project.

Peripherals Input-output and secondary storage devices that represent the means by which data is input, stored, retrieved, and output from the computer.

Peripheral storage See Secondary storage.

Personal computing Computer use for an individual instead of a group of individuals or for an organization.

PERT Program Evaluation and Review Technique. A graphical management tool for defining and interrelating on a time scale the jobs and events that must take place to accomplish desired objectives. The interdependency of tasks establishes a network in which the longest path through the network is the critical path that determines the duration of the overall project. In contrast to CPM, PERT has the ability to develop probability estimates for each activity, and for the critical path.

Physical data base design Designing the physical layout and determining the devices which will contain the data.

Physical design Physical system design is concerned with the conversion of the logical system design into a form that can be processed by the computer economically and effectively. Generally, physical system design takes place in Phase III of the system development process and determines the organization of files and the devices to be used.

Physical file A physical unit such as a reel of magnetic tape.

Physical record A block of data stored contiguously on a device or medium such as magnetic disk or tape.

Picosecond One-trillionth of a second.

PL/1 A general purpose data processing language that is suitable for both scientific and business applications. PL/1 combines many of the features of FORTRAN and COBOL, and has a wide range of possible applications; however, it is relatively complex and not universally used.

Pointer A field in a record which gives the address (identifier) of another record that is logically related to the first.

Point of sale recorders A device that is used to input sales data at the time when a sale is executed. Generally, a point of sale recorder uses optical or magnetic reading techniques.

Polling A procedure that contacts terminals in a network.

Positional value The value that is found by raising the base of the number system used to the power of the position. For example, in the decimal system the zero (or units) position has positional value 10^0 or 1, and the first (or tens) position has positional value 10^1, etc.

Postimplementation audit Analyzing a system to insure that the design objectives were accomplished.

Present value analysis An analysis that takes into account the time value of money. Present value is the equivalent value now of future dollars discounted back from a specified future date to the present date at a given rate of compound interest.

Primary storage The storage that is considered an integral part of the CPU. It contains both the computer program(s) and the data to be processed by the program(s).

Problem-oriented language A programming language designed for ease of problem definition and problem solution for specific classes of problems.

Procedure-oriented language A programming language designed for convenience in expressing the technique or sequence of steps required to carry out a process or flow. It is usually a source language and is usually not machine oriented.

Process flowchart A flowchart used in the early 1900s to portray physical flow of materials, products, and often clerical activities.

Processing specification A document, prepared by the system analyst, that delineates approximate procedures for computer processing data.

Program An explicit set of steps or instructions that directs the computer and coordinates the operation of the various hardware components.

Programmable calculator Small desk-top minicomputers used for solving problems.

Program evaluation and review technique See PERT.

Programmer-oriented flowcharts Those flowcharts that use the terminology, symbols, and terms generally required by a programmer in developing a computer application.

Protocol A set of rules for data communication in a data communications network.

Pseudocode English-like description of the processing steps in a computer program.

Punched card A card that is punched with a pattern of holes to represent information. The punched card is commonly used as an input-output medium for digital computers. The punched holes are sensed electrically by wire brushes, mechanically by metal feelers, or photoelectrically.

Punched paper tape Paper tape on which a pattern of holes or cuts is used to represent data.

Query language Languages designed to facilitate inquiries into a data base. A high level, English like language to enable users to formulate their own inquiries into a system.

Random access See Direct access.

Randomizing See Key transformation.

Random access memory (RAM) See random processing.

Random processing The processing of transactions in the order in which they occur. Used in direct access file organization.

Read-only memory (ROM) Memory modules where instructions can be read but not written.

Reasonableness check A means of verifying data to insure that it does not exceed the limit prescribed by reason.

Record A set of related data items or fields, pertaining to a particular item, unit, or entity.

Record key See Identifier.

Recording density The number of characters or symbols recorded or stored in a unit of length, area, or volume.

Redundancy In data transmission, it refers to parity bits and checks added to the message to assist in determining the accuracy of transmitted digits or words.

Register A device for the temporary storage of data or instructions to facilitate arithmetical, logical, or transfer operations.

Report file Set of records extracted from data in master files, used to prepare reports.

Return on investment (ROI) analysis An analysis to determine the expected return on monies invested. It is derived by dividing savings (income) by the cost of an investment. Return on investment is a useful management tool utilized in the ranking of various investment alternatives.

Rotational delay time In accessing a disk, it is that time necessary for the disk to rotate until the desired sector (or record) is positioned at the read-write head.

RPG Report Program Generator. A data processing language

designed for relatively simple business applications in which there is a need for generating routine business reports.

Run manual The complete documentation of a specific program used in a particular run.

Scalar In an array, a scalar is a single element of data, usually a number.

Scientific application Computer application which pertains to the sciences. For instance, airframe stress analysis, guidance and flight control, matrix inversion, and blood count analysis.

Secondary storage A storage that supplements primary storage. Secondary storage devices include magnetic disk units, magnetic drums, and magnetic tape. Secondary storage is characterized by slower speed of operation and correspondingly lower cost than those related to primary storage.

Sector A portion of a track (from a magnetic disk) whose shape is similar to a slice of pie. Each track is equally divided into sectors, in which each sector may have its own distinct address.

Selector channel A channel that is used where high-speed devices are to be attached to a system. A single channel can operate only one input-output device at a time. Two or more channels connected to any computer system provide the ability to read, write, and compute from multiple input-output devices.

Sequential access A file organization in which items of information become available only in a one after the other sequence, whether or not all the information or only some of it is desired. That is, it is necessary to start at a given reference point and to examine each record in sequence until the desired record is located.

Sequential file A file in which records are arranged in ascending or descending order according to a key that may be numeric, alphabetic, or alphanumeric. To locate a specific record it is necessary to start at a given reference point and to examine each record in sequence until the desired record is located.

Sign check A means of verifying data to ascertain the appropriateness of the algebraic sign.

Simple parity check In data transmission, it is an error detection technique, in which a bit is added to each character to make the total number of one bits in each character transmitted either odd or even. Each character is then checked for correct parity at the receiving end. Simple parity check will not detect errors involving an even number of bits, and does not permit error correction.

Simplex In data transmission, it is a transmission mode that permits transmission of data in one direction only.

Small business computer A small computer designed for business applications.

Software Computer programs and related techniques that bridge the gap between a user's problems, on one hand, and strictly hardware functions and requirements, on the other. Software includes programming languages and translators, operating systems, and applications programs.

Sorting The arranging of a list (or file) of data into a desired sequence.

Source computer The computer that is utilized to translate source programs into object programs for computer execution.

Source symbol marking Coding merchandise with machine readable symbols.

Special-purpose flowchart A flowchart designed for a specific function. The terminology utilized restricts its use to a special purpose.

Storage device See Storage unit.

Storage unit A device into which data may be inserted, in which it may be retained, and from which it may be retrieved.

Stored program A set of instructions contained in main memory that directs the operation of a computer without human intervention.

Structure charts A top-down design and documentation technique that depicts the modules of the program and their relationships.

Structured programming A programming method that utilizes top-down design and three basic control structures to simplify development, testing and modification.

Structured programming A technique for designing and coding computer programs that reduces complexity.

Subprogram A part of a larger program that can be compiled independently.

Subrouting A sequence of statements that may be used in one or more computer programs and/or at one or more points in a computer program.

Supercomputer Fastest, most powerful computers available. Used by large research laboratories, on-line reservation networks, etc.

Supervisor A routine that controls and coordinates all operations in the computer system. The supervisor organizes and regulates the flow of work, and provides translations among languages, diagnoses of human mistakes, priority assignments, equipment malfunctions, and opens and closes files, as well as other housekeeping details.

Switched service See Dialed service.

Symbolic addresses An address, or label chosen for convenience by a programmer to specify a storage location in the context of a particular program.

Synchronous data transmission In this type of data transmission, the sending and receiving terminals are kept in constant synchronization by data sets. Synchronizing information is transmitted in the modulated signal, and special timing circuitry is used in the receiving station.

Synergism The concept that the whole is equal to more than the sum of its parts. For example, man and computer together can produce more than either can produce alone.

Synonyms Record keys or identifiers that generate the same storage addresses. In other words, synonyms require a search of two or more areas before location of the desired record is attained.

Syntax error An error in the usage of the programming language utilized.

System An organized collection of parts or elements united by regulated interaction and designed or required to accomplish a specific purpose or objective. Every system involes (1) input, (2) processing, and (3) output.

System analysis Examination of a system and delineation of resources (personnel, equipment, materials, and facilities) required for proper operation of the system.

System analyst An individual who analyzes a system to determine where improvements can be made.

System designer An individual who converts system requirements into a set of specifications which allow it to be computer-processed.

System feasibility analysis The process of evaluating the advantages versus the costs of converting a manual operation to computer processing or to a more sophisticated level of computing.

System software Consists of operating system, utility programs, programming languages and their supporting compilers and assemblers.

System survey The initial phase of the system development cycle which documents company history, external environment, objectives and policies, and delineates the master plan.

System tests Actual running of all applications (modules) for the complete system, using actual or hypothetical data and analyzing the results. System tests are designed for purposes of testing the accuracy, capability, and adequacy of an entire system.

Table An organized collection of data, usually arranged in an array where each item in the array is uniquely identifiable by some label or by its relative position. Items in a table are easier to locate or identify, and thus provide a ready reference.

Telecommunications See Data communication system.

Teleprocessing See Data communication system.

Terminal In data communication systems, a terminal is a

point at which data can enter or leave the communication network.

Third generation system design approach A systems development approach that concentrates on studying the organization as a whole, giving priority to the life-stream activities of the firm.

Time-sharing system An on-line system in which many users share availability of a remote central computer.

Top-down design/programming The concept of starting from the top and then providing successive levels of detail (as opposed to bottom up design or programming).

Track The portion of a moving memory medium (such as tape, disk, or drum) which passes beneath, and is accessible to a particular read-write head position. In a disk or drum, tracks run in a circular manner whereas tracks in tapes run lengthwise.

Transaction An exchange between a terminal and a computer that accomplishes a particular action or result.

Transaction file Set of records resulting from transaction that affect the status of items in the master file. It is used to update the master file.

Translator A routine, program, or device capable of directing the translation or transformation of statements or their equivalent codes in one language to equivalent statements or their equivalent codes in another language.

Unconditional branch instruction An instruction that is always executed each time the computer encounters it. The unconditional branch instruction causes the computer to branch to another location in the program—either a higher or lower address.

User-oriented flowchart Those flowcharts that use the terminology, symbols, and terms that permit verification of logic by the user.

Utility program A general-purpose program, supplied by a manufacturer with his equipment, for executing standard or typical operations, such as sorting, indexing, translating, assembling, compiling, or merging.

Variable A symbol whose numeric value changes from one repetition of a program to the next, or changes within each repetition of a program.

Variable word length A computer word in which the number of characters in a given word is variable and subject to the discretion of the programmer. Each character is addressable, which permits control of word lengths.

Vertically oriented systems Management systems that provide pertinent information to various levels of management, for example, a market forecasting system for strategic level management.

Video display A device that uses a cathode-ray tube (CRT) and permits on-line visual display of data. Display units are widely used where it is necessary to provide direct access to computer files.

Video Mask Programmed forms on a cathode ray tube with blanks to be filled in.

Virtual storage Storage space that may be regarded as part of addressable main memory, although the addresses may exceed the actual capacity of main memory. The size of virtual storage is limited by the addressing scheme of the computer and by the amount of secondary storage available, but not by the actual number of main storage locations.

Visual display See Video display.

Voiceband In data transmission, it is used to denote facilities capable of transmitting data over voice-frequency telephone channels.

Voice response unit A device that permits computer output in the form of recorded or synthesized human voice.

Wideband See Broadband.

Word A set of characters that occupies one storage location and is treated by the computer circuits as a unit and is transported as such. Word lengths are fixed or variable, depending on the particular computer and program.

Word processing Systems which emphasize the processing of words and textual material rather than numeric data.

Zoned decimal A decimal representation in EBCDIC in which each character is encoded as an eight-bit character, utilizing both the zone and numeric bits for each decimal digit. The zone bits represent the sign of the number, that is, a bit pattern of 1111 in the zone portion represents an unsigned number, 1100 represents a positive number, and 1101 represents a negative number.

INDEX